Lecture Notes in Artificial Intelligence 4386

Edited by J. G. Carbonell and J. Siekmann

Subseries of Lecture Notes in Computer Science

T0217361

Pablo Noriega   Javier Vázquez-Salceda
Guido Boella   Olivier Boissier
Virginia Dignum   Nicoletta Fornara
Eric Matson (Eds.)

Coordination, Organizations, Institutions, and Norms in Agent Systems II

AAMAS 2006 and ECAI 2006
International Workshops, COIN 2006
Hakodate, Japan, May 9, 2006
Riva del Garda, Italy, August 28, 2006
Revised Selected Papers

 Springer

Series Editors

Jaime G. Carbonell, Carnegie Mellon University, Pittsburgh, PA, USA
Jörg Siekmann, University of Saarland, Saarbrücken, Germany

Volume Editors

Pablo Noriega
Instituto de Investigación en Inteligencia Artificial, CSIC, Barcelona, Spain
E-mail: pablo@iiia.csic.es

Javier Vázquez-Salceda
Universitat Politècnica de Catalunya, Barcelona, Spain, E-mail: jvazquez@lsi.upc.edu

Guido Boella
Università di Torino, Torino, Italy, E-mail: guido@di.unito.it

Olivier Boissier
Ecole Nationale Supérieure des Mines, Saint-Etienne, France
E-mail: Olivier.Boissier@emse.fr

Virginia Dignum
Universiteit Utrecht, Utrecht, The Netherlands, E-mail: virginia@cs.uu.nl

Nicoletta Fornara
Università della Svizzera Italiana, Lugano, Switzerland
E-mail: nicoletta.fornara@lu.unisi.ch

Eric Matson
Wright State University, Dayton, OH, USA, E-mail: eric.matson@wright.edu

Library of Congress Control Number: 2007932915

CR Subject Classification (1998): I.2.1, D.2, F.3, D.1, C.2.4, D.3

LNCS Sublibrary: SL 7 – Artificial Intelligence

ISSN	0302-9743
ISBN-10	3-540-74457-6 Springer Berlin Heidelberg New York
ISBN-13	978-3-540-74457-3 Springer Berlin Heidelberg New York

Springer is a part of Springer Science+Business Media

springer.com

© Springer-Verlag Berlin Heidelberg 2007
Printed in Germany

Typesetting: Camera-ready by author, data conversion by Scientific Publishing Services, Chennai, India
Printed on acid-free paper   SPIN: 12113002   06/3180   5 4 3 2 1 0

Preface

In recent years, social and organizational aspects of agency have become major research topics in MAS. Recent applications of MAS on Web services, grid computing and ubiquitous computing highlight the need for using these aspects in order to ensure social order within such environments. Openness, heterogeneity, and scalability of MAS, in turn, pose new demands on traditional MAS interaction models and bring forward the need to look into the environment where agents interact and at different ways of constraining or regulating interactions. Consequently, the view of coordination and governance has been expanding to entertain not only an agent-centric perspective but societal and organization-centric views as well.

The overall problem of analyzing the social, legal, economic, and technological dimensions of agent organizations, and the co-evolution of agent interactions, provide theoretically demanding and interdisciplinary research questions at different levels of abstraction. The MAS research community has addressed these issues from different perspectives that have gradually become more cohesive around the four notions in the title to the workshop: coordination, organization, institutions, and norms. The COIN workshops are thus designed to consolidate the subject by providing focus events that reach researchers from diverse communities working in related topics and facilitate more systematic discussion of themes that have been treated from various perspectives.

This year, the COIN workshops were hosted during AAMAS 2006, (on June 9, in Hakodate, Japan) and ECAI 2006 (on August 28, in Riva del Garda, Italy). The papers contained in this volume are the revised versions of a selection of those that were presented in these workshops.

We want to express our gratitude to the Program Committee members, the additional reviewers, the participants of workshops, and most particularly to the authors for their respective contributions. We also want to thank the organizers of the Fifth International Joint Conference on Autonomous Agents and Multi-agent Systems in Hakodate and of the 17th European Conference in Artificial Intelligence in Riva del Garda, for hosting and supporting the organization of the workshops, Finally, we would also like to acknowledge the encouragement and support from Springer, in the person of Alfred Hofmann, for the publication of this second volume of COIN workshops.

COIN@AAMAS06: Virginia Dignum
Nicoletta Fornara
Pablo Noriega
COIN@ECAI06: Guido Boella
Olivier Boissier
Eric Matson
Javier Vázquez-Salceda

Vorwort

Organization

COIN@AAMAS06 Program Committee

Guido Boella	Università di Torino, Italy
Olivier Boissier	ENS Mines Saint-Etienne, France
Stephen Cranefield	University of Otago, New Zealand
Frank Dignum	Utrecht University, The Netherlands
Carl Hewitt	MIT, USA
Catholijn Jonker	Radboud University Nijmegen, The Netherlands
Christian Lemaître	Universidad Autónoma Metropolitana, Mexico
Gabriela Lindemann	Humboldt University in Berlin, Germany
Henrique Lopes Cardoso	Universidade do Porto, Portugal
Fabiola López y López	Benemérita Universidad Autónoma de Puebla, Mexico
Michael Luck	University of Southampton, UK
Eric Matson	Wright State University, USA
Eugenio Oliveira	Universidade do Porto, Portugal
Andrea Omicini	Università di Bologna, Italy
Anja Oskamp	Free University Amsterdam, The Netherlands
Sascha Ossowski	University Rey Juan Carlos, Spain
Julian Padget	University of Bath, UK
Adrian Perreau de Pinninck	IIIA-CSIC, Spain
Alessandro Provetti	Università degli Studi di Messina, Italy
Luciano dos Reis Coutinho	University of Sao Paulo, Brazil
Ana Paula Rocha	Universidade do Porto, Portugal
Juan Antonio Rodríguez Aguilar	IIIA-CSIC, Spain
Rossella Rubino	Università di Bologna, Italy
Franco Salvetti	Università degli Studi di Messina, Italy
Jaime Simão Sichman	University of Sao Paulo, Brazil
Carles Sierra	IIIA-CSIC, Spain
Liz Sonenberg	University of Melbourne, Australia
Wamberto Vasconcelos	University of Aberdeen, UK
Javier Vázquez-Salceda	Universitat Politècnica de Catalunya, Spain
Mario Verdicchio	Politecnico di Milano, Italy
Marina de Vos	University of Bath, UK
Pinar Yolum	Bogazici University, Turkey
Franco Zambonelli	Università di Modena e Reggio Emilia, Italy

COIN@ECAI06 Program Committee

Ulises Cortés	Universitat Politècnica de Catalunya, Spain
Yves Demazeau	LEIBNIZ, France
Virginia Dignum	University of Utrecht, The Netherlands
Jomi Fred Hubner	FURB Blumenau, Brazil
Catholijn Jonker	Radboud Universiteit Nijmegen, The Netherlands
Victor Lesser	University of Massachussetts-Amherst, USA
Gabriela Lindemann	Humboldt University, Germany
Pablo Noriega	IIIA-CSIC, Spain
Andrea Omicini	University of Bologna, Italy
Sascha Ossowski	University Rey Juan Carlos, Spain
Julian Padget	University of Bath, UK
Juan Manuel Serrano	University Rey Juan Carlos, Spain
Onn Shehory	IBM Research Labs, Isreal
Jaime Simão Sichman	University of Sao Paulo, Brazil
Catherine Tessier	ONERA, France
Leender van der Torre	University of Luxembourg, Luxembourg

Workshop Organizers

Guido Boella	Università di Torino, Dipartimento di Informatica, Turin, Italy guido@di.unito.it
Olivier Boissier	Ecole Nationale Supérieure des Mines, Saint-Etienne, France, Olivier.Boissier@emse.fr
Virginia Dignum	Institute for Computing and Information Sciences, Utrecht University, The Netherlands, virginia@cs.uu.nl
Nicoletta Fornara	Università della Svizzera Italiana (University of Lugano) Faculty of Communication Sciences, Lugano, Switzerland fornaran@lu.unisi.ch
Eric Matson	Department of Computer Science and Engineering, Wright State University, Dayton, Ohio, USA, eric.matson@wright.edu
Pablo Noriega	Instituto de Investigación en Inteligencia Artificial, Consejo Superior de Investigaciones Científicas, Barcelona, Spain pablo@iiia.csic.es
Javier Vázquez-Salceda	Universitat Politècnica de Catalunya, Departament de Llenguatges i Sistemes Informàtics, Barcelona, Spain jvazquez@lsi.upc.edu

Table of Contents

IV   NORM EVOLUTION AND DYNAMICS

V   AUTONOMY, COORDINATION AND SOCIAL ORDER

Part I
MODELLING AND ANALYZING ORGANIZATIONS

Structural Aspects of the Evaluation of Agent Organizations

Davide Grossi[1], Frank Dignum[1], Virginia Dignum[1], Mehdi Dastani[1],
and Làmber Royakkers[2]

[1]Institute of Information and Computing Sciences, Utrecht University,
Utrecht, The Netherlands
{davide,dignum,virginia,mehdi}@cs.uu.nl
[2]Department of Technology Management, Eindhoven University of Technology,
Eindhoven, The Netherlands
L.M.M.Royakkers@tm.tue.nl

Abstract. A multi-agent system can be analyzed and specified as an organization consisting of roles and their relations. The performance of an organization depends on many factors among which the type of its organizational structure, i.e., the set of relations holding between its roles. This work focuses on the structure of organizations and addresses the issue of the analysis, evaluation, and comparison of organizational structures which can contribute to develop general methods for the assessment of multi-agent systems' performance. Specifically, quantitative concepts from graph theory are used to provide numerical analyses of organizational structures. It is argued that these analyzes can be used for evaluating to what extent an organizational structure exhibits some characteristic properties such as robustness, flexibility and efficiency.

1 Introduction

A great deal of ongoing research in the field of organization-based multi-agent systems (MAS) is devoted to comparing and evaluating different types of organizations and their performance. Work on these issues varies from surveys comparing organizational paradigms [6], to frameworks for representing and verifying organizational designs [7,19], to studies concerning properties and performance of specific types of organizations [13,17].

The present paper aims at contributing to the establishment of a number of techniques for evaluating MAS organizations and their performance. The notion of organization plays an important role in multi-agent systems, which is also reflected in many agent-oriented software methodologies (cf. GAIA, TROPOS). The performance of different organizations depends on organizations' characteristics such as robustness, flexibility, and efficiency. For example, hierarchies are known not to perform well in rapidly changing environments because of their poor flexibility. The paper is based on the intuition that a connection can be drawn between some of these characteristics and graph-theoretical properties of the structure of organizations. For example, flexibility depends on how strongly the roles in the organization are connected with one another. The notion of flexibility, though complex and multi-faceted, can definitely be correlated

P. Noriega et al. (Eds.): COIN 2006 Workshops, LNAI 4386, pp. 3–18, 2007.
© Springer-Verlag Berlin Heidelberg 2007

with structural aspects of the organization. Intuitively, the more are the connections between the roles in the organization, the more flexible is the organization. The point is to relate the notion of flexibility to precise properties of the organizational structure. Given an organization, can we say it is flexible? And how flexible? Is it more flexible than another one as far as structure is concerned? How can a designer foster flexibility in a MAS just working on its structure? These types of questions constitute, in a nutshell, the target of the present work.

We claim that an investigation of this connection is important for the development of appropriate methods for comparing and evaluating different types of organizations and their performances. In order to tackle the evaluation problem, "the space of organizational options must be mapped, and their relative benefits and costs understood" [6], and to provide such a "map" a rigorous analysis of organizational structure plays a crucial role. The perspective chosen consists thus in addressing the evaluation issue from a structural perspective, that is to say, analyzing the organizational structure of MAS and providing a way to rigorously describe the pros and cons of them which lie in their structures.

We will proceed as follows. Firstly (Section 3), building on the results presented in [3] (briefly recapitulated in Section 2) we investigate a number of simple equations which can provide ways of measuring to what extent a given organizational structure enjoys some specific graph-theoretical properties. For instance, to what degree is the structure connected? These measures already provide a way to evaluate, in an exact fashion, the adherence of organizational structures to structural constraints a designer might take into consideration. Secondly (Section 4), the proposed measures are linked to commonly used criteria for the classification and evaluation of organizations. The criteria on which we focus are robustness, flexibility and efficiency. We show then (Section 5) how these criteria can conflict with each other, and how to ground a structural analysis of these conflicts as well. Conclusions follow in Section 6.

2   Organizational Structure

2.1   Some Terminology

Before getting started it is worth recollecting some standard graph theoretical notions which will be used in the proceeding of the paper. An R_k-path (of length n) is a sequence $\langle x_1, ..., x_{n+1} \rangle$ of distinct elements of $Roles$ s.t. $\forall x_i \; 1 \leq i \leq n$, $(x_i, x_{i+1}) \in R_k$. A R_k-semipath (of length n) is a sequence $\langle x_1, ..., x_{n+1} \rangle$ of distinct elements of $Roles$ s.t. $\forall x_i \; 1 \leq i \leq n$, $(x_i, x_{i+1}) \in R_k$ or $(x_{i+1}, x_i) \in R_k$. A $source$ in $Roles$ is an element s s.t. $\forall d \in Roles$ with $d \neq s$ there exists a R_k-path from s to d. The $indegree$ $id_k(d)$ of a point d in structure k is the number of elements d_1 s.t. $(d_1, d) \in R_k$. The $outdegree$ $od_k(d)$ of a point d in structure k is the number of elements d_1 s.t. $(d, d_1) \in R_k$. We say a point d to be incident w.r.t. a k link if $id_k(d) \leq 1$, and it is said to have emanating k links if $od_k(d) \leq 1$.

2.2   Representing Organizational Structures

In [3] a view on organizational structure has been proposed, inspired by foundational work on the theory of organizations [11,15], which is based on the claim that organizations do not exhibit only one structural dimension, but rather a multiplicity of interrelated dimensions, the dimensions of *power, coordination* and *control*. A natural way of modeling this notion of organizational structure is via directed graphs, which we represent here as systems of relations.

Definition 1. (Organizational structure)
An organizational structure OS is a tuple:

$$\langle Roles, R_{Pow}, R_{Coord}, R_{Contr} \rangle$$

where Roles is the finite set of roles, and $R_{Pow}, R_{Coord}, R_{Contr}$ are three irreflexive binary relations on Roles characterizing the Power, respectively, the Coordination and the Control structures.

For every R_k s.t. $k \in \{Pow, Coord, Contr\}$, we denote with $Roles_k$ the smallest subset of $Roles$ such that, if $(x, y) \in R_k$ then $x, y \in Roles_k$. In other words, sets $Roles_k$ denote the set of roles involved in the structural dimension k. Each digraph $\langle Roles_k, R_k \rangle$ in OS will be also referred to as the *structural dimension k of OS*.

Some observations are in order. First, it is worth noticing that in [3] the enactment relations between agents and roles are also included under the notion of organizational structure . In that work, it was necessary to include agents in the explicit representation of the structure in order to give an account of the effects that structural links bear on agents' performance. That study proposes also a formal analysis of the meaning of structural links in terms of the effects that they have on the activities of the agents playing roles in the organization. To briefly recapitulate it, the *power structure* defines the task delegation patterns possible within the organization. The *coordination structure* concerns the flow of knowledge within the organization, and the *control structure* has finally to do with the task recovery functions of the organization. In other words, the existence of a power link between role a and role b implies that every delegation of tasks from agent a (agent enacting role a) to agent b (agent enacting role b) ends up in the creation of an obligation directed to agent b. If a and b are connected via a coordination link, then every information act from a to b ends up in creating the corresponding knowledge in agent b. Finally, a control link between a and b implies that agent a has to monitor the activities of agent b, possibly taking over the tasks of agent b which have not been accomplished. In the present work however, such concern about the "semantics" of the structural links is left aside, and the main focus is settled only on the structural configurations linking the roles of the organization. This emphasizes also the generality of the method proposed here. In fact, the technical results that are going to be presented in Section 3 abstract from the meaning attached to the links, and can thus be applied to any kind of organizational structure representable in the fashion of Definition 1.

Second, we consider the roles on which the organizational structure ranges (i.e., the elements of set $Roles$) to be enacted by one and only one agent. The reason for this choice is illustrated by the following example. Suppose we need to model an organization for a soccer team implementing a 4-3-3 strategy. in such a way that the organizational structure inherent in the strategy is made explicit. Three roles can be defined in every team: 'attacker', 'defender' and 'midfielder', which are connected by appropriate power, control and coordination relations. An option would be to model the organization via imposing complex enactment constraints such as: "the role 'attacker' should be enacted by three agents such that the first agent should communicate with the third one, the second agent should monitor the first and third ones, etc.". However, this would make implicit in the enactment constraints the power, coordination and control links that are present between all the various attackers in the 4-3-3 strategy. A better option would be to explicitly define three new roles, which can be seen as specializations of the 'attacker' role and which can be enacted by only one agent. The organizational links existing between these three new roles could thus be made explicit, and the resulting organizational structure satisfactorily modeled. This is the perspective we assume here. In practice, this boils down to a modeling issue: if two agents enacting a same role have to be connected by power coordination or control links, then two different roles have to be specified which substitute the first one and which are played by only one agent. This finer level of granularity is essential in order to suitably evaluate the adherence of the organizations to desired criteria, which constitute the primary target of the paper: for example, is the 4-3-3 organization flexible? An analysis at a level where roles do not specify the precise relative positions of all agents with respect to all the structural dimensions would fall short, missing many relevant structural links. It follows from this distinction that a study of the organizational structure ranging on role types would abstract from those power, coordination, and control links that might be present between role tokens specializing the same role type (for instance the three attackers in a 4-3-3 strategy). Here we are instead interested in the analysis of structure at the level of the actual agents' positions within the organization, and thus at a finer level of granularity. The elements of the set *Roles* in an *OS* are then to be considered role tokens. In the rest of the paper, if not stated otherwise, we use the word role intending role-token.

Finally, besides the analysis of the power, coordination and control dimensions, [3] proposes a number of 'soundness' properties of organizational structures, which concern the interplay between the different structural dimensions.

Definition 2. (Sound *OS*)
A sound organizational structure is a tuple: $\langle Roles, R_{Pow}, R_{Coord}, R_{Contr} \rangle$ *where Roles is the finite set of roles, and* $R_{Pow}, R_{Coord}, R_{Contr}$ *are three irreflexive binary relations on Roles such that* $\forall r, s \in Roles$:

$$(r, s) \in R_{Pow} \Rightarrow \text{ there exists a } R_{Coord}\text{-path from } r \text{ to } s;$$
$$(r, s) \in R_{Pow} \Rightarrow \text{ there exists a } t \in Roles \text{ s.t. } R_{Contr}(t, s).$$

The occurrence of a power relation between role r and role s requires: the existence of a (finite) coordination path from r to s so that effective informative actions can transmit the relevant knowledge of agents enacting role r to agents enacting role s; and the existence of at least one element t (which, notice, might be r itself) which is in a control relation with s.

3 Measuring Structure

This section presents some equations measuring specific graph-theoretical aspects of organizational structures[1].

---

[1] Equations 2, 3 and 4 below are an adaptation of equations presented in [8].

3.1 Completeness, Connectedness, Economy

Completeness and connectedness of an OS have to do with how strongly roles are linked with one another within one of the structural dimensions k. How much does the given structure approximate the structure where all directed links are present (*completeness*)? And how much is the given structure split in fragments (*connectedness*)?

$$\text{Completeness}_k(OS) = \frac{|R_k|}{|Roles_k| * (|Roles_k| - 1)} \tag{1}$$

$$\text{Connectedness}_k(OS) = 1 - \frac{|\text{DISCON}_k|}{|Roles_k| * (|Roles_k| - 1)} \tag{2}$$

with $|R_k| > 0$ and DISCON_k is the set of ordered pairs (x, y) of $Roles_k$ s.t. there is neither a R_k-semipath from x to y nor from y to x, i.e., the set of disconnected ordered pairs of the structural dimension $\langle Roles_k, R_k \rangle$. The condition $|R_k| > 0$ states that the structural dimension k does indeed exist. If the structure does not exist it cannot be measured. As a consequence, $\text{Completeness}_k > 0$. Stating that $\text{Completeness}_k(OS) = 0$ means thus that $R_k = \emptyset$ and hence that no structure at all is given. In practice, formula 1 measures the fraction of the actual links of the dimension $\langle Roles_k, R_k \rangle$ on all the available ones and formula 2 measures how 'not disconnected' that dimension is. With respect to connectedness, an important notion is that of cutpoint or, in an organizational reading, *liason role* [4], i.e., a role whose removal decreases the connectedness of the structure.

The *economy* of a given OS expresses a kind of balance between the two concerns of keeping the structure connected and of minimizing the number of links, i.e., minimizing completeness:

$$\text{Economy}_k(OS) =$$

$$1 - \frac{|R_k| - (|Roles_k| - 1)}{|Roles_k| * (|Roles_k| - 1) - (|Roles_k| - 1)} \tag{3}$$

with $|R_k| > 0$. The equation is based on the intuition according to which the most 'economical' digraph of n points consists of $n - 1$ links, i.e., the minimum number of links which is still sufficient to keep the digraph connected. Indeed, the nominator of the fraction, consists of the number of links in the structural dimension k which are in excess or in defect w.r.t. the optimum of $n - 1$ links. The denominator denotes instead the absolute number of links in excess in k. If $|R_k| = n - 1$ then the value of $\text{Economy}_k(OS)$ is optimal, i.e., equal to 1. The equation measures, therefore, how much k is 'not expensive' in terms of links. Notice that $\text{Economy}_k(OS) = 1$ does not imply $\text{Connectedness}_k(OS) = 1$, it does only imply that there are enough links in R_k for it to be possibly connected. If the existence of symmetric links in R_k is assumed, then $n - 1$ links are clearly not enough any more for guaranteeing connectedness. On the other hand, notice also that $\text{Economy}_k(OS)$ can assume a value greater than 1. That indicates a sort of '*over-efficiency*' of k. In this case, it is easy to see that, if $\text{Economy}_k(OS) > 1$ then $\text{Connectedness}_k(OS) < 1$. In other words, if the economy measures of OS is lower than the optimal value 1, then OS has more links than the ones necessary for OS to be connected. If economy is instead higher than the optimal value 1, than there are in OS too few links for it to be connected.

3.2   Unilaterality, Univocity, Flatness

The properties of unilaterality and univocity express the tendency of an OS to display, respectively, an orientation in its links (*unilaterality*), and the absence of redundant links ending up in the same role (*univocity*). Do the links of an OS always have a 'direction' or does the OS allow, so to say, 'peer-to-peer' connections? And how many of those connections are such that no role has more than one incident link of the same structural dimension?

$$\text{Unilaterality}_k(OS) = 1 - \frac{|\text{SIM}_k|}{|R_k|} \tag{4}$$

$$\text{Univocity}_k(OS) = \frac{|\text{IN}_k|}{|Roles_k|} \tag{5}$$

$$\text{Flatness}_k(OS) = 1 - \frac{|\text{CUT}_k|}{|Roles_k|} \tag{6}$$

with $|R_k| > 0$ and SIM_k denotes the set of links (x, y) in R_k s.t. (y, x) is also in R_k, i.e., $|\text{SIM}_k|$ is twice the number of symmetric links in k; IN_k denotes the set of roles x in $Roles_k$ s.t. $id_k(x) = 1$ or $id_k(x) = 0$, i.e., the set of roles which either have indegree equal to 1 in k or they are a source of k or of some subgraphs of k; and CUT_k denotes the set of roles x s.t. $od_k(x) \leq 1$ and $id_k(x) \leq 1$, that is to say, the set of roles which are at the same time addresser and addressee of k links. Intuitively, equation 4 measures how much asymmetry is present in k, while equation 5 measures how much a dimension k is univocal or "non ambiguous". The most univocal structures are assumed to be either the ones in which every point, except the source, has one and only one incident link (like in trees), or the ones in which exactly all points have only one incident link (like in cycles). Finally, equation 6 measures the relative amount of points in dimension k which are not intermediate point in a k-path, in other words the amount of points the removal of which would not determine a cut in any k-path. Obviously, the lowest value of flatness is provided by cycles.

Intuitively, unilaterality has to do with the level of subordination present in a structure. Consider the R_{Coord} dimension. The higher the number of unilaterality, the lower the amount of 'peer-to-peer' information exchange within OS. Univocity has to do with the level of conflict and redundancies of a given structure. Consider the R_{Pow} dimension. The higher the level of univocity, the more unambiguous is the chain of commands, as well as the more fragile once a link happens to be removed. See also [2] for similar investigations on this issue. Flatness instead, has to do with the length of paths available within a given structure. We will see in Section 4 that long paths of the control dimension can be useful in order to implement levels of control on the controller roles themselves.

3.3   Detour, Overlap, Cover and Chain

The properties we address in this section do not concern structural dimensions taken in isolation, like the one just investigated, but instead how the different dimensions of an OS interact with one another. This constitutes a crucial undertaking, though hardly investigated [4].

The properties we call *detour* and *overlap* regard the degree to which a structural dimension j 'follows' a structural dimension k, meaning by this the degree to which j establishes corresponding paths for each link of k, so that the roles that are related by R_k links are the same as those that are related by R_j-paths.

$$\text{Detour}_{jk}(OS) = \frac{|\text{PATH}_{jk}|}{|R_k|} \qquad (7)$$

with $|R_k| > 0$ and the set PATH_{jk} is defined as the set of ordered pairs (x, y) s.t. $(x, y) \in R_k$ and there exists a R_j-path from x to y. Equation 7 measures the relative amount of R_j-paths between the elements of $Roles_k$ which have the same direction of the links in R_k. A special case of detour is the overlap. In fact, to measure how much does a dimension j overlap with a dimension k, it suffices to define a set LINK_{jk} corresponding to a PATH_{jk} where the R_j-paths are of length 1, i.e., simple links, and hence: $\text{LINK}_{jk} \equiv R_k \cap R_j$. A set LINK_{jk} consists then of all the pairs (x, y) which are in R_k and in R_j, that is to say, of all x, y which are linked in R_k and in R_j.

$$\text{Overlap}_{jk}(OS) = \frac{|\text{LINK}_{jk}|}{|R_k|} \qquad (8)$$

with $|R_k| > 0$. Intuitively, the more j-pairs correspond to k-pairs, the more j overlaps k in OS.

The property we call *in-cover* concerns the extent to which all the incident roles of k are also incident roles of a dimension j. In other words, we say that a dimension j *in-covers* a dimension k if all the roles which are addressees of a k link, are also addressees of a j link.

$$\text{InCover}_{jk}(OS) = \frac{|\text{IN}_j^+ \cap \text{IN}_k^+|}{|\text{IN}_k^+|} \qquad (9)$$

with $|R_k| > 0$ and the set IN_i^+ is defined as the set of all elements x in $Roles_i$ such that $id_i(x) \leq 1$. The equation describes then how many of the incident roles of k are also incident roles in j.

The usefulness of these measures for capturing aspects of the structural interplay can already be shown in relation with Definition 2. Readers might have noticed that, via the equations just exposed, it is possible to provide a quantification of the degree to which a given OS adheres to the soundness principle concerning the interplay of the three dimensions of power, coordination and control. In fact, if we have $\text{Detour}_{Coord-Power}(OS) = 1$ and $\text{InCover}_{Contr-Pow}(OS) = 1$ then, following Definition 2, OS is sound. Lower degrees of these measures would thus determine lower adherence to the soundness principle. Notice also that maximum soundness is trivially obtained via an overlap of both coordination and control structures on the power structure: that is to say, if $\text{Overlap}_{Coord-Power}(OS) = 1$ and $\text{Overlap}_{Contr-Power}(OS) = 1$, then OS is (maximally) sound.

Equation 9 can be easily modified in order to capture analogous properties which we call *out-cover* and *chain*. The first one concerns the extent to which all the roles with emanating links in a dimension k are also roles with emanating links in a dimension j.

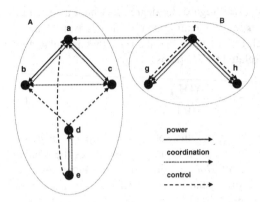

	Pow	Coord	Contr
Compl.$_k(OS)$	$\frac{5}{56}$	$\frac{11}{56}$	$\frac{5}{56}$
Conn.$_k(OS)$	$\frac{1}{4}$	$\frac{31}{56}$	$\frac{26}{56}$
Econ.$_k(OS)$	$\frac{51}{49}$	$\frac{45}{49}$	$\frac{51}{49}$
Unil.$_k(OS)$	1	$\frac{3}{11}$	1
Univ.$_kOS$	1	$\frac{5}{8}$	1
Flat.$_kOS$	1	$\frac{1}{2}$	1

power
coordination
control

	Coord-Pow	Contr-Pow	Pow-Contr	Coord-Contr	Contr-Coord	Pow-Coord
Detour$_{jk}(OS)$	1	$\frac{2}{5}$	$\frac{2}{5}$	$\frac{2}{5}$	$\frac{2}{9}$	$\frac{4}{9}$
Overlap$_{jk}(OS)$	1	$\frac{2}{5}$	$\frac{2}{5}$	$\frac{2}{5}$	$\frac{2}{9}$	$\frac{5}{9}$
InCover$_{jk}(OS)$	1	$\frac{4}{5}$	$\frac{4}{5}$	1	$\frac{5}{6}$	$\frac{5}{6}$
OutCover$_{jk}(OS)$	1	$\frac{2}{3}$	$\frac{2}{3}$	$\frac{2}{3}$	$\frac{2}{5}$	$\frac{3}{5}$
Chain$_{jk}(OS)$	$\frac{2}{3}$	$\frac{1}{3}$	$\frac{1}{3}$	$\frac{1}{3}$	$\frac{3}{5}$	$\frac{2}{5}$

Fig. 1. Example of structural measures

The second one concerns the extent to which a dimension j is 'incident' to the emanating links in a dimension k, in the sense that the roles with incident links in j contain the roles with emanating links in k.

$$\text{OutCover}_{jk}(OS) = \frac{|\text{OUT}_j^+ \cap \text{OUT}_k^+|}{|\text{OUT}_k^+|}, \tag{10}$$

$$\text{Chain}_{jk}(OS) = \frac{|\text{IN}_j^+ \cap \text{OUT}_k^+|}{|\text{OUT}_k^+|}, \tag{11}$$

with $|R_k| > 0$, IN_i^+ is as defined above and OUT_i^+ is the set of all elements x in $Roles_i$ such that $od_i(x) \leq 1$. Notice that the chain measure can be viewed as an inter-structural version of the flatness measure.

Before ending the section, it is worth noticing that all structural measures defined above range between 0 and 1 except economy which can get values higher than 1. Despite this, we saw that the optimal value of Economy$_k(OS)$ is still 1 (higher values determine over-efficiency). Whether a given OS enjoys a property at its optimal level, can therefore be handled as a matter of approximation of the corresponding measure to 1: the more Economy$_k(OS)$ approximates value 1 the more OS enjoys economy, etc.

3.4   An Example

In order to illustrate the above measures, an example is here provided and discussed. Consider the OS depicted in Figure 1. It is specified as follows:

$Roles = \{a, b, c, d, e, f, g, h\}$,
$R_{Pow} = \{(a, b), (a, c), (e, d), (f, g), (f, h)\}$,
$R_{Coord} = \{(a, b), (a, c), (b, a), (c, a), (b, c), (c, b), (e, d), (f, g), (f, h)\}$,
$R_{Contr} = \{(d, b), (e, a), (d, c), (f, g), (f, h)\}$.
We then have that: $Roles_{Pow} = Roles_{Coord} = Roles_{Contr} = \{a, b, c, d, e, f, g, h\}$.

Such an OS specifies an organization where two substructures A and B are connected via a symmetric coordination link. It is what we may call, following [6], a form of *federation*.

Substructure B is a typical form of highly centralized hierarchy: all connections move from the source f to the subordinated roles g and h. Indeed, it exhibits the optimal level of *efficiency, unilaterality, univocity* and *flatness* (equal to 1) for all three structural dimensions. Completeness and connectedness are also the same for all three dimensions, respectively equal to $\frac{2}{6}$ and to 1. Besides, there is a full reciprocal *overlap* (equal to 1) of all the three dimensions which, as showed above in Section 3.3, implies the soundness of the structure.

Substructure A, instead, displays a slightly more complex pattern. It hides two disconnected power hierarchies composed by roles a, b and c and, respectively, roles d and e. In fact, we have that Completeness$_{Pow}(A) = \frac{3}{20}$ and Connectedness$_{Pow}(A) = \frac{7}{10}$. Besides, the coordination structure is much more complete than the power one (Completeness$_{Coord}(A) = \frac{7}{20}$). This is due to the full connection holding between roles a, b and c. As to the interplay of the different dimensions in A, it is easily seen that OS is not maximally sound since InCover$_{Contr-Pow}(A) = \frac{2}{3}$. This is due to the fact that role d is not object of control although it is subordinated, in the power structure, to role e. In case e would delegate to d a task, a failure in accomplishing this task would not be recovered. This would definitely constitute a weak spot in an organization designed according to this structure. Interestingly, there is minimum overlap between R_{Contr} and R_{Pow}: Overlap$_{Contr-Pow}(A) = 0$. This embodies a sort of complete "*separation of concerns*" between the power and the control dimensions, in the sense that controller roles are never in a power position with respect to the controlled roles. This is obviously a sensible design requirement for preventing connivances between controllers and roles in power positions. On the other hand, OutCover$_{Pow-Contr}(A) = \frac{1}{2}$ and OutCover$_{Coord-Contr}(A) = \frac{1}{2}$ show that, although no role is at the same time in a power and in a control position w.r.t. the same roles, there are controllers in A (one out of two) which have the possibility to delegate tasks and communicate with other roles (role e). Worth noticing is also the following: Chain$_{Contr-Pow}(A) = \frac{1}{2}$, that is, one out of two roles in a power position are subjected to control. Interestingly, the only uncontrolled role in a power position is the controller role e itself, and in fact no control of the controller is implemented: Flatness$_{Contr}(A) = 1$.

After discussing the two substructures in isolation we focus now on the federation OS emerging by the joining of the two substructures via a symmetric coordination link between roles a and f. The resulting structural measures of OS are the one listed in figure 1. Let us comment upon them. First of all, none of the three dimensions is connected (with coordination being the most connected among the three). This means that within each dimension, there exist unrelated clusters of roles. In particular, the roles in a controlling position within substructure A cannot communicate with the rest of the federation. It follows that all dimensions happen to display high values of economy and even over-efficiency, like in the case of power and control. As to the degree of unilaterality and univocity, power and control enjoy a degree equal to 1, and they thus display typically hierarchical features. On the other hand, coordination is highly reciprocal except, as we saw, within substructure B and it maintains a high degree of univocity keeping therefore a low level of redundancies in coordination as well. As to the interplay between the different dimensions, OS inherits the flaw of substructure A which prevents it from enjoying the maximum degree of measure InCover$_{Contr-Pow}$, jeopardizing soundness. Coordination, instead, fully overlaps power guaranteeing the necessary flow of communication after the delegation activity. In the tables in Figure 1 more measures concerning OS are provided which, for reasons of space limitation, cannot be commented upon here.

4   Criteria and Structure

As the example showed, the structural measures captured in equations (1)-(11) would be already enough for a quantified comparison of organizational structures. What is still lacking, is to give those measures an 'organizational meaning', so to say, in terms of the criteria of robustness, flexibility and efficiency.

In this section we ground such a connection. The structural measures captured in equations (1)-(5) and (7)-(11) are used to provide hints about the adherence of a given organizational structure to criteria commonly utilized for the classification of organizations. Questions we aim at shedding light on are of the type: Is the coordination structure flexible (enough)? Is the power structure efficient (enough)? Is the interplay between power and control structure robust (enough)? etc.

Notice that we do not claim that those notions can be understood only on the basis of structural considerations. We rather address what, just by looking at the structure of an organization, can be said about its robustness, flexibility and efficiency. As a matter of fact, considerations about structure have always been relevant both in organizational sciences and multi-agent systems for explaining why, for instance, a network is more flexible than a hierarchy. Here, we try to ground this kind of considerations on a more solid and fully-fledged base.

Before doing this, it is important to stress that the structural analysis of the general criteria of robustness, flexibility, and efficiency presupposes the semantics of structural links exposed in [3] and summarized in Section 2.

4.1   Robustness

"Robustness is simply a measure of how stable the yield is in the face of anticipated risks. That is, the maintenance of some desired system characteristics despite fluctuations in the behavior of its component parts or its environment [...]. Adding robustness thus adds complexity" [18].

Robustness asks for redundancies in the structural dimensions used for dividing tasks within an organizations, i.e., the power and the coordination structures. Redundancy for a power structure means low values of the Univocity$_{Pow}$ measure, and for a coordination structure also a low degree of the Unilaterality$_{Coord}$ in order to allow for symmetric coordination links. In particular, symmetric coordination links can substitute broken power links allowing for bilateral negotiations of tasks to replace direct delegation. Therefore, a high Overlap$_{Coord-Pow}$ would be a sign of robustness.

For the same reasons the control structure plays an important role for the robustness of an organization allowing for failure detection and reaction. It can be required that each role in the power and coordination structures is controlled, suggesting a high degree of the following measures: Chain$_{Contr-Pow}$, i.e., the control of agents in power positions; Chain$_{Contr-Coord}$, i.e., the control of roles from which coordination links depart; InCover$_{Contr-Coord}$, i.e., the control of roles to which coordination links are directed. Furthermore, every role in the control structure can be required to have a high in-degree (every role is monitored by many other roles), which corresponds to a low level of Univocity$_{Contr}$. The number of control levels can also be increased, so that as many controllers as possible are, in turn, controlled. This has to do with the well-known "control of the controllers" issue which we already touched upon in [3] and corresponds to a low degree of Flatness$_{Contr}$ (long control paths are enabled).

On the other hand, a good control structure is of no use if the controlling roles have no capabilities or no power or coordination connections to follow up on perceived failures. This can be fostered via high values of, respectively, OutCover$_{Pow-Contr}$ and OutCover$_{Pow-Coord}$. In addition, the coordination structure determines how well information can disseminate over the organization. For robustness it is important that information about failures can spread to the roles that can take appropriate action. Also this structure can serve as a back up for a failure of the power structure. So, one can easily claim that the more complete and more connected (Completeness$_{Coord}$ and Connectedness$_{Coord}$) the coordination structure is the more robust the organization is.

To sum up, the level of robustness of an organization, from the point of view of its organizational structure, can be evaluated considering the following structural measures:

Completeness$_{Coord}$	1	Overlap$_{Coord-Pow}$	1
Connectedness$_{Coord}$	1	Chain$_{Contr-Pow}$	1
Univocity$_{Pow}$	0	Chain$_{Contr-Coord}$	1
Unilaterality$_{Coord}$	0	InCover$_{Contr-Coord}$	1
Univocity$_{Contr}$	0	OutCover$_{Pow-Contr}$	1
Flatness$_{Contr}$	0	OutCover$_{Pow-Coord}$	1

The 1 and 0 symbol indicate the value which is considered to maximize robustness with respect to that measure. For instance, the maximum enhancement of robustness obtainable via modification of the connectedness measure is yielded by value 1. In other words, the more Connectedness$_{Coord}$ approximates 1, the more the structure is robust. As to univocity the optimal value for increasing robustness is instead 0.

Getting back to the organizational structure OS discussed in the example above (Section 3.4), we see that the robustness criterion is not its forte. Nevertheless it does score well in the robustness-related measures concerning the interaction between the structures:

$$\text{OutCover}_{Pow-Contr}(OS) = \tfrac{2}{3}, \text{OutCover}_{Pow-Coord}(OS) = \tfrac{3}{5},$$
$$\text{Chain}_{Contr-Coord}(OS) = \tfrac{3}{5} \text{ and InCover}_{Contr-Coord}(OS) = \tfrac{5}{6}.$$

4.2 Flexibility

"Flexible organizations are a looser co-operative association than classic hierarchical organizations. [...] Flexible organizations are continually in flux and are able to adapt in a flexible way to changing circumstances" [14].

To make it more concrete, we look at the flexibility of an organizational structure as its ability to cope with changing tasks. It is clear that the capabilities required for the enactment of each role constitute a crucial issue. If all roles require the capability to perform any task at any moment, then all roles would be designed to cope with any different type of task. The actual structure does not really matter in this case, because no matter how a task is distributed over roles and how it is controlled it would be anyway performed. Given that the organization is sound, the information about the task is appropriately distributed, control is properly configured and the organization is thus as flexible as it can be.

Assuming a diversified distribution of capabilities among roles, flexibility of an organization amounts to decomposing a task in subtasks such that for every subtask a role can be found which is held to be capable to perform that subtask. This can be done via delegation through the power structure. However, an articulated power structure hinders flexibility constraining the distribution of tasks to predisposed patterns. This suggests that, for enhancing flexibility at a structural level, low degrees of both Completeness$_{Pow}$ and Connectedness$_{Pow}$ are required. Besides, it is worth noticing that a given power structure assumes that the role having the power to delegate a task is at least capable to perform those operations on the task that are needed before it can be delegated. This can be some preprocessing of a task or a decomposition of a task or even just a determination to which role the task should be delegated. Whenever a role does not have the capability to perform this operation for a new task, the processing of the task halts. Even if the subordinate roles could perform the task they would not get it and thus the task would not be performed.

The control structure might alleviate this effect in that it can function as a link between different parts of the power structure. Whenever an agent enacting a role in the power structure fails on (the distribution of) a task, its controller should react and have the power to redistribute the task, structurally: high values of Chain$_{Contr-Pow}$ and OutCover$_{Pow-Contr}$.

Network organizations and teams, instead, where no power structure exists, are commonly indicated as the paradigmatic example of flexible organizations [12]. In this type of organizations the specification of the capabilities required for each role cannot be complete since the nature of the tasks the organization has to fulfill is not exhaustively known in advance. What becomes essential is therefore a coordination structure through which the knowledge, concerning which agent might be capable to handle the new task, flows within the whole organization. The more roles are connected through this structure the more likely the right agent can be found to perform a new task. Completeness and connectivity (Completeness$_{Coord}$ and Connectedness$_{Coord}$) are thus directly linked also to the enhancement of the flexibility of an organization.

To recapitulate, these are the relevant measures for flexibility:

Completeness$_{Pow}$	0	Completeness$_{Coord}$	1
Connectedness$_{Pow}$	0	Connectedness$_{Coord}$	1
Chain$_{Contr-Pow}$	1	OutCover$_{Pow-Contr}$	1

Again, 1 and 0 indicate the measures' values which are considered to maximize flexibility.

With respect to the flexibility of the structure OS in the example, we see that it has indeed a small power structure (connectedness and completeness are very low) and a reasonably connected coordination structure (= $\frac{31}{56}$). These two aspects both enhance flexibility. This is indeed what we would expect, being OS a form of "federation", that is, a form of organization which retains some purely hierarchical aspects (in its substructures) but exhibiting better flexibility. It scores well also w.r.t. the OutCover measure between power and control: OutCover$_{Pow-Contr} = \frac{2}{3}$.

4.3   Efficiency

According to [1], efficiency mostly refers to the amount of resources used by the organization to perform its tasks. Organizational structure plays a role in this sense, since "links are not without cost in a social systems" [8].

There is a general assumption that high specialization of roles leads to more efficient performance; it is the old principle of the *division of labour*[2]. Within organizational theory as well as within AOSE (Agent Oriented Software Engineering) it is however known that there is a balance between specializing (and thus creating more roles) and the overhead this generates in the coordination of the tasks. Having less roles in the organizational structure leads to higher efficiency. But having too few roles leads to lower efficiency due to less appropriate performances of the tasks by the roles.

The existence of a power structure guarantees efficient distribution of tasks, and a tree is the most efficient structure to cover all roles. Such a structure is obtained imposing value 1 for all the following measures: Connectedness$_{Pow}$ (a disconnected power structure generates fragments with independent power), Economy$_{Pow}$ (maximum economy without over-efficiency), Unilaterality$_{Pow}$ (no peer-to-peer connections) and Univocity$_{Pow}$ (no conflicts in the chain of command). If every role is specialized to an extreme that all the capabilities required by the roles are disjunct, then every task can be distributed in only one way within the organization. Given that there is only one way of distributing the task, one can use a power structure reaching all roles to efficiently effectuate this.

---

[2] "The greatest improvement in the productive powers of labour [...] seem to have been the effects of the division of labour" ([16] p. 9).

As to coordination and control, economy (Economy) should also be required to be 1 in order to minimize the amount of links. Besides, the most efficient way in order to guarantee soundness (Definition 2) consists in mirroring the power dimension, therefore obtaining high levels for all measures of overlap, that is: Overlap w.r.t. the related dimensions of $Coord - Pow$, $Contr - Pow$, as well as $Pow - Coord$ and $Pow - Contr$ (overlap needs to hold in both directions in order to enforce coincidence). This keeps the number of links minimal and avoids the creation of further roles with mere coordination and control tasks. It follows that a fully hierarchical organization (such as substructure B described in the example of Section 3.4) where all structures follow the same pattern forms the most efficient organization possible.

These are the thus the measures we consider to be related to efficiency:

Connectedness$_{Pow}$	1	Unilaterality$_{Pow}$	1
Economy$_{Pow}$	1	Univocity$_{Pow}$	1
Economy$_{Coord}$	1	Economy$_{Contr}$	1
Overlap$_{Coord-Pow}$	1	Overlap$_{Contr-Pow}$	1
Overlap$_{Pow-Coord}$	1	Overlap$_{Pow-Contr}$	1

Again, 1 and 0 indicate the value which is considered to maximize efficiency with respect to the measure at issue.

The structure OS of the example incorporates a very efficient power structure: unilaterality and univocity are optimal (equal to 1) as well as the overlap between coordination and power. On the other hand, the power structure covers only a small fraction of the whole organization (Connectedness$_{Pow}(OS) = \frac{1}{4}$). As a consequence, distribution of tasks via delegation can only partially take place.

5   Tuning Structural Measures to Organizational Properties

At this stage the obvious question is whether organizations can be designed which maximize the adherence to all three properties at the same time. From a structural point of view and as intuition suggests, it is easy to show that this is not possible. Consider, for instance, the coordination structure. In fact, efficiency increases when Economy$_{Coord}$ approximates 1. Maximum robustness and flexibility both require Economy$_{Coord}$ equal to 0, while maximum efficiency requires Economy$_{Coord}$ equal to 1:

	Robust	Flexible	Efficient
Economy$_{Coord}$	0	0	1

Intuitively, both robustness and flexibility increase the number of structural links and thus the costs of the organizational overhead, while efficiency reduces these overhead costs. Similar problems exist, for instance, for the power structure. The robustness criterion requires as many redundancies as possible, and therefore low levels of univocity, while flexibility demands the structure to be as small as possible and therefore with very low degrees of completeness. A number of similar incompatibilities can be detected and mathematically investigated.

Since it is not possible to maximize the adherence to all properties at the same time, the point consists then in finding suitable compromise solutions.

A good option might be, for instance, to maximize all structural features at the same time getting a structure which exhibits Pareto efficiency w.r.t. the allocation of values to equations (1)-(11): an assignment of value to every equation should be found such that no other assignment exists which attributes a better value to one of the equations. This would be a typical compromise solution. Although for many applications this can be a good way to go, such a Pareto efficient structure would adhere to a reasonable extent to each criterion, but it would not exhibit optimal values in any of the investigated measures. A circumstance in which this solution would be sensible is when the environment is expected to change often while the organizational structure is not able to adapt. In that case a middle of the road solution can provide reasonable performances over time.

However, when the environment does not change that frequently (i.e. it is known in which kind of environment the organization should function) the issue amounts to what in organization theory is called "*synthesis problems*", that is, the questions concerning "which structures are best suited to solve optimally certain types of problems" [5]. Should for instance flexibility be privileged over efficiency? In other words, choices should be made between the concurrent criteria. An extensive analysis of the interdependencies between equations (1)-(11) could provide useful insights on this type of issues.

6   Conclusions and Future Work

The work addressed the issue of the influence of organizational structures on the performance of organizations, aiming at providing a rigorous method for analyzing, comparing and evaluating different types of structures. We proceeded as follows. First, making use of graph theory, we provided a number of meaningful measures for quantifying the adherence of organizational structures to specific structural features. Second, these measures have been used to ground a numerical analysis of the key organizational properties of robustness, efficiency and flexibility. Third, it has been shown that such an analysis pose the ground for an exact investigation of the extent to which those properties can conflict with each other, providing interesting information for a more aware design of organizational structures.

In future work we plan to extended this method in order to incorporate more structural measures and to account for more organizational criteria like, for example, the scalability of an organizational structure. Another issue worth a detailed investigation concerns the way the equations proposed in this work are related to each other also constitutes an issue worth pursuing in future researches. Finally, the framework and its results should be compared in details with approaches developed in the field of management sciences, such as [9,10], which bear many similarities both in purposes and technical solutions.

Acknowledgments. We would like to thank Dr. Juan A. Rodríguez-Aguilar for the useful pointers to relevant literature.

References

1. Etzioni, A.: Modern Organizations. Prentice-Hall, Englewood Cliffs (1964)
2. Friedell, M.F.: Organizations as semilattices. American Sociological Review 32, 46–54 (1967)
3. Grossi, D., Dignum, F., Dastani, M., Royakkers, L.: Foundations of organizational structures in multiagent systems. In: Proceedings of AAMAS'05, Fourth International Joint Conference on Autonomous Agents and Multiagent Systems, July 2005, pp. 690–697. ACM Press, New York (2005)
4. Harary, F.: Graph theoretic methods in the management sciences. Managemenet Science 5(4), 387–403 (1959)
5. Harary, F.: Status and contrastatus. Sociometry 22, 23–43 (1959)
6. Horling, B., Lesser, V.: A Survey of Multi-Agent Organizational Paradigms. Computer Science Technical Report 04-45, University of Massachusetts (May 2004)
7. Horling, B., Lesser, V.: Using ODML to model and design organizations for multi-agent systems. In: Boissier, O., Dignum, V., Matson, E., Sichman, J., Utrecht (eds.) Proceedings ofthe International Workshop on Organizations in Multi-Agent Systems (OOOP). AAMAS'05 (July 2005)
8. Krackhardt, D.: Graph theoretical dimensions of informal organizations. In: Carley, C.M., Prietula, M.J. (eds.) Computational Organization Theory, pp. 89–110. Lawrence Erlbaum Associates, Mahwah (1994)
9. Malone, T.W.: Modeling coordination in organizations and markets. Management Sciences 33(10), 1317–1332 (1987)
10. Malone, T.W., Smith, S.A.: Modeling the performance of organizational structures. Operational Research 36(3), 421–436 (1988)
11. Morgenstern, O.: Prolegomena to a theory of organizations. Manuscript (1951)
12. Powell, W.W.: Neither market nor hierarchy: Network forms of organizations. Research in Organizational Behavior 12, 295–336 (1990)
13. Scerri, P., Xu, Y., Liao, E., Lai, J., Sycara, K.: Scaling teamwork to very large teams. In: Proceedings of the Third International Joint Conference on Autonomous Agents and Multiagent Systems (AAMAS'04), ACM Press, New York (July 2004)
14. Schoemaker, M.: Identity in flexible organizations: Experiences. Dutch Organizations Creativity and Innovation Management 12 (December 2003)
15. Selznick, P.: Foundations of the theory of organization. American Sociological Review 13, 25–35 (1948)
16. Smith, A.: An Inquiry into the Nature and Causes of the Wealth of Nations. Methuen and Co, London (1776)
17. So, Y., Chon, K.: A performance model for tree-structuresd multiagent organizations in faulty environments. In: Boissier, O., Dignum, V., Matson, E., Sichman, J., Utrecht (eds.) Proceedings ofthe International Workshop on Organizations in Multi-Agent Systems (OOOP). AAMAS'05, July 2005 (2005)
18. Stimson, W.: The Robust Organization: Transforming Your Company Using Adaptive Design. Irwin Professional Publishing (1996)
19. van der Broek, E.L., Jonker, C.M., Sharpanskykh, A., Treur, J., Yolum, P.: Formal modeling and analysis of organizations. In: Boissier, O., Padget, J., Dignum, V., Lindemann, G., Matson, E., Ossowski, S., Sichman, J.S., Vázquez-Salceda, J. (eds.) Coordination, Organizations, Institutions, and Norms in Multi-Agent Systems. LNCS (LNAI), vol. 3913, pp. 18–34. Springer, Heidelberg (2006)

Integrating Trust in Virtual Organisations*

Ramón Hermoso, Holger Billhardt, and Sascha Ossowski

Artificial Intelligence Group
DATCCCIA - ESCET
University Rey Juan Carlos
{ramon.hermoso,holger.billhardt,sascha.ossowski}@urjc.es

Abstract. Organisational models cannot only be used to structure multiagent systems but also to express behaviour constraints for agents in open environments. However, sometimes these behaviour constraints cannot be exhaustively enforced, and some agents may transgress the norms put forward by a Virtual Organisation. This poses an additional burden on agents, as they cannot be sure that their acquaintances will behave as prescribed. Trust and reputation mechanisms are of particular relevance to this respect, as they are commonly used to infer expectations of future behaviour from past interactions.

In this paper we argue that, on the one hand, the a priori structure of Virtual Organisations can be useful to improve the efficiency of trust and reputation mechanisms, and that, on the other hand, such mechanisms provide relevant information for agents that are part of Virtual Organisations. For this purpose, we identify relevant aspects of existing organisational (meta-)models, and outline a reputation mechanism for Virtual Organisations that integrates these aspects. The dynamics of this mechanism is illustrated by an example.

1 Introduction

It is commonly agreed that the notion of organisation is of foremost importance to Multiagent Systems (MAS). In particular, organisational concepts are heavily used in the field of Agent-oriented Software Engineering [26]. In fact, it is tempting to maintain a tight coupling between a MAS, and the relevant features of the (human) organisation that it models, during the whole design process. Organisational concepts are often used as first-class abstractions that provide *structure* to the different models and stages of MAS design, and thus help designers to cope with high levels of complexity that MAS applications usually need to cope with [15].

When shifting the attention to *open* MAS, the *coercive* facets of organisational models gain relevance. Organisational abstractions are conceived as something aimed at limiting the freedom of choice of otherwise autonomous agents: once an agent freely chooses to enter an organisation in a certain position, playing certain

---

* The present work was partly funded by the Spanish Ministry of Education and Science under grant TIC2003-08763-C02-02.

P. Noriega et al. (Eds.): COIN 2006 Workshops, LNAI 4386, pp. 19–31, 2007.

roles, etc., it is supposed to behave in accordance with prescriptions attached to those concepts. Often, these prescriptions are complemented by a more general set of *norms* [23][3]. We refer to open MAS with these characteristics as *Virtual Organisations* (VOs) [19].

VOs differ in the way that prescriptions are enforced. Several approaches provide mechanisms to make it *impossible* for agents to transgress norms (e.g. by providing specific "governor" agents [6], or by integrating "filtering" mechanisms into MAS infrastructures [14]). However, especially for large-scale VOs this is a rather difficult and computationally expensive task. An alternative approach is to endow the VO with *incentive* mechanisms that, in general, make it too costly for agents to deviate from the prescribed behaviour (e.g. by means of installing incomplete but sufficiently effective detection and penalisation mechanisms for potential transgressors) [4]. Still, in the latter case, from the standpoint of an individual agent there is a significantly higher degree of uncertainty as to whether its organisational acquaintances will effectively behave in accordance with the organisational norms.

Several authors have investigated trust and reputation mechanisms that provide agents with *expectations* about the future behaviour of their acquaintances based on their interaction history within the MAS [11,2,18]. However, most mechanisms aim at supporting the emergence of overlay networks of trust relations in otherwise poorly structured systems. We believe that, on the one hand, the a priori structure of VOs can be useful to improve the efficiency of reputation mechanisms, and that, on the other hand, such mechanisms can be quite useful for an agent's decision-making. This is particularly true for agents that are part of (and have to act to attain their individual goals within) VOs with "soft" enforcement mechanisms.

In this paper we present first results of our work in progress, aimed at integrating the structuring and coercive facets of organisational abstractions into trust and reputation mechanisms for VOs. In Section 2 we point to relevant aspects of previous work in the fields of organisational models and trust and reputation mechanisms. Section 3 outlines our proposal for building up and maintaining a trust model that takes into account organisational concepts, and shows how it can guide an agent's decision-making in a VO. We present an example of how to apply those mechanisms within a particular VO in Section 4. Finally, we conclude summarising our proposal, compare it to approaches by other authors, and outline future lines of work.

2   Background

There is a wide range of organisational (meta-) models aimed at describing basic organisational concepts and their interrelation in the context of MAS [7,10,20,13]. There is a common agreement that the notion of *role* is central for linking agents to an organisational model. Roles are sometimes defined by the *actions* they can perform, but usually they are characterised by the types of *social interactions* to which they contribute. The latter term does not primarily refer to the interaction protocols that agents engage in, but rather to the social functionality that such interactions shall achieve. In this sense, we assume that VOs define roles and specify the interactions (functionalities) in which each role can participate.

Several meta-models allow for *specialisation* relations among essential organisational concepts. In the organisational model underlying the FIPA-ACL, for instance, *information exchange* interactions are a special kind of *request* interaction, where the requested action is a communicative action of type *inform* (e.g., [21]). In much the same way, the *informer* role involved in this interaction can be conceived as a specialisation of the *requester* role. In summary, organisational models often contain *taxonomies* of concept types, e.g., for roles or for interactions. Such taxonomies can be provided to the agents participating in an organisation – for instance, as an organisational service.

Finally, it is worth noting that many organisational models allow for certain types of *aggregation* relations. Different notions of *groups* – conceived as collections of agents – [7,13], or collections of interaction protocols [9] are examples of such composed concepts. In a similar sense, the proper *organisation* itself as the aggregation of all its participating agents can be conceived as an individual unit.

There are many recent proposals for reputation mechanisms and approaches to evaluate trust in *peer-to-peer* systems in general (e.g. [25,2]), and MAS in particular (e.g. [11,24,18]). Sabater and Sierra [17] consider reputation to have two different dimensions of influence: an *individual dimension* measuring local reputation – evaluated from direct interactions– and a *social dimension* evaluated from direct interactions and from the opinions from the society. In this paper, we will follow the proposal by Ramchurn et al. [16] regarding basic concepts of trust-based systems: *confidence* is a local rating based on direct interactions; *reputation* is a rating based on opinions of others; and *trust* is a rating built as a result from combining.

3   Trust Mechanisms in Virtual Organisations

Although VOs may limit the freedom of choice of agents, especially in less regulated organisations agents will still be confronted with the problem of deciding appropriate counterparts for their interactions according to their own beliefs and goals. Hence, trust and reputation mechanisms should be added as an additional layer on top of the organisational layer of a MAS as it is presented in Figure 1.

Not only a trust layer is useful for VOs. Also VOs provide a new viewpoint to trust and reputation mechanisms; organisational structures can help to get more reliable trust evaluations. In the following sections we present, first, an adaptation of standard trust and reputation mechanisms to VOs. Then we show how an agent can use knowledge about the organisational structure to infer confidence in an issue if no previous experience is available.

Fig. 1. Layered-network model for MAS

3.1   Basic Trust Model for Virtual Organisation

As described in Section 2, it seems reasonable to assume that a minimal organisational model defines at least roles and interactions, and that every agent
participating in the VO plays at least one defined role. Furthermore, we assume
that agents participating in an VO know the organisational structure, i.e. they
know the roles other agents are playing within the organisation as well as the
interactions that are defined for each role.

In line with other approaches [12,24,17,16], we base our trust model on the
notions of confidence and reputation. A typical situation is that an agent A
wants to evaluate the trustworthiness of some other agent B – playing the role
R – in the interaction I. This trustworthiness is denoted as $t_A(\langle B, R, I \rangle)$, with
$t_A(\langle B, R, I \rangle) \in [0..1]$, and it measures the trust of A in B (playing role R) being
a "good" counterpart in the interaction I. In order to build trust, agents can
rely on two different measures: their own confidence, and the social reputation
of an issue.

Confidence, $c_A(\langle B, R, I \rangle)$, is obtained from A's own experience when interacting with agent B playing role R in past interactions of type I. Confidence values
for past interactions are stored in the agent's *local interaction table* (LIT). This
table contains one entry for each counterpart agent, playing a particular role,
with which the agent has interacted in a particular interaction[1]. LIT_A denotes
agent A's LIT. An example is given in table 1.

Each entry in a *local interaction table* LIT contains the following elements: i)
the Agent/Role/Interaction identifier $\langle X, Y, Z \rangle$, ii) the confidence value for the issue $(c_A(\langle X, Y, Z \rangle))$, and iii) a reliability value $(r(c_A(\langle X, Y, Z \rangle)))$. The confidence
value may be obtained from some function that evaluates past experiences on
the same issue. We suppose $c_A(\langle X, Y, Z \rangle) \in [0..1]$ and higher values to represent
higher confidence. Reliability $(r(c_A(\langle X, Y, Z \rangle)))$ measures how certain an agent is
about its own confidence in issue $\langle X, Y, Z \rangle$. We suppose $r(c_A(\langle X, Y, Z \rangle)) \in [0..1]$.
Furthermore, we assume that $r(c_A(\langle X, Y, Z \rangle)) = 0$ for any tuple $\langle B, R, I \rangle$ not
belonging to LIT_A.

---

[1] Depending on computational restrictions, the table may resume all past events or
just the recent interactions the agent was involved in.

Table 1. An agent's local interactions table (LIT_A)

$\langle X, Y, Z \rangle$	$c_A(\langle X, Y, Z \rangle)$	$r(c_A(\langle X, Y, Z \rangle))$
$\langle a_2, r_5, i_1 \rangle$	0.5	0.3
$\langle a_4, r_1, i_2 \rangle$	0.7	0.8
$\langle a_2, r_3, i_1 \rangle$	0.9	0.5
$\vdots$	$\vdots$	$\vdots$
$\langle a_9, r_2, i_5 \rangle$	0.4	0.7

Reliability can be computed, for example, as proposed by Huynh, Jennings and Shadbolt [11,12], by taking into account the number of interactions a confidence value is based on and the variability of the individual values across past experiences.

An agent may build trust directly form its confidence value or it may combine confidence with the social reputation of an issue. The latter is especially necessary if an agent has no experience on an issue or if its confidence is not sufficiently reliable. An agent can obtain the social reputation of an issue by asking other agents about their opinion on that issue. Agents that have been asked for their opinion return the corresponding confidence and reliability values from their LIT. Based on confidence and reputation, the trust A has in the issue $\langle B, R, I \rangle$ can be defined in the following way:

$$
t_A(\langle B, R, I \rangle) = \begin{cases} c_A(\langle B, R, I \rangle), & if \ \ r(c_A(\langle B, R, I \rangle)) > TR_A \\ \dfrac{\sum_{A_k \in RA} c_{A_k}(\langle B, R, I \rangle) \cdot w_{A_k}(c_{A_k}(\langle B, R, I \rangle))}{\sum_{A_k \in RA} w_{A_k}(c_{A_k}(\langle B, R, I \rangle))} & otherwise \end{cases} \quad (1)
$$

Using this formula, trust will be measured at a scale $[0..1]$. TR_A is a threshold for the reliability of A's own confidence values. If the reliability is below TR_A, $t_A(\langle B, R, I \rangle)$ is calculated as the weighted mean of the confidence values received from a set of *recommender agents* (RA). Agent A itself belongs to RA. $w_{A_k}(c_{A_k}(\langle B, R, I \rangle))$ is the weight given to agent A_k's confidence on issue $\langle B, R, I \rangle$. This weight can be calculated as follows:

$$
w_{A_k}(c_{A_k}(\langle B, R, I \rangle)) = \begin{cases} r(c_{A_k}(\langle B, R, I \rangle)) \cdot \alpha, & if \ \ A_k = A \\ r(c_{A_k}(\langle B, R, I \rangle)) \cdot (1 - \alpha), & otherwise \end{cases} \quad (2)
$$

where $\alpha \in [0..1]$ is a parameter specifying the importance given to A's own confidence value. For values of $\alpha > 0.5$, an agent relies stronger on its own experience than on the opinions obtained form others.

One problem of reputation mechanisms is to determine the recommender agents that should be asked for their opinion about an issue $\langle B, R, I \rangle$. In a VO an agent A can take advantage of the organisational structures in order to decide which agents it should ask for their opinion. In fact, good recommenders may be other agents that play the same role as A. The reason is twofold. First, agents playing the same role in an organisation will have the similar goals and, hence, it is likely that they have a similar subjective opinion about the trustworthiness of possible counterparts. Second, A probably wants to evaluate the trustworthiness of an issue $\langle B, R, I \rangle$ because A's own role can participate in the interaction I. Thus, it is likely that other agents, playing the same role as A, will already have some experience with interaction I and possibly with the particular agent B.

3.2   Confidence and Trust for Organisational Structures

In the following sections we propose alternative ways to build an agent's confidence in an issue. We only concentrate on confidence values obtained from an agent's own experiences. The use of the proposed approaches in combination with social reputation in order to build trust is straight forward.

Agents accumulate past experiences in form of atomic confidence values for Agent/Role/Interaction tuples in their LIT. This information may be used to calculate confidence (and trust) values for other organisational elements by accumulating the corresponding entries in an agent's LIT.

Agent/role confidence evaluates an agent's trust in a specific role within the organisation. It measures the confidence an agent A has in agent B playing a role R and can be calculated by compiling past experiences from any type of interaction where A and B (playing role R) have met:

$$c_A(\langle B, R, \_ \rangle) = \frac{\sum_{\langle B, R, \_ \rangle_i \in LIT_A} c_A(\langle B, R, \_ \rangle_i) \cdot r(c_A(\langle B, R, \_ \rangle_i))}{\sum_{\langle B, R, \_ \rangle_i \in LIT_A} r(c_A(\langle B, R, \_ \rangle_i))} \qquad (3)$$

The notation $\langle B, R, \_ \rangle$ refers to tuples for a fixed agent B and a fixed role R regardless the interaction. Agent/role confidence may be used as an additional evidence measure when calculating $t_A(\langle B, R, I \rangle)$. However, more importantly it provides a manner to evaluate $c_A(\langle B, R, I \rangle)$ (and $t_A(\langle B, R, I \rangle)$) if agent A has none or not enough experience regarding the issue $\langle B, R, I \rangle$, that is, if $r(c_A(\langle B, R, I \rangle)) < TR_A$. The importance increases if none of the agents in the organisation has had any experience regarding the issue $\langle B, R, I \rangle$, and therefore, none of the agents could give any (reliable) recommendation. In such a scenario, $c_A(\langle B, R, \_ \rangle)$ can provide a valuable approximation of $c_A(\langle B, R, I \rangle)$ for any interaction I.

In a similar way, agents can compute *agent confidence* $(c_A(\langle B, \_, \_ \rangle))$ – the (global) confidence agent A has in agent B. Agent confidence values can provide a second level of approximation when building $t_A(\langle B, R, I \rangle)$. They may be used as an alternative for $c_A(\langle B, R, I \rangle)$ if there is not even enough expertise for a reliable confidence $c_A(\langle B, R, \rangle)$. In a more general environment with agents possibly participating in several organisations, agent confidence may also be used as a gauge to authorise agents to join an organisation.

Equation 3 can be adapted to calculate *role confidence* $(c_A(\langle \_, R, \_ \rangle))$ and *interaction confidence* $(c_A(\langle \_, \_, I \rangle))$.[2] Role confidence measures an agents confidence in a specific role within an organisation. It could be used as a default confidence value assigned to agents that just entered an organisation playing a

---

[2] It is also possible to compute *agent/interaction confidence* values $(c_A(\langle B, \_, I \rangle))$. However, we do not consider this measure very useful.

specific role and, thus, for which there are no confidence values available. Interaction confidence provides an estimation of the trust in a concrete interaction within an organisation despite the actual agents that have participated in the interaction. Interaction confidence may be used as a means to choose between several alternative interactions an agent could participate in.

Role and interaction confidence have an additional importance for VOs. They evaluate certain parts of an organisation at the institutional level, that is, independently on the agents actually participating in the organisation. From the institutional point of view, role and interaction confidence can be used to identify deficiencies in the organisational structure and functioning. From the outside, both measures can be used to evaluate parts of an organisation or an organisation as a whole.

Confidence (and trust) values can also be aggregated for groups of agents – either in general or in relation to one or more interactions or roles. Suppose, an agent A intends to evaluate a group of agents ($AG = \{B_1, B_2, ..., B_n\}$), for instance, in order to decide whether to join them or not. The value can be estimated from A's experience about past interactions in which also agents belonging to AG participated. The confidence an agent A has in the group AG with regard to an interaction I is defined as follows:

$$c_A(\langle AG, \_, I \rangle) = \frac{\sum_{\langle B,\_,I \rangle_i \in LIT_A \wedge B \in AG} c_A(\langle B, \_, I \rangle_i) \cdot r(c_A(\langle B, \_, I \rangle_i))}{\sum_{\langle B,\_,I \rangle_i \in LIT_A \wedge B \in AG} r(c_A(\langle B, \_, I \rangle_i))} \qquad (4)$$

In a similar way it is possible to compute the confidence in a group of agents in general ($c_A(\langle AG, \_, \_ \rangle)$), or in a group of agents with respect to a specific set of roles and/or interactions.

Finally, considering AG to be the set of all agents participating in a specific organisation, then $c_A(\langle AG, \_, \_ \rangle)$ specifies the confidence in that organisation – measured as the aggregation of the confidence values for all participating agents. Organisation confidence may have a special importance in open MAS with where several VOs compete with each other.

3.3   Confidence Inference Using Role and Interaction Similarities

In the previous subsection we have proposed to use the agent/role confidence $c_A(\langle B, R, \_ \rangle)$ (or $c_A(\langle B, \_, \_ \rangle)$) as an estimation for $c_A(\langle B, R, I \rangle)$ if agent A has no reliable experience about issue $\langle B, R, \_ \rangle$. This approach is based on the hypothesis that, in general, agents behave in a similar way in all interactions related to the same role. Formally, we assume that for any interaction I', with $I' \neq I$, the value $c_A(\langle B, R, I' \rangle)$ is an approximation for $c_A(\langle B, R, I \rangle)$. Refining this idea, it seems reasonable to assume that the more similar I' and I the more similar will be the values $c_A(\langle B, R, I' \rangle)$ and $c_A(\langle B, R, I \rangle)$. And the same actually applies to roles. Using this idea, confidence values accumulated for similar agent/role/interaction tuples may provide evidence for the value of $c_A(\langle B, R, I \rangle)$.

We propose the following equation for calculating confidence:

$$c_A(\langle B, R, I \rangle) = \frac{\sum_{\langle B', R', I' \rangle \in LIT_A} c_A(\langle B', R', I' \rangle) \cdot r(c_A(\langle B', R', I' \rangle)) \cdot sim(\langle B', R', I' \rangle, \langle B, R, I \rangle)}{\sum_{\langle B', R', I' \rangle \in LIT_A} r(c_A(\langle B', R', I' \rangle_i)) \cdot sim(\langle B', R', I' \rangle, \langle B, R, I \rangle)}$$

(5)

Using equation 5, each entry from agent A's LIT has an influence in the calculation of $c_A(\langle B, R, I \rangle)$. The weight given to an entry is determined by the similarity of the agent/role/interaction key to the key $\langle B, R, I \rangle$ and by the reliability of the confidence value. $sim(\langle B', R', I' \rangle, \langle B, R, I \rangle)$ can be computed as the weighted sum of the similarities of the individual elements (agent, role, and interaction), as defined in the following equation:

$$sim(\langle B', R', I' \rangle, \langle B, R, I \rangle) = \alpha \cdot sim_A(B, B') + \beta \cdot sim_R(R, R') + \gamma \cdot sim_I(I, I') \quad (6)$$

where $sim_A(B, B')$, $sim_R(R, R')$, $sim_I(I, I') \in [0..1]$ measure the similarity between the agents, roles and interactions, respectively. α, β and γ, with $\alpha + \beta + \gamma = 1$, are parameters specifying the sensibility regarding the individual similarities. Assuming that only confidence values for the same agent are taken into account, $sim_A(B, B')$ is defined as follows:

$$sim_A(B, B') = \begin{cases} 1, & if \ B = B' \\ 0, & otherwise \end{cases} \quad (7)$$

As argued in Section 2, many organisational models include taxonomies of roles and/or interactions. If this is the case, $sim_R(R, R')$ and $sim_I(I, I')$ can be implemented by *closeness functions* that estimate the similarity between two concepts on the basis of their closeness in the concept hierarchy.

Equations 3 and 5 can be used as an additional indicator for $t_A(\langle B, R, I \rangle)$. If an agent has no reliable experience about a particular agent/role/interaction issue, they can be used to estimate trust without the necessity to rely on the opinions of other agents. Thus, the proposed model makes agents less dependent on others, which is an important issue especially in VOs that do not provide mechanisms to keep its members from cheating.

4   An Example

In this section we illustrate our approach with an example taken from the University domain. This and other examples have been successfully tested (but not included in this paper) using a testbed called *TOAST* [8]. Suppose a School of Computer Science whose members play roles out of the taxonomy shown in Figure 2. Furthermore, suppose that the social functionalities provided by the organisation are summarised in the interaction taxonomy illustrated in Figure 3.

Suppose an agent a, playing the role *Student*, has just finished its first year at the university and wants to enrol in the second year. Suppose a wants to enrol in the subject *Artificial Intelligence (AI)* and suppose there are two different lecturers giving AI classes: L_1 and L_2. Agent a has to decide one of those lecturers to

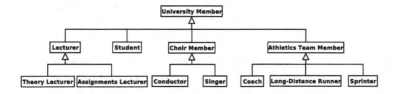

Fig. 2. Role taxonomy provided by University organisation

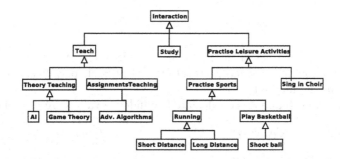

Fig. 3. Interaction taxonomy provided by University organisation

Table 2. Agent a's local interaction table

$\langle X, Y, Z \rangle$	$c_a(\langle X, Y, Z \rangle)$	$r(c_a(\langle X, Y, Z \rangle))$
$\langle L_7, Th.Lecturer, Teach \rangle$	0.1	0.3
$\langle L_2, Th.Lecturer, Teach\_GameTheory \rangle$	0.9	0.3
$\langle S_7, Student, Study \rangle$	0.7	0.5
$\langle S_7, Sprinter, Running \rangle$	0.3	0.7
$\langle L_1, Ass.Lecturer, Teach\_AdvancedAlgorithms \rangle$	0.8	0.9
$\langle L_2, Lecturer, Teach\_GameTheoryAssignments \rangle$	0.3	0.8
$\langle L_1, Th.Lecturer, Teach \rangle$	0.7	0.5
$\langle L_1, Singer, Sing\_In\_Choir \rangle$	0.5	0.5
$\langle S_4, Student, Study \rangle$	0.7	0.8

attend his/her classes. In order to make this decision agent a can use its experience stored in form of confidence values in its LIT. This LIT is shown in Table 2.

As it can be seen in Table 2, agent a has no direct experience , that is, no confidence values, for the issues $\langle L_1, Lecturer, Teach_{AI} \rangle$ and $\langle L_2, Lecturer, Teach_{AI} \rangle$. However, using knowledge about the organisation, agent a could assess the expression $c_a(\langle L_1/L_2, Lecturer, \_ \rangle)$ as an approximation for the desired confidence values. In doing so, the agent obtains:

$$c_a(\langle L_1, Lecturer, \_ \rangle) = novalue \qquad c_a(\langle L_2, Lecturer, \_ \rangle) = 0.3.$$

Observe that there is no possible rating for $c_a(\langle L_1, Lecturer, \_ \rangle)$ since there is no matching between tuple $\langle L_1, Lecturer, \_ \rangle$ and any other tuple in LIT_A.

In this case, as a second approximation, agent a could calculate agent confidence:

$$c_a(\langle L_1, \_, \_\rangle) = 0.56 \qquad c_a(\langle L_2, \_, \_\rangle) = 0.46.$$

This approximation, however, would not only count the confidence in L_1 and L_2 as teachers, but also, for example, the confidence in L_1 as a *Singer* in the *Choir*. Hence, it would be better to calculate $c_a(\langle L_1/L_2, Lecturer, Teach_{AI}\rangle)$ using equation 5. In order to do that, the agent could use the following simple equation to calculate the similarity between roles and interactions, respectively:

$$sim_{R/I}(x, y) = 1 - \frac{h_i}{h_{MAX}} \tag{8}$$

where x, y are either roles or interactions, h_i is the number of nodes between x and y in the taxonomy, and h_{MAX} is the longest possible path between any pair of elements in the hierarchy tree.

Using equations 5 and 8 the calculated confidence values are the following:

$$c_a(\langle L_1, Lecturer, Teach_{AI}\rangle) = 0.61 \qquad c_a(\langle L_2, Lecturer, Teach_{AI}\rangle) = 0.54,$$

(We have set $\alpha = 0.5, \beta = 0.35$ and $\gamma = 0.15$.) Based on these values, agent a decides to attend the classes from lecturer L_1.

5   Conclusion

In this paper we have presented results of our work in progress, aimed at integrating organisational facets into trust mechanisms. We have emphasised the problem of finding "good" counterparts, even if no previous interactions have been performed. The proposed trust model takes into account key concepts of organisational models, such as *roles* and *interactions*, as well as the their aggregation in *groups* or *organisations*. We have also endowed our model with inference capabilities exploiting *taxonomies* of concept types provided by VOs.

In contrast to other approaches to trust systems (most of them based on reputation distribution), we have presented a way of evaluating trust at a local level that emphasizes the different experiences of agents from past interactions. The model proposed by Sabater and Sierra [18] incorporates *social networks* (social relations between agents) as a key factor for reputation ratings. Moreover their approach considers a hierarchical ontology structure in order to obtain different kinds of reputation. However, they do not take into account the effect of super-concepts for the estimation of similarity ratings.

Abdul-Rahman and Hailes [1] propose a trust model for virtual communities but use qualitative ratings for estimating trust. They focus on evaluating trust from past expertise and reputation coming from *recommender agents* without considering explicitly VO structures.

The FIRE model proposed by Huynh, Jennings and Shadbold [11] is also concerned with *interaction trust* and *role-based trust*. As in our approach, the former is built from direct experience of an agent, while the latter is the rating that results from role-based relationships between agents. Nevertheless, the FIRE model does not consider inference on VO structures.

The trust model by Ramchurn et al. [16] is based on direct and indirect multi-agent interactions for establishing contracts between agents in electronic institutions[5]. Still, it does not account for VOs with "soft" enforcement mechanisms, where norms and behaviour rules can be transgressed.

We have also designed and developed a testbed [8] that allow us to simulate VOs with different trust models (included proposed in this paper), so as to gain experimental evidence regarding their behaviours in different situations. It will also allow us to come up with a more quantitative comparison to other approaches. In future work, we will investigate how different agents behaviours (honest, incompetent, malicious, etc.) can affect the overall VO performance using the proposed trust model. Furthermore, we will look into different ways of applying more accurate similarity functions to uise with structural taxonomies, e.g., [22] as well.

References

1. Abdul-Rahman, A., Hailes, S.: Supporting trust in virtual communities. In: HICSS (2000)
2. Aberer, K., Despotovic, Z.: Managing trust in a peer-2-peer information system. In: CIKM '01: Proceedings of the tenth international Conference on Information and Knowledge Management, pp. 310–317. ACM Press, New York, USA (2001)
3. Camino, A.G., Aguilar, J.A.R., Sierra, C., Vasconcelos, W.: Norm-oriented programming of electronic institutions: A rule-based approach. In: Noriega, P., Vázquez-Salceda, J., Boella, G., Boissier, O., Dignum, V., Fornara, N., Matson, E. (eds.) COIN 2006. LNCS(LNAI), vol. 4386, pp. 177–193. Springer, Heidelberg (2007)
4. Grossi, D., Aldewereld, H., Dignum, F.: Ubi lex, ibi poena: Designing norm enforcement in e-institutions. In: Noriega, P., Vázquez-Salceda, J., Boella, G., Boissier, O., Dignum, V., Fornara, N., Matson, E. (eds.) COIN 2006. LNCS(LNAI), vol. 4386, pp. 101–114. Springer, Heidelberg (2007)
5. Esteva, M., Rodriguez, J.A., Sierra, C., Garcia, P., Arcos, J.L.: On the formal specifications of electronic institutions. In: Sierra, C., Dignum, F.P.M. (eds.) Agent Mediated Electronic Commerce. LNCS (LNAI), vol. 1991, pp. 126–147. Springer, Heidelberg (2001)
6. Esteva, M., Rosell, B., Rodríguez-Aguilar, J.A., Arcos, J.L.: AMELI: An agent-based middleware for electronic institutions. In: Proceedings of the Third International Joint Conference on Autonomous Agents and Multiagent Systems, vol. 1, pp. 236–243 (2004)
7. Ferber, J., Gutknecht, O.: A meta-model for the analysis of organizations in multi-agent systems. In: Demazeau, Y. (ed.) Proceedings of the Third International Conference on Multi-Agent Systems (ICMAS'98), Paris, France, July 1998, pp. 128–135. IEEE Press, Los Alamitos (1998)
8. Hermoso, R., Billhardt, H., Centeno, R., Ossowski, S.: Effective use of organisational abstractions for confidence models. In: Proceedings of 7th Annual International Workshop Engineering Societies in the Agents World, pp. 246–261 (2006)

9. Hermoso, R., Ortiz, R., Saugar, S., Serrano, J.M.: Instrumentación de sistemas multi-agente mediante un entorno organizativo/lingüístico: Un caso práctico. In: Moreno, J.C.G., Morales, P.C., Mestras, J.P. (eds.) I Taller en Desarrollo de Sistemas Multiagente (DESMA-2004), Málaga, November 2004, pp. 72–83 (2004)

10. Hübner, J.F., Sichman, J.S., Boissier, O.: Using the moise+ for a cooperative framework of mas reorganisation. In: Bazzan, A.L.C., Labidi, S. (eds.) SBIA 2004. LNCS (LNAI), vol. 3171, pp. 506–515. Springer, Heidelberg (2004)

11. Huynh, T.D., Jennings, N.R., Shadbolt, N.R.: Developing an integrated trust and reputation model for open multi-agent systems. In: Falcone, R., Barber, S., Sabater, J., Singh, M. (eds.) AAMAS-04 Workshop on Trust in Agent Societies (2004)

12. Huynh, T.D., Jennings, N.R., Shadbolt, N.R.: FIRE: An integrated trust and reputation model for open multi-agent systems. In: Proceedings of the 16th European Conference on Artificial Intelligence (ECAI) (2004)

13. Odell, J., Nodine, M.H., Levy, R.: A metamodel for agents, roles, and groups. In: Odell, J.J., Giorgini, P., Müller, J.P. (eds.) AOSE 2004. LNCS, vol. 3382, pp. 78–92. Springer, Heidelberg (2005)

14. Omicini, A., Ossowski, S., Ricci, A.: Coordination infrastructures in the engineering of multiagent systems. In: Bergenti, F., Gleizes, M.-P., Zambonelli, F. (eds.) Methodologies and Software Engineering for Agent Systems: The Agent-Oriented Software Engineering Handbook, June 2004, ch. 14, pp. 273–296. Kluwer Academic Publishers, Dordrecht (2004)

15. Omicini, A., Ossowski, S.: Objective versus subjective coordination in the engineering of agent systems. In: Klusch, M., Bergamaschi, S., Edwards, P., Petta, P. (eds.) Intelligent Information Agents. LNCS (LNAI), vol. 2586, pp. 179–202. Springer, Heidelberg (2003)

16. Ramchurn, S.D., Sierra, C., Godó, L., Jennings, N.R.: A computational trust model for multi-agent interactions based on confidence and reputation. In: Proceedings of 6th International Workshop of Deception, Fraud and Trust in Agent Societies, pp. 69–75 (2003)

17. Sabater, J., Sierra, C.: REGRET: a reputation model for gregarious societies. In: Müller, J.P., Andre, E., Sen, S., Frasson, C. (eds.) Proceedings of the Fifth International Conference on Autonomous Agents, Montreal, Canada, pp. 194–195. ACM Press, New York (2001)

18. Sabater, J., Sierra, C.: Reputation and social network analysis in multi-agent systems. In: AAMAS '02: Proceedings of the first international joint conference on Autonomous agents and multiagent systems, pp. 475–482. ACM Press, New York, USA (2002)

19. Schumacher, M., Ossowski, S.: The governing environment. In: Weyns, D., Parunak, H.V.D., Michel, F. (eds.) E4MAS 2005. LNCS (LNAI), vol. 3830, pp. 88–104. Springer, Heidelberg (2006)

20. Serrano, J.M., Ossowski, S., Fernández, A.: The pragmatics of software agents - analysis and design of agent communication languages. In: Klusch, M., Bergamaschi, S., Edwards, P., Petta, P. (eds.) Intelligent Information Agents. LNCS (LNAI), vol. 2586, pp. 234–274. Springer, Heidelberg (2003)

21. Serrano, J.M., Ossowski, S.: On the impact of agent communication languages on the implementation of agent systems. In: Klusch, M., Ossowski, S., Kashyap, V., Unland, R. (eds.) CIA 2004. LNCS (LNAI), vol. 3191, Springer, Heidelberg (2004)

22. Sierra, C., Debenham, J.: Trust and honour in information-based agency. In: Proceedings of the Fifth International Joint Conference on Autonomous Agents and Multiagent Systems, AAMAS 2006, pp. 1225–1232 (2006)

23. Vázquez-Salceda, J., Dignum, V., Dignum, F.: Organizing multiagent systems. Autonomous Agents and Multi-Agent Systems 11(3), 307–360 (2005)
24. Yu, B., Singh, M.P.: An evidential model of distributed reputation management. In: AAMAS '02: Proceedings of the first international joint conference on Autonomous agents and multiagent systems, pp. 294–301. ACM Press, New York, USA (2002)
25. Yu, B., Singh, M.P., Sycara, K.: Developing trust in large-scale peer-to-peer systems. In: Proceedings of First IEEE Symposium on Multi-Agent Security and Survivability, pp. 1–10. IEEE Computer Society Press, Los Alamitos (2004)
26. Zambonelli, F., Jennings, N.R., Wooldridge, M.: Organizational abstractions for the analysis and design of multi-agent systems. In: Ciancarini, P., Wooldridge, M.J. (eds.) AOSE 2000. LNCS, vol. 1957, pp. 235–252. Springer, Heidelberg (2001)

Coordinating Tasks in Agent Organizations
Or: Can We Ask You to Read This Paper?

Virginia Dignum and Frank Dignum

Dept. Information and Computing Sciences, Utrecht University,
The Netherlands
{virginia,dignum}@cs.uu.nl

Abstract. Support for new forms of organization and social interaction requires understanding the influence of structure on behavior. Goal dependencies indicate some relationship between roles, through which actions can be coordinated. Social relationships determine different types of power links between roles. Efficient coordination requires that goal dependency and power structure are well tuned to each other. In this paper, we will investigate what is the exact nature of this relationship between roles in an organization and what are the consequences of different structure forms. We will also see what is the difference if the relations are not hierarchical but organized through a market or network structure.

1   Introduction

One of the main issues in agent organizations is the specification of coordination mechanisms between agents playing roles in a regulated social environment. Coordination can be defined as the process of managing dependencies between activities [16]. One way to coordinate is to manage functional dependencies. In this sense, which is the most commonly used in Multi-Agent Systems (MAS) research, coordination refers to the allocations of tasks to agents, such that common goals are achieved. Coming forth from Organizational Theory, another way to manage dependencies, considers the supervision and collaboration relations between actors. In this sense, coordination refers to the specification of power and authority relations between agents. Although the two perspectives are interrelated, they are based on different concepts and views on organizations, and their differences are not explicitly accounted for in most MAS models.

In this paper, we discuss the implications of the coordination type to the dependencies between roles. Given that one role depends on another to achieve a goal, the realization of that goal will depend on the social relationship between the roles, that is, whether the role has power over the other role. We distinguish between hierarchical, network and market social relationships between roles. Although role hierarchies can be thought of in terms of hierarchical organizations, we argue that the reason to call an organization hierarchical is not just because the roles are structured in some kind of a hierarchy (or tree), but has more bearing on the type of coordination used between roles that are related. A tree shaped organization usually also indicates that the roles coordinate in a hierarchical way (through commands), but this is not necessarily so. Even in such an organization, each role might offer a task to its "subordinates" (using something like contract net and a market mechanism) instead of delegating it.

P. Noriega et al. (Eds.): COIN 2006 Workshops, LNAI 4386, pp. 32–47, 2007.

The paper is organized as follows. In sections 2 and 3 we introduce both perspectives on coordination: from Organizational Theory as the representation of the social structure, and from MAS as the specification of task relationships. In section 4, we describe how the concept of role can integrate both views, by means of role dependencies and coordination types. Section 5 shows the consequences of this integration for the semantics of the role-based coordination model. Finally, we present our conclusions and directions for future research in section 6.

2   Social Structure

Support for social interaction and organizational structure requires understanding the influence of structure on behavior. Sociology and Organizational Theory have since long investigated social structures as the medium for human activities. In this section, we will describe relevant research in those fields on the topic of organizational structure. In the following sections, we will draw from these insight to analyze and model MAS organization.

Behavior and structure are interleaved; people go through a socialization process and become dependent on the existing social structures, but at the same time structures are modified by their activities. Giddens' *structuration theory* offers an account of social life in terms of structure and agency [13]. Giddens argues that order, or structure, is primarily created as a medium for practical activity. This instantiation of practical activity is not based on a even distribution of power and resources, but asymmetry and domination are, in fact, part of the natural order. Different power relations between actors and the utilization of different resources are at the basis of the development of particular structural principles. It is useful to consider groups and organizations from a structuration perspective because doing so: (a) helps one understand the relative balance of deterministic influences and willful choices that characterize groups; (b) suggests possibilities for how members may be able to exercise more influence than they otherwise think themselves capable of.

An organizational structure has essentially two objectives [9]: First, it facilitates the flow of information within the organization in order to re duce the uncertainty of decision making. Secondly, the structure of the organization should integrate organizational behavior across the parts of the organization so it is coordinated.

Relationships between and within organizations are developed for the exchange of goods, resources, information and so on. Williamson argues that the transaction costs are determinant for the organizational model [23]. Transaction costs will rise when the unpredictability and uncertainty of events increases, and/or when transactions require very specific investments, and/or when the risk of opportunistic behavior of partners is high. When transaction costs are high, societies tend to choose a hierarchical model in order to control the transaction process. If transaction costs are low, that is, are straightforward, non- repetitive and require no transaction-specific investments, then the market is the optimal choice. Powell introduces networks as another possible coordination model [20]. Networks stress the interdependence between different organizational actors and pay a lot of attention to the development and maintenance of (communicative) relationships, and the definition of rules and norms of conduct within the network. At the same time, actors are independent, have their own interests, and can be allied to different networks. That is, transaction costs and interdependencies in organizational relationships determine different models for organizational coordination.

Central in the way coordination is described is the concept of role. Role theory bridges social psychology, sociology, and anthropology [1], and recently has interested agent researchers. Its central concern has been with patterns of conduct, that is, expectations, identities, and social positions; and with context and social structure. Fox et al. introduce an organizational taxonomy which includes organizations, organizational goals, roles, and authority [12]. Agents can play roles, which potentially give them authority over other agents playing other roles. Empowerment and authority are recognized as critical aspects, since these identify which roles (and hence which agents) are enabled to perform which actions.

3   Coordination in MAS

Multi-agent coordination, defined as managing interdependencies between activities, addresses the special issues arising from the dependency relationships between multiple agents tasks. Task coordination in MAS has concentrated on developing coordination mechanism which facilitates dynamic collaboration between agents, with the goal of satisfying in some specified sense both local and global system objectives. The coordination structure must support the task-solving process using a generic mediation mechanism and should provide communication protocols to link the agents having common interests.

In Distributed Artificial Intelligence (DAI), coordination approaches are often based on contracting. The most famous example of these is the Contract Net Protocol (CNP) [22] for decentralized task allocation. CNP was designed to handle applications with a natural spatial distribution. By employing standard interaction mechanisms, the agents in the MAS can expect certain behavior. The behavior of each individual is determined to a great extent by the requirements of these interaction patterns. Roles provide both the building blocks for agent social systems and the requirements by which agents interact. Each agent is linked to other agents by the roles it plays by virtue of the applications functional requirements which are based on the expectations that the application has of the agent [17].

Such contract-based approaches assume the possibility for direct communication between agents. However, direct interaction and explicit communication are not always the best approaches to achieve coherent systemic behavior in the context of MAS and Agent Organizations (cf. stygmergy or mediation infrasctuctures). Omicini et al. have proposed the notion of coordination artifacts to deal with indirect interaction. Coordination artifacts are runtime abstractions encapsulating and providing a coordination service, to be exploited by agents in a certain social context [19]. In particular, they are suitable tools for modelling and engineering the Behavioral Implicit Communication (BIC) approach [2], which allows a wide spectrum of coordination problems for intelligent agents to be modelled without relying on direct communication.

In our approach, organizational structures can be seen as a kind of coordination artifacts. By using the structure, agents are able to coordinate their behavior with each other and following the expectations of the organization's design. The more is made explicit in the coordination structure, the less need agents have to communicate in order to coordinate. Organizational structure in MAS has been defined as that "what persists when agents enter or leave an organization, i.e. the relationships that makes an aggregate of elements a whole" [11]. A social structure may be explicitly implemented in the form of a social coordination artifact existing independently of the implementations of the agents, may be realized as part of the implementations of the agents, or may exist only intangibly, in the form of the policies or organizational rules followed by the agents during interaction.Much of this work has strong roots on the organizational forms identified in organization theory [8]. Basically the same three paradigms as in Organizational Science have proved to be most popular among MAS developers: hierarchy, market-oriented and team-centric, or network, organizations.

Finally, several researchers have recognized that the design of agent societies can benefit from abstractions analogous to those employed by our robust and relatively successful societies and organizations. Normative systems are increasingly being proposed in agent research cope with the challenge of social order, as to decide on a course of action when unexpected or undesired events occur (cf. [5,10]). Norms and conventions specify the behavior that society members are expected to conform to and are suitable means for decentralized control.

4   Roles and Dependencies

The main idea behind Agent Organizations is that interactions occur not just by accident but aim at achieving some desired global goals. Global goals are external to each individual participant (or agent) but can only be reached by the interaction of those participants. The design of agent organizations must capture on the one hand, the structure and requirements of the society owners, and on the other hand, must assume that participating agents must be available that are able and interested in enacting society roles. Several authors have proposed different models that consider organization as a first-class abstraction and use roles to model organizational positions. The remainder of this paper is based on the OperA model. However, most our claims can be related to other approaches as well.

The OperA Model for agent organizations [7] integrates a top-down specification of the society objectives and global structure, with a dynamic fulfillment of roles and interactions by independent participants. That is, the model separates the description of the structure and global behavior of the domain from the specification of the individual entities that populate the domain. Agents are actors that perform role(s) described by the society design. The agent's own capabilities and aims determine the specific way an agent enacts its role(s). An OperA model can be thought of as a kind of abstract protocol that governs how member agents should act according to social requirements. In this paper, we will only describe a few elements of the organizational model. In the next sections, we discuss how this model for agent coordination, based on organizational theory, can be used for social and task dependencies between roles.

4.1   Roles

Roles identify the activities and services necessary to achieve social objectives and enable to abstract from the specific individuals that will eventually perform them. From a society design perspective, roles provide the building blocks for agent systems that can perform the role, and from the agent design perspective, roles specify the expectations of the society with respect to the agent's activity in the society. Roles also define normative behavioral repertoires for agents [18]. That is, a role is the abstract representation of a policy, service or function. In OperA, roles are described in terms of *objectives* and *sub-objectives* (that is, what is an actor of the role expected to achieve) and *norms* (that is, how is an actor expected to behave). Furthermore, role descriptions also specify the *rights* associated with the role and the *type* of enactment of the role, that is, whether it is an institutional role (which behavior is controlled by the society) or an external role.

The specification of objectives and sub-objectives can be more or less restrictive on the actor performance. The more the aspects that are fixed in the specification, the less the freedom an agent enacting the role has to decide on how to achieve the role objectives and interpret its norms. Following the ideas of [15], we call such expressions *landmarks*. Formally, landmarks are conjunctions of logical expressions that are true in a state. Intuitively, landmarks provide a description of a place or situation, which is enough to identify it but without prescribing any specific process. Several different specific actions can bring about the same state, and therefore, landmarks represent actually families of protocols. The use of landmarks to describe activity, enables the actors to choose the best applicable actions, according to their goals and capabilities. The level of specification of landmarks determines the degree of freedom the actors have about their performance.

Role objectives are thus states of affairs expected to be achieved in the environment. Once a society model is animated, the objectives of a role are expected to be executed by the agent(s) enacting that role, that is, role objectives should become part of the goals of the enacting agent. Intuitively, role objectives enable the 'link' between society objectives and agent goals. At this level of abstraction, role objectives do not have a fixed semantics since roles are not performative entities but mere 'placeholders' for actors. The actual semantics of objectives depend on the way objectives are treated and assumed by the agent acting the role and on the semantics of agent goals in the agent model.

Definition 1 (Role Objective). *Represented by ρ, is a predicate describing an ideal state (or set of states) for the role. P_r is the set of objectives of role r.*   □

Roles are identified by their objectives, that is, different roles have different objectives and all roles must have at least one objective. Formally:

1. $\forall r_1, r_2 : r_1 = r_2 \Leftrightarrow P_{r_1} = P_{r_2}$
2. $\forall r : P_r \neq \{\}$

A role objective ρ can be further described by specifying a set of sub-objectives that must hold in order to achieve objective ρ. Sub-objectives give an indication of how an objective is to be achieved, that is, describe the states that are part of any plan that an agent enacting the role can specify to achieve that objective. Sub-objectives abstract from any temporal issues that must be present in a plan, and as such must not be equated with plans. Intuitively, sub-objectives are objectives that contribute to the realization of another objective. That is, if $\Pi_\rho = \{\rho_1, ..., \rho_n\}$ is a set of sub-objectives for ρ, the realization of all sub-objectives in Π_ρ yields the realization of ρ. Furthermore, for each objective ρ, the trivial set of sub-objectives ρ is defined.

For example, in a Conference Organization, the objective of the PC-member role is to review papers submitted to the conference, that is, to be in a state in which there are review reports for all the papers assigned to her. Sub-objectives of that objective are (a) to have read the paper, (b) to have written the review report, and, (c) to have sent the report to the organizers. How an actor of the PC-member role is going to achieve this, and indeed if she herself will do it (e.g. she can ask a student to read the paper and make the review report) is not, in this situation, a concern of the society.

4.2   Coordination Types

Different application contexts exhibit different needs with respect to coordination, and the choice of a coordination model will have great impact on the design of the agent society. The implications of the coordination type to the architecture and design of agent societies have usually not been considered. Societies depend on a facilitation layer that provides the social backbone of the organization [4]. Facilitation activities deal with the functioning of the society itself and are related to the underlying coordination model.The social coordination model is used to specify the facilitation framework for an agent society. In this paper, we distinguish between three coordination models: hierarchies, markets and networks, which result in different frameworks for agent societies.

Hierarchies are very effective at addressing issues of scale, in particular if the domain can easily be decomposed along some dimension. In a hierarchy, interaction lines are well defined and the facilitation level assumes the function of global control of the society and coordination of interaction with the outside world. In a hierarchy, agents are cooperative, not motivated by self interest and all contribute to a common global goal. Coordination is achieved through command and control lines. **Market** models that typically arise in e-business applications allow agents to coordinate activities without ceding authority to other agents. In markets, agents are self-interested (i.e. determine and follow their own goals) and value their freedom of association and own judgement above security and trust issues. Openness is thus a feature of markets. Facilitation in markets is, in the most extreme case, limited to identification and matchmaking activities, but usually also includes the specification of some trusted third party, such as a bank. Interaction in markets occurs through communication and negotiation. Finally, teams or **networks** are efficient when working on large-grained tasks which require coordinated capabilities of more that one agent, but require higher communication capabilities. Network organizations are built around general patterns of interaction or contracts. Relationships are dependent on clear communication patterns and social norms. Agents in a network society are still self-interested but are willing to trade some of their freedom to obtain secure relations and trust. Therefore, agents need to enter a social contract with the network society in which they commit themselves to act within and according to the norms and rules of the society. The society is responsible to make its rules and norms known to potential members. Coordination is achieved by mutual interest, possibly using trusted third parties, and according to well-defined rules and sanctions.

The coordination model determines interaction patterns and functionality of the facilitation layer of the society, that is, the interaction primitives and agent roles necessary to implement the facilitation layer that are specific to each type of society (market, network or hierarchy). Moreover, coordination models provide a framework to express interaction between the activities of agents and the behavior of the system [3].

4.3   Dependencies Between Roles

The notion of role is closely related to those of cooperation and coordination. The way tasks, or objectives, are allocated to roles determines the dependencies between them. These dependencies describe how agents enacting the roles should interact and contribute to the realization of the objectives of each other. That is, an objective of a role can be delegated to, or requested from, other roles. The dependency relation between roles r_1 and r_2 for objective γ of r_1, represented by $r_1 \succeq_\rho r_2$, indicates that objective ρ can be passed to r_2, that is, that r_2 can realize objective ρ for r_1.

Definition 2 (Role dependency). *A dependency relation $r_1 \succeq_\rho r_2$ describes the fact that role r_1 depends on role r_2 to realize (sub)objective ρ. The relation $\succeq_\rho \in R \times R$ is reflexive and transitive. That is, for all $r_1, r_2, r_3 \in R$,*

1. $r_1 \succeq_\rho r_1$
2. $r_1 \succeq_\rho r_2$ and $r_2 \succeq_\rho r_3$ implies $r_1 \succeq_\rho r_3$.   □

In OperA, roles are organized as a partially ordered set, represented as $\Re = (R, \succeq)$ that reflects role dependencies. A dependency graph represents the dependency relations between roles. Nodes in a dependency graph are roles in the agent society. Arcs are labelled with the objectives of the parent role for which realization the parent role depends on the child role. There can be more than one arc between two nodes, representing the fact that the parent role depends on the child role for more than one of its objectives. The root of the graph is the society itself, represented as a super-role, and contains the global objectives of the society, which are then decomposed into role objectives distributed along the role tree. The dependency graph for the Conference Organization is displayed in figure 1. For example, the arc labelled *paper−reviewed*, r, between nodes $PCchair$, C, and $PCmember$, M, represents the role dependency $C \succeq_r M$. Note that this graph does not have to be a tree. It should only be partially ordered (to avoid circular dependencies).

Considering that dependencies require interaction between two actors in order to establish how to pass the objective from one actor to the other, it is necessary to describe how this interaction occurs. In OperA, this is determined by the three coordination types discussed in the previous section: hierarchy, market and network. The way the objective ρ in a dependency relation $r_1 \succeq_\rho r_2$ is actually passed between r_1 and r_2 depends on the coordination type of the society:

- In hierarchies, the parent role demands the realization of its sub-objectives from its children. In this case, the enactor of a children role can not decide which objectives it will get but must accept whichever objectives are delegated to it by its parent role. Hierarchical dependencies are represented by $r_1 \succeq_\rho^H r_2$.
- In markets, a parent role can request the performance of objectives by the child role; the child role decides whether it will offer to perform it and the parent role will then decide whether allocation is desired and which instance of the child role

Fig. 1. Role dependencies in the conference society

will get to realize the objective. In this case, the enactors of a child role can choose which objectives of its parent they will offer to perform, such that it best fits its own private goals. Market dependencies are represented by $r_1 \succeq_\rho^M r_2$.

– In a network, both situations can happen. That is, an objective can either be delegated by the parent role or offered by the child role, which defines a kind of equivalence relation between related roles in a network. This can depend on prior agreements between the agents, or be negotiated for each specific situation. Network dependencies are represented by $r_1 \succeq_\rho^N r_2$.

Role dependencies illustrated in figure 1 are therefore interpreted in different ways depending on the coordination type holding in the society. For instance, in the case of an hierarchy, the relation $C \succeq_r M$, indicates that agents enacting the role $PCchair$, C, will delegate the objective $paper-reviewed$, r, to an enactor of role $PCmember$, M. In a market dependency relation, enactors of $PCmember$ can bid for objective review-paper to the enactor of $PCchair$, that is, a PC member can choose which papers they want to review and apply for those to the Program Chair. In a network, a dependency relation represents a request that can be initiated either by the parent or the child roles.

5   Role Dependencies and Coordination

One of the main issues in OperA is the specification of coordination between role enacting agents in a regulated society environment. Therefore, the representation of relationships between roles is one of crucial importance. Role dependencies indicate the relations between roles through which objectives can be passed. In this section, we discuss in more detail what are consequences of the type of coordination mechanism to the interaction between roles, and how they influence the semantics of the communication between agents. Our focus is not the implementation of coordination mechanisms, such as for example the work on coordination artifacts [19], but we mostly concerned with the conceptual level of communication. How exactly the concepts and relationships we identify below will be taken over in multi-agent systems will be object of further study.

5.1   Relationship Types

In organizational systems, it is usual to organize roles in a inheritance, or *is-a*, hierarchy. In such hierarchies, child roles inherit the characteristics (attributes, rights, norms) of its parent roles. However, other relationships can hold between roles. Dependency relations in OperA are not inheritance relations, but define the links through which objectives can be delegated to other roles. Coordination of behavior is relatively easy when dependencies are defined hierarchically, in which case when an agent i enacts a role that is superior to the role that agent j enacts, a request from i will result in an obligation for j. In networks and markets, however, coordination requires some more effort. Hierarchical organizations are thus very efficient, in that, task allocation occurs with no need for negotiation, given the power relations between agents. On the other hand, networks are more flexible, in that agents can negotiate task allocation between them so that they can attempt to obtain a most preferred assignment of objectives fitting with their own goals. In general, one can identify three different reasons for an agent j to commit itself to a request from another agent i [6]:

- **Power:** j accepts a request from i because of some domination relationship between i and j. This type of relation is standard in hierarchical societies, but can also be explicitly defined between two specific roles, in other types of societies. Power relations, represented by $power(i, j, \varphi)$, indicate that i has power over j for φ.
- **Authorization:** when j has committed itself to i for a certain service, a request from i leads to an obligation when the conditions are met. This relation is established by mutual agreement, e.g. in a (previous) interaction, for a certain time and under certain conditions. Although authorization relations can happen in any type of society, they are typical of networks (e.g. where participants can negotiate different approaches to goal realization in each situation). Authorization relations, represented by $auth(i, j, \varphi)$, mean that i has the authorization to request j to do φ.
- **Charity:** j will answer a request from i without having any explicit relation to i that forces it to do so. An obligation arises when agent j communicates its acceptance of the request.

The main difference between power and authorization relationships is that power is structurally determined and, for a great extent, static; that is, power relations are not influenced by the actions of the agents. On the other hand, authorization relations can be created by negotiation between agents; that is, an agent can decide to authorize another agent to request from it a certain action or resource. In the following, we describe the implications of power and authorization relations over the interaction behavior of the agents. For a complete description of the semantics, we refer the reader to [7]. Charity relations do not have a specific operator, since such relations are completely dependent on the 'personality' of the agent establishing such relation, and cannot thus be influenced or negotiated.

Definition 3 (Power relation). *Given agents i, j and roles r_1, r_2:*
$$\forall i, j, r_1, r_2 : rea(i, r_1) \wedge rea(j, r_2) \wedge r_1 \succeq_{\varphi}^{H} r_2 \rightarrow power(i, j, \varphi) \qquad \square$$

The above definition just states that $r_1 \succeq_{\varphi}^{H} r_2$, the hierarchical dependency relation between roles r_1 and r_2 gives rise to a power relation $power(i, j, \varphi)$ between agents

i and j whenever $rea(i, r_1)$ and $rea(j, r_2)$. Where the role enacting agent relation, $rea(i, r_1)$, means that agent i performs role r_1.

The expression $power(i, j, \varphi)$ means informally that i has the power to force j to achieve φ. Power relations are *reflexive*, i.e. each agent has power over itself, and often, but not always, also *transitive*, that is, if $power(i, j, \varphi)$ and $power(j, k, \varphi)$ then $power(i, k, \varphi)$. Moreover, power to demand φ implies power to demand all what can be derived from φ. Formally, the following axiom holds for the power relation:

Definition 4 (Properties of power relation). *Given expression φ and a role i, the following axioms hold:*

1. $\models \forall i : power(i, i, \varphi)$.
2. $\models \forall i, j : power(i, j, \varphi) \wedge (\varphi \rightarrow \psi) \rightarrow power(i, j, \psi)$ □

Authorization relations describe situations when power can be (temporarily) effective. Informally, an authorization, $auth(i, j, \varphi)$ means that i has the authorization to order j to achieve φ. In fact, authorization establishes an agreed power relation of i over j for φ. Consequently, authorization relations always hold in the case of a power relation. That is, if an agent i has power with respect to φ over agent j, then agent i is also authorized to request j to achieve φ. Formally, the following axiom holds for the power relation:

Definition 5 (Authorization relation). *Given expression φ and agents i and j, the following axiom holds:*

$\models \forall \varphi, i, j : power(i, j, \varphi) \rightarrow auth(i, j, request(i, j, \varphi))$. □

(We will more formally introduce the $request$ speech act in the next section.)

As we saw above, in hierarchical dependencies between roles, the power relation is implicit in the dependency. Unfortunately, in the case of markets and hierarchies one cannot specify ways to define authorization relations in similar ways. Authorization relations can still be defined between roles but this requires a communicative process between those roles in order to establish such authorization and its implications. In the following section we will describe these communication processes.

5.2   Realizing Coordination

It is usual to describe communication between agents fulfilling roles in terms of speech acts [21]. The illocution of a speech act is the content of the message that the speaker intends to be recognized by the hearer as what the speaker intends to be doing (informing, requesting, agreeing, etc.) Many different illocutions can be defined, however for the purpose of this paper, we assume *accept*, *propose*, and *request* to be basic illocutions that can be uttered by agents fulfilling roles in an agent society. The illocutionary force of a speech act depends on the social relationship between the agents. That is, speech acts have different effects depending on the type of social dependency between the agents. For example, a request to agent x has another force whether it is done by an agent with power over x, than by any other agent.

Definition 6 (Syntax of Communicative Acts). *Given a domain language L_D the set of all communicative acts, $Comm_D$, on L_D, is defined as:*

- $ill(i, j, \varphi) \in Comm_D$, *where* $ill \in \{request, accept\}$, *$i$: speaker, j: hearer and $\varphi \in L_D$.*

- $propose(i, j, \varphi, \psi) \in Comm_D$, where i: speaker, j: hearer and $\varphi, \psi \in L_D$.
- If $\iota \in Comm_D$ then also $ill(i, j, \iota), ill(i, j, \neg\iota) \in Comm_D$. $\qquad\qquad\square$

The request is intuitively used to get another agent to realize a certain state φ. The propose is used to offer to realize φ in return for the other agent realizing ψ. This can be seen as a kind of conditional commitment. The accept is used to positively answer a request without authorization (as in the charity relation) or to accept a proposal. The intended effects of communicative acts are described more formally in definition 7 by means of deontic operators, and using the dependency relations between agents. These axioms describe how obligations can arise for an agent: by means of a request based on a power or authorization relation, or by (conditionally) committing itself through a propose action. We do not formally introduce the dynamic deontic logic used in this semantics, but only mention the intuition behind the basic constructs of the dynamic and deontic operators. In dynamic logic $[\alpha]\varphi$ indicates that the performance of action α leads to a state in which φ holds. The deontic logic uses a conditional obligation operator $O_{ij}(\varphi|\psi)$ indexed by the debtor and creditor of the obligation. The debtor i is obliged towards the creditor j to establish φ under the condition that ψ holds. We refer the reader to [6] for a more formal semantics of these operators.

Definition 7 (Axioms for communicative acts). *The formal semantics of basic speech acts are:*

1. $\models auth(i, j, request(i, j, \varphi)) \rightarrow [request(i, j, \varphi)]O_{ji}\varphi$
2. $\models [request(i, j, \varphi); accept(j, i, request(i, j, \varphi))]O_{ji}\varphi$
3. $\models [propose(i, j, \varphi, \psi)]O_{ij}(\varphi|auth(i, j, request(i, j, \psi)))$
4. $\models [propose(i, j, \varphi, \psi); accept(j, i, propose(i, j, \varphi, \psi))](O_{ij}\varphi \wedge auth(i, j, request(i, j, \psi)))$ $\qquad\square$

Informally, the first axiom says that if i is authorized than its request to j to achieve φ leads to an obligation of j to achieve φ. The second axiom states that a similar result can be achieved by a request of i followed by an accept of j. In this case no authorization is necessary. The propose leads to a conditional obligation for the proposer. In fact, this formalization of the propose is the most simple form to establish a contract between i and j. It leads possibly to an obligation on one side and a potential obligation (an authorization to create an obligation) on the other side. Through nesting of operators we can incorporate a whole set of conditional authorizations for both sides in ψ.

The last axiom states that if a proposal is accepted than the obligation and authorization become reality.

The above axioms can be combined with the definitions of the previous section to reflect that in hierarchical dependencies, power relations define authorization relations and therefore imply the realization of the intended state of affairs. That is:

$$r_1 \succeq^H_\varphi r_2 \wedge rea(i, r_1) \wedge rea(j, r_2) \rightarrow [request(i, j, \varphi)]O_{j,i}\varphi$$

This explains the efficiency of hierarchical organizations on getting things done. In networks and market organizations authorization is not automatically granted between different roles and must be established by a (more or less) complex communicative process. This process can be described by a sequence of proposals and contra-proposals between the interested parties in order to determine the conditions of authorization.

Such proposal acts can be seen as a kind of conditional commitment, in which each party says "I'll commit to achieve X for you (or commit to do X) provided that you give me authorization to request you to achieve Y (or you commit to do Y upon request)".

Different market mechanisms have been designed in order to describe how a proposal process should run. A well known standard is the Contract Net Protocol that basically says that an agent should put forward a call for proposals (request for X) which can be answered by any other agent. By accepting one of these proposals, the requesting agent is establishing an obligation to the proposing agent to fulfil X. The process of achieving role dependencies in market organizations is basically as follows:

$$(r_1 \succeq_\varphi^M r_2 \wedge rea(i, r_1) \wedge (\forall j \in G : rea(j, r_2))) \rightarrow$$
$$[request(i, G, \varphi); propose(j \in G, i, \varphi, true);$$
$$accept(i, j, propose(j, i, \varphi, true))]O_{j,i}\varphi$$

The above formula contains some liberal notation to avoid complications necessary to correctly express speech acts directed to a group and answers from members of that group. Notice also that the formula above only describes the state of affairs necessary to achieve an obligation to realize goal φ and abstracts from price issues. These can be thought to be part of the formula φ which should then be read as $\varphi \equiv \phi \wedge gave(i, j, price)$, and ignores negotiation iterations between the agents enacting roles r_1 and r_2.

Whereas hierarchies follow strict power relations and markets usually are guided by well defined interaction standards, as the one exemplified above, network organizations are traditionally fairly *'informal'* in the way relations are established between different roles. On the other hand, once a relation between different roles is formed those tend to last for some time and often be intensified as more (successful) goal delegations occur between those roles. Trust and a common desire to realize certain global objectives are the drive of networks, which see different roles as equals in power to establish relations. In practice, interactions in a network function in terms of exchange of favors, or promises to exchange favors. That is, agent A agrees to do X for agent B, expecting to be able at some time to request B to do something else for A. Proposal negotiations are often more complex than in markets because both parties must agree on the needs of each side. Formally, this can be seen as:

$$r_1 \succeq_\varphi^N r_2 \wedge rea(i, r_1) \wedge rea(j, r_2) \rightarrow$$
$$[request(i, j, \varphi); propose(j, i, \varphi, \psi)]$$
$$(auth(j, i, request(j, i, \psi)) \rightarrow O_{j,i}\varphi)$$

The crux in the above formula is of course the part: $auth(j, i, request(j, i, \psi))$. This authorization has to be established by agent i. So, it needs at least another communication step here. This can be a simple accept by agent i. However, the establishment of this authorization might also involve a more intricate negotiation between i and j.

To illustrate the effect of communication between roles in different organization types, we will use the example of the dependency for the objective paper review, r, between agent c enacting the role of Program Chair, C, and agent m enacting the role of PC member, M. Different social dependencies give rise to different attitudes concerning the communication:

- In a hierarchical relation, $C \succeq_r^H M$, the power relation $power(c, m, r)$ holds. Therefore, after $request(c, m, r)$ the obligation $O_{m,c}r$ holds.
- In a market relation, $C \succeq_r^M M$, after $request(c, m, r))$ an explicit proposal from m to do r and its acceptance by c is necessary in order to have the obligation. That is, the following (minimal) dialog must occur:

  $c : request(c, M, r)$

  $m : propose(m, c, r, true)$

  $c : accept(c, m, r)$

  $\therefore O_{m,c}r$

- In a network relation, $C \succeq_r^N M$, not only m has to accept the request, but also c has to agree to a counter request from m (in a conference setting, this would typically be a request to extend the review deadline, e). This can be represented by the following dialog:

  $c : request(c, M, r)$

  $m : propose(m, c, r, e)$

  $c : accept(c, m, propose(m, c, r, e))$

  $\therefore O_{m,c}r \wedge auth(m, c, request(m, c, e))$

The main difference between the market and network situations is the amount of deliberation needed to reach the obligation. Whereas in a market relation, the program chair agent just has to evaluate the proposals on the exact paper review request it had made, in a network situation, the program chair agent will also need that capability to evaluate the new proposal, and possibly enter a negotiation on the deadline extension parameter as well.

5.3   Implications of Coordination

In the previous section, we have introduced the differences in task delegation that result from different types of coordination in organizations. From a coordination perspective hierarchical relations are most efficient in achieving the delegation of tasks. They need only one message to achieve the delegation. It seems that the network type is the least efficient to achieve the delegation of a task, basically, because it allows for some more negotiation on counter-activities. However, as remarked before the final agreement usually encompasses more than one interaction. In the example above it could e.g. result in authorization for the PC chair to ask the PC member to review papers on his favorite topics for the next 3 years, while not giving him more than 3 papers each time and at least 5 weeks for reviewing. As a consequence of this agreement the PC chair only needs to send a request in the next 2 years (just like if there would be a power relation) to achieve the obligation to review a paper. This means that the costs of the current coordination effort should be spread over 3 years to compare with the other mechanisms. Most likely the average coordination costs per year will then be lower than that of the market mechanism that requires the explicit propose and accept part every time.

Note that in the above we only considered the coordination costs (in terms of the number of messages that have to be send after each other (parallel messages to or from a group count for one)). However, from an organizational perspective we are, of course, mainly interested in getting the actual task done. So, we should also take a look at the costs of performing the task once it is delegated to the agent that should actually perform it. In our formalism (as in reality) the task delegation, no matter which mechanism is used, results in an obligation. There is therefore no absolute guarantee that the task will indeed be done, as the agent is free to not fulfil its obligations. The requesting agent should be able to evaluate the capabilities and availability of the requested agent in order to maximize the certainty of task achievement. Moreover, mechanisms for controlling the realization of tasks are needed. We will not go into the latter aspect here but see [14] for further discussion.

In a hierarchy the requesting agent needs to have all the information available to determine the best possible agent for a task. So, it needs to know the capabilities, efficiency, capacity and current workload of all agents. When task requirements and agent capabilities are fairly stable, then it is quite feasible for the delegating agents to maintain this information. In this case the requesting agent just needs to determine the best agent for the task and a request leads to the obligation to do it. However, if tasks and agents change rapidly, or if the requesting agent does not have the capability to evaluate either the task requirements of the capabilities and availability of the agents, then the obligation that follows the request may stay unfulfilled and the requesting agent is then forced to perform the task itself or negotiate realization with other agents, as in the market or network cases. The decision for a certain coordination type is dependent on the characteristics of the agents and of the environment.

It is exactly for situations where the delegating agent cannot maintain all information about the other agents that market mechanisms are meant for. The proposals of the agents answering a request (implicitly) carry the information that the agent needs to make the best possible choice for delegating the task. If an agent is not capable to perform the task it will not answer with a propose. If it is already very busy it will propose to perform the task later, or slow. The delegating agent only needs to compare the proposals to find the best one every time. Because the resulting obligations only hold for the current transaction, the agents are capable to choose the best option every time, based on the most up-to-date information. So, the overhead in coordination costs might be paid back through more efficient distribution of the tasks.

As before, the networks have an intermediate position between hierarchies and markets. In networks, besides the agreement concerning the initial request, usually further interaction will happen (concerning the realization of the counter request). The interest in maintaining such long-time relation with the requested agent is often one of the reasons for the requesting agent to enter a negotiation on the counter proposal (see the example above). In this way long-time relations between agents are achieved, without the inflexibility of a hierarchy. However, if one foresees that the environment will change rapidly, this longer term relationships may not be very useful. E.g. if the topics of the conference change every year it is no use to make an agreement for a PC member to review papers on a fixed topic for several years (because he might have nothing to do next year). The network mechanism is especially suited for situations where agents might not always be available (the system is not (completely) closed or agents have multiple tasks for different organizations) while the environment is relatively stable.

In the previous paragraphs we analyzed the properties of hierarchical, market and network relations. Often organizations as a whole are said to be of one of these three types.

Although often the relationships within an organization tend to be of the same kind it is worth observing that we did not assume that all relations within an organization are of the same kind. One could e.g. have hierarchical relations between the general chair role and the PC chair role and local organizer role, while the relation between the PC chair role and the PC member role is of a market type. In this way one can optimally combine the coordination mechanisms for optimal efficiency and utility of the organization.

6   Conclusion

In this paper we have argued that organizational structures are important for MAS. In line with other current research we think that these structures need to exist outside the individual agents in order to ensure the achievement of objectives of the organization that rise above the individual agent level. By having explicit organizational structures we also ensure the stability of the organization over a longer period of time.

We have shown that the organizational structure consists of several inter-related elements. We have concentrated mostly on the role dependencies that arise from the dependencies between the objectives of those roles. These dependencies seem to indicate the basic needs of coordination between the roles. Moreover we have shown that the basic coordination types from organizational theory (market, hierarchy and network) are also very useful for MAS design. Starting from the dependencies between roles that follow from their objectives, these coordination types determine how the interaction between the dependent roles is shaped. The coordination type of the organization also influences the type of facilitation roles that are needed in that organization, such as a matchmaker for a market and a gate keeper for a network organization.

In the last section we made a start on determining how some characteristics of the coordination types and the environment determine the best structure to be used for a MAS in a particular environment. Although we base our theory on the formal theory underlying the OperA model, we will use simulations to check for the organizational characteristics that will benefit the organization best in a certain environment.

The main objective of this paper is to present an interconnected view over the many facets of organization and coordination. We present an initial model for linking coordination to organizational structure in terms of the interpretation of communicative acts depending on the dependencies between the roles agents are enacting in the organization. Future research will focus on the validation and application of the model and will lead to more grounded results. In particular, we will use the ideas proposed in [14] to analyze the performance of different organizational structures.

Acknowledgements. The research of the first author is funded by the Netherlands Organization for Scientific Research (NWO), through Veni-grant 639.021.509.

References

1. Biddle, B.: Role Theory: Concepts and Research. Krieger Publishing Co. (1979)
2. Castelfranchi, C.: Silent agents: From observation to tacit communication. In: Proc. of WS on Agent Tracking: Modelling Other Agents from Observations (2004)

3. Ciancarini, P., Omicini, A., Zambonelli, F.: Coordination models for multi-agent systems. AgentLink News 3 (July 1999)
4. Dellarocas, C.: Contractual agent societies: Negotiated shared context and social control. In: Proc. Workshop on Norms and Institutions in MAS, Autonomous Agents (2000)
5. Dignum, F.: Autonomous agents with norms. AI & Law 7, 69–79 (1999)
6. Dignum, F., Weigand, H.: Communication and deontic logic. In: Wieringa, R., Feenstra, R. (eds.) Information Systems - Correctness and Reusability. Selected papers from the IS-CORE Workshop, pp. 242–260. World Scientific Publishing Co., Singapore (1995)
7. Dignum, V.: A Model for Organizational Interaction: based on Agents, founded in Logic. SIKS Dissertation Series 2004-1. Utrecht University, PhD Thesis (2004)
8. Dignum, V., Dignum, F.: Structures for agent organizations. In: Proc. of KIMAS'05, IEEE Press, Los Alamitos (2005)
9. Duncan, R.: What is the right organizational structure: Decision tree analyis provides the answer. Organizational Dynamics, 59–80 (Winter, 1979)
10. Esteva, M., Padget, J., Sierra, C.: Formalizing a language for institutions and norms. In: Meyer, J.-J.C., Tambe, M. (eds.) ATAL 2001. LNCS (LNAI), vol. 2333, Springer, Heidelberg (2002)
11. Ferber, J., Gutknecht, O., Michel, F.: From agents to organizations: An organizational view of multi-agent systems. In: Giorgini, P., Müller, J.P., Odell, J.J. (eds.) Agent-Oriented Software Engineering IV. LNCS, vol. 2935, Springer, Heidelberg (2004)
12. Fox, M., Barbuceanu, M., Gruniger, M., Lin, J.: An organizational ontology for enterprise modeling. In: Prietula, M., Carley, K., Gasser, L. (eds.) Simulating Organizations: Conceptual Models of Institutions and Groups, MIT Press, Cambridge (1998)
13. Giddens, A.: The Constitution of Society: Outline of the Theory of Structure. Univ. California Press (1984)
14. Grossi, D., Dignum, F., Dignum, V., Dastani, M., Royakkers, L.: Structural aspects of the evaluation of agent organizations. LNCS, vol. 4386, pp. 3–19. Springer, Heidelberg (2007)
15. Kumar, S., Huber, M., Cohen, P., McGee, D.: Towards a formalism for conversation protocols using joint intention theory. Computational Intelligence Journal 18(2) (2002)
16. Malone, T., Crowston, K.: The interdisciplinary study of coordination. ACM Computing Surveys 26(1) (March 1994)
17. Odell, J., Nodine, M., Levy, R.: A metamodel for agents, roles, and groups. In: Giorgini, P., Müller, J.P., Odell, J.J. (eds.) Agent-Oriented Software Engineering IV. LNCS, vol. 2935, Springer, Heidelberg (2004)
18. Odell, J., Van Dyke Parunak, H., Fleischer, M.: The role of roles in designing effective agent organizations. In: Garcia, A.F., de Lucena, C.J.P., Zambonelli, F., Omicini, A., Castro, J. (eds.) Software Engineering for Large-Scale Multi-Agent Systems. LNCS, vol. 2603, Springer, Heidelberg (2003)
19. Omicini, A., Ricci, A., Viroli, M., Castelfranchi, C., Tummolini, L.: Coordination artifacts: Environment-based coordination for intelligent agents. In: Jennings, N., et al. (eds.) AAMAS 2004, pp. 286–293. ACM Press, New York, USA (2004)
20. Powell, W.: Neither market nor hierarchy: Network forms of organisation. Research in Organisational Behavior 12, 295–336 (1990)
21. Searle, J.: Speech Acts: an Essay in the Philosophy of Language. Cambridge U Press, Cambridge (1969)
22. Smith, R.: The contract net protocol: High-lever communication and control in a distributed problem solver. IEEE Transactions on Computers C-29(12), 1014–1113 (1980)
23. Williamson, O.: Markets and hierarchies: Analysis and Antitrust Implications. Free Press, New York (1975)

Redesign of Organizations as a Basis
for Organizational Change

Mark Hoogendoorn[1], Catholijn M. Jonker[2], and Jan Treur[1]

[1] Vrije Universiteit Amsterdam, Department of Artificial Intelligence,
De Boelelaan 1081a, 1081 HV Amsterdam, The Netherlands
{mhoogen,treur}@cs.vu.nl
[2] Radboud University Nijmegen, Nijmegen Institute for Cognition and Information
Montessorilaan 3, 6525 HR Nijmegen, The Netherlands
C.Jonker@nici.ru.nl

Abstract. Artificial Intelligence has contributed (formal) design models and software support tools to application areas such as architecture, engineering and software design This paper explores the effectiveness of applying design models to the area of organization (re)design. To that purpose a component-based model for (re)design of organizations is presented as a specialization of an existing generic design model. Using recently developed formalizations within Organization Theory organization models are described as design object descriptions, and organization goals as design requirements. A design process specification is presented that models the redesign process for an organization that adapts to changes in the environment. The formally specified and implemented approach to organization redesign thus obtained has been tested for a well-known historical case study from the Organization Theory literature.

1 Introduction

Organizations are created to smoothen processes in all aspects of society, even in the artificial societies of software agents. From a design perspective organizations have goals to be achieved or maintained that serve as requirements for their functioning. The behavior of the elements or parts of the organization and their interaction together should result in overall organization behavior that fulfills the goals of the organization. Environmental circumstances impose constraints on the organization with respect to the way its goals can be fulfilled. As the environment changes over time, so do these constraints. To adapt to such changes in constraints, the organization might have to change itself. From a design perspective the changing constraints can be interpreted as changing requirements for a redesign problem.

Within the area of AI and Design, in the last decade formally specified generic models for (re)design processes have been developed; e.g., [1, 4]. Application of a generic redesign model to the area of organizations requires specialized knowledge on: (1) organization goals; (2) how to derive refined requirements from such goals given a variable environment; (3) the current design object description, and (4) what components for a design object satisfy which requirements. A redesign process results in a new design object description as a modification of the existing one and a specification of changed (new) design requirements.

P. Noriega et al. (Eds.): COIN 2006 Workshops, LNAI 4386, pp. 48–64, 2007.

A redesign process as formally modeled in [4] involves generation and modification steps both for the specification of the requirement set and for the design object description. A formal model of a redesign process thus requires formalizations of design objects, design requirements, and of the dynamics of redesign processes. This paper proposes such formalizations for the area of organizational (re)design, in the context of a component based model for (re)design of organizations. Formalized organization models [5,10,11,14,18] serve as design object descriptions. Formalizations of organizational behavior are used for design requirements specifications [10,11,14,18]. Finally, for design process dynamics a formalization is used as put forward in [1]. The resulting approach contributes to the organization redesign domain in that it facilitates formal modeling, simulation and verification of the redesign process, supported by modeling and analysis tools.

Section 2 gives the component-based model for the design and redesign process and describes the types of domain specific knowledge needed in such a process. Section 3 addresses the formalization of design object descriptions by means of an organization model format in which different components and aggregation levels are distinguished. In Section 4 the relation between goals, changing environment and requirements is described, illustrated for cases described in Organization Theory. Section 5 presents the method of requirements refinement and shows a specific example. Thereafter, Section 6 presents examples of design object that are known to satisfy certain design requirements, and Section 7 presents generic properties which enable an evaluation of the successfulness of the whole (re)design process. Section 8 presents simulation results of the model, and finally Section 9 is a discussion.

2   A Component-Based Model for (Re)design of Organizations

This Section presents a component-based generic model for design of organizations based on requirements manipulation and design object description manipulation. The component-based model presented draws inspiration from [4] and was specified within the DESIRE [3] framework. It is composed of three components, see Figure 1:

- RQSM, for Requirement Qualification Set Manipulation, acquires requirements, for example, by elicitation from managers within a company. Within RQSM the appropriate requirements are determined in relation to the goals set for the organization and the current environmental conditions. After having selected a set of requirements, these are refined to more specific ones.
- DODM, for Design Object Description Manipulation, creates a design object description based on the (specific) requirements received from RQSM. In order to do this, a number of alternative solutions known to satisfy the requirements are generated and according to certain strategic knowledge one of those is selected.
- Design Process Coordination (DPC) is the coordinating component for the design process. The component determines the global design strategy (e.g., [4]) and can evaluate whether the design process is proceeding according to plan.

Information exchange possibilities are represented by the links between input and output of the components and the input and output of the model. Input and output are represented by the small boxes left and right of components.

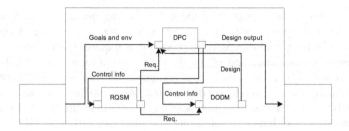

Fig. 1. Top level of the design model

The next sections describe the three components in more detail. The model as described here, is a generic design model for organizational design without application- or domain-specific knowledge. In later sections such knowledge is specified for a case study.

RQSM. This component is composed of two sub-components, namely Requirements Sets Generation and Requirements Set Selection, see Figure 2.

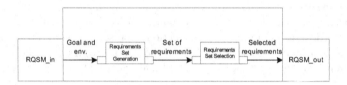

Fig. 2. Components within RQSM

The component Requirements Sets Generation receives as an input the current environmental conditions and the organizational goals. The sub-component contains knowledge on what requirements entail fulfillment of organizational goals given the environmental conditions. Such knowledge can be depicted in the form of AND/OR trees as shown in Figure 3.

If for example E1 is observed, requirement R1 is an example of a requirement that, when fulfilled, guarantees to satisfy goal G under environmental conditions E1. If the environment changes to situation E2, the requirement has to change as well; the example tree shows how R1 can be changed to requirement R2 that guarantees G under the new environmental conditions E2. Note that these environmental conditions can be defined as an abstraction of the potentially infinite actual environment. This resembles how a manager would define such requirements, for instance by just looking at a few specific aspect of the environment, and basing his/her requirement for the organization on those. After a requirement is determined, it can be refined in order to obtain requirements on a more specific level. Making such a requirement more specific can result in several options being generated. For example, it might be possible to establish a certain market share by having the best quality products but also by having the lowest priced products. After having refined each of the requirements, all possible sets of refined requirements are forwarded to the component Requirements Set Selection.

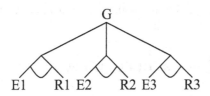

Fig. 3. Example AND/OR tree relating environmental conditions and requirements to a goal

After the component Requirements Set Selection has received the alternative sets of requirements its task is to select one of those alternatives, and to forward it to the component DODM which will in turn find a suitable organization design for such a requirement set. Different selection methods exist, e.g., explicit ranking, on the basis of strategic knowledge. Such strategic knowledge can for example be based on the source of requirements: requirements that originate from users can for example be preferred over those derived by default rules which are in turn preferred over requirements derived from previous requirements (see [12]).

DODM. This component receives a set of refined requirements from RQSM, which is handled by two sub-components, Design Object Description Generation and Design Object Description Selection. The design object descriptions are descriptions of designs of the organization, including both structural aspects as behavioral aspects.

Design Object Description Generation receives the requirements and delivers descriptions of possible alternative design objects (i.e., organization design descriptions), such that the (specific) requirements as received from RQSM are satisfied. To establish satisfaction, knowledge is needed that specifies what part of a design object contributes to fulfillment of a specific requirement. If, for example, the requirement is to produce products of the highest quality, then a satisfactory design is an organization having a department dedicated to checking quality and repairing of production errors. Again, there can be many possibilities available that satisfy the requirements. All alternatives found are forwarded to the component Design Object Description Selection.

The component Design Object Description Selection can use several criteria to choose the optimal design, such as operational costs effectiveness, and production time effectiveness. In order to make such a selection, the component has (strategic) knowledge concerning these aspects. It might for example know the typical price for hiring an agent for a particular role. Eventually, the component outputs a new design for the organization.

DPC. The component DPC is the component which determines the global design strategy and oversees whether the design process proceeds according to plan. Two different tasks are distinguished. DPC checks whether a design object description determined by DODM satisfies the refined requirements. It might for example be the case that the combination of two suitable design object parts causes a conflict. In case the refined requirements are not satisfied control information is passed to DODM stating that an alternative should be found (e.g., taking a different branch of an OR tree). In case these refined requirements are satisfied whereas the high-level requirements are not, the requirements refining process has failed, therefore control information is given to RQSM to refine the requirements in another way (again by for example taking another OR branch).

3 Organization Models as Design Objects

An organizational structure defines different elements in an organization and relations between them. The dynamics of these different elements can be characterized by sets of dynamic properties. An organizational structure has the aim to keep the overall dynamics of the organization manageable; therefore the structural relations between the different elements within the organizational structure have to impose relationships or dependencies between their dynamics; cf. [18]. In the introduction to their book Lomi and Larsen [20] emphasize the importance of such relationships:

- 'given a set of assumptions about (different forms of) individual behavior, how can the aggregate properties of a system be determined (or predicted) that are generated by the repeated interaction among those individual units?'
- 'given observable regularities in the behavior of a composite system, which rules and procedures - if adopted by the individual units- induce and sustain these regularities?'

Both views and problems require means to express relationships between dynamics of different elements and different levels of aggregation within an organization. In [20] two levels are mentioned: the level of the organization as a whole versus the level of the units. Also in the development of MOISE [11,12,14] an emphasis is put on relating dynamics to structure. Within MOISE dynamics is described at the level of units by the goals, actions, plans and resources allocated to roles to obtain the organization's task as a whole. Specification of the task as a whole may involve achieving a final (goal) state, or an ongoing process (maintenance goals) and an associated plan specification.

The approach in this paper is illustrated for the AGR [9] organization modeling approach. Figure 4 shows an example organization modeled using AGR. Within AGR organization models three aggregation levels are distinguished: (1) the organization as a whole; the highest aggregation level, denoted by the big oval, (2) the level of a group denoted by the middle size ovals, and (3) the level of a role within a group denoted by the smallest ovals. Solid arrows denote transfer between roles within a group; dashed lines denote inter-group interactions. This format is adopted to formalize organization models as design object descriptions. In addition, behavioral properties of elements of an organization are part of a design object description. TTL [17] is used to express such behavioral properties.

In TTL state ontology is a specification (in order-sorted logic) of a vocabulary. A state for ontology Ont is an assignment of truth-values {true, false} to the set At(Ont) of ground atoms expressed in terms of Ont. The *set of all possible states* for state ontology Ont is denoted by STATES(Ont). The set of *state properties* STATPROP(Ont) for state ontology Ont is the set of all propositions over ground atoms from At(Ont). A fixed *time frame* T is assumed which is linearly ordered. A *trace* or *trajectory* γ over a state ontology Ont and time frame T is a mapping $\gamma : T \rightarrow$ STATES(Ont), i.e., a sequence of states γ_t (t ∈ T) in STATES(Ont). The set of all traces over state ontology Ont is denoted by TRACES(Ont). Depending on the application, the time frame T may be dense (e.g., the real numbers), or discrete (e.g., the set of integers or natural numbers or a finite initial segment of the natural numbers), or any other form, as long as it has a linear ordering. The set of *dynamic properties* DYNPROP(Σ) is the set of temporal statements that can be formulated with respect to traces based on the state ontology Ont in the following manner.

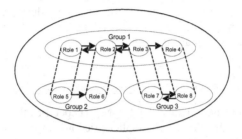

Fig. 4. An AGR Organization Structure

Given a trace γ over state ontology Ont, the state in γ at time point t is denoted by state(γ, t). These states can be related to state properties via the formally defined satisfaction relation ⊨, comparable to the Holds-predicate in the Situation Calculus: state(γ, t) ⊨ p denotes that state property p holds in trace γ at time t. Based on these statements, dynamic properties can be formulated in a formal manner in a sorted first-order predicate logic, using quantifiers over time and traces and the usual first-order logical connectives such as ¬, ∧, ∨, ⇒, ∀, ∃. A special software environment has been developed for TTL, featuring both a Property Editor for building and editing TTL properties and a Checking Tool that enables formal verification of such properties against a set of (simulated or empirical) traces.

4 RQSM: Changing Requirements Upon Environmental Change

Organizational requirements change due to changing environmental circumstances. The circumstances are input to RQSM. The general pattern is follows. A certain organizational goal G (e.g. sufficient demand) is no longer reached, due to an environmental change, say from E1 to E2. In the old situation requirement R1 was sufficient to guarantee G under environmental condition E1: E1 & R1 ⇒ G. Here R1 is a requirement expressing a relation which states that under the condition E1 the organization is able to achieve G. The change from E1 to E2 makes that requirement R1, which is still fulfilled but has become insufficient, is to be replaced by a new, stronger requirement R2 which expresses that under environment E2 goal G can be achieved; therefore: E2 & R2 ⇒ G. Thus, the organization is triggered to change to fulfill R2 and as a consequence fulfill goal G again.

Jaffee [16] distinguishes several classes of external triggers for organizational change: triggers in the organization's *input*, (e.g., changes in the resources or suppliers), and triggers in *enabling / constraining factors* such as government/labor rules and (new) technology. Government regulations for workers might affect human resource practices and composition of the workforce. Concerning labor aspects, the union might demand a reduction from 40 to 36 hours a week, which naturally causes organizational change. Examples of input triggers are *resources* that run out, becoming a lot more expensive, *customers* whose demands decrease for the good being produced, and *competitors* changing their production methods causing more efficient production for products within the same product group. Another example of an input-base external trigger is the case that at time t *suppliers* increase their price of a product P, which is used by the organization for the production, from M_1 to M_2. A formal form of this environmental condition is specified in E1 using the Temporal Trace Language (TTL) as explained in Section 3.

E1(P, M, t): Supplier Price
∃R:REAL state(γ, t) |= environmental_condition(price(P, R), pos) & R ≤ M

Before the environmental change, E1(P1, M_1, t) specifies the relevant property of the environment. After the change of supplier price however, this property no longer holds whereas E1(P1, M_2, t) does hold. The overall goal to be maintained within the organization is to keep the demand of product P above a threshold D. A formal specification of the goal is presented in OP1.

OP1(P, D, t): Sufficient demand
∃I:INTEGER state(γ, t) |= environmental_condition(customer_demand(P, I), pos) & I ≥ D

The requirement imposed for the organization is to maintain the goal of keeping demand for product P2 above D, in the new situation given the environmental condition of the price M for product P1 which is needed for the production of P2. This requirement is specified below in property R.

R(P1, P2, M, D): Maintain demand
∀t :TIME [state(γ, t) |= needed_for_production_of(P1, P2) & E1(P1, M, t)] ⇒ OP1(P2, D, t)

Before the change in the environment, requirement R1 which is R(P1, P2, M_1, D) was sufficient to ensure the goal being reached. After the change however, this requirement is still satisfied but might be insufficient to ensure the goal. This is due to the fact that the environmental condition E1 in the antecedent of E1 & R1 ⇒ G does not hold, and hence, cannot be used to entail G (although the requirement R1 is fulfilled all the time). The requirement is therefore withdrawn and replaced by the requirement R2 which is R(P1, P2, M_2, D). This R2, however, is not necessarily satisfied and may require an organizational change to enable fulfillment.

5   RQSM: Refining Requirements Based on Interlevel Relations

To fulfill requirements at the level of the organization as a whole as discussed in Section 4, parts of the organization need to behave adequately (see also the central challenges put forward by Lomi and Larsen [20] as discussed in Section 2). Based on this idea, in this paper dynamics of an organization are characterized by sets of dynamic properties for the respective elements and aggregation levels of the organization. An important issue is how organizational structure (the design object description determined in DODM) relates to (mathematically defined) relationships between these sets of dynamic properties for the different elements and aggregation levels within an organization (cf. [18]). Preferably such relations between sets of dynamic properties would be of a logical nature; this would allow the use of logical methods to analyze, verify and validate organization behavior in relation to organization structure. Indeed, following [18], in the approach presented below, logical relationships between sets of dynamic properties of elements in an organization turn out an adequate manner to (mathematically) express such dynamic cross-element or cross-level relationships.

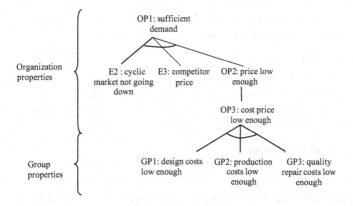

Fig. 5. Hierarchy of Organizational and Group properties

Figure 5 shows an example of a hierarchy of dynamic properties for an organization producing certain products, the properties follow field observations at the Ford Motor Company in 1980 described in [25]. The overall organizational goal is to maintain sufficient demand for the goods being produced, as was also the case in OP1 in Section 4. The organization has separate departments for design, production and quality control, which are modeled as groups in the organization. The highest levels represent organizational properties or goals at the aggregation level of the organization as a whole, whereas the lowest level shown here represents properties at the aggregation level of the groups. Note that the fact that these are group properties already restricts the design of the object in DODM, which makes the process less complex.

A definition for each of the properties in Figure 5 is presented below. Notice that this hierarchy could easily be extended by other aspects (e.g., of quality of the products as a reason for the demand decreasing or not). Property OP1 is described in Section 4. One of the environmental conditions is that the cyclic market is not going down for a product P at time t in case the demand for the product group as a whole (i.e., all goods produced by different companies in this particular category) is not going down.

E2(P, t): Cyclic market not going down
  $\forall$G:PRODUCT_GROUP, l1,l2:INTEGER
  [state(γ, t) |= belongs_to_product_group(P, G) &
    state(γ, (t-1)) |= environmental_condition(customer_demand(G, l1), pos) &
    state(γ, t) |= environmental_condition(customer_demand(G, l2), pos)]
  $\Rightarrow$ l2 $\geq$ l1

Furthermore, an environmental condition E3 poses a requirement on the price of competitors in the form of the average price of products within the product group to which product P belongs. These prices should not be higher than V:

E3(P, V, t): Competitor Price
∀G:PRODUCT_GROUP, V1:REAL [[state(γ, t) |= belongs_to_product_group(P, G) &
state(γ, t) |= environmental_condition(average_price(G,V1), pos)] ⇒ V1 ≥ V]

To achieve goal OP1 given environmental conditions E2 and E3, the price of the products being produced by the organization should be low enough, which in turn is the requirement posed on the organization. Prices are considered low enough for a product P at time t in case the price for the product is equal or below the average price level within the product group (i.e. prices are ≤ V as set above).

OP2(P, V, t): Price low enough
∀G:PRODUCT_GROUP, V1:REAL [state(γ, t) |= price(P, V1)] ⇒ V1 ≤ V

Whether the price is low enough depends on the cost price for the particular product P at time t, which purely depends on the costs for the different groups within the organization, as expressed in the group properties (GP's).

OP3(P, V, t): Cost price low enough
∀V1,V2,V3:REAL [state(γ, t) |= design_cost(P, V1) & state(γ, t) |= production_cost(P, V2) &
state(γ, t) |= quality_repair_cost(P, V3)] ⇒ V1+V2+V3 ≤ V

Finally, the individual group properties can be specified such that the costs of each group are below a certain value. The division of such costs over groups is a refinement choice. An example decision could be to allow only a small percentage of the costs for quality repair and to divide the brunt of the costs equally over production and design. Each group should meet their individual requirements. First of all, design costs should be low enough:

GP1(P, V1, t): Design costs low enough
∀Q:REAL [state(γ, t) |= design_cost(P, Q)] ⇒ Q ≤ V1

Also, the production costs for product P should be low enough:

GP2(P, V2, t): Production costs low enough
∀Q:REAL [state(γ, t) |= production_cost(P, Q)] ⇒ Q ≤ V2

Finally, quality repair costs should be low enough for product P:

GP3(P, V3, t): Quality repair costs low enough
∀Q:REAL [state(γ, t) |= quality_repair_cost(P, Q)] ⇒ Q ≤ V3

After having generated all options in RQSM, selection knowledge is used to select one of the available options. In this paper, such selection knowledge is not further addressed. The output of RQSM is, however, of the form selected_basic_refinement_set(RS) where RS is a name for a requirements set. The elements within this set are defined as follows: in_selected_basic_refinement_set(R, RS) where R is a requirement, as the ones shown above, and RS is the selected basic refinement set.

6 DODM: Constructing Design Objects

As stated in Section 2, DODM contains a library of templates for (parts of) design objects which are known to satisfy certain requirements (of the form as specified in the last paragraph of the previous section). For the case study, the DODM library contains two templates. One of those is a template in which a mass production system is used to produce goods. Such a system produces goods at reasonable production costs but at high quality repair costs. The template for mass production includes a group of production workers (e.g. a production worker for attaching a wheel to a car). The mass production template also contains a quality repair department of considerable size with quality repair worker roles.

The second template in the library is a lean production organization. Lean production has no quality repair costs, since there is no separate quality repair department. The production costs are at the same level as the production costs for mass production organizations. In the lean production method (see e.g. [25]), multi-task production workers are present which perform several tasks, and also handle errors in case they are observed. As a result of such immediate error detection and correction, a quality repair department is not present within a lean production model.

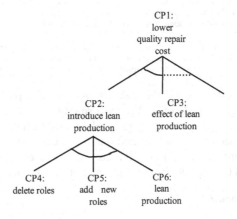

Fig. 6. Redesign options specified in the form of an AND/OR tree

Figure 6 shows an example AND/OR tree for DODM (focusing at lean production as a solution) in which options for changes in a design object not satisfying the requirement that design costs are low enough. The specific changes in the design object are presented below. First of all, the highest level property states that design costs will at least at the required level within a duration d:

CP1(P, D, t):Lower Quality Repair Costs
∀V1,V2:REAL [state(γ, t) |= selected_basic_requirement_in(GP3(P, V1, t), RS) &
state(γ, t) |= DOD_includes(D, quality_repair_cost(P, V2)) & V1 < V2]
⇒ ∃t2:TIME > t, V3:REAL [t2 < t+d & state(γ, t2) |=DOD_includes(D,quality_repair_cost(P, V3)) & V3 ≤ V1]

On a lower level, property CP2(P, D, t) specifies the introduction of lean production into an organization. This reduces the quality repair costs to 0 as shown by CP3(P, D, t).

Although more options are possible for reducing quality repair costs, shown by the dots in Figure 6, these are not addressed in this paper.

CP2(P, D, t): Introduce Lean Production
∀V1,V2:REAL [state(γ, t) |= selected_basic_requirement_in(GP3(P, V1, t), RS) &
state(γ, t) |= DOD_includes(D, design_cost(P, R2)) & V1 < V2]
⇒ ∃t2:TIME > t [t2 < t + d & state(γ, t2) |= DOD_includes(D, lean_production_method(P))]

CP3(P, D, t): Effect of Lean Production
[state(γ, t) |= DOD_includes(D, lean_production_method(P)) ⇒
state(γ, t) |= DOD_includes(D, quality_repair_cost(P, 0))]

Introducing a lean production system entails that within the production process the specialized roles for mass-production and quality repair department are deleted.

CP4(P, D, t): Delete Roles
∀R1,R2:REAL [state(γ, t) |= DOD_includes(D, lean_production_method(P))
⇒   ∃t2:TIME > t [t2 < t + d &
state(γ,t2)|= ¬DOD_includes(D,exists_role(spec_production_worker)) &
state(γ, t2)|= ¬DOD_includes(D,exists_group(quality_repair_group))]]

Moreover, roles are created that perform multiple tasks, and teams are created such that the roles combined in the team have all the abilities to make a car.

CP5(P, D, t): Add New Roles
∀R1,R2:REAL [state(γ, t) |= DOD_includes(D, lean_production_method(P))
⇒   ∃t2:TIME > t, ∀A:AGENT
[t2 < t + d & state(γ, t2) |= DOD_includes(D, exists_role(multi_task_production_worker)) &
state(γ, t2) |= DOD_includes(D, previously_allocated_to(A, spec_production_worker, production_group)) &
state(γ, t2) |= DOD_includes(D, allocated_to(A, multi_task_production_worker, production_group))]]

Agents that were allocated to the deleted roles in the production process are allocated to the newly formed roles. Agents formerly allocated to a role in quality repair are fired. Once the system is organized in this fashion, quality repair in a separate department becomes obsolete, and quality repair costs are down to 0 as the production workers are now performing the task. CP6 expresses that the measures as described in CP4 and CP5 results in a lean production method for the product P:

CP6(P, D, t): Lean Production
∀A:AGENT
[state(γ, t) |= ¬ DOD_includes(D, exists_role(spec_production_worker)) &
state(γ, t) |= ¬ DOD_includes(D, exists_group(quality_repair_group)) &
state(γ, t) |= DOD_includes(D, exists_role(multi_task_production_worker)) &
state(γ, t) |= DOD_includes(D, previously_allocated_to(A, spec_production_worker, production_group))
state(γ, t) |= DOD_includes(D, allocated_to(A, multi_task_production_worker, production_group))]
⇒ ∃t2:TIME < t + d state(γ, t2) |= DOD_includes(D,lean_production_method(P))

After such options for (re)design of the object have been generated based on the requirements, selection knowledge is used to select one of the options that have been generated. This knowledge is not addressed in this paper. Eventually, DODM outputs a design object description of the form selected_DOD_output(D) where D is the design object description. Furthermore to identify properties of the DOD or its parts, output of the form in_selected_DOD_output(P,D) is generated where P is a property of (a part of) the DOD and D is the selected DOD. This is based on the internal information represented in the form of DOD_includes(D, P).

7   (Re)design Process Evaluation

This section addresses the evaluation of the whole design process. The overall design process is successful when both RQSM and DODM show the proper behavior.

RQSM shows the proper behavior in case it generates requirements, and these requirements indeed result in the goal set for the organization being met. Such properties are formulated in a formal form below.

RQSM_generate

If RQSM receives new environmental conditions on its input, then RQSM eventually generates a set of requirements

∀t:TIME, γ:TRACE, E:ENV_COND [[state(γ, t, input(RQSM)) |= environment_property(E) &
  ¬∃t':TIME < t [state(γ, t', input(RQSM)) |= environment_property(E)]]
⇒ ∃t2:TIME > t, G:GOAL, RS:REQUIREMENT_SET [state(γ, t2, output(RQSM)) |= main_requirement(G) &
      state(γ, t2, output(RQSM)) |= selected_basic_refinement_set(RS)]]

RQSM_successful

If RQSM generates requirements, then the combination of these requirements entail the goal set for the organization.

∀t:TIME, γ:TRACE, RS :REQUIREMENT_SET, G :GOAL
[[state(γ, t, output(RQSM)) |= main_requirement(G) &
  state(γ, t, output(RQSM)) |= selected_basic_refinement_set(RS)] ⇒ entails_goal(RS, G)]

DODM shows the proper behavior in case it first of all generates a design object description in case a new requirement set is received. Besides simply generating such a design object description, the object also needs to satisfy the requirements received on its input.

DODM_generate

If DODM receives a new requirements set on its input, then DODM eventually generates a design object description as output.

∀t:TIME, γ:TRACE, RS :REQUIREMENTS_SET
[state(γ, t, input(DODM)) |= selected_basic_refinement_set(RS) &
  ¬∃t':TIME < t [state(γ, t', input(DODM)) |= selected_basic_refinement_set(RS)]
⇒ ∃t2:TIME, D:DESIGN_OBJECT_DESCRIPTION
  state(γ, t2, output(DODM)) |= selected_DOD_output(D)]

DODM_successful

If DODM generates a design object description as output, then the design object description satisfies the requirements set on the input of DODM.

∀t:TIME, γ:TRACE, R :REQUIREMENT_SET,
  D:DESIGN_OBJECT_DESCRIPTION
[state(γ, t, input(DODM)) |= selected_basic_refinement_set(R) &
  state(γ, t, output(DODM)) |= selected_DOD_output(D)]
⇒ fulfills_requirements(D, R)

---

8   Simulation Results

In order to show the functioning of the model presented above, simulation runs have been performed based on the properties as identified in Sections 4-6 using the component-based design presented in Section 2. As a scenario for the case study, a sudden decrease of competitor price is inserted as an event into the simulation

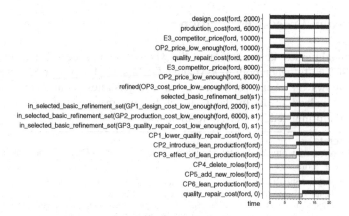

Fig. 7. Case study simulation results

(following [25]). Figure 7 shows a partial trace of the simulation results. In the figure, the left side shows the atoms that occur during the simulation whereas the right side shows a timeline where a dark gray box indicates an atom being true at that particular time point and a light gray box indicates the atom is false.

The figure shows the following. Initially, the different cost factors for the ford design object are the following: design_cost(ford, 2000); production_cost(ford, 6000); quality_repair_cost(ford, 2000). This perfectly fulfills the requirement that price is considered to be low enough in case it is at most 10000 as expressed in OP2 at that time point: OP2_price_low_enough(ford, 10000) . This requirement is sufficient to guarantee the goal OP1 (as expressed in Figure 5) due to the environmental condition E3 that competitor price for products within the same product group as ford are at that exact same level: E3_competitor_price(ford, 10000). Furthermore, the cyclic market should not be going down (E2) which is left constant during this simulation. Suddenly however, the environment changes, the price of competing cars drops to 8000: E3_competitor_price(ford, 8000). The current property OP2 is now insufficient to guarantee the overall goal OP1 being satisfied, therefore, a redesign process is activated. RQSM determines a new requirement for the design object, namely that prices should be below 8000, the competitor car price:OP2_price_low_enough(ford, 8000). Other options might be possible as well, but are not addressed in the simulation. The requirement is refined, first of all by expressing that the cost price should be low enough: refined(OP3_cost_price_low_enough(ford, 8000)). This results in a selected basic refinement that quality repair costs should become 0 whereas design and production costs can remain 2000 and 6000 respectively, as shown in the requirements part of the selected refinement s1:

in_selected_basic_refinement_set(GP1_design_cost_low_enough(ford, 2000), s1);
in_selected_basic_refinement_set(GP2_production_cost_low_enough(ford, 6000), s1);
in_selected_basic_refinement_set(GP1_quality_repair_cost_low_enough(ford,0),s1).

Since these are basic refinements, they are passed to DODM in order to find templates appropriate for these basic requirements. DODM observes that quality repair costs for the current design object are too high, and therefore starts to use the tree as expressed in Figure 6, refining the exact changes to be performed on the design object more and more. First the introduction of the lean production system is chosen, as expressed in CP2. Thereafter, the more concrete changes are determined, namely the deletion of the specialized production worker roles, the addition of new multi-task roles, and the insertion of the new behavior of those roles: CP4_delete_roles(ford); CP5_add_new_roles(ford); CP6_lean_production(ford). Note that in the simulation the actual contents of such properties are more concrete (in the form of current DOD descriptions), however, these are not presented here for the sake of brevity. Finally, after the actual changes have been performed for the design object, quality repair costs drop to 0, and the goal is therefore satisfied again: quality_repair_cost(ford, 0). To see whether the properties as expressed in Section 7 hold for the simulation trace, first of all, the RQSM_generate and DODM_generate properties have been checked against the trace shown in Figure 7 using a software tool called the TTL Checker [17]. Both properties were shown to hold for the trace. In order to see whether the refinement process within RQSM is properly performed, the tree used for the simulation as presented before in Section 5 has been formally proven by means of the SMV model checker [22]. The results indeed show that the lowest level properties entail the goal given the environmental conditions. Furthermore, to prove the successfulness of DODM, the property hierarchy shown in Figure 6 has also been proven by the SMV model checker which shows that introducing lean production in a design object indeed results in canceling the quality repair costs, which satisfied the property DODM_successful. As a result, the DODM_successful property is satisfied as well as the RQSM_successful property in case the components indeed generate the output based on these property hierarchies.

9 Discussion

Organizations aim to meet their organizational goals. Monitoring whether events occur that endanger fulfillment of these goals enables organizations to consciously adapt and survive. Adaptation is essential once an organizational goal becomes unreachable. This paper views such a change as a (re)design process. A component-based formal generic model for design developed within the area of AI and Design is specialized into a model for organization (re)design.

Formalizations developed within Organization Theory and AI (or computational organization theory), have proved suitable for the description of organization models as design object descriptions, and organization goals as design requirements. Furthermore, different types of specialized knowledge have been identified: (1) about main organization goals and their relation for given environmental conditions to organization requirements, (2) about refinement of organization requirements, (3) about design object descriptions, and (4) which components for a design object description satisfy which requirements. The generic design model was instantiated with such types of knowledge to constitute a specialized component-based model for (re)design of organizations. Example properties have been taken from a well known case in Organization Theory on the introduction of lean production [25].

This paper focuses on external triggers for organizational change. Triggers are related to specific goals that play the role of design requirements which the organizational change should comply to. These requirements tend to be high-level goals and lack the detail needed for specifying how an organization should change.

Therefore, design requirement refinement is used based on requirements hierarchies. Such hierarchies relate objectives of the organization (e.g., high demand for cars) to organizational change properties at different organizational levels (e.g., change in some departments). Thus, they relate triggers at the level of the organization to properties at the level of parts (groups) within the organization. For example, that a certain type of car is not selling according to the goals set is related to the costs of quality repair. Requirements hierarchies help to localize where to change the organization. High-level goals for an organization as well as goals for organizational redesign have been related to low-level executable properties. Formal verification has been performed, showing satisfaction of the non-leaf properties in the property tree.

When comparing the approach to previous work in redesign of organizations a main strength is the formal description of the whole redesign process in terms of a generic redesign model for organizations. In the field of management for example (e.g., [7]), only informal descriptions are given of redesign processes. Systems Theory (e.g., [23]), addresses goal oriented behavior. The gap observed between actual and desired state of a system causes redesign, which corresponds with the approach taken in this paper. Formalizations by means of property hierarchies are, however, not present, therefore formal verification as done in this paper cannot be performed.

In [13] a general diagnosis engine is presented which drives adaptation processes within multi-agent organizations using the TAEMS modeling language as the primary representation of organizational information. In the design of the diagnostic engine three distinct layers are identified: symptoms, diagnosis, and reactions which in the approach presented in this paper roughly correspond to Section 4, 5, and 6 respectively. The implementation of these elements differs in both approaches. The goals and requirements in this paper are explicitly connected to each other. Once an organizational goal is observed not to be fulfilled, such a dissatisfaction is related directly to a goal for change. In the approach presented in [13] lacks such an explicit relation between goals and error diagnosis. Furthermore, this paper also introduces an approach to diagnose whether the whole reorganization process was successful, which is not the case in [13]. [6] explores dynamic reorganization of agent societies and focuses on changes to the structure of an organization, this paper presents an approach that enables such a dynamic reorganization.

[15] presents an approach which aims to archive adaptive real-time performance through reorganizations of the society. As a domain of application, production systems are used throughout that paper. Whereas that paper focuses on adaptive agents, this paper concentrates on adaptation of an organizational model that abstracts from agents and specifies elements on the level of roles the agents can fulfill.

The work presented in this paper can also be compared with the work on institutions as a way to describe multi-agent organizations. In [8] an institution is said to structure interactions and enforce individual and social behavior by obliging everybody to act according to norms, and a formalization language is introduced for such an institution. The approach to use dynamic expressions as a restriction of the behavior of agents allocated to that role used in this paper is also expressive enough to describe such norms. For example, in [21] an example of a norms is the following: "Students are prohibited from sitting the exam if they have not completed the assignment". Such a norm can easily be formulated in terms of a dynamic property for the student role. The approach presented in this paper could therefore also be applied to institutions and normative organizations. In [2] an adaptation mechanism of norms is proposed using an evolutionary approach contrary to the pre-specified knowledge assumed in this paper. Such an evolutionary approach can be incorporated in RQSM and DODM, allowing them to derive requirements and design objects for certain environmental conditions and goals without using pre-specified knowledge.

Finally, in the field of coalition formation (see e.g. [19, 24]), the main purpose of forming a coalition is to perform a task that cannot be performed by a single agent. That work can be combined with our approach by addressing the problem of the allocation of agents to roles, after the change of the organizational model by the approach presented in this paper.

References

1. Bosse, T., Jonker, C.M., Treur, J.: Analysis of Design Process Dynamics. In: de Mantaras, R.L., Saitta, L. (eds.) Proceedings of the 16th European Conference on Artificial Intelligence, ECAI'04, pp. 293–297 (2004)
2. Bou, E., Lopez-Sanchez, M., Rodriguez-Aguilar, J.A.: Towards Self-Configuration in Automatic Electronic Institutions. LNCS, vol. 4386, pp. 247–263. Springer, Heidelberg (2007)
3. Brazier, F.M.T., Jonker, C.M., Treur, J.: Principles of Component-Based Design of Intelligent Agents. Data and Knowledge Engineering 41, 1–28 (2002)
4. Brazier, F.M.T., van Langen, P.H.G., Treur, J.: Strategic knowledge in design: a compositional approach. Knowledge-Based Systems 11, 405–415 (1998)
5. Ciancarini, P., Wooldridge, M.J. (eds.): AOSE 2000. LNCS, vol. 1957. Springer, Heidelberg (2001)
6. Dignum, V., Sonenberg, L., Dignum, F.: Dynamic Reorganization of Agent Societies. In: Proc. of CEAS: Workshop on Coordination in Emergent Agent Societies at ECAI 2004 (2004)
7. Douglas, C.: Organization redesign: the current state and projected trends. Management Decision 37(8) (1999)
8. Esteva, M., Padget, J., Sierra, C.: Formalizing a language for institutions and norms. In: Meyer, J.-J.C., Tambe, M. (eds.) ATAL 2001. LNCS (LNAI), vol. 2333, pp. 348–366. Springer, Heidelberg (2002)
9. Ferber, J., Gutknecht, O.: A meta-model for the analysis and design of organisations in multi-agent systems. In: Proceedings of the Third International Conference on Multi-Agent Systems (ICMAS'98), pp. 128–135. IEEE Computer Society Press, Los Alamitos (1998)
10. Hannoun, M., Sichman, J.S., Boissier, O., Sayettat, C.: Dependence Relations between Roles in a Multi-Agent System: Towards the Detection of Inconsistencies in Organization. In: Sichman, J.S., Conte, R., Gilbert, N. (eds.) Multi-Agent Systems and Agent-Based Simulation. LNCS (LNAI), vol. 1534, pp. 169–182. Springer, Heidelberg (1998)
11. Hannoun, M., Boissier, O., Sichman, J.S., Sayettat, C.: MOISE: An organizational model for multi-agent systems. In: Monard, M.C., Sichman, J.S. (eds.) SBIA 2000 and IBERAMIA 2000. LNCS (LNAI), vol. 1952, pp. 152–161. Springer, Heidelberg (2000)
12. Haroud, D., Boulanger, S., Gelle, E., Smith, I.F.C.: Strategies for conflict management in preliminary engineering design. In: Proceeding of the AID 1994 Workshop Conflict Management in Design (1994)

13. Horling, B., Benyo, B., Lesser, V.: Using Self-Diagnosis to Adapt Organizational Structures. In: Muller, J.P., Ander, E., Sen, S., Frasson, C. (eds.) Proceedings of the Fifth International Conference on Autonomous Agents, pp. 529–536. ACM Press, New York (2001)
14. Hubner, J.F., Sichman, J.S., Boissier, O.: A Model for the Structural, Functional and Deontic Specification of Organizations in Multiagent Systems. In: Proc. 16th Brazilian Symposium on Artificial Intelligence (SBIA'02), Porto de Galinhas, Brasil (2002) Extended abstract in: Castelfranchi, C., Johnson, W.L. (eds.) Proc. of the First International Joint Conference on Autonomous Agents and Multi-Agent Systems, AAMAS'02. pp. 501–502, ACM Press, New York (2002)
15. Ishida, T., Yokoo, M., Gasser, L.: An Organizational Approach to Adaptive Production System. In: Proceedings of the 8th National Conference on Artificial Intelligence, Boston, USA, pp. 52–58 (1990)
16. Jaffee, D.: Organization Theory: Tension and Change. McGraw-Hill Publishers, New York (2001)
17. Jonker, C.M., Treur, J.: Compositional verification of multi-agent systems: a formal analysis of pro-activeness and reactiveness. Int. J. of Cooperative Information Systems 11, 51–92 (2002)
18. Jonker, C.M., Treur, J.: Relating Structure and Dynamics in an Organisation Model. In: Sichman, J.S., Bousquet, F., Davidsson, P. (eds.) MABS 2002. LNCS (LNAI), vol. 2581, pp. 50–69. Springer, Heidelberg (2003)
19. Klusch, M., Gerber, A.: Dynamic Coalition Formation among Rational Agents. IEEE Intelligent Systems 17(3), 42–47 (2002)
20. Lomi, A., Larsen, E.R.: Dynamics of Organizations: Computational Modeling and Organization Theories. AAAI Press, Menlo Park (2001)
21. McCallum, M., Vasconcelos, W.W., Norman, T.J.: Verification and Analysis of Organisational Change. In: Boissier, O., Dignum, V., Matson, E., Sichman, J. (eds.) Proc. 1st OOOP Workshop, pp. 91–106 (2005)
22. McMillan, K.: Symbolic Model Checking: An approach to the state explosion problem. Kluwer Academic Publishers, Dordrecht (1993)
23. Rapoport, A.: General System Theory. Abacus Press (1986)
24. Shehory, O., Kraus, S.: Task allocation via coalition formation among autonomous agents. In: Proceedings of IJCAI 1995, pp. 655–661 (1995)
25. Womack, J.P., Jones, D.T., Roos, D.: The Machine That Changed The World: The Story of Lean Production. HarperCollins Publishers, New York (1991)

Part II
MODELLING AND ANALYZING INSTITUTIONS

Specifying and Reasoning About Multiple Institutions

Owen Cliffe, Marina De Vos, and Julian Padget

Department of Computer Science
University of Bath, BATH BA2 7AY, UK
{occ,mdv,jap}@cs.bath.ac.uk

Abstract. Correctly specifying the behaviour of normative systems such as contracts and institutions is a troublesome problem. Designers are faced with two concurrent, difficult tasks: firstly specifying the relationships (over time) of agents' actions and their effects, and secondly combining this model with another that captures the agents' permissions and obligations. In this paper we present our model and operational semantics for specifying individual and collective institutions and outline a declarative action language for describing them. We demonstrate, by way of an example, how this may be used to enable the analysis of institutional specifications either for simply visualising possible outcomes or for checking for absence or presence of certain (un)desirable correctness properties.

1 Introduction

Institutions have long been studied in the multi agent systems community as a means for capturing the *social semantics* of interactions among agents. While a lot of work [16, 19, 20, 18, 7, 17, 1, 5, 5] has focused on modelling single institutions, nobody so far has addressed the issue of modelling multiple interacting institutions. In this case, particular aspects of a society may be modelled individually and then combined to give a richer model, leading to the possibility of using institutions as a means for abstraction (capturing increasing levels of specificity at lower levels) and also as a means for delegation (whereby one institution relies on the behaviour of another to augment its function). A good example is a contract violation which is considered as a breach of civil law. The contract and the civil law are themselves independent entities, and one could argue that a formal contract exists without the force of law, however the presence of this institution leads to more force behind the contract—that is, a victim of contract violation may have a reasonable expectation that the violator will be sanctioned elsewhere.

Action languages have evolved over recent years as a means of providing declarative, human-readable descriptions of the effects of actions and events. In [10] Gelfond and Lifschitz summarise action languages thus: *"Abstract Action languages are formal models of parts of the natural language that are used for talking about the effects of actions."* The semantics of action languages are typically described over a transition system where each state (or situation) is composed of the valuations of zero or more fluents and each transition is modelled by one or more action symbols.

Action languages are typically used for the analysis of situations and in this case, the action language describes a model of the situation which can then be queried to determine various properties. An intuitive and elegant way of doing this is to map the action

P. Noriega et al. (Eds.): COIN 2006 Workshops, LNAI 4386, pp. 67–85, 2007.

language to an answer set program. Answer set programming (ASP) is a logic programming language that admits reasoning about possible world views in the absence of complete information. Due to its formal semantics, and combined with efficient heuristic solvers, answer set programming, provides an excellent basis from which derived models may be queried. More information about answer set programming and its applications can be found in [3].

In this paper, we extend the formal specification of single institutions in [4] to multi-institutions. We present a top-down approach to virtual multi-institutions, in which external normative concepts are represented in forms that at the same time designers may analyse (off-line) and about which agents may reason (on-line). Instead of using ASP directly (as in [5, 4]), we introduce an action language designed for multi-institutions. The use of the action language makes generating the ASP code less open to human coding error, and perhaps more importantly easier to understand and create without losing either expressiveness or a formal basis for the language by narrowing the semantic gap.

2   Multi-institutions

2.1   The Single Institution

To provide some context for the theory that follows, this section begins with a brief overview of institutions and the terms that we use. As outlined in the introduction the essential characteristics of an institution are captured in its norms with varying degrees of specificity. What agents do or say is constrained by the institutional context, so that irrelevant actions or communications are ignored, and relevant ones advance the interaction, cause an agent to acquire an obligation, or through a violation, invite a sanction. But while that serves to capture the agent's point of view, what about the (institutional) environment? How are actions to be observed, how are obligations to be recorded and their satisfaction enforced, and how are violations to be detected and the corresponding sanctions to be applied?

The model we propose is based on the concept of *Observable Events* that capture notions of the physical world — "shoot somebody" — and *Institutional Events* that are those generated by society — "murder" — but which only have meaning within a given social context. While observable events are clearly observable, institutional ones are not, so how do they come into being? Searle [12] describes the creation of an institutional state of affairs through *Conventional Generation*, whereby an event in one context *Counts As* the occurrence of another event in a second context. Taking the physical world as the first context and by defining conditions in terms of states, institutional events may be created that count as the presence of states or the occurrence of events in the institutional world.

Thus, we model an institution as a set of *institutional states* that evolve over time subject to the occurrence of *events*, where an institutional state is a set of *institutional fluents* that may be held to be true at some instant. Furthermore, we may separate such fluents into *domain* fluents, that depend on the institution being modelled, such as "A owns something", and *normative fluents* that are common to all specifications and may be classified as follows:

- **Institutional Power:** This represents the institutional capability for an event to be brought about meaningfully, and hence change some fluents in the institutional state. Without institutional power, the event may not be brought about and has no effect; for example, a marriage ceremony will only bring about the married state, if the person performing the ceremony is empowered so to do.
- **Permission:** Each permission fluent captures the property that some event may occur without violation. If an event occurs, and that event is not permitted, then a *violation event* is generated.
- **Obligation:** Obligation fluents are modelled as the dual of permission. An obligation fluent states that a particular event is obliged to occur before a given deadline event (such as a timeout) and is associated with a specified violation. If an obligation fluent holds and the obliged event occurs then the obligation is said to be satisfied. If the corresponding deadline event occurs then the obligation is said to be violated and the specified violation event is generated.

Events can be classified into: (i) a set of observable events, being those events external to the institution which may be brought about independently from the institution and (ii) a set of *institutional events* which may be broken down into *violation events* and *institutional actions*; these events may only be brought about if they are generated by the institutional semantics. Finally we have a set of institutional rules which associate the occurrence of events with some effects in the subsequent state. These can be divided into: (i) *generation rules* which account for the conventional generation of events. Each generation rule associates the satisfaction of some conditions in the current institutional state and the occurrence of an (observed or institutional) event with a generated institutional event. For example: "A wedding ceremony counts as civil marriage only if the couple have a licence". The generating and generated events are taken by the institution to have occured simultaneously. (ii) *consequence rules*, each of which associates the satisfaction of some conditions in the current institutional state and the occurrence of an event in the institution or the world to the change in state of one or more fluents in the next institution state. For example: "Submitting a paper to a conference grants permission for the paper to be redistributed by the conference organisers".

Violation and sanction play an important role in the specification of institutions. Violations may arise either from explicit generation, from the occurrence of a nonpermitted event, or from the failure to fulfil an obligation. In these cases sanctions that may include obligations on violating agents or other agents and/or changes in agents' permission to do certain actions, may then simply be expressed as consequences of the occurrence of the associated violation event in the subsequent institutional state.

2.2 Combining Institutions

Institutions are not necessarily separate entities; several of them could operate within the same context, agents can participate in a number of them at the same time and perhaps more interestingly institutions themselves can be governed by institutions. In this section we investigate how such relationships can be established. To our knowledge we are the first to examine this topic.

Just as agents have the right to join in or stay out of an institution, it should be up to the institution to allow other institiutions to change directly or indirectly its state. In other words, it needs to put in place a mechanism of empowerment that allows institutions to bring about events and to initiate and terminate fluents within the institution.

Providing other institutions with the power to bring about certain events within the institution can easily be supported using the existing single institutional framework by quantifying the institutional power with the institution that is given the power. Since verifying empowerment is already part of event generation for a single institution, we do not need to change event generation in the presence of multiple institutions.

Things are different, when we want to empower institutions to change directly each others' state, because as for single institutions, empowerment only ranges over events. In the presence of multi-instititutions, we need to introduce two new empowerments: one for initialising and one for terminating fluents. These two institutional powers will then be used in conjunctions with the consequence rules to determine the next state of the institution.

2.3 Operational Specification

The model. Each multi-institution specification $\mathcal{M}$ is characterised by the institutions $\mathcal{I}$ that constitute it. Thus, $\mathcal{M} = \langle \mathcal{I}_1, \ldots, \mathcal{I}_n \rangle$ is a sequence of individual institutions $\mathcal{I}_i$. Each of these institutions is a five-tuple $\mathcal{I}_i := \langle \mathcal{E}_i, \mathcal{F}_i, \mathcal{C}_i, \mathcal{G}_i, \Delta_i \rangle$ with institutional Events ($\mathcal{E}_i$), Fluents ($\mathcal{F}_i$), Consequences ($\mathcal{C}_i$), Event Generation ($\mathcal{G}_i$) and Initial State (Δ_i). In the following subsections we discuss the various parts in more detail and their effect on the multi-institution $\mathcal{M}$.

Institutional Events. Each institution $\mathcal{I}_i$ defines a set of event signatures $e \in \mathcal{E}_i$, to denote the types of event that may occur. $\mathcal{E}_i$ comprises two disjoint subsets, $\mathcal{E}_{obs}^i$ denoting *observable events* and $\mathcal{E}_{inst}^i$ denoting *institutional events*. We break institutional events down further into the disjoint subsets: *institutional actions* $\mathcal{E}_{instact}^i$ and *violation events* $\mathcal{E}_{viol}^i$. We define $\mathcal{E}_{viol}^i$ such that $\forall e \in \mathcal{E}_{instact}^i \cdot \mathrm{viol}(e) \in \mathcal{E}_{viol}^i$: that is each institutional action has a corresponding violation event $\mathrm{viol}(e)$ in $\mathcal{E}_{viol}^i$ which may arise from performing e when it is not permitted. Other violations can be added to indicate agents have not behaved as they should have, e.g. fulfilling an obligation.

We assume that the individual institutions have disjoint sets of events $\mathcal{E}_i$[1]. We define the set of all events of the multi-institution $\mathcal{M}$, by $\mathcal{E}_{\mathcal{M}} = \bigcup_{i=1}^{n} \mathcal{E}_i$. We define $\mathcal{E}_{inst}^{\mathcal{M}}$, $\mathcal{E}_{obs}^{\mathcal{M}}$, $\mathcal{E}_{instact}^{\mathcal{M}}$ and $\mathcal{E}_{viol}^{\mathcal{M}}$ in a similar fashion. To obtain the corresponding institution for any event e, we define the function $\rho : \mathcal{E}_{\mathcal{M}} \to \mathbb{N}$ such that $\rho(e) = i$ when $e \in \mathcal{E}_i$.

Institutional Fluents. Each institution $\mathcal{I}_i$ defines a set of *Domain Fluents* denoted $\mathcal{D}_i$ which is a set of fluents modelling the context in which the institution is operational. In addition to the domain fluents, we define a number of disjoint sets of boolean fluents, $\mathcal{W}_i$, $\mathcal{P}_i$, $\mathcal{O}_i$, $\mathcal{S}_i$ and $\mathcal{T}_i$, indicating different types of *normative fluents*. Together, these disjoint sets of domain fluents and normative fluents form the *Institutional Fluents* $\mathcal{F}_i$ ($\mathcal{F}_i = \mathcal{W}_i \cup \mathcal{P}_i \cup \mathcal{O}_i \cup \mathcal{S}_i \cup \mathcal{T}_i \cup \mathcal{D}_i$). The set of all available fluents in the multi-institution $\mathcal{M}$ is denoted as $\mathcal{F}_{\mathcal{M}}$ ($\mathcal{F}_{\mathcal{M}} = \bigcup_{j=1}^{n} \mathcal{F}_j$).

---

[1] This may seem as a limitation, especially when the observable events are conscerned, but it is not. We are modelling events from the viewpoint of an institution and not from the events themselves.

$\mathcal{W}_i$ A set of institutional powers of the form $pow(j, e) : 1 \le j \le n, e \in \mathcal{E}^i_{instact}$ where each power fluent denotes the capability of some event e to be brought about in the institution.

$\mathcal{P}_i$ A set of action permissions: $perm(e) : e \in \mathcal{E}^i_{instact}$ where each permission fluent denotes that it is permitted for action e to be brought about. An event is not explicitly forbidden, instead this is implicitly represented through the absence of permission for that event to occur.

$\mathcal{O}_i$ A set of obligations, of the form $obl(e, d, v) : e \in \mathcal{E}_i, d \in \mathcal{E}_i, v \in \mathcal{E}_{inst}$ where each obligation fluent denotes that action e should be brought about before the occurrence of event d or be subject to the violation v. Note that v need not necessarily be a violation, but any event which represents the failure to satisfy the obligation.

$\mathcal{S}_i$ A set of institutional initiating powers of the form $inipow(j, f): 1 \le j \le n$, where $f \in \mathcal{D}_i$ denotes that institution j is empowered to initiate some domain fluent f in institution i.

$\mathcal{T}_i$ A set of institutional terminating powers of the form $termpow(j, f): 1 \le j \le n$, where $f \in \mathcal{D}_i$ denotes that institution j is empowered to terminate some fluent f in institution i.

The state of an institution at a certain time is determined by those institutional fluents that are valid at that time. So a state S is a subset of $\mathcal{F}$. A fluent f which is not valid is denoted as $\neg f$. This notation can be extended to sets of fluents.

The set of all possible *institutional states* of institution $\mathcal{I}_i$ is denoted as Σ_i with $\Sigma_i = 2^{\mathcal{F}_i}$. It is important to note that not all those states will actually be reachable in an institution. The state of the multi-institution $\mathcal{M}$ is modelled as a sequence $\langle S_1, \ldots, S_n \rangle$ with $S_i \in \Sigma_i$. The state of all possible states for $\mathcal{M}$ is defined as $\Sigma_\mathcal{M} = \Sigma_1 \times \ldots \times \Sigma_n$.

Events can have the same effect on a number of states. Borrowing a book from a library will result in the obligation to bring it back regardless of how many books are currently on loan. To facilitate this, we introduce the concept of *State Formulae* to capture a collection of states that satisfy certain properties in that they either contain certain fluents or they do not. The set of all state formulae is denoted as $\mathcal{X}_i$ with $\mathcal{X}_i = 2^{\mathcal{F}_i \cup \neg \mathcal{F}_i}$, where $\neg \mathcal{F}_i$ is the negation of each fluent in $\mathcal{F}_i$.

Consequences. Each institution $\mathcal{I}_i$ defines the function $\mathcal{C}_i$ which describes which fluents are initiated and terminated by the occurrence of a certain event in a state matching some criteria. The function is expressed as $\mathcal{C}_i : \mathcal{X}_i \times \mathcal{E}_i \to 2^{\mathcal{F}_\mathcal{M}} \times 2^{\mathcal{F}_\mathcal{M}}$. Given $X \in \mathcal{X}_i$ and $e \in events_i$, $C_i(X, e) = (\mathcal{C}_i^\uparrow(X, e), \mathcal{C}_i^\downarrow(X, e))$ with $\mathcal{C}_i^\uparrow(X, e)$ containing those fluents which are initiated by the event e in a state matching X and $\mathcal{C}_i^\downarrow(X, e)$ collecting those fluents which are terminated by event e in a state matching X. Notice that the consequence relation can indicate which events can cause fluents to change in the state of institutions different from itself. This will only take effect if the institution is empowered to do so.

Event Generation. Each institution $\mathcal{I}_i$ defines an event generation function $\mathcal{G}_i$ which describes when the occurrence of one event *counts as* the occurrence of another:
$$\mathcal{G}_i : \mathcal{X}_i \times \mathcal{E}_i \to 2^{\mathcal{E}^\mathcal{M}_{inst}}.$$

Initial State. Each institution $\mathcal{I}_i$ defines the set $\Delta_i \subseteq \mathcal{F}_i$ which denotes the set of fluents that should hold when the institution is created.

The initial state of the multi-institution $\mathcal{M}$ is the sequence $\Delta_{\mathcal{M}} = \langle \Delta_1, \ldots, \Delta_n \rangle$.

2.4 Semantics

During the lifetime of an institution, its state changes due to events that take place. Each observable event possibly generates more events which in turn could create further events. Each of these events could have an effect on the current state. The combined effect of these events determines the next state.

States. We define the semantics of a multi-institution $\mathcal{M}$ over a set of states $\Sigma_{\mathcal{M}}$. Each $S \in \Sigma_{\mathcal{M}}$ consists of a sequence containing a state $S_i \in \Sigma_i$ for each institution $\mathcal{I}_i$ in $\mathcal{M}$. Each state S_i is a set of fluents in $\mathcal{F}_i$ which are held to be true at a given time. We say that $S \in \Sigma_{\mathcal{M}}$ satisfies fluent $f \in \mathcal{F}_i$, denoted $S \models f$, when $f \in S_i$. It satisfies its negation $\neg f$, when $f \notin S_i$. This notation can be extended to sets $X \subseteq \mathcal{X}_i$ in the following way: $S \models X$ iff $\forall x \in X \cdot S \models x$.

Event Generation. In order to model event generation we define function which describes which events are generated in a given state. $\mathrm{GR} : \Sigma_{\mathcal{M}} \times 2^{\mathcal{E}_{\mathcal{M}}} \to \mathcal{E}_{\mathcal{M}}$. Given a state S and a set of of events E, $\mathrm{GR}(S, E)$ includes all of the events which must be generated by the occurrence of events E in state S and is defined as follows:

$$
\begin{aligned}
\mathrm{GR}(S, E) = \{ e \in \mathcal{E} \mid \; & e \in E & \textbf{or} \\
& \exists\, e' \in E \text{ s.t. } j = \rho(e'), X \in \mathcal{X}_j, e \in G_j(X, e') \cdot S_{\rho(e)} \models \mathrm{pow}(j, e) \wedge S \models X \; & \textbf{or} \\
& \exists\, e' \in E, X \in \mathcal{X}_{\rho(e)}, e \in G_{\rho(e)}(X, e') \cdot e \in \mathcal{E}^{\rho(e)}_{viol} \wedge S \models X & \textbf{or} \\
& \exists\, e' \in E \cdot e = viol(e'), S \models \neg\,\mathrm{perm}(e') & \textbf{or} \\
& \exists\, e' \in \mathcal{E}_{\rho(e)}, d \in E \cdot S \models \mathrm{obl}(e', d, e) \}
\end{aligned}
$$

The first condition ensures that events remain generated. The second is responsible for generating those events that are both prescribed by the institutions' event generator and empowered. The third condition deals with violations specified by the event generator, while the fourth generates violations as consequences of events that were not permitted. The final conditions deals with obligations that are not met.

It is easy to see that $\mathrm{GR}(S, E)$ is a monotonic function. This implies that for any given state and a set of events, we can obtain a fixpoint $\mathrm{GR}^{\omega}(S, E)$. In our multi-institutional model, generated events arise from the performance of one *observable event* $e_{obs} \in \mathcal{E}^{\mathcal{M}}_{obs}$ in a given state S. So, to obtain all events that originate from this one event in this state, we simply need $\mathrm{GR}^{\omega}(S, \{e_{obs}\})$.

Event Effects. Each fluent is either valid or not in each state of the institution it belongs to. The status of these fluents changes over time according to which generated events have occurred in the previous transition. Events can have two sorts of effects regarding fluents: fluents can be initiated (they become true in the next state) or they can be terminated (they cease to be true in the next state). The combination of all effects generated in a state defines the state transition. The state transition function captures inertia, so all fluents that are not affected in the current state remain valid in the next state.

As mentioned above, given an observable event e_{obs} all events that could have an effect on the state S, are obtained by $GR^\omega(S, \{e_{obs}\})$.

A fluent can be initiated either by any event in the same institution, or by any event in another institution which initiates the fluent, if that institution has the power to initiate the fluent.

$$\text{INIT}(S, e_{obs}) = \{\, p \in \mathcal{F}_\mathcal{M} \mid \exists\, e \in GR^\omega(S, \{e_{obs}\}), i = \rho(e), X \in \mathcal{X}_i.$$
$$p \in \mathcal{F}_i, p \in \mathcal{C}_i^\uparrow(X, e), S \models X \text{ or}$$
$$p \in \mathcal{F}_j, \mathcal{I}_j \neq \mathcal{I}_j, p \in \mathcal{C}_i^\uparrow(X, e), S \models X, S \models \text{inipow}(i, p)\}$$

A fluent can be terminated either by an event in the same institution, or by an event in another institution given permission, or if it is a fulfilled obligation in any institution of the multi-institution.

$$\text{TERM}(S, e_{obs}) = \{p \in \mathcal{F}_\mathcal{M} \mid \exists\, e \in GR^\omega(S, \{e_{obs}\}), i = \rho(e), X \in \mathcal{X}_i.$$
$$p \in \mathcal{F}_i, p \in \mathcal{C}^\downarrow(i, X)e, S \models X \qquad\qquad\qquad \text{or}$$
$$p \in \mathcal{F}_j, \mathcal{I}_j \neq \mathcal{I}_j, p \in \mathcal{C}_i^\downarrow(X, e), S \models X, S \models \text{termpow}(i, p) \text{ or}$$
$$p = \text{obl}(e, d, v) \in \mathcal{F}_\mathcal{M} \wedge p \in S \qquad\qquad\qquad \text{or}$$
$$p = \text{obl}(e', e, v) \in \mathcal{F}_\mathcal{M} \wedge p \in S\}$$

Now that we know which fluents need adding or deleting we can define the transition function $TR : \Sigma_\mathcal{M} \times \mathcal{E}_{obs}^\mathcal{M} \to \Sigma_\mathcal{M}$ as $TR(\{S_1, \ldots, S_n\}, e_{obs}) = \{S_1', \ldots, S_n'\}$ such that $S_i' = \{p \in \mathcal{F}_i \mid p \in S, p \notin \text{TERM}(S, e_{obs}) \text{ or } p \in \text{INIT}(S, e_{obs})\}$.

The first condition models inertia: all fluents which are asserted in the current state persist into the next state, unless they are terminated. The second condition includes fluents which are initiated in the current state.

Ordered Traces. Now that we have defined how states may be generated from a previous state and a single observable event, we may define traces and their state evaluations:

- An *ordered trace* is defined as a sequence of observable events $\langle e_0, e_1, \ldots, e_n \rangle$ with $e_i \in \mathcal{E}_{obs}^\mathcal{M}, 0 \leq i \leq n$
- The *evaluation of an ordered trace* for a given starting state S_0 is a sequence $\langle S_0, S_1, \ldots S_{n+1} \rangle$ such that $S_{i+1} = TR(S_i, e_i)$
- Ordered traces and their evaluations allow us to monitor or investigate the evolution of an institution over time. They provide us with the data necessary to answer most queries one might have about a certain (multi-)institution.

2.5   A Simple Example: Borrowing

This institution (formalised in Fig. 1) describes when agents may borrow money, when they must pay it back and when they are permitted to leave the interaction. The norm described by the protocol is that when money is borrowed it must be paid back before the agent leaves. Note that the observable events in this institution are not generated by the agents but by the environment in which this institution operates. Also note that the agents will only receive empowerment to leave the institution as soon as they borrow from the institution (line 8). This is to indicate that is useless to leave an agreement before you even started.

Given set of agents $Agents$, and multi-institution $\mathcal{M}$ s.t. $a \in Agents, \mathcal{I}_{bor}, \mathcal{I}_i \in \mathcal{M}$:

$$\mathcal{E}_{obs}^{bor} = \{\texttt{msg\_borrow}(a), \texttt{msg\_payback}(a), \texttt{msg\_leave}(a)\} \tag{1}$$

$$\mathcal{E}_{instact}^{bor} = \{\texttt{borrow}(a), \texttt{payback}(a), \texttt{leave}(a)\} \tag{2}$$

$$\mathcal{E}_{viol}^{bor} = \{\texttt{viol}(e) \mid e \in \mathcal{E}_{obs}^{b} \cup \mathcal{E}_{instact}^{bor}\} \cup \{nonpay(a)\} \tag{3}$$

$$\mathcal{D}_{bor} = \{\texttt{loan}(a)\} \tag{4}$$

$$\mathcal{W}_{bor} = \{\text{pow}(i, e) \mid e \in \mathcal{E}_{instact}^{bor}\} \tag{5}$$

$$\mathcal{P}_{bor} = \{\text{perm}(e) \mid e \in \mathcal{E}_{obs}^{bor} \cup \mathcal{E}_{instact}^{bor}\} \tag{6}$$

$$\mathcal{O}_{bor} = \{\text{obl}(e, d, v) \mid e, d \in \mathcal{E}_{obs}^{bor} \cup \mathcal{E}_{instact}^{bor}, v \in \mathcal{E}_{inst}^{bor}\} \tag{7}$$

$\mathcal{C}_{bor}^{\uparrow}(\mathcal{X}, \mathcal{E}_{\mathcal{M}}):$ $\langle\{\}, \texttt{borrow}(a)\rangle \mapsto$ $\{\text{obl}(\texttt{payback}(a), \texttt{leave}(a), nonpay(a)),$
       $\text{pow}(bor, \texttt{payback}(a)), \text{pow}(bor, \texttt{leave}(a)),$
       $\texttt{loan}(a)\}$ (8)

$\mathcal{C}_{bor}^{\downarrow}(\mathcal{X}, \mathcal{E}_{\mathcal{M}}):$ $\langle\{\}, \texttt{borrow}(a)\rangle \mapsto$ $\{\text{pow}(bor, \texttt{borrow}(a))\}$ (9)

       $\langle\{\}, \texttt{payback}(a)\rangle \mapsto$ $\{\text{pow}(bor, \texttt{payback}(a)), \text{pow}(bor, \texttt{leave}(a)),$
       $\texttt{loan}(a)\}$ (10)

       $\langle\{\}, \texttt{leave}(a), \rangle \mapsto$ $\{\text{pow}(bor, \texttt{payback}(a)), \text{pow}(bor, \texttt{leave}(a))\}$ (11)

$\mathcal{G}_{bor}(\mathcal{X}, \mathcal{E}_{\mathcal{M}}):$ $\langle\{\}, \texttt{msg\_borrow}(a)\rangle \mapsto \{\texttt{borrow}(a)\}$ (12)

       $\langle\{\}, \texttt{msg\_payback}(a)\rangle \mapsto \{\texttt{payback}(a)\}$ (13)

       $\langle\{\}, \texttt{msg\_leave}(a)\rangle \mapsto \{\texttt{leave}(a)\}$ (14)

$S_0^{bor} = \{\text{perm}(\texttt{msg\_borrow}(a)), \text{perm}(\texttt{msg\_payback}(a)),$
     $\text{perm}(\texttt{msg\_leave}(a)), \text{perm}(\texttt{borrow}(a)), \text{perm}(\texttt{payback}(a)),$
     $\text{perm}(\texttt{leave}(a)), \text{pow}(\texttt{borrow}(a))\}$ (15)

Fig. 1. The formal model of the borrowing scenario

The state transition diagram for an instance (with a single agent) of this contract is displayed in Fig. 4. Fluents that are true are included in each state and transitions are labelled with events (generated events are shown in square brackets).

3   InstAL: An Action Language for Describing Institutions

In this section we outline the syntax and semantics of our institutional action language InstAL.

3.1   Syntax

The syntax of our action language consists of a set of declarations which define the types, fluents and events which are supported by the institution and a set of rules which define the operational semantics of the institution. These are summarised by way of the borrowing institution described above.

Types. Each InstAL specification may contain zero or more types. Types describe a set of atoms which may be applied to the parameters of fluents and events in rule descriptions. The language defines four internal types which are grounded automatically by the contents of the specification: (i) The set of events: Event (ii) The set of institutions: Inst (iii) The set of all fluents Fluent (iv) The set of all domain fluents DFluent In the example we define one type Agent which ranges over the possible subjects of the contract;

```
type  Agent;
```

Event Declarations. Each specification may define zero or more event signatures, each of which describes the event's status (observable, action or violation), its (unique) name and the types of any parameters associated with the event.

We define three observable events (Fig. 1, 1) which denote messages associated with: a request to borrow money by an agent (msg_borrow(..)), a message describing that the money has been payed back (msg_payback(...)) and a message indicating an agent has left the situation (msg_leave(...)).

```
observable event msg_borrow(Agent);
observable event msg_payback(Agent);
observable event msg_leave(Agent);
```

We define four institutional events (Fig. 1, 2) which denote the effective achievement of borrowing and paying back money and leaving the contract. Additionally we define a violation event (Fig. 1, 3) nonpay(...) which is associated with an agent failing to repay borrowed money.

```
action event borrow(Agent);
action event payback(Agent);
action event leave(Agent);
violation event nonpay(Agent);
```

Fluents. Fluent declarations define institutional properties which may change over time. A fluent declaration consists of a fluent name, and zero or more fluent parameters, the types of which must be specified.

For instance the following declaration:fluent owns(Agent,Object); defines a fluent with name owns with two parameters which range over the types Agent and Object respectively.

In addition to fluents declared in a specification the following types of normative fluents are implicitly defined:

(i) pow(Inst,Event): A given institution is empowered to generated a given event (if no institution is specified then the institution in which the fluent is referenced is assumed).

(ii) initpow(Inst,DFluent),termpow(Inst,DFluent): A given (external) institution has the power to initiate or terminate a given fluent.

(iii) `perm(Event)`: A given event is permitted.

(iv) `obl(Event,Event,Event)` : A given obligation exists.

In the example we define a single institutional domain fluent (Fig. 1, 4) which represents the existence of a loan with respect to some agent.

```
fluent loan(Agent);
```

Rules. Each specification may contain zero or more rules, three types of which are available: (i) *Causal rules* which describe when fluents change in response to the occurrence of events. (ii) *Generation rules* which describe when events may be generated. (iii) *Initial rules* which describe the initial state of the institution.

A causal rule consists of (i) *a trigger event* which denotes the event which (may) activate the rule. (ii) *an operation* which indicates whether the rule initiates or terminates the fluents in the rule body. (iii) *a set of fluents* which are initiated or terminated by the rule. (iv) *a (possibly empty) condition* consisting of an expression describing fluents which must be true in order for the rule to have an effect.

In our example we define the effects of the successful occurrence of the `borrow(..)` event (Fig. 1, 8) as the termination of the power to perform further `borrow` events and creation of the power to pay back and leave the contract, and also the creation of an obligation for the agent to repay the debt before they leave the contract (lest they cause a `nonpay(...)` violation). Borrowing also initiates a loan for the borrowing agent.

```
borrow(A) initiates pow(payback(A)),pow(leave(A)),loan(A),
    obl(payback(A),leave(A),nonpay(A));
```

We similarly define that `borrow(...)` terminates the further power to borrow (Fig. 1, 9) (so borrowing may not occur while a loan exists). Both `payback(...)` and `leave(...)` terminate the power to both payback and leave (Fig. 1, 10-11).

```
borrow(A) terminates pow(borrow(A));
payback(A) terminates pow(payback(A)),pow(leave(A)),loan(A);
leave(A) terminates pow(payback(A)),pow(leave(A));
```

We define three generation rules which associate the performance of the three observable messages with the generation of the corresponding institutional events (Fig. 1, 12-14).

```
msg_borrow(A) generates borrow(A);
msg_payback(A) generates payback(A);
msg_leave(A) generates leave(A);
```

Finally we define the initial state (Fig. 1, 15), in this state all events are permitted, and borrowing is initially empowered.

```
initially perm(msg_borrow(A)),perm(msg_payback(A)),
    perm(msg_leave(A)),perm(borrow(A)),perm(payback(A)),
    perm(leave(A)),pow(borrow(A));
```

Static Properties. In addition to fluents which change over time, it is sometimes useful to refer to external properties which will not change during the execution of an institution, but are not known at the time of specification. As with fluents, static properties consist of a name and zero or more typed parameters, for instance the declaration: `static participant(Agent,Inst)` defines a static property with name `participant` and parameters which range over the types `Agent` and `Inst`. This static property indicates which agents are allowed to participate in the institution. It does not imply that the agents cannot come and go at run-time.

Variables. Variables are indicated in the language by capitalised strings and may appear in the parameters of fluents and events within rules or within expressions in the conditions of rules (such as `X!=Y`). Variables are locally scoped to each rule and each variable has a corresponding type, which is computed based on where (in the parameters of a given fluent or event reference) it occurs in the rule.

During processing, a rule containing variables is expanded into a set of rules containing all valid possible assignments of each variable. For example the rule: `sell(X,Y) terminates owns(X,Y);` would be implicitly expanded to variable free rules containing assignments for X and Y based on the parameter types of event `sell` and fluent `owns`. In the case where the condition of a rule rule contains variable expressions (i.e. `A=bob`) then only those variable expansions which satisfy the expressions are generated.

3.2 Model Evaluation

We evaluate properties of our models by performing a transformation of one or more InstAL specifications into answer set programs (see [3] for an extensive overview of answer set programming or [9] for an brief desciption). While the details of this transformation are omitted from this paper, we summarise the process here.

Models are evaluated by taking one or more (related) institutional specifications, a domain description which includes elements of the sets defined in `type` declarations and `static` declarations, a query (see below) and a maximum time interval. This information is then compiled into an answer set program of the form described in [4]. This program may then be solved using an answer set solver such as Smodels[2], yielding zero or more answer sets, each of which represents an ordered trace (up to the maximum time interval) of the institution which matches the query. These traces are then parsed and can be visualised individually or combined into state transition diagrams of the form seen in Figs. 4 and 5.

This process is sound and complete: all requested traces are found as answer sets and all answer sets are valid traces fulfilling the specified conditions. In general the computational complexity of answer set programming is σ_1^P (See [3] for more details). However, the specific chararistics of our program reduces this significantly.

Although ASP can theoretically cope with infinite time, its implementations cannot as the program needs to ground its variables in advance. This implies that we need to specify in advance the number of time steps about which one wishes to reason.

Two mechanisms for specifying queries on the properties of models may be used: (i) for simple queries such as "does it hold that this property is never (or ever) true in

---

[2] http://www.tcs.hut.fi/Software/smodels/

the model?" and "what is the state after the performance of this sequence of observable events?" we include a simple query language. In the first case `ever loan(a);` for example would produce all answer sets where a loan is created. (ii) In the second case: `after msg_borrow(a),fineAgent(a),msg_leave(a);` would yield a single answer set describing the series of states (including domain fluents, institution fluents and generated events) brought about by the occurrence of the specified actions. While this query language is useful for simple queries, it represents only a small subset of the possible queries which may be computed using our model. In light of this, queries may also be expressed directly as answer set program rules, for instance:

```
condition:- holdsat(loan(bob),I),not holdsat(loan(bob),J),
    before(I,J),instant(I),instant(J).
compute all { not condition }.
```

would return all traces where a loan was created at some time instant but never settled at some point in the future. In the simple example with a single agent `bob` above this query yields a single trace of length 2: `msg_borrow(bob),msg_leave(bob)` and associated fluents.

3.3   An Extended Example: Contract Enforcement

In the previous section we discussed a single specification of a simple institution for governing loans, however as is clear from Fig. 4 once an agent has violated a loan agreement by leaving before paying, no further action may be taken. In many cases in the real world such violations are delegated to a "higher power" which would impose a sanction. In the following example we demonstrate such an institution which provides a mechanism for enforcing the violation, not only in the borrowing example but also in a broad class of institutions where enforcement is required. [3]

The enforcement institution (*enf*) (formally described in Fig. 2) describes a single static property `participant(Agent,Inst)` (*Part* in Fig. 2) which defines when agents are participating in a contract, one domain fluent: `validContract(Inst)` (19) describes when a given institution is considered to be a valid (enforceable) contract. Six event types (17-18) are defined: (i) `submitContract(Inst)` must be generated by the institution in which sanctions are to be enforced. It generates an `acceptContract(..)` event if the submitted institution is not already considered a valid contract (27), and initiates `validContract(..)` for the accepted contract and the power for that contract to generate contract violations in the enforcement institution. (ii) `acceptContract (Inst)` describes when a contract is is treated as valid, initiating (23) the `valid Contract(i)` fluent also the power for the new contract to dissolve itself and generate contract violation events in the enforcement institution. (iii) `contractViolation (Agent)` must be generated by the contract and when generated, initiates an obligation in the enforcement institution to apply a sanction to that agent before the contract is terminated, or be subject to a `badViol` violation. (iv) `fineAgent(Agent)` is an observable event which stands for the imposition of a fine. In the case that a valid contract exists with this agent this event generates an `applySanction(..)` event (28) in the

---

[3] We omit the action language description of this example for space reasons. See `http://www.cs.bath.ac.uk/~occ/instal/` for the source of both examples.

Given set of agents $Agents$, contract participants $Part_i \subseteq Agents$ and institutions $\mathcal{M}$ s.t $a_i \in Part_i, enf, i \in \mathcal{M}$:

$$\mathcal{E}_{obs} = \{\texttt{fineAgent}(a_i)\} \tag{16}$$

$$\mathcal{E}_{instact} = \{\texttt{submitContract}(i), \texttt{acceptContract}(i), \texttt{dissolveContract}(i),$$
$$\texttt{contractViolation}(a_i, i), \texttt{applySanction}(a_i)\} \tag{17}$$

$$\mathcal{E}_{viol} = \{\texttt{badGov}\} \cup \{\texttt{viol}(e), e \in \mathcal{E}_{obs}^{enf} \cup \mathcal{E}_{instact}^{enf}\} \tag{18}$$

$$\mathcal{D} = \{\texttt{validContract}(i)\} \tag{19}$$

$$\mathcal{W}^{enf} = \{\text{pow}(i, e), e \in \mathcal{E}_{instact}^{enf}\} \tag{20}$$

$$\mathcal{P}^{enf} = \{\text{perm}(e), e \in \mathcal{E}_{obs}^{enf} \cup \mathcal{E}_{instact}^{enf}\} \tag{21}$$

$$\mathcal{O}^{enf} = \{\text{obl}(e, d, v), e, d \in \mathcal{E}_{obs}^{enf} \cup \mathcal{E}_{instact}^{enf}, v \in \mathcal{E}_{inst}^{enf}\} \tag{22}$$

$\mathcal{C}_{enf}^{\uparrow}(\mathcal{X}, \mathcal{E}_{\mathcal{M}}) :$

$$\langle\{\}, \texttt{acceptContract}(i)\rangle \mapsto$$
$$\{\texttt{validContract}(i), \text{pow}(i, \texttt{dissolveContract}(i)),$$
$$\text{pow}(i, \texttt{contractViolation}(a_i, i))\} \tag{23}$$

$$\langle\{\texttt{validContract}(i)\}, \texttt{contractViolation}(a_i, i)\rangle \mapsto$$
$$\{\text{pow}(enf, \texttt{applySanction}(a_i)), \text{perm}(\texttt{fineAgent}(a_i))$$
$$\text{obl}(\texttt{applySanction}(a_i), \texttt{dissolveContract}(i), \texttt{badGov})\} \tag{24}$$

$\mathcal{C}_{enf}^{\downarrow}(\mathcal{X}, \mathcal{E}_{\mathcal{M}}) :$

$$\langle\{\}, \texttt{dissolveContract}(i)\rangle \mapsto$$
$$\{\texttt{validContract}(i), \text{pow}(i, \texttt{dissolveContract}(i)),$$
$$\text{pow}(i, \texttt{contractViolation}(a_i, i))\}, \text{perm}(\texttt{fineAgent}(a_i)) \tag{25}$$
$$\text{pow}(enf, \texttt{applySanction}(a_i))$$

$$\langle\{\}, \texttt{applySanction}(a_i)\rangle \mapsto \{\text{perm}(\texttt{fineAgent}(a_i))$$
$$\text{pow}(enf, \texttt{applySanction}(a_i)) \tag{26}$$

$\mathcal{G}_{enf}(\mathcal{X}, \mathcal{E}_{\mathcal{M}}) :$

$$\langle\{\neg\texttt{validContract}(i)\}, \texttt{submitContract}(i)\rangle \mapsto$$
$$\{\texttt{acceptContract}(i)\} \tag{27}$$

$$\langle\{\}, \texttt{fineAgent}(a_i)\rangle \mapsto \{\texttt{applySanction}(a_i)\} \tag{28}$$

$$S_0^{enf} = \{\text{pow}(enf, \texttt{acceptContract}(i)), \text{pow}(i, \texttt{submitContract}(i)),$$
$$\text{perm}(\texttt{submitContract}(i)), \text{perm}(\texttt{acceptContract}(i)), \tag{29}$$
$$\text{perm}(\texttt{dissolveContract}(i)), \text{perm}(\texttt{applySanction}(a_i))\}$$

Fig. 2. The enforcement institution $enf \in \mathcal{M}$

institution (if this event is empowered). (v) `dissolveContract(Inst)` terminates all powers granted to the contract by its acceptance and also terminates the validity of the contract (25).

In order to make the borrowing contract enforceable by this institution we extend it as follows (Formalised in Fig. 3): borrowing money creates a contract in the enforcement institution (33), paying back money dissolves the contract (34), not paying back the money generates a contract violation (32) and fining an agent in the enforcement

Given a set of agents *Agents* and institutions $\mathcal{M}$ s.t. $a \in$ *Agents* and $bor \in \mathcal{M}$:

$$\mathcal{C}^{\uparrow}_{bor}(\mathcal{X}, \mathcal{E}_{\mathcal{M}})' : \ \langle\{\}, \texttt{acceptContract}(bor)\rangle \ \mapsto \{\text{pow}(e, \texttt{payback}(a))\} \qquad (30)$$

$$\mathcal{C}^{\downarrow}_{bor}(\mathcal{X}, \mathcal{E}_{\mathcal{M}})' : \langle\{\}, \texttt{dissolveContract}(bor)\rangle \mapsto \{\text{pow}(e, \texttt{payback}(a))\} \qquad (31)$$

$$\mathcal{G}_{bor}(\mathcal{X}, \mathcal{E}_{\mathcal{M}})' : \ \langle\{\}, \texttt{nopay}(a),\rangle \ \mapsto \{\texttt{contractViolation}(bor, a)\} \qquad (32)$$

$$\langle\{\}, \texttt{borrow}(a)\rangle \ \mapsto \{\texttt{submitContract}(bor)\} \qquad (33)$$

$$\langle\{\}, \texttt{payback}(a)\rangle \ \mapsto \{\texttt{dissolveContract}(bor)\} \qquad (34)$$

$$\langle\{\}, \texttt{fineAgent}(a)\rangle \mapsto \{\texttt{payback}(a)\} \qquad (35)$$

Fig. 3. Extensions of the borrowing scenario for contract enforcement

institution pays back the debt (35). Additionally the creation and dissolution of a contract in the enforcement institution initiate and terminate the power for that institution to pay back debts (30-31) finally the initial state is extended to permit and empower the generation of re-payment (not shown).

Fig. 5 shows the reachable states for a combined model (with one borrower) of the enforcement and borrowing institutions. The ASP query in Section 3.2 above, yields no answer sets, indicating that there are no traces in the generated model (up to the search length) where a loan is not repaid.

4   Discussion and Related Work

The use of common-sense reasoning tools such as action languages and answer set programing for reasoning about normative systems and agent-based systems in general has been studied extensively in the literature and a complete analysis is beyond the scope of this paper, however a number of recent studies merit discussion.

The Event Calculus (EC) [14, 15] is a declarative logic that reinterprets the Situation Calculus to capture when and how states change in response to external events. EC has been used to model both the behaviour of commitments [22] among agents in order to build interaction protocols, corresponding to the regulatory aspects of the work described above, as well as more general social models such as those described in [13]. From a technical point of view, our approach essentially has a kind of duality compared to EC, in that the basis for the model is events rather than states. In itself, this offers no technical advantage although we believe that being able to express violations in terms of events rather than states better captures their nature. More significant are the consequences of the grounding in ASP: (i) For the most part the state and event models are equivalent with respect to properties such as induction and abduction, but non-monotonicity is inherent in ASP and so resort to the tricky process of circumscription is avoided. (ii) Likewise, reasoning about defaults requires no special treatment in ASP. (iii) The consequence rules of our specification have equivalents in EC, but the event generation rules do not. (iv) The state of a fluent is determined by its truth-value

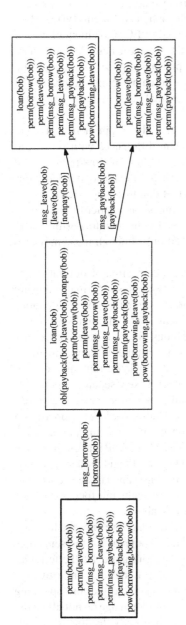

Fig. 4. Reachable states of Borrowing institution for a given agent 'bob'

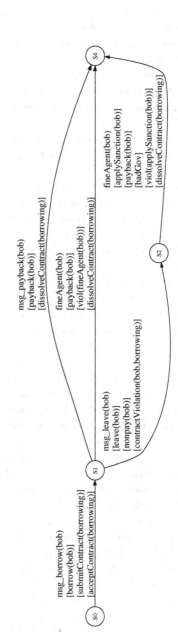

Fig. 5. States of the combined borrowing and enforcement institution

in the ASP interpretation, whereas EC (typically) has to encode this explicitly using two predicates. (v) Inertia in EC is axiomatic, whereas in our approach it follows from the application of the TR operator—although there is a strong syntactic similarity (perhaps compounded by using the same terminology!) the philosophy is different. (vi) ASP allows a wider variety of queries than is typically provided in EC implementations but space constraints do not allow the full illustration of this aspect here. We also note that, EC is much more general, in that it is aimed at capturing arbitrary narrative, while the InstAL language we have presented is more like a domain-specific language that allows only the expression of institutional issues and in that sense is more restrictive than EC.

[8] use EC to represent the specification of contracts. Their approach of dealing with contract is similar to ours but with some important differences with respect to the broader picture of multi-institutions: (i) any formalisation of pow/permissions/ obligation is ommitted from their specification and left as domain dependent concepts which are modelled using XML (ii) this means that that their approach does not have conventional generation of events/obligations/permissions explicitly, only their effects (iii) in their work the authors are just concerned with monitoring the state, not investigating other properties (i.e. planning/verificaition), although these may also be possible.

Artikis et al. in [1, 2, 13] describe a system for the specification of normative social systems in terms of power, empowerment and obligation. This is formalized using both the event calculus [14] and a subset of the action language $C+$ [6]. The notions of power and empowerment are equivalent in both systems, but additionally we introduces violation as events and our modelling of obligations differs in that (i) they are deadline-sensitive, and (ii) can raise a violation if they are not met in time. Violations greatly improve the capacity to model institutions, but it should be remembered that institutional modelling was (apparently) not Artikis's goal. Likewise, although the interpretation of $C+$ using the CCalc tool gives rise to similar reasoning capabilities (with similar complexity) to ASP, we believe our approach, including violations, provides a more intuitive and natural way of expressing social constraints involving temporal aspects. A further advantage is in the formulation of queries, where ASP makes it possible to encode queries similar to those found in (bounded) temporal logic model checking, whereas, as noted above, queries on action languages are constrained by the action language implementation. The other notable difference is once again, our focus on events rather than states, which we have discussed at some length above.

The syntax and underlying semantics of the action language we present here are similar to those of the $C+$ language in [6]. Besides internal support for the semantics of institutions our approach specifies the effects of actions (in particular the termination of inertial fluents) in a different way. For example, in $C+$ the rules "a causes f.a causes ¬f" will necessarily lead to a being non-executable, the corresponding statements a initiates f; a terminates f in our language do not effect the ability of a to occur or be generated and can be handled consistently (leading to f holding immediately after a); this is similar to the treatment of fluents in the event calculus [14]. The choice of our semantics stems from a desire to assimilate actions in the real world rather than model them accurately, in which case, the institution should be able to generate consistently a consequent institutional state (albeit one in which no effect has occurred), regardless of the originating event.

While their work does not consider multiple institutions, $C+$ could be used for this purpose. This would, however come at the cost of the semantic and syntactic checking of the institutional extensions which we provide. $C+$ does offer some syntactic extensions, which would lead more concise specifications. Of particular interest are *multivalued fluents* (where a fluent is multi-valued rather than boolean) and *Dynamic laws* e.g. "caused f1 if f2 " which allow for the state of fluents to be expressed indirectly as a function of other (inertial) fluents. The integration of either of these features into InstAL appears straightforward and is left for future work.

4.1   Related Papers in This Volume

The paper by Viganò and Colombetti [21] focusses on two key elements: (i) A language for the definition of and (ii) verification of, social aspects of MAS in respect of normative systems and electronic institutions, building on Colombetti's work on ontological decomposition of institutions and on Searle's model of constructed social reality.

The basis for the work is the concept of status functions that capture institutional facts (including roles, such as buyer and refinement of roles, such as auction winner) and deontic positions (sic). Status functions are only reified when needed to verify the legitimacy of an action and as such constitute institutional objects, rather than observables, in contrast to the event-based approach described here and in the related work. The language, called FIEVeL, accounts for obligation, permission and power — although the authors call this authorization. Obligations are temporal conditions that may be tested in contrast to their nature as observable objects in the institution/environment as described here. FIEVeL permits off-line verification by translation into Promela (the input language for SPIN) and hence LTL model checking, while the system we have presented, based on ASP, permits checking and presentation of results in terms of institutional fluents at the domain level. The use of model checking demonstrates how correctness properties, e.g. desirable outcomes, of protocols can be verified off-line.

Grossi *et al* [11] explore a classification of norms into three kinds: substantive norms that are generally high-level in nature and not directly enforceable, check norms that specify how to verify substantive norms and reactive norms that define how violations are to be sanctioned. Particularly relevant to this paper are the check norms that the authors view as so-called *sub-institutions* that carry out regular or continuous monitoring in respect of the upholding of the substantive norm. These sub-institutions could potentially be specified in the language we have outlined and then combined with the rest of the system, using the multi-institution approach described here. There is a further intriguing parallel in the observation of deep normative structures that capture multiple levels of combinations of regimentation and enforcement, where the latter is essentially delegation to the next level.

References

[1] Artikis, A., Sergot, M., Pitt, J.: An executable specification of an argumentation protocol. In: Proceedings of conference on artificial intelligence and law (icail), pp. 1–11. ACM Press, New York (2003)

[2] Artikis, A., Sergot, M., Pitt, J.: Specifying electronic societies with the Causal Calculator. In: Giunchiglia, F., Odell, J.J., Weiss, G. (eds.) AOSE 2002. LNCS, vol. 2585, Springer, Heidelberg (2003)

[3] Baral, C.: Knowledge Representation, Reasoning and Declarative Problem Solving. Cambridge Press, Cambridge (2003)

[4] Cliffe, O., De Vos, M., Padget, J.: Answer set programming for representing and reasoning about virtual institutions. Computational Logic in Multi-Agent Systems (CLIMA-VII) (to appear)

[5] Cliffe, O., De Vos, M., Padget, J.: Specifying and analysing agent-based social institutions using answer set programming. In: Boissier, O., Padget, J., Dignum, V., Lindemann, G., Matson, E., Ossowski, S., Sichman, J.S., Vázquez-Salceda, J. (eds.) Coordination, Organizations, Institutions, and Norms in Multi-Agent Systems. LNCS (LNAI), vol. 3913, pp. 99–113. Springer, Heidelberg (2006)

[6] Giunchiglia, E., Lee, J., Lifschitz, V., McCain, N., Turner, H.: Nonmonotonic causal theories. Artificial Intelligence 153, 49–104 (2004)

[7] Esteva, M., Padget, J., Sierra, C.: Formalizing a language for institutions and norms. In: Meyer, J.-J.C., Tambe, M. (eds.) ATAL 2001. LNCS (LNAI), vol. 2333, Springer, Heidelberg (2002)

[8] Farrell, A.D.H., Sergot, M.J., Sallé, M., Bartolini, C.: Using the event calculus for tracking the normative state of contracts. International Journal of Cooperative Information Systems 14(2 & 3), 99–129 (2005)

[9] Gelfond, M., Lifschitz, V.: The stable model semantics for logic programming. In: Proc. of fifth logic programming symposium, pp. 1070–1080. MIT Press, Cambridge (1988)

[10] Gelfond, M., Lifschitz, V.: Action languages. Electron. Trans. Artif. Intell. 2, 193–210 (1998)

[11] Grossi, D., Aldewereld, H., Dignum, F.: Ubi lex, ibi poena: Designing norm enforcement in e-institutions. LNCS, vol. 4386, pp. 110–123. Springer, Heidelberg (2007)

[12] Searle, J.R.: The Construction of Social Reality. Allen Lane, The Penguin Press (1995)

[13] Kamara, L., Artikis, A., Neville, B., Pitt, J.: Simulating computational societies. In: Petta, P., Tolksdorf, R., Zambonelli, F. (eds.) ESAW 2002. LNCS (LNAI), vol. 2577, pp. 53–67. Springer, Heidelberg (2003)

[14] Kowalski, R., Sergot, M.: A logic-based calculus of events. New Gen. Comput. 4(1), 67–95 (1986)

[15] Kowalski, R.A., Sadri, F.: Reconciling the event calculus with the situation calculus. Journal of Logic Programming 31(1–3), 39–58 (1997)

[16] Noriega, P.: Agent mediated auctions: The Fishmarket Metaphor. PhD thesis, Universitat Autonoma de Barcelona (1997)

[17] Padget, J., Bradford, R.: A π-calculus model of the spanish fishmarket. In: Noriega, P., Sierra, C. (eds.) AMET 1998 and AMEC 1998. LNCS (LNAI), vol. 1571, pp. 166–188. Springer, Heidelberg (1999)

[18] Rodríguez, J.-A., Noriega, P., Sierra, C., Padget, J.: FM96.5 A Java-based Electronic Auction House. In: Proceedings of 2nd Conference on Practical Applications of Intelligent Agents and MultiAgent Technology (PAAM'97), London, UK, April 1997, pp. 207–224 (1997), ISBN 0-9525554-6-8

[19] Rodriguez-Aguilar, J.A.: On the Design and Construction of Agent-mediated Institutions. PhD thesis, Universitat Autonoma de Barcelona (2001)

[20] Vázquez-Salceda, J.: The role of Norms and Electronic Institutions in Multi-Agent Systems applied to complex domains. PhD thesis, Technical University of Catalonia (2003)

[21] Viganò, F., Colombetti, M.: Specification and verification of institutions through status functions. LNCS, vol. 4386, pp. 125–141. Springer, Heidelberg (2007)

[22] Yolum, P., Singh, M.P.: Flexible protocol specification and execution: applying event calculus planning using commitments. In: AAMAS '02: Proceedings of the first international joint conference on Autonomous agents and multiagent systems, pp. 527–534. ACM Press, New York (2002)

Controlling an Interactive Game with a Multi-agent Based Normative Organisational Model

Benjamin Gâteau[1,2], Olivier Boissier[2], Djamel Khadraoui[1], and Eric Dubois[1]

[1] CITI/CRP Henri Tudor
29 Av. John F. Kennedy L-1855 Luxembourg – G.-D. of Luxembourg
{forename.name}@tudor.lu
[2] SMA/G2I/ENSM Saint-Etienne
158, Cours Fauriel F-42023 Saint-Etienne Cedex 02 – France
boissier@emse.fr

Abstract. Interactive multimedia applications are whelming to increase realism in their content and scenes with which users interact. To this aim, autonomous agents are increasingly used to implement the objects composing the scene. Although autonomy brings flexibility and realism in the animation, it has to be controlled in order to conform to the global behaviour targeted by the designer of the application. Multi-agent based organisational models are good candidates to specify "rights" and "duties" of agents with respect to the intended behaviour. In this paper we present $\mathcal{M}\text{OISE}^{Inst}$, a meta-model aiming at representing normative organisations of agents according to four points of view: structural, functional, contextual and normative. We show how this model is suited to control an application of interactive TV game show where avatars are based on agents.

1 Introduction

For a long time, the interactive multimedia animation domain has specified multimedia objects' behaviours in such a rigid manner that they could not behave in a non-expected way [1]. Recently, with the development of interactive TV (iTV), more flexible and realistic scenes and contents are required. Multimedia objects start to be considered as autonomous agents allowing the definition of scenarii in which they would act by adapting themselves to the context [2]. However the content designers need also to be able to constrain and to control the resulting autonomy and unpredictability introduced in their scenes according to a preestablished scenario. Thus, iTV requires models and tools to define multimedia contents in which, on one side, objects may be autonomous, and, on the other side, control and regulation of the scenes are possible and made explicit.

To this aim, we turn to multi-agent technologies. They offer the possibility to bring more adaptability by modelling multimedia objects as agents. Their adaptability in the scene results from the agents ability to modify their behaviours according to their own goals, to the other objects or to the environment in which they are situated. In order to control and regulate their behaviour as the designer has intended to, we have chosen organisational models (e.g. [3,4]) and different proposals of e-institution middleware (e.g. [5,6]). This later provides useful mechanisms to control and enforce the system global laws.

P. Noriega et al. (Eds.): COIN 2006 Workshops, LNAI 4386, pp. 86–100, 2007.

In order to cope with the requirements of our application, we have developed a normative organisation meta-model, $\mathcal{M}\text{OISE}^{Inst}$ and an e-institution middleware, $\mathcal{S}\text{YNAI}$. $\mathcal{M}\text{OISE}^{Inst}$ offers the possibility to represent both the rights and duties of agents. It is expressive enough to tackle with the modelling of organisations controlling agents evolving in multimedia contents. In this paper, we focus on $\mathcal{M}\text{OISE}^{Inst}$. A brief description of $\mathcal{S}\text{YNAI}$ is given in Sec. 2.2. To illustrate our approach, we use an iTV game issued from the European ITEA Jules Verne Project.

In section 2, we present the requirements for the above mentioned application of iTV game. We also give an overview of the underlying framework in which this application has been implemented. We then describe in details the different components of the $\mathcal{M}\text{OISE}^{Inst}$ meta-model, illustrating them with the application. Finally, before concluding, section 5 compares our work to other organisational models and e-institutions.

2   Motivations

We will present the general architecture of the normative framework in which our application has been implemented. This framework provides the application with the mechanisms to interpret and use the $\mathcal{M}\text{OISE}^{Inst}$ model. Before its presentation we describe the main scenario that has motivated the analysis and development of the $\mathcal{M}\text{OISE}^{Inst}$ organisational model.

2.1   Interactive Game

Let's consider, a team of televiewers. Each one is equipped with hardware (remote control and set-top-box) and software developed within the Jules Verne project. They participate to an iTV game consisting in a "questions–answers". Being at home, each televiewer is represented in the TV game by an Avatar (cf. Fig. 1). The Avatar is directly controlled by the user. The Avatars team is opposed to a team of real players. The QuizMaster is a virtual assistant that automatically regulates the game.

As in all collective games, the purpose is to constrain players to adopt a team behaviour and to respect rules. Avatars should take into account the game's rules. However teleplayers do not know each other and do not, a priori, intend to play collectively. To make the game appealing for televiewers, nothing must prevent them to behave individually and to violate some rules of the game. For instance, in the second round the televiewer who plays the "History" role has to answer only certain questions with same label but he can also use his Avatar to answer in spite of that. While not being autonomous regarding their user as in [7], Avatars must be autonomous regarding the game's rules governing the scene. We require them to be dependent of the game in term of skills but we want them to be independent of the rules of the game so that they could be easily changed.

However, the scene must be controlled with the different rules governing the game: Avatars should behave under the explicit control of the set of rules representing the game rules coupled with explicit sanctions (e.g. if the player answers while he is not authorised to, his good answer brings less points than it could and a bad answer makes him lose points). Thus while being able to decide to answer whereas it is not his turn, the televiewer will take the risk to be punished via the iTV scene in which it is playing by the mediation of his Avatar. In this application, one more requirement must be considered concerning the evolution of the rules controlling the game: rules change according to rounds of the game. Thus, the designer must be able to describe explicitly the evolution of the game.

2.2   Electronic Institution of Interactive Games Regulation

In order to define rights and duties of autonomous and generic agents by means of unambiguous specifications, we use electronic Institutions. To this aim, we need to represent the rights and duties of the agents in the context of the game round in which they are situated and to control their consequently behaviour. However, this representation should preserve the agent's decision capability on one hand, and on the other hand, it should be used to enforce and control the agents' behaviour in case of non respect.

Whereas the first point is considered in normative deliberative agents [8], the second point is addressed by Electronic Institutions that have been introduced these last years in multi-agent domain [9], and in e-commerce in particular [10], where the purpose was to introduce trust among agents during their transactions [5] through an external confident. In human societies an institution defines a set of artificial constraints that articulate agent interactions [11]. These rules enclose all kinds of informal or formal constraints that human beings use to interact. Current approaches propose the modelling of these rules through normative systems [12,13]. These ones define an institution as a set of agents which behave according to some norms taking into account their possible violation.

In the same way we define an Electronic Institution for Interactive Games as an autonomous agents' *organisation* in which their behaviours are ruled by *norms* and controlled by an *arbitration system*. The role of this arbitration system consists in rewarding or punishing agents when they respect or not their commitments.

The interactive game is thus composed of two layers (see Fig. 1): (i) the multi-agent interactive game in which Avatars evolve as autonomous agents, (ii) an institutional multi-agent middleware called $\mathcal{S}$YNAI (**SY**stem of **N**ormative **A**gents for **I**nstitution) dedicated to the management of the organisation and to the arbitration. Both layers use a normative organisational model described with the $\mathcal{M}\text{OISE}^{Inst}$ language which is an extension to $\mathcal{M}\text{OISE}^+$ [14]. The institutional middleware reads this specification in order to supervise and control the agents in accordance.

The architecture of the Avatars is thus equipped with the ability to represent and reason on the organisation and norms described with $\mathcal{M}\text{OISE}^{Inst}$. Avatars have the possibility to decide to take it into account or not. By themselves Avatars can't generate or choose goals, plans and execute actions without the help of their user. They are just an "interface" with the user proposing him a choice between what is intended by the organisation in which they operate and all the possibilities in terms of goals, plans and actions offered to a user.

The agents are executed on the SACI platform [15]. In this paper we mainly focus on the presentation of $\mathcal{M}\text{OISE}^{Inst}$. In this ITV Game, emotions are treated in a rather simplistic manner in the sense that no model of personality or social roles are used. This was not the focus of this work as is the case for instance in PsychSim [16].

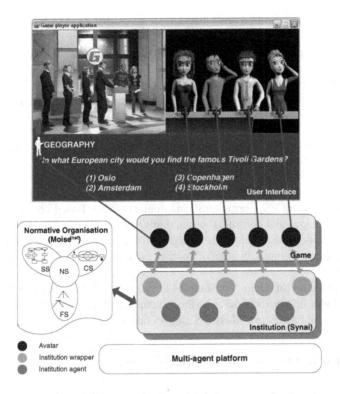

Fig. 1. Global view of the E-Institution for an i-TV game show specification

2.3 General View of $\mathcal{M}\text{OISE}^{Inst}$

$\mathcal{M}\text{OISE}^{Inst}$ extends the $\mathcal{M}\text{OISE}^{+}$ organisational model (**M**odel of **O**rganization for mult**I**agent **S**yst**E**m) [14]. $\mathcal{M}\text{OISE}^{+}$ allows to specify the global expected functioning (functional specification) of an agents organisation as well as the structure of this organisation in terms of *roles*, *groups* and *links* (structural specification). A deontic specification expresses permissions, obligations and prohibitions of missions referring to the functional specification with respect to the structural specification roles. As shown in [17], this explicit split of representations enlarges and facilitates the reorganisation task in MAS.

To take into account the requirements presented in the scenario such as, for instance, the need to structure the rules according to the game rounds, we have extended the three existing specifications of $\mathcal{M}\text{OISE}^{+}$ and have added a specification to describe the a priori dynamic of the system. $\mathcal{M}\text{OISE}^{Inst}$ is thus composed of (see Institution Specification in Fig. 1):

- A structural specification (SS) that defines the roles that agents will play, the links between these roles and the groups to which agents playing roles should participate to and where interactions take place;

- A functional specification (FS) that defines goals that have to be achieved in the system;
- A contextual specification (CS) that defines the transitions and contexts influencing the evolution of the organisation;
- A normative specification (NS) that extends and replace the $\mathcal{M}$OISE$^+$ deontic specification. It defines clearly rights and duties of roles and groups on a mission (set of goals) in specific contexts.

These four specifications form the Organisational Specification (OS), i.e. representation of organisation independent of the agents that are executing in the system. The Organisation is an instance of the OS and is built from the set of agents that have adopted roles according to the SS of the OS, interacting within groups, activating missions according to the current FS, norms (NS) and contexts (CS). Based on this the $\mathcal{S}$YNAI middleware manages and controls the functioning of this Organisation by the way of different events corresponding to the entry/exit of agents of the Organisation, adoption/leaving roles or groups, change of context, commitment to missions, achievement of goals, etc.

Focus is made on the main contributions of $\mathcal{M}$OISE^{Inst} that consist in CS and NS. However we will first quickly describe the structural and functional specifications that define the general framework where CS and NS take place.

3   Structural and Functional Specifications

Structural and functional specifications of $\mathcal{M}$OISE^{Inst} come from $\mathcal{M}$OISE$^+$. Due to lack of space we will not go into details here. The interested reader may refer to [14]. However, in order to figure out a global view of both specifications, we describe the OS built for the scenario described in section 2.1.

3.1   Structural Specification

The $\mathcal{M}$OISE^{Inst} structural specification (SS) represents the structure of an organisation in terms of *roles*, *groups* and *links* between roles. A set of *cardinalities* constrain roles and groups.

Groups of the Avatars application (see Fig. 2) defines the first level of structuration of a game and are: "Team" which structures the Avatars and "Game" structuring the Avatars, the QuizMaster's agents and the Avatars waiting for a place in the team. A group specification gt is represented by a set of no abstract roles that may be played in groups created from gt, a set of sub-groups of gt, intra and inter-group links and cardinalities. Cardinalities express minimum and maximum number of roles that have to be played in the group gt. They also express minimum and maximum number of sub-groups that have to be instanciated in gt and minimum and maximum number of agents having to play a role in gt.

In our application, root group is "Game" and its only one sub-group is "Team". We will detail their roles, their links and their cardinalities in the following.

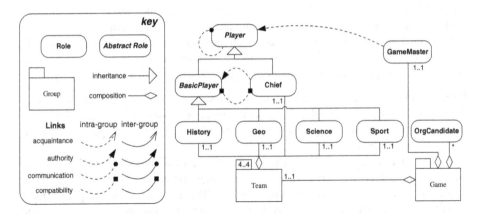

Fig. 2. Structural Specification of the iTV Game

Roles of the example are "Player", "BasicPlayer", "Chief", "History", "Geo", "Sport", "Science", "GameMaster" and "OrgCandidate". Inheritance link between roles permit to specialize definition of roles. If a role r' inherits a role r with $r \neq r'$, then r' receives some properties (implication into links and norm for instance) from r, and r' is a sub-role of r. An *abstract role* is a role that can not be played by an agent.

In our case, the *group* "Team" is composed of the roles "History", "Geo", "Sport", "Science" and "Chief". It means that the Avatars could play these roles relevant to the Question/Answer Game by participating to an instance of group "Team". Besides the "Chief" role inherits from the "Player" role and roles "History", "Geo", "Sport" and "Science" inherit from "BasicPlayer" role. At last, the group "Game" is composed of "GameMaster" and "OrgCandidate" roles. "GameMaster" is the role played by the QuizMaster virtual assistant. The role "OrgCandidate" can be played by an agent in order to join the team and to play another role.

Links constrain directly agents and are specified by their source and target roles and their type. Types are *acquaintance, communication, authority* and *compatibility*. An acquaintance link authorises the agents playing source role to have a representation of the agents playing target role. A communication link authorises the agents playing source role to communicate with the agents playing target role. An authority link authorises the agents playing source role to control the agents playing target role. A compatibility link authorises agents playing source role to also play target role. An authority link implies a communication link which implies itself an acquaintance link.

Inheritance between roles implies links' inheritance that means if r_s is the source role of an acquaintance link and r_t is the target of this link, and r'_s inherits from r_s then r'_s is also the source of an acquaintance link where r_t is the target role. The same reasoning can be done with the target role.

The SS of the Avatars application specifies thus an authority link between the "GameMaster" and the "Player" role that means that all inheriting roles from "Player" are under the authority of the "GameMaster". Agents playing roles inherited from the "Player" role is authorised to communicate with other agents playing roles also inherited from "Player". The agent playing the "Chief" role is authorised to control the agents playing "History", "Geo", "Sport" or "Science" roles and is also authorised to play one of these roles because of the compatibility link between these two roles. All links defined here are intra-group links which means that roles of the links must be in the same instance of group "Team". For instance, an agent playing the role "Chief" in the group $Team_1$ does not have authority on basic players from a group $Team_2$.

Cardinalities specify the number of agents allowed to play a role in gt for a role cardinality. A sub-group cardinality specifies the number of sub-group instances allowed by the group gt. At last, an agent cardinality specifies the number of agents allowed to play a role in group gt.

For instance, in group "Team", cardinality '1..1' on the composition links imposes that "History", "Geo", "Sport", "Science" and "Chief" roles can be adopted by only one Avatar at the same time. Thus given the compatibility link, one agent can play at most two of those five roles. In order to avoid that an agent playing the "Chief" role could play several roles of kind "BasicPlayer", the group cardinality '4..4' bearing on group "Team", states that any well formed instance of this group may contain four and only four Avatars. At last, since we can have a lots of candidate wanting to join the team, the cardinality is '*'.

3.2 Functional Specification

The $\mathcal{M}\text{OISE}^{Inst}$ functional specification (FS) expresses the global functioning of the system as a set of social schemes. A *social scheme* is composed of collective goals bound together by plans and of missions.

As in [18], goals may be decomposed or not into sub-goals (plan) until primitive actions. The aim is to delegate to the agents the choice of the way to achieve goals. The composition of sub-goals into plan uses three operators:

- *sequence* ("$g1 = g2, g3$") which means that the goal $g1$ will be achieved if the goal $g2$ is achieved and after that also the goal $g3$ is achieved;
- *choice* ("$g4 = g5 \mid g6$") which means that the goal $g4$ will be achieved if one and only one of the goals $g5$ or $g6$ is achieved;
- *parallelism* ("$g7 = g8 \parallel g9$") which means that the goal $g7$ will be achieved if both goals $g8$ and $g9$ are achieved, but they can be achieved in parallel.

According to their roles (see below) agents may adopt a goal and achieve it alone or in cooperation with other agents. The achievement of a goal is monitored and controlled by the $\mathcal{S}$YNAI middleware. It will activate other goals in accordance to the evolution of the plan of the activated social scheme. Missions express the a priori grouping of the goals composing social schemes into sets according to the way the designer wants the global plan to be achieved by different agents. The link between those sets of goals and the agents will be expressed within the NS that will bind roles or groups to missions.

The main goal of the Avatars application FS is to play a game. That's why as shown in Fig. 3, the root goal of the "Functional Scheme" is "Game played". This latter has just one sub-goal which is achieved when all questions are handled. In order to handle

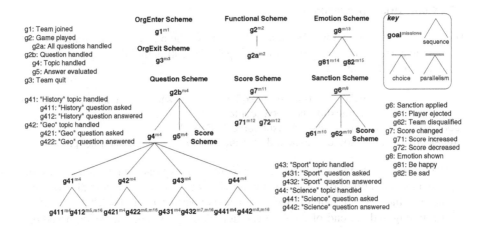

Fig. 3. Functional Specification of the iTV Game

a question, a "Question Scheme" instance must be executed, and so the "Question handled" goal must be achieved. Its plan is a sequential achievement of goals "g4", "g5" and of the root goal of the "Score Scheme" because a scheme may be reused within other social schemes. The goal "Topic handled" is achieved when a question with a topic chosen between *history*, *geography*, *science* and *sport* is asked and an answer to this question is given. The "Score Scheme" is dedicated to the management of the scoring during the game and consists in choosing between increasing or decreasing the score. The "Emotion Scheme" consists in choosing to show either an happy Avatar or a sad one. The "Sanction Scheme" describes penalties or rewards that agents may have. The root goal of this scheme consisting in applying a sanction "Sanction applied" is split into "Player ejected" sub-goal to exclude a player, "Team disqualified" sub-goal to make the other team win and "Score Scheme" to change the score. The "OrgEnter Scheme" (resp. "OrgExit Scheme") defines the behaviour to join (resp. leave) a team.

4   Contextual and Normative Specifications

Thanks to SS and FS, we are able now to describe and specify the global architecture and the global functioning of an organisation. However as shown by several works in multi-agent domain, multi-agent applications are often situated in dynamic environment. Depending on the evolution, the designer may be able to express at design-time some constraints on the changes that could occur in the organisation. For instance, in our application, the game execution is structured according to rounds that impose changes on the rules governing it. The satisfaction of this requirement is captured by the Contextual Specification (CS) of $\mathcal{MOISE}^{Inst}$. After its presentation, we will focus on the Normative Specification (NS) of $\mathcal{MOISE}^{Inst}$ that is used to glue all specifications in a coherent and normative organisation.

4.1   Contextual Specification

The contextual specification (CS) of an OS describes the a priori set of contexts occupied by the corresponding Organisation during the execution life of the system. The CS is defined in BNF as follows:

⟨CS⟩   ::= '(CS' :context ⟨contextDesc⟩* :transition ⟨transition⟩ :initialCtxt
              ⟨contextId⟩ :finalCtxt ⟨contextId⟩ ')'
⟨contextDesc⟩ ::= '(':id ⟨contextId⟩ [:subcontext ⟨CS⟩*]')'
⟨transition⟩ ::= '(':source ⟨contextId⟩ :target ⟨contextId⟩ [:event ⟨eventId⟩]']')'

- ⟨contextDesc⟩ is the specification of a context, i.e. global state occupied by the Organisation during runtime. It is referenced with an identity ⟨contextId⟩ which is used in the NS (see below). Special contexts :initialCtxt and :finalCtxt express the beginning and the end of the CS evolution. A context could be decomposed into sub-contexts (sub-CS). These sub-contexts may evolve in parallel.
- ⟨transition⟩ defines a one way transition from a source context to a target context. The trigger of the transition is done by the production in the Organisation of an event ⟨event⟩. Events are application dependant. They are produced and monitored by SYNAI. In our case, for the iTV game, the following events have been defined: *beginG* and *endG* corresponding to the start and the end of the game, *chgR* corresponding to a new round, *chgT* produced by a change of turn of team to answer and *avT* if the game starts with a question for Avatars (teleplayers) or *hmT* for Humans players.

In Fig. 4, we can see the CS of our application. The organisation will start in context "Begin". In this context, as we will see below in the NS, the Avatars are authorised to join their team, i.e. to play the role "OrgCandidate". Out of this context, it is forbidden to join the team. The context "Game" is decomposed into three sub-contexts corresponding to the different rounds encountered during the game. The context "Game" will be used in the definition of the basic rules of the game while the three sub-contexts corresponding to the different rounds will be used in the definition of the specific rules governing these rounds. The "Game" context is also decomposed into two sub-contexts corresponding to the players' turn. A round sub-context and a turn sub-context can be active at the same time. Let's notice that the macro-context "Game" is active in all its

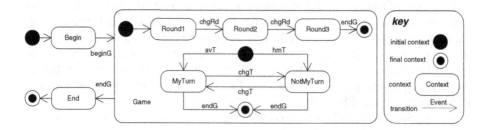

Fig. 4. Contextual Specification of the iTV Game

sub-contexts. This property ensures that the rules defined in the "Game" context stay valid and active in sub-contexts.

Finally the last context is the one in which Avatars quit their team. As stated before this specification permits to clearly define contexts in which rights and duties of Avatars could be totally different. This is what we outline in the next section.

4.2 Normative Specification

We turn now to the definition of the NS. It is composed of norms (see Fig. 1) that glue together the SS, FS and CS.

In the Multi-Agent System domain, norms are defined differently according to their use (constraints, obligations, goals). In $\mathcal{M}\text{OISE}^{Inst}$, a norm will define a right (i.e. *permission*) or a duty (i.e. *obligation*, *prohibition*) for a role or a group to execute a *mission* in a particular *context* and during a given *time*. This is supervised by an *issuer* which can apply a *sanction* on the *bearer* if the norm is not respected. A norm is active when the *context* referred in the norm equals the current organisation context. A norm is valid as long as its *condition* is satisfied. A norm could be respected or violated as long as it is active and valid. We represent a norm as the following expression

$$norm : \varphi \rightarrow op(cont, issuer, bearer, m, sanc, w, tc)$$

where:

- φ is the condition that defines the particular state of the Organisation in which the norm may be valid. As long as φ is satisfied, the norm is valid. A condition could be a composition of sub-conditions structured with logical operator such as AND and OR. A primitive condition consists in:
  - a predicate that is application dependant such as *sad* or *happy* which test if an Avatar shows a sad or happy face;
  - a predicate related to the life cycle of the organization such as *number* or *cardinalityMax* which respectively access the number of agents being part of a group and the maximum number of agents that a group may accept;
  - a predicate related to the functioning of the institution itself such as *violated* which tests if the norm is violated.

  A primitive condition is a test on a function result that $\mathcal{S}$YNAI agents execute.
- $op \in \{O, P, F\}$ defines if the norm is an obligation (O), a permission (P) or a prohibition (F);
- *cont* refers to a context of the CS in which the norm becomes active (see below). As a context could be composed of sub-CS, if a norm is active in a context then it is also active in sub-CS' contexts. For instance, if a norm is defined for the "Game" context, the norm will be active when the Organisation will be in the "Round1", "Round2" and "Round3" contexts and will be also active in the "MyTurn" and "NotMyTurn" contexts.
- *issuer* and *bearer* refer to structural entities of the SS (i.e. the whole groups and roles) from which the norm is issued and on which it is applied. The *issuer* of the norms is also the role or the group that checks the respect of the norm. Composition and inheritance that are defined in the SS among groups and roles have consequence on norms:

- When the *bearer* is a group, all roles taking place in this group in the SS, become the *bearer* of this norm. For instance, the prohibition for the "Team" group to answer a question when it is not its turn, is applied on all the roles ("History", "Science", "Geo", "Sport", "Chief") being part of this group. Idem for the norm's *issuer*.
- If the norm's *bearer* is a role r all roles inheriting from r are also concerned by the norm. For instance, if a norm oblige the "Player" role to answer a question, "BasicPlayer" and "Chief" are also obliged to answer a question, and "History", "Science", "Geo" and "Sport" roles are also obliged to answer a question. Idem for the norm's *issuer*.
- If the norm's *bearer* is a group gt then all sub-groups composing gt are concerned by the norm. For instance, if a norm concerns the "Game" group, the norm concerns also the "Team" group. As a consequence, if a norm concerns "Game" and "Team" groups, it concerns also roles belonging to both groups i.e. "History", "Science", "Geo", "Sport", "Chief", "GameMaster" and "OrgCandidate". Idem for the norm's *issuer*.

Let us notice that the expression of norms refers to the notions of roles and groups and not to agents themselves. In this way, the norm expressions are independent of the kinds of agents that could populate the system at one time.

- m refers to a mission of the FS concerned by the norm.
- *sanc* contains the reference of a different norm in the NS. It expresses a "sanction" to apply in case of norm violation. If *norm* specifies a sanction *sanc*, then the norm *sanc* must specify a condition $\varphi = violated(norm)$.
- w defines a priority used for solving conflicts between norms in case of incoherence [19], when for instance an agent could be constrained by two contradictory norms[1].
- tc specifies when the norm is valid: before ('<'), while ('=') or after ('>') a date.

Condition φ, context *con*, sanction *sanc*, weight w and time constraint tc are optional.

The norms of iTV Game application are shown in Fig. 5. The column "context" refers to the CS (see Fig. 4). Column "w" contains the weight of the norms. Column "issuer" and "bearer" refers to the roles and groups as defined in Fig. 2. Column "deOp" contains the deontic operator. Column "mission" contains the missions id specified in FS (see upper right of the goals in Fig. 3). Sanctions referring to the NS are written in column "sanction".

The norms allow us to define game rules as well as what happens before and after the game. For instance, norms N01 to N04 constrain the management of the organisation by defining when it's possible to join and to quit the team. N01 states that *any agent playing the "OrgCandidate" role is obliged to join a team (instance of "Team" group) in case there is still a role to play in this team*. According to the "context" field, this norm is valid as long as the Organisation is in the "Begin" context. The norm N02 is used to manage the end of the game by stating that *any agent playing a role in the "Team" group is obliged to quit the team (instance of "Team" group) when the*

---

[1] Even, if this field is not satisfactory in case of two norms having the same weight, it was sufficient in our application. Future works will have to consider this issue.

context	id	w.	condition	issuer	bearer	deOp	mission	deadline	sanction
Begin	N01	1	nb(Team)<max(Team)	Supervisor	OrgCandidate	O	m1	---	---
End	N02	1	---	Supervisor	Team	O	m3	---	---
Game	N03	1	---	Supervisor	OrgCandidate	F	m1	---	N17
Game	N04	1	---	Supervisor	Team	F	m3	---	---
Game	N05	1	---	Supervisor	GameMaster	O	m2	---	---
Game	N06	1	---	Supervisor	GameMaster	O	m4	---	---
Game	N07	1	---	Supervisor	Team	P	m13	---	---
Game	N08	2	---	Supervisor	Team	F	m16	---	N18
Round1	N09	3	---	Supervisor	Team	P	m16	< answer_delay	---
Round2	N11	1	---	Supervisor	History	P	m5	< answer_delay	---
Round2	N12	1	---	Supervisor	Geo	P	m6	< answer_delay	---
Round2	N13	1	---	Supervisor	Sport	P	m7	< answer_delay	---
Round2	N14	3	---	Supervisor	Science	P	m8	< answer_delay	---
Round3	N10	1	---	Supervisor	Chief	P	m16	< answer_delay	---
NotMyTurn	N15	1	---	Supervisor	Team	F	m16	---	---
NotMyTurn	N16	1	---	Supervisor	Team	F	m14	---	---
Game	N17	1	violated(N02)	Supervisor	GameMaster	O	m9	---	---
Game	N18	1	violated(N08)	Supervisor	GameMaster	O	m11	---	---

Fig. 5. Normative Specification of the iTV Game

Organisation is in the "End" context. Moreover in the "Game" context, agents playing the "OrgCandidate" role are forbidden to join a team and agents playing a role in the "Team" group are forbidden to quit the team.

The norm N03 has a sanction which is expressed as the norm N17 stating that *in case of violation of N03, any agent playing the "GameMaster" role has to eject the agent playing the "OrgCandidate" role.* Let us notice that the mission expressed in this normative expression refers to a mission expressed in the "Sanction" Scheme of the FS.

Other norms constrain the functioning of the game by defining the game's rules. For instance, as long as the Organisation is in the "Game" context, according to N05 and N06 *any agent playing the "GameMaster" role is obliged to ask question and to evaluate the answer* (see missions m2 and m4 in Functional Scheme). According to N07, *any member of a team (which means any agent playing a role belonging to the "Team" group) is forbidden to answer a question during the game.* Exceptions to this prohibition are set by defining specific norms in the context of the different rounds occurring during the game: when the Organisation is in the first and third rounds, N09 and N10 permit any agent playing respectively a role belonging to the "Team" group and the role "Chief" to answer all questions during the answer delay. When the Organisation is in the second round, four norms (N11, N12, N13, N14) allow concerned roles to answer question. Exceptions are expressed by defining for same context, role and mission a different priority ("weight").

Finally norms N15 and N16 forbid the team to answer a question or to show an happy face when the Organisation is in the "NotMyTurn" context which means the question is asked to the opponent team.

5 Related Works

In the different works on organisations [3,4] agents can be constrained to play roles and to belong to groups. Sometimes we can influence the agents behaviour by defining social contracts from an organisation. Contracts can concern either two agents or an agent and the society in which it evolves [20,21].

Since the origin of $\mathcal{M}$OISE$^+$ and its evolution into $\mathcal{M}$OISE^{Inst}, other specifications of normative organisations and e-institutions have been defined in the MAS domain. In ISLANDER [6], an Institution Definition Language (IDL) is proposed. It is mainly focused on the specification of interactions and protocols that take part to the definition of scenes. The agents have to follow the protocols to evolve in a scene. In our case, interactions are not described in terms of performatives and protocols: we are mainly concerned with the global coordination for the achievement of goals by the agents. However, even if we don't define performative structure as in [9], our CS is similar to the scene model which is defined in their work. Compared to $\mathcal{M}$OISE^{Inst}, their specification of role hierarchy is minimal in the sense that we can only define roles and inheritance and compatibility between roles. Their definition of norms don't contain sanctions.

As in ISLANDER, the OMNI platform [22] aims at defining in a complex manner the context in which agents interact. Thus, no specification of the global functioning in terms of plans or execution schemes are defined. It defines on one hand an organisational dimension and on the other hand a normative dimension. As in our case this normative dimension glue all the concepts in the definition of norms in the sense that roles, groups, scenes and interactions are seen as norms.

In this paper, the norm definition that we use, is derived from several works. The deontic logic is used to differentiate a right (permission) of a duty (obligation) which define the limits for the agents behaviour like in [5]. Inspired by [20] we completed the constraint resulting from the norm with a deadline and an activation condition. We also added a norm issuer.

6   Conclusion and Perspectives

We have proposed in this paper the $\mathcal{M}$OISE^{Inst} model which is an extension of $\mathcal{M}$OISE$^+$. This model is considered as a normative organisation specifying the rights and duties of agents operating in an organisation as norms expressed are seen as relations between roles or groups and missions in a given context.

Contrary to existing models, $\mathcal{M}$OISE^{Inst} takes into consideration the whole specification points of view (structural, functional, contextual and normative). All these specifications are essential description and representations for building our iTV application. To enlarge the scope of this model, we plan to incorporate an ontological specification (like OMNI) or an interaction specification (like ISLANDER) the same way as the other specifications are integrated in the model.

Acknowledgement

These research works are funded by the University of Luxembourg through the LIASIT project.

References

1. Oechslein, C., Klgl, F., Herrler, R., Puppe, F.: Uml for behavior-oriented multi-agent simulations. In: Dunin-Keplicz, B., Nawarecki, E. (eds.) CEEMAS 2001. LNCS (LNAI), vol. 2296, Springer, Heidelberg (2002)
2. Renault, S., Meinkohn, F., Khadraoui, D., Blandin, P.: Reactive and adaptive multimedia object approach for interactive and immersive applications. In: Proceedings of the International Conference on Information & Communication Technologies: From Theory to Applications, Damascus, Syria (2004)
3. Ferber, J., Gutknecht, O.: A meta-model for the analysis and design of organizations in multi-agent systems. In: Proceedings of the Third International Conference on Multi-Agent Systems (ICMAS98), pp. 128–135. IEEE Computer Society Press, Los Alamitos (1998)
4. Dignum, V., Meyer, J., Weigand, H., Dignum, F.: An organizational-oriented model for agent societies. In: Lindemann, G., Moldt, D., Paolucci, M. (eds.) RASTA 2002. LNCS (LNAI), vol. 2934, Springer, Heidelberg (2004)
5. Dignum, F.: Agents, markets, institutions, and protocols. In: Sierra, C., Dignum, F.P.M. (eds.) Agent Mediated Electronic Commerce. LNCS (LNAI), vol. 1991, Springer, Heidelberg (2001)
6. Esteva, M., de la Cruz, D., Sierra, C.: Islander: an electronic institutions editor. In: 1rst international joint conference on autonomous agents and multiagent systems (AAMAS'02), vol. 3, pp. 1045–1052. ACM Press, New York (2002)
7. Scerri, P., Pynadath, D.V., Tambe, M.: Why the elf acted autonomously: Towards a theory of adjustable autonomy. In: Castelfranchi, C., Johnson, W. (eds.) Proceedings of the First International Joint Conference on Autonomous Agents and Multi-Agent Systems (AAMAS 2002), ACM Press, New York (2002)
8. Castelfranchi, C., Dignum, F., Jonker, C.M., Treur, J.: Deliberative normative agents: Principles and architecture. In: Jennings, N.R. (ed.) ATAL 1999. LNCS, vol. 1757, pp. 3–540. Springer, Heidelberg (2000)
9. Esteva, M., Rodriguez-Aguilar, J.A., Sierra, C., Garcia, P., Arcos, J.L.: On the formal specification of electronic institutions. In: Sierra, C., Dignum, F.P.M. (eds.) Agent Mediated Electronic Commerce. LNCS (LNAI), vol. 1991, Springer, Heidelberg (2001)
10. Sierra, C., Rodriguez-Aguilar, J.A., Blanco-Vigil, P.N., Arcos-Rosell, J.L., Esteva-Vivancos, M.: Engineering multi-agent systems as electronic institutions. UPGRADE - The European Journal for the Informatics Professional V(4), 33–39 (2004)
11. North, D.C.: Institutions, Institutional Change and Economic Performance. In: Political Economy of Institutions and Decisions, Cambridge University Press, Cambridge (1990)
12. Papendick, S., Wellner, J., Dilger, W.: Normative behavior based on emergent invariant expectations. In: Proceedings of the Second Workshop on Norms and Institutions in MAS, 5th International Conference on Autonomous Agents, Montreal, Canada (2001)
13. López y López, F., Luck, M., d'Inverno, M.: Normative agent reasoning in dynamic societies. In: Jennings, N.R., Sierra, C., Sonenberg, L., Tambe, M. (eds.) 3rd international joint conference on Autonomous Agents & Multi-Agent Systems (AAMAS), Columbia University, New York City - USA, 19-23 July 2004, vol. 2, pp. 732–739. ACM Press, New York (2004)
14. Hübner, J.F., Sichman, J.S., Boissier, O.: A model for the structural, functional, and deontic specification of organizations in multiagent systems. In: Bittencourt, G., Ramalho, G.L. (eds.) SBIA 2002. LNCS (LNAI), vol. 2507, pp. 118–128. Springer, Heidelberg (2002)
15. Hübner, J.F., Sichman, J.S.: Saci: Uma ferramenta para implementação e monitoração da comunicação entre agentes. In: Monard, M.C., Sichman, J.S. (eds.) International Joint Conference, 7th Ibero-American Conference on AI, 15th Brazilian Symposium on AI (Open Discussion Track), São Carlos, ICMC/USP, pp. 47–56 (2000)

16. Marsella, S.C., Pynadath, D.V., Read, S.J.: Psychsim: Agent-based modeling of social inter-actions and influence. In: ICCM (2004)
17. Hübner, J.F., Sichman, J.S., Boissier, O.: Using the $\mathcal{M}$OISE$^+$ model for a cooperative frame-work of mas reorganisation. In: Bazzan, A.L.C., Labidi, S. (eds.) SBIA 2004. LNCS (LNAI), vol. 3171, pp. 506–515. Springer, Heidelberg (2004)
18. Tambe, M., Pynadath, D.V., Chauvat, N., Das, A., Kaminka, G.A.: Adaptive agent integra-tion architectures for heterogeneous team members. In: Fourth International Conference on Multi-Agent Systems (ICMAS-2000), pp. 301–308 (2000)
19. Kollingbaum, M.J., Norman, T.J., Preece, A., Sleeman, D.: Norm conflicts and inconsisten-cies in virtual organisations. LNCS, vol. 4386, pp. 264–278. Springer, Heidelberg (2007)
20. Salle, M.: Electronic contract framework for contractual agents. In: Proceedings of the 15th Conference of the Canadian Society for Computational Studies of Intelligence on Advances in Artificial Intelligence, pp. 349–353. Springer, Heidelberg (2002)
21. Dellarocas, C.: Contractual agent societies: Negotiated shared context and social control in open multi-agent systems. In: Proceedings of the Workshop on Norms and Institutions in Multi-Agent Systems, 4th International Conference on Multi-Agent Systems (Agents-2000), Barcelona, Spain (2000)
22. Vázquez-Salceda, J., Dignum, V., Dignum, F.: Organizing multiagent systems. Autonomous Agents and Multi-Agent Systems 11(3), 307–360 (2005)

Ubi Lex, Ibi Poena:
Designing Norm Enforcement in E-Institutions

Davide Grossi, Huib Aldewereld, and Frank Dignum

Institute of Information and Computing Sciences, Utrecht University,
Utrecht, The Netherlands
{davide,huib,dignum}@cs.uu.nl

Abstract. The viability of the application of the e-Institution paradigm
for obtaining overall desired behavior in open multiagent systems (MAS)
lies in the possibility of bringing the norms of the institution to have an
actual impact on the MAS. Institutional norms have to be *implemented*
in the society. The paper addresses two possible views on implementing
norms, the so-called *regimentation* of norms, and the *enforcement* of
norms, with particular attention to this last one. Aim of the paper is to
provide a theory for the understanding of the notion of enforcement and
for the design of enforcement mechanisms in e-Institutions.

1 Introduction

The purpose of electronic institutions (e-Institutions) is to guarantee the overall behavior of an open multi-agent system (MAS) to exhibit desired properties
without compromising the agents' autonomy, aiming in particular at easing interactions and enhancing trust between agents [11]. This is accomplished through
norms directed to the agents in the society which specify the behavior that the
institution expects from the agents. As such, institutions can be seen as normative systems [1], i.e., as sets of norms.

Institutions do not have access to the internal states of the agents and hence,
they cannot modify them in order to avoid any incongruence between the goals
of the agents and the norms of the institutions. Therefore, the problem arises of
how to let those norms have an effective influence on the activities of the agents.
This is the problem of *norm implementation*. This issue consists of two main
aspects.

First, there is an *interpretation* issue concerning the concepts used in the
formulation of the norms in terms of the ontology used at the society level. It is
well-known feature of normative codifications (especially in legal systems) to be
"open-textured" [6] or abstract, that is, to be in need of interpretation in order for
them to be translated into norms which are meaningful for the regulated society.
This is what we have called the "ontological" aspect of norm implementation
[4] or, to use terminology common in legal and social theory, the "constitutive"
aspect [9]. For instance, an institution might require personal data to be treated
according to specific procedures. The notion of "personal data" is of an abstract

P. Noriega et al. (Eds.): COIN 2006 Workshops, LNAI 4386, pp. 101–114, 2007.

nature and, in order for the norms concerning the treatment of personal data to be implemented, a clear specification of what *counts as* personal data in the given institution should be made precise. Much attention to this issue has been dedicated by the authors in previous work (see for instance [5,4]). The present paper will leave the problem of the interpretation of norm codifications aside.

Second, there is the issue concerning the design of appropriate "enforcement mechanisms" required to push the society toward the compliance to the norms of the institution. For instance, if personal data is not treated in accordance to the institutional regulation, the institution should trigger some kind of reaction. This broad notion of "institutional reaction" corresponds to what we call here enforcement.

The present paper focuses on this last point, aiming at discussing a theory for understanding the implementation of norms in institutions and the design of enforcement mechanisms.

The core of the enforcement implementation strategy presented in this paper is summarized in the saying "Ubi lex ibi poena" ("where there is law, there is sanction"). In other words, if norms are to be enforced, then the institution should specify and handle sanctions for every possible violation of the norms. The paper is trying to give some answers around two concrete questions about enforcement: How do institutions handle violations and specify enforcement mechanisms? And how should sanctions be designed in order to be effective for the enforcement of norms in eInstitutions?

In Section 2 we discuss different enforcement strategies (regimentation vs. reaction). The effect of these different enforcement strategies on the society are discussed in Section 3. In Section 4 we discuss what are the possible sanctions that an institution can take in a society consisting of software agents. In Section 5 we give some conclusions and areas for future work.

2   Dealing with Violations

There exists an obvious way in which the compliance to the norms of an institution can be implemented, namely by making the violation of the norms impossible. When this is the case we talk about *regimentation* ([7]): norm compliance is unavoidable, and hence, with respect to what is stated by the norms of the institution, the space of the agents' autonomy is strongly limited. This typically happens in e-commerce: when shopping on the web, you cannot get your goods delivered before giving consent for using your credit card number for paying those goods.

Regimentation guarantees the compliance of the society to the norms of the institution. However, it has been argued, for instance in [2], that violations can be functional for the society as a whole. Even stronger, if no violation can occur, if nothing can go wrong, it does not make sense any more to talk about norms at all. From the agent point of view, a regimented norm, is just a fact.

With *enforcement* we mean the *reaction* that the institution specifies to respond to a violation of its norms. Enforcement presupposes, therefore, the possibility of violation. Institutions aim at regulating the behavior of agents through norms, but it is commonplace that norms are useless if the violation of those norms is ignored (to quote the Romans again: "*ubi culpa est, ibi poena subesse debet*", that is, "where there is a violation, there must be a sanction"). In other words, the enforcement of a norm by an institution requires the institution to be in the condition of recognizing the occurrence of violations of that norm in the society and to react upon them. Not surprisingly, this *check-react* enforcement mechanism is specified by means of more norms. Enforcement is sought through further regulating the domain, i.e., adding norms imposing checks and norms specifying reactions to the occurrences of a given violation. Regulations on tax evasion are a typical example in this sense: tax payment is impossible to be regimented but checks, which could detect possible violations, are made obligatory. Once the detection takes place, precise reactions are also specified and made obligatory.

On the basis of these considerations, we can isolate three types of norms involved in the specification of institutions. In fact, the whole statute of an institution could be analyzed in terms of sets of norms of these types. There is a set of *substantive norms* which consists of those norms which describe the society's behavior desired by the institution, and there is a set of *enforcement norms* consisting of norms regulating checks and reactions on violations of other norms.

The following is an example inspired by the domain concerning the policies for data protection followed by the Spanish National Transplant Organization in the organ allocation process [10].

Example 1. (Types of norms for the specification of institutions)

Substantive norm. "The National Transplant Organization is not allowed to use racial data for allocating organs to patients".
Check norm. "The inspecting authority should perform random checks of the compliance to the previous norm every two months ...".
Reaction norm. "If racial data are used in the allocation process, then the hospital has to be fined accordingly."

The enforcement activity can thus be split in two sub-activities: check and reaction. *Check norms* deserve some further comments. They specify the way the institution is supposed to perceive the occurrence of violations. Needless to say, this can happen in many different ways. Either directly, via random checks, like in the above example; or via constant monitoring activity, like a referee in a sport match. Or indirectly, allowing agents to denounce the occurrence of a violation and then verifying their claim. This last checking activity is of an intrinsically more complex nature, calling for the establishment of tribunal-like sub-institutions within the main institution. It would be appropriate, in this case, to talk about check *sub-institutions* rather than *check norms*. For the present paper, we leave these complexities aside focusing rather on direct forms of checks.

Via such a normatively specified enforcement of the substantive norms, the enforcement issue is just lifted up to the set of enforcement norms because, if not

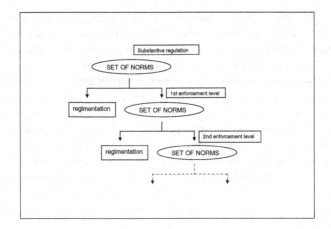

Fig. 1. Norms implementation between regimentation and enforcement

regimented, those norms could be violated and be thus in need of enforcement. In principle, this pattern could be endlessly iterated unless there exists a final enforcement level, whose norms are all regimented, or whose violations are not punished (see Figure 1).

As a matter of fact, such a cascade is precisely how real human institutions seem to be organized, where several levels of enforcement regulations may be recognized. Violations on the last level are not considered. I.e. rulings of a supreme court are supposed to be final (even though they might be violating a norm). In this sense it seems very interesting that instead of a full regimentation, the devising of a deep (i.e. structured on more enforcement levels) normative guided reaction appears to offer an efficient implementation strategy, granting at the same time a certain institutional flexibility and the room for institutional change and development. It is finally important to notice that, although we have somehow drawn a neat line between the regimentation approach and the approach leaving the possibility of violations open, an institution will most likely choose for a mixed approach deciding to regiment a (small) number of norms, and to enforce the others. We will expand on this crucial issue in the next section.

3   Different Enforcements, Different Societies

The way in which we have framed institutional implementations of norm enforcement offers a straightforward ground for showing in what precisely enforcement strategies can differ, and what kind of impact they have on societies. Consider the following most common cases:

1. A set of norms is implemented via direct regimentation;
2. A set of norms is implemented via regimentation of the set of first level enforcement norms, i.e. all occurrences of violations of the substantive regulation are sanctioned;

3. A set of norms is implemented via regimentation of the set of reaction norms of the second enforcement level, while the violation of check norms of this level is ignored.

In Case 1 violation is impossible. In Case 2 violation is possible but the reaction is absolutely certain. This would result in creating perfect deterrents. Agents would violate the norms only if they consider the benefits obtained via violating the norm higher than the disadvantages originating by the institutional reaction.

It is clear that only in Case 3 it is possible to violate a substantive norm without any reaction on that precise violation to occur. This can happen because of a failure in complying with the corresponding check norm or with the reaction norm at the first enforcement level. If the violation of the substantive norms does not happen to be detected at the first enforcement level, then no reaction at all would follow, because at the second enforcement level only the reaction norms of the first level are regimented. This happens, for instance, when one does not get caught by the police while exceeding speed limits (they were not checking): a violation occurs which is not detected and, as a consequence, no reaction is taken. If, on the other hand, the violation of the substantive norms is detected, but still no reaction is undertaken, then the second enforcement level would automatically detect this violation occurred at the first enforcement level and react to it. This would correspond to the (unrealistic) case of police agents who are automatically sanctioned when they detect a violation of speed limits and they do not issue a fine.

3.1   An Example

In the previous section we sketched how institutions can implement norm enforcement over different levels of regimentation. When designing an institution this would lead to the question concerning the number of levels the institution should use. What are the consequences for the society when one, two, three, or more levels are used? In this section this question is elaborated upon by means of a simple example. We take into consideration three possible implementation strategies of an institution that two agents can use in order to play a chess match.

Example 2. (Electronic chess)
Let us first consider what happens in an electronic chess match. Players cannot move pieces other than in the way prescribed by the rules of the game, that means that they cannot violate them: the set of actions they can perform within the game is limited, and each of these actions is norm compliant. There is no possibility for them to move the rook as if it were a bishop. For these reasons electronic versions of the game of chess constitute a clear example of *regimentation* of a substantive regulation. Agents cannot do anything else than playing chess according to the rules.

It is instructive to notice that the AMELI framework [3] falls under this category. In fact, in AMELI every agent is coupled with an institutional agent, the "governor", which acts as a filter on the agent's activities letting only allowed actions to actually take place. Governors are, as such, an excellent example of norm implementation based on the full regimentation of the set of substantive norms. It provides for a clear and protected environment. However, it is not very flexible to change (all possible moves of the game in every situation must be known beforehand).

Example 3. (Chess with flawless referee agent)
A variation on the previous example would be the use of an automatic agent referee regimenting the first enforcement level norms. Such a referee would always recognize violations and react to them. What would be the difference of this implementation of the chess institution with respect to the one described before? In that implementation, the agents could not do anything but play chess, while here they would have a wider range of actions at their disposal such as, for instance, making illegal moves on purpose in order to distract the opponent or to signal something.

The resulting games would therefore be quite different from the one implemented in the previous example, even though the set of substantial rules (the rules of chess) is the same.

Example 4. (Chess with referee agent)
Consider now how a chess match in a standard live contest is devised. The two players are not subjected to any regimentation: there is no limitation of the set of actions available. They have the possibility to move rooks as bishops, thus violating the rules of chess. However, there is a further set of norms stating precisely how to react to a violation. There might for example be a third party involved, namely a referee, whose task is to detect violations and react to them in specific ways, or to whom suspected violations can be reported by the players. We can then think of a norm, addressed to the referee, stating that the referee ought to check what happens on the chessboard (check norm), to signal an occurring violation and to intervene in the game suspending it and ordering the faulting player to retract its move (reaction norms).

Nevertheless, this might not be enough. Violations can indeed occur also at this level and the same implementation problem is then shifted to the first enforcement level. What should happen if the referee does not detect a move that is not allowed, or does not sanction a player? A further set of norms siding, this time, the first enforcement regulation provides answers to these questions. A new enforcement level, namely a *second enforcement level*, is therefore added. This can be a contest committee which is obliged to annul a game vitiated by referee's faults and so on. As already noticed, reactive levels can in principle be added *ad infinitum*, but they are, of course, *de facto* limited. For a chess contest, two reactive levels could be reasonably enough to grant a regular chess match. However, they are not enough in an absolute sense. It is possible that the last reactive level does not behave in the expected way (reconsidering the example, suppose that the committee does not annul an irregular match), at least as far as it is also not fully regimented.

What are the new opportunities in this situation? Notice that in this situation players might violate the norms without being noticed (and sanctioned). Therefore the simple fact that a player does not violate the rules might already give him extra credit with his opponent. A notion like "trust" suddenly might become important in this game. In general, the possible reasons for making a (illegal) move have again multiplied as well as the interpretation of them. Therefore, again, the game is enriched even though the basic rules remain the same.

By means of this example we tried to illustrate how different implementation strategies of the same substantive set of norms can actually give rise to radically different institutions and therefore to considerably different systems. The natural question arising is then: what would be, given a society and a set of substantive norms, the most sensible implementation strategy? And more crucially, why to allow for violations instead of choosing for a full regimentation?

3.2 E-Institutions: To Regiment or to Enforce?

The implementation of a set of (substantive) norms can be obtained either via regimentation or via the specification of an enforcement activity to be carried out by the institution. Enforcement specification takes place normatively, i.e., via adding more norms to the prior set which, thus, also require implementation. Schematically, suppose S to be the set of to-be-implemented norms, $Regiment(X)$ to denote the set of norms from X which are regimented, and $Enforce(X)$ to denote the set of norms containing X together with all the norms specifying the enforcement of X ($X \subseteq Enforce(X)$). The implementation of S can be formally defined as follows:

$$Implement(S) = Enforce(S \setminus Regiment(S)).$$

In other words, to implement a set of norms amounts to implement the set of unregimented norms together with their enforcement. This definition clearly states that the implementation of a set of norms yields a set of norms, and this is, in a nutshell, one of the main theses we are upholding here. In some sense, it is very difficult to get rid of the normative reality. The only possibility is via regimentation. In fact:

$$\text{If } Regiment(S) \equiv S \text{ then } Implement(S) \equiv \emptyset.$$

Instead:

$$\text{If } Regiment(S) \subset S \text{ then } \emptyset \subset Implement(S)$$

which means that the implementation operation should be applied again on $Implement(S)$.

This analysis has been led by the consideration of human institutions, but when it comes to electronic ones, some more assumptions can be made.

First of all, for human institutions it can be accepted that the violation of some norms can remain in principle ignored (see Example 4), this is not the case for e-Institutions. No designer would accept the possibility of norms the violation of which would not trigger any reaction.

Secondly, for e-Institutions, one enforcement level (level one of Figure 1) is enough. The reason is that when implementing unregimented norms, we would expect the enforcement agents to be explicitly programmed by the designer of the institution, and therefore we would assume them to act in perfect accordance with the principles of the institution itself.[1]

Based on these considerations we can consider Example 4 as too rich (and unrealistic) in the perspective of e-Institutions. If an institution has to be designed for agents to play chess, than the possibility of an unreliable referee can be reasonably ruled out assuming that the designer of the institution would program appropriate referee agents.[2] Only two implementation choices are therefore to be considered realistic:

1. Either all substantive norms are regimented: $Regiment(S) \equiv S$. In this case no checking and reacting activities are necessary like in Example 2.
2. Or some (possibly all) norms are left unregimented ($Regiment(S) \subset S$), while what is regimented is just their enforcement like in Example 3, that is: $Regiment(Enforce(S \setminus Regiment(S))$.

The question amounts then to: "when is it better to choose 1 over 2 or vice versa?" In general, the preference for 2 over 1 can be dictated by two factors.

Complexity of the regimented activities. Regimentation can considerably raise the complexity of the activities that agents carry out within the institution, so that for an agent to pursue its goals it would be necessary to go through too complex procedures. This is illustrated by a simple example: consider a postal service in which the deliverer should wait for the addressee to open his/her parcels and confirm the content has been delivered in the desired state. This would rule out the possibility of deliveries of damaged parcels, but it would also make the delivery process considerably slower and inconvenient for the agents which should always be present at the delivery. In other words, regimentation can thus give rise to computationally demanding activities (see [12]) both for the institution itself, and for the agents acting within it. Formally analogous scenarios can be devised especially in the eCommerce domain, where the possibility of simple and quick transactions can be a highly desired feature.

---

[1] It is instructive to notice that this is not the case in human institutions, where the enforcement is always outsourced, in the sense that no agent can be assumed to be "programmed" by the institution: for instance, enforcement agents such as policemen do maintain private goals and believes completely inaccessible from an institutional perspective. This is why, in human institutions, the nesting of many more that just one enforcement levels is the rule.

[2] These are of course contingent assumptions on the actual state of the art in MAS and e-Institutions. Future developments in these fields would make them become possibly obsolete. It can indeed be thought of e-Institutions hiring external agents and delegating to them the enforcement activity.

This aspect has directly to do with the delicate balance between the two fundamental goals of e-Institutions, i.e, increase trust in agents' transactions and facilitate those transactions [11]. The point is that, although via regimentation the highest level of trust can be achieved, agents' interaction can end up being not facilitated at all.

Usefulness of the violations. As we have seen in Example 3 the possibility for agents to violate the substantive regulation would allow for activities which would otherwise be impossible. The agent can choose to violate the regulation and possibly incur in a sanction in order to pursue some specific goals. In Example 3 agents playing chess in an institution with a flawless referee would actually have the possibility to use a wider variety of strategies for winning the game by trying to distract the opponent via performing invalid moves. Alternatively, suppose a reputation value to be attached to each chess-playing agent so that the less often they violate the norms the higher reputation they get. In this case, the possibility to violate the norms enables also the possibility to introduce a reputation value system which might be useful for further purposes: for instance, a high reputation value might be required to access chess tournaments.

In the end, allowing for violations results in a higher flexibility of the e-Institutions which might happen to serve more purposes than the one for which it was designed. This can be a desirable feature especially in domains where more e-Institutions operate on the same society.

4   Sanctions in E-Institutions

When using an enforcement mechanism to implement norms in an e-Institution, as argued in the previous sections, sanctions need to be specified to define the institution's reaction to the violations of the norms. Violations that do not trigger any reaction have no sensible meaning in an e-Institution. In previous literature (cf. [11,8]) several kinds of sanctions have been proposed, mostly influenced by sanctions used in human institutions. Some of the sanctions involve, e.g. bans, dismissal, reputation or trust influences, fines to the agent or its owner, etc. However, when designing an e-Institution not all human sanctions make sense, like, for instance, incarceration, which is a common sanction for humans, but no direct electronic equivalent of this sanction appears useful. In general there are two ways of sanctioning agents which make sense: 1) limiting the future actions of the agents, or 2) executing an action on behalf of the agents.

The first option includes, but is not limited to, sanctions such as bans and fines that are meant to restrict the agent in doing actions that are needed for it to achieve its goals (the money spent on the fine was actually meant to buy goods in an auction; the ban prevented the agent from making a bid before the auction closed). The second kind of sanctions are those where the institution changes some information (resource) pertaining to the agent which usually can only be changed by the agent itself. This might consist in changing the reputation of the agent or in paying bills on behalf of the agent, because either the agent has granted the institution this power upon entering (by signing a contract that states that the institution has the authority to issue payments on behalf of the agent in case of violations), or because the agent had to pay a deposit when it entered the institution (the deposit is then used to pay the bills and any fines that might arise).

Whatever type of sanction is chosen they are there to serve a purpose. In the following we examine the purpose of sanctions. We look at what sanctions are supposed to do and how the complexity of the agents in the institution can influence the choice of sanctions.

4.1 A Taxonomy of Sanctions

Sanctions serve different purposes in different institutions. However, there is a general purpose to sanctions that holds for all institutional environments: sanctions are there to discourage agents from taking actions that are considered unwanted or illegal by the institution. Sanctions can be viewed as a deterrents, making agents less keen on performing these unwanted and illegal actions. To achieve this discouraging effect on the agents in the institution, sanctions are designed to limit the future actions of agents. For instance, fines influence the possibilities of the agent, since they make it harder for the agent to get the items it requires as the agent has less money to spend (which, of course, only really restricts the agent if it had a limited budget and the agent's owner ordered the agent to obtain lots of items). Similarly, reputation changes might limit the actions of an agent as it might influence the outcome of future negotiations and interactions.

Next to their discouraging effect, sanctions might also be used as a compensation to those most affected by the violation of the norm. In order to provide some satisfaction or compensation to those harmed by the violation, the violating agent is sanctioned. For instance, an agent might become obliged, after violating a norm, to pay an amount of money to the affected agent(s) as compensation. This difference between using sanctions as a deterrence and as a compensation signifies a difference in the role of the institution when applying the sanction. Sanctions that are solely used as a discouragement are sanctions that are applied by the institution itself, and therefore benefit the institution itself (the fines are payed to the institution, bans are applied solely to maintain order in the system). When sanctions are applied to provide a compensation to those harmed (note that the sanction will also retain its deterring nature), the institution becomes a mediator instead, interacting between the agent who committed the violation and the rest of the society.

Another difference in sanctions, as mentioned in [12], is whether the sanction is of direct or indirect nature. Direct sanctions are those that influence the agent immediately and are noticeable directly. These include fines, bans and other "corporeal" sanctions. Indirect sanctions, on the other hand, influence the agent on a kind of meta-level, such as reputation changes or trust related sanctions. Those sanctions might not be noticeable immediately but can influence the agent for a longer period of time. Combinations of both types of sanctions can be used as well.

The choice between using a sanction merely as deterrence or adding a compensational value to it depends on the norm and domain in question. If the violation of the norm harms other agents, and these 'victims' require support to overcome this harm, a compensation might seem appropriate. However, if the norm only affects the institution, no compensation is needed. Similarly, the choice between the usage of direct and indirect sanctions is entirely up to the domain and norm in question. If indirect sanctions have an equal deterring value as direct sanctions, indirect sanctions can be used just as well. In a domain, however, where reputation plays no role, an indirect sanction (in this case, lowering the agents reputation value) has no value and a direct sanction should be used instead.

4.2 Sanctions and Types of Agents

Whatever purpose the sanctions might serve in a certain institution, the complexity of the agents in the system must be understood to determine the effectiveness of the sanction. A system that is trying to discourage agents from violating the norms by applying bans might be quite successful when the agents in the system feel bad about being banned, or are unable to complete their goals because of the ban. However, if the agents do not mind the ban the sanction fails its purpose.

The hierarchy of types of agents' autonomy developed in [13] can be used to distinguish, for each level of autonomy, what the impact of sanctions can be and what sanctions are suitable for the cognitive structure of the agent. The hierarchy of [13] distinguishes the following types of autonomy in agents (also see figure 2):

Type I Reactive Agents: Agents whose autonomy completely resides in the combination of environmental cues and system properties.

Type II Plan Autonomous Agents: Agents that are autonomous in their choosing the sequences of actions (plans) to obtain goals. The goals itself are either inherent to the agent or triggered by requests from other agents.

Type III Goal Autonomous Agents: Agents that are autonomous in making decisions about goals (which have become their interests), enabling them to choose their "prevailing interest", considering its goals. It determines which states of the world are desired, given the goal satisfaction and its goal priority.

Type IV Norm Autonomous Agents: Agents with the capabilities to choose goals that are legitimate to pursue, based on the norms of the system. Moreover, norm autonomous agents are equipped to judge the legitimacy of its own and other agents' goals.

The lower level agents, i.e. types I to III, have no idea of a sanction (they have no conception of what a sanction is). To these agents, a sanction applied by the system is nothing more than an environmental reaction to the situation at hand (or to the action they have just performed). This makes informing the agents about the norms a bit harder, as the norms need to be translated to situational causal effects that are triggered by actions in various situations. The sanctions become a necessary causal effect of the actions prohibited by the norms. However, directing and controlling the agents is a bit easier for the lower types of agents,

Fig. 2. A Taxonomy of Autonomy

as punishing agents by making them unable to reach their goal is easy for agents of types I and II. These agents can easily be prevented to achieve their goals by making them unable to do an action (making the sanction not as much a punishment for the agent, but more an incentive for the developer to redesign the agent to become norm-compliant). This is a bit harder for agents of type III , as these agents are more capable of coming up with alternative ways to achieve their goal (or can pursue alternative goals, making the punishment less effective).

Type IV agents are even a bigger problem, since they have a clear conception about what a sanction is and when a sanction will be applied. These agents can reason about the results of their actions in a normative manner, i.e. they take the norms into account to determine if an action in a certain situation is acceptable or if it will trigger a violation. This means that if a type IV agent violates a norm, the agent has probably reasoned that violating the norm is the only or the most efficient way to achieve it's goal, and a punishment is therefore only an increase in cost for the agent doing the action (while this increased cost has been fully taken into account in the decision of the agent). Moreover, since agents of type IV have the same capabilities as agents of type III, the sanctions loose even more of their deterring effectiveness.

A big problem, however, is that no guarantees can be given whether the sanction has the right effect on all the agents possibly joining the institution. To design sanctions to work for agents, assumptions about the inner working of the agents have to be made; what effect will the sanction have on them? Will they replan and try again, or will the sanction make them sorry about what they did?

In human institutions, such assumptions about the inner process of humans can be made, and such assumptions are correct most of the time (we know how most of us think, react to certain stimuli etc.). Sanctions applied in human institutions are based on these assumptions to work as an effective deterrent, as humans tend to dislike spending time in prison or paying fines applied after violating a norm. Even alternative punishments, such as being put under probation, which can be seen merely as a warning, work for humans, as they apply to the moral sense of the perpetrator. For agents, however, this kind of reaction is not assured. Agents are programmed by different developers, making them heterogeneous in nature. This heterogeneity also means that the inner workings of agents can be very different between agents. Since one cannot assume that all agents work in a similar manner or have the same beliefs in certain situations, it makes designing sanctions that are really punishments for all agents very hard. Using, for instance, probations in agent environments makes no sense, since most agents will not consider this sanction to be a warning.

If, however, one can assume that (the majority of) Type IV agents are programmed in such a manner that they will try to be norm-compliant, sanctioning these agents becomes a bit easier as the sanction is no longer seen by these agents just as a necessary causal effect to a prohibited action but as something undesirable in itself. This would mean that a norm breaking action is just less preferred by such agents than other norm-compliant actions (even if the norm-compliant action is more costly) because of the agent's desire to be norm-compliant. Sanctions can in this case rely on an intrinsic deterrence effect allowing for the specification of less drastic institutional reactions to violations (for instance fines instead of bans). However, if the willingness of agents to be norm-compliant cannot be guaranteed, the normative awareness with which Type IV agents are endowed cannot be exploited and they will have to be sanctioned in the same way as Type III agents.

5   Conclusions

In this paper we have explored two related problems that have to be solved when implementing norms in e-Institutions. First is the decision between enforcement of norms through regimentation or through reaction. An interesting first observation is that implementing norms actually implies adding more norms (albeit of a slightly different nature). Of course all conceivable levels of enforcement norms are possible. However, we have seen that in most situations the best is to have one level of enforcement norms in e-Institutions due to the fact that enforcing agents are centrally controlled (and programmed).

The second question addressed in this paper was which sanctions are useful as reaction to violations. We have shown that, although many mechanisms are based on human society, not all human-based sanctions make sense in an e-Institution. A first classification of different types of sanctions is given, but many issues still remain open. One of the first issues to be addressed is how to choose the most effective sanction from an institutional point of view. This would both deter agents from violating norms too easily, but also facilitate normal transactions between agents as much as possible.

References

1. Alchourrón, C.E., Bulygin, E.: Normative Systems. Springer, Wien (1986)
2. Castelfranchi, C.: Formalizing the informal?: Dynamic social order, botton-up social control, and spontaneous normative relations. Journal of Applied Logic 1(1-2), 47–92 (2004)

3. Esteva, M., Rodríguez-Aguilar, J.A., Rosell, B., Arcos, J.L.: AMELI: An agent-based middleware for electronic institutions. In: Third International Joint Conference on Autonomous Agents and Multi-agent Systems, New York, US, July 2004 (2004)
4. Grossi, D., Aldewereld, H., Vázquez-Salceda, J., Dignum, F.: Ontological aspects of the implementation of norms in agent-based electronic institutions. Computational & Mathematical Organization Theory 12(2-3), 251–275 (2006)
5. Grossi, D., Dignum, F., Meyer, J.-J.Ch.: Contextual terminologies. In: Toni, F., Torroni, P. (eds.) Computational Logic in Multi-Agent Systems. LNCS (LNAI), vol. 3900, pp. 284–302. Springer, Heidelberg (2006)
6. Hart, H.L.A.: The Concept of Law. Clarendon Press, Oxford (1961)
7. Jones, A.J.I., Sergot, M.: On the characterization of law and computer systems. Deontic Logic in Computer Science, 275–307 (1993)
8. Pasquier, P., Flores, R.A., Chaib-draa, B.: Modelling flexible social commitments and their enforcement. In: Gleizes, M.-P., Omicini, A., Zambonelli, F. (eds.) ESAW 2004. LNCS (LNAI), vol. 3451, pp. 153–165. Springer, Heidelberg (2005)
9. Searle, J.: The Construction of Social Reality. Free Press (1995)
10. Ley 30/1979, de 27 de octubre, sobre extracción y transplante de órganos. Boletín Oficial del Estado 266 (April 29, 1986)
11. Vázquez-Salceda, J.: The role of Norms and Electronic Institutions in Multi-Agent Systems. Birkhuser Verlag AG (2004)
12. Vázquez-Salceda, J., Aldewereld, H., Dignum, F.: Norms in multiagent systems: from theory to practice. International Journal of Computer Systems Science & Engineering 20(4), 95–114 (2004)
13. Verhagen, H.: Norm Autonomous Agents. PhD thesis, The Royal Institute of Technology and Stockholm University (2000)

Specification and Verification of Institutions Through Status Functions[*]

Francesco Viganò[1] and Marco Colombetti[1,2]

[1] Università della Svizzera italiana, via G. Buffi 13, 6900 Lugano, Switzerland
{francesco.vigano,marco.colombetti}@lu.unisi.ch
[2] Politecnico di Milano, piazza Leonardo Da Vinci 32, Milano, Italy
marco.colombetti@polimi.it

Abstract. Institutions have been proposed as a means to regulate open interaction systems by introducing a set of norms (involving deontic positions like authorizations, obligations, prohibitions, and permissions) and to define the ontology of the context in which agents interact. To better clarify the interdependence existing among deontic positions and the ontology defined by each institution, in this paper we propose to model institutions in terms of status functions imposed on agents and defined as aggregates of deontic positions. We present a metamodel which describes the concepts necessary to specify an institution and FIEVeL, a language that can be used to formalize institutions. Finally, we discuss how to automatically translate FIEVeL specifications into the input language of the SPIN model checker and the kind of properties that it is possible to check.

1 Introduction

Following the ideas presented in [17], institutions have been put forward as a means for regulating open interaction systems where agents' internal states cannot be accessed or agents are implemented by different parties. *Norms* play a fundamental role in the design and management of open systems, because they create positive expectations in the outcomes of such systems and make more predictable the behavior of other agents which are assumed to be autonomous. To introduce norms in open multiagent systems, in [7,3,13,10] the authors propose to model such systems in terms of *electronic institutions*, a formalism developed to design protocols and which can be used to automatically enforce them as explained in [6].

From a different perspective, but with similar objectives, in [20,22] *normative systems* have been proposed to describe agents behavior in terms of obligations, prohibitions, and permissions when it is not possible to assume that agents will behave according to the expected behavior. In any case, institutions and normative systems have been essentially applied to define interaction protocols [7,4,9,20,24]: for this reason, we will exemplify our approach with examples taken by a widely used interaction protocol, the English Auction, which allows us to exemplify and compare our approach with other attempts to formalize institutions.

---

[*] Supported by Swiss National Science Foundation project 200020-109525, "Artificial Institutions: specification and verification of open distributed interaction frameworks."

P. Noriega et al. (Eds.): COIN 2006 Workshops, LNAI 4386, pp. 115–129, 2007.
© Springer-Verlag Berlin Heidelberg 2007

Following the analysis of institutional reality presented in [21], in [9,24] we have suggested that institutions not only define norms, but also the *ontology* of the interaction context. For instance, the institution of the English Auction defines the very concept of winning an auction, which also implies that the winner ought to follow a set of norms. In [9,24] institutional attributes assigned to entities and norms are combined to describe the interaction context and the protocol.

While in [4,9,20,24] institutional states are described and are assumed to exist independently of agents' deontic positions (authorizations, obligations, etc.), following Searle [21] we think that, with the exception of institutional facts related with the creation of meaning, institutional facts cannot be described or exist without deontic positions. In fact, when an agent modifies or creates a new institutional fact, it is actually modifying an authorization or creating new obligations for another agent or for itself. For instance, when the auctioneer declares a new current price, participants are authorized only to make higher bids.

According to Searle [21], institutional facts are built thanks to the ability of agents to collectively impose new statuses, named *status functions*[1], on objects, events or agents. When a new status function is imposed on an agent (or an object) by a community of agents, it holds certain positions and performs certain functions independently of its physical features. Moreover, since institutional objects represent the continuous possibility of agents' activities [21], imposed status functions become manifest only when they are necessary to perform actions. Therefore, when agents impose a new status function, they are actually creating new possibilities of action for agents themselves.

Starting from this theory of institutional reality, we propose to model all institutional facts, even those imposed on events and objects, in terms of status functions imposed on agents, which are named *agent status functions*. In particular, we describe agent status functions in terms of deontic positions, which represent what actions are authorized, obliged, forbidden, or permitted for an agent. In doing so, institutional events can be characterized in terms of what status functions are imposed or revoked, which helps to clarify how each institutional event changes agents' deontic positions.

Once we have formalized an institution, we have also to ensure that our specification is sound and allows agents to reach the desired states of affairs. Furthermore, as soon as institutions become complex, without the aid of automated techniques it is prohibitive to foresee all possible evolutions and states in which the institution may evolve. For this reason in this paper we also consider how to verify institutions by applying model-checking techniques [2,19]. Automated formal verification should be considered as an important step in the development of institutions, because it can increase the reliability of institutions by ensuring that agents will be provided with all the needed powers to fulfill their objectives and that they will not be subject to contradictory or undesired norms.

The remainder of this paper is so structured: in Section 2 we define a metamodel of institutional reality based on the concept of status functions. In Section 3 we briefly

---

[1] As in [21] we use the term *function* to refer to i) a *position* or an *action* for which an agent or a thing is specially fitted or ii) to a *status* imposed on agents or things independently of their specific physical features (status function). Therefore, we do not use the term function in its mathematical sense.

present the syntax and the semantics of FIEVeL, a language that can be used not only to model institutions, but also also to verify such specifications. In Section 4 we show how FIEVeL specifications can be translated into Promela (*Pro*cess *Me*ta *La*nguage), the input language of the SPIN model checker [12], while in Section 5 we discuss what kind of properties can be checked in our current implementation. Finally in Section 6 we present an evaluation of our approach and a comparison with other works in the field of institutions and normative systems.

2   The Institution Metamodel

Many researches on institutions share several common or strongly related notions such as the concepts of role, norms, and authorization [4,9,10,20]. In this section we introduce our institution metamodel to enhance a comparison with other works and to explain what are the key concepts that we perceive as essential to specify an institution, the relationships existing between them and their intended meaning.

As shown in Figure 1, our metamodel is based on the notion of *agent status function*, that is, a status imposed on an agent and recognized as existing by a set of agents. Typical examples of status functions are not only the concept of auctioneer, participant, or winner of an auction, but also being the owner of a good, being the husband or the wife of somebody. The concept of status function shares several features with the concept of role as it has been discussed in the literature (refer to [1,16] for an overview). Despite that, we prefer to use the term status function for three reasons: (i) the term role has been used with different meanings and it has been characterized in terms of very different concepts such as mental states, tasks, duties, etc; (ii) the term status function better represents the fact that we are concerned with status assigned to agents to perform several functions and whose existence depends on those agents that recognize them as

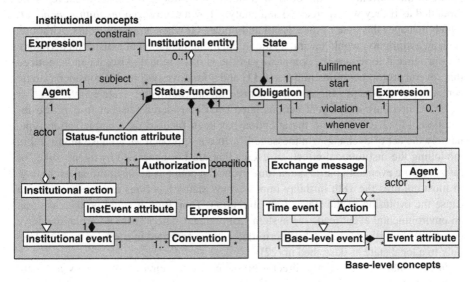

Fig. 1. The institution metamodel

existing; (iii) the concept of status function is broader than the concept of role as used, for example, in [1]. In fact, it seems to be difficult to describe in terms of a "preexisting organization" being the owner of a good or being under age, while it is quite natural to regard them as status functions imposed by a group of agents.

We define status functions as possibly empty aggregates of *deontic positions* that can be expressed in terms of two main concepts, *authorizations* (also named *institutionalized power* [14,20]) and *obligations*. An obligation is characterized by a *state* and by four *expressions* (*whenever*, *start*, *fulfillment*, and *violation*) which are used to specify conditional obligations and when an obligation should be considered fulfilled or violated (more details can be found in [23]). An obligation is created because a status function is imposed, changes its state when its conditions are satisfied, and eventually reaches a final state (*inactive*) either because its expressions are evaluated to true or because it is associated to a revoked status function. Obligations can be also used to express prohibitions by specifying suitable violation expression, while we do not define a specific construct to explicitly represent the fact that an agent is permitted to perform an action as in [4,10,20]. Instead, as in [24] we consider that every action, if it is not prohibited, is also permitted.

Interdependent status functions are declared within *institutional entities* which enforce on a group of status functions a set of *constraints* (e.g. an auctioneer cannot be also a participant). Moreover, institutional entities define cardinality constraints, like "an auction is composed by an auctioneer and a set of participants".

Base-level events reflect changes that are produced in the physical world or that are relative to lower level institutions, like *time* events and *exchange message* events. We do not name these kinds of events "physical" because, strictly speaking, most events are somehow dependent on language and therefore institutional [21]. Despite that, in most cases the deontic positions we want to model are not affected by the institutional nature of those events, and therefore we can ignore it. In FIEVeL base-level events are modelled as if they were perceived and analyzed by a centralized *institution manager*, which manages the state of the system and updates it when an event occurs. Although such an assumption would be unrealistic in the implementation of a distributed system, we introduce it to reduce the complexity of the verified model. Also, it can be noticed that several prototypes of institutions [6,11] and normative systems [8] consider a single centralized component which makes the institutional (normative) state evolve.

In the literature only agent actions have been considered relevant to describe institutions [4,9,20,22,24], and the attention has been focused on a single action type, namely the act of exchanging a message [7]. In our approach we are also interested in modelling the institutional effects of events that are not generated by agents, like for instance time events. In particular, a time event can count as an institutional event (e.g. in most cultures the 18th birthday imposes new status functions on a person) or can cause the evolution of the state of an obligation. Therefore, it could be the case that an environmental event leads the system from a legal state (where no violations have occurred) to an illegal state, while permitted actions executed in a legal state must lead only to a legal state as described in [22].

Institutional events are not directly produced by the environment or by an agent thanks to its own capabilities, because their effects need to be recognized by a set of agents. Instead, institutional events happen because agents accept that when certain base-level events occur, if certain contextual conditions are satisfied, they *count as* institutional events. Therefore, there exists an ontological difference among base-level events and institutional events: while the former exist because they correspond to certain physical changes, the latter exist because they are recognized as existing by a community of agents.

In [9] we discussed what kind of contextual conditions are relevant to model that an agent action counts as an institutional action. In particular, we single out the following conditions: (i) there must exist a convention, namely a message type, binding the agent action to the institutional action; (ii) the system must satisfy the preconditions associated to the institutional action; (iii) the agent must be authorized to perform the institutional action. In this paper we extend the treatment of the count-as relation by considering institutional events in general. Therefore, the act of exchanging a message cannot be taken as our unique primitive to specify conventions. Instead, any base-level event can be used to define a new convention. As in [9] a precondition must be satisfied, although here preconditions are expressed in terms of the existence or absence of certain status functions. Finally, in the case of institutional actions, the agent must also be authorized. If all these conditions are satisfied, a base-level event counts as an institutional action and its effects take place, which means that certain status functions will be assigned or revoked.

3   FIEVeL

Figure 1 not only depicts our metamodel of institutions, but it actually represents the abstract syntax of FIEVeL (*F*unctions for *I*nstitutionalized *E*nvironments *V*erification *L*anguage), a language that has been defined to *model* institutions in terms of the concepts introduced by our metamodel and to *verify* them by applying model-checking techniques [2,19]. For this reason, FIEVeL has been designed to limit the *state explosion problem* [2] and to be translated into Promela, the input language of the SPIN model checker [12]. In the following of this Section we will discuss the formal framework we have developed to define the semantics of FIEVeL and we will exemplify FIEVeL constructs by reporting few fragments extracted by our specification of the English Auction institution. More details about the formal semantics of FIEVeL, its grammar and the full specification of the English Auction can be found in [23].

A FIEVeL specification may be composed of several institutions that are concurrently executed, although at the moment FIEVeL does not allow the development of interdependent institutions, that is, institutions whose state and evolution directly depend on the state of another institution. A FIEVeL specification is composed by four main sections:

- *basic-domain definition*, where a designer can define new basic types by specifying them as subsets of built-in basic types or by enumerating their elements. FIEVeL defines few built-in basic types, like integers (*int*), agent identifiers (*AID*), and objects identifiers (*OID*). User defined basic types can then be used to define complex types (status functions, events, etc.).

- *base-events definitions*, where a designer can list all the relevant events. In particular, messages are constituted by a *message type* and a (possible empty) set of attributes, which can affect the institutions defined in the current specification. At the moment FIEVeL assumes that all messages belong to a single type of communicative acts, namely, *declarations* [9].

- *institution definitions*, where for each institution it is possible to specify a set of institutional entities and status functions, a possibly empty set of constraints on them, and a set of conventions binding base-level events to the performance of several institutional-events. In Figure 2 it can be noticed that preconditions of institutional events are specified in terms of the existence or absence of certain status functions, while their effects are expressed by assigning (or revoking) several status functions on agents. As in [15], an institutional event describes some changes among two consecutive states representing which "variables" have been modified and their new values.

- *model definition*, where elements composing each basic domain and the initial state of the system, described by imposing certain status functions on agents, are defined. Domain elements are specified because SPIN is able to verify only finite models.

In Figure 2 we report a few fragments of our specification of the English Auction institution, showing that an auctioneer that has received at least one offer (represented by OFFERED status function) is not only authorized to declare the current winner if no agent can still make a bid (INROUND), but since then it is also obliged to do so before the next time instant has elapsed. The action *currentWinner* is conventionally bound to the exchange of a message of type *decCurrentWinner* and, if the agent indicated as winner of the round is the first which has offered the highest price, therefore that agent is declared *current winner* and offers relative to the previous round are cancelled.

In FIEVeL time is considered as a component of the system. Two consecutive time events t_i and t_{i+1} may be separated by a sequence (possible empty) of other base level events, which are assumed to occur at time t_i. Hence the institutional state may change due, for instance, to message-exchange events even if the time variable does not change. Therefore, time aspects are regarded in two distinct ways: (i) as in classical temporal logic, to define *qualitative* properties (e.g. it is always the case that an auctioneer cannot win an auction), and (ii) as in RTTL [18] to express *quantitative* properties (e.g. the auctioneer must open the auction before two minutes since now).

Every FIEVeL specification corresponds to an *ideal* transition system characterized by a *many sorted first-order signature* where every transition represents all institutional effects (institutional events, fulfillment of obligations, etc) associated with a base-level event. Actually, the generation of such transition system is not only computationally expensive, but it would also lead to a huge number of Promela code lines. In fact, due to several limitations of SPIN, for every institution instance we should generate a transition for each possible combination of base-level events, institutional-events, and obligation state changes. For this reason, instead of calculating the ideal transition system, we prefer to derive a *computational* transition system, such that each transition partially represents the institutional effects of an event, so that summing the effects of a sequence of transitions we can reach the same institutional state.

```
basic-types:
   priceD subtype-of int;
base-events :
  message decOffer(agent : AID, price : priceD, num : int);
    ...
institution EnglishAuctionInstitution {
  institutional-entity englishAuction {
    ...
    [0,ALL] status-function OFFERED (bidder: AID,
    price: priceD, num: int) {
    key: bidder;
      authorizations:
        currentWinner c <- not exists x in INROUND [true];
      deontic-specification:
        obligation(not exists x in INROUND[true],done(currentWinner),
          activation-time>1);
    }// OFFERED
      ...
    constraints:
      AUCTIONEER disjoint PARTICIPANT;
  }// entity
conventions:
    exch-Msg(decCurrentWinner (ag,pr,r)) =c=> currentWinner(ag,pr,r);
      ...
  institutional-events:
    institutional-action currentWinner(agent : AID,
    price : priceD, n: int):
    pre: (exists o in OFFERED[((o.subject = actor and o.bidder=agent)
      and (o.price=price and o.num=n))] and forall x in OFFERED
      [(x.price < price or (x.price=price and n<=x.num))]);
    eff: p in PARTICIPANT -X->
          assign(p.subject, CURWINNER(price))[p.subject = agent],
        o in OFFERED -X->
          revoke(o.subject, OFFERED(o.agent, o.price, o.n))[true];
    ...
}// institution
model-definition:
  basic-domains:
    AID={aid_0,aid_1,aid_2};
    ...
  institutions:
    EnglishAuctionInstitution initial-state:
      assign(aid_0,AUCTIONEER());
      ...
```

Fig. 2. Fragments of the English Auction institution specification

To demonstrate that we can build a computational transition system which simulates the ideal system, that is, satisfies the same properties we want to verify, let $M = (S, S_0, R, V)$ be a Kripke structure over a set AP of atomic propositions such that S is a finite nonempty set of *states*, $S_0 \subseteq S$ is a finite nonempty set of *initial states*, R is a total relation on S, and V is a valuation function associating a value in $\{0, 1\}$ at each atomic proposition p in AP for each state. In the sequel we write π_k for the k-th state of path $\pi = s_0, s_1, s_2, \dots$ and π^k for the suffix of π starting at state π_k, that is, the sequence $s_k, s_{k+1}, s_{k+2}, \dots$ Π stands for the set of all paths in M, while Π_0 represents the set of all initialized paths in M, that is, the set of all paths whose first state is an initial state (formally: $\Pi_0 = \{\pi \in \Pi \mid \pi_0 \in S_0\}$).

Let $\widehat{M}$ be a second Kripke structure defined over a set of atomic proposition $\widehat{AP}$ such that $AP \subseteq \widehat{AP}$; we define a relation $Z \subseteq \Pi \times \widehat{\Pi}$ such that $(\pi, \widehat{\pi}) \in Z$ if and only if for each proposition $p \in AP$:

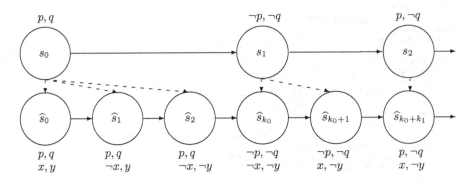

Fig. 3. Simulation relation among paths of different models with respect to propositions p and q. Dashed arrows represent the Z relation.

1. $V(\pi_0, p) = \widehat{V}(\widehat{\pi}_0, p)$;
2. there exists a $k > 0$ such that:
   (a) $V(\pi_1, p) = \widehat{V}(\widehat{\pi}_k, p)$;
   (b) for every $0 < r < k$ $V(\pi_0, p) = \widehat{V}(\widehat{\pi}_r, p)$;
   (c) $(\pi^1, \widehat{\pi}^k) \in Z$.

Let us consider a Kripke structure M characterized by a set $AP = \{p, q\}$ of atomic propositions and let $\widehat{M}$ be a second Kripke structure defined over $\widehat{AP} = \{p, q, x, y\}$. Figure 3 depicts two paths π and $\widehat{\pi}$ related by the Z relation ($(\pi, \widehat{\pi}) \in Z$). The reader can observe that: (i) the valuation of common propositions p and q is the same in the first state; (ii) there exists a segment of length k_0 such that state $\widehat{\pi}_{k_0}$ has the same valuation of π_1 and all other states of the segment have the same valuation of state π_0; the suffix $\widehat{\pi}^{k_0}$ is related by Z to the suffix of π starting from π_1.

Path $\widehat{\pi}$ is therefore emulating the behavior of path π by simulating each transition on path π with a finite sequence of transitions, such that it keeps unchanged the truth values of common atomic propositions until it changes them in a single step. Intuitively, we can imagine building a path $\widehat{\pi}$ by taking path π and inserting between two consecutive states (π_i, π_{i+1}) a new set of intermediate states which are characterized by the same valuation function of state π_i.

It can be demonstrated (see [23]) that if for each $\pi \in \Pi_0$ exists a $\widehat{\pi} \in \widehat{\Pi}_0$ such that $(\pi, \widehat{\pi}) \in Z$, and for each $\widehat{\pi} \in \widehat{\Pi}_0$ exists a $\pi \in \Pi_0$ such that $(\pi, \widehat{\pi}) \in Z$, for each temporal formula φ composed by atomic propositions belonging to AP and which does not contain the *next* temporal operator, $M \models \varphi$ with respect to initialized paths Π_0 if and only if $\widehat{M} \models \varphi$ with respect to $\widehat{\Pi}_0$. This result can be extended to transition systems (see [23]) and it means that given an *ideal* transition system which corresponds to a FIEVeL specification, we can build a *computational* transition system which preserves all temporal properties of the *ideal* system. It can be observed that to obtain this result we have to renounce to the *next* operator, which does not represent a problem considering that not even SPIN supports it for efficiency reasons. Although in [5] the *next* temporal operator has been used to specify interaction protocols, we think that its use is problematic if we consider as possible events not only message exchanges but also time events, since it is not longer ensured that the next state is due to a message exchange. For this reason, we think that renouncing to the *next* operator in the specification of an institution is a sensible choice.

4   Translating FIEVeL into Promela

A Promela specification is composed by a set of *processes* and *global variables* that can be described by defining new *process types* and *record structures*. Essentially a Promela process is constituted by a set of statements, which can be *simple statements*, like assignments, or *compound statements*, like selection (if) and repetition (do). Each statement is characterized by an *enabling condition* and a *postcondition*. Promela imposes severe restrictions on what can be specified in a precondition, therefore, to overcome such limitations and to increase the expressiveness of FIEVeL without producing an huge number of intermediate states, we chose to use embedded C code to evaluate preconditions of transitions and to compute reachable states. The SPIN model checker adopts an interleaving semantics, which means that when several processes have executable statements, it randomly chooses one of them and executes it. When all enabling conditions are evaluated to false, two special preconditions (also named guards) timeout and else, are evaluated to *true*. In particular, else is enabled only if all transitions at the process level cannot be executed, while timeout is evaluated to true only if no process has an enabled transition. In this brief overview we have just introduced a few concepts that are necessary for the sake of the present discussion, while further details can be found in [12].

To model check FIEVeL specifications we have defined an automatic translation of FIEVeL into Promela which proceeds as follows. First, status functions, institutional entities, obligations, base events, and institutional events are translated into a set of type definitions, which are then used to declare a set of variables representing the state of the system. According to the framework discussed in Section 3, in Promela we identify two groups of variables, one representing the *current institutional state* and another which is exploited to generate the *next institutional state*.

Each institution contained in a FIEVeL specification is then translated into a new process definition according to the pattern represented in Figure 4. Each process instance is associated to an identifier to bind the process with an appropriate set of variables representing its state. Every process representing an institution consists of a main loop, which is enabled whenever a new base event is generated. For the sake of simplicity, we can imagine that the process contains an inner loop where each statement represents an institutional event or an obligation state transition. Actually, to further reduce the number of intermediate transitions and to generate a more compact Promela code, our current implementation introduces several improvements that have not been reported in Figure 4.

```
proctype institutionProc(int id) {
  do
  :: (nextEvent.analyzed[id]==FALSE)->
    do
    :: (condition_inst_event_x1 || condition_inst_event_x2)->
       apply_effects(next_event);
    ...
    :: (condition_inst_event_y1 || condition_inst_event_y2)->
       apply_effects(next_event);
    :: ((next_obligation.state==inactive) &&
        (start_obligation && obligation.state==unfired)->
        next_obligation.state=unfired;
    ::else -> break;
    od
    nextEvent.analyzed[id]=TRUE;
  od
}
```

Fig. 4. Translation pattern for processes representing institutions

As discussed in Sections 2 and 3, institutional states evolve because base-level events happen and they count-as institutional events. To model base level events, we define a new process, named *eventGenerator*, which generates actions and events as if they were produced by agents or the environment. Actually, since we are concerned with the analysis and verification of institutional reality, at each stage we only consider those events that, according to the institutional state of the system, can count as an institutional event and we randomly generate one of them. The general structure of an *eventGenerator* is represented in Figure 5.

Finally we declare an *init* process to generate the initial state of the system according to the model-definition section of a FIEVeL specification. Essentially, the *init* process sets the initial values of the variables and for each institution instance creates a process of the corresponding process type.

To intuitively show that our translation respects the framework depicted in Section 3, we can observe that the *eventGenerator* is executed only when no other process has an enabled statement, as guaranteed by the timeout guard. Since it is activated, the *eventGenerator* updates the *current state* with the values contained in the *next state* variables, calculates the truth value of a set of propositions representing count-as conditions (preconditions and authorizations) and finally, if it is possible and if a *termination condition* has not been reached, generates a new event. Finally, it sets the next base-level event, which also means that *analyzed* variables are set to *false*, and since then all other processes can be executed. Therefore, according to the process structures presented in Figure 4 and Figure 5, we ensure that whenever an *eventGenerator* is executed, any other process cannot be interleaved. Also, we guarantee that the *eventGenerator* is executed only when all institution instances have generated the next institutional state by considering all possible institutional transitions (count-as, institutional-event effects, and obligation transitions), such that current state variables can be updated with the new calculated values.

An important aspect of our translation of FIEVeL into Promela is that we can directly check LTL properties, instead of writing assertions embedded in the Promela code. As a consequence, properties definition results significantly simplified and it can be

```
proctype eventGenerator(){
  do
  :: timeout ->
    curr_state=next_state;
    updateConditions();
    if
    :: !(end_condition)->
      if
      :: (true) -> next_event = timer; next_time++;
      :: condition_event1 -> next_event = event1;
      :: condition_event2 -> next_event = event2;
      ...
      :: condition_event -> next_event = event;
      fi
    fi
  od
}
```

Fig. 5. The structure of an eventGenerator process

automated, although at the moment this feature has not been implemented yet in our tool.

5   Verifying Institutions

Once an institution has been defined with FIEVeL and translated into Promela, we think that there are two main types of properties that must be verified, *soundness properties* and *domain specific properties*. Soundness properties represent general desirable properties of institutions which stem from the metamodel: for example, the soundness of an institution specification requires the consistency of the set of deontic-positions associated to a status function (*weak consistency*) and the consistency of all the obligation of status functions that may be assigned to an agent (*strong consistency*). Instead, domain specific properties stem from peculiar features of the specified model and regard the functionality of an institution: for instance, we may check if it is possible that a participant is declared to be the winner of an auction. In the following we exemplify our approach by defining several LTL properties and by showing how they can be verified with SPIN.

Soundness properties are often defined to guarantee the rationality of an institution. For instance, an institutional event must eventually happen in at least one execution. By checking the *satisfiability* of the following formula, where we combine FIEVeL expressions with temporal operators, we can verify that an event of type *current_winner_is* must happen in least one execution:

$$\mathbf{F}\,happens(current\_winner\_is)$$

Temporal operators and FIEVeL expressions can be combined because we assume that semantics domains are fixed at all states of our system. The SPIN model checker only admits propositional symbols into LTL formulae [12], hence we must introduce new propositional symbols corresponding to FIEVeL expressions. For instance, the *happens* expression reported above is translated as follows:

```
#define happens_currentWinner (lastEvent.EAI_currentWinner_==true)
```

If the property does not hold, the model checker returns a counterexample, which shows a possible trace that violates it.

To conclude this section we report an example of a domain specific property that allows us to verify that desired institutional states may be reached, which implies that our specification defines all the institutional actions and authorizations needed for the correct evolution of the system. For instance, we may want to check that only a participant can become the winner of an auction. This requirement also means that an auctioneer cannot win an auction and that any participant may eventually become the winner. These properties are formalized as follows:

$$\mathbf{G}\neg(auctioneer \wedge winner) \tag{1}$$

$$\mathbf{F}(participant \wedge winner) \tag{2}$$

By verifying if property 1 is *valid* and if property 2 is *satisfiable* and by analyzing the generated counterexamples, we discovered and fixed an error in an earlier version of our specification of the English Auction. In fact, the effects of the institutional action *current_winner_is* were accidentally specified such that the status function of current-winner was assigned to the actor of that action, instead of to the agent declared to be the winner (see Section 3). Clearly, given that such action is authorized only for the auctioneer, in that specification only an auctioneer could win an auction.

To provide the reader with a feeling of the computational costs of our approach, we report results obtained during the verification of property 1 on a desktop PC with installed Windows and equipped with a pentium 3.0 GHz and 512 MB of RAM. Clearly, results reported in Table 1 are severely influenced by the small amount of memory we had at our disposal. Despite that, we consider our results interesting, considered the complexity of the specification and compared with our experience in the verification of systems specified in Promela.

Table 1 reports our experiments, where "HCm" indicates that we have applied the Hash Compression mode while "*" represents the fact that the verification process requires more than 500 seconds and therefore it has been interrupted. Analyzing results showed in Table 1, we can observe that the number of agents and prices, but especially the number of possible time events contribute to a very fast growth of time and memory required to verify the property. This is essentially due to two different factors, one relative to our framework and one which depends on the chosen example. The representation of time as an explicit variable of the system somehow introduces an explicit counter, which leads the model checker to consider as different similar states which just differ in the value of the clock. In our formalization of the English Auction the order in which agents make their bids is associated to each OFFERED status function (see Section 3), so that the auctioneer is able to declare a *current winner* even if two agents have offered the same price during a round (the first agent that has bid the highest price is declared to be the current winner). Clearly, keeping trace of the relative order of offers contributes to increasing the number of possible paths that the model checker has to consider, and hence the amount of required memory and time.

Table 1. Time and memory required to verify $\mathbf{G}\neg(auctioneer \wedge winner)$. Results are reported showing the size of the considered models.

Agents	Time events	Prices	Memory (MB)	Time (sec)	HCm memory (MB)	HCm time (sec)
3	2	5	94.71	4	4.96	2
3	2	6	155.78	7	6.60	4
3	2	7	252.90	12	8.65	8
4	2	5	150.03	10	5.79	6
4	2	6	257.40	18	7.43	14
4	2	7	421.32	123	9.47	23
3	3	5	309.85	16	9.47	10
3	3	6	511.60	374	13.98	13
3	3	7	*	*	20.53	25
4	3	5	505.60	165	10.70	23
4	3	6	*	*	15.62	43
4	3	7	*	*	23.00	56
4	4	7	*	*	52.10	147
4	5	7	*	*	109.05	444

6   Discussion and Conclusions

In this paper we have presented a framework for verifying institutional reality based on the notion of status function, which is regarded as a possibly empty aggregate of authorizations and obligations. Our approach is motivated by the fact that institutional events modify institutional facts and, as a consequence, agents authorizations and obligations are changed. For this reason, we chose to characterize institutional events in terms of imposition and revocation of agent status functions, which are taken as our basic concept. We have also introduced FIEVeL, a language which allows to specify artificial institutions in terms of the concepts of our metamodel. We have also briefly discussed how FIEVeL specifications can be translated into Promela, such that soundness properties can be defined and model-checked with SPIN.

Several attempts have been previously carried out to apply model checking techniques and tools to verify *electronic institutions*, a formalism proposed in [7] to specify institutions. Roughly speaking, the language defined in [7] describes institutions as finite automata, and starting from this point [13] and [3] focus their attention on properties of finite automata (e.g. "it is always possible to reach a final state"), while they do not take into account norms. Instead, in our approach the attention is essentially focused on verifying properties of institutional states, described in terms of status functions, which are intrinsically related with norms of the system and thereby on checking whether norms and authorizations defined by the designer are consistent. In this respect, our approach is more similar to the one presented in [4], where answer set programming techniques are applied to represent and analyze institutions. In [4] the authors distinguish among *institutional domain facts* and *normative facts* (obligations, institutionalized powers, and permissions), while in this paper we proposed a unified view of institutional domain and normative facts. Indeed, we claim that institutional facts are such only because they imply new normative facts for the interacting agents, which also represents a significant difference with respect to our previous attempts to model institutional reality [9,24].

As [4,24], in [20] several key concepts like authorizations, obligations and prohibition are used to model institutional reality. It can be observed that the formalism used in [20] to specify institutions (named *normative systems*) does not provide any abstraction to describe that every institutional action must be authorized in order to be successfully executed. Instead, the authors must specify this fact for every single action and for every role defined by the institution. Therefore, the definition of a metamodel provides a significant advantage, especially when many status function (or roles, using the terminology of [20]) are authorized to perform the same institutional action. Furthermore, the definition of an automatic translation of FIEVeL into Promela allows us to verify our specification, while in [20] the authors must rely on "systematic runs".

We plan to extend our metamodel, and consequently FIEVeL, to model different interdependent institutions like in [24], which raises, among others, two interesting research problems: first, how to model interdependencies among different contexts, and second, how to design an institution which somehow depends on another institution.

References

1. Boella, G., van der Torre, L.: The Ontological Properties of Social Roles: Definitional Dependence, Powers and Roles Playing Roles. In: Proceedings of the ICAIL05 Workshop on Legal Ontologies and Artificial Intelligence Techniques (2005)
2. Clarke, E.M., Grumberg, O., Peled, D.: Model Checking. MIT Press, Cambridge, MA (1999)
3. Cliffe, O., Padget, J.: A Framework For Checking Interactions Within Agent Institutions. In: Proceedings of the ECAI Workshop on Model Checking and Artificial Intelligence (MoChart I) (2002)
4. Cliffe, O., Vos, M.D., Padget, J.: Specifying and Analysing Agent-based Social Institutions using Answer Set Programming. In: Boissier, O., Padget, J., Dignum, V., Lindemann, G., Matson, E., Ossowski, S., Sichman, J.S., Vázquez-Salceda, J. (eds.) Coordination, Organizations, Institutions, and Norms in Multi-Agent Systems. LNCS (LNAI), vol. 3913, pp. 99–113. Springer, Heidelberg (2006)
5. Endriss, U.: Temporal Logics for Representing Agent Communication Protocols. In: Dignum, F., van Eijk, R.M., Flores, R. (eds.) AC 2005. LNCS (LNAI), vol. 3859, Springer, Heidelberg (2006)
6. Esteva, M., Rodríguez-Aguilar, J.A., Rosell, B., Arcos, J.L.: AMELI: An Agent-based Middleware for Electronic Institutions. In: Jennings, N.R., Sierra, C., Sonenberg, L., Tambe, M. (eds.) Proceedings of the 3rd International Joint Conference on Autonomous Agents and Multi-Agent Systems (AAMAS 2004), pp. 236–243. ACM Press, New York (2004)
7. Esteva, M., Rodríguez-Aguilar, J.A., Sierra, C., Garcia, P., Arcos, J.L.: On the Formal Specification of Electronic Institutions. In: Sierra, C., Dignum, F.P.M. (eds.) Agent Mediated Electronic Commerce. LNCS (LNAI), vol. 1991, pp. 126–147. Springer, Heidelberg (2001)
8. Farrell, A.D.H., Sergot, M.J., Sallé, M., Bartolini, C.: Using the Event Calculus for Tracking the Normative State of Contracts. Journal of Cooperative Information Systems 14(2-3), 99–129 (2005)
9. Fornara, N., Viganò, F., Colombetti, M.: Agent Communication and Institutional Reality. In: van Eijk, R.M., Huget, M.-P., Dignum, F.P.M. (eds.) AC 2004. LNCS (LNAI), vol. 3396, pp. 1–17. Springer, Heidelberg (2005)

10. Garcia-Camino, A., Noriega, P., Rodriguez-Aguilar, J.A.: Implementing norms in electronic institutions. In: Proceedings of the 4th International Joint Conference on Autonomous agents and Multi-Agent Systems (AAMAS 2005), pp. 667–673. ACM Press, New York (2005)

11. García-Camino, A., Rodríguez-Aguilar, J.A., Sierra, C., Vasconcelos, W.W.: A distributed architecture for norm-aware agent societies. In: Baldoni, M., Endriss, U., Omicini, A., Torroni, P. (eds.) DALT 2005. LNCS (LNAI), vol. 3904, pp. 89–105. Springer, Heidelberg (2006)

12. Holzmann, G.: The SPIN Model Checker: Primer and Reference Manual. Addison-Wesley, Reading (2003)

13. Huget, M.-P., Esteva, M., Phelps, S., Sierra, C., Wooldridge, M.: Model Checking Electronic Institutions. In: Proceedings of the ECAI Workshop on Model Checking and Artificial Intelligence (MoChArt I) (2002)

14. Jones, A., Sergot, M.J.: A formal characterisation of institutionalised power. Journal of the IGPL 4(3), 429–445 (1996)

15. Kowalski, R.A., Sergot, M.J.: A Logic-based Calculus of Events. New Generation Computing 4, 67–95 (1986)

16. Masolo, C., Vieu, L., Bottazzi, E., Catenacci, C., Ferrario, R., Gangemi, A., Guarino, N.: Social Roles and their Descriptions. In: Dubois, D., Welty, C., Williams, M. (eds.) Proceedings of the Ninth International Conference on the Principles of Knowledge Representation and Reasoning (KR2004), pp. 267–277 (2004)

17. North, D.: Institutions, Institutional Change and Economics Performance. Cambridge University Press, Cambridge, United Kingdom (1990)

18. Ostroff, J.S.: Modelling, specifying and verifying real-time temporal interval logic. In: Proceedings of the IEEE Symposium on Real-Time Systems, New York, IEEE Press, Los Alamitos (1987)

19. Peled, D.: Software reliability methods. Texts in Computer Science. Springer, New York, NJ USA (2001)

20. Pitt, J., Kamara, L., Sergot, M., Artikis, A.: Formalization of a voting protocol for virtual organizations. In: Proceedings of the 4th International Joint Conference on Autonomous agents and Multi-Agent Systems (AAMAS 2005), pp. 373–380. ACM Press, New York, USA (2005)

21. Searle, J.R.: The construction of social reality. Free Press, New York, USA (1995)

22. Sergot, M.J.: Modelling unreliable and untrustworthy agent behaviour. In: Dunin-Keplicz, B., Jankowski, A., Skowron, A., Szczuka, M. (eds.) Monitoring, Security, and Rescue Techniques in Multiagent Systems. Advances in Soft Computing, pp. 161–178. Springer, Heidelberg (2005)

23. Viganò, F.: FIEVeL, a Language for the Specification and Verification of Institutions. Technical Report 3, Institute for Communication Technologies, Università della Svizzera Italiana (2006)

24. Viganò, F., Fornara, N., Colombetti, M.: An Event Driven Approach to Norms in Artificial Institutions. In: Boissier, O., Padget, J., Dignum, V., Lindemann, G., Matson, E., Ossowski, S., Sichman, J.S., Vázquez-Salceda, J. (eds.) Coordination, Organizations, Institutions, and Norms in Multi-Agent Systems. LNCS (LNAI), vol. 3913, pp. 142–154. Springer, Heidelberg (2006)

Part III
NORMATIVE MODELS AND ISSUES

Spatially Distributed Normative Objects

Fabio Y. Okuyama[1], Rafael H. Bordini[2], and Antônio Carlos da Rocha Costa[3]

[1] Universidade Federal do Rio Grande do Sul, Brazil
okuyama@inf.ufrgs.br
[2] University of Durham, United Kingdom
R.Bordini@durham.ac.uk
[3] Universidade Católica de Pelotas, Brazil
rocha@atlas.ucpel.tche.br

Abstract. Organisational structures for multi-agent systems are usually defined independently of any spatial or temporal structure. Therefore, when the multi-agent system is situated in a spatial environment, there is usually a conceptual gap between the definition of the system's organisational structures and the definition of the environment. In this paper, we focus on a mechanism for the spatial distribution of an organization's normative information. Spatially distributing the normative information over the environment is a natural way to simplify the definition of organisational structures and the development of large-scale multi-agent systems. By distributing the normative information in different spatial locations, we allow agents to directly access the relevant information needed in each environmental context. We extend our previous work on a language for modelling multi-agent environments in order to allow for the definition of spatially distributed norms in the form of *normative objects*.

1 Introduction

The environment is an important part of a Multi-Agent System (MAS), specially for systems of situated agents. Situated multi-agent systems are usually designed as a set of agents, together with the environment where they operate, their social structures, and the possible interactions among these components. In previous works, we introduced a language that allows MAS designers to describe, at a high conceptual level, environments for situated multi-agent systems [11,1]. The language is called ELMS, and was created to be part of a platform for the development of (social) simulations based on multi-agent systems.

In this paper, we present extensions to the ELMS language which allow the distribution of normative information over an environment, construing what we call *situated norms*. In particular, we introduce here the notion of spatially distributed *normative objects*, which facilitates the modelling of various real-world situations, particularly for simulation, but more generally the coordination of large-scale multi-agent systems too, through situated norms.

To understand the notions of normative object and situated norm, consider the posters one typically sees in public places (such as libraries or bars) saying "Please be quiet" or "No smoking in this area". Human societies often resort to this mechanism for decentralising the burden of regulating social behaviour; people then adopt such situated

P. Noriega et al. (Eds.): COIN 2006 Workshops, LNAI 4386, pp. 133–146, 2007.

norms whenever they have visual access to such posters. This should be equally efficient for computational systems because it avoids the need for providing a complete,
exhaustive representation of all social norms in a single public structure, known to all
agents, as it is usually the case in current approaches to agent organisations.

Another extension we have introduced to our environment description language is the
notion of normative places, which are zones where the normative objects and situated
norms are relevant. As an example, consider a research group where there are agents
with the role *principal researcher* whose main objective is to supervise the research of
agents playing the *research student* role; such research can be conducted both at the
laboratory or at the library. The interactions at the laboratory are to be outlined in the
spatial scene of the laboratory space. The information about how to behave in a library
is defined in the library spatial scene, where all researchers will also assume the role of
library users. Normative information relevant for each such site (and each place within
each site) can be made accessible to the agents with the help of normative objects.

In summary, the extensions we introduce here support situated norms and leaves the
necessary room for the inclusion of group structures that are spatially situated within a
(simulated) physical environment. This is done using two means: first, *normative objects*, which are objects that can contain normative information; and second, a normative principle for *situated norms*, conceived as a special form of conditional rule, where
an explicit condition on an agent's perception of a normative object appears: 'When
playing the relevant role and being physically situated within the confines referred by
a situated norm $\mathcal{N}$ expressed in a normative object previously perceived, the agent is
required to reason about following norm $\mathcal{N}$; otherwise, it is excused from reason about
it'. Also, normative objects may be directed towards a specific role in a given organisation. We can thus model things such as a sign saying that students are not allowed
beyond the library desk (while members of staff are).

In the next section, we briefly present our platform and the various component languages we use to model multi-agent systems. In Section 3, we briefly review how an
environment should be modelled using our approach. In Sections 4 and 5, we present
and discuss the normative extensions that we introduce in this paper. We then illustrate our approach with an example in Section 6; the example is based on the scenario
presented in [4]. We discuss related work in Section 7, then conclude the paper.

2   The MAS-SOC Platform

One of the main goals of the MAS-SOC simulation platform (**M**ulti-**A**gent **S**imulation
for the **SOC**ial Sciences)is to provide a framework for the creation of agent-based simulations which do not require too much experience in programming from users, yet
allowing the use of state-of-the-art agent technologies. In particular, it should allow for
the design and implementation of simulations with *cognitive* agents.

In our approach, an agent's individual reasoning is specified in an extended version
of AgentSpeak [13], as interpreted by *Jason*, an *open source* agent platform[1] based
on Java [2]. The extensions allow, among other things, the use of speech-act based

---

[1] Available at http://jason.sf.net

agent communication, and there is ongoing work to allow the use of ontologies and of organisational structures as part of a *Jason* multi-agent system.

The environments where agents are situated are specified in ELMS, a language we have designed for the description of multi-agent environments [11]. For more details on MAS-SOC, refer to [1]. We here concentrate on the ELMS extensions to describe basic organisational structures and social norms, and to relate an organisational structure and the relevant normative aspects to the spatial structures defined within the physical environment.

3   Modelling Physical Environments with ELMS

As presented in [11], we developed ELMS (**E**nvironment Description **L**anguage for **M**ulti-Agent **S**imulation) as a means to describe environments and to execute simulated environments. Agents in a multi-agent system interact with the environment where they are situated and interact with each other (possibly through the shared environment). Therefore, the environment has an important role in a multi-agent system, whether the environment is the Internet, the real world, or some simulated environment.

We understand as environment modelling, the modelling of external aspects that an agent needs as input to its reasoning and for deciding on its course of action. Further, it is necessary to model explicitly the physical actions and perceptions that the agents are capable of in a given environment. Below we briefly review how a physical environment is described using this language.

To define an environment using ELMS, the following classes of constructs can be used:

– **Agent Body:** the agent's characteristics that are perceptible to other agents. Agent "bodies" are defined by a set of properties that characterise it and are perceptible to other agents. Such properties are represented as *string*, *integer*, *float*, and *boolean* values. Each "body" is associated with a set of actions that the agent is allowed to perform and of environment properties that the agent can perceive.
– **Agent Sensorial Capabilities (Perception):** the environment properties that will be perceptible to each agent at a given time, and under given specific circumstances.
– **Agent Effective Capacities (Actions):** the actions that an agent is able to perform in order to change the current state of the environment. These actions are defined as assignments of values to the attributes of entities in the environment[2]. The production (i.e., instantiation) of previously defined resources (i.e., objects), and the consumption (i.e., deletion) of existing instances can also be part of an action description.
– **Physical Environment Objects (Resources):** the objects/resources that are present in the environment. Although objects and resources can have conceptual differences, they are represented by the same structure in ELMS. Agents interact with objects through their actions in the environment. Object structures are defined by a set of properties that are relevant to the modelling and may be perceived by an agent. In the same way as the properties of the "bodies" of the agents, the properties of objects are also represented by *string*, *integer*, *float*, and *boolean* values.

---

[2] Note that agent bodies are also properties of the environment.

Each object can also be associated with a set of reactions that may happen as consequence of an agent's actions.

- **Object Reactions:** the objects can "react", under specific circumstances, in order to respond to actions performed by the agents in the environment. Such reactions are given as the assignment of values to properties, the creation of previously defined object instances, and the deletion of existing object instances.
- **Space Structure (Grid):** the space is (optionally) divided into cells forming a grid that represents the spatial structure of the environment. When a grid is used, it can be defined in 2 or 3 dimensions. As for resources, each cell can have reactions associated to it. Although the specified set of reactions apply to all of the cells, this does not mean that all cells will behave equally, since they may be in different contexts (i.e., each cell has independent attributes, thus having different contents and, clearly, different positions, which can all affect the particular reactions).

3.1 Notes on Environment Descriptions

- **Perceptions:** agents do not normally have complete access to the environment. Perception of the environment will not normally give complete and accurate information about the whole environment and the other agents in it. However, since such restriction is not imposed by the ELMS model itself, designers can choose to create fully accessible environments if this is appropriate for a particular application.
- **Actions:** actions defined here are assumed to be atomic, as the action chaining or planning is meant to be part of the "mind" of the agent
- **Reactions:** all object reactions triggered by some change in the environment are executed in a single simulation cycle. This is different from agent actions, as each agent can execute only one action per cycle.

Additionally to the constructs mentioned above, the following operational constructs are used in our approach to model the (simulated) physical environment.

- **Constructors:** Each agent and resource may need to be initialised at the moment of its instantiation. This is defined by a list of initial value assignment to its attributes.
- **Observables:** A list of environment properties whose values are to be displayed/logged; these are the specific properties of a simulation that the user wants to observe/analyse.

The simulation of the environment itself is done by a process that controls the access and changes made to the data structure that represents the environment; the process is called the *environment controller*. The data structure that represents the environment is generated by the ELMS interpreter from a specification in ELMS given as input. In each simulation cycle, the environment controller sends to all agents currently taking part in the simulation the percepts to which they have access (as specified in ELMS). Recall that ELMS environments are designed for cognitive agents, so perception is transmitted in messages as a list of ground logical facts. After sending perception, the process waits for the actions that the agents have chosen to perform in that simulation cycle and then execute the actions, changing the environment data structures accordingly.

4   Normative Objects and Situated Norms

Typically, environments will have some objects aimed at informing agents about norms, give some advice, or warn about potential dangers. For example, a poster fixed on a wall of a library asking for "silence" is an object of the environment, but also informs about a norm that should be respected within that space. Another example are traffic signs, which give advice about directions or regulate priorities in crossings. The existence of such signs, that we call *normative objects*, implies the existence of a regulating code in such context, that we call *situated norms*.

In the examples above, the norms are only meant to be followed within certain boundaries of space or time and lose their effect completely if those space and time restrictions are not met, which is the initial motivation for situated norms. Another important advantage of modelling some norms as situated norms is the fact that the spatial context where the norm is to be followed is immediately determined. Thus, the norm can be "pre-compiled" to its situated form, making it easier for the agents to operationalise the norm, and also facilitating the verification of norm compliance.

For example a norm that says "Be kind to the elderly", may be quite hard to operationalise and verify, in general. However, in a fixed spatial context such as a bus or train, with the norm contextualised as "Give up your seat for the elderly", or in a street crossing, with the norm contextualised as "Help elderly people to cross the street", the norm would be much more easily interpreted by the agents, and verified by any norm compliance checking mechanism.

It is important to remark that the norm-abiding behaviour is not related to the existence of a normative object. Beyond the existence of such object, it is necessary for the agent to perceive the normative object, and autonomous agents will also reason about whether to follow or not the norm stated by the normative object.

4.1   Normative Objects and Situated Norms in ELMS

In the extended version of ELMS, normative objects are "readable" by agents under specific individual conditions: an agent is able to read a specific rule if it has the specific ability to perceive the type of object in which the rule is written at its given location. In the most typical case, the condition is simply being physically close to the object.

Normative objects can be defined before the simulation starts, or can be created dynamically during the simulation. Each normative object can be placed in a normative place (see below), in the spatial grid of the environment. The conditions under which the normative objects can be perceived are defined by the simulation designer using the usual ELMS constructs for defining perception capabilities and their conditions.

The normative information in a normative object is "read" by an agent through its perception ability. Besides the norm itself, it may contain meta-information, e.g., which agent or institution created the norm. In ELMS, normative objects should have at least the following properties:

- **Type:** the type of the normative information contained in the object; it determines the level of importance (e.g., a warning, an obligation, a direction);
- **Issued by:** where the power underlying the norm comes from (e.g., an agent, a group, an institution).

- **Norm:** a string that represents the normative information; this should be in the format of AgentSpeak predicates in the case of MAS-SOC environments, or whatever format the targeted agents will be able to understand.
- **Placement:** the set of normative spaces where the normative information applies. If omitted, the object is assumed to be accessible from anywhere, but normally under conditions determined by the designer; see the next item.
- **Condition:** conditions under which the normative information can be perceived. The conditions can be associated with groups, roles, abilities, and current physical placement and orientation of agents and objects.
- **Id:** identification string for eventual deletion/edition of the normative object.

We now briefly describe how the agents will receive normative information from normative objects. Whenever the agent position is such that access to the normative object is accessible, and the **Condition** is satisfied, the agent will receive perception of the form:

rule([PLACE],[GROUP],[ISSUED BY],[NORM])
Ex: rule(home, family, parents, obligation(child,play(TOY),tidy(TOY)))

The example above can be read as: "This is rule in group *family*, issued by the *parents*, with application at the normative place *home* (see below), that says: if the action *play(TOY)* is done by an agent of role *child*, then it is an obligation of that agent to do *tidy(TOY)* as well".

A rule like that would not normally be posted on a sign in a family home, but it illustrates the more general idea of situated norms as norms that apply within given environmental locations.

4.2 Normative Places in ELMS

Considering the ideas discussed above about normative objects and situated norms, ELMS descriptions of an environment (based on the concepts of agent bodies, objects, and an optional grid) need to be extended with the notion of *normative places*, i.e., a set of cells where an organisational activity occurs under the conditions of a set of situated norms.

A *normative place* can be defined in ELMS simply by its name and the set of cells that are part of it. A normative place may have intersections with other normative places, or even be contained within another normative place. For example, a normative place "school" may have a large set of cells where some of those cells refer to a normative place "classroom" and others to its "library". A normative place allows for the definition of the spatial location where certain situated norms are valid and relevant, as it will be exemplified in the next section.

In order to facilitate the definition of repetitive normative place structures, classes of normative places can be first defined and then instantiated in specific positions of the grid. The place "home" in the previous section is an example of a normative place. Other examples of such definitions and instantiations are as follows:

```
<NORMATIVE-PLACE-TYPE NAME="library"/>

<NORMATIVE-PLACE-TYPE NAME="classroom"/>

<PLACE NAME="lib1" NORMATIVE-PLACE-TYPE="library">
     <CELL X="0" Y="0"/>
     <CELL X="0" Y="1"/>
</PLACE>

<PLACE NAME="cr1" NORMATIVE-PLACE-TYPE="classroom">
     <CELL X="2" Y="0">
</PLACE>
```

5   MAS-SOC Modelling of Organisations Governed by Situated Norms

As the MAS-SOC platform does not enforce a particular agent-oriented software engineering methodology, designers can use the one they prefer. It is possible to model a multi-agent system that will have an ELMS environment using any approach: starting from the system organisation (top-down), or starting from the agent interactions (bottom-up).

In both approaches, the modelling of the organisational structures and the agents' reasoning need fine tuning to achieve the desired results. To have a stable point on which to base the tuning-up of the agents' reasoning or the organisational model, we have suggest the use of an explicitly defined environment description written in the ELMS language and the concepts presented in the Section 3. The environment is an important part of an multi-agent system, and although it can be very dynamic, in regards to design it is usually the most "stable" part of the system.

Based on these observations, we suggest that the multi-agent system modelling starts with the environment definition, followed by the definition of the normative places. The environment modelling is achieved by:

1. Definition of which kinds of action each type of agent is able to perform in the environment. Actions typically produce effects over objects of the environment or other agents.

2. Based on the changes that the agents' effective capabilities are able to make in the environment and the objectives of the simulation, the size and granularity of the grid can be determined. For example, how many cells an agent can move within one action or simulation cycle, and in how many simulation cycles the agent would be able to traverse the simulated space.

3. Based on the granularity and size of the spatial environment, the sensorial capabilities of the agents can be modelled, defining for example in which range an agent can detect other agents or objects.

4. Based on an agent's sensorial capabilities and on its typical activities, it should be possible to define which attributes of that agent is important to declare as accessible to other agents. For example, if agents identify each other's role by the colour of their uniform, the "agent body" should have an attribute that represent the colour of the agent's uniform.

5. The types of objects or resources present in the environment should also be modelled based on which attributes will be perceptible by the agents and which actions can affect them.
6. Finally, instances of the agent and object classes should be placed in the environment, determining its initial state.

The definition of the environment should be followed by the definition of normative places and then by the definition of the spatially distributed normative objects, as follows:

1. Together with the object types placed in the environment, the types of normative places within the environment can also be defined.
2. By instantiating normative places into sets of cells, *normative places* are created.
3. Then, based the set of activities that can possibly be performed in each type of normative place, the norms that are relevant to that type of place can be defined.
4. Finally, the types of *normative objects* can be defined and instantiated in the normative places, defining the locations where situated norms can be perceived.

Using the environment as a basis, the agents' reasoning capabilities can then be defined so as to help agents achieve their objectives as well as the objective of the groups in which they participate. Also, the detailed definitions of possible organisational structures can be fine-tuned, in order to have the system achieving its overall objectives. In MAS-SOC, we use AgentSpeak to define the practical reasoning for each agent; in particular, we use the extended version of AgentSpeak as interpreted by *Jason*; for details, see [3].

6   Example

Below we give an example showing how normative objects are defined using our approach. It is based on the scenario presented in [4], a scenario in which the agents are placed on an environment where they may eat the food they find, challenge other agents for their food, or move in search of food.

In this scenario, an agent owns any food item that is near to itself (at a distance of up to 2 cells). The agents can "see" food and other agents in a radius of 1 cell, but can sense food in a radius of 2 cells. The physical space is represented by a grid of 10×10 cells.

The norms used in that scenario essentially concern the respect for the ownership of a food item, which means they prescribe non-aggressive behaviour. In the original scenario, the norms were valid throughout the grid, but in this example norms are valid only within normative places, as indicated by normative objects.

A shortened version of the physical environment description in ELMS is given below.

```
<!DOCTYPE ENVIRONMENT SYSTEM "elms.dtd">
<ENVIRONMENT NAME = "NORMATIVE">
    <DEFGRID SIZEX="10" SIZEY = "10"/>

    <RESOURCE NAME="food">
      <STRING  ownner = "none">
    </RESOURCE>
```

```
<AGENT_BODY NAME="agent">
    <INTEGER NAME = "id"> "SELF" </INTEGER>
    <PERCEPTIONS>
        <ITEM NAME = "vision"/>
        <ITEM NAME = "sense_food">
    </PERCEPTIONS>
    <ACTIONS>
        <ITEM NAME = "walk"/>
        <ITEM NAME = "attack"/>
        <ITEM NAME = "eat"/>
    </ACTIONS>
</AGENT_BODY>

<PERCEPTION NAME="vision">
    <CELL_ATT ATTRIBUTE="CONTENTS" ABSOLUTE="TRUE">
        <X> +0</X>
        <Y> +0</Y>
    </CELL_ATT>
    <CELL_ATT ATTRIBUTE="CONTENTS" ABSOLUTE="TRUE">
        <X> +1</X>
        <Y> +0</Y>
    </CELL_ATT>
    <!-- shortened-->
</PERCEPTION>

<PERCEPTION NAME="sense_food">
    <!-- shortened-->
</PERCEPTION>

<ACTION NAME="eat">
    <PARAMETER NAME = "FOOD_ID" TYPE="INTEGER" />
    <!-- shortened-->
</ACTION>

<ACTION NAME="walk">
    <!-- shortened-->
</ACTION>

<ACTION NAME="attack">
    <!-- shortened-->
</ACTION>

<INITIALIZATION>
    <!-- instantiation and placement of
         food and agents -->
</INITIALIZATION>
</ENVIRONMENT>
```

In the code excerpt above, the grid size is defined, then food is defined as an environment resource, then a generic type of agent body is defined. The agent body is defined as being capable of two types of perception — vision and food sensing – and being able to perform three types of actions: walk, attack, and eat. The vision perception allows the agent to perceive the contents of the current cell and the 4 neighbouring cells, while sense_food allows it to perceive food within a 2-cell radius.

For this example, the grid is partitioned in four normative places of equal sizes, and the normative objects are defined and placed only in the upper-left and upper-right quadrants, as shown in the code excerpt below:

```
<NORMATIVE-PLACE-TYPE NAME="food-protected"/>

<PLACE NAME="upper-left" NORMATIVE-PLACE-TYPE="food-protected">
    <CELL X="0" Y="0"/><CELL X="1" Y="0"/>
    <!-- shortened-->
```

```
      <CELL X="3" Y="4"/><CELL X="4" Y="4"/>
   </PLACE>

   <PLACE NAME="upper-right" NORMATIVE-PLACE-TYPE="food-protected">
      <CELL X="5" Y="0"/><CELL X="6" Y="0"/>
      <!-- shortened-->
      <CELL X="8" Y="4"/><CELL X="9" Y="4"/>
   </PLACE>

   <PLACE NAME="lower-left" NORMATIVE-PLACE-TYPE="null">
      <CELL X="0" Y="5"/><CELL X="1" Y="5"/>
      <!-- shortened-->
      <CELL X="3" Y="9"/><CELL X="4" Y="9"/>
   </PLACE>

   <PLACE NAME="lower-right" NORMATIVE-PLACE-TYPE="null">
      <CELL X="5" Y="4"/><CELL X="6" Y="4"/>
      <!-- shortened-->
      <CELL X="8" Y="9"/><CELL X="9" Y="9"/>
   </PLACE>

   <NORMATIVE_OBJECT ID="norm1" TYPE="prohibition" PLACE = "upper-left">
      <NORM>prohibited(true,attack(SELF,AGENT))</NORM>
   </NORM_OBJ>

   <NORMATIVE_OBJECT ID="norm2" TYPE="prohibition" PLACE = "upper-right">
      <NORM>prohibited(not(owned(FOOD,SELF)),eat(SELF,FOOD))</NORM>
   </NORM_OBJ>
```

The norms in the above example are very simple, and are given simply to illustrate how they can be modelled in our approach. For instance, norm1 says that an agent ought not to attack (steal food from) another agent, while norm2 says that the agent ought not to eat a food item that is not owned by itself.

Clearly, the agents' behaviour will be different in the four quadrants of the environment:

- in the upper-left quadrant, an agent is barred from eating food that belongs to another agent (since the situated norm states that an agent is prohibited from stealing food);
- in the upper-right quadrant, agents are supposedly prohibited of doing that, but not effectively, since the situated norm only prohibits the eating of food that is not owned by the agent itself rather than the stealing of food, so an agent can eat food that previously belonged to another agent if it first manages to steal that food;
- the lower quadrants (both left and right) are lawless areas, where agents are completely free to attack each other and to eat anyone else's food.

Notice that prohibited is used as a conditional deontic operator, with two arguments: the first argument is a condition to be tested, the second argument is the action that is prohibited.

7 Related Work

The notion of artifacts [16] and coordination artifacts [12] resembles our notion of *normative objects*. As defined in [12], coordination artifacts are abstractions meant to improve the automation of coordination activities, being the building blocks to create effective shared collaborative working environments. They are defined as runtime abstractions that encapsulate and provide a coordination service to the agents. Artifacts [16] were presented as a generalisation of coordination artifacts. Artifacts are an abstraction to represent tools, services, objects and entities in a multi-agent environment.

As building blocks for environment modelling, artifacts encapsulate the features of the environment as services to be used by the agents. The main objective of a coordination artifacts is to be used as an abstraction of an environmental coordination service provided to the agents. However, coordination artifacts express normative rules only implicitly, through their practical effects on the actions of the agents, and so their normative impact does not require any normative reasoning from the part of the agents. In our work, rather than having a general notion of objects that by their (physical) properties facilitate coordination, *normative objects* are objects used specifically to store *symbolic* information that can be interpreted by agents, so that they can become aware of norms that should be followed within a well-defined location.

Our choice has the advantage of keeping open the possibility of agent autonomy, as suggested in [5]. Agents are, in principle, able to decide whether to follow the norms or not, when trying to be effective in the pursuit of their goals. This is something that is not possible if an agent's action can only happen if in accordance to norms enforced by coordination mechanisms.

Another important difference is that *normative objects* are spatially distributed over a physical environment, with a spatial scope where they apply, and closely tied to the part of the organisation that is physically located in that space. While the objective of the coordination artifacts is to remove the burden of coordination from the agents, our work tries to simplify the way designers can guide the behaviour of each individual agent as they move around an environment where organisations are spatially located; this allows agents to adapt the way they behave in different social contexts.

In [8], the authors present the AGRE model, an extension to the previous AGR model. These latest extensions allow the definition of structures that represents the physical space. The approach defines organisational structures (i.e., groups) and the physical structures (i.e., areas) as "specialisations" of a generic space. The social structures are not contextualised in the space as they are in our work, leaving the social and physical structures quite unrelated.

In ELMS, however, it is not possible to explicitly define social structures, even though it would be possible to implicitly define them through the norms. This is because the aim of ELMS is, as mentioned earlier, to allow for environmental infrastructures compatible with existing approaches to organisational modelling, not for the modelling of organisations as such; the combination of ELMS with existing approaches to modelling organisations is planned as future work.

Another important series of related work is that on Electronic Institutions [9]. The internal working of an electronic institutions is given (in a simplified view) as a state-machine where each state is called a "scene". Each scene specifies the set of roles that agents may perform in it, and a "conversation protocol" that the agents should follow when interacting in the scene. To traverse the series of scenes that constitute the operation of the electronic institution, agents must do a sequence of actions in each scene, and also to commit to certain actions in certain scenes, as the result of their having performed certain other actions in certain other scenes. Our notion of normative space was inspired by such notion of scene, through giving it a physical, spatial content.

Similar to the electronic institutions approach, there is work on *computational institutions* [14], which are defined as virtual organisations ruled by constitutive norms and regulative norms. In computational institutions, organisational modelling uses the abstraction of coordination artifacts as building blocks, in a way that is very similar to our use of normative objects in spatially distributed organizations, but still keeping implicit in coordination artifacts the normative content imposed on the agents.

8   Conclusions

In this paper we have extended the ELMS language for describing environments with the means to define normative structures that make part of an environment representation. There are currently many approaches to modelling and implementing multi-agent systems: some are top-down approaches with focus on the organisations, while bottom-up approaches focus on the agents. We believe that including environment modelling at the initial stages of both approaches would help the modelling and implementation of multi-agent systems. To help such modelling, we have proposed an approach with an explicit environment description which now also includes the notions of *situated norms*, *normative places*, and (spatially distributed) *normative objects*.

It is important to note that our work is not an approach for modelling the organisational dimension of a multi-agent system. With the definition of *normative places*, where group structures would be inserted, we intend to fill a conceptual gap between the usual ways in which organisations and physical environments are modelled. In future work, with the integration of current means for defining organisational structures with ELMS, and thus with the possibility of associating them to normative places, we hope to contribute to a more integrated approach to designing and implementing the various aspects of multi-agent systems: concentrating on one particular organisation section at a time, specially if it is an organisation section attached to a spatial location, makes it easier for designers to define the groups, roles and agent behaviour that should operate in that particular organisation section.

By distributing the normative information in the environment, it is possible to partition the environment in a functional way, thus helping the structured definition of large simulations, norms being associated only with the places where they are meant to be followed. It is also more efficient (by taking advantage of natural distribution) to have norms spread in an environment than having them in a repository made available for the whole society, as it is usually the case.

We believe that an explicit environment description is an important part of a multi-agent system because it is a stable point from where the agent reasoning and the organisational structures can be fine-tuned so as to facilitate the development of agents and organisations that can achieve their goals. The notion of *spatially distributed normative objects* that we have introduced here can be a good solution connecting definitions of organisations and definitions of environments. Additionally, distributing the organisational/normative information can facilitate the modelling of large organisations.

It is interesting to note that, being conditioned on the possibility of checking the existence of a normative object, the normative reasoning required from agents that deal with normative objects is necessarily of a non-monotonic nature, and the experience of programming such reasoning in AgentSpeak is something we plan to experiment with in the future. Also as future work, we intend to allow a normative place to be associated with group structures, creating a connection between the organisational structures and the physical environment. We plan to make possible such association for any existing approach to agent organisations, such as $\mathcal{M}\text{OISE}^+$ [10], OperA/OMNI [15], GAIA [17], or approaches based on electronic institutions [6,7]. The recursive nature of normative places may not be compatible, however, with some of such approaches to organisation, where the (possibly implicit) system of normative rules has no provision for a recursive structure in its operation.

Acknowledgements

This work was partially supported by CNPq, CAPES, and FAPERGS. Rafael Bordini gratefully acknowledges the support of The Nuffield Foundation (grant number NAL/01065/G). The authors greatly benefited from the comments and suggestions that arose in the discussions during the presentation of the paper at the COIN@ECAI2006 workshop in Riva del Garda.

References

1. Bordini, R.H., da Rocha Costa, A.C., Hübner, J.F., Moreira, Á.F., Okuyama, F.Y., Vieira, R.: MAS-SOC: a social simulation platform based on agent-oriented programming. Journal of Artificial Societies and Social Simulation 8(3) (2005)
2. Bordini, R.H., Hübner, J.F., et al.: Jason: A Java-based Interpreter for an Extended Version of AgentSpeak, manual, release version 0.9 edn. (July 2006),
   http://jason.sourceforge.net/
3. Bordini, R.H., Hübner, J.F., Vieira, R.: Jason and the Golden Fleece of agent-oriented programming. In: Bordini, R.H., Dastani, M., Dix, J., Seghrouchni, A.E.F. (eds.) Multi-Agent Programming: Languages, Platforms and Applications, ch. 1, Springer, Heidelberg (2005)
4. Castelfranchi, C., Conte, R., Paolucci, M.: Normative reputation and the costs of compliance. Journal of Artificial Societies and Social Simulation 1(3) (1998),
   http://www.soc.surrey.ac.uk/JASSS/1/3/3.html
5. Castelfranchi, C., Dignum, F., Jonker, C.M., Treur, J.: Deliberative normative agents: Principles and architecture. In: Jennings, N.R. (ed.) ATAL 1999. LNCS, vol. 1757, pp. 364–378. Springer, Heidelberg (2000)
6. Esteva, M., de la Cruz, D., Sierra, C.: Islander: an electronic institutions editor. In: AAMAS, pp. 1045–1052. ACM Press, New York (2002)
7. Esteva, M., Rosell, B., Rodríguez-Aguilar, J.A., Arcos, J.L.: Ameli: An agent-based middleware for electronic institutions. In: AAMAS, pp. 236–243. IEEE Computer Society, Los Alamitos (2004)
8. Ferber, J., Michel, F., Báez-Barranco, J.-A.: Agre: Integrating environments with organizations. In: Weyns, D., Parunak, H.V.D., Michel, F. (eds.) E4MAS 2004. LNCS (LNAI), vol. 3374, pp. 48–56. Springer, Heidelberg (2005)
9. Garcia-Camino, A., Noriega, P., Rodríguez-Aguilar, J.A.: Implementing norms in electronic institutions. In: Dignum, F., Dignum, V., Koenig, S., Kraus, S., Singh, M.P., Wooldridge, M. (eds.) AAMAS, pp. 667–673. ACM Press, New York (2005)

10. Hübner, J.F., Sichman, J.S., Boissier, O.: MOISE$^+$: Towards a structural, functional, and deontic model for MAS organization. In: Proceedings of the First International Joint Conference on Autonomous Agents and Multi-Agent Systems (AAMAS'2002), Bologna, Italy (2002)

11. Okuyama, F.Y., Bordini, R.H., da Rocha Costa, A.C.: ELMS: An environment description language for multi-agent simulations. In: Weyns, D., van Dyke Parunak, H., Michel, F. (eds.) E4MAS 2004. LNCS (LNAI), vol. 3374, pp. 91–108. Springer, Heidelberg (2005)

12. Omicini, A., Ricci, A., Viroli, M., Castelfranchi, C., Tummolini, L.: Coordination artifacts: Environment-based coordination for intelligent agents. In: AAMAS'04 (2004)

13. Rao, A.S.: AgentSpeak(L): BDI agents speak out in a logical computable language. In: Perram, J., Van de Velde, W. (eds.) MAAMAW 1996. LNCS, vol. 1038, Springer, Heidelberg (1996)

14. Rubino, R., Omicini, A., Denti, E.: Computational institutions for modelling norm-regulated MAS: An approach based on coordination artifacts. In: Boissier, O., Padget, J., Dignum, V., Lindemann, G., Matson, E., Ossowski, S., Sichman, J.S., Vázquez-Salceda, J. (eds.) Coordination, Organizations, Institutions, and Norms in Multi-Agent Systems. LNCS (LNAI), vol. 3913, pp. 127–141. Springer, Heidelberg (2006)

15. Vázquez-Salceda, J., Dignum, V., Dignum, F.: Organizing multiagent systems. Autonomous Agents and Multi-Agent Systems 11(3), 307–360 (2005)

16. Viroli, M., Omicini, A., Ricci, A.: Engineering MAS environment with artifacts. In: Weyns, D., Parunak, H.V.D., Michel, F. (eds.) E4MAS 2005. LNCS (LNAI), vol. 3830, pp. 62–77. Springer, Heidelberg (2006)

17. Wooldridge, M., Jennings, N.R., Kinny, D.: The GAIA methodology for agent-oriented analysis and design. Autonomous Agents and Multi-Agent Systems 3(3), 285–312 (2000)

Informing Regulatory Dynamics in Open MASs

Carolina Felicíssimo[1], Ricardo Choren[2], Jean-Pierre Briot[1,3], and Carlos Lucena[1]

[1] DI, PUC-Rio, Rua M. de São Vicente, 225, Gávea Rio de Janeiro, RJ, 22453-900, Brasil
{cfelicissimo,lucena}@inf.puc-rio.br
[2] SE-8, IME - Pca General Tiburcio 80, 22290-270, Rio de Janeiro RJ, Brazil
choren@de9.ime.eb.br
[3] LIP6 - 8 rue du Capitaine Scott, 75015 Paris, France
jean-pierre.briot@lip6.fr

Abstract. We believe that, in the near future, all multi-agent systems (MASs) will be open, permitting agents to migrate among MASs to obtain resources or services not found locally. In this scenario, open MASs should be enhanced with norms for restricting agents' actions and, thus, avoiding unexpected behavior. In this work, we present a case study where an open MAS is enhanced with contextual norms. Agents from this MAS are continuously supported with precise norm information, according to their contexts (*implicit situational information*) and, then, can make better decisions. Although the presented case study is simple, it clearly shows different levels of norm abstractions and how agents can be influenced by norms while acting in a regulated open MASs.

1 Introduction

Multi-agent systems (MASs) have emerged as a powerful technology for developing information systems that clearly require several goal-oriented problem-solving entities [25]. Information systems tend to be formed of autonomous entities and without centralized control [21]. Following this direction, we believe that, in the near future, all MASs will be open and composed of many sets of heterogeneous self-interested agents, migrating among MASs for obtaining resources or services not found locally. Because agents' actions will probably deviate from expected behavior according to individual goals, regulatory mechanisms will be a mandatory feature of open MASs.

Important works concerning regulations in open MASs, as [1], [6], [15], [16], [17], have been proposed recently. However, in these works, it is missed a precise mechanism for explicitly regarding different levels of norm abstractions. Consequently, it is hard to define and evolve specific norms. We are currently working on an approach for supporting contextual regulation in open MASs. Our approach, called DynaCROM (*dynamic contextual regulation information provision in open MASs*) [9], [10], [11], [12], continuously provides precise norm information for agents according to their contexts. DynaCROM is based on a top-down modeling of contextual norms, on a meta-ontology for representing norm semantics and on a rule inference engine for composing related contextual norms. Furthermore, DynaCROM implementation can be summarized as an agent behavior, independent of agents' original codes.

P. Noriega et al. (Eds.): COIN 2006 Workshops, LNAI 4386, pp. 147–162, 2007.
© Springer-Verlag Berlin Heidelberg 2007

Norm-aware agents can use DynaCROM answers (updated contextual norm information) to make better decisions and, thus, achieve their goals faster. Developers of regulations in open MASs can use DynaCROM as a flexible solution for defining, updating and managing contextual norms.

The structure of this paper is organized as follows. Section 2 briefly presents DynaCROM. Section 3 describes a case study where agents are continuously supported with contextual norm information and, then, make decisions based on this information. Section 4 compares DynaCROM with related works. Finally, Section 5 concludes the work and outlines directions for future works.

2 Norm-Aware Open Multi-agent Systems

MASs are generally made up of environments, organizations and agents [24]. Environments [37] are discrete computational locations (similar to places in the physical world) that provide conditions for agents to inhabit it. Organizations [13] are social locations where groups of agents play roles inside it. Roles are abstractions that define a set of related tasks for agents achieving their designed goals [34]. Agents interact with others, from the same or different organizations and environments.

Environments, organizations, roles and agent interactions suggest different contexts found in MASs. Contexts can be defined as pieces of information that characterize the situation of participants [7]. Context-aware systems use contexts to provide relevant information and/or services to their users, where relevancy depends on the users' tasks [7]. In our definition, a regulated context-aware MASs is a MASs that continuously provides updated contextual norm information to their agents.

Researches into context-aware applications suggest top-down architectures for modeling contextual information [26]. Thus, DynaCROM suggests to model norms of open MASs according to the *Environment*, *Organization*, *Role* and *Interaction* contexts. These *regulatory contexts* are differentiated by their boundaries. Environment *norms* are applied to all agents in a regulated environment. *Organization norms* are applied to all agents in a regulated organization. *Role norms* are applied to all agents playing a regulated role. *Interaction norms* are applied to all agents involved in a regulated interaction.

DynaCROM regulatory contexts and their data (norms) are explicitly represented by an ontology, which provides a meaningful understanding for heterogeneous agents from open MASs. For the DynaCROM ontology, the following definitions are valid: an *ontology* is a conceptual model that embodies shared conceptualizations of a given domain [19]; a *contextual ontology* is an ontology that represents contextual information [3]; and, a *contextual normative ontology* is an ontology that represents contextual norm information.

Fig. 1 illustrates the DynaCROM ontology. It is made up of six related concepts. The *Action* concept encompasses all instances of regulated actions. The *Penalty* concept encompasses all instances of fines to be applied when norms are not fulfilled. The *Norm* concept encompasses all instances of norms from all regulatory contexts. The *Environment* concept encompasses all instances of regulated environments; and, each environment encompasses its associated norms and its owner environment (the environment it belongs to). The *Organization* concept encompasses all instances of regulated organizations; and, each organization encompasses its associated norms, main organization (the organization to which it is associated) and environment. The *Role* concept encompasses all instances of regulated roles; and, each role encompasses its associated norms and organization.

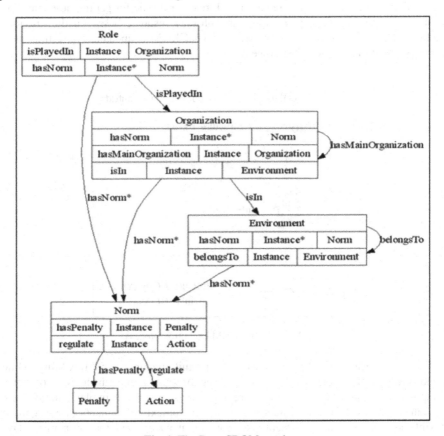

Fig. 1. The DynaCROM ontology

Norms should control environments, organizations, agent roles and agent interactions by defining which actions are *permitted*, *obliged* and *prohibited*. A *permitted norm* defines that an act is allowed to be performed; an *obliged norm* defines that an act must be performed; and a *prohibited norm* defines that an act must not be performed. While regulating open MASs from different domains, the DynaCROM ontology must be instantiated with particular domain instances and it can be extended with domain concepts and interaction norms. Interaction norms should be implemented by following a representation pattern, from the Semantic Web Best Practices document [30]. This pattern defines that the relation object itself must be represented by a created concept that links the other concepts from the relation (i.e., reification of the relationship). So, in DynaCROM ontologies, an interaction norm should be represented by a new Norm sub-concept linking two Role concepts.

Norms from related regulatory contexts should be easily composed during systems' run-time. For this, DynaCROM uses rules and a rule inference engine for both composing related contextual norms and informing them to agents. DynaCROM execution process can be summarized by the following tasks: read the ontology instance for getting data and how concepts are structured; read a rule file for getting how concepts must be composed; and, finally, infer an ontology instance based on the previous readings. Thus, all information provided by DynaCROM is updated. Fig. 2 illustrates an overview of the DynaCROM process.

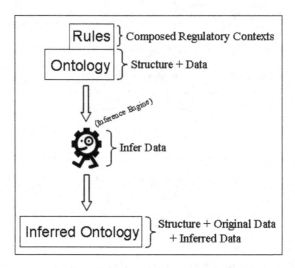

Fig. 2. The DynaCROM execution process

The main idea behind using rules is to permit dynamics and flexibility while compositing related contextual norms. Instead of spread implementations of norm compositions in agents' codes and in regulated systems, these implementations are centralized in a rule file. Furthermore, modular context refinements allow a more flexible system, providing a better support to manage regulatory dynamics. DynaCROM offers a simple way to manage norm evolutions, without the need to stop the system execution, in two different cases. The first case is when norms need to be added, updated or deleted. For this case, simply updating the ontology instance makes the evolution done. The second case is when new compositions of contextual norms are desired. For this case, simply updating the specific rules for the new compositions concludes the evolution.

3 Case Study

The domain of multinational corporations is used to present our case study. This domain was chosen because it well illustrates important implicit contextual information found in MASs. In our case study, a regulated open MASs continuously provides updated contextual norm information, permitting agents to make better decisions.

The world of our case study is created as follows: Canada and the United States of America are environments located in the North America environment; Argentina, Brazil and Chile are environments located in the South America environment; Hpie Canada and Hpie Argentina organizations are branches from the Hpie main organization; Dellie Brazil and Dellie Chile organizations are branches from the Dellie main organization; Dellie organizations have the supplier, manufacturer and customer roles; and, Hpie organizations have the supplier, manufacturer, distributor, retailer and customer roles. All entities from our world are illustrated in Fig. 3.

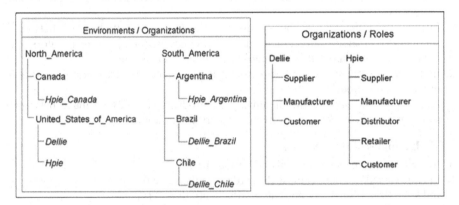

Fig. 3. The environments, organizations and roles from our case study

3.1   Examples of Environment, Organization, Role and Interaction Norms

Normally, organizations do not make their norms public because they are of strategic importance to their businesses. Because of this, based on the available information collected from several corporate Web sites, we created norms for our environments, organizations, roles and agent interactions and classified them according to our four regulatory contexts.

3.1.1   Examples of Environment Norms

a. In North America, the price of a finished good from every organization has a percentage of its price (depending on the seller's location) added as taxes if the delivery is immediate (carry-out) or if the delivery address is in the seller's location.
b. In Canada, a finished good from every organization has 15% of the price value added as taxes if the delivery is immediate (carry-out) or if the delivery address is in Canada.
c. In the state of the Dellie headquarters (in the United States of America), a finished good from every organization has 8% of the price value added as taxes if the delivery is immediate (carry-out) or if the delivery address is in the state of the Dellie headquarters.

d. In the state of the Hpie headquarters (in the United States of America), a finished good from every organization has 5% of the price value added as taxes if the delivery is immediate (carry-out) or if the delivery address is in the state of the Hpie headquarters.
e. In South America, taxes are included in the price of every finished good.

3.1.2 Examples of Organization Norms

a. Hpie organizations have to follow the direct sales to customer model, i.e. sales of the organization's products can only be made between: suppliers and manufacturers, or manufacturers and distributors, or distributors and retailers, or retailers and customers.
b. In Hpie Argentina, sales of the organization's products can only be made between: suppliers and manufacturers, or manufacturers and distributors, or distributors and retailers, or distributors and customers, or retailers and customers.
c. In Dellie organizations, only suppliers and manufacturers are permitted to sell organization's products to customers.
d. In Dellie Chile, sales of the organization's products can only be made between: suppliers and manufacturers, or manufacturers and customers.

3.1.3 Examples of Role Norms

a. In Dellie, customers receive only complete orders.
b. In Hpie Canada, suppliers must ship orders on their due dates.
c. In Dellie Brazil, suppliers must ship orders until their due dates.
d. In Dellie Brazil, customers must receive orders until one day after their due dates.
e. In Hpie Argentina, customers must make a down payment of 10% for every order placed.

3.1.4 Examples of Interaction Norms

a. In Dellie, manufacturers can pay in up to 30 days after they receive their orders from suppliers.
b. In Dellie Brazil, manufacturers have a 10% discount off the total price of their orders if the payment to their suppliers is made in cash.
c. In Hpie Canada, suppliers can ship incomplete orders to manufacturers.

For our case study, the DynaCROM ontology was extended for representing the interaction norms 3.1.4a, 3.1.4b and 3.1.4c, and the following roles: supplier, manufacturer, distributor, retailer and customer. Then, the extended ontology was instantiated for representing all the norms written above. Fig. 4, Fig. 5, Fig. 6 and Fig. 7 illustrate different parts of the DynaCROM ontology instance created for our case study.

3.2 Applying Environment, Organization, Role and Interaction Norms

The following five subsections present different issues resulting from the application of contextual norms. Subsections 3.2.1 and 3.2.2 present scenarios where norm-aware agents make decisions based on given norm information. Subsections 3.2.3 and 3.2.4 exemplify, respectively, restriction and relaxation of contextual norms. Subsection 3.2.5 exemplifies how composition of contextual norms can generate conflicts.

3.2.1 A Scenario Where Customers Need Their Orders in Due Dates

For exemplifying how norm-aware agents can make decisions based on given norm information, a scenario is given with a customer in North America looking for Hpie products. This customer needs his orders on the due dates. For minimizing delivery expenses, the customer will choose to buy in Hpie or in Hpie Canada (Hpie organizations in North America) depending on their current norms. Fig. 4 illustrates the current norms related to the Hpie and Hpie Canada contexts.

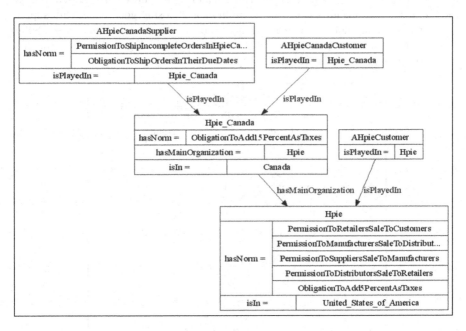

Fig. 4. Hpie and Hpie Canada organization norms

If the customer decides to buy in Hpie (being "*AHpieCustomer*"), he is restricted to buying products only from retailers (organization norm 3.1.2a), but he pays only 5% of the price value as taxes if the delivery is immediate (carry-out) or if the delivery address is in the state of the Hpie headquarters (environment norm 3.1.1d).

If the customer decides to buy in Hpie Canada (being "*AHpieCanadaCustomer*"), he has to pay 15% of the price value as taxes if the delivery is immediately (carry-out) or if the delivery address is in Canada (environment norm 3.1.1b). In Hpie Canada, the customer can also buy direct from suppliers and, doing that, he has the guarantee that his orders will be shipped on their due dates (role norm 3.1.3b). However, if Hpie Canada is also regulated through Hpie norms (its main organization norms), the customer is restricted to buying products only from retailers (organization norm 3.1.2a), but he pays only 5% of the price value if the delivery is immediate (carry-out) or if the delivery address is in the state of the Hpie headquarters (environment norm 3.1.1d).

Because Hpie and Hpie Canada are organizations in North America, both are also regulated through the North America environment norm 3.1.1a. This norm is more general than the environment norms 3.1.1b and 3.1.1d and, thus, does not affect the current regulation.

3.2.2 A Scenario Where Manufacturers Look for Good Deals with Suppliers

For another example of how norm-aware agents can make decisions based on given norm information, a scenario is given with a manufacturer in North America looking for suppliers. This manufacturer has flexibility for choosing good deals with suppliers. For minimizing delivery expenses, the customer can choose to buy with Dellie, Hpie or Hpie Canada suppliers (North America suppliers). Fig. 5 illustrates the current norms related to the Dellie context.

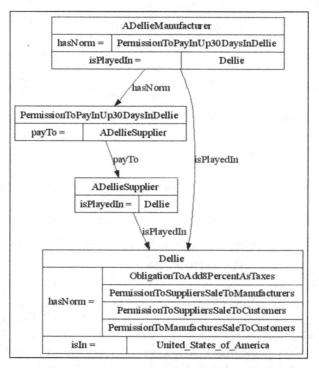

Fig. 5. Dellie organization norms and Dellie manufacturer and supplier role norms

If the manufacturer decides to buy in Dellie with one of the Dellie suppliers (being *"ADellieManufacturer"*), he has the benefit payoff being able to pay in up to 30 days after he receives his orders (interaction norm 3.1.4a). Besides this, he pays 8% of the price value as taxes if the delivery is immediately (carry-out) or if the delivery address is in the state of the Dellie headquarters (environment norm 3.1.1c).

If the manufacturer decides to buy in Hpie Canada with one of the Hpie Canada suppliers (being *"AHpieCanadaManufacturer"*), he has the permission to receive incomplete orders before their due dates (interaction norm 3.1.4c). However, he has to pay 15% of the price value as taxes if the delivery is immediate (carry-out) or if the deliver address is in Canada (environment norm 3.1.1b).

If the manufacturer decides to buy in Hpie with one of the Hpie suppliers (being "*AHpieManufacturer*"), he pays only 5% of the price value as taxes if the delivery is immediate (carry-out) or if the delivery address is in the state of the Hpie headquarters (environment norm 3.1.1d).

3.2.3 A Scenario Where Norms Are Restricted

For exemplifying restriction of contextual norms, a scenario is given with organization norms 3.1.2a and 3.1.2b. Hpie Argentina is regulated through the organization norm 3.1.2b, but as Hpie is its main organization, it is also regulated through the Hpie organization norm 3.1.2a. Thus, by the composition of contextual norms, Hpie Argentina distributors are no longer allowed to sell directly to customers. This scenario is illustrated in the left side of Fig. 6. (note that the dashed norm from the left side of Fig. 6. – "*PermissionToDistributorsSaleToCustomers*" – is not presented in Hpie).

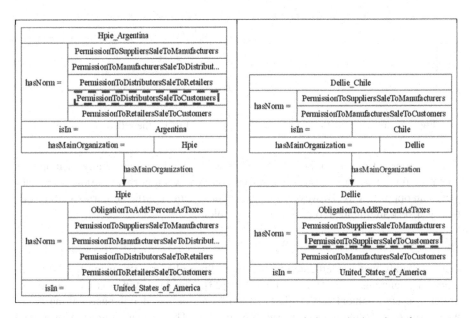

Fig. 6. Compositions of contextual norms resulting in restriction and relaxation of norms

3.2.4 A Scenario Where Norms Are Relaxed

For exemplifying relaxation of contextual norms, a scenario is given with organization norms 3.1.2d and 3.1.2c. Dellie Chile is regulated through the organization norm 3.1.2d, but as Dellie is its main organization, it is also regulated through the Dellie organization norm 3.1.2c. Thus, by the composition of contextual norms, Dellie Chile suppliers are now allowed to sell direct to customers. This scenario is illustrated in the right side of Fig. 6. (note that the dashed norm from the right side of Fig. 6. – "*PermissionToSuppliersSaleToCustomers*" – is only presented in Dellie).

3.2.5 A Scenario Where Norms Are Conflicting

For exemplifying how composition of contextual norms can generate conflicts, a scenario is given with the role norm 3.1.3c, from Dellie Brazil suppliers, and with the role norm 3.1.3d, from Dellie Brazil customers. These norms state the same subject (deadline to ship orders) in an opposite way. The role norm 3.1.3c states that suppliers are obliged to ship orders until their due dates, but the role norm 3.1.3d states that customers can receive their orders until one day after their due dates. Fig. 7 illustrates this scenario.

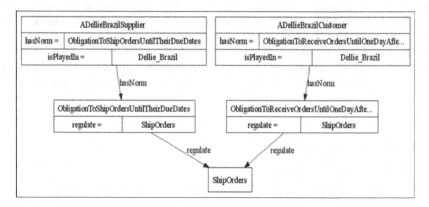

Fig. 7. Compositions of role norms resulting in a conflict for the action of ship orders

It is important to remark here that, in this work, we do not make any assumptions about the problem of how to resolve raised conflicts when norms state the same subject in an opposite way. However, we suggest enhancing conflicted norms with priorities, as a very simple idea to minimize the problem.

3.3 Case Study Implementation

Our case study was implemented inside the Eclipse platform [8], using the Java programming language [18] and the Jena API [23]. The Jena API was used as a programmatic environment for OWL [27] and as a rule-based inference engine (rules were written according to the Jena rule syntax [23]). The Protégé Editor [31] was used to extend and instantiate the DynaCROM ontology. Our agents were implemented in JADE [22], extending its *Agent class* with both an attribute for agents' locations and two specific behaviors. One behavior, called *Migratory*, makes agents move randomly from one location to another. The other behavior, called *Normative*, continuously informs agents about their current contextual norms. Once an agent migrates, its location attribute is updated and, consequently, the answers from the *Normative* behavior change, informing the new contextual norms to which the agent is currently bound. Fig. 8 illustrates the code responsible for adding the *Migratory* and *Normative* behaviors inside our JADE agents.

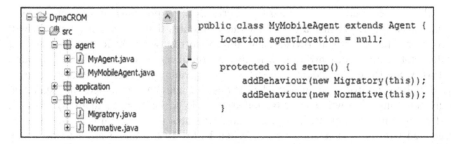

Fig. 8. Adding the *Migratory* and *Normative* behaviors inside our agents

JADE containers were used for representing the abstractions of environments and organizations. North America, South America, Canada, the United States of America, Argentina, Brazil, Chile, Dellie, Hpie, Hpie Canada, Hpie Argentina, Dellie Brazil and Dellie Chile are all the JADE containers created for our case study. These containers offer the technical support for agents with the *Migratory* behavior change locations. Fig. 9 illustrates the JADE containers for the United States of America, Canada, Brazil and Chile environments with some agents inside them. For instance, in Brazil there is an agent, called *"*****MobileAgent1"*, with the *Migratory* and *Normative* behaviors. Once this agent migrates, its location attribute is updated. Subsequently, the *Normative* behavior gets the new agent location and, then, informs the contextual norms to which it is currently bound.

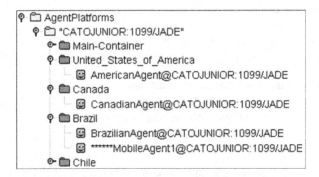

Fig. 9. Part of our system's world implemented as Jade containers

Our *Normative* behavior uses rules for compositions and retrievals of contextual norms. These rules are *ontology-driven*, i.e. they are created based on how DynaCROM regulatory concepts are linked to each other (see the structure of its ontology in Fig. 1). Rules can be activated and deactivated, at run time, for changing the current compositions of contextual norms. To activate rules, it is necessary to remove rules' comment marks; to deactivate rules, it is necessary to insert rules' comment marks, both from a rule file.

All the rules used for the scenarios described in the previous subsections are presented in Table 1. When **Rule 1** is activated, it states that a given environment will also be regulated with its owner environment norms; when **Rule 2** is activated, it states that a given organization will also be regulated with its main organization norms; when **Rule 3** is activated, it states that a given organization will also be regulated with its environment norms; when **Rules 1**, **2** and **3** are activated, they state that a given organization will also be regulated with the norms from its main organization and environment; when **Rule 4** is activated, it states that a given role will also be regulated with its organization norms. When **Rules 1**, **2**, **3** and **4** are activated, they state that a given role will also be regulated with the norms from its organization, its organization's main organization and environments.

Table 1. Rules for compositions of contextual norms

Rule 1- [ruleForEnvironmentWithOwnerEnvironmentNorm:
    (?Environment *belongsTo* ?OwnerEnvironment)
    (?OwnerEnvironment *hasNorm* ?OwnerEnvironmentNorm)
     -> (?Environment *hasNorm* ?OwnerEnvironmentNorm)]

Rule 2- [ruleForOrganizationWithMainOrganizationNorm:
    (?Organization hasMainOrganization ?MainOrganization)
    (?MainOrganization hasNorm ?MainOrganizationNorm)
     -> (?Organization hasNorm ?MainOrganizationNorm)]

Rule 3- [ruleForOrganizationWithEnvironmentNorm:
    (?Organization isIn ?Environment)
    (?Environment hasNorm ?EnvironmentNorm)
     -> (?Organization hasNorm ?EnvironmentNorm)]

Rule 4- [ruleForRoleWithOrganizationNorm:
    (?Role isPlayedIn ?Organization)
    (?Organization hasNorm ?OrganizationNorm)
     -> (?Role hasNorm ?OrganizationNorm)]

The *Normative* behavior represents the core of DynaCROM. This is because this behavior is responsible for implementing the DynaCROM execution process (illustrated in Fig. 2). The most important part of this implementation is presented in Table 2. The DynaCROM process starts when the "*getOntModel()*" method (see line 8) retrieves both the ontology structure (related regulatory contexts) and data (norms). The defined compositions of contextual norms are defined by activations and deactivations of rules written in the "*rulesToComposeNorms.rules*" file (called in line 4). The "*reasoner*" variable (see line 5) represents the rule-based inference engine which, based on the retrieved ontology instance and active rules, automatically deduces the defined compositions of contextual norms. This result is kept in the "*inferredModel*" variable (see line 7), which will be used by DynaCROM for continuously informing agents about their updated contextual norms.

Table 2. The core of the DynaCROM implementation

Model m = ModelFactory.createDefaultModel();	(1)
Resource configuration = m.createResource();	(2)
configuration.addProperty (ReasonerVocabulary.PROPruleSet,	(3)
ontologyDir.concat ("rulesToComposeNorms.rules"));	(4)
Reasoner reasoner =	(5)
GenericRuleReasonerFactory.theInstance().create(configuration);	(6)
InfModel inferredModel =	(7)
ModelFactory.createInfModel(reasoner, this.getOntModel());	(8)

4 Related Work

Our work was compared to OMNI (*Organizational Model for Normative Institutions*) [35]. OMNI is a framework for modeling agent organizations in three levels of abstractions: the *Abstract Level*, which has the statutes of the organization to be modeled, the definitions of terms that are generic for any organization and the ontology of the model itself; the *Concrete Level*, which refines the meanings defined in the previous level, in terms of norms and rules, roles, landmarks and concrete ontological concepts; and, finally, the *Implementation Level*, which has the Normative and Organizational dimensions implemented in a given multi-agent architecture with the mechanisms for role enactment and for norm enforcement.

Comparing our work with OMNI, both define a meta-ontology with a taxonomy for regulations in open MASs and use norms to recommend right and wrong behavior. The use of norms can inspire trust in regulated MASs. One difference is that, in OMNI, enforcement is carried out by any internal agents from the system while in our work it can be carried out by some trusted agents or by some system's enforcement mechanisms. A second difference, and the most important, is that in OMNI the idea of regulatory contexts is not explicit and separated in different levels of abstractions, especially for the environment and role norm contexts. Our approach is based on the environment, organization, role and interaction regulatory contexts to simplify the enforcement and evolution processes. For instance, the social structure of an organization in OMNI describes, in the same level of abstraction, norms for roles and groups of roles. Group of roles is used to specify norms that hold for all roles in the group. We use the organization regulatory context to specify organization norms that hold for all roles from an organization and use the role regulatory context to specify role norms, both regulatory contexts from different levels of abstractions.

In [16], a distributed architecture for endowing MASs with a social layer is proposed. This architecture explicitly represents and manages normative positions via rules. Every external agent from the architecture has a *dedicated governor agent* connected to it, enforcing the norms of executed events. DynaCROM also uses rules to manage normative agent positions, but executed actions, instead of executed events, are the focus of the regulation. Moreover, DynaCROM provides a more precise mechanism for regulation, while permitting the use of contextual norms. Furthermore, each agent can be enhanced with a normative behavior for continuously informing its contextual norms instead of having many extra monitoring agents.

5 Conclusion

In this work, we focused on a case study for exemplifying different issues resulting from the application of contextual norms. It was presented two scenarios where norm-aware agents make decisions based on given norm information and three scenarios where compositions of contextual norms result in restrictions, relaxations and conflicts. For the case study, we used our DynaCROM solution for continuously informing the current contextual norms of agents from an open MAS. Norm-aware agents use DynaCROM answers (updated contextual norms) to make better decisions and, thus, achieve their goals faster. Developers of regulations in open MASs use DynaCROM as a flexible solution for updating systems' norms at run-time.

DynaCROM has being used in three different application domains. For the domain of ubiquitous computing [20], [33] DynaCROM is supporting the implementation of context-aware pervasive mobile applications [36]. Instead of using JADE containers for simulating environments and organizations, we are using MoCA (Mobile Collaboration Architecture) [32] for delivering updated real location information of mobile devices. MoCA infers mobile devices' locations based on the intensity of their signals to 802.11 network access points. DynaCROM uses MoCA answers (device locations) for continuously apply the contextual norms of agents found in the mobile devices. For the domain of next-generation wireless communications [2], DynaCROM is being used in an example where it automatically changes prices and other parameter values (based on pre-defined rules) according to overloads in regulated networks. The idea is to keep balancing the use of network bandwidths by distributing clients in particular networks. Clients will be guided to always use a not overload network by following pricing discounts. Thus, only changing the domain instance of DynaCROM rules and data, developers can better distribute clients in their regulated networks. For the domain of Brazilian navy [4], DynaCROM has being used for dynamically determinate the better ship routes based on climate and other pre-defined conditions.

For future work, we are currently testing DynaCROM with the LGI [28], [29] and SCAAR [5] frameworks, both specific for norm enforcement. The idea is to use DynaCROM for continuously feeding the enforcement framework with the information of agent contextual norms and expect from this framework the enforcement of norms. Concerning our rule solution, we are planning to use the JESS rule engine [14] instead of the JENA engine [23], mainly addressing issues such as ease-of-use, expressiveness and reasoning. We are also planning to use JADEX instead of JADE for enhancing BDI agents with DynaCROM answers. We aim to discover how we can interfere in agents' beliefs, which are, normally, pre-defined during the design phase.

Acknowledgments

This work was partially funded by the projects ESSMA (CNPq 552068/2002-0) and EMACA (CAPES/COFECUB 482/05 PP 016/04), and by CNPq individual grants.

References

1. Artikis, A.: Executable Specification of Open Norm-Governed Computational Systems. PhD thesis, Imperial College London (2003)
2. Berezdivin, R., Breinig, R., Topp, R.: Next-generation wireless communications concepts and technologies. IEEE Communications Magazine 40, 108–116 (2002)
3. Bouquet, P., Giunchiglia, F., van Harmelen, F., Serafini, L., Stuckenschmidt, H.: C-OWL: Contextualizing Ontologies. In: Fensel, D., Sycara, K.P., Mylopoulos, J. (eds.) ISWC 2003. LNCS, vol. 2870, pp. 164–179. Springer, Heidelberg (2003)
4. Brazilian Navy: Accessed in (October 2006), https://www.mar.mil.br/
5. Chopinaud, C., Fallah-Seghrouchn, A.E., Taillibert, P.: Prevention of Harmful Behaviors Within Cognitive and Autonomous. In: The Proc. of the 17th European Conference on Artificial Intelligence (ECAI 2006), Italy, pp. 205–209 (2006), ISBN: 1-58603-642-4
6. Cliffe, O., de Vos, M., Padget, J.: Specifying and Reasoning about Multiple Institutions. LNCS, vol. 4386, pp. 73–92. Springer, Heidelberg (2007)
7. Dey, A.: Understanding and using context. Personal and Ubiquitous Computing 5(1), 4–7 (2001)
8. Eclipse: Accessed in (October 2006), http://www.eclipse.org/
9. Felicíssimo, C.H.: Dynamic Contextual Regulations in Open Multi-agent Systems. In: Cruz, I., Decker, S., Allemang, D., Preist, C., Schwabe, D., Mika, P., Uschold, M., Aroyo, L. (eds.) ISWC 2006. LNCS, vol. 4273, pp. 974–975. Springer, Heidelberg (2006)
10. Felicíssimo, C.H., de Lucena, C.J.P., Briot, J.-P., Choren, R.: Regulating Open Multi-Agent Systems with DynaCROM. In: The Second Workshop on Software Engineering for Agent-oriented Systems (SEAS 2006), Brazil (2006)
11. Felicíssimo, C.H., de Lucena, C.J.P., Briot, J.-P., Choren, R.: An Approach for Contextual Regulations in Open MAS. In: The Eight International Bi-Conference Workshop on Agent Oriented Information Systems (AOIS-2006) at AAMAS, Hakodate, Japan (2006)
12. Felicíssimo, C.H., de Lucena, C., Carvalho, G., Paes, R.: Normative Ontologies to Define Regulations over Roles in Open Multi-Agent Systems. In: AAAI Fall Symposium TR FS-05-08, USA (2005), ISBN 978-1-57735-254-9
13. Ferber, J., Gutknecht, O., Michael, F.: From Agents to Organizations: an Organization View of Multi-Agent Systems. In: Giorgini, P., Müller, J.P., Odell, J.J. (eds.) Agent-Oriented Software Engineering IV. LNCS, vol. 2935, Springer, Heidelberg (2004)
14. Friedman-Hill, E.: Jess, the Rule Engine for the Java Platform. At Sandia National Laboratories. Accessed in (October 2006), http://herzberg.ca.sandia.gov/
15. Gaertner, D., Clark, K., Sergot, M.: Ballroom etiquette: a case study for norm-governed multi-agent systems. LNCS, vol. 4386, pp. 228–243. Springer, Heidelberg (2007)
16. Garcia-Camino, A., Rodriguez-Aguilar, J.-A., Sierra, C., Vasconcelos, W.: A Distributed Architecture for Norm-Aware Agent Societies. In: Baldoni, M., Endriss, U., Omicini, A., Torroni, P. (eds.) DALT 2005. LNCS (LNAI), vol. 3904, Springer, Heidelberg (2006)
17. García-Camino, A., Rodriguez-Aguilar, J.-A., Sierra, C., Vasconcelos, W.: Norm-Oriented Programming of Electronic Institutions: A Rule-based Approach. LNCS, vol. 4386, pp. 192–207. Springer, Heidelberg (2007)
18. Gosling, J., Joy, B., Junior, G.L.S., Bracha, G.: The Java Language Specification. Accessed in (October 2006), http://java.sun.com/, ISBN 0-201-31008-2
19. Gruber, T.R.: A translation approach to portable ontology specifications. Knowledge Acquisition 5(2), 199–220 (1993)

20. Henricksen, K., Indulska, J.: Developing context-aware pervasive computing applications: Models and approach. In: Pervasive and Mobile Computing, Elsevier, Amsterdam (in press)
21. Hewitt, C.: Open Information Systems Semantics for Distributed Artificial Intelligence. Artificial Intelligence 47(1-3), 79–106 (1991)
22. JADE: Accessed in (October 2006), http://jade.tilab.com/
23. Jena: Accessed in (October 2006), http://jena.sourceforge.net/
24. Jennings, N.R.: On Agent-Based Software Engineering. AI 117(2), 277–296 (2000)
25. Jennings, N., Sycara, K., Wooldridge, M.: A Roadmap of Agent Research and Development. Journal of Agents and Multi-Agent Systems 1, 7–38 (1998)
26. Khedr, M., Karmouch, A.: ACAI: Agent-Based Context-aware Infrastructure for Spontaneous Applications. Journal of Network & Computer Applications 28(1), 19–44 (1995)
27. McGuinness, D.L., Harmelen, F.v.: OWL Web Ontology Language Overview. Accessed in (October 2006), http://www.w3.org/TR/owl-features/
28. Minsky, N.H.: The imposition of protocols over open distributed systems. IEEE Transactions on Software Engineering, USA (1991)
29. Minsky, N.H.: LGI. Accessed in (November 2006), http://www.moses.rutgers.edu/
30. Noy, N., Rector, A. (eds.): Defining N-ary Relations on the Semantic Web: Use with Individuals. Accessed in (October 2006), http://www.w3.org/TR/swbp-n-aryRelations/
31. Protégé: Accessed in (October 2006), http://protege.stanford.edu/
32. Rubinsztejn, H.K., Endler, M., Sacramento, V., Gonçalves, K., Nascimento, F.N.: Support for context-aware collaboration. MATA 2004 5(10), 34–47 (2004)
33. Soldatos, J., Pandis, I., Stamatis, K., Polymenakos, L., Crowley, J.L.: Agent based middleware infrastructure for autonomous context-aware ubiquitous computing services. Journal of Computer Communications (2006)
34. Thomas, G., e Williams, A.B.: Roles in the Context of Multiagent Task Relationships. AAAI Fall Symposium TR FS-05-08. USA (2005), ISBN 978-1-57735-254-9
35. Vázquez-Salceda, J., Dignum, V., Dignum, F.: Organizing Multiagent Systems. Journal of Autonomous Agents and Multi-Agent Systems 11(3), 307–360 (2005)
36. Viterbo, J., Felicissimo, C., Briot, J.-P., Endler, M., Lucena, C.: Applying Regulation to Ubiquitous Computing Environments. In: The Second Workshop on Software Engineering for Agent-oriented Systems (SEAS 2006), Brazil (2006)
37. Weyns, D., Parunak, H.V.D., Michel, F., Holvoet, T., Ferber, J.: Environments for Multi-agent Systems: State-of-the-Art and Research Challenges. In: Weyns, D., Parunak, H.V.D., Michel, F. (eds.) E4MAS 2004. LNCS (LNAI), vol. 3374, pp. 1–47. Springer, Heidelberg (2005)

Operationalisation of Norms for Electronic Institutions

Huib Aldewereld[1], Frank Dignum[1], Andrés García-Camino[2], Pablo Noriega[2],
Juan Antonio Rodríguez-Aguilar[2], and Carles Sierra[2]

[1] Institute of Information and Computing Sciences, Utrecht University,
The Netherlands
{huib,dignum}@cs.uu.nl

[2] Artificial Intelligence Research Institute, IIIA, Spanish Council for Scientific
Research, CSIC, Campus de la UAB, Barcelona, Spain
{andres,pablo,jar,sierra}@iiia.csic.es

Abstract. Agent-mediated electronic institutions belong to a new and promising field where interactions among agents are regulated by means of a set of explicit norms. Current implementations of such open-agent systems are, however, mostly using constraints on the behaviour of the agents, thereby severely limiting the autonomy of the agents. In this paper we propose an extension to electronic institutions to allow for a flexible enforcement of norms, and manners to help overcome the difficulties of translating abstract norms for the use of implementation.

1 Introduction

Agent-mediated institutions, introduced in [16,17], are open agent systems that allow heterogeneous agents to enter and perform tasks. Because of this heterogeneous nature of the agents joining the electronic institution (e-institution), measures have to be taken to control and regulate the behaviour of these agents. These measures are needed to improve and guarantee the safety and stability of the system, as agents joining the institution might, (un)intentionally, break the system by behaving in non-expected or non-accepted manners. It has been widely accepted that norms can be used to ensure this safety, since norms, can be used for defining the legality and illegality of actions (and states) in e-institutions [4].

For these norms to be used in the e-institutions, thereby regulating the agents joining the institution, enforcement mechanisms must be devised to implement the norms in the institution, ensuring its safety. There is, however, a big gap between the theoretical work on norms and the practice of e-institutions. In this paper we will try to bridge this gap from both sides.

From the implementation side we will extend current implementations of norm enforcement through constraints on unwanted behaviour [7] by mechanisms that can detect violations of norms and react to these violations. This will allow the agents in e-institutions more freedom and flexibility, while still complying to the norms.

P. Noriega et al. (Eds.): COIN 2006 Workshops, LNAI 4386, pp. 163–176, 2007.

On the theoretical side work on normative systems (mainly focussed on deontic frameworks [14,5]) is mostly *declarative in nature* while using very abstract notions of norms. Norms are specified in a general way abstracting from specific actions or parties and thus being on the one hand very generally applicable while in the other hand being very vague and ambiguous compared to a concrete situation in an institution. The implementation of norms and norm enforcement in e-institutions, as mentioned above, require norms to have an *operational semantics* that is concrete and that connects with the ontology of the institutional actions. Recent approaches on normative systems have begun to research and express this operational meaning of norms, as seen in [18,2,15,10]. These approaches represent norms and their operational meaning, but are not conclusive on how the implementation in an agent system, such as an e-institution, should be obtained. In this paper we extend this work, by proposing a "translation" from the operational approach proposed in [18] to elements usable for norm enforcement in AMELI. Moreover we will show that the approaches from [15] and [2] can be translated in this formalism as well.

In this paper we assume institutions to be defined as a set of norms, which are to be enforced by a distributed set of (internal) agents. Secondly we assume that the norms can sometimes be violated by agents in order to keep their autonomy, which can also be functional for the system as a whole as argued in [3]. The violation of norms is handled from the organisational point of view by violation and sanction mechanisms. And finally, we assume that the internal state of agents is neither visible, nor controllable from an institution's point of view, which, basically, means that enforcement of norms needs to be done by the detection of violations and the reacting to these violations, and that we can only use the observable behaviour of agents to detect the violations.

The remainder of this paper is organised as follows. In the next section we give a short discussion on a formal view of electronic institutions. In sections 3 and 4 we introduce the syntax and semantics of the mechanism used for expressing and handling the violation of norms, while in section 5 we give a translation from the norm frame of [18] into this enforcement mechanism. In section 6 we give a tentative comparison on how this enforcement method can be applied to other normative approaches, and in section 7 we indicate some issues in the translation process of norms to implementation.

2   Electronic Institutions

Electronic institutions, as we consider them [6,16,17], shape agent environments that restrict the behaviour of agents to ensure that agents interact in safe conditions. E-institutions constrain agent behaviour by defining the valid sequences of (dialogical) interactions that agents can have to attain their goals.

The dialogical framework defines all the conventions required to make interaction between two or more agents possible. Moreover, it defines what the participant roles within the e-institution and the relationships among them will be. We take interactions to be a sequence of speech acts between two or more parties. Formally, we express speech acts as illocutionary formulas of the form: $\iota(speaker, hearer, \phi, t)$. The speech acts that we use start with an illocutionary particle (ι), which can be "declare", "request", "promise", etc., that a *speaker* addresses to a *hearer*, at time t, whose content ϕ is expressed in some object language whose vocabulary stems from an e-institution's ontology.

A *dialogical framework* encompasses all the illocutions available to the agents in a given institution. Formally,

Definition 1. *A dialogical framework is a tuple $DF = \langle O, L_O, P, R, R_S \rangle$ where O stands for an ontology (vocabulary); L_O stands for a content language to express the information exchanged between agents using ontology O; P is the set of illocutionary particles; R is the set of roles; R_S is the set of relationships over roles.*

For each activity in an institution, interactions between agents are articulated through agent group meetings, which we call *scenes*. A scene is a role-based multi-agent protocol specification. A scene defines the valid sequences of interactions among agents enacting different roles. It is defined as a directed graph where each node stands for scene state and each edge connecting two states is labelled by an illocution scheme. An illocution scheme is an illocutionary formula with some unbound variables. At run-time, agents playing different roles make a scene evolve by uttering illocutions that match the illocution schemes connecting states. Each scene maintains the context of the interaction, that is how the dialogue is evolving, i.e. which have been the uttered illocutions and how the illocution schemes have been instantiated.

Definition 2. *A scene is a tuple $S = \langle s, R, DF, W, w_0, W_f, \Theta, \lambda, min, Max \rangle$ where s is the scene identifier; R is the set of scene roles; DF is a dialogical framework; W is the set of scene states; $w_0 \in W$ is the initial state; $W_f \subseteq W$ is the set of final states; $\theta \subseteq W \times W$ is a set of directed edges; $\lambda : \theta \longrightarrow \mathcal{L}^*_{DF}$ is a labelling function, which maps each edge to an illocution scheme in the pattern language of the DF dialogical framework $\mathcal{L}^*_{DF}$; $min, Max; \mathbb{R} \longrightarrow \mathbb{N}$ $min(r)$ and $Max(r)$ are, respectively, the minimum and the maximum number of agents that must and can play each role $r \in R$.*

The activities in an e-institution are the composition of multiple, distinct, possibly concurrent, dialogical activities, each one involving different groups of agents playing different roles. A performative structure can be seen as a network of scenes, whose connections are mediated by transitions (a special type of scene), and determines the role-flow policy among the different scenes by showing how agents, depending on their roles and prevailing commitments, may get into different scenes, and showing when new scenes will be started. The performative structure defines the possible order of execution of the interaction protocols (*scenes*). It also allows agent synchronisation, and scene interleaved execution.

Definition 3. *A performative structure is a tuple $PS = \langle S, T, s_0, s_\Omega, E, f_L, f_T, f_E^O, \mu \rangle$ where S is a finite, non-empty set of scenes; T is a finite, non-empty set of transitions; $s_0 \in S$ is the initial scene; $s_\Omega \in S$ is the final scene; $E = E^I \cup E^O$*

is a set of edge identifiers where $E^I \subseteq S \times T$ is a set of edges from scenes to transitions and $E^O \subseteq T \times S$ is a set of edges from transitions to scenes; $f_L : E \longrightarrow DNF_{2^{V_A \times R}}$ maps each edge to a disjunctive normal form of pairs of agent variable and role identifier representing the edge label; $f_T : T \longrightarrow \mathcal{T}$ maps each transition to its type; $f_E^O : E^O \longrightarrow \mathcal{E}$ maps each edge to its type; $\mu : S \longrightarrow \{0, 1\}$ sets if a scene can be multiply instantiated at execution time;

The institutional state consists of the list of scene executions (described by their participating agents and interaction context) along with the participating agents' state (represented by their observable attributes).

3   Integrity and Dialogical Constraints

As mentioned in the introduction, we want to extend the AMELI formalism with mechanisms to implement norms by means of a distributed set of agents. To achieve this we need mechanisms to detect violations and react to these violations. This is accomplished by using, respectively, integrity constraints and dialogical constraints. The main idea is that integrity constraints are checked by the institution to detect and register all violations, i.e. the passing from a legal state to an illegal state. The dialogical constraints express the obligation of the enforcing agents to act according to the violations detected, i.e. sanction the responsible agent. The dialogical constraints themselves are part of the internal enforcing agents.

Due to the fact that the internal agents should be designed to follow the norms of the institution, we might assume that internal agents will always act according to the dialogical constraints specified. However, the internal agents might not be responsible for the enforcement of all the norms in the system, we can specify integrity constraints that express when a dialogical constraint (which is in a sense an obligation to enforce) has been violated, i.e. a violation has occurred, but no action has been taken by the enforcing agent to punish the violator. In theory, complex hierarchical structures of enforcement chains (institutions enforcing the enforcement within another institution, etc.) are possible with the approach presented in this paper, but we are not going to discuss them in this paper.

Before enforcement can take place, norm violations have to be detected. This is done by specifying integrity constraints, extracted from previous work [8]:

Definition 4. *Integrity constraints are first-order formulas of the form*

$$\left(\bigwedge_{i=1}^{n} uttered(s_i, w_{k_i}, \textbf{\textit{i}}_{l_i}) \wedge \bigwedge_{j=0}^{m} e_j \right) \Rightarrow \bot$$

where s_i are scene identifiers or variables, w_{k_i} is a state k_i of scene s_i or a variable, $\textbf{\textit{i}}_{l_i}$ is an illocution scheme l_i matching the schema labelling an outgoing arc from w_{k_i} and e_j are boolean expressions over variables from uttered predicates.

These integrity constraints define sets of situations that *should not* occur within an e-institution. The meaning of these constraints is that if grounded illocutions matching the illocution schemes $i_{l_1}, \ldots, i_{l_n}$ are uttered in the corresponding scenes and states, and expressions $e_1, \ldots, e_m$ are satisfied, then a violation ($\bot$)occurs afterwards. We use the "$\Rightarrow$" to indicate that it is not really an implication, but some temporal order is involved.

Since agents can violate norms, the integrity constraints are not enough. We need to specify which actions are to be taken by the enforcers after the violation has been detected. In a sense, the violation of a norm by agents within the e-institution obliges the enforcers to perform actions, namely to punish the agent breaking the norm. This "obligation to enforce" is expressed by means of a dialogical constraint:

Definition 5. *Dialogical constraints are first-order formulas of the form:*

$$\left(\bigwedge_{i=1}^{n} uttered(s_i, w_{k_i}, i^*_{l_i}) \wedge \bigwedge_{j=0}^{m} e_j \right) \Rightarrow$$

$$\left(\bigwedge_{i=1}^{n'} uttered(s'_i, w'_{k_i}, i'^*_{l_i}) \wedge \bigwedge_{j=0}^{m'} e_j \right)$$

where s_i, s'_i are scene identifiers or variables, w_{k_i}, w'_{k_i} are variables or states of scenes s_i and s'_i respectively, $i^*_{l_i}$, $i'^*_{l_i}$ are illocution schemes l_i matching the schema labelling an outgoing arc from w_{k_i} of scenes s_i and s'_i respectively, and e_j, e'_j are boolean expressions over variables from uttered predicates. These boolean expressions can include functions to check the state of the institution.

The intuitive meaning of a dialogical constraint is that if grounded illocutions matching $i^*_{l_1}, \ldots, i^*_{l_n}$ are uttered in the corresponding scene states, and the expressions $e_1, \ldots, e_m$ are satisfied, then, grounded illocutions matching $i'^*_{l_1}, \ldots, i'^*_{l_n}$ satisfying the expressions $e'_1, \ldots, e'_{m'}$ must be uttered in the corresponding scene states as well. Dialogical constraints assume a temporal ordering: the left-hand side illocutions must be uttered prior to the illocutions on the right-hand side, i.e. the illocutions on the left should have time stamps which precede those of the illocutions on the right.

The dialogical constraints point out the actions to perform in the enforcement of a violated norm. For instance,

$$uttered(S,W,inform(A,Role,all,Role2,smoke,T)) \Rightarrow$$
$$uttered(S,W,inform(B,enforcer,A,Role,decrement(credit,50),T')) \wedge T' > T$$

shows an example of a dialogical constraint which expresses that every agent "A" playing any role "Role" that smokes in a scene should be sanctioned (since smoking is illegal). Whenever an agent performs the action of smoke, an "enforcer" agent "B" is obliged to decrement its credit by 50.

The integrity constraints are then implemented in the infrastructure of the e-institutions, thereby providing the means to detect violations of norms, where the dialogical constraints are implemented in the enforcing agents which use them to determine the illocutions that should be uttered when a norm has been violated.

4 Semantics

In this section we present the semantics of the integrity constraints, used for detecting violations, and the dialogical constraints, used for specifying enforcement, which we introduced in the previous section. In the definitions below we use the standard concept of *substitution* (denoted by σ) to relate a set of values (first-order terms denoted τ) to a set of variables (denoted x, y, z) in a computation [1,9]. We use $\phi \cdot \sigma$ to denote the formula ϕ on which the substitution σ has been performed.

We conceive the notion of state (Δ) in an electronic institution as the set of illocutions uttered (expressions of the form $uttered(s, w, i)$) and the boolean expressions that hold during its enactment. The execution of the institution would be divided into two different, alternating rounds: event addition and processing. Firstly, we start the execution with a (possibly empty) initial state where agents' illocutions are added. Secondly, the rules are executed evolving the state adding inconsistency marks or obligations. Then, we again start the event addition round and so on. The semantics of the integrity constraints are defined as relationships (s_{IC}) between the current state Δ and the next state Δ'. Let us first look at the utterances and boolean expressions that are used in the constraints. An utterance holds iff it is uttered in the current state:

Definition 6. $S(\Delta, uttered(s, w, i), \sigma)$ holds iff $uttered(s \cdot \sigma, w \cdot \sigma, i \cdot \sigma) \in \Delta$

The semantics of Boolean expressions are defined as follows:

Definition 7. $S(\Delta, \tau_1 \rhd \tau_2, \sigma)$ holds iff $\tau_1 \cdot \sigma \rhd \tau_2 \cdot \sigma$ holds. Where $\rhd \in \{=, \neq, >, <, \geq, \leq\}$ with their usual meaning.

Conjunctions used in the constraints are satisfied in the normal way:

Definition 8. $S(\Delta, (\bigwedge_{i=1}^{n} \phi_i), \sigma)$ holds iff $S(\Delta, \phi_i, \sigma)$, $1 \leq i \leq n, n \in \mathbb{N}$, hold.

In the following we use u as an abbreviation of: $\bigwedge_{i=1}^{n} uttered(s_i, w_{k_i}, i_{l_i}) \wedge \bigwedge_{j=0}^{m} e_j$

Integrity constraints define the violations of the norms. An integrity constraint is applicable to the institutional state (Δ), and thus introducing a violation ($\bot$), iff the conjunction of utterances and boolean expressions holds in Δ:

Definition 9. $s_{IC}(\Delta, u \cdot \sigma \Rightarrow \bot, \Delta \cup \{\bot\})$ holds iff $S(\Delta, u, \sigma)$ hold.

An integrity constraint does not introduce a violation, if either the utterances or the boolean expressions do not hold in Δ, i.e. the integrity constraint is not applicable:

Definition 10. $s_{IC}(\Delta, u \cdot \sigma \Rightarrow \bot, \Delta)$ *holds iff* $S(\Delta, u, \sigma)$ *does not hold.*

Dialogical constraints introduce obligations to enforce, based on the violations detected by integrity constraints. We define the semantics of dialogical constraints as relationships (s_{DC}) between current state Δ and the next state Δ'. A dialogical constraint is applicable to a state Δ, thus introducing an obligation to enforce, iff the conjunction of utterances and boolean expressions holds in Δ:

Definition 11. $s_{DC}(\Delta, u \cdot \sigma \Rightarrow u' \cdot \sigma, \Delta \cup \{u' \cdot \sigma\})$ *holds iff* $S(\Delta, u, \sigma)$ *holds.*

A dialogical constraint does not introduce an obligation to enforce iff the conjunction of utterances or the conjunction of boolean expression does not hold in Δ:

Definition 12. $s_{DC}(\Delta, u \cdot \sigma \Rightarrow u' \cdot \sigma, \Delta)$ *holds iff* $S(\Delta, u, \sigma)$ *does not hold.*

Note that definitions 9 and 10 can be seen as a kind of special cases of definitions 11 and 12. We chose to treat them separate, because the temporal flavor (and implementation) of the dialogical constraints is much bigger than of the integrity constraints. From the semantics we can straightforwardly implement an interpreter in Prolog as done in [11]. This interpreter would evolve the state of enactment of an institution by adding inconsistency marks, based on violations detected through the integrity constraints, or obligations to enforce, based on the specified dialogical constraints.

In the current AMELI framework, agent interactions are mediated by a special kind of agents called *governors*. These governors regulate the agents' illocutions following the specification of electronic institutions, i.e. they only forward illocutions that match the illocution scheme of an outgoing arc of the current state of the scene. By including the interpreter mentioned above, we improve the governors by allowing them to regulate according to more expressive and flexible specifications of electronic institutions.

5   Implementing Norms

The operational approach to norms expressed in [18] that tries to implement norms from an institutional perspective, that is to say enforcing norms by means of detecting violations and reacting to such violations, views norms as a manner to describe how someone should behave, i.e., they define obligations, permissions and prohibitions also known as the *declarative meaning of norms* (cf. [5,14]). Since a system needs responses to the violations that occur, the norms in this approach are viewed as a frame which includes not only this declarative meaning of the norm but also a definition of the responses to violations to the norms, which are known as sanctions and repairs (also known as the *operational meaning of the norm*). In [18] this norm frame is defined as follows:

Definition 13 (Norms)

$$
\begin{aligned}
\text{NORM} &:= \text{NORM\_CONDITION,VIOLATION\_CONDITION,} \\
& \quad \text{DETECTION\_MECHANISM,SANCTION,REPAIRS} \\
\text{VIOLATION\_CONDITION} &:= formula \\
\text{DETECTION\_MECHANISM} &:= \{action\ expressions\} \\
\text{SANCTION} &:= \text{PLAN} \\
\text{REPAIRS} &:= \text{PLAN} \\
\text{PLAN} &:= action\ expression \mid action\ expression\ ; \text{PLAN}
\end{aligned}
$$

The norm condition is the declarative norm, as obtained from, for instance, the legal domain (see definition 14 for a description of what these norm conditions can be. The other fields in this norm description are; 1) the *violation condition* which is a formula defining when the norm is violated, 2) the *detection mechanism* which describes the mechanisms included in the agent platform that can be used for detecting violations, 3) the *sanction* which defines the actions that are used to punish the agent(s) violating the norm, and 4) the *repairs* which is a set of actions that are used for recovering the system after the occurrence of a violation.

Definition 14 (Norm Condition)

$$
\begin{aligned}
\text{NORM\_CONDITION} &:= N(a,S\ \langle\text{IF}\ C\rangle) \mid \text{OBLIGED}(a\text{ENFORCE}(N(a,S\ \langle\text{IF}\ C\rangle))) \\
N &:= \text{OBLIGED} \mid \text{PERMITTED} \mid \text{FORBIDDEN} \\
S &:= P \mid \text{DO } A \mid P\ \text{TIME } D \mid \text{DO } A\ \text{TIME } D \\
C &:= formula \\
P &:= predicate \\
A &:= action\ expression \\
\text{TIME} &:= \text{BEFORE} \mid \text{AFTER}
\end{aligned}
$$

As definition 14 shows, norms can either be permissions, obligations or prohibitions. Moreover, norms can be related to actions or to predicates (states). Through the condition (C) and deadline (D), norms can be made applicable to certain situations only (conditions and deadlines are considered optional).

Before we can use norms specified in the formalism described above, we need to translate the abstract predicates and actions into corresponding concrete utterances and scenes that are specified in the definition of the institution. For instance, a norm such as

OBLIGED(($buyer$ DO $pay(Price,seller)$) IF $done(buyer,won(Item,Price))$)

should be translated into utterances as used in e-institutions:

$uttered(payment,W,inform(A,buyer,B,payee,pay(Item,Price),T))$
$uttered(auction,w2,inform(C,auctioneer,A,buyer,won(Item,Price),T'))$

We will get back to this issue in section 7. For now we will assume that some translation from, e.g., OBLIGED((a DOA) IF C) into OBLIGED($utter(S,W,I)$IF C) can be given, taking into account that the state S and world W of the institution will correspond to the applicable state meant by the norm, and that I is an illocution performed by a to implement action A. We can use the DETECTION_MECHANISM description to assist in the translation.

Once the norms are contextualised, we can map them to integrity constraints, as specified in the previous section, which we use to check whether violations occur. This mapping of the contextualised norm conditions to integrity constraints can be done by the use of the following table:

Norm	Translation
FORBIDDEN($utter(s,w,i)$)	$uttered(s,w,i){\to}\bot$
OBLIGED($utter(s,w,i)$ IF C)	$(C\wedge\neg uttered(s,w,i)){\to}\bot$
FORBIDDEN($utter(s,w,i)$ IF C)	$(C\wedge uttered(s,w,i)){\to}\bot$
OBLIGED($utter(s,w,i)$ BEFORE D)	$(\nexists T{:}uttered(s,w,i(T))\wedge T{<}D){\to}\bot$
OBLIGED($utter(s,w,i)$ AFTER D)	$(\nexists T{:}uttered(s,w,i(T))\wedge T{>}D){\to}\bot$
FORBIDDEN($utter(s,w,i)$ BEFORE D)	$(\exists T{:}uttered(s,w,i(T))\wedge T{<}D){\to}\bot$
FORBIDDEN($utter(s,w,i)$ AFTER D)	$(\exists T{:}uttered(s,w,i(T))\wedge T{>}D){\to}\bot$

An observant reader should note that permissions are left out of this translation, since permissions cannot be violated, and therefore cannot be specified as an integrity constraint. Unconditional obligations are also not in this table, since these would mean that agents are obliged to utter a certain illocution all the time, which is not meaningful. Likewise, obligations that should be satisfied after a specific point in time are not very useful either, since these can never be violated. This can, however, be adapted by including another deadline before which the obligation has to be fulfilled, which would mean that, in most cases, the obligation should be fulfilled before the institution ends.

The VIOLATION_CONDITION of a norm is translated into a conjunction of boolean expressions that can be checked in the institution.

Finally, the SANCTION and REPAIR of a norm as described in the norm framework should both be translated to (a sequence of utterances plus boolean constraints) for the enforcer agents. This will create the dialogical constraints to be used by the enforcing agents to determine which actions should be performed when a norm is violated.

6   Other Normative Approaches

In this section we give a tentative comparison between the approach just mentioned and the norm frameworks introduced in [2] and [15]. Given the concepts seemingly in those frameworks we show how we think norms from these frameworks can be implemented using the language given in section 3.

6.1   Norms in Z

In [15] Luck et al. proposed a framework for norms that could be integrated into their multiagent systems. Like the framework of the previous section it identifies the addressee, normative goal, punishments and context of norms (in the previous approach these were, respectively, the role a, the predicate P or action A, the sanctions and the (temporal) condition C or D). The norm frame in [15] expands this with the concepts of beneficiaries, exceptions and rewards, which were left implicit in the approach of the previous section. Additionally, their norm frame also specifies that for norms the inclusion of an addressee, a context and a normative goal are mandatory, and, moreover, it shows that the sets defining the context and the exceptions, as well as the sets of rewards and punishments, are disjoint. Note that punishments and rewards in this norm frame are specified as goals which are to be achieved by norm enforcing agents, that is to say, when the norm is violated the norm enforcing agents of the system are obliged to fulfil the punishment-goal to punish the agent violating the norm.

Using the language introduced in section 3 we can again show that norms specified in this norm frame can be operationalised for use in e-institutions. After contextualisation, the norms can be automatically translated to integrity constraints and inference rules.

The contextualisation of the norms as specified above includes linking the addressee, beneficiaries (if present) and normative goal to the correct corresponding utterance, as well as identifying the predicates used in the e-institution to express the context and exceptions. After this contextualisation the norms can easily be translated into the following integrity constraint to detect violations of the norm:

$$(context \land \sim exception \land \neg goal') \rightarrow \perp$$

where *context* and *exception* are predicates obtained through the contextualisation for specifying the context and exceptions mentioned in the norm, *goal'* is the contextualised normative goal (thus including the addressee and possible beneficiaries), and the $\sim$ operator is for expressing negation-as-failure (since no exceptions might be given).

If punishments and rewards are specified, the following dialogical constraints can be defined:

$$(context \land \sim exception \land \neg goal') \Rightarrow punishment$$

$$(context \land \sim exception \land goal') \Rightarrow reward$$

which define that *punishment* should be executed by an enforcing agent when the specified condition (i.e. the violation of the norm) occurs while a reward should be given when agents comply to the norm.

6.2   Event Calculus Norms

In [2] Artikis et al. propose the use of event calculus for the specification of norm based protocols. The event calculus is a formalism to represent reasoning about actions or events and their effects in a logic programming framework. It is based on a many-sorted first-order predicate calculus.

Predicates that change along time are called *fluents*. Obligations, permissions, empowerments, capabilities and sanctions are formalised by means of the following fluents: $obl(Ag, Act)$, $per(Ag, Act)$, $pow(Ag, Act)$, $can(Ag, Act)$ and $sanction(Ag)$. In the example of [2], prohibitions are not formalised as fluents since they assume that every action that is not permitted is forbidden by default.

The expression below shows an example of an obligation specified in Event Calculus extracted from [2]. The obligation that C revokes the floor holds at time T if C enacts the role of chair and the floor is granted to someone else different from the best candidate.

$$\mathsf{holdsAt}(obl(C, revoke\_floor(C)) = \mathsf{true}, T) \leftarrow$$
$$\quad role\_of(C, chair)$$
$$\quad \mathsf{holdsAt}(status = granted(S, T'), T), (T \geq T'),$$
$$\quad \mathsf{holdsAt}(best\_candidate = S', T), (S \neq S')$$

If we translate all the *holdsAt* predicates into *uttered* predicates, we can translate the obligations of the example by including the rest of conditions in the LHS of the integrity constraints:

$$(uttered(s, w, inform(A, R, B, R', best\_candidate(S'))) \wedge$$
$$uttered(s, w, inform(C, chair, S, candidate, granted(S))) \wedge$$
$$S \neq S') \Rightarrow utter(s, w, inform(C, chair, A, R'', revoke\_floor))$$

However, since there is no concrete definition of a norm, we cannot state that Artikis' approach is fully translatable into integrity constraints and dialogical constraints.

Although event calculus models time, the deontic fluents specified in the example of [2] are not enough to inform an agent about all types of duties. For instance, to inform an agent that it is obliged to perform an action before a deadline, it is necessary to show the agent the obligation fluent and the part of the theory that models the violation of the deadline.

7   Contextualising Norms

In previous sections we have mentioned that norms need to be contextualised in order to be used in e-institutions. This contextualisation is, in a sense, interpreting the abstract norm from the institution's point of view such that it is usable for implementation. In the example that we used earlier this interpretation was quite clear. However, if we regard institutional norms that are derived (or translated) from human laws and regulations, the contextualisation becomes much harder, as laws contain vague and ambiguous concepts that cannot always be related to a single integrity constraint. In order to implement such norms with a high level of abstraction two steps must be taken: 1) interpreting the abstract concepts and link them to concrete concepts used in the institution, and 2) adding procedural information and artifacts to the institution to simplify (or allow) the enforcement of the norm. In this section we examine both these elements.

7.1   Ontological Interpretations of Concepts

The first step of the contextualisation of norms is to connect abstract concepts appearing in the norm to concepts used in the institution. Consider the following norm of an auction house, expressing the obligation to identify oneself upon entering an auction:

OBLIGED(($participant$ DO $identify$) IF ($participant$ DO $enter(auction)$))

The action $identify$ in this norm has an abstract meaning and can be implemented in various different manners. To implement this norm the meaning of this abstract action must be defined, which is done by connecting the abstract action to concrete action(s), e.g. through the use of a *counts-as* operator [12,13]:

[$participant$ DO $give(certificate,manager)$ AND
$manager$ DO $check(certificate)$] COUNTS-AS $participant$ DO $identify$

describing that giving an identification certificate to the auction manager, and the manager checking this certificate (both actions defined in the institution!) is seen as an implementation of the *identify* action. Each institution can define its own relations between abstract and concrete concepts (depending on the available concrete concepts) using the counts-as relation.

Thus implementing these counts-as definitions is achieved by extending the existing ontology of the institution. This ontology consists of all the concrete concepts used in the institution. It is extended with the abstract concepts that are used in the norms and the relation between the abstract and concrete concepts using the counts-as relation as done above.

7.2   Introducing Procedural Information

After interpreting the abstract concepts of the norm, the norm can be implemented by means of integrity and dialogical constraints as mentioned in sections 3 and 4. In some cases, though, trying to detect a violation would be computationally hard or totally infeasible from the institution's point of view. Moreover, there might be norms for which a recovery from a violation is difficult or costly.

In both cases, the norm should be modified in (logically or morally equivalent) norms such that it either becomes feasible to detect the violation, or protect the system from very harmful violations. This process of contextualising norms can be done in two ways. Either the norm is translated into smaller and simpler norms which are easier to check but ensure the compliance of the original norm, or the norm is translated into a set of constraints that ensure the compliance.

Consider the following norm in an auction house, expressing that as an agent bids on an item it has to pay for the item if it won the auction:

OBLIGED(($buyer$ DO $pay(Price,seller)$) IF $done(buyer,won(Item,Price))$)

Violations of this norm occur, for instance, because the agent does not have enough money to pay, the agent does not want the item anymore or the agent simply disconnects (unintentionally or on purpose). Although the violation of this norm can be detected easily, sanctioning the agent and repairing the situation might be difficult (especially if the agent disconnects). To avoid these situations, one can choose to implement this norm by means of a constraint; upon entering the institution all agents have to deposit an amount of money (for security) that they will get back when leaving the institution if no violations have occurred:

OBLIGED(($agent$ DO $pay(Security\_Fee)$) IF $done(agent, enter(Institution))$)

However, if a violation of the mentioned norm occurs, this money can be used to pay for the items, thereby sanctioning the agent. This means that our original norm has been implemented by introducing a norm that is easier to enforce (i.e. agents are obliged to pay security before entering), which generates the constraint (or mechanism) that is used for enforcing the original norm. Thus, instead of implementing one norm which was hard to enforce, we have implemented two norms (which were derived from the original norm) that are easily enforced.

8   Conclusions

Previous implementations of electronic institutions enforced norms by ensuring that the agents joining the system followed a pre-defined protocol, thereby guaranteeing norm compliance of the agents. As this approach severely limits the autonomy of the agents, a more flexible enforcement was desired. This paper proposes the use of integrity constraints and dialogical constraints to implement such a flexible enforcement of norms. This norm enforcement is based on the detection of and reacting to the violations of norms.

In order for any kind of norm enforcement to be implemented, abstract norms need to be expanded with an operational meaning, as the declarative nature of abstract norms only defines what is legal/illegal, but never expresses how this legality/illegality is obtained/averted. In [18] we introduced several mechanisms for operationalising norms, where we annotated norms (expressed in deontic logic) with operational aspects, like sanctions and repairs. In this paper we have used this normative frame to design an implementation scheme usable for implementing norm enforcement in electronic institutions. However, before norms can be implemented using this scheme, the norms need to be contextualised. This contextualisation is 1) connecting the abstract concepts of the norm to the concrete concepts used in the institution, and 2) extending the norm with additional procedural information before attempting to implement it. The contextualisation of the norms is, in fact, a further operationalisation of the norms, where, in contrast to declarative norms (which never change the world), the second step of this operationalisation changes the world in order to enforce the norm.

Acknowledgements

The first author of this paper was supported by the Netherlands Organisation for Scientific Research (NWO) under project number 634.000.017. This paper was also partially supported by the Spanish Science and Technology Ministry as part of the Web-i-2 project (TIC-2003-08763-C02-00) and the IEA project (TIN2006-15662-C02-01).

References

1. Apt, K.R.: From Logic Programming to Prolog. Prentice-Hall, UK (1997)
2. Artikis, A., Kamara, L., Pitt, J., Sergot, M.: A protocol for resource sharing in norm-governed ad hoc networks. In: Leite, J.A., Omicini, A., Torroni, P., Yolum, P. (eds.) DALT 2004. LNCS (LNAI), vol. 3476, Springer, Heidelberg (2005)
3. Castelfranchi, C.: Formalizing the informal?: Dynamic social order, bottom-up social control, and spontaneous normative relations. Journal of Applied Logic 1(1-2), 47–92 (2003)
4. Dignum, F.: Abstract norms and electronic institutions. In: Lindemann, G., Moldt, D., Paolucci, M. (eds.) RASTA 2002. LNCS (LNAI), vol. 2934, pp. 93–104. Springer, Heidelberg (2004)
5. Dignum, F., Broersen, J., Dignum, V., Meyer, J.-J.C.: Meeting the Deadline: Why, When and How. In: Hinchey, M.G., Rash, J.L., Truszkowski, W.F., Rouff, C.A. (eds.) FAABS 2004. LNCS (LNAI), vol. 3228, Springer, Heidelberg (2004)
6. Esteva, M.: Electronic Institutions: from specification to development. Number 19 in IIIA Monograph Series. PhD Thesis (2003)
7. Esteva, M., Rodríguez-Aguilar, J., Rosell, B., Arcos, J.: AMELI: An Agent-based Middleware for Electronic Institutions. In: Third International Joint Conference on Autonomous Agents and Multi-agent Systems, New York, US, July 2004 (2004)
8. Esteva, M., Vasconcelos, W., Sierra, C., Rodríguez-Aguilar, J.: Verifying norm consistency in electronic institutions. In: Proc. of The AAAI-04 Workshop on Agent Organizations: Theory and Practice (ATOP), San Jose, California, July 2004 (2004)
9. Fitting, M.: First-Order Logic and Automated Theorem Proving. Springer, New York, USA (1990)
10. García-Camino, A., Rodríguez-Aguillar, J.: Implementing norms in electronic institutions. In: Proceedings of the 4th Int. Joint Conf. on Autonomous Agents & Multi Agent Systems (AAMAS-05), Utrecht, The Netherlands, July 2005 (2005)
11. García-Camino, A., Rodríguez-Aguillar, J., Sierra, C., Vasconcelos, W.: A distributed architecture for norm-aware agent societies. In: Baldoni, M., Endriss, U., Omicini, A., Torroni, P. (eds.) DALT 2005. LNCS (LNAI), vol. 3904, Springer, Heidelberg (2006)
12. Grossi, D., Aldewereld, H., Vázquez-Salceda, J., Dignum, F.: Ontological aspects of the implementation of norms in agent-based electronic institutions. Computational and Mathematical Organization Theory (to appear)
13. Grossi, D., Dignum, F., Meyer, J.-J.C.: Contextual taxonomies. In: Leite, J.A., Torroni, P. (eds.) Computational Logic in Multi-Agent Systems. LNCS (LNAI), vol. 3487, pp. 2–17. Springer, Heidelberg (2005)
14. Lomuscio, A.R., Nute, D. (eds.): DEON 2004. LNCS (LNAI), vol. 3065. Springer, Heidelberg (2004)
15. López y López, F., Luck, M.: Towards a Model of the Dynamics of Normative Multi-Agent Systems. In: Lindemann, G., Moldt, D., Paolucci, M. (eds.) RASTA 2002. LNCS (LNAI), vol. 2934, pp. 175–194. Springer, Heidelberg (2004)
16. Noriega, P.: Agent-Mediated Auctions: The Fishmarket Metaphor. Number 8 in IIIA Monograph Series. PhD Thesis (1997)
17. Rodriguez-Aguilar, J.A.: On the Design and Construction of Agent-mediated Electronic Institutions. Number 14 in IIIA Monograph Series. PhD Thesis (2001)
18. Vázquez-Salceda, J., Aldewereld, H., Dignum, F.: Implementing norms in multi-agent systems. In: Lindemann, G., Denzinger, J., Timm, I.J., Unland, R. (eds.) MATES 2004. LNCS (LNAI), vol. 3187, pp. 313–327. Springer, Heidelberg (2004)

Norm-Oriented Programming of Electronic Institutions: A Rule-Based Approach

Andrés García-Camino[1], Juan-Antonio Rodríguez-Aguilar[1], Carles Sierra[1], and Wamberto Vasconcelos[2]

[1] IIIA-CSIC, Campus UAB, 08193 Bellaterra, Spain
{andres,jar,sierra}@iiia.csic.es
[2] Dept. of Computing Science, University of Aberdeen,
Aberdeen AB24 3UE, United Kingdom
wvasconcelos@acm.org

Abstract. Norms constitute a powerful coordination mechanism among heterogeneous agents. We propose means to specify and explicitly manage the normative positions of agents (permissions, prohibitions and obligations), with which distinct deontic notions and their relationships can be captured. Our rule-based formalism includes constraints for more expressiveness and precision and allows the norm-oriented programming of electronic institutions: normative aspects are given a precise computational interpretation. Our formalism has been conceived as a machine language to which other higher-level normative languages can be mapped, allowing their execution.

1 Introduction

A major challenge in multi-agent system (MAS) research is the design and implementation of *open* multi-agent systems in which coordination must be achieved among agents defined with different languages by several designers who may not trust each other. Norms can be used for this purpose as a means to regulate the observable behaviour of agents as they interact in pursuit of their goals [1,2,3]. There is a wealth of socio-philosophical and logic-theoretical literature on the subject of norms (*e.g.*, [4,5]), and, more recently, much attention is being paid to more pragmatic and implementational aspects of norms, that is, how norms can be given a computational interpretation and how norms can be factored in in the design and execution of MASs (e.g. [6,7,8,9,10]).

A normative position [4] is the "social burden" associated with individual agents, that is, their obligations, permissions and prohibitions. Depending on what agents do, their normative positions may change – for instance, permissions/prohibitions can be revoked or obligations, once fulfilled, may be removed. Ideally, norms, once captured via some suitable formalism, should be directly executed, thus realising a computational, normative environment wherein agents interact. This is what we mean by *norm-oriented programming*. We try to make headway along this direction by introducing an executable language to specify

P. Noriega et al. (Eds.): COIN 2006 Workshops, LNAI 4386, pp. 177–193, 2007.
© Springer-Verlag Berlin Heidelberg 2007

agents' *normative positions* and manage their changes as agents interact via speech acts [11].

In this paper we present a language that acts as a "machine language" for norms on top of which different, higher-level normative languages can be accommodated. This language can represent distinct flavours of deontic notions and relationships. Although our language is rule-based, we achieve greater flexibility, expressiveness and precision than production systems by allowing constraints to be part of our rules and states of affairs. In this way, normative positions can be further refined. For instance, picture a selling agent that is obliged to deliver a good satisfying some quality requirements before a deadline. Notice that both the quality requirements and the delivery deadline can be regarded as constraints that must be considered as part of the obligations. Thus, when the agent delivers the good satisfying all the constraints, we should regard the obligation as fulfilled. Notice too that since the deadline might eventually be changed, we also require the capability of modifying constraints at run-time. Hence, constraints are considered as first-class citizens in our language.

Although in this paper we restrict to a particular class of MASs, namely electronic institutions [12], our work sets the foundations to specify and implement open regulated MASs via norms.

The structure of this paper is as follows. In the next section we present desirable properties of normative languages. In section 3 we propose a simple normative language that covers all these requirements along with a sketch of an implementation of an interpreter. Section 4 summarises electronic institutions and explains how we capture normative positions of participating agents. We put our language to use by specifying the Dutch Auction protocol in section 5. In section 6 we contrast our approach with a sample of other contemporary work. Finally, we draw conclusions and outline future work in section 7.

2   Norm-Oriented MAS: Desiderata

Our main goal is to produce a language that supports the specification of coordination mechanisms in multi-agent systems by means of norms. For this purpose, we identify below the desirable features we expect in candidate languages.

Explicit Management of normative positions. We take the stance that we cannot refer to agents' mentalistic notions, but only to their observable actions and their normative positions. Notice that as a result of agents' observable, social interactions, their normative positions [4] change. Hence, the first requirement of our language is to support the *explicit management* of agents' normative positions.

General purpose. Turning our attention to theoretical models of norms, we notice that there is a plethora of deontic logics with different axioms to establish relationships among deontic notions. Thus, we require that our language captures different deontic notions along with their relationships. In other words, the language must be of *general purpose* so that it helps MAS designers to encode any axiomatisation, and thus specify the widest range of normative systems as possible.

Pragmatic. In a sense, we pursue a "machine language" for norms on top of which higher-level languages may be accommodated. Along this direction, and from a language designer's point of view, it is fundamental to identify the *norm patterns* (*e.g.*, conditional obligation, time-based permissions and prohibitions, continuous obligation, and so on) in the literature to ensure that the language supports their encoding – this is demonstrated in section 6. In this way, not only shall we be guaranteeing the expressiveness of our language, but also addressing pragmatic concerns by providing *design patterns* to guide and ease MAS design.

Declarative. In order to ease MAS programming, we shall also require our language to be *declarative*, with an implicit execution mechanism to reduce the number of issues designers ought to concentrate on. As an additional benefit, we expect its declarative nature to facilitate verification of properties of the specifications.

3   A Rule Language for Norms

In this section we introduce a rule language for the explicit management of norms associated with a population of agents. Our rule-based language allow us to represent changes in an elegant way and also fulfils the requirement that a normative language should be declarative. The rules depict how normative positions change as agents interact with each other. We achieve greater flexibility, expressiveness and precision by allowing *constraints* [13] to be part of our rules – such constraints associate further restrictions with permissions, prohibitions and obligations.

The building blocks of our language are first-order terms (denoted as τ) and implicitly, universally quantified atomic formulae (denoted as α) without free variables . We shall make use of numbers and arithmetic functions to build terms; arithmetic functions may appear infix, following their usual conventions[1]. We also employ arithmetic relations (*e.g.*, $=$, $\neq$, and so on) as predicate symbols, and these will appear in their usual infix notation with their usual meaning. Atomic formulae with arithmetic relations represent *constraints* on their variables and have a special status, as we explain below. We give a definition of our constraints, a subset of atomic formulae:

Definition 1. *A constraint γ is an atomic formula of the form $\tau \lhd \tau'$, where $\lhd \in \{=, \neq, >, \geq, <, \leq\}$.*

We need to differentiate ordinary atomic formula from constraints. We shall use α' to denote atomic formulae that are *not* constraints.

---

[1] We adopt Prolog's convention using strings starting with a capital letter to represent variables and strings starting with a small letter to represent constants.

Intuitively, a state of affairs is a set of atomic formulae. As we will show below, they can store the state of the environment[2], observable agent attributes and the normative positions of agents:

Definition 2. *A state of affairs $\Delta = \{\alpha_0, \ldots, \alpha_n\}$ is a a finite and possibly empty set of implicitly, universally quantified atomic formulae $\alpha_i, 0 \leq i \leq n, n \in \mathbb{N}$.*

Our rules are constructs of the form $LHS \rightsquigarrow RHS$, where LHS contains a representation of parts of the current state of affairs which, if they hold, will cause the rule to be triggered. RHS depicts the updates to the current state of affairs, yielding the next state of affairs. The grammar in Fig. 1 defines our rules, where x is a variable name and LHS^* is a LHS without set constructors (see below). The Us represent the updates: they add (via operator $\oplus$) or remove (via operator $\ominus$) atomic formulae αs. Furthermore, we make use of a special kind of term, called a *set constructor*, represented as $\{\alpha' \mid LHS^*\}$. This construct is useful when we need to refer to all α's for which LHS^* holds, e.g., $\{p(A, B) \mid A > 20 \wedge B < 100\}$ is the set of atomic formulae $p(A, B)$ such that $A > 20$ and $B < 100$.

$$
\begin{aligned}
R &::= LHS \rightsquigarrow RHS \\
LHS &::= LHS \wedge LHS \mid \neg LHS \mid Lit \\
RHS &::= U \bullet RHS \mid U \\
Lit &::= \alpha \mid x = \{\alpha' \mid LHS^*\} \\
U &::= \oplus\alpha \mid \ominus\alpha
\end{aligned}
$$

Fig. 1. Grammar for Rules

We need to refer to the set of constraints that belongs to a state of affairs. We call $\Gamma = \{\gamma_0, \ldots, \gamma_n\}$ the set of all constraints in Δ.

Definition 3. *Given a state of affairs Δ, relationship $constrs(\Delta, \Gamma)$ holds iff Γ is the smallest set such that for every constraint $\gamma \in \Delta$ then $\gamma \in \Gamma$.*

In the definitions below we rely on the concept of *substitution*, that is, the set of values for variables in a computation, as well as the concept of its application to a term [14]. We now define the semantics of our rules as relationships between states of affairs: rules map an existing state of affairs to a new state of affairs. We adopt the usual semantics of production rules, that is, we exhaustively apply each rule by matching its LHS against the current state of affairs and use the values of variables obtained in this match to instantiate the RHS via $\mathbf{s}^*$.

Definition 4. $\mathbf{s}^*(\Delta, LHS \rightsquigarrow RHS, \Delta')$ *holds iff* $\mathbf{s}_l^*(\Delta, LHS, \{\sigma_1, \ldots, \sigma_n\})$ *and* $\mathbf{s}_r(\Delta, RHS \cdot \sigma_i, \Delta'), 1 \leq i \leq n, n \in \mathbb{N}$, *hold.*

That is, two states of affairs Δ and Δ' are related by a rule $LHS \rightsquigarrow RHS$ if, and only if, we obtain all different substitutions $\{\sigma_1, \ldots, \sigma_n\}$ that make the left-hand

---

[2] We refer to the *state of the environment* as the set of atomic formulae that represent the aspects of the environment in a given point in time.

side match Δ and apply these substitutions to RHS (that is, $RHS \cdot \sigma_i$) in order to build Δ'.

Our rules are *exhaustively* applied on the state of affairs thus considering all matching atomic formulae. We thus need relationship $\mathbf{s}_l^*(\Delta, LHS, \Sigma)$ which obtains in $\Sigma = \{\sigma_0, \ldots, \sigma_n\}$ all possible matches of the left-hand side of a rule:

Definition 5. $\mathbf{s}_l^*(\Delta, LHS, \Sigma)$ *holds, iff* $\Sigma = \{\sigma_1, \ldots, \sigma_n\}$ *is the largest non-empty set such that* $\mathbf{s}_l(\Delta, LHS, \sigma_i), 1 \leq i \leq n, n \in I\!N$, *holds.*

We now define the semantics of the LHS of a rule:

Definition 6. $\mathbf{s}_l(\Delta, LHS, \sigma)$ *holds between state* Δ, *the left-hand side of a rule* LHS *and a substitution* σ *depending on the format of* LHS:

1. $\mathbf{s}_l(\Delta, LHS \wedge LHS', \sigma)$ *holds iff* $\mathbf{s}_l(\Delta, LHS, \sigma')$ *and* $\mathbf{s}_l(\Delta, LHS', \sigma'')$ *hold and* $\sigma = \sigma' \cup \sigma''$.
2. $\mathbf{s}_l(\Delta, \neg LHS, \sigma)$ *holds iff* $\mathbf{s}_l(\Delta, LHS, \sigma)$ *does not hold.*
3. $\mathbf{s}_l(\Delta, \alpha', \sigma)$ *holds iff* $\alpha' \cdot \sigma \in \Delta$ *and* $constrs(\Delta, \Gamma)$ *and* $satisfiable(\Gamma \cdot \sigma)$ *hold.*
4. $\mathbf{s}_l(\Delta, \gamma, \sigma)$ *holds iff* $constrs(\Delta, \Gamma)$ *and* $satisfiable((\Gamma \cup \{\gamma\}) \cdot \sigma)$ *hold.*
5. $\mathbf{s}_l(\Delta, x = \{\alpha' \mid LHS'\}, \sigma)$ *holds iff* $\sigma = \{x/\{\alpha' \cdot \sigma_1, \ldots, \alpha' \cdot \sigma_n\}\}$ *for the largest* $n \in I\!N$ *such that* $\mathbf{s}_l(\Delta, \alpha' \wedge LHS', \sigma_i), 1 \leq i \leq n$

Cases 1-3 depict the semantics of atomic formulae and how their individual substitutions are combined to provide the semantics for a conjunction. Case 4 formalises the semantics of our constraints when they appear on the left-hand side of a rule: we apply the substitution σ to them (thus reflecting any values of variables given by the matchings of atomic formula), then check satisfiability of constraints [3]. Case 5 specifies the semantics for *set constructors*: x is the set of atomic formulae that satisfy the conditions of the set constructor.

Definition 7. *Relation* $\mathbf{s}_r(\Delta, RHS, \Delta')$ *mapping a state* Δ, *the right-hand side of a rule* RHS *and a new state* Δ' *is defined as:*

1. $\mathbf{s}_r(\Delta, (\mathsf{U} \bullet RHS), \Delta')$ *holds iff both* $\mathbf{s}_r(\Delta, \mathsf{U}, \Delta_1)$ *and* $\mathbf{s}_r(\Delta_1, RHS, \Delta')$ *hold.*
2. $\mathbf{s}_r(\Delta, \oplus \alpha', \Delta')$ *holds iff* $\Delta' = \Delta \cup \{\alpha'\}$.
3. $\mathbf{s}_r(\Delta, \oplus \gamma, \Delta') = \mathbf{true}$ *iff* $constrs(\Delta, \Gamma)$ *and* $satisfiable(\Gamma \cup \{\gamma\})$ *hold and* $\Delta' = \Delta \cup \{\gamma\}$.
4. $\mathbf{s}_r(\Delta, \ominus \alpha, \Delta')$ *holds iff* $\Delta' = \Delta \setminus \{\alpha\}$

Case 1 decomposes a conjunction and builds the new state by merging the partial states of each update. Case 2 cater for the insertion of atomic formulae α' which do not conform to the syntax of constraints. Case 3 defines how a constraint is added to a state Δ: the new constraint is checked whether it can be satisfied with constraints Γ and then it is added to Δ'. Case 4 cater for the removal of atomic formulae.

We extend $\mathbf{s}^*$ to handle sequences of rules: $\mathbf{s}^*(\Delta_0, \langle R_1, \ldots, R_n \rangle, \Delta_n)$ holds iff $\mathbf{s}^*(\Delta_{i-1}, R_i, \Delta_i), 1 \leq i \leq n$ hold.

---

[3] Our work builds on standard technologies for constraint solving – in particular, we have been experimenting with SICStus Prolog constraint satisfaction libraries.

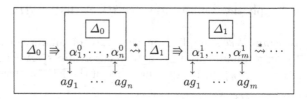

Fig. 2. Semantics as a Sequence of Δ's

The semantics above define an infinite sequence of states $\langle \Delta_0, \Delta_1, \ldots \rangle$ if $\mathbf{s}^*(\Delta_i, \{\mathsf{R}_1, \ldots, \mathsf{R}_n\}, \Delta_{i+1})$, that is, Δ_{i+1} (obtained by applying the rules to Δ_i) is used to obtain Δ_{i+2} and so on. Fig. 2 illustrates how this sequence can accommodate the intervention of agents sending/receiving messages. The diagram shows an initial state Δ_0 (possibly empty) that is offered (represented by "$\Rightarrow$") to a set of agents $\{ag_1, \ldots, ag_n\}$. These agents exchange messages, adding a record (via "$\updownarrow$") $\{\alpha_1^0, \ldots, \alpha_n^0\}$ of these messages to Δ_0. After the agents add their utterances, then the rules are exhaustively applied (represented by "$\overset{*}{\rightsquigarrow}$") to $\Delta_0 \cup \{\alpha_1^0, \ldots, \alpha_n^0\}$. The resulting state Δ_1 is, on its turn, offered to agents, and so on.

3.1 Implementation

The semantics above provide a basis for the implementation of our rule interpreter. Although we have implemented it with SICStus Prolog we show such interpreter in Fig. 3 as a logic program, interspersed with built-in Prolog predicates; for easy referencing, we show each clause with a number on its left.

---

1. $\mathbf{s}^*(\Delta, Rules, \Delta') \leftarrow$
   $\mathrm{findall}(\langle RHS, \Sigma \rangle, (\mathrm{member}((LHS \rightsquigarrow RHS), Rules), \mathbf{s}_l^*(\Delta, LHS, \Sigma)), RHSs),$
   $\mathbf{s}_r'(\Delta, RHSs, \Delta')$
2. $\mathbf{s}_l^*(\Delta, LHS, \Sigma) \leftarrow \mathrm{findall}(\sigma, \mathbf{s}_l(\Delta, LHS, \sigma), \Sigma)$
3. $\mathbf{s}_l(\Delta, (LHS \wedge LHS'), \sigma) \leftarrow \mathbf{s}_l(\Delta, LHS, \sigma'), \mathbf{s}_l(\Delta, LHS', \sigma''), \mathrm{union}(\sigma', \sigma'', \sigma)$
4. $\mathbf{s}_l(\Delta, \neg LHS, \sigma) \leftarrow \neg \, \mathbf{s}_l(\Delta, LHS, \sigma)$
5. $\mathbf{s}_l(\Delta, \alpha', \sigma) \leftarrow \mathrm{member}(\alpha' \cdot \sigma, \Delta), constrs(\Delta, \Gamma), \mathrm{satisfiable}(\Gamma \cdot \sigma)$
6. $\mathbf{s}_l(\Delta, \gamma, \sigma) \leftarrow constrs(\Delta, \Gamma), \mathrm{satisfiable}([\gamma \mid \Gamma] \cdot \sigma)$
7. $\mathbf{s}_l(\Delta, x = \{\alpha' \mid LHS'\}, \{x/AllAlphas\}) \leftarrow \mathrm{findall}(\alpha' \cdot \sigma, \mathbf{s}_l(\Delta, \alpha' \wedge LHS', \sigma), AllAlphas)$
8. $\mathbf{s}_r'(\Delta, [\,], \Delta') \leftarrow \Delta = \Delta'$
9. $\mathbf{s}_r'(\Delta, [\langle RHS, \Sigma \rangle \mid RHSs], \Delta') \leftarrow \mathbf{s}_r''(\Delta, RHS, \Sigma, \Delta''), \mathbf{s}_r'(\Delta'', RHSs, \Delta')$
10. $\mathbf{s}_r''(\Delta, RHS, [\,], \Delta') \leftarrow \Delta = \Delta'$
11. $\mathbf{s}_r''(\Delta, RHS, [\sigma \mid \Sigma], \Delta') \leftarrow \mathbf{s}_r(\Delta, RHS \cdot \sigma, \Delta''), \mathbf{s}_r''(\Delta'', RHS, \Sigma, \Delta')$
12. $\mathbf{s}_r(\Delta, (U \bullet RHS), \Delta') \leftarrow \mathbf{s}_r(\Delta, U, \Delta_1), \mathbf{s}_r(\Delta_1, RHS, \Delta')$
13. $\mathbf{s}_r(\Delta, \oplus\alpha', [\alpha' \mid \Delta]) \leftarrow$
14. $\mathbf{s}_r(\Delta, \ominus\alpha, \Delta') \leftarrow \mathrm{delete}(\Delta, \alpha, \Delta')$
15. $\mathbf{s}_r(\Delta, \oplus\gamma, [\gamma \mid \Delta]) \leftarrow constrs(\Delta, \Gamma), \mathrm{satisfiable}([\gamma \mid \Gamma])$

Fig. 3. An Interpreter for Rules

Clause 1 contains the top-most definition: given an existing Δ and a set of rules $Rules$, it obtains the next state Δ' by finding all those rules in $Rules$ (picked by the `member` built-in) whose LHS holds in Δ (checked via the auxiliary definition $\mathbf{s}_l^*$). This clause then uses the RHS of those rules with their respective sets of substitutions Σ as the arguments of $\mathbf{s}'_r$ to finally obtain Δ'. Clause 2 implements $\mathbf{s}^*_l$: it finds all the different ways that the left-hand side LHS of a rule can be matched in Δ – the individual σ's are stored in sets Σ of substitutions, as a result of the `findall/3` execution. Clauses 8 and 9 show how $\mathbf{s}'_r$ computes the new state from a list $RHSs$ of pairs $\langle RHS, \Sigma \rangle$ (obtained in the second body goal of clause 1): it picks out each pair $\langle RHS, \Sigma \rangle$ and uses $\mathbf{s}''_r$ (clauses 10 and 11) to compute each intermediate state of affairs after applying the RHS to Δ via predicate $\mathbf{s}_r$ for all the substitutions in Σ. Clauses 3-7 and 12-15 are, respectively, adaptations of the cases depicted in Def. 6 and Def. 7.

4   Electronic Institutions

Our work extends *electronic institutions* (EIs) [12], providing them with an explicit normative layer. There are two major features in EIs: the *states* and *illocutions* (*i.e.*, messages) uttered (*i.e.*, sent) by those agents taking part in the EI. The states are connected via edges labelled with the illocutions that ought to be sent at that particular point in the EI. Another important feature in EIs are the agents' *roles*: these are labels that allow agents with the same role to be treated collectively thus helping engineers abstract away from individuals. We define below the class of illocutions we aim at – these are a special kind of term:

Definition 8. *Illocutions* I *are terms* $p(ag, r, ag', r', \tau, t)$ *where* p *is an illocutionary particle (e.g., ask); ag, ag'* *are agent identifiers;* r, r' *are role labels;* τ *is a term with the actual content of the message and* $t \in \mathbb{N}$ *is a time stamp.*

We shall refer to illocutions that may have uninstantiated (free) variables as *illocution schemes*, denoted by $\bar{\mathsf{I}}$.

Another important concept in EIs we employ here is that of a *scene*. Scenes offer means to break down larger protocols into smaller ones with specific purposes. We can uniquely refer to the point of the protocol where an illocution I was uttered by the pair (s, w) where s is a scene name and w is the state from which an edge labelled with $\bar{\mathsf{I}}$ leads to another state.

An institutional state is a state of affairs that stores all utterances during the execution of a MAS, also keeping a record of the state of the environment, all observable attributes of agents and all obligations, permissions and prohibitions associated with the agents that constitute their normative positions.

We differentiate seven kinds of atomic formulae in our institutional states Δ, with the following intuitive meanings:

1. $oav(o, a, v)$ – object (or agent) o has an attribute a with value v.
2. $att(s, w, \mathsf{I})$ – an agent attempted to get illocution I accepted at state w of scene s.
3. $utt(s, w, \mathsf{I})$ – I was accepted as a legal utterance at w of s.
4. $ctr(s, w, t_s)$ – the execution of scene s reached state w at time t_s.
5. $obl(s, w, \bar{\mathsf{I}})$ – $\bar{\mathsf{I}}$ ought to be uttered at w of s.
6. $per(s, w, \bar{\mathsf{I}})$ – $\bar{\mathsf{I}}$ is *permitted* to be uttered at w of s.
7. $prh(s, w, \bar{\mathsf{I}})$ – $\bar{\mathsf{I}}$ is *prohibited* at w of s.

We only allow fully ground attributes, illocutions and state control formulae (cases 1-4 above) to be present[4]; however, in formulae 5-7 s and w may be variables and $\bar{I}$ may contain variables. We shall use formulae 4 to represent state change in a scene in relation to a global clock. We shall use formulae 5–7 above to represent normative positions of agents within EIs.

We do not "hardwire" deontic notions in our semantics: the predicates above represent deontic operators but not their relationships. These are captured with rules (also called in this context institutional rules), conferring the generality claimed on section 2 on our approach as different deontic relationships can be forged, as we show below. We can confer different grades of enforcement on EIs . On the one hand, we can transform only legal attempts into accepted utterances:

$$\begin{pmatrix} att(S,\,W,\,I)\wedge \\ per(S,\,W,\,I)\wedge\neg\,prh(S,\,W,\,I) \end{pmatrix} \rightsquigarrow \begin{pmatrix} \ominus att(S,\,W,\,I)\bullet \\ \oplus utt(S,\,W,\,I) \end{pmatrix} \tag{1}$$

This rule states that if an agent attempts to say something and it is permitted and not prohibited, then that attempt becomes a (confirmed) utterance. On the other hand, we can allow agents to do certain illegal actions under more harsh penalties:

$$\begin{pmatrix} att(S,\,W,\,inform(Ag_1,\,R,\,Ag_2,\,R',\,info(Ag_3,\,C),\,T))\wedge \\ Ag_1\neq Ag_2 \wedge Ag_1\neq Ag_3 \wedge Ag_2 \neq Ag_3 \end{pmatrix}$$
$$\rightsquigarrow \tag{2}$$
$$\begin{pmatrix} \ominus att(S,\,W,\,inform(Ag_1,\,R,\,Ag_2,\,R',\,info(Ag_3,\,C),\,T))\bullet \\ \oplus utt(S,\,W,\,inform(Ag_1,\,R,\,Ag_2,\,R',\,info(Ag_3,\,C),\,T)) \end{pmatrix}$$

The rule above states that if an agent attempts to reveal to Ag_2 (secret) information about agent Ag_3, it is accepted without taking into account if it is forbidden or not. In both cases (rules 1 and 2), we can punish agents that violate prohibitions. Although we can address all forbidden utterances if we use a variable as the third parameter of att and prh, the following rule punishes only the revelation of beliefs of third parties:

$$\begin{pmatrix} att(S,\,W,\,inform(Ag_1,\,R,\,Ag_2,\,R',\,info(Ag_3,\,C),\,T))\wedge \\ Ag_1\neq Ag_2 \wedge Ag_1\neq Ag_3 \wedge Ag_2 \neq Ag_3\wedge \\ prh(S,\,W,\,inform(Ag_1,\,R,\,Ag_2,\,R',\,info(Ag_3,\,C),\,T))\wedge \\ oav(Ag_1,\,rep,\,V_{Rep})\wedge(V'_{Rep}=V_{Rep}-10) \end{pmatrix}$$
$$\rightsquigarrow$$
$$\left(\ominus oav(Ag_1,\,rep,\,V_{Rep})\bullet\oplus oav(Ag_1,\,rep,\,V'_{Rep})\right)$$

The rule above states that when agent Ag_1 tries to reveal to Ag_2 information about agent Ag_3, it gets punished. Notice that agents can be punished by decreasing the value of any of their observable attributes. But only for exemplifying purposes, we use here an attribute called rep (for reputation) that models in which degree an agent is norm compliant. In the example, the punish consists

---

[4] We allow agents to utter whatever they want (via att formulae). However, the illegal utterances may be discarded and/or may cause sanctions, depending on the deontic notions we want or need to implement. The utt formulae are thus *confirmations* of the att formulae.

in decreasing the trust of agents to share information with Ag_1, that is, the value of Ag_1's reputation is decreased by 10.

5   Example: The Dutch Auction

We now illustrate the pragmatics of our norm-oriented language, as required in section 2, by specifying, with the rules of Fig. 4, the auction protocol for a fish market as described in [15]. In the fish market several scenes [12] take place simultaneously, at different locations, but with some causal continuity. The principal scene is the auction itself, where buyers bid for boxes of fish that are presented by an auctioneer who calls prices in descending order, the so-called *downward bidding protocol*, a variation of the traditional Dutch auction protocol that proceeds as follows: 1. The auctioneer chooses a good out of a lot of goods that is sorted according to the order in which sellers deliver their goods to the sellers' admitter; 2. With a chosen good, the auctioneer opens a *bidding round* by quoting offers downward from the good's starting price, previously fixed by a sellers' admitter, as long as these price quotations are above a *reserve price* previously defined by the seller; 3. For each price the auctioneer calls, several situations might arise during the open round described below. 4. The first three steps repeat until there are no more goods left.

The situations arising in step 3 are:

Multiple bids – Several buyers submit their bids at the current price. In this case, a collision comes about, the good is not sold to any buyer, and the auctioneer restarts the round at a higher price;

One bid – Only one buyer submits a bid at the current price. The good is sold to this buyer whenever his credit can support his bid. Otherwise, the round is restarted by the auctioneer at a higher price, the unsuccessful bidder is fined;

No bids – No buyer submits a bid at the current price. If the reserve price has not been reached yet, the auctioneer quotes a new price obtained by decreasing the current price according to the price step. Otherwise, the auctioneer declares the good as *withdrawn* and closes the round.

5.1   Proposed Solution

  I. **Multiple bids** – it obliges the auctioneer to inform the buyers, whenever a collision comes about, about the collision and to restart the bidding round at a higher price (in this case, 120% of the collision price). Notice that X will hold all the utterances at scene *dutch* and state w_4 issued by buyer agents that bid for an item It at price P at time T_0 after the last offer. We obtain the last offers by checking that there are no further offers whose time-stamps are greater than the time-stamp of the first one. If the number of illocutions in X is greater than one, the rule fires the obligation above;

 II. **One bid/winner determination** – If only one bid has occurred during the current bidding round and the credit of the bidding agent is greater than or equal to the price of the good in auction, the rule adds the obligation for the auctioneer to inform all the buyers about the sale.

$(X = \{ \alpha_0 | \alpha_1 \wedge \neg (\alpha_2 \wedge T_2 > T_1) \wedge T_0 > T_1 \} \wedge | X | > 1) \rightsquigarrow (\oplus \alpha_3 \bullet \oplus \alpha_4 \bullet \oplus (P_2 > P * 1.2))$

$where \begin{cases} \alpha_0 = utt(dutch, w_4, inform(A_1, buyer, Au, auct, bid(It, P), T_0)) \\ \alpha_1 = utt(dutch, w_3, inform(Au, auct, all, buyer, offer(It, P), T_1)), \\ \alpha_2 = utt(dutch, w_3, inform(Au, auct, all, buyer, offer(It, P), T_2)) \\ \alpha_3 = obl(dutch, w_5, inform(Au, auct, all, buyer, collision(It, P), T_2)) \\ \alpha_4 = obl(dutch, w_3, inform(Au, auct, all, buyer, offer(It, P_2), T_3)) \end{cases}$ (I)

$\begin{pmatrix} X = \{ \alpha_0 | \alpha_1 \wedge \neg (\alpha_2 \wedge T_2 > T_1) \wedge T_0 > T_1 \} \wedge \\ | X | = 1 \wedge oav(A_1, credit, C) \wedge C \geq P \end{pmatrix} \rightsquigarrow (\oplus \alpha_3)$

$where \begin{cases} \alpha_0 = utt(dutch, w_4, inform(A_1, buyer, Au, auct, bid(It, P), T_0)) \\ \alpha_1 = utt(dutch, w_3, inform(Au, auct, all, buyer, offer(It, P), T_1)), \\ \alpha_2 = utt(dutch, w_3, inform(Au, auct, all, buyer, offer(It, P), T_2)) \\ \alpha_3 = obl(dutch, w_5, inform(Au, auct, all, buyer, sold(It, P, A_1), T_4)) \end{cases}$ (II)

$(\alpha_0 \wedge \neg (\alpha_1 \wedge T2 > T) \wedge oav(Ag, credit, C) \wedge C < P) \rightsquigarrow (\oplus \alpha_2)$

$where \begin{cases} \alpha_0 = utt(dutch, w_3, inform(Au, auct, A, buyer, offer(It, P), T)) \\ \alpha_1 = utt(dutch, w_3, inform(Au, auct, A, buyer, offer(It, P), T_2)) \\ \alpha_2 = prh(dutch, w_4, inform(A, buyer, Au, auct, bid(It, P_2), T_3)) \end{cases}$ (III)

$\begin{pmatrix} X = \{ \alpha_0 | \alpha_1 \wedge \neg (\alpha_2 \wedge T_2 > T_1) \wedge T_0 > T_1 \} \wedge \\ | X | = 1 \wedge oav(A_1, credit, C) \wedge C < P \end{pmatrix} \rightsquigarrow \begin{pmatrix} \ominus oav(A_1, credit, C) \bullet \\ \oplus oav(A_1, credit, C_2) \bullet \oplus \alpha_3 \bullet \\ \oplus (C_2 = C - P * 0.1) \bullet \oplus (P_2 = P * 1.2) \end{pmatrix}$

$where \begin{cases} \alpha_0 = utt(dutch, w_4, inform(A_1, buyer, Au, auct, bid(It, P), T_0)) \\ \alpha_1 = utt(dutch, w_3, inform(Au, auct, all, buyer, offer(It, P), T_1)), \\ \alpha_2 = utt(dutch, w_3, inform(Au, auct, all, buyer, offer(It, P), T_2)) \\ \alpha_3 = obl(dutch, w_5, inform(Au, auct, all, buyer, offer(It, P_2), T_3)) \end{cases}$ (IV)

$\begin{pmatrix} ctr(dutch, w_5, T_n) \wedge \alpha_0 \wedge \neg (\alpha_1 \wedge T_2 > T) \wedge \\ timeout(dutch, w_4, w_5, T_3) \wedge T_3 > T \wedge \\ oav(IT, reservation\_price, RP) \wedge \\ oav(IT, decrement\_rate, DR) \wedge RP < P - DR \end{pmatrix} \rightsquigarrow \begin{pmatrix} \oplus \alpha_2 \bullet \\ \oplus (P2 = P - DR) \end{pmatrix}$

$where \begin{cases} \alpha_0 = utt(dutch, w3, inform(Au, auct, all, buyer, offer(IT, P), T)) \\ \alpha_1 = utt(dutch, w3, inform(Au, auct, all, buyer, offer(IT, P), T_2)) \\ \alpha_2 = obl(dutch, w5, inform(Au, auct, all, buyer, offer(IT, P2), T_4)) \end{cases}$ (V)

$\begin{pmatrix} ctr(dutch, w_5, T_n) \wedge \alpha_0 \wedge \neg (\alpha_1 \wedge T_2 > T) \wedge \\ timeout(dutch, w_4, w_5, T_3) \wedge T_3 > T \wedge oav(It, reservation\_price, RP) \wedge \\ oav(It, decrement\_rate, DR) \wedge RP \geq P - DR \end{pmatrix} \rightsquigarrow (\oplus \alpha_2)$

$where \begin{cases} \alpha_0 = utt(dutch, w_3, inform(Au, auct, all, buyer, offer(It, P), T)) \\ \alpha_1 = utt(dutch, w_3, inform(Au, auct, all, buyer, offer(It, P), T_2)) \\ \alpha_2 = obl(dutch, w_5, inform(Au, auct, all, buyer, withdrawn(It), T_3)) \end{cases}$ (VI)

Fig. 4. Rules for the Dutch Auction Protocol

III. **Prevention** – It prevents agents from issuing bids they cannot afford (their credit is insufficient) and states that if agent Ag's credit is less than P (the last offer the auctioneer called for item It, at state w_3 of scene $dutch$), then agent Ag is prohibited to bid.

IV. **Punishment** – It punishes agents when issuing a winning bid they cannot pay for. More precisely, the rule punishes an agent A_1 by decreasing his credit of 10% of the value of the good being auctioned. The oav predicate on the LHS of the rule represents the current credit of the offending agent. The rule also adds an obligation for the auctioneer to restart the bidding

round and the constraint that the new offer should be greater than 120%
of the old price.

V. **No bids/New Price** – It checks if there were no bids and the next price
is greater than the reservation price. If so, it adds the obligation for the
auctioneer to start a new bidding round. Rule 5 checks that the current
scene state is w_5, whether a timeout has expired after the last offer and
whether the new price is greater than the reservation price. If so, the rule
adds the obligation for the auctioneer to offer the item at a lower price. By
retrieving the last offer we gather the last offer price. By checking the *oav*
predicates we gather the values of the reservation price and the decrement
rate for item *It*.

VI. **No bids/withdrawal** – It checks if there were no bids and the next price
is less than the reservation price, then adds the obligation for the auctioneer
to withdraw the item. Rule 6 checks that the current institutional state is
w_5, whether a timeout has occurred after the last offer and whether the
new offer price is greater than the reservation price. If the *LHS* holds, the
rule fires to add the obligation for the auctioneer to withdraw the item. By
checking the last offer we gather the last offer price. By checking the *oav*
predicates we gather the values of the reservation price and the decrement
rate for the price of item *It*.

6   Comparison with Other Normative Languages

In this section we compare our proposal with other normative languages in the
literature. We concentrate on different approaches, explaining how we can capture a wide range of normative notions from these formalisms using our rule
language. In doing so, we can provide an *implementation* for some of these formalisms.

A norm from [16] is composed of several parts: the norm condition is the
declarative description of the norm and the context in which it applies; the *violation condition* (a formula defining when the norm is violated); the *detection
mechanism* describing the mechanisms that can be used for detecting violations;
3) the *sanctions* defined as actions to punish the agents' violation of the norm;
and the *repairs* (a set of actions that are used for recovering the system after
the occurrence of a violation). Through the condition (IF) and temporal operators (BEFORE and AFTER), which are considered optional, norms can be made
applicable only to certain situations. Temporal operators can be applied to a
deadline or to an action or predicate.

Norms as defined in [16] can be translated into our rules by specifying the
violation conditions on the *LHS* and sanctions and repairs on the *RHS*. Since
we consider illocutions as the only actions that can be performed in an electronic
institution, actions need to be translated into illocutions uttering that the action
has been done. We call this operation *contextualisation*. In general, the translation of the norms of [16] into our rules is straightforward. The permission of an
action is translated as a rule that converts the attempt to utter illocution, *i.e.*,

$att(S, W, I)$, into the illocution being uttered, *i.e.*, $utt(S, W, I)$. The prohibition of an action can be translated into a rule that ignores the attempt to utter the illocution, and, optionally, a sanction to the violation can be imposed. The obligation of an action needs to be translated into two rules, *viz.*, a rule to sanction an agent when it does not fulfil an obligation (*i.e.*, not uttering the expected illocution at the right scene and state), and a rule to remove the obligation once it is fulfilled. The translation of temporal clauses (**BEFORE** and **AFTER**) can be achieved by adding to the LHS of the rule the condition that the time in which the attempt is done has to be less (or greater) than the deadline.

Although the work in [3] proposes a framework that covers several topics of normative multi-agent systems we shall focus on its definition of norm, in which *addressees* stands for the set of agents that have to comply with the norm; *beneficiaries* stands for the set of agents that profit from the compliance of the norm; *normativegoals* stands for the set of goals that ought to be achieved by addressee agents; *rewards* are received by addressee agents if they satisfy the normative goals; *punishments* are imposed to addressee agent when they do not satisfy the normative goals; *context* specifies the preconditions to apply the norm and *exceptions* when it is not applicable. Notice that a norm must always have addressees, normative goals and a context; *rewards* and *punishments* are disjoint sets, and *context* and *exceptions* too.

A norm from [3] can be translated into the following rule schema to detect its violation:

$$(\textit{context} \ \wedge \neg \ \textit{exception} \wedge \neg \ \textit{goal}') \rightsquigarrow \textit{punishments}$$

where *context* and *exception* are predicates obtained through contextualisation[5] for specifying the context and exceptions mentioned in the norm, *goal'* is the contextualised normative goal (which includes the addressee and possible beneficiaries). Component *punishments* are contextualised actions obtained from the norm. This rule captures that in a particular context which is not an exception of the norm and whose goal has not yet been fulfilled the actions defined by *punishments* should be executed.

Rewards can also be specified via the rule schema:

$$(\textit{context} \ \wedge \neg \ \textit{exception} \wedge \textit{goal}') \rightsquigarrow \textit{rewards}$$

where *rewards* are also contextualised actions obtained from the norm. This rule specifies that a reward should be given when *addressee* agents comply with the norm, which is when the norm is applicable and the contextualised normative goal (*goal'*) has been achieved.

Event calculus is used in [6] for the specification of protocols. Event calculus is a formalism to represent reasoning about actions or events and their effects in a logic programming framework and is based on a many-sorted first-order predicate calculus. Predicates that change with time are called *fluents*. In [6] obligations, permissions, empowerments, capabilities and sanctions are formalised by means

---

[5] Recall that contextualisation is the process of transforming actions into illocutions stating that actions have been brought about.

of fluents – prohibitions are not formalised in [6] as a fluent since they assume that every action not permitted is forbidden by default. If we translate all the *holdsAt* predicates into *utt* predicates, we can translate the obligations and permissions of [6] by including the rest of conditions in the *LHS* of the normative rules. However, since there is no concrete definition of norm, we cannot state that the approach in [6] is fully translatable into our rules.

Although event calculus models time, the deontic fluents specified in the example of [6] are not enough to inform an agent about all types of duties. For instance, to inform an agent that it is obliged to perform an action before a deadline, it is necessary to show the agent the obligation fluent and the part of the theory that models the violation of the deadline.

In [7] we find a proposal to represent norms via rules written in a modal logic with temporal operators called hyMITL$^\pm$. It combines CTL$^\pm$ with Metric Interval Temporal Logic (MITL) as well as features of hybrid logics. That proposal uses the technique of formula progression from the TLPlan planning system to monitor social expectations until they are fulfilled or violated.

Intuitively, our rules capture formulae $\mathsf{AG}^+(LHS \to \mathsf{X}^+ RHS)$ where *LHS* and *RHS* are atomic formulae without temporal operators. As we build the next state of affairs by applying the operations on the *RHS* of the fired rules, we cannot use any other temporal operator in the *RHS* of our rules. Furthermore, since our state of affairs has non-monotonic features we cannot reason over the past of any formulae. We can only do it with predicates with time-stamps, like the *utt* predicate, that are not removed from the state of affairs.

We can capture the meaning of the X^- operator when it is used on the *LHS* of the hyMITL rule: $\mathsf{X}^- \phi$ is intuitively equivalent to $ctr(S, W, T_s) \land \phi(T_0) \land T_0 = T_s - 1$. Moreover, we can also translate the U^+ operator when it is used in the *RHS* of the hyMITL rule: $\phi \, \mathsf{U}^+ \psi$ is roughly equivalent to $\psi \rightsquigarrow \ominus\phi$. Although we cannot use all the temporal operators on the *RHS* of our rules, we can obtain equivalent results by imposing certain restrictions in the set of rules. $\mathsf{F}^+\phi$ can be achieved if $\oplus\phi$ appears on the *RHS* of a rule and it is possible that the rule fires. $\mathsf{G}^+\phi$ can be achieved after ϕ is added and no rule that could fire removes it. Time intervals can be translated into comparisons of time-points as shown in the previous example.

In [17] the language Social Integrity Constraints (SIC) is proposed. This language's constructs check whether some events have occurred and some conditions hold to add new expectations, optionally with constraints. Although syntactically their language is very similar to ours, they are semantically different. Different from their use of abduction and Constraint Handling Rules (CHR) to execute their expectations, we use a forward chaining approach. Despite the fact that expectations they use are quite similar to obligations and they mention how expectations are treated, that is, what happens when an expectation is fulfilled or when it is not, and state the possibility of SICs being violated, no mechanism to regulate agents' behaviour like the punishment of offending agents or repairing actions are offered.

The work in [8] proposes the Object Constraint Language (OCL) for the specification of artificial institutions. The example of this work commits an auctioneer not to declare a price lower than the agreed reservation price. As shown in section 5, we can also express (rule VI) the case that the auctioneer is obliged to withdraw the good when the call price becomes lower than the reservation price. As for [8], we cannot perform an exhaustive analysis of the language because neither the syntax nor the semantics are specified.

The approach in [18] uses Answer Set Programming (ASP) [19] for the specification and analysis of agent-based social institutions. They state that ASP overcomes many Prolog limitations since, instead of calculating only the first possible solution, it provides all answers to a query. Although ASP is suitable for institution analysis, it may not be so efficient as required for institution execution since only one answer is needed, *viz.*, the next state of affairs.

As for institution modelling, they include institutional facts and actions, permissions, prohibitions, obligations (only) with deadline, violations and institutional power. The latter, not included in our EI model: it specifies that a certain agent is empowered to perform a specified institutional action in a given institution. However, they do not include the possibility of rewarding for norm compliance nor managing other constraints than deadlines.

The work in [9] reports on the translation of the normative language presented in [16] into Jess rules to monitor and enforce norms. This language captures the deontic notions of permission, prohibition and obligation in several cases: absolute norms, conditional norms, norms with deadline and norms in temporal relation with another event. Absolute norms are directly translated into Jess facts; conditional norms are directly translated into rules that add the deontic facts when the condition holds; norms with deadline are translated into rules that add conditional norms after the deadline has passed. Finally, norms in temporal relation with other events are translated into rules that check if those events have occurred.

Our proposal bears strong similarities with the work reported in [20] where norms are represented as rules of a production system. We notice that our rules can express their notions of contracts and their monitoring (*i.e.*, fulfilment and violation of obligations). However, in [20] constraints can only be used to depict the left-hand side of a rule, that is, the situation(s) when a rule is applicable – constraints are not manipulated the way we do. Furthermore, in that work there is no indication as to how individual agents will know about their normative situation; a diagram introduces the architecture, but it is not clear who/what will apply the rules to update the normative aspects of the system nor how agents synchronise their activities.

After analysing all these approaches we have found some norm patterns that they have in common. Norms can be conditional or can have temporal constraints, that is, they establish relationships between time-points or events or they hold periodically. Our rules can capture the patterns from rather disparate formalisms, thus fulfilling the requirement of general purpose mentioned in section 2.

7   Conclusions and Future Work

In this paper we have introduced a formalism for the explicit management of the normative position of agents in electronic institutions. Ours is a rule language in which constraints can be specified and changed at run-time, conferring expressiveness and precision on our constructs. The semantics of our formalism defines a kind of production system in which rules are exhaustively applied to a state of affairs, leading to the next state of affairs. The normative positions are updated via rules, depending on the messages agents send.

Our formalism addresses the points of a desiderata for normative languages introduced in section 2. We have explored our proposal in this paper by specifying a version of the Dutch Auction protocol. We illustrate how our language can provide other (higher-level) normative languages with a computational model (*i.e.*, an *implementation*) thus making it possible for normative languages proposed with more theoretical concerns in mind to become executable.

Although our language is not as expressive as the language of [7] since we cannot represent all the temporal modalities, our language is not a language for checking properties of a system but for specifying its behaviour.

Furthermore, we notice that although our implementation directly captures the proposed formal semantics, it is not as efficient as other implementations for rule-based systems, such as the Rete algorithm [21].

As for future work, we would like to overcome the efficiency issue by providing an implementation based on the Rete algorithm.

We would also like to generalise our language to cope with arbitrary actions, rather than just speech acts among agents – this would allow our work to address any type of open multi-agent system. We would also like to improve the semantics of the language in order to support the use of temporal operators for the management of time.

Our semantics describe a transition system similar to the one presented in [22] – we would like to carry out a careful comparison between that work and our operational semantics.

An interesting avenue of investigation is to endow agents with reasoning abilities over our rules. Such reasoning, possibly using resource-bounded forward and backward chaining mechanisms, would allow agents to anticipate the effects of their actions, that is, the punishments or rewards for, respectively, norm violation and norm compliance.

We also want to investigate the verification of norms (along the lines of our work in [23]) expressed in our rule language, with a view to detecting, for instance, obligations that cannot be fulfilled, prohibitions that will prevent progress, inconsistencies and so on.

Acknowledgements. This work was partially funded by the Spanish Education and Science Ministry as part of the projects TIN2006-15662-C02-01 and 2006-5-0I-099. García-Camino enjoys an I3P grant from the Spanish Council for Scientific Research (CSIC).

References

1. Wooldridge, M.: An Introduction to Multiagent Systems. John Wiley & Sons, Chichester, UK (2002)
2. Dignum, F.: Autonomous Agents with Norms. Artificial Intelligence and Law 7(1), 69–79 (1999)
3. López y López, F.: Social Power and Norms: Impact on agent behaviour. PhD thesis, Univ. of Southampton (2003)
4. Sergot, M.: A Computational Theory of Normative Positions. ACM Trans. Comput. Logic 2(4), 581–622 (2001)
5. Shoham, Y., Tennenholtz, M.: On Social Laws for Artificial Agent Societies: Offline Design. Artificial Intelligence 73(1-2), 231–252 (1995)
6. Artikis, A., Kamara, L., Pitt, J., Sergot, M.: A Protocol for Resource Sharing in Norm-Governed Ad Hoc Networks. In: Leite, J.A., Omicini, A., Torroni, P., Yolum, p. (eds.) DALT 2004. LNCS (LNAI), vol. 3476, Springer, Heidelberg (2005)
7. Cranefield, S.: A Rule Language for Modelling and Monitoring Social Expectations in Multi-Agent Systems. Technical Report 2005/01, Univ. of Otago (2005)
8. Fornara, N., Viganò, F., Colombetti, M.: An Event Driven Approach to Norms in Artificial Institutions. In: Boissier, O., Padget, J., Dignum, V., Lindemann, G., Matson, E., Ossowski, S., Sichman, J.S., Vázquez-Salceda, J. (eds.) Coordination, Organizations, Institutions, and Norms in Multi-Agent Systems. LNCS (LNAI), vol. 3913, pp. 142–154. Springer, Heidelberg (2006)
9. García-Camino, A., Noriega, P., Rodríguez-Aguilar, J.A.: Implementing Norms in Electronic Institutions. In: Procs. 4th AAMAS (2005)
10. García-Camino, A., Rodríguez-Aguilar, J.A., Sierra, C., Vasconcelos, W.: A Distributed Architecture for Norm-Aware Agent Societies. In: Baldoni, M., Endriss, U., Omicini, A., Torroni, P. (eds.) DALT 2005. LNCS (LNAI), vol. 3904, Springer, Heidelberg (2006)
11. Searle, J.: Speech Acts, An Essay in the Philosophy of Language. Cambridge University Press, Cambridge (1969)
12. Esteva, M.: Electronic Institutions: from Specification to Development. PhD thesis, Universitat Politècnica de Catalunya (UPC), IIIA monography vol. 19 (2003)
13. Jaffar, J., Maher, M.J.: Constraint Logic Programming: A Survey. Journal of Logic Progr. 19/20, 503–581 (1994)
14. Fitting, M.: First-Order Logic and Automated Theorem Proving. Springer, New York, USA (1990)
15. Noriega, P.: Agent-Mediated Auctions: The Fishmarket Metaphor. PhD thesis, Universitat Autònoma de Barcelona (UAB), IIIA monography vol. 8 (1997)
16. Vázquez-Salceda, J., Aldewereld, H., Dignum, F.: Implementing Norms in Multiagent Systems. In: Lindemann, G., Denzinger, J., Timm, I.J., Unland, R. (eds.) MATES 2004. LNCS (LNAI), vol. 3187, Springer, Heidelberg (2004)
17. Alberti, M., Gavanelli, M., Lamma, E., Mello, P., Torroni, P.: Specification and Verification of Agent Interactions using Integrity Social Constraints. Technical Report DEIS-LIA-006-03, University of Bologna (2003)
18. Cliffe, O., De Vos, M., Padget, J.: Specifying and Analysing Agent-based Social Institutions using Answer Set Programming. In: Boissier, O., Padget, J., Dignum, V., Lindemann, G., Matson, E., Ossowski, S., Sichman, J.S., Vázquez-Salceda, J. (eds.) Coordination, Organizations, Institutions, and Norms in Multi-Agent Systems. LNCS (LNAI), vol. 3913, pp. 99–113. Springer, Heidelberg (2006)

19. Baral, C.: Knowledge Representation, Reasoning and Declarative Problem Solving. Cambridge Press, Cambridge (2003)
20. Lopes Cardoso, H., Oliveira, E.: Towards an Institutional Environment using Norms for Contract Performance. LNCS (LNAI). Springer, Heidelberg (in press)
21. Forgy, C.: Rete: a fast algorithm for the many pattern/many object pattern match problem. Artificial Intelligence 19(1), 17–37 (1982)
22. Gelfond, M., Lifschitz, V.: Representing action and change by logic programs. Journal of Logic Programming 17, 301–321 (1993)
23. Vasconcelos, W.W.: Norm Verification and Analysis of Electronic Institutions. In: Leite, J.A., Omicini, A., Torroni, P., Yolum, P. (eds.) DALT 2004. LNCS (LNAI), vol. 3476, Springer, Heidelberg (2005)

An Agent-Based Model for Hierarchical Organizations

Luis Erasmo Montealegre Vázquez and Fabiola López y López

Facultad de Ciencias de la Computación
Benemérita Universidad Autónoma de Puebla
montealegreluis@gmail.com, fabiola.lopez@siu.buap.mx

Abstract. Hierarchical structures have been widely used by human organizations because they provide the natural means to delegate tasks, to reduce communication lines and to control the activities performed into them. This has motivated the development of different approaches to automate many of the activities that take place in hierarchical organizations. Recent frameworks, such as Gaia, AALAADIN, HarmonIA and OperA, among others, have considered the agent paradigm to do so without taking into account that organizations are dynamic entities that evolve with the time and, consequently, agents must adapt to changes. Here we develop a model for flexible and open hierarchical organizations where agents can dynamically adapt themselves to organizational changes.

1 Introduction

The deployment of Internet and the middleware available to build distributed applications provide the tools needed to automate many of the tasks that are carried out into organizations. To do so, a paradigm to allow the representation of both the elements that comprise an organization and the processes that occur within it, is needed. Since humans are a key element in any organization and computational agents are conceived as software entities acting on behalf of users, multi-agent systems (MAS) have been considered a suitable paradigm to represent any kind of social group [1].

A big effort has been made to introduce organizational concepts into the analysis and design of multi-agent systems. Examples of this can be found in models such as AALAADIN [2], MOISE [3], and MaSE [4]. All of them are based on concepts such as roles, groups and structures. In addition, there are methodologies based in organizational concepts like Gaia [5]. An extension to Gaia, the GaiaExOA methodology [6], includes organizational patterns to promote the reusability of design models. Some other models such as HarmonIA [7] and OperA [8] have dealt with open systems and self-interested agent behavior. HarmonIA is a framework to model electronic organizations from the abstract level where norms are defined to the final protocols and procedures that implement those norms [7]. OperA is a framework for the specification of multi-agent systems that distinguishes between the mechanisms through which the structure

P. Noriega et al. (Eds.): COIN 2006 Workshops, LNAI 4386, pp. 194–211, 2007.

and the global behavior of the model is described and coordinated, and the aims and the behavior of the agents that populate the model [8].

Hierarchical structures have been widespread by human organizations because they provide a natural way to delegate tasks, to reduce communication lines and to control the behavior of each member in an organization. Moreover, in hierarchical organizations, as in any type of organization, services are provided either to other organizations or to individuals, well-defined roles are established for every member and organizational objectives are set since the beginning. However, organizations are complex and dynamic by nature, they can be redesigned and re-engineered, consequently the way the agents and the coordination structure adapt and change over the time may affect the organizational performance [9]. This paper presents our first results to address this problem.

Here, we have developed a model for *open hierarchical organizations* by taking a framework for normative agents [10] as the base. In our model, each member of the organization is considered as a *normative agent* [11], capable of reasoning about the responsibilities and benefits it acquires acting as a member of an organization. We have used *positions profiles* [12] to represent *functional positions* (or roles) and *hierarchical structures*. Since normative agents can *modify its behavior* according to the changes in the legislation by rejecting or adopting *new norms*, we have used norms in the definition of position profiles to represent *dynamical functional positions*. Thus, *agents can adapt to organizational changes at runtime* by updating the set of norms that defines their position profile. This makes possible the implementation of *flexible and dynamic organizations*. Our work also takes many concepts from different social theories such as the classic and the neoclassic administration theory [13,14] as well as the human relationships theory [15]. We have used the *administrative process* [14] to *coordinate*, to *monitor* and to *control* the activities of the agents in the organization. The model is mainly intended *to facilitate the implementation of agent-based hierarchical organizations that may help us to automate human organizations*. In our model one or several agents may act on behalf of a human member of an organization.

The model is represented by using the Unified Modeling Language (*UML*) [16] because it has been widespread and it has become a *standard de facto* within the software development industry. This paper is organized as follows. In Section 2, we present the UML representation of the different elements of normative multi-agent systems. Section 3 describes each element in the model for agent-based hierarchical organizations. In Section 4, we develop the classical example of a conference organization [8,5] by using our model, in order to show its applicability. Finally, in Section 5 we present our conclusions and future work.

2   Normative Multi-Agent Systems

We have used the normative framework for agent-based systems developed by López, Luck and d'Inverno [10] as the basis of our model. In this section we present a summary of the main components, details can be found elsewhere [11,17,18,19].

2.1 Norms

According to [10], norms are the mechanisms through which societies regulate the behavior of their members. The model of a norm, which representation is shown in Figure 1, includes the following components:

- *Normative goals.* These are the goals prescribed by a norm.
- *Addressee agents.* These agents must comply the normative goals.
- *Beneficiaries agents.* These agents might result benefited from norm compliance.
- *Context.* It represents the conditions to activate a norm.
- *Exceptions.* These are the situations where the agents are not forced to fulfill a norm.
- *Punishments.* They model the penalties applied to the agents that do not satisfy the normative goals.
- *Rewards.* Rewards are given to the agents that comply the norms.

Norms may be created by the agent designer as built-in norms, they can be the result of agreements between agents, or can be elaborated by a complex legal system [11]. Here, we assume that norms have already been created. Norms can be divided into categories in several ways, like in [20] where norms are classified according to their *context* into environment, organization, role and interaction laws, for instance. Hereafter, we adhere to the position of López, Luck and d'Inverno [10] and we will use the term *norm* as an *umbrella term* to cover every type of norm ranging from obligations and permissions to social commitments and social codes. We also recognize that although norms can be created in different ways and for different purposes, all of them share the same structure as described before. Categories of norms can be found in [11,18].

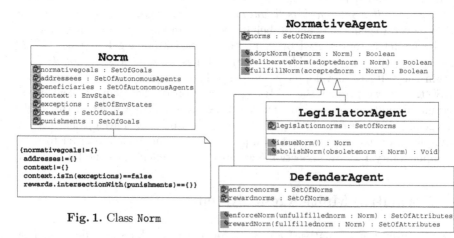

Fig. 1. Class Norm

Fig. 2. Types of agents in a NMAS

2.2   Normative Agents

A *normative agent* is an autonomous agent able to adopt, to deliberate and to comply with norms on the basis of its own goals and preferences. A better description of these kind of agents can be found in [19]. Due to space constraints we do not present the UML specification for attributes, goals, environmental states, and autonomous agents, but it can be found elsewhere in [21]. Figure 2 describes a normative agent which is supposed to inherit from an autonomous agent class. In a Normative Multi-Agent System (NMAS) there are agents entitled to *legislate* and therefore to create new norms (see class LegislatorAgent), and there are agents entitled to give *rewards* or to apply *punishments* to other agents according to the compliance of norms (observe class DefenderAgent). The UML representation of these agents is also shown in Figure 2. A NMAS [11] must include the following elements (illustrated graphically in Figure 3).

- A set of agent *members* able to reason about the norms.
- A set of *legislator* agents.
- A set of norm *defender* agents.
- A set of *norms* directed to regulate the behavior of the agents.
- A set of norms whose purpose is to *enforce* and to determine the fulfillment of the most recent set of norms.
- A set of norms directed to promote the fulfillment of norms through *rewards*.
- A set of emitted norms to allow the *creation* and the *abolition* of norms.

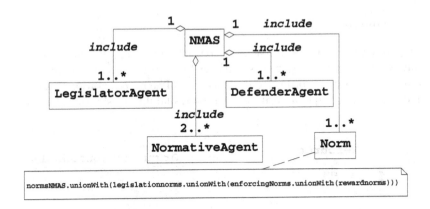

Fig. 3. Class NMAS

When systems regulated by norms are populated by autonomous agents, neither can all norms be considered in advance (since *new conflicts among agents may surge, and consequently new norms may be needed*), nor can compliance with norms be guaranteed (*since agents can decide not to comply norms*). Thus, these systems must include mechanisms to deal with the modification and creation of norms as well as with the unpredictable normative behavior of agents. That is

the case of the last three sets of norms described above, which are intended to
be used by legislators and defenders to address such problems. Further details
are given in [10].

3 An Agent-Based Hierarchical Organization

In this section we use the model of NMAS and some concepts taken from administrative theories to develop a model for hierarchical organizations. A *human
organization* is a goal-oriented social entity consisting of a group of persons and
designed to obtain results, to generate utilities and to provide social satisfaction. It is structured deliberately because its structure suggests the division of
labor in such a way that it can be used to assign the execution of tasks among
its members [13]. The neoclassic administrative theory [14] adds some elements
to the formal concept of organization and defines it as *a set of functional and
hierarchical positions oriented to the production of goods and services.*

Translating these definitions to an *agent-based hierarchical organization* we
can define it as a NMAS where agent's activities are coordinated with the purpose of reaching organizational goals and, in this way, to offer some services.
In addition, an agent-based hierarchical organization has a set of functional
positions which describes a hierarchical structure. This structure is used to coordinate the activities of the agents within the organization. Before providing
a model for hierarchical organizations we describe some organizational concepts
that will be used later on.

3.1 Resources

In order to provide services and achieve goals *a human organization* needs several
resources. Similarly, an *agent-based hierarchical organization* requires a set of
resources to operate according to its objectives. The representation of a resource
includes a name, a type, a location, and its availability as shown in Figure 4.

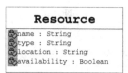

Fig. 4. Class `Resource`

Fig. 5. Class `OrganizationalGoal`

3.2 Organizational Goals

Every *human organization* exists not only to reach objectives and to produce
results (lending some service) but also to obtain profits [14]. In a similar way,
an *agent-based hierarchical organization* is designed to reach goals, to offer services and to obtain profits. Viewing the organization as a unit, the goals of an

agent-based hierarchical organization are defined as a set of desired states. Each organizational goal has associated some elements, such as a plan to reach that goal, and a leader whose mission is to *coordinate* and consequently to *ensure* the achievement of the organizational goal. This leader must be a legislator, because it must make changes in legislation in the case of *recurrent and unexpected conflicts among agents* or due to *effectiveness reasons*. Its representation is shown in Figure 5. The plans related to goals will be further described in Section 3.7. Whereas, position profiles will be described in Section 3.5.

3.3   Organizational Services

Human organizations are intended to provide services to both organizations and individuals [14]. In an *agent-based organization*, a service is defined as the set of capacities or resources of a software entity, which can be accessed through the network by external entities such as individual agents, people or other agent-based organizations. Our representation of a service is like the one shown in Figure 6. It includes an identifier, a set of goals, a description (which helps the client to decide whether to contract the service or not), a plan, and a leader which must be a defender agent, because it is the one responsible of guaranteeing the service through norm compliance. Due to space constraints the process to verify the fulfillment or the violation of a norm in a NMAS is not explained here, but it can be found elsewhere in [11].

3.4   Contracts

A contract represents *rights* and *obligations* for the participants in it. *An obligation is a norm* which infringement is always penalized. To specify a *right* we need a *pair of norms*, one specifying what must be done and another specifying a reward to the addressee of the first norm. This relation between norms has been called *interlocked norms* and the concept is better explained in [10]. Thus, we can represent a contract by using sets of norms. In this way norms specify the things that must be done to consider a service as fulfilled. A contract consists of an identifier for the service, the identifiers of the participants, and the set of obligations directed to the service providers (delivered product, deadlines, etc.). The *normative goals of these obligations must match the service goals*, otherwise the service cannot be guaranteed, i. e. the fulfillment of the service goals is an obligation for the service providers, they are responsible of achieving the desired results specified in the contract. A contract also includes the set of obligations associated to clients (payment, for instance). Therefore, obligations of both clients and providers *benefit* their counterpart agents with *rewards* and/or *contribute* to reach their goals when fulfilling the contract norms. Designing contracts in this way let the agent decide whether to join the society or not as described in [22]. The remaining contract details are not discussed in this paper. However, details about the specification of contracts can be found elsewhere [8,23,24].

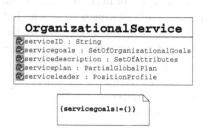

Fig. 6. Class `OrganizationalService`

Fig. 7. Class `Contract`

3.5   Position Profiles

In order to *represent the hierarchy* of an organization we have used the *functional positions analysis*, as described in [12]. A functional position analysis consists of a *header* which includes the organization's general information (name, address, etc.); an *identification for the position*, this includes all the information required to identify the positions (a key for the position, a hierarchical level, the amount of employees performing that position, the immediate inferior and superior positions, etc.); a *generic description*, here all the position activities are defined in terms of goals; a *specific description*, this describes in detail all the activities of the profile (i.e activities are ordered chronologically and according to their importance); a *specification for the position*, it is derived from the position's description and emphasizes the minimum requirements to perform the position (abilities, responsibilities, effort and working conditions); and a *position profile*, which contains all the information collected during the analysis. A position profile is intended firstly, to identify a functional position in a hierarchy, secondly, to describe the set of obligations and rights related to a position, and thirdly, to determine the authority and communication paths, i. e. to specify the superior and the set of inferior elements regarding to a given position.

A role is an abstract description of an entity's expected function [25]. Roles have been represented in [3] as a set of forbidden/authorized goals to achieve, plans to follow, actions to execute and resources to use. In [4] a role defines the tasks that must be accomplished in order to achieve the role's targets. In HarmonIA [7] a role is a set of rules which define constraints to ensure that desired states are kept or achieved, and acceptable behaviors are performed, i. e. rules define the actions that are accepted. In OperA [8] roles are described in terms of objectives and norms which specify the rights associated with the role, and the type of enactment of the role (institutional or external). Here we use the term *position profile* for describing a role, its main difference and advantage over other models is that our role model include norms in its definition. Thereby, agents can modify a position profile (role) by adopting new norms or updating its current set of norms at runtime.

As mentioned before, in an *agent-based hierarchical organization*, the position profiles are defined by using norms. It can be done due to the possibility of designing norms to specify authority (by means of benefits) and responsibility (by means of obligations). The class `PositionProfilet` shown in Figure 8 depicts the elements needed to define a *profile for a functional position* [12]. A profile must include a profile key and a profile identifier. It also specifies the sets of norms representing the obligations and the responsibilities included in a profile, as well as the set of position profiles representing its subordinates and the position profile representing its superior. The usage of these attribues will be detailed in Section 4. It is necessary to emphasize that *every organizational goal must be an obligation for at least one position profile* (the goal's leader profile). There is a relation between profiles and services similar to the one between organizational goals and profiles. *Service goals must be an obligation for the leader and/or its subordinates.* These two constraints can be explained as follows. Think for instance, in the organization of a conference (see Section 4 for further details). One goal for this organization is to review the papers submitted, this is the PC members' main obligation, they have to review at least one paper, i.e. there is a *norm* in their *profiles* which *aim* is to review the papers assigned to them. These constraints must apply for every organizational goal, otherwise it is not possible to guarantee the proper operation of the organization.

3.6 Organizational Agents

This section aims to determine the characteristics and the capabilities of an organizational agent. An *organizational agent* must exhibit abilities to do certain activities or to obtain goals (autonomous agents). It must recognize and fulfill the norms of the organization (normative agents). It must adopt one or several functional positions, which are defined by position profiles; it must recognize the authority lines of an organization and it must have access to some resources (organizational agents). Thus, we have modelled the class `OrganizationalAgent` as a specialization of the class `NormativeAgent`. In the case of organizational agents which are also authorities, they must be represented by inheriting from either `LegislatorAgent` or `DefenderAgent` classes. The `OrganizationalAgent` class also defines the position profiles that an agent is currently performing as well as the resources to which an agent has access to. Figure 9 shows how an organizational agent is represented.

3.7 Administrative Process

A *human organization* can offer more than one service. The notion of service needs the knowledge of the administrative process functions [14]. Each service defines an administrative process. The administrative process consists of four interrelated activities as Figure 10 shows.

1. *Planning.* In this phase the objectives of a service or organizational goal are determined.
2. *Organization.* The output of this phase is a plan, which is the result of the decomposition of an organizational goal into sub-goals. These sub-goals

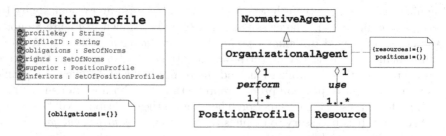

Fig. 8. Class PositionProfile   **Fig. 9.** Class OrganizationalAgent

are assigned to specific position profiles. A plan also defines the *conditions* or states under which it can be applied and the *consequences* or the states reached after the plan has been effectively finished (like in a STRIPS planner [26]), as well as the resources required to achieve a goal or to provide a service. A plan is depicted as Figure 11 shows. An important restriction related to plans must be highlighted. *All the sub-goals of a plan must be in the obligations of the set of normative goals of the participants profiles.*

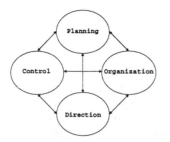

Fig. 10. The administrative process

Fig. 11. Class PartialGlobalPlan

3. *Direction.* This activity involves the processes through which an administrator tries to influence its subordinates, to make them behave according to the expectations and to reach the organizational goals. In our approach, it is done by establishing performance standards. A performance standard is modelled as an organizational goal.
4. *Control.* The activity of control supervises the organizational activities by comparing the current performance (the goals achieved in a given moment) with the established standard, and executes remedial actions, if needed.

In an *agent-based hierarchical organization* we can achieve coordination by using the administrative process functions and the position profiles.

3.8   Administrative Agents

As mentioned before, we have used the administrative process as a coordination mechanism. Then, we must recognize and describe the types of agents capable of performing the functions of the administrative process (see Figure 12).

- *Administrator.* It is an agent with certain authority over other agents. Its main capabilities are focused on *planning* and *directive* activities.
- *Supervisor.* This agent verifies the fulfillment of other agents' obligations, this activity is intended to achieve the organizational goals. This type of agent is capable of performing activities of *supervision* and *control.*

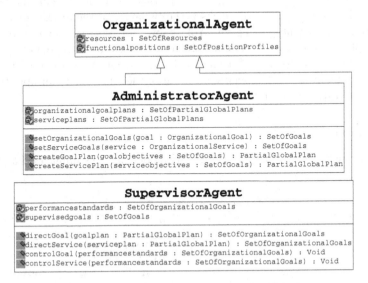

Fig. 12. Administrator and supervisor agents

An *administrator* must be able to establish the objectives of a goal or service as stated by the first administrative activity: planning. This is done by the methods `setOrganizationalGoals` and `setServiceGoals`. An administrator can also generate *plans* (i. e. it can perform the second administrative activity: organization) by using the methods `createGoalPlan` to satisfy a goal and `createServicePlan` to provide a service. This type of agent is a specialization of the class `LegislatorAgent` because it is responsible of applying changes in legislation in order to coordinate an organizational goal or service as mentioned in Section 3.2. The activity of direction is carried out by a *supervisor* by means of the methods `directGoal` and `directService`. These methods take the plan of a service or goal to establish the expected performance standards. A supervisor can reward or enforce the fulfillment or violation of norms since it is the one in charge of monitoring the agents' behavior in order to assure the achievement of the organizational objectives, thus a supervisor must inherit from class `DefenderAgent`. The activity of control is implemented by the methods `controlGoal` and `controlService`. Both of them verify if performance standards have been reached and execute a remedial action if needed.

Previous organizational models [4,3,2],do not define a supervisor agent. This agent is necessary because the agents in an open organization can act in a *self-interested* way, and therefore, as the workers of a human organization, they will try to satisfy their *individual goals* [15]. The individual goals and the motivations (preferences) of agents allow them to choose which norms to fulfill. Thus, we need a means to control the unexpected and undesirable behavior of agents, with the purpose of preserving the good performance of the organization. This control is exerted by the supervisor agent. The idea of this kind of agent appears in the HarmonIA framework [7]. There, an institutional role is defined, the *police agent*, which is an agent that checks if the behavior of the other agents follows the norms. The agent playing this role knows all the roles, and consequently the complete set of rules that define them. Once again, our model of supervisor is better in the sense that if a change in legislation may occur it would not affect the effectiveness of supervision, because the supervisor can update its set of monitored norms at runtime.

3.9   Global View

The relations between the elements of our model can be summarized as follows.

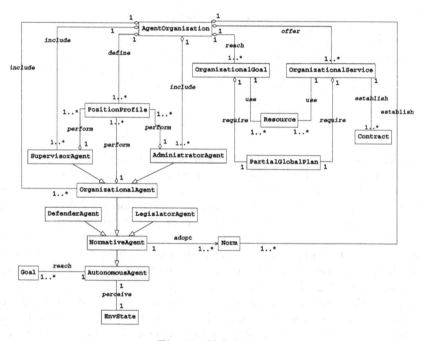

Fig. 13. Global view

An *agent-based hierarchical organization* consists of a set of *organizational agents* able to perform the administrative process activities (the agents *supervisor* and *administrator*). An organizational agent is the specialization of a *normative agent*. A normative agent can be a *defender* or a *legislator*. A normative agent is the specialization of an *autonomous agent*, which is defined as a BDI agent capable of reaching *goals* and perceiving an *environment*. An agent-based organization aims to offer *services* and to achieve *organizational goals*. These services and goals need to use various *resources* and require the elaboration of a *plan*. A service associates a *contract* for each client of an organization. An agent-based organization defines *position profiles* which are performed by organizational agents. The organization establishes *norms* to regulate the behavior of agents. This description is depicted in the UML diagram shown in Figure 13.

4   The Applicability of the Model

In order to show the applicability of our model, we have developed the example of a conference organization, previously done in [8] and [5]. Due to the lack of space, we will only compare our model with OperA [8]. The UML use case diagram for our organization is shown in Figure 14. The functional positions in this example are: the organizer, the PC chairs, the PC members, the local chairs, and the session chairs. The organizational service provided by this society is to organize a conference. To organize a conference, it is necessary to review the papers submitted. This service is described in the instance of the Figure 15. It includes the identifier for the service, it also describes the goals of the service. Each one of these goals have associated a set of goals which must be previously achieved. These goals are aimed to show the *dependency* between service's goals. They also define the *importance* of each goal, because they dictate which goal must be reached first. It means that in order to review a paper it must be assigned first, then it must be read and a report must be written, finally, this report must be sent to the leader of the service. Additional information related to the participation of the client in the conference is also given (the date and the place where the conference will take place). It also has a plan and a profile, which acts as the service leader, associated. Once the author has decided to contract the service, an instance like the one shown in Figure 16 is created. It includes the identifier for the service and an identifier for both the client and the provider, it also describes the obligations that the author, as a client, must

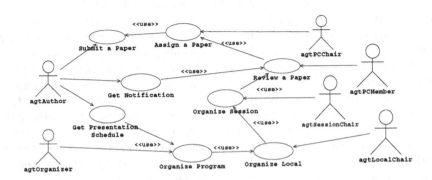

Fig. 14. Use case diagram

```
srvReviewPaper : OrganizationalService
serviceID = "RVW"
servicegoals = {
  {paperAssigned(Paper,Reviewer,Deadline),{}},
  {read(Paper),{golPaperAssigned}},
  {reportWritten(Paper,Report),{goalReadPaper}},
  {reviewReceived(serviceleader,Paper,Report),
                          {golReportWritten}},
  {paperReviewed(paper,report),
                          {golReviewReceived}}}
servicedescription = {hostCity(CityName),
                presentationDate(Month,Year)}
serviceplan = plnReviewPaper
serviceleader = prfPCChair
```

Fig. 15. Service `srvReviewPaper`

```
ctrAuthorContract : Contract
serviceID = "srvReviewPaper"
participantsID = {authorID,conferencename}
obligationsprovider = {nrmAssignPaper,
                          nrmReviewPaper}
obligationsclient = {nrmAssistConference,
                nrmAcceptNotificationResult}
```

Fig. 16. Contract `ctrAuthorContract`

accept. In this case its obligation is to accept the reviewing results (negative or positive), and to attend the conference in the case the paper is accepted. On the other hand, the organization, as a service provider, is obliged to assign the paper to a reviewer, who consequently, must review the paper.

In [8] a role is defined as a set of objectives, a set of sub-objectives, a set of rights, a set of norms and a type. In our model, that role corresponds to the class `PositionProfile`. Figure 17 shows the instance for the PC member profile. The profile key is PCM, which identifies the profile in general. The profile identifier gives a unique identifier to the agent performing that profile. The attributes `superior` and `inferiors`, have been defined in order to represent the organization's hierarchical structure. The profile for the PC member indicates that it's superior is the profile PC Chair, and that it has no inferiors, which means that this profile is the lowest in the hierarchy, because it has no subordinates. Conversely when a profile has no superior, it means that it is highest in the hierarchy. Therefore, these attributes describe the hierarchical levels of the organization being modelled. Following the example developed in [8], the obligations given to `pfrPCMember`, are defined by the norms `nrmReviewPaper` and `nrmRefuseColleague`. Figure 18 shows the instance diagram for the norm `nrmReviewPaper`. The normative goals for the norm are: to review the paper, to make a written report of the paper, and to send the report to the PC member in charge. Those actions will lead the agent to the state `paperReviewed(Paper,Report)`. These goals have some other goals associated which tell the agent which goals have to be reached first, starting from the most important, which has no goals associated, to the least. In other words, *the goals' importance of the profile defines individual goal dependency.* Observe that these goals are a subset of the goals of the service. This implies a dependency between the profiles `prfPCMember` and `prfPCChair`. Observe that the context of the norm `nrmReviewPaper` is the goal `paperAssigned(Paper, Reviewer,Deadline)` which is the goal of the norm `nrmAssignPaper` which is directed to the profile `prfPCChair`. This means that a paper cannot be reviewed until that paper is assigned to a PC member. Due to space constraints neither the profile nor the norm mentioned above are depicted here.

To model the processes done in organizations, OperA uses scene scripts. A scene script serves as a blueprint for the actual interactions between actors [8].

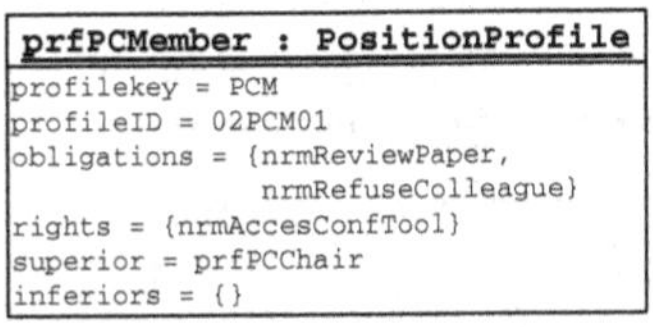

```
prfPCMember : PositionProfile
profilekey = PCM
profileID = 02PCM01
obligations = {nrmReviewPaper,
               nrmRefuseColleague}
rights = {nrmAccesConfTool}
superior = prfPCChair
inferiors = {}
```

Fig. 17. Position profile prfPCMember

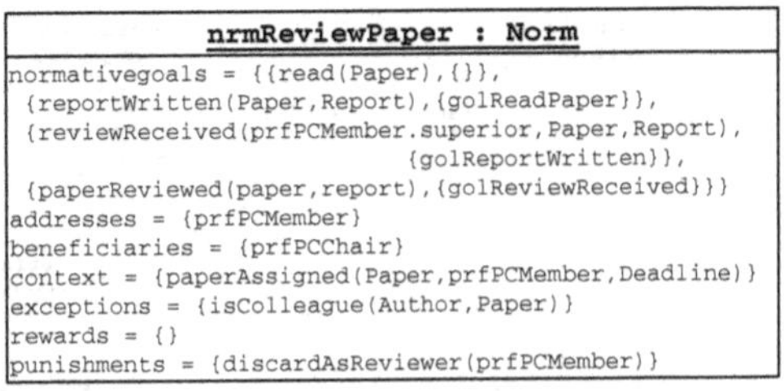

```
nrmReviewPaper : Norm
normativegoals = {{read(Paper),{}},
  {reportWritten(Paper,Report),{golReadPaper}},
  {reviewReceived(prfPCMember.superior,Paper,Report),
                            {golReportWritten}},
  {paperReviewed(paper,report),{golReviewReceived}}}
addresses = {prfPCMember}
beneficiaries = {prfPCChair}
context = {paperAssigned(Paper,prfPCMember,Deadline)}
exceptions = {isColleague(Author,Paper)}
rewards = {}
punishments = {discardAsReviewer(prfPCMember)}
```

Fig. 18. Norm nrmReviewPaper

A *scene script is equivalent* to the activities of *planning and direction* of the administrative process. In what follows we describe the administrative process done when a paper is reviewed, by using UML sequence diagrams. The use case begins when an author uploads a paper to the *ConfMaster Tool*, this action changes the environment in the organization by adding the predicate newPaper(Author,Paper). This induces the deliberation process of the agent enacting the position profile prfOrganizer who is the leader of the organizational service (agtOrganizer). The current environmental state matches the context of the norm nrmCoordinateReviewProcess which is defined in the profile prfOrganizer. Service's goals are the goals of the norm activated. The agent agtOrganizer creates a new organizational goal oglReviewPaper, which aim is to review the paper recently sent. To do so, the organizer uses method setOrganizationalGoal which returns the set of sub-goals for the organizational goal (see Figure 12), these goals are the same defined in the goals of the service (assign and read the paper and write and deliver the report as Figure 15 shows). This method corresponds to the first activity in the administrative process. Once the sub-goals are established, the organizer uses method createGoalPlan, which creates the partial global plan to achieve the organizational goal. Thus, the agent agtOrganizer get its inferiors' position profiles, to choose the profile that best fits the sub-goals. This decision is taken based on the *obligations' normative goals* of the profile. Then, the agent creates a plan establishing the set of sub-goals, the set of position profiles, the set of resources required, and the context for the plan, in order to add that plan to the organization's set of plans. Once a resource is assigned to an agent performing a profile, it is no longer available to any other until the goal plan has been achieved or the plan has been discarded. These actions correspond to the second administrative process activity (See Figure 19).

The following example is intended to show, the actions taken when some agents do not comply with their obligations. In OperA [8] this can be done by monitoring the contracts of the role enactors, but not specific activities or mechanism are defined. Verification of norm compliance is an optional clause in the contract that specifies by whom and how the norm will be verified and which are the actions to be executed if norms are ignored. In HarmoniA norm compliance is verified by the police agents as mentioned in Section 3.8. In the approach presented in [27] the verification of norm compliance is done by checking the

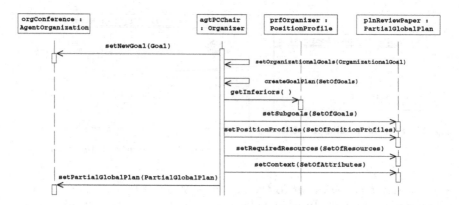

Fig. 19. Planning and organizing a global goal

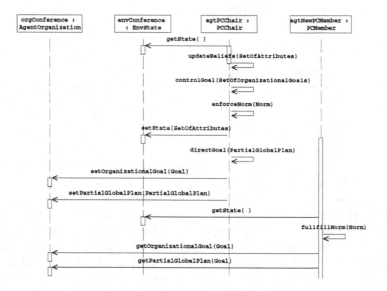

Fig. 20. Directing and controlling a global goal

safety and the *liveness* properties of protocols. The former states that if there is no steps in a protocol that violate any norm, the protocol will not violate any of the norms as a whole [27], the latter checks if the protocol achieves a specific goal at its end.

Here, the actions to verify norm compliance are implemented using the activities of control and direction. If the agent PC member decides not to fulfill the norm `nrmRefuseColleague`, the following process is initiated. The PC chair detects that a PC member did not comply with norm `nrmRefuseColleague`, and uses its method `controlGoal`, which takes the set of organizational goals that cannot be reached, and decides whether to apply a corrective action or not.

A corrective action can be either, the issue or the enforcement of a norm, the modification of either a global plan or a global goal, or the creation of a contingency plan among other actions. This undesirable behavior, activates method `enforceNorm`, by applying the punishment associated. In our example, it produces the activation of method `directGoal`, which creates a contingency plan, by adding a new global goal directed to a new reviewer, i. e. other agent performing the PC member position profile, this new agent gets both the new plan and the new goal directed to it. Figure 20 illustrates these activities.

Here we have proposed a norm-based model to represent hierarchical organizations which main difference with other models, and specifically with OperA is its *flexibility*. Autonomous normative agents are designed in such a way that changes in norms and the issuance of new ones does not produce any harm to the effectiveness of the whole system, since agents can adopt new norms and update its current set of norms. Therefore, the implementation of dynamical position profiles (or roles) is possible, this can also lead us to represent flexible organizations. This flexibility is extended to the mechanisms of supervision and verification of norm compliance, since changes in norms are updated by supervisor and defender agents at runtime.

5   Conclusions

We have presented a model for hierarchical organizations based on a normative framework for agent-based systems [10]. The model comprises elements from the administrative area [13,14] like, the administrative process, which defines the set of internal actions performed when an organization needs to provide a service or to reach some organizational goals. The model defines suitable agents to support and to perform the administrative process functions. It also provides a representation for a position profile, which is used to make a functional position analysis in human organizations [12]. Just as in human organizations [15] our model also represents the norms that control the behavior of their members [11]. The usage of norms in the definition of the position profiles allow to adapt agent's behavior at runtime. The model can be used to represent and to automate the procedures that are present in human organizations. So, we can make possible the implementation of human-like organizations open and heterogeneous, based on normative multi-agent systems. This implementation can be done by using the middleware available until now and the services can be provided through the Internet. In this paper we have assumed that the organization is already formed, details concerning to the creation of the system such as, how are the norms created, how the agents enter or leave the organization or how are they selected to perform a position profile (by using a trust mechanism as the one described in [28], for instance), etc., as well as more specific details related to the implementation of the model are beyond the scope of this paper, however these issues conform our proposal for future research.

References

1. Luck, M., McBurney, P., Shehory, O., Willmott, S.: Agent Technology: Computing as Interaction (A Roadmap for Agent Based Computing). AgentLink (2005)
2. Ferber, J., Gutknecht, O.: A meta-model for the analysis and design of organizations in multi-agent systems. In: Proceedings of the Third International Conference on Multi-Agent Systems (ICMAS98), pp. 128–135 (1998)
3. Hannoun, M., Boissier, O., Sichman, J.S., Sayettat, C.: MOISE: An organizational model for multi-agent systems. In: Monard, M.C., Sichman, J.S. (eds.) SBIA 2000 and IBERAMIA 2000. LNCS (LNAI), vol. 1952, pp. 156–165. Springer, Heidelberg (2000)
4. DeLoach, S.A., Wood, M.F., Sparkman, C.H.: Multiagent systems engineering. International Journal of Software Engineering and Knowledge Engineering 11(3), 231–258 (2001)
5. Zambonelli, F., Jennings, N.R., Wooldridge, M.: Developing multiagent systems: The gaia methodology. ACM Transaction on Software Engineering Methodology 12(3), 317–370 (2003)
6. Gonzalez-Palacios, J., Luck, M.: A framework for patterns in gaia: A case-study with organisations. In: Odell, J.J., Giorgini, P., Müller, J.P. (eds.) AOSE 2004. LNCS, vol. 3382, pp. 174–188. Springer, Heidelberg (2005)
7. Vázquez-Salceda, J.: Thesis: The role of norms and electronic institutions in multi-agent systems applied to complex domains. The harmonia framework. AI Communications 16(3), 209–212 (2003)
8. Dignum, V.: A model for organizational interaction: based on agents, founded in logic. PhD thesis, Utrecht University (2003)
9. Carley, K.M., Gasser, L.: Computational organization theory. In: Weiss, G. (ed.) Multiagent systems: A modern Approach to Distributed Artificial Intelligence, pp. 299–330. MIT Press, Cambridge (1999)
10. López, F., Luck, M., d' Inverno, M.: A normative framework for agent-based systems. In: NorMAS '05: Proceedings of the Symposium on Normative Multiagent Systems, The Society for the Study of Artificial Intelligence and the Simulation of Behaviour, pp. 24–35 (2005)
11. López, F., Luck, M.: A model of normative multi-agent systems and dynamic relationships. In: Lindemann, G., Moldt, D., Paolucci, M. (eds.) RASTA 2002. LNCS (LNAI), vol. 2934, pp. 259–280. Springer, Heidelberg (2004)
12. Gama, E.: In: Bases para el Análisis de los Puestos. Manual Moderno, ch. 4, pp. 59–89 (1992)
13. Chiavenato, I.: Teoría Clásica de la Administración. In: Introducción a la Teoría General de la Administración, pp. 88–112. McGraw-Hill, New York (2000)
14. Chiavenato, I.: Teoría Neoclásica de la Administración. In: Introducción a la Teoría General de la Administración, pp. 201–250. McGraw-Hill, New York (2000)
15. Chiavenato, I.: Implicaciones de la Teoría de las Relaciones Humanas. In: Introducción a la Teoría General de la Administración, pp. 141–196. McGraw-Hill, New York (2000)
16. Rumbaugh, J., Jacobson, I., Booch, G.: Unified Modeling Language Reference Manual. Addison-Wesley, Reading (1998)
17. López, F., Luck, M., d' Inverno, M.: Constraining autonomy through norms. In: AAMAS '02: Proceedings of the First International Joint Conference on Autonomous Agents and Multiagent Systems, pp. 674–681. ACM Press, New York (2002)

18. López, F., Luck, M.: Modelling norms for autonomous agents. In: Chavez, E., Favela, J., Mejia, M., Oliart, A. (eds.) ENC '03: Proceedings of the Fourth Mexican International Conference on Computer Science, Washington, DC, USA, pp. 238–245. IEEE Computer Society Press, Los Alamitos (2003)
19. López, F., Arenas, A.: An architecture for autonomous normative agents. In: ENC '04: Proceedings of the Fifth Mexican International Conference in Computer Science (ENC'04), Washington, DC, USA, pp. 96–103. IEEE Computer Society Press, Los Alamitos (2004)
20. Felicíssimo, C., Choren, R., Briot, J.P., Lucena, C.: Supporting regulatory dynamics in open mas. LNCS, vol. 4386, pp. 140–155. Springer, Heidelberg (2007)
21. Montealegre, L.: Modelado de organizaciones jerárquicas usando sistemas multiagentes normativos. Master's thesis, Benemérita Universidad Autónoma de Puebla (2005)
22. López, F., Luck, M., d'Inverno, M.: Normative agent reasoning in dynamic societies. In: Jennings, N., Sierra, C., Sonenberg, L., Tambe, M. (eds.) AAMAS '04: Proceedings of the Third International Joint Conference on Autonomous Agents and Multiagent Systems. LNCS (LNAI), vol. 3394, pp. 732–739. IEEE Computer Society, Los Alamitos (2004)
23. Boella, G., van der Torre, L.: Contracts as legal institutions in organizations of autonomous agents. In: Proceedings of the 3rd International Joint Conference on Autonomous Agents and Multiagent Systems, pp. 948–955 (2004)
24. Sandholm, T., Lesser, V.: Leveled-commitment contracting: A backtracking instrument for multiagent systems. AI Magazine 23(3), 89–100 (2002)
25. Kendall, E.: Agent roles and role models: New abstractions for intelligent agent system analysis and design. In: Proceedings of the International Workshop on Intelligent Agents in Information and Process Management, Bremen, Germany, September 1998 (1998)
26. Russell, S., Norving, P.: Artificial Intelligence. A Modern Approach. Prentice Hall, Englewood Cliffs, NJ (1995)
27. Aldewereld, H., Vázquez-Salceda, J., Dignum, F., Meyer, J.: Verifying norm compliancy of protocols. In: Boissier, O., Padget, J., Dignum, V., Lindemann, G., Matson, E., Ossowski, S., Sichman, J.S., Vázquez-Salceda, J. (eds.) Coordination, Organizations, Institutions, and Norms in Multi-Agent Systems. LNCS (LNAI), vol. 3913, pp. 127–141. Springer, Heidelberg (2006)
28. Hermoso, R., Billhardt, H., Ossowski, S.: Integrating trust in virtual organisations. LNCS, vol. 4386, pp. 17–29. Springer, Heidelberg (2007)

Ballroom etiquette: A Case Study for Norm-Governed Multi-Agent Systems

Dorian Gaertner*, Keith Clark, and Marek Sergot

Imperial College London, SW7 2AZ, United Kingdom

Abstract. We present a case study which describes a ballroom as a social institution with autonomous dancer agents constrained by sets of norms and conventions that coordinate the behaviour of the participants. We provide a representation for the interaction protocols as finite state machines and a new way of formalising the associated norms in a logic programming language. Furthermore, we report on recent and ongoing work on an architecture for normative systems of this kind which allows agents to dynamically download interaction protocols and operational norms to guide their behaviour. Finally, we outline an alternative approach for representing the *institutional state* in a virtual, distributed fashion in the agents' private belief stores.

1 Introduction

We present the main elements of a norm-governed multi-agent system which simulates a ballroom for social dancing. It is intended as a case study to explore the specification and implementation of a wide class of norm-governed multi-agent systems. Agents in the ballroom form commitments by negotiating according to specified protocols and conventions. The fulfilment of these commitments, and other aspects of the agents' interactions, are further guided and constrained by norms of conduct expressing what behaviours are socially acceptable (or 'legal'). These protocols and norms together constitute the ballroom *etiquette*[1]. Our assumption is that all ballroom etiquette has general common features, and an ontology in terms of which the norms can be expressed, though the details will vary from one specific ballroom to another. Our aim is to provide an implementation in which agents joining a computational society (here, a ballroom) are provided with an executable representation of the applicable norms which they use in their internal decision-making procedures.

Clark and McCabe [7] have used the ballroom example to demonstrate features of the agent programming language Go!, and its support for multi-threaded agents with inter-agent communication and coordination via messages. Although the agents are quite simple, this scenario encompasses key behavioural features

---

* The first author undertook part of this work while at the Artificial Intelligence Research Institute (IIIA) in Bellaterra, Spain.

[1] *Etiquette:* the customs or rules governing behaviour regarded as correct or acceptable in social or official life. [Collins dictionary]

P. Noriega et al. (Eds.): COIN 2006 Workshops, LNAI 4386, pp. 212–226, 2007.

of agents: autonomy, adaptability and responsibility. However, in that implementation the norms governing the dancers' interactions — the protocols used to negotiate commitments, and the conventions that govern how commitments are fulfilled — are implicit in the code. These implicit norms are hard-coded which makes their modification cumbersome and time-consuming.

We have constructed a version in which these norms are *explicit*, providing a case study for specifying and implementing a multi-agent system (MAS) in which agents take account of and deliberate about the norms that regulate their behaviour. Like Artikis et al. [2,3], Ossowski [16], and many others, we accept that organisational and legal elements of open agent systems, the semantics of agent communication, and social and normative relations generally, must be externally visible and not embedded in the internal state of individual member agents. However, we also want to address how individual agents can take into account the existence of norms in their internal decision making procedures. While this aspect has been analysed thoroughly for individual normative agents by Boella and Lesmo [4] and Castelfranchi et al. [6] and others, the institutional view of norms for multi-agent systems is only just beginning to receive attention (but see *e.g.* [14,17]).

In the present version we assume that agents always fulfil their commitments and comply with any other applicable norms, as in the original implementation by Clark and McCabe. In future versions we will remove this assumption, so as to explore mechanisms for enforcing and encouraging norm compliance, sanctioning and other reparational procedures, and the associated auditing infrastructure. These topics will not be covered in this paper.

In the next section, we describe the ballroom simulation in more detail. We provide examples of the protocols and norms, their representation, and requirements for their implementation in Sections 3 and 4. In Section 5 we outline an agent architecture in which agents can download interaction protocols together with the applicable norms and conventions expressed in a common ontology when they join the ballroom. Section 6 then introduces a way of modelling the institutional state in a virtual fashion, in which each agent maintains its own representation of the relevant state of the institution as part of its internal beliefs. Section 7 presents related work and Section 8 concludes.

2   The Simulation

As a springboard for this research we are using a ballroom simulation devised by Clark and McCabe [7] that consists of a dance floor and a bar area. In this simulation, male and female agents participate in social dancing and negotiate over which partner to dance with for the next dance of a certain kind. The agents are multi-threaded in the sense that their reactive and deliberative behaviours are executed concurrently. Agents communicate and coordinate their behaviour using their beliefs, intentions and desires which are modelled using dynamic memory stores. The band, represented by an additional agent, plays one of six different types of dance deciding randomly which dance to play next. Once a negotiation between two dancers concludes in an agreement between them to dance the next polka, say, both dancers are committed to indeed perform the next polka together.

Dancer agents can arrive and leave the dance hall at any time — while the band is playing or during the negotiation phase. When a new dancer agent arrives, it registers with the directory server (which is a facilitator used by the dancer agents to discover potential partners) its gender and a list of its desires. These include the desire to dance n_1 dances of type D_1, n_2 dances of type D_2, and so on, and to go to the bar when dances of type D_3 are played. The directory server then announces the arrival of a new dancer agent to the others and informs the new dancer about what were the *initial* desires of the other agents that are present. This information might not coincide with the current desires of the other dancers due to the fact that it is the dancers themselves, rather than the directory server, which keep track of (their beliefs about) other dancers' changing desires. For example, while agent Bob may have been informed that agent Alice initially desired to dance two tangos, he is generally unaware that she may already have fulfilled these desires (unless it was he himself who has danced the tango with her twice, in which case he will have updated his beliefs accordingly). The prototype application is written in Go!, a multi-paradigm programming language for agent applications. Go! has logic programming features such as relations and action procedure definitions for imperative programming [7]. It is multi-threaded and uses asynchronous message-passing for inter-agent communication. Threads within the same agent can also communicate using Prolog-style dynamic relations as shared memory, in the manner of a Linda [5] tuple store.

The simulation cycles through two phases. In *phase one*, the band plays a tune of type D (randomly chosen from the set of dance types). In the Go! implementation, the band announces that it is about to play a dance of type D by broadcasting a start D message. Dancers who have a joint commitment to dance the next D dance together, then exchange messages as part of a handshake protocol and begin to dance. Dancers who have a joint commitment to go to the bar together at the next D dance, exchange messages and go to the bar. The end of the dance is signalled when the band announces (again by way of message broadcast) that it has stopped playing.

In *phase two*, which takes place between dances, the dancer agents negotiate to form commitments to dance the next time the band plays a particular type of dance, say a waltz, or to go to the bar area the next time some type of dance, say a polka, is played. At the next dance interval the beliefs, desires and intentions of the dancer will almost certainly have changed. Even if they are the same, a re-negotiation with the same female may now have a different outcome because of changes in her mental state. The negotiations in phase two follow fixed protocols, the details of which will vary from one dance hall to another and will be looked at in the next section.

3   Negotiation Protocols

In order to coordinate what to dance, when, and with whom, agents need to negotiate. In the simplest form, this involves one agent inviting another agent to dance, who then accepts or declines. In general however, negotiations can be much more complex and have to follow certain protocols which define valid interactions.

Example variations. The dance simulation we described above restricts the ability to negotiate to times when the band is not playing. This is not necessarily a fixed feature of all dance halls. In some dance halls one may want to allow negotiations to take place at any time, or perhaps only when the band is not playing except if both dancers are at the bar.

Another characteristic of a negotiation is the initiator. In the original simulation the female never takes the initiative. A female dancer has to wait for an initial proposal from a male and thereafter can make counter proposals about a different dance or about going to the bar, depending on her current desires and commitments.

Our approach supports a wider range of negotiation protocols, according to the type of dance hall. In a *ladies' choice discotheque*, for example, the female dancer can and should take the initiative. This is easily implemented by changing the protocol. Other possible variations involve disallowing counter proposals, or requiring a dancer to accept any proposal to dance, irrespective of its desires, as long as it does not conflict with existing commitments. One could also imagine a ballroom, in which dancers must negotiate via some intermediary. As mentioned before, a dancer agent can participate in many simultaneous negotiations by spawning auxiliary negotiation threads, subject to the 'good faith' principle outlined below. We may wish to impose further restrictions, so that agents can negotiate with only one other agent at a time, for example.

Commitments. We assume that agents do not dance/go to the bar unless they have a commitment to do so. Furthermore, in the present version of the system, dancers always fulfil their commitments, i.e. they will always dance/go to the bar, if they have a commitment to do so. Thus dancer agents should never make commitments regarding a particular type of dance with more than one partner at a time. It also follows that each agent has at most n dance commitments at any given time, where n is the number of different dance types, since commitments are always taken to be for the actions to be performed the next time the band announces a particular type of dance.

Good faith principle. Dancers can participate in many negotiations concurrently, but only in accordance with a *principle of good faith* whereby (a) they never initiate, accept or counter-propose a new negotiation concerning the next dance of type D when already participating in a negotiation about dance type D with another agent, and (b) they never propose or accept a commitment concerning dance type D when they already have a commitment regarding dance type D with another agent. There are several assumptions about the nature of the negotiation protocol that are implicit in this good faith principle: one aim of our case study is to make them explicit.

Representation. Negotiations follow a particular protocol which is specified by the system designer when formalising the interaction of agents. These protocols are represented as *Finite-State-Machines* and instantiated by the agents when required. One example protocol and the simplified messages passed between the negotiation participants is given in Figure 1. Note that Dance, Dance2 and Dance3 are variables instantiated such that Dance $\neq$ Dance2 etc. and that in this example, only female dancers can suggest drinking at the bar.

After the negotiations are finished and the band has announced it has started to play a certain dance (a polka, say) the dancing phase is executed (as explained in Section 2). Agents who have a joint commitment to action, triggered by the announcement, enter another exchange of messages. There, another protocol regulates the interaction between male and female dancers similar to the notion of a hand-shake. The male reminds the female of their mutual commitment and the female acknowledges him and the action, to dance or go to the bar, begins. If their agreement was to go drinking at the bar when the next polka is played, then their interaction will vary accordingly. Once the band stops playing, the dancing or drinking stops and another round of negotiations begins. Finally, the band announces the end of the evening and agents follow a protocol that governs how they bid farewell to each other.

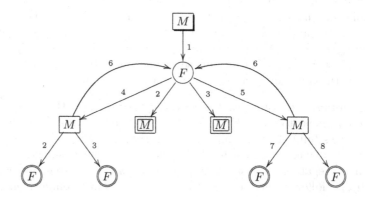

Fig. 1. Simplified example protocol which allows agents to counter-propose

(1) willyouDance(Dance)	(5) barWhen(Dance2)
(2) okDance()	(6) willyouDance(Dance3)
(3) sorryDance()	(7) okBar()
(4) willyouDance(Dance2)	(8) sorryBar()

To summarise, there are three stages in the simulation that are controlled by a protocol (negotiation, hand-shake and farewell) but these protocols are no longer hard-wired into the agents' code. Instead they are downloaded dynamically, in a sense that will become clear in Section 5.

4   Norms

For the purposes of this paper, we will follow a commonly accepted usage and classify norms broadly into two general categories: *constitutive norms* and *behavioural norms* (or norms of conduct).

Constitutive norms specify (1) the conventional-institutional meaning of messages and other communicative acts within a given institution (that a message 'Will you dance the tango?' is an expression of an 'offer to dance', that a message 'Yes' is an expression of an 'acceptance to dance' depending on context, and so on), (2) the protocols and procedures which define what kinds of acts are meaningful or 'valid' according to context (that an 'acceptance' following a (valid) 'offer' forms a 'commitment', that an 'offer' by one party can be followed by a 'counter-offer' by the other party in a negotiation, that the parties in a negotiation must take turns in exchanging messages, and so on), and (3) other more general forms of what are sometimes called 'qualification norms' which define how institutional facts, such as 'band is playing', are determined from observable facts ('brute facts' in Searle's terminology) such as a 'started playing' message having been broadcast by the band agent and no 'stopped playing' message having been broadcast in the meantime. A wide variety of formalisms for expressing constitutive norms have been reported in the literature. We discuss the choices we have made in our current implementation in the following section.

Behavioural norms specify what actions are permitted and obligatory. They may be further classified according to whether we take a "bird's eye" perspective from the system designer's point of view or whether we take a genuinely agent-centric perspective. We will not elaborate further on that distinction here. As already mentioned, in the present version of our system we assume for simplicity that all agents comply with the applicable behavioural norms: agents do not perform actions that are not permitted, and always perform actions that are obligatory. We plan to remove this simplification in later versions.

Although apparently simple, the ballroom example has a very rich and varied set of possible norms, of both kinds. Some are straightforwardly constitutive, some are clearly behavioural, and some, in their natural language formulation, can be interpreted in different ways. We list here some examples with a brief discussion in each case.

Some constitutive norms:

- Dance partner (and negotiation partner) must be of opposite sex — this may not apply in certain dance halls. It may be that a male agent sends a message to another male agent offering to dance but that message is not a valid offer according to the constitutive norms in force in the ballroom. We might want to add a further behavioural norm to say that it is not *permitted* for a male dancer to send a message that offers to dance to another male agent, but that is a *separate* level of specification.

- A female must wait to be approached by a male dancer: only a male agent can (has the institutional *power* to) initiate a negotiation to dance — this can also vary according to the dance hall. Again, it is possible that a female agent sends a message attempting to initiate a negotiation but this is not a meaningful message according to the constitutive rules in force. As a separate level of specification, we might add another norm to the effect that females are not permitted to send such messages.
- Negotiations only take place when the band is not playing. In other dance halls, negotiations can take place at any time, or perhaps only at the bar when the band is playing. Messages offering to dance can be sent while the band is playing but they are not offers to dance according to the constitutive norms. It is a separate question whether the dance hall permits such messages to be sent.

Some behavioural norms:

- An agent must fulfil all its commitments to dance/go to the bar (if it has a chance to do so).
- An agent should not leave the dance hall while it has unfulfilled commitments. In future versions we will allow agents to negotiate about the release from commitments but we do not support that refinement yet.
- Always accept a request for a dance if it does not conflict with existing commitments. (This does not apply in all dance halls.) Here there is an obligation on an agent to exercise its powers, as defined in the constitutive norms, in a particular way.
- Do not dance more than three consecutive dances with the same partner. (In the present version, agents do not maintain an explicit history of all previous dances but this can be easily added by extending the belief state of an agent.)
- At a wedding dance, all male agents must dance at least once with their mother-in-law. (In the present version, agents negotiate only about the next dance of a particular type. In future versions we want to introduce an element of planning, say regarding the next but one waltz.)

In the present version, agents always fulfil their commitments, and comply with all obligations. In future versions, we plan to distinguish between *deliberate* violation of an obligation (such as when an agent chooses not to fulfil its commitment to dance) and *practically unavoidable* violations (such as when an agent is prevented from fulfilling its commitment to dance, for example because of physical restrictions on the size of the dance floor, inability to complete the required hand-shaking protocol in the time available, and so on).

Some norms, in their natural language formulation, can be interpreted either as constitutive norms, or as behavioural norms, or as a combination of the two.

For example: the principle of 'good faith' introduced in Section 3 requires that an agent X does not propose to dance a tango with Y when it already has a commitment to dance a tango, or is already negotiating to dance a tango, with another agent Y'. Should this be represented as a constitutive norm or as a behavioural norm? If we view it as a constitutive norm, we are saying that a message from X to Y proposing to dance a tango is not valid when X has a (potentially) conflicting commitment to dance with Y'. Depending on what other norms are in force, the recipient Y may have obligations to accept offers from X, or to send counter-proposals, or rejections, according to its other commitments. But how is the recipient Y to determine whether X's offer is valid? In order to do that, it would need to know what other commitments X has made, and even what other negotiations X is currently engaged in. This is clearly impractical, unless we have some kind of central server which records all messages exchanged and to which agents can refer to determine what is currently valid and what is not. This is something we want to avoid. The alternative is to say that all proposals from X are constitutionally valid (as long as they are correctly formed) whether or not X is currently committed to dancing the tango or is engaged in negotiations to do so. Instead, we say that there is a behavioural norm which forbids X from sending (valid) offers to dance the tango in these circumstances. Y can proceed in its decision-making without access to X's other commitments and negotiations; the obligation is on X to ensure that the 'good faith' principle is complied with.

5   Architecture

In this section, we will outline an agent architecture that supports normative agents of a heterogeneous kind. While we assume that, in order to participate in the ballroom, dancers have an understanding of concepts from an underlying ontology (as outlined in [8]), the agents are not required to have the norms hard-wired into their code. Instead, they *download* the interaction protocols together with explicit norms and conventions when they join the ballroom. The choice of ontology language is not important in our present discussion.

In order to understand the protocol annotation, agents need to know the semantics of *role names* and the institutional meaning of messages sent and received. The interpretation of a message 'Will you dance the tango?' as expressing an offer to dance, and the specific conditions under which it is a valid offer to dance, are part of the (constitutive) norms of the ballroom etiquette. In this paper we will refer to the institutional meaning of a message as its *purpose*. We are aware that this term is rather overloaded, but it seems natural and intuitive in the present context. Since each transition in the protocol graph corresponds to the sending of a message, we annotate the protocol arc with the corresponding 'purpose'. Furthermore, not every agent can use every transition, so role labels are used to restrict certain transitions.

When an agent decides, depending on its current goal, to invoke a communication with another agent, the protocol tells it what messages to send subject to

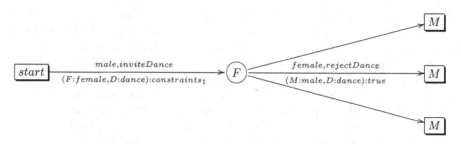

Fig. 2. Part of a proposal protocol with annotated arcs

certain norms. It can only send the message if it has the correct role and fulfils all the norms associated with the transition in question. These norms are expressed using an ontology of specific relations and the interface to this ontology needs to be understood by each dancer.

An example could be a norm limiting the number of dances a dancer can perform with the same partner to six. It uses the predicate `dancesPerPartner(P,N)`, which has to be implemented by each agent and provides access to its mental state. This particular predicate unifies N with the number of dances that the agent has already danced with partner P.

```
canStillDanceWith(P) :-
        dancesPerPartner(P, N),
        N < 6.
```

The norm `canStillDanceWith(P)` is not violated, if this number is less than six. In a different ballroom, this number may vary or indeed the norm may not be present at all. The predicate `dancesPerPartner` is an example of the relations we termed *introspective predicates*. Each participating agent is required to provide definitions for each of these predicates, which then access the current mental state of the agent. These definitions are agent specific and can be implemented in a variety of ways thus allowing for more autonomy when designing agents. Even architectural differences can be accounted for at this level (*e.g.* a predicate will have different implementations depending on whether or not the agent operates in a multi-threaded fashion). Another example introspective predicate is `bandResting`. In the absence of a central authority that logs when the band starts and stops to play, each agent needs to keep track of this itself and the predicate is true, if the agent currently believes that the band is not playing.

Thus, the ontology comprises the top-level set of relations (those that express the normative conditions used in the protocol) and the introspective predicates (those that access the mental state of the agent and are used in the rules defining the top-level relations).

In Figure 2, we illustrate a part of the protocol from Figure 1. The arcs between states of the protocol are annotated with a role, a purpose, several parameters and a set of constraints. The introspective predicates can be used here directly to constrain a transition or they can be used in the description of an explicit norm that has been downloaded by the dancer.

For example, an agent can go from the start state to the next state if it has the role *male* by sending a message which has the purpose *inviteDance*. The actual illocution used by the agent is provided by the protocol so that agents do not have to know them as long as they understand the *purposes*. An agent obtains this illocution by providing two things: a binding for the variable F (of type female) and a binding for the variable D (of type dance). The constraints denoted by *constraints1* in Figure 2 further restrict the applicability of this transition. They are made up of introspective predicates and some of the downloaded conventions. In the example, *constraints1* could be:

`canStillDanceWith(P), bandResting, notCommittedNorm(D)`

A different transition that leaves the state annotated with F can only be traversed by a *female* agent who intends to reject an offer. The female dancer needs to provide the identity of the male who approached her and the dance in question in order to form a valid rejection message (using the appropriate illocution provided by the protocol). However, there are no further constraints associated with this transition (indicated by the *true* constraint).

Summarising, we can see that the path an agent takes through the protocol graph is influenced by its desires, biases and preferences as well as the constraints on the protocol and the norms and conventions it downloaded.

6   Virtual, Distributed Institutional State

In common with previous work (see *e.g.* [3,12] among others), we use the term *institutional state* to refer to the set of obligations, permissions, and other institutional facts (such as 'band is playing' or 'X can send an offer') current at any given time. An implementation of a MAS then provides some mechanism to maintain and evolve this institutional state and verify actions with respect to it. In many implementations, this is done by providing a central server external to the agents but perhaps physically distributed, to which agents refer to obtain authoritative information about the current institutional state (see e.g. [1,12]). In García-Camino et al. [12] *governor agents* are used to intercept messages from agents. They are forwarded to the intended recipients and recorded as communications in the institutional state only if they conform to the norms specified in the current institutional state. These governor agents act as filters, stopping agents from acting in prohibited ways (by restricting its autonomy) but they cannot enforce obligations.

We are using the ballroom case study to develop an alternative approach, intended to be complementary to the methods summarised above, which we believe is more appropriate in some applications of norm-governed MAS. Like Robertson in [18], we argue that centralised control is not always needed. Instead of storing the institutional state externally, whether centralised or in a distributed manner, every agent in the system is responsible for maintaining its own partial view of the current institutional state. This is intended to provide a much lighter and more flexible mechanism for enforcing norm compliance and also allows agents to determine how to conform to norms without resorting to governor agents. Conceptually, there is an institutional state, but it is not represented explicitly (except perhaps for auditing purposes which might be desirable in some applications).

Our ballroom scenario is one example of a society which can operate without central control or norm enforcement. If an institution has sanctions, compensations and/or reparatory mechanisms, then it needs some form of auditing to objectively test its participants' claims. The more it relies on such mechanisms, the more important it is to have some central authority. Conversely, societies that have more implicit norm enforcement (via reputation and trust) are less reliant on strict, authoritarian enforcement.

Since each agent is responsible for maintaining its own beliefs about the evolving institutional state, these beliefs may differ from the actual institutional state. We make two remarks about this.

- In order to be effective, both in terms of impact and in terms of execution time, norms (both constitutive and behavioural) that apply to agents must be formulated in terms of facts that an agent can observe directly or obtain via simple communication with other agents. We have already discussed one such example in previous sections, where we argued that the recipient of a message (an offer to dance the tango, for example) could not be expected to have information about the sender's other commitments or ongoing negotiations.
- We imagine it will be possible to verify formally that an agent's implementation of the required norm interpreter will yield correct beliefs about the institutional state (correct with respect to the conceptual institutional state), on the assumption that all relevant actions are monitored reliably. We believe a certification process of this kind can be made practicable, in some cases at least. Experimentation with other possible methods is one of the main topics of the next phase of the development.

We have several promising candidate formalisms for representing agents' beliefs about the institutional state. In particular we are investigating the use of $nC+$ [20], an adapted version of the action language $(C+)^{++}$ [21] for this purpose.

7   Related Work

Electronic institutions have attracted a lot of attention amongst AI researchers recently. Thus far they have been used in the domain of e-Commerce, most notably in the form of auctions [10,15,19] and allocation processes [23,24]. Frameworks have been developed which help with the specification of organisational requirements and verification of electronic institutions. Two examples are OMNI [24] and ISLANDER [10,19].

We have used the ISLANDER formalism and associated specification tool to design the ballroom as an electronic institution. This work has been undertaken in collaboration with Sierra, Noriega, Rodríguez-Aguilar and García-Camino and will be reported elsewhere.

Grossi et al. [13] note that ontologies are used to relate the abstract concepts in which the norms of an institution are defined to the concrete application. They introduce the notion of contextual ontology and formally characterise it using a description logic. We avoid the need to translate from norms expressed in an abstract way to operational norms by making the conventions and norms downloadable at run-time. Agents still need to be aware of concepts from an ontology, but in our case these concepts are limited to role names, purposes and introspective predicates.

As we have pointed out in the introductory section, there has been a lot of research on normative agents, some of which pre-dates the work on the institutional view on norms (i.e. [4,6,9]). Our work attempts to take into account the institutional responsibilities as well as internal beliefs and desires when choosing a course of action for each agent. The agent architecture we outlined facilitates this by providing a way to combine external norms with internal mental states.

8   Summary and Future Work

The aim of this paper was to present a novel and rich case study for investigating normative behaviour in multi-agent systems. We described a ballroom simulation where interaction protocol templates can be downloaded at run-time together with a representation of behavioural norms and conventions associated with them. We outlined an agent architecture that incorporates these ideas and suggested that for some multi-agent systems no central regulatory authority is needed, and can be replaced by a virtual representation where each agent is responsible for maintaining its own partial view of the relevant institutional state. A main aim of our experiments with this example is to determine more precisely the relative merits and disadvantages of this approach, and to identify the classes of applications in which it can be used.

The fundamental issues we raised in this paper must be taken into account when trying to make norms operational in a distributed environment. We hope to stimulate scientific discussions with our thoughts and will continue to work with the ballroom scenario in a variety of ways. Below, we describe some of our ideas.

In order to achieve full norm-awareness, agents need to be able to reason about norms. In some cases, they will adopt a norm and in others they will not. This depends a lot on their current beliefs, desires and intentions. For example, a female agent, who believes strongly in emancipation is unlikely to adopt a norm that says *'A female has to wait to be approached by a male dancer'*. We are currently working on relating a norm or potential commitment to the BDI modalities (for preliminary results, the interested reader is referred to the BDI+C architecture [11]). The ballroom scenario can then be used to investigate norm adoption by simulating different ballrooms with different conventions and allowing the agent to choose which ballroom to go to depending on its agreement with the conventions.

A second line of research is to investigate more formally the openness of the system. In a fully open system that makes as few assumptions about the agents' capabilities as possible, the conventions will need to be expressed in an XML-like ontology language (like OWL) for agents to read and reason about them (using an OWL reasoners like [22]). Queries such as *'Can I still dance with X?'* will need to be answered by an external, institutional service. The feasibility of this approach has to be contrasted to our de-centralised (but less open) approach where introspective predicates are used.

We are currently also working on extensions which include planning (allowing agents to commit further into the future), standing obligations (the mother-in-law example) and action histories (implemented using a variant of the Event Calculus as in [3]). All of these will clearly complicate the internal representation of an agent and lead to modifications of our system.

The ballroom example may seem at first sight to be unrealistically simple, a toy example that offers few practical insights. This is not so. As we have tried to indicate in the paper, the example exhibits a very wide and varied range of issues, of exactly the kind that are to be encountered in practical applications of norm-governed multi-agent systems. A multiple-auction application, for instance, shares many of the same features. What is deliberately simple in the ballroom example is the implementation of the agents' internal decision making procedures not connected to the representation of norms – in the example, how to dance a specific number of dances, and how to select potential partners. This allows us to focus on the primary question of interest, which is the representation and possible operationalisations of norms. We are confident that lessons learned from experiments with the ballroom example will be directly applicable in practical applications.

Acknowledgements

The first author is partially supported by a PhD bursary from the Engineering and Physical Sciences Research Council (EPSRC) of the United Kingdom. He also received a scholarship from Fujitsu Laboratories of America and is grateful for a student grant from the Spanish Scientific Research Council through the Web-i(2) project (CSIC PI 2004-5 0E 133).

References

1. Artikis, A.: Executable Specification of Open Norm-Governed Computational Systems. PhD thesis, Imperial Colllege London (2003)
2. Artikis, A., Kamara, L., Pitt, J.V., Sergot, M.J.: A protocol for resource sharing in norm-governed ad hoc networks. In: Leite, J.A., Omicini, A., Torroni, P., Yolum, P. (eds.) DALT 2004. LNCS (LNAI), vol. 3476, Springer, Heidelberg (2005)

3. Artikis, A., Pitt, J.V., Sergot, M.J.: Animated specifications of computational societies. In: Castelfranchi, C., Johnson, W.L. (eds.) Proceedings of the first international joint conference on Autonomous agents and multiagent systems (AAMAS 2002), pp. 1053–1061. ACM Press, New York (2002)
4. Boella, G., Lesmo, L.: Deliberate normative agents. In: Conte, R., Dellarocas, C. (eds.) Social order in MAS, Kluwer Academic Publishers, Dordrecht (2001)
5. Carriero, N., Gelernter, D.: Linda in context. Communications of the ACM 32(4), 444–458 (1989)
6. Castelfranchi, C., Dignum, F., Jonker, C.M., Treur, J.: Deliberative normative agents: Principles and architecture. In: Agent Theories, Architectures, and Languages, pp. 364–378 (1999)
7. Clark, K.L., McCabe, F.G.: Go! - a multi-paradigm programming language for implementing multi-threaded agents. Annals of Mathemathics and Artificial Intelligence 41(2-4), 171–206 (2004)
8. Clark, K.L., McCabe, F.G.: Ontology schema for an agent belief store. International Journal Of Human Computer Studies (to appear)
9. Conte, R., Falcone, R., Sartor, G.: Introduction: Agents and norms: How to fill the gap? Artificial Intelligence and Law 7, 1–15 (1999)
10. Esteva, M.: Electronic Institutions: from specification to development. PhD thesis, Institut d'Investigació en Intelligència Artificial, Bellaterra, Spain (2003)
11. Gaertner, D., Noriega, P., Sierra, C.: Extending the BDI architecture with commitments. In: Proceedings of the Ninth Internation Conference of the Catalan Asscociation for Artificial Intelligence, Perpignan, France (2006)
12. García-Camino, A., Rodríguez-Aguilar, J.A., Sierra, C., Vasconcelos, W.: A distributed architecture for norm-aware agent societies. In: Baldoni, M., Endriss, U., Omicini, A., Torroni, P. (eds.) DALT 2005. LNCS (LNAI), vol. 3904, Springer, Heidelberg (2006)
13. Grossi, D., Aldewereld, H., Vázquez-Salceda, J., Dignum, F.: Ontological aspects of the implementation of norms in agent-based electronic institutions. In: Proceedings of NorMAS'05, First International Symposium on Normative Multiagent Systems, Hatfield, April 2005 (2005)
14. Lopéz y Lopéz, F., Luck, M.: Modelling norms for autonomous agents. In: Mejia, M., Chavez, E., Favela, J., Oliart, A. (eds.) Proceedings of the Fourth Mexican International Conference on Computer Science (ENC'03), pp. 238–245. IEEE Computer Society Press, Los Alamitos (2003)
15. Noriega, P.: Agent Mediated Auctions: The Fishmarket Metaphor. PhD thesis, Universitat Autònoma de Barcelona (1997)
16. Ossowski, S.: Coordination in Artificial Agent Societies: Social Structure and its Implications for Autonomous Problem-Solving Agents. In: Distibuted Artificial Intelligence. Lecture Notes on Artificial Intelligence, vol. 1535, pp. 48–55. Springer, Heidelberg (1999)
17. Panzarasa, P., Jennings, N.R., Norman, T.J.: Formalising collaborative decision-making and practical reasoning in multi-agent systems. Journal of Logic and Computation 12(1), 55–117 (2002)
18. Robertson, D.: A lightweight coordination calculus for agent systems. In: Leite, J.A., Omicini, A., Torroni, P., Yolum, P. (eds.) DALT 2004. LNCS (LNAI), vol. 3476, pp. 183–197. Springer, Heidelberg (2005)
19. Rodríguez-Aguilar, J.A.: On the Design and Construction of Agent-mediated Electronic Institutions. PhD thesis, Institut d'Investigació en Intelligéncia Artificial (2003)

20. Sergot, M., Craven, R.: The deontic component of action language nC+. In: Goble, L., Meyer, J.-J.C. (eds.) DEON 2006. LNCS (LNAI), vol. 4048, pp. 222–237. Springer, Heidelberg (2006)
21. Sergot, M.J.: $(\mathcal{C}+)^{++}$: An action language for modelling norms and institutions. Technical Report 2004/8, Department of Computing, Imperial College London (2004)
22. Sirin, E., Parsia, B., Grau, B.C., Kalyanpur, A., Katz, Y.: Pellet: A practical OWL-DL reasoner. Journal of Web Semantics (submitted for publication)
23. Vázquez-Salceda, J.: The Role of Norms and Electronic Institutions in Multi-Agent Systems. Birkhaeuser Verlag (2004)
24. Vazquez-Salceda, J., Dignum, V., Dignum, F.: Organizing multiagent systems. Autonomous Agents and Multi-Agent Systems 11(3), 307–360 (2005)

Part IV
NORM EVOLUTION AND DYNAMICS

Towards Self-configuration in Autonomic Electronic Institutions

Eva Bou[1], Maite López-Sánchez[2], and Juan Antonio Rodríguez-Aguilar[1]

[1] IIIA - CSIC Artificial Intelligence Research Institute, Campus UAB 08193
Bellaterra, Spain
{ebm,jar}@iiia.csic.es
[2] WAI, Volume Visualization and Artificial Intelligence, MAiA Dept., Universitat de
Barcelona
maite@maia.ub.es

Abstract. Electronic institutions (EIs) have been proposed as a means of regulating open agent societies. EIs define the rules of the game in agent societies by fixing what agents are permitted and forbidden to do and under what circumstances. And yet, there is the need for EIs to adapt their regulations to comply with their goals despite coping with varying populations of self-interested agents. In this paper we focus on the extension of EIs with autonomic capabilities to allow them to yield a dynamical answer to changing circumstances through the adaptation of their norms.

1   Introduction

The growing complexity of advanced information systems in the recent years, characterized by being distributed, open and dynamical, has given rise to interest in the development of systems capable of self-management. Such systems are known as self-* systems [1], where the * sign indicates a variety of properties: self-organization, self-configuration, self-diagnosis, self-repair, etc. A particular approximation to the construction of self-* systems is represented by the vision of autonomic computing [2], which constitutes an approximation to computing systems with a minimal human interference. Some of the many characteristics of autonomic systems are: it must configure and reconfigure itself automatically under changing (and unpredictable) conditions; it must aim at optimizing its inner workings, monitoring its components and adjusting its processings in order to achieve its goals; it must be able to diagnose the causes of its eventual malfunctions and reparate itself; it must act in accordance to and operate into a heterogeneous and open environment.

In what follows we argue that are EIs [3] a particular type of self-* system. When looking at computer-mediated interactions we regard Electronic Institutions (EI) as regulated virtual environments wherein the relevant interactions among participating agents take place. EIs have proved to be valuable to develop open agent systems [4]. However, the challenges of building open systems

P. Noriega et al. (Eds.): COIN 2006 Workshops, LNAI 4386, pp. 229–244, 2007.
© Springer-Verlag Berlin Heidelberg 2007

are still considerable, not only because of the inherent complexity involved in having adequate interoperation of heterogeneous agents, but also because the need for adapting regulations to comply with institutional goals despite varying agents' behaviors. Particularly, when dealing with self-interested agents.

The main goal of this work consists in studying how to endow an EI with autonomic capabilities that alllow it to yield a dynamical answer to changing circumstances through the adaptation of its regulations. Among all the characteristics that define an autonomic system we will focus on the study of self-configuration as pointed out in [2] as a second characteristic: "An autonomic computing system must configure and reconfigure itself under varying (and in the future, even unpredictable) conditions. System configuration or "setup" must occur automatically, as well as dynamic adjustments to that configuration to best handle changing environments".

The paper is organized as follows. In section 2 we introduce the notion of autonomic electronic institution as an extension of the classic notion of electronic institution along with a general model for norm adaptation. Section 3 details a case study to be employed as a scenario wherein to test the model presented in section 2. Section 4 provides some preliminary, empirical results. Finally, section 5 summarizes some conclusions and outlines paths to future research.

2   Autonomic Electronic Institutions

The idea behind EIs [5] is to mirror the role traditional institutions play in the establishment of "the rules of the game"–a set of conventions that articulate agents' interactions– but in our case applied to agents (be them human or software) that interact through messages whose (socially relevant) effects are known to interacting parties. The essential roles EIs play are both descriptive and prescriptive: the institution makes the conventions explicit to participants, and it warrants their compliance. EIs involve a conceptual framework to describe agent interactions as well as an engineering framework [6] to specify and deploy actual interaction environments.

Although EIs can be regarded as the computational counterpart of human institutions for open agent systems, there are several aspects in which they are nowadays lacking. According to North [7] human institutions are not static; they may evolve over time by altering, eliminating or incorporating norms. In this way, institutions can adapt to societal changes. Nonetheless, neither the current notion of EI in [3] nor the engineering framework in [6] support norm adaptation so that an EI can self-configure. Thus, in what follows we study how to extend the current notion of EI in [3] to support self-configuration.

First of all, notice that in order for norms to adapt, we believe that a "rational" view of EIs must be adopted (likewise the rational view of organizations in [8]) and thus consider that *EIs seek specific goals*. Hence, EIs continuously adapt their norms to fulfill their goals. Furthermore, we assume that an EI is *situated* in some environment that may be either totally or partially observable by the EI and its participating agents.

With this in mind, we observe that according to [3] an EI is solely composed of: a dialogic framework establishing the common language and ontology to be employed by participating agents; a performative structure defining its activities along with their relationships; and a set of norms defining the consequences of agents' actions. From this follows that further elements are required in order to incorporate the fundamental notions of goal and norm transition as captured by the following definition of *autonomic electronic institution*.

Definition 1. *Given a finite set of agents A, we define an Autonomic Electronic Institution (AEI) as a tuple* $\langle PS, N, DF, G, P_i, P_e, P_a, V, \delta \rangle$ *where:*

- *PS stands for a performative structure;*
- *N stands for a finite set of norms;*
- *DF stands for a dialogic framework;*
- *G stands for a finite set of institutional goals;*
- $P_i = \langle i_1, \ldots, i_s \rangle$ *stands for the values of a finite set of institutional properties, where* $i_j \in \mathbb{R}$, $1 \leq j \leq s$ *contains the value of the j-th property;*
- $P_e = \langle e_1, \ldots, e_r \rangle$ *stands for the values of the environment properties, where each* e_j *is a vector,* $e_j \in \mathbb{R}^{n_j}$ $1 \leq j \leq r$ *contains the value of the j-th property;*
- $P_a = \langle a_1, \ldots, a_n \rangle$ *stands for the values that characterize the institutional state of the agents in A, where* $a_j = \langle a_{j_1}, \ldots, a_{j_m} \rangle$ $1 \leq j \leq n$ *stands for the institutional state of agent* A_j;
- *V stands for a finite set of reference values; and*
- $\delta : PS \times N \times G \times V \to PS \times N$ *stands for a normative transition function that maps a performative structure and a set of norms into a new performative structure and a new set of norms given a set of goals and a set of values for the reference variables.*

Notice that a major challenge in the design of an AEI is to learn a *normative transition function*, δ, that ensures the achievement of its institutional goals under changing conditions. Next, we dissect the new elements composing an AEI.

An AEI employs norms to constrain agents' behaviors and to assess the consequences of their actions within the scope of the institution. Although there is a plethora of formalizations of the notion of norm in the literature, in this paper we adhere to a simple definition of norms as effect propositions as defined in [9]:

Definition 2. *An effect proposition is an expression of the form*

$$A \text{ causes } F \text{ if } P_1, \ldots, P_n$$

Where A is an action name, and each of $F, P_1, \ldots, P_n (n \geq 0)$ is a fluent expression. About this proposition we say that it describes the effect of A on F, and that $P_1, \ldots, P_n$ are its preconditions. If n = 0, we will drop if and write simply A causes F. From this definition, changing a norm amounts to changing either its pre-conditions, or its effect(s), or both.

Agents participating in an AEI have their social interactions mediated by the institution according to its norms. As a consequence of his interactions, only the *institutional (social) state* of an agent can change since an AEI has no access whatsoever to the inner state of any participating agent. Therefore, given a finite set of participating agents $A = \{A_1, \ldots, A_n\}$ where $n \in \mathbb{N}$, each agent $A_i \in A$ can be fully characterized by his institutional state, represented as a tuple of observable values $\langle a_{i_1}, \ldots, a_{i_m} \rangle$ where $a_{i_j} \in \mathbb{R}$ $1 \leq j \leq m$. Thus, the actions of an agent within an AEI may change his institutional state according to the institutional norms.

The main objective of an AEI is to accomplish its goals. For this purpose, and AEI will adapt its norms. We assume that the institution can observe the environment, the institutional state of the agents participating in the institution, and its own state to assess whether its goals are accomplished or not. Thus, from the observation of environment properties(P_e), institutional properties (P_i), and agents' institutional properties (P_a), an AEI obtains the reference values required to determine the fulfillment of goals. Formally, the reference values are defined as a vector $V = \langle v_1, \ldots, v_q \rangle$ where each v_j results from applying a function h_j upon the agents' properties, the environmental properties and/or the institutional properties; $v_j = h_j(P_a, P_e, P_i)$, $1 \leq j \leq q$.

Finally, we can turn our attention to institutional goals. An example of institutional goal for the Traffic Regulation Authority could be to keep the number of accidents below a given threshold. In other words, to ensure that a reference values satisfies some constraint.

Formally we define the goals of an AEI as a finite set of constraints $G = \{c_1, \ldots, c_p\}$ where each c_i is defined as an expression $g_i(V) \lhd [m_i, M_i]$ where $m_i, M_i \in \mathbb{R}$, $\lhd$ stands for either $\in$ or $\notin$, and g_i is a function over the reference values. In this manner, each goal is a constraint upon the reference values where each pair m_i and M_i defines an interval associated to the constraint. Thus, the institution achieves its goals if all $g_i(V)$ values satisfy their corresponding constraints of being within (or not) their associated intervals.

2.1 Norm Adaptation

A major challenge in the design of an AEI is to learn a *normative transition function* that allows to accomplish institutional goals under changing situations. In this work, we concentrate on norm adaptation and therefore we consider that there is no definition of performative structure. Thus, institutional goals must be accomplished through norms, which will be the only means of regulating agents' actions. We are considering the *normative transition function* defined in 1 in a more simple way, $\delta : N \times G \times V \to N$, namely as a normative transition function that maps a set of norms into a new set of norms.

From the definition 2 of norm, changing a norm amounts to changing either its pre-conditions, or its effects, or both. Norms can be parameterized, and therefore we propose that each norm, $N_i \in N$, has a set of parameters $\langle p_{i_1}, \ldots, p_{i_m} \rangle \in \mathbb{R}^{i_m}$. Notice that when the parameters of the norms are associated to the pre-conditions and/or to the effects, changing the values of these parameters means changing the norm. When we refer to change the norms or to adapt the norms we are referring to change or to adapt the values of the parameters of the norms. Norms have associated parametres that can be changed to increase its persuasiveness depending on the agent population behavior. We propose to learn the *normative transition function* by exploring the space of parameter values in search for the ones that best accomplish goals for a given population of agents. In this manner, if we can automatically adapt norms to the global behavior of an agent population, then, we can repeat it for a number of different agent populations and thus characterize the overall *normative transition function*.

Figure 1 describes how this learning process is performed for a given population of agents (A) using an evolutionary approach. We have an initial set of individuals ($\langle I_1, .., I_n \rangle$), where each individual represents a set of norm parameters ($\{ \langle p_{11}, .., p_{1m} \rangle , ..., \langle p_{i1}, .., p_{im} \rangle \}$). The institution performs a simulation for each individual with the population of agents A, so that the norms represented by each individual can be evaluated according to the institutional goals (*Norm evaluation*).Finally, the AEI compiles the evaluations of all individuals in order to perform the *Norm adaptation* process that results with a new set of individuals (*New norms*) to be used as an initial set of individuals for next step in the learning process.

Since we are working with a complex system, we propose use an evolutionary approach for learning due to the fact that the institutional objective function can be naturally mapped to the fitness function and an evolutionary approach provides a solution good enough. Notice that the AEI does not learn any agent parameter, it learns the best parameters by simulation for a certain population of agents, that is whose values will be changed by the normative transition function and by the PS transition function. It is a first step learning where the AEI learns by simulation the best parameters for a list of populations, thus, in a next step the AEI could use this learning in a real environment to adapt itself to any population of agents (e.g., using Case-Based Reasoning (CBR) problem solving technique).

3 Case Study: Traffic Control

Traffic control is a well-known problem that has been approached from different perspectives, which range from macro simulation for road net design [10] to traffic flow improvement by means of multi-agent systems [11]. We tackle this problem from the Electronic Institutions point of view, and therefore, this section is devoted to specify how traffic control can be mapped into Autonomic Electronic Institutions.

In this manner, we consider the Traffic Regulation Authority as an Autonomic Electronic Institution, and cars moving along the road network as agents inside the institution. Considering this set-up, traffic norms regulated by Traffic Authorities can therefore be translated in a straight forward manner into norms belonging to the Electronic Institution. Norms within this normative environment

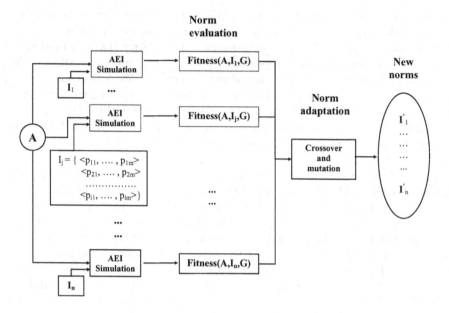

Fig. 1. Example of an step in norm adaptation using an evolutionary approach

are thus related to actions performed by cars (in fact, in our case, they are always restricted to that). Additionally, norms do have associated penalties that are imposed to those cars refusing or failing to follow them. In our case study, we assume that the Traffic Authority is always aware of norm violations: cars may or may not respect rules, but they are not able to avoid the consequences of their application. Furthermore, our Electronic Institution is able to change norms based on its goals – just as traffic authorities do modify their traffic rules– and, therefore, it is considered to be autonomic.

Our AEI sets up a normative environment where cars do have a limited amount of credit (just as some real world driving license credit systems) so that norm offenses cause credit reductions. The number of points subtracted for each traffic norm violation is specified by the sanction associated to each norm, and this sanction can be changed by the regulation authority (that is, our AEI) if its change leads –or contributes to– the accomplishment of goals. Eventually, those cars without any remaining points are forbidden to circulate. On the other hand, we assume a non-closed world, so expelled cars are replaced by new ones having the total amount of points.

Getting into more detail, we focus on a two-road junction. It is a very restrictive problem setting, but it is complex enough to allow us to tackle the problem without losing control of all the factors that may influence the results. In particular, no traffic signals (neither yield or stop signals nor traffic lights) are considered, therefore, cars must only coordinate by following the traffic norms imposed by the AEI. Our institution is required to define these traffic norms based on general goals such as minimization of the number of accidents or deadlock avoidance.

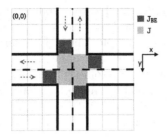

Fig. 2. Grid environment representation of a 2-lane road junction

We model the environment as a grid composed by road and field cells. Road cells define 2 orthogonal roads that intersect in the center (see figure 2). Discretization granularity is such that cars have the size of a cell. As section 3.2 details, our model has been developed with the Simma tool [12]. Although the number of road lanes can be changed parametrically, henceforth we assume the 2-lane case. Next subsections are devoted to define this "toy problem" and present our solution proposal in terms of it. But before that, we introduce some nomenclature definitions:

- A_i: an agent i, agents correspond to cars.
- t: time step. Our model considers discrete time steps (ticks).
- (J_x, J_y): size in x, y of our road junction area.
- J: inner road junction area with (x_0^J, y_0^J) as top left cell inside it
  $J = \{(x, y) \mid x \in [x_0^J, x_0^J + J_x - 1], \ y \in [y_0^J, y_0^J + J_y - 1]\}$
  Considering the 4 J cells in the junction area of Figure 2:
  $J = \{(x_0^J, y_0^J), (x_0^J + 1, y_0^J), (x_0^J, y_0^J + 1), (x_0^J + 1, y_0^J + 1)\}$.
- J_{BE}: Junction Boundary Entrance, set of cells surrounding the junction that can be used by cars to access it. They correspond to cells near by the junction that belong to incoming lanes. Figure 2 depicts $J_{BE} = \{(x_0^J, y_0^J - 1), (x_0^J - 1, y_0^J + J_y - 1), (x_0^J + J_x - 1, y_0^J + J_y), (x_0^J + J_x, y_0^J))\}$.
  Nevertheless, the concept of boundary is not restricted to adjacent cells: a car can be also considered to be coming into the junction if it is located one –or even a few– cells away from the junction.
- (x_i^t, y_i^t): position of car A_i at time t, where $(x, y) \in \mathbb{N} \times \mathbb{N}$ stands for a cell in the grid.
- (h_{ix}^t, h_{iy}^t): heading of car A_i, which is located in (x, y) at time t. Heading directions run along x, y axes and are considered to be positive when the car moves right or down respectively. In our orthogonal environment, heading values are: 1 if moving right or down; −1 if left or up; and 0 otherwise (i.e., the car is not driving in the axe direction). In this manner, car4's heading on the right road of figure 3 is (-1,0).

3.1   AEI Specification

Environment. As mentioned above, we consider the environment to be a grid. This grid is composed of cells, which can represent roads or fields. The main difference among these two types is that road cells can contain cars. Indeed, cars move among road cells along time.

Figure 2 depicts a 8×8 grid example. The top left corner of the grid represents the origin in the x, y axes. Thus, in the example, cell positions range from (0,0) in the origin up to (7,7) at the bottom-right corner. Additionally, a cell is a road if one of its x, y coordinates belong to J inner junction area (see previous definition).

We define this grid environment as:

$$P_e = \langle (x, y, \alpha, r, d_x, d_y) \mid 0 \leq x \leq max_x, \ 0 \leq y \leq max_y,$$
$$\alpha \subseteq P(A), \ r \in [0,1], \ d_x \in [-1,0,1], \ d_y \in [-1,0,1] \ \rangle$$

being x and y the cell position, α defines the set of agents inside the grid cell (x,y), r indicates whether this cell represents a road or not, and, in case it is a road, d_x and d_y stand for the lane direction, whose values are the same as the ones for car headings. Noticie that the institution can observe the environment properties along time, we use P_e^t to refer the values of the grid environment at a specific time t. This discretized environment can be observed both by the institution and cars. The institution observes and keeps track of its evolution along time, whilst cars do have locality restrictions on their observations.

Agents. We consider $A = \langle A_1, ..., A_n \rangle$ to be a finite set of n agents in the institution. As mentioned before, agents correspond to cars that move inside the grid environment, with the restriction that they can only move within road cells. Additionally, agents are given an account of points which decreases with traffic offenses. The institution forbids agents to drive without points in their accounts. The institution can observe the $P_a = \langle a_1, \ldots, a_n \rangle$ agents' institutional properties, where

$$a_i = \langle x_i, \ y_i, \ h_{ix}, \ h_{iy}, \ speed_i, \ indicator_i, \ offenses_i,$$
$$accidents_i, \ distance_i, \ points_i \rangle$$

These properties stand for: car A_i's position within the grid, its heading, its speed, whether the car is indicating a trajectory change for the next time step (that is, if it has the intention to turn, to stop or to move backwards), the norms being currently violated by A_i, wether the car is involved in an accident, the distance between the car and the car ahead of it; and, finally, agent A_i's point account. Notice that the institution can observe the agent properties along time, we use a_i^t to refer the agent A_i's properties at a specific time t.

Reference values. In addition to car properties, the institution is able to extract reference values from the observable properties of the environment, the participating agents and the institution. Thus, these reference values are computed as a compound of other observed values. Considering our road junction case study, we identity different reference values:

$$V = \langle num\_collisions, \ num\_crashed, \ num\_offenses,$$
$$num\_blocked \rangle$$

where **num_collisions** indicates total number of collisions for last t_w ticks ($0 \leq t_w \leq t_{now}$):

$$num\_collisions = \sum_{t=t_{now}-t_w}^{t_{now}} \sum_{e \in P_e^t} f(e_{\alpha^t})$$

being P_e^t the values of the grid environment at time t, e_{α^t} the α^t component of element $e \in P_e^t$ and

$$f(e_{\alpha^t}) = \begin{cases} 1 & if \ |e_{\alpha^t}| > 1 \\ 0 & otherwise \end{cases}.$$

Furthermore, *num_crashed* counts the number of cars involved in accidents for last t_w ticks, *num_offenses* indicates the total number of offenses accumulated by all agents during last t_w ticks, and finally, *num_blocked* shows how many cars have been blocked by other cars for last t_w ticks.

Goals. Goals are institutional goals. The aim of the traffic authority institution is to accomplish as many goals as possible. The institution tries to accomplish these goals by defining a set of norms (see subsection 3.1).

Institutional goals are defined as constraints upon a combination of reference values. Considering our scenario, we define restrictions as intervals of acceptable values for the previous defined reference values (V) so that we consider the institution accomplishes its goals if V values are within their corresponding intervals. In fact, the aim is to minimize the number of accidents, the number of traffic offenses, as well as the number of blocked cars by establishing the list of institutional goals G as:

$G = \langle$ *num_collisions* $\in [0, MaxCollisions]$, *num_crashed* $\in [0, MaxCrashed]$,
    num_offenses $\in [0, MaxOffenses]$, *num_blocked* $\in [0, MaxBlocked]$ $\rangle$

Norms. Autonomic Electronic Institutions try to accomplish goals by defining norms. Norms have associated penalties that are imposed to those cars refusing or failing to follow them. These penalties can be parameterized to increase its persuasiveness depending on the agent population behavior.

Considering a road junction without traffic signals, priorities become basic to avoid collisions. We consider, as in most continental Europe, that the default priority is to give way to the right. This norm prevents a car A_i located on the Junction Boundary Entrance (J_{BE}) to move forward or to turn left whenever there is another car A_j on its right. For example, car 1 in figure 3 must wait for car 2 on its right, which must also wait for car 3 at the bottom J_{BE}. The formalization in table 1 can be read as follows: "if car A_i moves from a position in J_{BE} at time $t - 1$ to its next heading position at time t without indicating a right turn, and if it performs this action when having a car A_j at the J_{BE} on its right, then the institution will fine A_i by decreasing its points by a certain amount" (see figure 4).

Where the predicate **in**$(a_i, Region, t)$ in table 1 is equivalent to $\exists (x, y, \alpha^t, r, d_x, d_y) \in E^t$ so that $(x, y) \in Region \ and \ a_i \in \alpha^t$ and **right**(a_i, a_j, t) is a boolean function that returns true if car a_j is located at J_{BE} area on the right side of car a_i. For the 2-lane J_{BE} case in Figure 2, it corresponds to the formula: $(x_i^t - h_{iy}^t + h_{ix}^t J_x, \ y_i^t + h_{ix}^t + h_{iy}^t J_y) = (x_j^t, y_j^t)$.

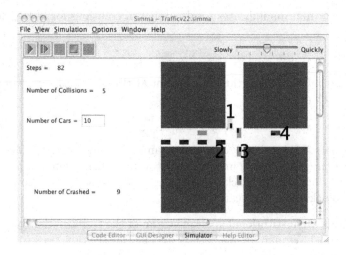

Fig. 3. Priority to give way to the right (Simma tool screenshot)

Table 1. Right priority norm

Action	$in(a_i, J_{BE}, t-1) \wedge$ $in(a_i, (x_i^{t-1} + h_{ix}^{t-1}, y_i^{t-1} + h_{iy}^{t-1}), t) \wedge$ $\neg indicator(a_i, right, t-1)$
Pre-conditions	$right(a_i, a_j, t-1)$
Consequence	$points_i^t = points_i^t - fine$

Other norms, such as deadlock avoidance or junction blocking prevention have been considered and implemented. Nevertheless, due to the lack of space, we cannot detail them.

3.2 Experimental Settings and Design

As a proof of concept of our proposal in section 2.1, we have designed an experimental setting that implements the traffic case study. In this preliminary experiment we consider a single normative goal ($num\_collisions$) and the right priority norm in table 1, which is parameterized by its fine (i.e., points to subtract to the car falling to follow the norm).

The 2-road junction traffic model has been developed with Simma [12], a graphical MAS simulation tool shown in Figure 3, in such way that both environment and agents can be easily changed. In our experimental settings, we have

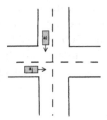

Fig. 4. Priority to give way to the right

modeled the environment as a 16×16 grid where both crossing roads have 2 lanes with opposite directions. Additionally, the environment is populated with 10 cars, having 40 points each.

Our institution can observe the agents properties for each tick and can keep a record of them in order to refer to past ticks. In fact, the institution usually determines traffic offenses by analyzing agent actions along time. Agent actions are observed through consecutive car positions and indicators (notice that the usage of indicators is compulsory for cars in this problem set up). During our discrete event simulation, the institution replaces those cars running out of points by new cars, so that the cars' population is kept constant. Cars follow random trajectories at a constant 1-cell/tick speed and they collision if two or more cars run into the same cell. In that case, the involved cars do remain for two ticks in that cell before they can start following a new trajectory.

Cars correspond to agents without learning skills. They just move based on their trajectories and institutional norms. Agents have local information about their environment (i.e., grid surrounding cells) and know whether their next moves will violate a norm and what fine will be thus applied. Agents decide whether to comply with a norm based on three parameters: $\langle fulfill\_prob,$ $high\_punishment,\ inc\_prob \rangle$. Being $fulfill\_prob \in [0,1]$ the probability of complying with norms that is initially assigned to each agent, $high\_punishment \in \mathbb{N}$ the fine threshold that causes an agent to consider a fine to be high enough to reconsider the norm compliance, and $inc\_prob \in [0,1]$ the probability increment that is added to $fulfill\_prob$ when the fine threshold is surpassed by the norm being violated. In summary, agents decide whether they keep moving regardless of violated norms or they stop in order to comply with norms based on a probability that is computed as: $final\_prob = fulfill\_prob + inc\_prob$ when $fine > high\_punishment$.

Our goal is to adapt norms to agent behaviors by applying Genetic Algorithms (GA)[1] to accomplish the institutional goal, to minimize the total number of collisions. We propose learn the norms by different agent populations behavior by simulation. Once specified what are the different agent populations behavior, a genetic algorithm is running by each population of agents. We use 10 individuals in each step of the genetic algorithm, where each individual is a set of parameters. Therefore, norm adaptation is implemented as a learning process

---

[1] We use GAlib [13], a C++ library of genetic algorithm components.

of the "best" norm parameters. To evaluate an individual we run 10 times the simulator with the set of parameters of the individual. The simulator run the AEI model explained above during 5000 ticks. Thus, norm quality is given by a fitness function that considers the number of collisions, which is computed as an average of 10 different 5000-tick-long simulations for each model setting.

4   Results

From the experimental settings specified above, we have run experiments for three different agent populations. These populations are characterized by their norm compliance parameters, being $fulfill\_prob = 0.5$ and $inc\_prob = 0.4$ for the three of them whereas $high\_punishment$ varies from 5 for the first, to 10 for the second, up to 14 for the third (see table 2).

Since the right priority norm contributes to reduce accidents, our AEI must learn how to vary its fine parameter to increase its persuasiveness for agents, and eventually, to accomplish the normative goal of minimizing the total number of collisions. As to shows table 2, our experiments have resulted in that our AEI learned a fine of 14, 12, and 15 for each respective population. In all three cases, the learned fine is larger than the population's $high\_punishment$ value, and therefore, the goal is successfully reached[2]. In this manner, we can state the AEI success in learning the norms that better accomplish its goal.

Table 2. Learning results for three different agent populations

Parameters	population1	population2	population3
$fulfill\_prob$	0.5	0.5	0.5
$high\_punishment$	5	10	14
inc_prob	0.4	0.4	0.4
Learned fine	**14**	**12**	**15**

Next figure 5 gives some more detail about the performance of agent populations for different norm fine values. First chart compares the number of collisions per 100 ticks when the fine is 4 with the resulting number of collisions when it is 14, which is the learnt value for agents with a $high\_punishment$ threshold equal to 5. Analogously, second and third charts compare results between value 4 and learnt values 12 and 15 respectively (which, again, are learnt when the corresponding agent populations have 10 and 14 threshold values). For all three cases, we can observe that the number of collisions for fine 4 keep above the ones for learnt fines. It is so both in average and along the curve that results from a simulation of 5000 ticks. As expected, the reason is that value 4 is smaller than the $high\_punishment$ values for all three agent populations. Additionally, we can also observe that the deviation in the number of collisions is smaller as well.

---

[2] Notice that, due to the agent's behavior, any fine value higher that the population $high\_punishment$ value will be equally successful.

Population 1: <0.5, 5, 0.4>

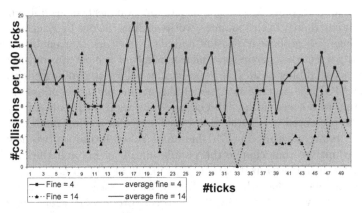

Population 2: <0.5, 10, 0.4>

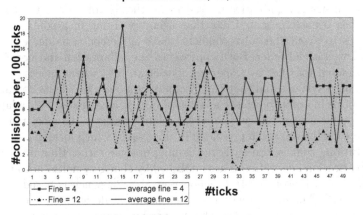

Population 3: <0.5, 14, 0.4>

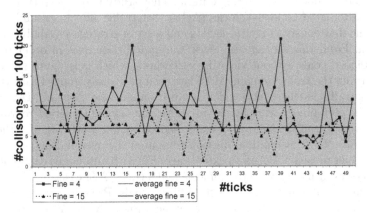

Fig. 5. Number of collisions per 100 ticks along a 5000-tick simulation

5 Discussion and Future Work

Within the area of Multi-Agent Systems, adaptation has been usually envisioned as an agent capability. In this manner, works such as the one by Excelente-Toledo and Jennings [14] propose a decision making framework that enables agents to dynamically select the coordination mechanism that is most appropriate to their circumstances. Hübner et al. [15] propose a model for controlling adaptation by using the $\mathcal{M}$OISE+ organization model. Agents in this model adapt their MAS organization to both environmental changes and their own goals. In [16] Gasser and Ishida presented a general distributed problem-solving model which can reorganize its architecture, in [17] Ishida and Yokoo introduce two new reorganization primitives that change the population of agents and the distribution of knowledge in an organization; and Horling et al. [18] propose an approach where the members adapt their own organizational structures at runtime. Norman et al. [19], within the CONOISE project, propose an agent-based model for dynamic formation of virtual organisations. However all these approaches are based on agent capabilities instead of on the use of norms. On the other hand, it has been long stated [20] that agents working in a common society need norms to avoid and solve conflicts, make agreements, reduce complexity, or to achieve a social order. Both approaches –i.e. adaptation and norms– have been considered together by Lopez-y-Lopez et al. [21], where agents can adapt to norm-based systems and they can even autonomously decide its commitment to obey norms in order to achieve associated institutional goals. This adaptation from the point of view of agents in these related works is the most remarkable difference with the approach presented in this paper, which focuses on adapting the institution –that is, the authority issuing norms– rather than adapting the agents. Institution adaptation is accomplished by changing norms autonomously (as opposite to the work by Hoogendoorn et al. [22], which is based on design considerations). Therefore, we do not select norms at design stages as it is done by Fitoussi and Tennenholtz [23], who do it so by proposing the notions of minimality and simplicity as selecting criteria. They study two basic settings, which include Automated-Guided-Vehicles (AGV) with traffic laws, by assuming an environment that consists of (two) agents and a set of strategies available to (each of) them. From this set, agents devise the appropriate ones in order to reach their assigned goals without violating social laws, which must be respected.

Regarding the traffic domain, MAS has been previously applied to it [11] [24] [25]. But traffic has been also widely studied outside the scope of MAS, for example, the preliminary work by [26] used Strongly Typed Genetic Programming (STGP) to controll the timings of traffic signals within a network of orthogonal intersections. Their evaluation function computed the overall delay.

This paper presents AEI as an extension of EIs with autonomic capabilities. In order to test our model, we have implemented a traffic AEI case study, where the AEI learns a traffic norm in order to fulfill its goals. Preliminary results in this paper provide soundness to our AEI approach. Recently, we have extended the AEI definition [27] in order to include a *performative structure transition function* in order to adapt performative structures. We are also currently performing the same experiments with other norms and with more goals. As future work, and since this basically represents a centralized scenario, we plan to develop a more complex traffic network, allowing us to propose a decentralized approach where different areas (i.e., junctions) are regulated by different institutions. Additionally, we are interested in studying how institutional norms and agent strategies may co-evolve. Nevertheless, this will require to extend the agents so that they become able to adapt to institutional changes. Nevertheless, we plan to extend both our traffic model and the institutional adaptation capabilities so that the AEI will not only learn the most appropriate norms for a given agent population, but it will be able to adapt to any change in the population.

Acknowledgements

This work was partially funded by the Spanish Science and Technology Ministry as part of the Web-i-2 project (TIC-2003-08763-C02-01) and by the Spanish Education and Science Ministry as part of the TIN2006-15662-C02-01 and the 2006-5-0I-099 projects. The first author enjoys an FPI grant (BES-2004-4335) from the Spanish Education and Science Ministry.

References

1. Luck, M., McBurney, P., Shehory, O., Willmott, S.: Agentlink Roadmap. Agenlink.org (2005)
2. Kephart, J.O., Chess, D.M.: The vision of autonomic computing. IEEE Computer 36(1), 41–50 (2003)
3. Esteva, M.: Electronic Institutions: from specification to development. IIIA PhD Monography, vol. 19 (2003)
4. Jennings, N.R., Sycara, K., Wooldridge, M.: A roadmap of agent research and development. Autonomous Agents and Multi-agent Systems 1, 275–306 (1998)
5. Noriega, P.: Agent-Mediated Auctions: The Fishmarket Metaphor. IIIA Phd Monography, vol. 8 (1997)
6. Arcos, J.L., Esteva, M., Noriega, P., Rodríguez-Aguilar, J.A., Sierra, C.: Engineering open environments with electronic institutions. Engineering Applications of Artificial Intelligence 18, 191–204 (2005)
7. North, D.: Institutions, Institutional Change and Economics Perfomance. Cambridge U. P., Cambridge (1990)
8. Etzioni, A.: Modern Organizations. Prentice-Hall, Englewood Cliffs, NJ (1964)
9. Gelfond, M., Lifschitz, V.: Representing action and change by logic programs. Journal of Logic Programming 17, 301–321 (1993)
10. Yang, Q.: A Simulation Laboratory for Evaluation of Dynamic Traffic Management Systems. PhD thesis, MIT (1997)
11. Luke, S., Cioffi-Revilla, C., Panait, L., Sullivan, K.: Mason: A new multi-agent simulation toolkit. In: Proceedings of the 2004 SwarmFest Workshop, p. 8 (2004)
12. López-Sánchez, M., Noria, X., Rodríguez-Aguilar, J.A., Gilbert, N.: Multi-agent based simulation of news digital markets. International Journal of Computer Science and Applications 2(1), 7–14 (2005)

13. Wall, M.: GAlib, A C++ Library of Genetic Algorithm Components. Massachusetts Institute of Technology (MIT), http://lancet.mit.edu/ga/
14. Excelente-Toledo, C.B., Jennings, N.R.: The dynamic selection of coordination mechanisms. Autonomous Agents and Multi-Agent Systems 9(1-2), 55–85 (2004)
15. Hübner, J.F., Sichman, J.S., Boissier, O.: Using the Moise+ for a cooperative framework of mas reorganisation. In: Bazzan, A.L.C., Labidi, S. (eds.) SBIA 2004. LNCS (LNAI), vol. 3171, pp. 506–515. Springer, Heidelberg (2004)
16. Gasser, L., Ishida, T.: A dynamic organizational architecture for adaptive problem solving. In: Proc. of AAAI-91, Anaheim, CA, pp. 185–190 (1991)
17. Ishida, T., Yokoo, M.: Organization self-design of distributed production systems. IEEE Trans. Knowl. Data Eng. 4(2), 123–134 (1992)
18. Horling, B., Benyo, B., Lesser, V.: Using Self-Diagnosis to Adapt Organizational Structures. In: Proceedings of the 5th International Conference on Autonomous Agents, pp. 529–536 (2001)
19. Norman, T.J., Preece, A., Chalmers, S., Jennings, N.R., Luck, M., Dang, V.D., Nguyen, T.D., Deora, V., Shao, J., Gray, W.A., Fiddian, N.J.: Conoise: Agent-based formation of virtual organisations. In: Gedeon, T.D., Fung, L.C.C. (eds.) AI 2003. LNCS (LNAI), vol. 2903, pp. 353–366. Springer, Heidelberg (2003)
20. Conte, R., Falcone, R., Sartor, G.: Agents and norms: How to fill the gap? Artificial Intelligence and Law 7, 1–15 (1999)
21. López-López, F., Luck, M., d'Inverno, M.: Constraining autonomy through norms. In: Alonso, E., Kudenko, D., Kazakov, D. (eds.) AAMAS '02: Proceedings of the 1st international joint conference on Autonomous agents and multiagent systems, pp. 674–681. ACM Press, New York, USA (2003)
22. Hoogendoorn, M., Jonker, C., Treur, J.: Redesign of organizations as a basis for organizational change. LNCS, vol. 4386, pp. 51–71. Springer, Heidelberg (2007)
23. Fitoussi, D., Tennenholtz, M.: Choosing social laws for multi-agent systems: Minimality and simplicity. Artificial Intelligence 119(1-2), 61–101 (2000)
24. Dresner, K., Stone, P.: Multiagent traffic management: An improved intersection control mechanism. In: The 4th International Joint Conference on Autonomous Agents and Multiagent Systems, pp. 471–477. ACM Press, New York (2005)
25. Doniec, A., Espié, S., Mandiau, R., Piechowiak, S.: Dealing with multi-agent coordination by anticipation: Application to the traffic simulation at junctions. In: EUMAS, pp. 478–479 (2005)
26. Montana, D.J., Czerwinski, S.: Evolving control laws for a network of traffic signals. In: Genetic Programming 1996: Proceedings of the 1st Annual Conference, Stanford University, CA, USA, pp. 333–338. MIT Press, Cambridge (1996)
27. Bou, E., López-Sánchez, M., Rodríguez-Aguilar, J.A.: Adaptation of Autonomic Electronic Institutions through norms and institutional agents. In: 7th Annual International Workshop Engineering Societies in the Agents World (ESAW'06), pp. 137–152 (2006)

Norm Conflicts and Inconsistencies in Virtual Organisations

Martin J. Kollingbaum, Timothy J. Norman, Alun Preece, and Derek Sleeman

Department of Computing Science, University of Aberdeen,
Aberdeen AB24 3UE, UK
{mkolling,tnorman,apreece,sleeman}@csd.abdn.ac.uk

Abstract. Organisation-oriented approaches to the formation of multi-agent systems use roles and norms to describe an agent's social position within an artificial society or Virtual Organisation. Norms are descriptive information for a role – they determine the obligations and social constraints for an agent's actions. A legal instrument for establishing such norms are contracts signed by agents when they adopt one or more roles. A common problem in open Virtual Organisations is the occurrence of conflicts between norms – agents may sign different contracts with conflicting norms or organisational changes may revoke permissions or enact dormant obligations. Agents that populate such Virtual Organisations can remain operational only if they are able to resolve such conflicts. In this paper, we discuss, how agents can identify these conflicts and resolve them.

1 Introduction

Organisation-oriented approaches to the formation of multi-agent systems assume that a community of agents form a Virtual Organisation. Its purpose is to facilitate resource sharing and problem solving among software and/or human agents [1,2]. Virtual Organisations are defined by a set of roles, inter-role relationships and norms describing the obligations and social constraints for agents adopting such roles. Agents are regarded as *signing a contract* with the rest of the community when they are recruited into a specific role – they commit to act according to the normative specification of a role. By adopting a set of norms, the agent finds itself in a specific *normative* position – it takes on a social burden in terms of specific norms. This implies that agents must be *norm-governed* – they must be able to reason about the obligations, permissions and prohibitions that characterise their role (or set of roles) within a specific organisational context.

Virtual organisations are situated in a changing world and may, therefore, need to adapt to changes. This dynamic nature of organisations has to be taken into account in the design of agents that are recruited into organisational structures. Due to the dynamic nature of coalitions, the agent's normative position can change – the agent may have to adopt additional norms or revise existing ones. Such a change can lead to *conflicts*: an agent wants to perform an action that is simultaneously allowed and forbidden. Or it can lead to *inconsistencies*: the agent may suddenly be forbidden to perform an action that may be essential for fulfilling one of its obligations.

P. Noriega et al. (Eds.): COIN 2006 Workshops, LNAI 4386, pp. 245–258, 2007.

The NoA model of norm-governed agency [3,4] is specifically designed to deal with such problems. NoA takes inspirations from classical BDI models [5], but has certain unique characteristics: (a) norms are first class entities that influence the practical reasoning of an agent and (b) a specific form of deliberation, called *informed deliberation* [6], is used that enables agents to efficiently identify and resolve norm conflicts and inconsistencies. An agent based on the NoA model will analyse whether it can fulfill its obligations in a *norm-consistent* way. The agent has to investigate whether (a) all options of actions for such an obligation are allowed, (b) least one of them or (c) whether the agent will be forced to violate any other norms if it wants to fulfill an obligation. NoA agents do not filter out options for action that are norm-inconsistent. Instead, the deliberation process of the agent is *informed* about conflicts between permissions and prohibitions and the consistency situation of obligations. With such a norm-informed deliberation, a NoA agent becomes *norm-autonomous* [7] – an agent can decide whether to honour its norms or act against them.

The concepts of norm conflict and consistency of obligations are related. The agent can perform actions and fulfill its obligations in a *norm-consistent* manner only if there are no *conflicts* within the set of norms – the agent must first resolve conflicts between permissions and prohibitions regarding actions in order to be able to create a *complete partitioning* of the options for actions for fulfilling obligations. Allowing conflicts in the first place has practical benefits in the engineering of multi-agent systems – exceptional situations do not have to be anticipated in advance, but the agents themselves are endowed to deal with them. In fact, we argue [6] that it is not possible to ensure that an agent will be conflict-free in even simple scenarios. For that, NoA introduces mechanisms for detecting and classifying conflicts and proposes conflict resolution strategies the agent can employ to disambiguate its normative position so that it can then decide and select actions for fulfilling its obligations.

This paper addresses the critical issue of the occurrence of norm conflicts and how agents can remain operative in the face of such conflicts. If there is a conflict, it has to be resolved by the agents involved. A set of conflict resolution strategies has been proposed in [3,4]. In this paper, we are interested how agents can *refine* their set of currently held norms (for example, via re-negotiating clauses in their contracts) in order to answer questions such as which obligations and prohibitions should be refined or removed or what additional permissions would ease a conflict situation and help an agent to remain operational.

2 Usage Scenario

A specific scenario is used to illustrate the importance of a normative approach to the use of Grid services. In this scenario, a research facility commits to achieve specific research goals for a company. Such a commitment has to be specified formally in the form of a contract to define the rights of the contracting partners. In our scenario, we assume that such a contract is established between the research facility and the company and includes an obligation for the researchers to deliver results of a specific analysis of a set of data. We also assume that this agreement describes a prohibition for the researchers to disclose any of these data (they have an obligation to observe confidentiality). In order to fulfill their obligation, they use services on the Grid to execute their scientific work. We assume that there are two different service providers operating on the Grid:

- a non-profit organisation provides the required service for free, but requires the user to make its data available for public use
- a commercial organisation provides the required service without such an obligation to disclose data, but the service itself is expensive

We assume that the fee for the commercial service is not covered by the budget of the research organisation – the contract with the industrial partner does not allow to spend money on such extra costs. The research organisation is, therefore, compelled to use the free service. This introduces a conflict, as the free service requires the data to be disclosed.

3   Norm-Governed Practical Reasoning

According to the model of norm-governed practical reasoning, as described in [3,4], NoA agents are motivated by obligations to achieve a state of affairs or to perform an action. NoA agents operate with a reactive planning mechanism, where capabilities of an agent are expressed as a set of pre-specified plans. These plans are adapted to the needs of a norm-governed reasoning – they include explicit effect specifications to allow an agent to reason about the normative consequences of possible actions. In the development of this model, specific attention was given to the fact that agents may be confronted with conflicting norms in open environments. A conflict would normally render an agent unable to act. Therefore, NoA includes a model of *informed* deliberation that provides the agent with information about classes of norm conflicts and proposes conflict resolution strategies. This guarantees that NoA agents remain operational in the face of such conflicts.

3.1   Conflicts and Inconsistencies

We describe an interference between obligations and prohibitions as *norm inconsistency* and the interference between permissions and prohibitions as *norm conflict*. In order to show how norms interfere, we have to investigate how norms are specified in NoA. The NoA norm specification language provides constructs to specify obligations, permissions and prohibitions. As NoA allows universally quantified variables within norm specifications, such specifications may address whole sets of states or actions:

```
obligation (r,perform shift("a","r",Z))
prohibition(r,perform shift("a",Y,Z))
```

Obviously, these two norms address sets of actions that possibly overlap – each of the norms is regarded as having a so-called *scope of influence*. By creating a graph over all partial and full instantiations of action (plan) shift, we can gain insights into these scopes of influence in more detail.

Figure 1 shows a part of a graph that outlines all partial and full instantiations of action shift(X,Y,Z). It also shows the *scope* of influence of the prohibition for

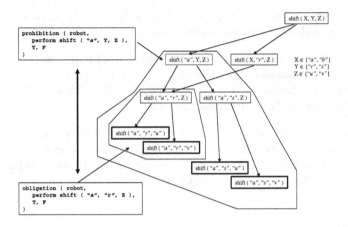

Fig. 1. Containment Relationship between Obligation and Prohibition

action shift("a",Y,Z). This prohibition is regarded to be explicitly specified for shift("a",Y,Z) and *propagated* to each node contained in its scope – each of these nodes represents a specific partial instantiation of shift(X,Y,Z) and each of these partial instantiations is regarded as being explicitly forbidden. The *instantiation set* in this depiction is the set of full instantiations that correspond to shift("a",Y,Z). They are regarded as *inheriting* their normative status from their antecedents and represent those actions that are *explicitly forbidden* because of the adoption of a prohibition that contains an activity specification that addresses a whole set of actions. The instantiation set represents the set of actions (or states) that are actually allowed or forbidden. With this representation, we can regard norms as being *explicitly* introduced for a specific partial instantiation of an action (or state), represented as a node in this graph, and being *propagated* to all nodes in the scope of the norm. Nodes are interconnected according to their (partial) instantiation, with leaf nodes in this graph representing full instantiations. We see that the scope of influence of the prohibition covers the scope of influence of the obligation – the obligation demands actions that are forbidden.

Conflicts and inconsistencies occur if norms are adopted with scopes of influence that overlap. In terms of the instantiation graph, norms are regarded as being introduced for different nodes within this graph at the same time, where (a) a norm addresses a specific partial instantiation of a state or action that is *contained* within the scope of another norm, (b) the scopes of two norms *intersect* or (c) a norm is adopted for a specific action that conflicts with norms adopted for states of affairs that are effects of this action. Three main categories of conflicts emerge [4]:

- *Containment*. The scope of a norm is contained within the scope of another norm. The norms themselves can be regarded as having a specialisation relationship – one norm contains an activity specification that addresses a subset of actions or states addressed by the second norm.
- *Intersection*. The scope of a norm intersects the scope of another norm. There is no specialisation relationship between the norms. The actions or states in the intersection of both scopes *inherit* both norms at the same time.

- *Indirect Conflict/Inconsistency.* As NoA distinguishes between the achievement of a state of affairs and the performance of an action explicitly, there can also be norms formulated that address either an action or a state. For example, an obligation is adopted that demands the performance of a set of actions (its scope of influence) and some of these actions may have effects (produce states of affairs) that are forbidden. This is regarded as an *indirect inconsistency*. In an analogous fashion, an *indirect conflict* may occur.

With respect to these characteristics of NoA, a definition of *norm-consistent action* can be given. If T_F describes the set of currently forbidden actions, S_F the currently forbidden states and S_O the set of states that the agent is obliged to achieve, then the execution of an action (plan) α, where α is not a currently forbidden action (T_F), is consistent with the current set of norms of an agent, if none of the effects of α, expressed as *effects*(α), is currently forbidden and none of the effects of α counteracts any obligation currently held by the agent (expressed as *neg_effects*(α)):

$$consistent(\alpha, T_F, S_F, S_O) \ \textit{iff} \quad p \notin T_F$$
$$and \ S_F \cap \textit{effects}(\alpha) = \emptyset$$
$$and \ S_O \cap \textit{neg\_effects}(\alpha) = \emptyset$$

With the definition of norm-consistent action and the concept of the scope of influence of a norm regarding these actions, the consistency of obligations can be determined. In NoA, we distinguish three so-called *levels of consistency* for obligations. If we describe with *options*(o) the set of options for action that would satisfy the obligation o and which represents the *scope of influence* for this obligation, then we can investigate the consistency of each element $\alpha \in options(o)$. There are three possible configurations for this set: (a) all elements in *options*(o) are consistent, (b) at least one element in *options*(o) is consistent or (c) all elements are inconsistent. According to these three possibilities, we introduce three so-called *consistency levels* for a specific obligation:

- *Strong Consistency.* An obligation is strongly consistent if all $\alpha \in options(o)$ are consistent.
- *Weak Consistency.* An obligation is weakly consistent if at least one candidate in the set *options*(o) is consistent.
- *Inconsistency.* An obligation is inconsistent if no candidate in the set *options*(o) is consistent.

With this consistency information, the agent can decide which actions to perform to remain in a situation of at least *weak consistency* regarding its obligations.

In accordance with our e-Science scenario, let us assume that the agent (representing the research institution) has signed a contract $C1$ (the research agent has to deliver a data analysis) (see figure 2) and, with that, committed to fulfil obligation O_{C1} and adhere to a prohibition F_{C1} (this can be, for example, a prohibition for the research agent to disclose data or to spend over budget). To fulfil its obligation, the agent has two Grid services available as options for action. To use one of these services, it has to accept a second contract $C2$ with one of the service providers. As outlined before, both service providers offer their services under conditions that counteract the original agreement between research agent and industrial partner. Let us assume that the agent does not have the capability to fulfil its obligation and, therefore, has to subcontract with one of the service providers. As pointed out in figure 2, contract $C2$ introduces a new obligation O_{C2}, which is regarded as conflicting with the prohibition F_{C1} of the original contract $C1$.

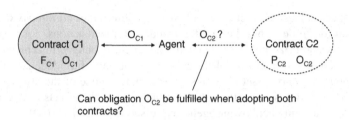

Can obligation O_{C2} be fulfilled when adopting both contracts?

Fig. 2. Agent Signs an Additional Contract

In this situation, the agent should re-negotiate one of these contracts. The contracting partners will try to change the norms specified within the contract. As our e-Science example shows, the research institution cannot act because of a conflict between obligations specified within different contracts. To resolve this conflict, certain obligations and prohibitions have to be changed. In our scenario, there are two options:

- the client lifts the non-disclosure agreement – with that, the contractee could use the free service;
- the client makes additional allowances in the agreed budget, which makes the use of a commercial service possible (the data does not have to be disclosed).

Both partners need information about the best course of action in such a negotiation. For the contracting partners, it is important to be informed about the normative situation – what are the conflicting norms and how obligations and prohibitions can be "relaxed" in order to allow additional options for action.

4   Norm Refinement

The goal of the re-negotiation of contracts is to create or extend a set of options for actions for a contracting agent that are *consistent* with respect to its obligations and prohibitions. In order to make such a decision, additional information is needed.

This reasoning of an agent can be supported by information derived from the instantiation graph. Inconsistency of an obligation means that the scope of influence of an obligation is completely contained within the scope of influence of a prohibition (see figure 1). To achieve a shift from inconsistency to, at least, weak consistency for an obligation, the scopes of influence have to be changed so that such a containment does not occur. There are three options:

– *Extending the Scope of Influence.* Change an obligation so that it becomes a motivator for additional actions that do not have any prohibitions.
– *Reducing the Scope of Influence.* Change a prohibition so that additional actions motivated by obligations become free of conflict.
– *Overriding prohibitions.* Introduce new permissions that override prohibitions to "allow" additional actions for the fulfilment of obligations.

To achieve a shift from this level of inconsistency to, at least, *weak consistency*, the *scope of influence* of either the obligation, the prohibition or both has to be changed. Figure 1 shows, that the two norm specifications can change their scope of influence by becoming either more specialised or more general. For example, if the prohibition forbids the action shift("a","s",Z) instead of the more general shift("a",Y,Z), no interference with the obligation would occur – the obligation would become *strongly consistent*. Similarly, if the obligations would be re-negotiated from shift("a","r",Z) to shift(X,Y,Z), then its set *options(o)* is extended and it becomes *weakly consistent*.

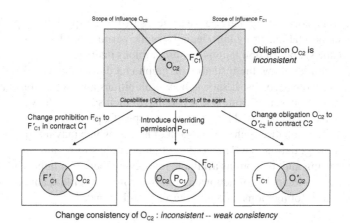

Fig. 3. Possible Changes to Norms to achieve a state of Weak Consistency

Figure 3 shows the transition from the initial situation of *inconsistency* to a situation of *weak consistency* by either re-negotiating F_{C1} to transform it into F'_{C1} (reducing its scope of influence) or re-negotiating O_{C2} to transform it into O'_{C2} (extending its scope of influence). Figure 3 also shows a third option. By introducing a new Permission P_{C1} with a scope of influence that intersects with the scope of F_{C1}, options for action can be made permitted to allow the fulfilment of obligation O_{C2}. The obligation O_{C2} is operating at a level of *weak consistency*. Translated into our e-Science example, the research agent will try to utilise the commercial service as an option for action, but has to re-negotiate additional budget allowances to cover the costs of its use. With that, it is able to fulfill its obligation of payment towards the commercial service.

To achieve *strong consistency*, those norms with intersecting scopes have to be separated completely. Figure 4 shows the transition from the left-most case of figure 3 into a

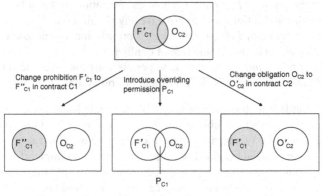

Fig. 4. Possible Changes to Norms to achieve a state of Strong Consistency

situation of strong consistency. This can be achieved by further specialising prohibitions or generalising obligations or by introducing specific permissions for those options for action, where the scopes of obligations and prohibitions intersect.

As these examples show, the instantiation graph is a device that can display issues of conflict and inconsistencies. It shows, how prohibitions and obligations have to be changed to achieve a partial or complete separation of their scopes or how the normative position of an agent can be eased by introducing a specific permission.

In order to operationalise such a refinement of norms, which may take place through a process of re-negotiation, the deliberation of an agent has to be informed about the problems occurring and the options available for solving them. An important device in NoA is the cross-referencing of actions and norms with a label that annotates actions with its *motivators* (obligations) and *prohibitors* prohibitions).

4.1 Labeling Actions

Actions are regarded as being motivated by obligations and may also be, at the same time, prohibited as well as permitted. The normative state of an action may, therefore, be determined by a set of obligations, permissions and prohibitions. In order to cross-reference actions with norms and to indicate potential interference between these norms, these three sets are used to construct a label for actions that contains a set of *motivators* and *prohibitors*. Obligations comprise the set of motivators. We assume that a conflict between a prohibition and permission is solved and that the set of prohibitors only contains prohibitions that are not in conflict with permissions (an overriding permission removes prohibitions from this set). We can describe a label for an action α as a tuple

$$l = \langle \alpha, MOTIVATORS, PROHIBITORS \rangle,$$

where

- α is the labelled candidate action for a set of motivating obligations
- *MOTIVATORS* is the set of obligations that motivate the consideration of this action as a candidate for execution, because (a) one of its effects achieves the state of affairs demanded by this obligation or (b) it is the action demanded by these obligations
- *PROHIBITORS* is the set of prohibitions or obligations that conflict with all the obligations in the set *MOTIVATORS*.

As an obligation may address a whole set of actions (see figure 1), it will be a motivator for these actions and, therefore, be an element of the set *MOTIVATORS* for each of these actions. A label for an action tries to accummulate information about conflicting norms in relation to an action. Therefore, the sets of motivators and prohibitors contain norms that are in conflict. In the set of motivators there may be obligations that are in conflict with only a subset of the prohibitors. To account for this situation, multiple labels have to be established for an action for each subset of obligations and prohibitors that are in conflict. If the set of prohibitors is empty, then a label expresses that an obligation is, at least, *weakly consistent*, as there is at least one option for action to fulfil this obligation without creating conflicts. If the set of prohibitors is empty in all labels, where an obligation occurs in the set of motivators, then this obligation is *strongly consistent*.

4.2   Detecting Conflicts

In investigating our previous example of an obligation,

```
obligation(r,perform shift("a","r",Z))
```

conflicting with a prohibition `prohibition(r,perform shift("a",Y,Z))`, we can conclude that there is a conflict between these norms if the terms representing the `shift` operation in both norm specifications can be unified. Consequently, a conflict can be resolved if the agent finds a substitution so that such a unification fails. For guiding the re-negotiation, the agent has to find the set $\Sigma^{failed} = \{\sigma_1,\ldots,\sigma_n\}$ where the σ_i, $1 \leq i \leq n$, are substitutions that are not unifiers for terms occurring in our norm specifications.

For example, if we assume $X \in \{"a","b","c"\}$, $Y \in \{"r","s","t"\}$ and $Z \in \{"u","v","w"\}$ for action `shift(X,Y,Z)`, then a substitution $\sigma = \{X/t_1, Y/t_2\}$ with $t_1 \in \{"b","c"\}$ and/or $t_2 \in \{"s","t"\}$ would be an appropriate argument for the agent to be proposed in its effort to refine either the prohibition or obligation.

The introduction of new permissions may be used to override prohibitors. A permission partially or completely overrides a prohibitor (covers parts of or the complete scope of influence), if the agent can find a substitution so that unification is successful. The agent has to find the set $\Sigma^{success} = \{\sigma_1,\ldots,\sigma_n\}$ where the σ_i, $1 \leq i \leq n$, are substitutions that are unifiers for terms occurring in our norm specifications. For example, if we assume $X \in \{"a","b","c"\}$, $Y \in \{"r","s","t"\}$ and $Z \in \{"u","v","w"\}$ for action `shift(X,Y,Z)`, then a substitution $\sigma = \{X/t_1, Y/t_2, Z/t_3\}$ with $t_1 \in \{"a"\}$ and $t_2 \in \{"r","s","t"\}$ and $t_2 \in \{"u","v","w"\}$ would be an appropriate proposal for a new permission.

In the set of prohibitors, only those prohibitions are contained that do not have a conflict with a permission. Therefore, if there is a conflict (for example, by introducing a permission that overrides a prohibition), then such a prohibition is removed from the set of prohibitors.

4.3   Options for Re-negotiation

The label expresses consistency for an action. As expressed before, an action is annotated with multiple labels, each displaying a conflict between obligations and prohibitions that expresses a situation of inconsistency for this action. An action is consistent if the set $PROHIBITORS$ is empty in all of its labels.

As outlined in figure 2, we assume a scenario where a new contract introduces a conflict. To simplify the explanations and avoid an overload with indexing, we assume that each contract introduces a single obligation, prohibition and / or permission and that each norm is indexed with a contract identifier to express the relationship between a norm and a contract.

$$l_{\alpha_1} = \langle \alpha_1, \{O_{C1}\}, \{\} \rangle$$
$$l_{\alpha_2} = \langle \alpha_2, \{O_{C3}\}, \{\} \rangle$$
$$l_{\alpha_3} = \langle \alpha_3, \{O_{C1}, O_{C2}\}, \{F_{C1}\} \rangle$$
$$l_{\alpha_4} = \langle \alpha_4, \{O_{C1}, O_{C3}\}, \{F_{C2}\} \rangle$$
$$l_{\alpha_5} = \langle \alpha_5, \{O_{C2}, O_{C3}\}, \{F_{C1}\} \rangle$$

In this scenario, a set of norms $N = \{O_{C1}, O_{C2}, O_{C3}, F_{C1}, F_{C2}, F_{C3}\}$ motivate and, partially, prohibit the performance of actions from the set of actions $A = \{\alpha_1, \ldots, \alpha_5\}$. For example, obligation O_{C1} can be fulfilled by candidate actions α_1, α_3 and α_4 – obligation O_{C1} is a motivator for these actions.

The goal of re-negotiation is to resolve conflicts in the set of norms that determine an agent's normative position. It must be possible for the agent to fulfil its obligations without violating other norms – all obligations have to be at least weakly consistent. To achieve this, the agent has to know which prohibitors to re-negotiate in order to resolve conflicts. In order to perform such an analysis, we will take a snapshot of the set of labels and investigate their sets of motivators and prohibitors.

As outlined before, a label with an empty set of prohibitors indicates that obligations in the set of motivators for this label are weakly consistent. As the scenario outlined above shows, actions α_1 and α_2 have a set of motivators only:

$$l_{\alpha_1} = \langle \alpha_1, \{O_{C1}\}, \{\} \rangle$$
$$l_{\alpha_2} = \langle \alpha_2, \{O_{C3}\}, \{\} \rangle$$

O_{C1} and O_{C3} are the motivators for actions α_1 and α_2. Their labels contain no prohibitors. Therefore, these two actions provide possibilities to fulfil these obligations without violating other norms – they make obligation O_{C1} and O_{C3} weakly consistent. With that, these two obligations do not have to be considered any more.

For a further analysis of the set of labels, all occurrences of these weakly consistent obligations are removed from the set of labels. If, after this cleanup, a label has an empty set of motivators, then this label will be removed from the set of labels. In our scenario, labels l_{α_1}, l_{α_2} and l_{α_4} are changed in this way and are removed:

$$l_{\alpha_3} = \langle \alpha_3, \{O_{C2}\}, \{F_{C1}\}\rangle$$
$$l_{\alpha_5} = \langle \alpha_5, \{O_{C2}\}, \{F_{C1}\}\rangle$$

The resulting set of labels can now be used to derive the minimal set of prohibitors that the agent has to re-negotiate in order to achieve weak consistency for all obligations. A procedure is employed here that will select a prohibitor according to *occurrence* – the prohibitor with the highest occurrence is chosen, removed from the remaining labels and added to a set R of prohibitors to be re-negotiated. Such a prohibitor has a relationship to a set of obligations and, therefore, has to be added to the set R together with its related obligations. In our scenario, set R contains prohibitor F_{C1} together with obligation O_{C2}:

$$R = \{\{F_{C1}, O_{C2}\}\}$$

In general, the removal of such a prohibitor from all the labels where it occurs will, again, leave some labels with empty sets of prohibitors. The cleanup step described before must be repeated and such labels deleted. After that, again, a new prohibitor with maximal occurrence has to be selected, added to set R and removed from labels. Both the cleanup step and the selection of a prohibitor has to be repeated until all labels are removed. This creates a set R of prohibitors for re-negotiation, where a precedence relationship $\prec$ exists between its members. The relationship of a prohibitor to its obligations has to be expressed accordingly:

$$R = \{\{F_1, O_1, \ldots, O_{m_1}\}, \ldots, \{F_n, O_1, \ldots, O_{m_n}\}\},$$

$$F_1 \prec F_2 \prec \ldots \prec F_n$$

Instead of selecting prohibitors according to *occurrence*, other criteria may be chosen for such a selection process. For example, the agent may hold a function

$$violate(F) : N \to \mathbb{R}$$

that calculates the cost of a violation of a specific prohibitor, which influences the selection in the elimination process described before.

5 Related Work

Norms have found increasing attention in the research community as a concept that drives the behaviour of agents within virtual societies. Conte and Castelfranchi [8,9] investigate in detail how agents within a society reason about norms regarding their actions and what motivates them to honour their obligations and prohibitions and fulfill their commitments. Conte et al. [8,7], argue that for a computational model of norm-governed agency, the internal representation of norms and normative attitudes, and models of reasoning about norms is a necessity. Norm-governed agents must be able to recognise norms as a social concept, represent them as mental objects and solve possible conflicts among them. Such agents should, in the words of [7], be truly *norm-autonomous* – they must know existing norms, learn / adopt new ones, negotiate norms with peers, convey / impose norms on other agents, control and monitor other agents' norm-governed behaviour, and be able to decide whether to obey or violate them. Panzarasa et al. [10,11] discuss the influence of a social context on the practical reasoning of an agent. They point out that the concept of *social commitment* as introduced by Castelfranchi and investigated by Cavendon and Sonenberg has to be extended to include issues of how social commitments and regulations inform and *shape* the internal mental attitudes of an agent to overcome the solipsistic nature of current BDI models. Work pursued by Broersen et al. [12], Dastani and van der Torre [13,14], the model of a normative agent described by Lopez et al. [15] and, specifically, the NoA system as presented in this paper and elsewhere [4,3] introduce concepts of norm influence into practical reasoning agent to make this transition from solipsistic to social agents. The NoA model of norm-governed agents takes strong inspirations from the work of Kanger [16], Lindahl [17] and Jones and Sergot [18,19] for the representation of *rights* and the concept of a *normative position*. Members of a society adopt these norms and, ideally, operate according to them. Adopted norms determine the social or normative position of an individual [17], expressing duties, powers, freedom etc. under specific legal circumstances. This normative position can change any time with new norms coming into existence or old ones removed. Relationships of power create organisational structures and hierarchies within a society, assigning specific roles to members of an organisation [18,20]. Dignum et al. [21] describe the three basic aspects in the modelling of virtual societies of agents: (a) the overall purpose of such a community of agents, (b) organisational structure based on a set of roles and (c) norms for regulating the actions and interactions of the agents adopting such roles. In line of our previous argument that the solipsistic nature of agents has to be overcome for virtual organisations, they emphasise as well the importance of introducing a *collective* perspective on an agent's actions in a specific role within a society - the agent cannot not be solely driven by internal motivations, but it has to be socially aware in its practical reasoning. As also described in [22], Agents take on roles and responsibilities and are determined in their actions by *external* influences in the form of social regulations and norms. Pacheco and Carmo [20] describe the modelling of complex organisations and organisational behaviour based on roles and normative concepts. The creation of virtual societies is based on contracts between agents. Such a contract describes the set of norms that specify roles and agents adopting such roles commit to act according to these norms. Pacheco and Carmo emphasise the importance of these contracts as the central element to bind agents into societies.

Organisational change and the impact of these social dynamics on the normative position of the agent, as addressed in previous work [23,4,24,3], also find attention in the work of Esteva et al. [25], Lopez and Luck [26] and Skarmeas [27]. Dastani et al. [28] investigate conflicts that can occur during the adoption of a role by an agent. Esteva et al. [25] present a computational approach for determining the consistency of an electronic institution. As shown in [4], the NoA model includes a detailed classification of conflict situations that *informs* the deliberation of the agent about problems of norm conflicts and inconsistencies between the agents actions and its norms and can be used to guide the re-negotiation of contracts. With that, a NoA agent does not require a conflict-free set of norms to be operable, as it is provided with conflict resolution strategies to deal with conflicting norm sets.

6 Conclusion

In case of a norm conflict, agents may have to re-negotiate their contracts. The goal of such a re-negotiation must be a guarantee that obligations can be fulfilled by actions that do not violate any prohibitions. The NoA model and architecture for norm-governed practical reasoning agents takes specific care to inform the agent about the *norm consistency* of its options for actions for fulfilling its obligations and provides resolution strategies for conflicts between norms. In this paper, we illustrate how this model of norm-consistent action and norm conflicts can be used to inform the agents in the re-negotiation of their contracts.

References

1. Foster, I., Kesselman, C., Tuecke, S.: The Anatomy of the Grid: Enabling Scalable Virtual Organizations. Int' J. Supercomputer Applications 15, 209–235 (2001)
2. Norman, T., Preece, A., Chalmers, S., Jennings, N., Luck, M., Dang, V., Nguyen, T., Deora, V., Shao, J., Gray, W., Fiddian, N.: Agent-based Formation of Virtual Organisations. Knowledge Based Systems 17, 103–111 (2004)
3. Kollingbaum, M.: Norm-governed Practical Reasoning Agents. PhD thesis, University of Aberdeen (2005)
4. Kollingbaum, M., Norman, T.: Strategies for Resolving Norm Conflict in Practical Reasoning. In: ECAI Workshop CEAS 2004 (2004)
5. Wooldridge, M.: An Introduction to MultiAgent Systems. John Wiley & Sons, LTD. Chichester (2002)
6. Kollingbaum, M., Norman, T.: Anticipating and Resolving Conflicts during Organisational Change, Technical Report AUCS/TR0505. Technical report, University of Aberdeen (2005)
7. Conte, R., Falcone, R., Sartor, G.: Agents and Norms: How to fill the Gap? Artificial Intelligence and Law 7 (1999)
8. Conte, R., Castelfranchi, C.: Cognitive and Social Action. UCL Press (1995)
9. Castelfranchi, C.: Modelling Social Action for AI Agents. Artificial Intelligence 103, 157–182 (1998)
10. Panzarasa, P., Norman, T., Jennings, N.: Modelling Sociality in the BDI Framework. In: Intelligent Agent Technology: Systems, Methodologies, and Tools. Proceedings of the First Asia-Pacific Conference on Intelligent Agent Technology. World Scientific Publishing, pp. 202–206 (1999)
11. Panzarasa, P., Jennings, N., Norman, T.: Social Mental Shaping: Modelling the Impact of Sociality on the Mental States of Autonomous Agents. Computational Intelligence 17, 738–782 (2001)
12. Broersen, J., Dastani, M., Hulstijn, J., Huang, Z., van der Torre, L.: The BOID architecture: Conflicts between Beliefs, Obligations, Intentions and Desires. In: Proceedings of Autonomous Agents 2001, pp. 9–16 (2001)
13. Dastani, M., van der Torre, L.: What is a normative Goal? In: Falcone, R., Barber, S., Korba, L., Singh, M.P. (eds.) AAMAS 2002. LNCS (LNAI), vol. 2631, Springer, Heidelberg (2002)

14. Dastani, M., van der Torre, L.: A Classification of Cognitive Agents. In: Proceedings of the 24th Annual Meeting of the Cognitive Science Society CogSci 2002, pp. 256–261 (2002)
15. Lopez y Lopez, F., Luck, M., dínverno, M.: Constraining autonomy through norms. In: Proceedings of the 1st International Joint Conference on Autonomous Agents and Multi-agent Systems, pp. 647–681 (2002)
16. Kanger, S., Kanger, H.: Rights and Parliamentarism. Theoria 32, 85–115 (1966)
17. Lindahl, L.: Position and Change: A Study in Law and Logic. D. Reidel Publishing Company (1977)
18. Jones, A., Sergot, M.: A Formal Characterisation of Institutionalised Power. Journal of the IGPL 4, 429–445 (1996)
19. Sergot, M.: A Computational Theory of Normative Positions. ACM Transactions on Computational Logic 2, 581–622 (2001)
20. Pacheco, O., Carmo, J.: A Role Based Model for the Normative Specification of Organized Collective Agency and Agents Interaction. Autonomous Agents and Multi-Agent Systems 6, 145–184 (2003)
21. Dignum, V., Meyer, J.J., Weigand, H., Dignum, F.: An Organization-Oriented Model for Agent Societies. In: Falcone, R., Barber, S., Korba, L., Singh, M.P. (eds.) AAMAS 2002. LNCS (LNAI), vol. 2631, Springer, Heidelberg (2003)
22. Dastani, M., Dignum, F., Dignum, V.: Organizations and Normative Agents. In: Proceedings of the 1st Eurasian Conference on Advances in Information and Communication Technology Eurasia ICT (2002)
23. Kollingbaum, M., Norman, T.: Norm Consistency in Practical Reasoning Agents. In: Dastany, M., Dix, J. (eds.) PROMAS Workshop on Programming Multiagent Systems (2003)
24. Kollingbaum, M., Norman, T.: Norm Adoption and Consistency in the NoA Agent Architecture. In: Dastani, M., Dix, J., El Fallah-Seghrouchni, A. (eds.) PROMAS 2003. LNCS (LNAI), vol. 3067, Springer, Heidelberg (2004)
25. Esteva, M., Vasconcelos, W., Sierra, C., Rodriguez-Aguilar, J.: Verifying Norm Consistency in Electronic Institutions. In: Proceedings of the AAAI 2004 Workshop on Agent Organisations: Theory and Practice (2004)
26. Lopez y Lopez, F., Luck, M.: Towards a Model of the Dynamics of Normative Multi-Agent Systems. In: Proceedings of the International Workshop on Regulated Agent-Based Social Systems: Theories and Applications RASTA'02, Bologna (2002)
27. Skarmeas, N.: Organisations through Roles and Agents. In: Proceedings of the International Workshop on the Design of Cooperative Systems COOP'95 (1995)
28. Dastani, M., Dignum, V., Dignum, F.: Role-assignment in open Agent Societies. In: Proceedings of the 2nd International Joint Conference on Autonomous Agents and Multiagent Systems (2003)

Using Dynamic Electronic Institutions to Enable Digital Business Ecosystems

Eduard Muntaner-Perich and Josep Lluís de la Rosa Esteva

Agents Research Lab, Edifici PIV, Campus de Montilivi, 17071
Universitat de Girona, Catalonia, Spain
{emuntane,peplluis}@eia.udg.cat

Abstract. In this paper, which is exploratory in nature, we introduce how to use Dynamic Electronic Institutions to enable Digital Business Ecosystems. A Digital Business Ecosystem is an evolutionary self-organising system aimed at creating a digital software environment for small organisations. These new forms of networked business require a multi-disciplinary approach based on biology, computer science and social sciences mechanisms and models. Our proposal is to use a multi-agent approach in combination with some social sciences metaphors. More specifically, we propose to imagine the digital environment of business ecosystems as an open agent system, and to study the spontaneous composition and adaptation of the different services and software components, by using Dynamic Electronic Institutions, which we have recently presented in our latest works. In this paper we present a brief summary of our previous work on dynamic institutions, and our first ideas on how to enable Digital Business Ecosystems.

Keywords: Open Agent Systems, Electronic Institutions, Coalition Formation, Digital Business Ecosystems, Normative Systems, Electronic Contracts.

1 Introduction

Businesses today are a highly interconnected network of companies, organisations, technologies, consumers, products and services. The degree of interactions in electronic business is becoming higher, and these interactions are becoming increasingly complex. In fact, the success of businesses is ever more dependent on the associations and relationships in the Market (business ecosystems).

The Digital Business Ecosystem (DBE) is the enabling technology for the business ecosystems. A Digital Business Ecosystem is defined as "an evolutionary self-organising system aimed at creating a digital software environment for small organisations that support the regional and local development by empowering open, distributed and adaptive technologies and evolutionary business models for small organisations growth" [1].

The concept of DBE has been coined initially in 2002 in Europe. Today the European vision of Digital Ecosystems is becoming mature ant currently there are two important related projects ongoing in Europe:

P. Noriega et al. (Eds.): COIN 2006 Workshops, LNAI 4386, pp. 259–273, 2007.

- The DBE Project [1,2]: the ideas behind the DBE project use mechanisms from living organisms like evolution, adaptation, autonomy, or self-organisation, to arrive at novel architectures, technologies and business processes, thus creating a network of digital business ecosystems for SMEs (Small and Medium size Enterprises) to improve their value networks and foster local economic development.
- The ONE Project [3]: the main objective of the ONE project is to enrich Digital Ecosystems with an open, decentralised negotiation environment and enabling tools that will allow organisations to create contract agreements (electronic contracts) for supplying complex, integrated services as a virtual organisation/coalition or temporary e-business unions.

The idea is that an open-source distributed environment will support the spontaneous composition and adaptation of services and software components (which include business rules and norms), in order to allow SMEs to cooperate in production of components and applications adapted to local business needs. A "digital environment" will be an environment populated by "digital species" like software components, applications, services, knowledge, business models, laws, etc. In Figure 1, an example of Digital Business Ecosystem is shown.

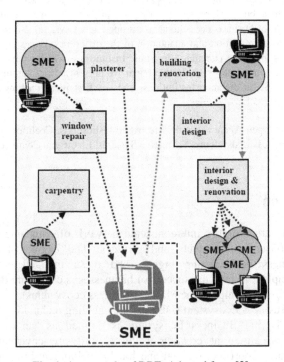

Fig. 1. An example of DBE. Adapted from [2].

The Digital Business Ecosystem concept is emerging as an innovative approach to support the adoption and development of ICTs [4]. A network of digital ecosystems, will offer opportunities of participation in the global economy to SMEs and also to less developed or remote areas. These new forms of dynamic business interactions and global cooperation among companies, organisations and business communities will foster local economic growth, and they will probably contribute to overcome the digital divide.

In the European case, SMEs represent the 99% of the total number of businesses, so they are a very important part of the European economy. The DBE Project aims to provide SMEs with new cost-effective technology paradigms and innovative uses of ICTs. This way, SMEs will be able to reduce their time to market, and to enlarge their business networks.

At this moment there are different European research groups and organisations working on the DBE Project and the ONE Project (Waterford Institute of Technology, Instituto Tecnológico de Aragón, Trinity College Dublin, London School of Economics, University of Girona, etc.). There is also some preliminary software for DBEs: DBE Execution Environment (ExE) [5] and DBE Studio [6]. But in our opinion, these projects are centred on the execution and management of DBEs, and we believe that there is a need to study the mechanisms which will allow the automatic composition and teamwork of the different components inside and among ecosystems.

These new forms of networked business will require a multi-disciplinary approach based on biology, computer science and social sciences mechanisms and models. The science team in the DBE project is working on an evolutionary environment by using a biological approach. Our proposal is to use a multi-agent approach in combination with some social sciences metaphors. More specifically, we propose to imagine the digital environment of the DBE as an open agent system, in which the components (agents) are not known a priori, can change over time, and can be heterogeneous (with different objectives, capabilities and behaviours).

But the use of open agent systems could cause some problems, because in this kind of systems, the emergent behaviour of the global system can become chaotic and unexpected. In critical applications this can be a significant problem, and it is evident that regulatory measures must be introduced to determine what things agents can and cannot do. Electronic institutions [7] could be an effective solution. They incorporate social and organisational abstractions into multi-agent systems; in fact they incorporate the rules of the game. But they have some limitations: they are based on medium to long-term associations between agents, they require a design phase performed by humans, and there are no mechanisms for automatic creation, reconfiguration and dissolution processes.

We argue, therefore, that the solution could be to study the spontaneous composition and adaptation of the different services and software components, by using Dynamic Electronic Institutions, which we have presented in our recent works [8, 9, 10].

This paper is organized as follows. In section 2 we explain the most important characteristics of electronic institutions, their key concepts and their main problems. In section 3 we explain our model and approach to Dynamic Electronic Institutions. Next, section 4 illustrates the connection points between dynamic institutions and DBE, and suggests a way for enabling DBEs by using dynamic institutions. Finally section 5 concludes with discussion and future research.

2 Electronic Institutions

From a social point of view, it is easy to observe that the interactions between people are often guided by institutions that help and provide us with structures for daily life tasks. Institutions structure incentives in human exchange (political, social, or economic). Institutions establish laws, norms and rules to respond to emergencies, disasters, et cetera. Somehow we could say that institutions represent the rules of the game in a society or, more formally, are the humanly devised constraints that shape human interaction [11].

The idea to use organisational metaphors to model systems was early proposed [12, 13]. These approaches suggest structuring the agent society with roles and relationships between agents. But the study of electronic institutions is a relatively recent field (the first approach was [14]). The main idea is simple, and it could be summarized by imagining groups of intelligent, autonomous and heterogeneous agents, which play different roles, and which interact with each other under a set of norms, with the purpose of satisfying individual goals and/or common goals. As a first impression, it could seem that these norms are a negative factor which adds constraints to the system, but in fact they reduce the complexity of the system, making the agents' behaviour more *predictable*.

Research in Distributed Artificial Intelligence (DAI), and more specifically, research in MAS, has focused on the individual behaviour of agents (agent-centred view). But this agent-centred perspective is not useful in complex systems like *open agent systems*, where their components (agents) are not known a priori, can change over time, and can be heterogeneous and exhibit very different behaviours. Open agent systems are also characterized by limited trust and conflicting individual goals. In these kinds of systems, this vision that is focused on the agent can cause the emergent behaviour of the global system to be chaotic and unexpected. In critical applications this can be a significant problem, and it is evident that is necessary to introduce regulatory measures which determine what things the agents can do, and what they cannot. It is here where the institutions acquire importance. Agent-centred approaches can be useful for closed and small systems, but they fail to design open systems [15, 16].

In Noriega's thesis [14], an abstraction of the notion of institution is introduced for the first time. He is also the first to use the term *agent-mediated electronic institution*, which he describes as: computational environments which allow heterogeneous agents to successfully interact among them, by imposing appropriate restrictions on their behaviours.

Continuing and extending the ideas of Noriega's thesis, there is Rodríguez-Aguilar [16] who emphasizes the need for a formal framework which allows to work with general electronic institutions.

From these first approaches to this area, to the actual lines of research, there have been different European research groups working on similar subjects, each one with its particular perspective and approach to the problem. At the moment, many efforts are dedicated to this research area. The proof of this is that in 2003, five PhD theses intimately related to this subject were presented. The theses are: [7,17,18,19,20].

These different approaches to electronic institutions have demonstrated how organisational approaches are useful in *open agent systems*, but in our opinion, they still have several problems and limitations. We have summarized these problems in the following list:

- All the approaches to electronic institutions are based on medium to long-term associations and dependencies between agents. This characteristic is useful in some application domains but it is a significant problem in other domains, where changes in tasks, in information and in resources make temporary associations (regulated by norms) necessary.
- Electronic institutions require a design phase (performed by humans). It is necessary to automate this design phase in order to allow the emergence of electronic institutions (without human intervention) in open agent systems.
- Agents can join and leave institutions, but how do these entrances and exits affect the institutions' norms and objectives? Could these norms and objectives change over time?
- When an institution has fulfilled all its objectives, how can it dissolve its components (agents)?

In our opinion, these problems and limitations can be studied and possibly solved with a coalition formation approach to electronic institutions, in order to develop dynamic electronic institutions. This is the main objective of our research. In the next section we present our model of dynamic electronic institutions and their lifecycle.

There is little previous work on dynamic electronic institutions: this idea has just recently been introduced as a challenge for agent-based computing. It first appeared when the term *dynamic electronic institution* appeared in a roadmap for agent technology [21].

3 Dynamic Electronic Institutions

We argue that Dynamic Electronic Institutions (DEIs from now on) can be described as follows: emergent associations of intelligent, autonomous and heterogeneous agents, which play different roles, and which are able to adopt a set of norms in order to interact with each other, with the aim of satisfying individual goals and/or common goals. These formations are dynamic in the sense that they can be automatically formed, reformed and dissolved, in order to constitute temporary electronic institutions on the fly. This type of institution should be able to adapt its norms and objectives dynamically in relation to its present members (agents).

There are several application domains that require short-term agent organisations or alliances, in which DEIs could be applied. Some of them are: Digital Business Ecosystems (we will study this application domain in the next section), B2B Electronic Commerce, Mobile Ad-Hoc Networks, simulation of Operations Other Than War (OOTW), etc.

In our opinion DEIs should have a lifecycle made up of by three phases: Formation, Foundation and Fulfilment (We call this lifecycle "3F cycle" [9]). Figure 2 depicts this cycle.

1. *Formation phase*: this is the coalition formation phase. Associations between agents which have the same (or similar) goals emerge. Other notions such as trust between agents should also be considered as important factors in the coalition formation phase. In order to allow agents to form coalitions, a coalition formation mechanism is necessary; this implies a protocol and strategies.

2. *Foundation phase*: the process of turning the coalition into a temporary electronic institution. This phase is the real challenge, because the process of turning the coalition into a temporary electronic institution is not a trivial problem. The foundation phase has never been studied before. Currently, we are focusing our work on this phase. We address this question in the next section.

3. *Fulfilment phase*: this is the dissolution phase. When the institution has fulfilled all its objectives, the association should be broken up. This phase occurs because the association is no longer needed, or because the institution is no longer making a profit. A dissolution process can also be considered after the formation phase. Within this phase the agents should distribute the profits obtained and store relevant information for future DEIs.

Within this lifecycle there are also the *re-formation* and the *re-foundation* processes as shown in Figure 2. The *re-formation* process facilitates reconfiguring the coalition when member changes occur, and the *re-foundation* process facilitates reconfiguring the institution when member changes occur.

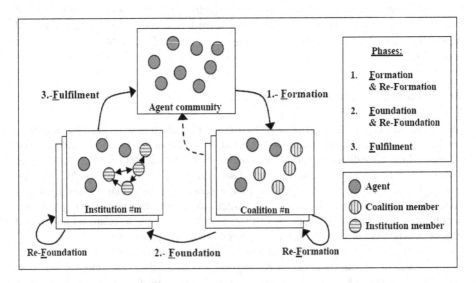

Fig. 2. DEI construction phases (3F cycle)

One of these three phases has been poorly studied in the past: the foundation phase (and the *re-foundation* process). At this moment, we are focusing our work on this phase.

3.1 The Foundation Phase

We define foundation as the process of turning a coalition into a temporary electronic institution. This phase is a real challenge because the process of turning the coalition into a temporary electronic institution is not a trivial problem. It requires the agents to adopt a set of norms that regulate their interactions. This must be an automated process, without any human intervention, so agents must be able to reason and negotiate at a high level.

Our perspective on this problem is that to construct an institution from zero without human intervention may be too difficult, so we argue that an approach based on using knowledge from previous cases (like Case Based Reasoning, CBR) could be interesting and useful for solving this issue (also for the *re-foundation problem*). Presently, we are directing our efforts in this direction.

The foundation phase can be represented as a black box in which a coalition is turned into an institution (Figure 3). In an ideal situation, the output of the black box for the foundation phase could be an ISLANDER specification of the institution [15]. Thus, AMELI [22] could be used for running the institution specified with ISLANDER. In our opinion these are the most complete and functional tools to work with electronic institutions.

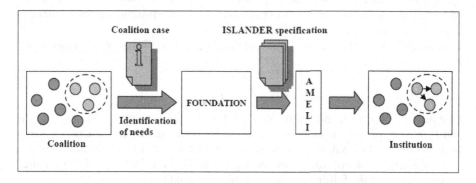

Fig. 3. The Foundation Phase represented using a black box

In our approach we are using Case-Based Reasoning. CBR is based on the idea that new problems are often similar to problems that have been encountered previously and that past solutions may be of use in the current situation.

A stored case refers to a problem situation and contains a description of a problem, and its solution, and a new case contains the description of the problem to be solved. Case-based reasoning is a cycle. There are four phases in the process: Retrieve, Reuse, Revise and Retain.

With a CBR approach to the foundation process, when a coalition has been formed and needs to turn itself into an institution, agents should consult their case databases in order to find the stored institution's specification that adapts best to the present situation, and should then make the pertinent reforms to the selected specification in order to obtain an institution that works correctly.

The CBR process should be done in a distributed way (each agent has its own stored institution cases, in relation to its own experience in the system) or in a centralized way (there is a central database with the stored institution cases. Previous-Institutions Base: PIB).

3.2 Formalisation of the Foundation Phase

In our system, a coalition can be expressed as a tuple C that consists of five components.

$$C = \{ A, T, O, het, tr \} \tag{1}$$

Where A is a finite set of agents. Each agent is also a tuple (that contains the agent's type, its objectives, its capabilities or tasks, and its private and public variables). T is the finite set of the types of the agents involved in the coalition. O is the finite set of the joint objectives of the agents involved in the coalition. Finally, there are two more components: het is a value that describes the heterogeneity of the coalition members. It must take into account the heterogeneity within types and the heterogeneity within objectives; and tr defines the trust mean value among the coalition members (it depends on the trust value between each pair of agents inside the coalition). All these components are used to create a *Coalition Case*, with the aim of finding the stored *Institution Case* (within the Previous-Institutions Base, PIB) that adapts best to the coalition.

A dynamic institution can be expressed as a tuple I that consists of six components.

$$I = \{ A, T, O, het, tr, IC \} \tag{2}$$

$$IC = \{ N, pr, ont, FC \}$$

Where the first five components (A, T, O, het, tr) are the same that in the coalition, and IC is a set of institutional components. IC is composed by four elements: N is a finite set of institutional norms (obligations, prohibitions and permissions), pr is a communication protocol, ont is an ontology, and FC is a finite set of the required conditions to start the fulfilment phase (Fulfilment Conditions).

With this formulation we can describe our CBR process for the foundation phase as a function called *Foundation*.

$$Foundation : C \times PIB \rightarrow IC \tag{3}$$

This function has two input parameters: a coalition C and a previous-institutions base PIB; and one output parameter: the institutional components IC which have to be adopted by the coalition in order to turn itself into an institution.

3.3 Exploratory Work

Our first exploratory work was focused on Operations Other Than War (OOTW) [8,10], which is a challenging problem because the task of planning humanitarian aid operations means that a large number of different types of organisations have to collaborate to solve problems in fast-changing environments [23]. Our first experiments were very simple [10], but the results were encouraging. They used a

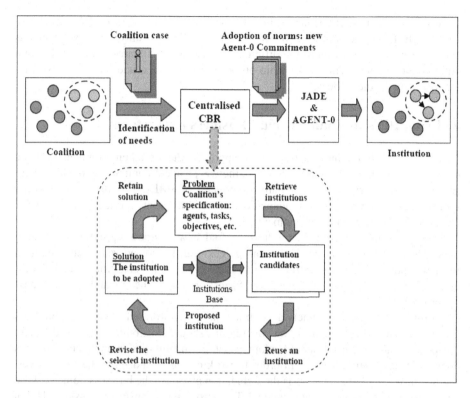

Fig. 4. A scheme of the foundation process within our exploratory work

centralized CBR approach on the OOTW domain, and showed that the foundation phase is feasible, and that the DEI lifecycle can be fully implemented.

Our first steps are based on a centralized CBR approach. We have used the JADE/Agent-0 framework [24], and our agents have a BDI architecture with a mental state composed of three mental categories: *Beliefs*, *Commitments* and *Capabilities*. Within our CBR mechanism, when a coalition has been formed and needs to turn itself into an institution, agents consult a centralized case database (Previous-Institutions Base, PIB) in order to find the stored institution's specification that adapts best to the present situation. Then the agents have to adopt the institutional components specified in the selected institution (at this moment we are only adopting norms) in order to turn the coalition into an institution. In our system, norms are adopted by taking on new commitments. Figure 4 shows a scheme of this process.

Our first experiments and results are encouraging but not yet decisive [10]; we have worked with our own framework, our own scenario, and our own examples, so we need to compare our results with other platforms and systems in order to validate them. The importance of these experiments is to show that the foundation phase is feasible, and that the DEI lifecycle can be fully implemented.

At this moment we are studying how to use our previous work on DEIs to enable Digital Business Ecosystems, or more specifically, to allow the spontaneous composition and adaptation of the different services and software components within digital environments. This is the main purpose of this paper, and in the next section we will focus on these ideas.

4   Using DEIs to Enable Digital Business Ecosystems

As we have said in the introduction, in our approach, the digital environment of DBEs is considered as an open agent system. So, there is an agent community in which there are the different services and software components of SMEs. The idea is to allow the spontaneous composition and adaptation of the different services and software components within digital environments.

These services and components have to find new business opportunities among them. Using our 3F cycle of DEIs, this process can be considered as the coalition formation phase. So, we are introducing an analogy between "coalition" and "business opportunity", and between "coalition formation" and the "search of business opportunities".

From our perspective, when a coalition has been formed (that is, a business opportunity has been found), an institution should be built, so the different components and services should adopt a set of institutional components (in this domain an electronic contract) in order to work correctly and fulfil their objectives. Using our 3F cycle, this process is the foundation phase. In the business domain, these temporary business unions are called UTEs (from the spanish expression "Union Temporal de Empresas"). A UTE is a legal form of temporary business cooperation set up for a specified period of time or for a specified project or service. UTEs allow several companies to operate together in one common project. This form of association is commonly used in engineering and construction projects.

This way, we are assuming some analogies between the DEIs and DBE domains (see Table 1).

Table 1. Analogies between Dynamic Electronic Institutions and Digital Business Ecosystems domains

Dynamic Electronic Institutions	Digital Business Ecosystems
Agent Community	Digital Environment
Coalition Formation	Search of Opportunities
Coalition	Business Opportunity
Institutional Components	Electronic Contract
Dynamic Institution	Temporary Business Union (UTE)

Figure 5 depicts the 3F cycle of DEIs with these new analogies from the DBE domain.

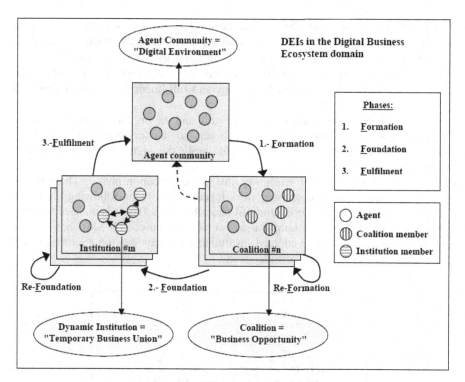

Fig. 5. DEI construction phases (3F cycle) with DBE analogies

In our opinion, the complete process should be divided in seven steps. Figure 6 shows these steps.

1. Search of opportunities (Formation): this is the coalition formation phase. The services and components within the digital environment have to find new business opportunities among them. Coalitions allow agents to perform tasks together that they would be unable to perform individually. Coalitions can be searched with respect to: agents' objectives, trust, etc. This phase has to be automatic and emergent. There are many works about coalition formation in business domains [25], but at this moment we are not interested in this phase, we are centring our research and our efforts on the foundation phase.
2. Analysis of the opportunity: when a business opportunity is found, the analysis and authorization (or rejection) of the user or manager is needed. Agents have to obtain authorization from their managers in order to continue the process.
3. Coalition establishment: when all authorizations have arrived, the coalition establishment can be done, with the purpose of preparing the foundation phase.
4. Temporary Business Union creation (Foundation): this is the foundation phase, the process of turning the coalition into a dynamic electronic institution, so in this domain, that means: turning the business opportunity into a temporary business union (UTE). Of course, the automatic adoption of norms and regulations is a hard

task, but as we have said before, our perspective on this problem is to use an approach based on using knowledge from previous cases. At this moment we are studying how to use our previous work on CBR to start our experiments with DBEs. In this domain the coalition should adopt the institutional components (norms and regulations, protocol, ontology and fulfilment conditions) through an electronic contract.

5. Acceptation: when the institution specification and the organisational mechanisms (institutional components) have been chosen, an authorization for each agent manager is required. This process could imply the signature of an electronic contract.

6. Temporary Business Union execution: this is the execution phase. The different software components and services work together as a team, following the norms that they have adopted, in order to fulfil their objectives. There is no need to create specific software for each temporal association, because each SME has its own software components. The adopted institution only provides the interactions and organisational mechanisms between them.

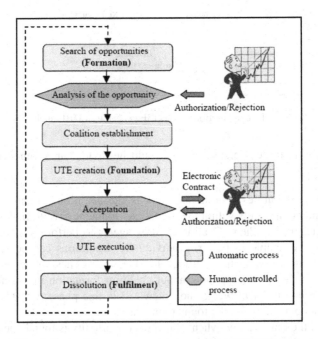

Fig. 6. Steps of the temporary business union (UTE) lifecycle

7. Dissolution (Fulfilment): when the temporary business union has fulfilled all its objectives, the association should be dissolved. This phase occurs because the association is no longer needed, or because the institution is no longer making a profit. This phase could imply the distribution of gains between agents, with respect to the electronic contract which has been adopted in the acceptation step.

5 Discussion and Conclusions

This article is a position paper that introduces some ideas on how to use Dynamic Electronic Institutions to enable Digital Business Ecosystems. This work is exploratory, and its main purpose is to find analogies between DBEs and DEIs, and to propose some research directions on how to use our previous work with DEIs in the Operations Other Than War domain in order to develop DBEs.

We have presented a brief summary of our previous work on DEIs: our general model, a possible formalisation for the foundation phase, and our first exploratory work. We have also presented our first ideas on how to enable DBEs, and finally we have introduced a possible set of steps for the DBE lifecycle.

Our approach, based on using dynamic institutions to enable digital business ecosystems, is closely related to the concept of Contractual Agent Societies [26], a metaphor for building open information systems where agents configure themselves automatically through a set of dynamically negotiated social contracts. In this approach, social contracts define the shared context of agent interactions, including ontologies, joint beliefs, joint goals, normative behaviours, etc.

We have not spoken about Virtual Organisations (VO, or Virtual Enterprises, VE) [25]. This concept is closely related to electronic institutions and coalition formation. In fact, in our opinion, virtual organisations could be described in terms of dynamic electronic institutions, although their architectures and implementations are usually directed to a specific application domain: B2B electronic commerce. We believe that in someway virtual organisations could be considered as a sub-group of dynamic electronic institutions which are more general. In [25] the authors work towards the development of an agent-based electronic institution providing a virtual normative environment that assists and regulates the creation and operation of VOs, through contract-related services. Their works confirm our idea, because they proof that VOs can be conceived as DEIs.

At this moment we are centring our efforts on the study of the foundation process (turning coalitions into institutions), which we have described in section 3. In the digital business ecosystems domain this process means to turn business opportunities (coalitions) into temporary business unions (dynamic institutions). We are using a CBR approach, but we do not rule out alternative approaches like meta-institutions or genetic algorithms.

There are several open issues in DEIs. These include works on the institutions' adaptivity and on the dissolution process (fulfilment phase). There is a recent work [27] that is focused on the extension of electronic institutions with autonomic capabilities to allow them to yield a dynamical answer to changing circumstances, through the adaptation of their norms. In our model this process is called re-foundation.

At this moment, we are involved in the ONE Project (Open Negotiation Environment [3]) and we would like to direct our research efforts toward developing DBE theory and technologies, by using our previous work and knowledge on DEIs.

Acknowledgments. This research was partially funded by EU project N° 34744 ONE: Open Negotiation Environment, FP6-2005-IST-5, ICT-for Networked Businesses.

References

1. DBE Project.: Conclusions of the brainstorming workshop on the Digital Ecosystem concept. Conclusions emerged from the 2002 cycle of workshops; Bruxelles (2002), (online document: http:// europa.eu.int/ information_society/ topics/ ebusiness/ godigital/ sme_research/doc/ ecowshop4oct.pdf)
2. DBE Project.: A micro-economic introduction to the DBE. DBE Induction Flash movie (2006), (online document: http://www.digital-ecosystem.org/ DBE_Main/ Members/ aenglishx/learn/ dbe_movies)
3. ONE Project.: Blog of the University of Girona (UdG) for the Project One (2006), (online blog: http://proj-one.blogspot.com/)
4. Dini, P., Nicolai, A.: DBE: The Digital Business Ecosystem: an introduction to the DBE project (2003), (online document: http://www.digital-ecosystems.org/ cluster/ dbe/ dbe_summary_cc.pdf)
5. Noguera, J.: ServENT user guide. Project documentation of the Swallow Project (DBE ExE), Sourceforge.net (2005)
6. McKitterick, D.: Getting on the DBE – The Basic Steps. Getting started with the DBE Studio. Digital-Ecosystems.org (2005)
7. Esteva, M.: Electronic Institutions: From specification to development. PhD thesis, Universitat Politècnica de Catalunya (2003)
8. Muntaner-Perich, E.: Towards Dynamic Electronic Institutions: from coalitions to institutions. Thesis proposal submitted to the University of Girona in Partial Fulfilment of the Requirements for the Advanced Studies Certificate in the Ph.D. program in Information Technologies. Girona (2005), http:// eia.udg.es/ %7eemuntane/ papers/ thesis_proposal.pdf
9. Muntaner-Perich, E., de la Rosa, J.L.: Dynamic Electronic Institutions: from agent coalitions to agent institutions. In: Hinchey, M.G., Rago, P., Rash, J.L., Rouff, C.A., Sterritt, R., Truszkowski, W. (eds.) WRAC 2005. LNCS (LNAI), vol. 3825, pp. 109–121. Springer, Heidelberg (2006)
10. Muntaner-Perich, E., de la Rosa, J.L., Carrillo, C., Delfín, S., Moreno, A.: Dynamic Electronic Institutions for Humanitarian Aid Simulation. Congrés Català d'Intel.ligència Artificial. In: Polit, M., Talbert, T., López, B., Meléndez, J. (eds.) Perpinyà, Octubre del 2006. Frontiers in Artificial Intelligence and Applications, vol. 146, p. 332 (2006)
11. North, D.C.: Economics and Cognitive Science. Economic History 9612002, Economics Working Paper Archive at WUSTL (1996)
12. Pattison, H.E., Corkill, D.D., Lesser, V.R.: Distributed Artificial Intelligence. In: Instantiating Descriptions of Organizational Structures, pp. 59–96. Pitman Publishers (1987)
13. Werner, E.: Distributed Artificial Intelligence. chapter Cooperating Agents: A Unified Theory of Communication and Social Structure, pp. 3–36. Pitman Publishers (1987)
14. Noriega, P.: Agent Mediated Auctions. The Fishmarket Metaphor. Ph.D.Thesis, Universitat Autònoma de Barcelona (1997)
15. Esteva, M., Rodríguez-Aguilar, J.A., Sierra, C., Garcia, P., Arcos, J.L.: On the Formal Specification of Electronic Institutions. IIIA, CSIC (2001)
16. Rodríguez-Aguilar, J.A.: On the design and construction of Agent-mediated Electronic Institutions. Ph.D. thesis, Universitat Autònoma de Barcelona (2001)
17. Dignum, V.: A model for organizational interaction. Based on Agents, Founded in Logic. Ph.D. Thesis, Utrecht University (2003)

18. Fornara, N.: Interaction and communication among autonomous agents in multiagent systems, Ph.D. Thesis, University of Lugano (2003)
19. López y López, F.: Social power and norms. Impact on Agent Behaviour. Ph.D. Thesis, University of Southampton (2003)
20. Vázquez-Salceda, J.: The role of Norms and Electronic Institutions in Multi-Agent Systems applied to complex domains. The HARMONIA framework. PhD thesis, Universitat Politècnica de Catalunya. Artificial Intelligence Dissertation Award, ECCAI (2003)
21. Luck, M., McBurney, P., Preist, C.: Agent Technology: Enabling Next generation Computing. A Roadmap for Agent Based Computing. AgentLink II (2003)
22. Sierra, C., Rodríguez-Aguilar, J.A., Noriega, P., Esteva, M., Arcos, J.L.: Engineering Multi-agent Systems as Electronic Institutions. Novática, 170 (July-August 2004)
23. Pechoucek, M., Barta, J., Mařík, V.: CPlanT: Coalition Planning Multi-Agent System for Humanitarian Relief Operations. Multi-Agent-Systems and Applications: pp. 363–376 (2001)
24. Muntaner-Perich, E., del Acebo, E., de la Rosa, J.L.: Rescatando AGENT-0. Una aproximación moderna a la Programación Orientada a Agentes. II Taller de Desarrollo en Sistemas Multiagente, DESMA'05. Primer Congreso Español de Informática, CEDI. Granada (2005)
25. Rocha, A.P., Lopes Cardoso, H., Oliveira, E.: Contributions to an Electronic Institution supporting Virtual Enterprises' life cycle. In: G. Putnik e M. M. Cunha (eds.), Virtual Enterprise Integration: Technological and Organizational Perspectives, Idea Group Inc. (in press, 2005)
26. Dellarocas, C.: Contractual Agent Societies: Negotiated shared context and social control in open multi-agent systems. In: Proc. WS on Norms and Institutions in Multi-Agent Systems, Autonomous Agents-2000, Barcelona (2000)
27. Bou, E., López-Sánchez, M., Rodríguez-Aguilar, J.A.: Towards Self-configuration in Autonomic Electronic Institutions. LNCS, vol. 4386, pp. 220–235. Springer, Heidelberg (2007)

A Peer-to-Peer Normative System to Achieve Social Order

Amandine Grizard[1], Laurent Vercouter[2], Tiberiu Stratulat[3], and Guillaume Muller[2]

[1] Institut Eurecom, Affective Social Computing Lab.,
2229 routes des crêtes, BP 193, F-06904 Sophia Antipolis, France
grizard@eurecom.fr
[2] École N.S. des Mines de Saint-Étienne, Multi-Agent System Dpt
158 cours Fauriel, F-42023 Saint-Étienne Cedex 02, France
{vercouter,muller}@emse.fr
[3] LIRMM
161 rue Ada, F-34392 Montpellier Cedex 5, France
stratulat@lirmm.fr

Abstract. Social order in distributed descentralised systems is claimed to be obtained by using social norms and social control. This paper presents a normative P2P architecture to obtain social order in multi-agent systems. We propose the use of two types of norms that coexist: rules and conventions. Rules describe the global normative constraints on autonomous agents, whilst conventions are local norms. Social control is obtained by providing a non-intrusive control infrastructure that helps the agents build reputation values based on their respect of norms. Some experiments are presented that show how communities are dynamically formed and how bad agents are socially excluded.

Introduction

In multi-agent systems the execution of global tasks strongly differs according to the centralised or decentralised nature of the system. Decentralisation implies that information, resources and agent capacities are distributed among the agents of the system and hence an agent cannot perform alone a global task. The most popular examples of decentralised multi-agent systems are peer-to-peer (P2P) networks used for file sharing. In such applications, agents must collaborate to index shared files and propagate queries for given files. It is also essential that all agents use compatible strategies for propagation (in most of the cases they use the same strategy) to ensure the correct termination of search algorithms.

Peer-to-peer systems illustrate how important it is in decentralised systems that each agent behaves well, that is to be compliant to some expected "good" behaviour, in order to cooperate with the others. If not, the activities of other agents can be blocked or corrupted. In peer-to-peer systems we usually consider that the agents have been downloaded from the same place and are coded by

P. Noriega et al. (Eds.): COIN 2006 Workshops, LNAI 4386, pp. 274–289, 2007.
© Springer-Verlag Berlin Heidelberg 2007

the same developers. It is then natural to consider that the agents will behave the same as expected. But if we consider decentralised multi-agent systems in general, this assumption is not realistic. Heterogeneity and autonomy are the required properties of the agents to build open and flexible systems and they rule out any assumption concerning the way they are constructed and behave. Moreover, the agents can no longer be controlled by central institutions which supervise their behavior since we consider decentralised systems.

C. Castelfranchi [1] also claimed that, in decentralised system, Social Order is achieved by the use of norms as rules of good behaviour and through *Social Control*. In order to preserve the openness and the flexibility of the system, norms are only external representations that should not be hard coded into the agents, since they are supposed to be dynamically created or modified. Norms also preserve the autonomy of the agents, since smart agents can reason on them, decide autonomously to respect or violate them and observe the behaviour of other agents if they are norm compliant. Social Control mainly refers to the fact that each agent is observed and controled by some other agents from the same system. However in the literature we find mainly trust mechanisms that are proposed to achieve it [2,3,4]. According to these works agents with bad behaviors are punished by social sanctions, get bad reputations and are excluded from the society.

In this paper we propose a peer to peer normative architecture to obtain social order in a decentralised system. The main contribution of our proposition is not on the formalism used to represent the norms nor on the representation and calculation of reputation but rather on the *integration* of norms within a trust model that allows agents to perform Social Control. We also provide some mechanisms to update existing norms when groups of agents feel the need for the system to evolve. The next section defines the concepts of norms used in this article and describe their formalization. Section 2 describes the architecture of a decentralised multi-agent system that performs social control and some experimental results are presented in section 3. Finally, we propose in section 4 a mechanism to adapt the content of some specific types of norms, called conventions and we conclude in the last section.

1   Norms and Control

In the area of agent-based systems, two important contradictory properties are needed: autonomy and control. Autonomy abstracts out the way an agent behaves when asked to solve a problem or execute a task. Control is necessary to be sure that autonomous agents behave according to the specifications formulated by someone on their behavior. In terms of degrees of freedom, the former relieves, the latter constrains.

Norms have been recently considered as being good candidate tools to design agent-based system and also to solve the paradoxical problem that confronts the preservation of the autonomy of the agents and the need of control. Getting its inspiration from social sciences, a norm is mainly a description of an (ideal) behavior that an agent or a group of agents is expected to display. The normative behavior is generally described by using deontic constraints, such as obligations, permissions and interdictions. Although there is no complete agreement on how to use norms in artificial systems, there are however two main trends [5]. The first considers a norm as a sort of specification of good behavior that, once identified, should be hard coded directly into the agents. The agents are by construction norm compliant or "regimented". The second trend adopts a more flexible perspective, where norms are considered as being only indications of an ideal behavior that could be adopted or not by an agent. In the case where the norm is not respected we talk about violation. In order to avoid the proliferation of unexpected behavior and therefore the chaos in the system, some of the works adopting the second perspective suggest the use of various structures that allow to sanction the deviating behavior and hence to "control" the agents.

In the literature two main categories of control structures are described: internal and external. Internal control is where an agent is able to identify by itself which is the good behavior to adopt according to an external reference. In this type of scenario we count on the agents' cognitive and learning capacities to understand and evaluate the normative behavior.

External control is where some external or institutional structures can interfere (even physically) with the agent and hence influence it to display the normative behavior. The behavior of an agent is interpreted and evaluated by others (authorities, group of agents, etc.) according to the norms governing the system wherein the agent acts.

1.1 Social Norms Revisited

In the domain of social sciences, R. Tuomela proposed a theory of social norms that characterizes communities in human societies [6]. For him a social norm has the form "An agent of the kind F in group G ought to perform task T in situation C". Such norms are further divided into rules (r-norms) and proper social norms (s-norms). The r-norms are the norms created by an authority or a body of agents that are authorized to represent the group. The obedience to the rules is made on an agreement-making basis and their violation is explicitly sanctioned. The governmental laws are examples of r-norms. The s-norms represent the conventions or the mutual beliefs about the right thing to do in a community. An agent obeys also to an s-norm because it believes that the other members of the community expect that. The sanction of an s-norm is only social: approval or disapproval and it can not be decided in advance.

The definition of both types of norms is given in terms of certain conditions. For instance a norm N of obligation which says "Everyone in G ought to perform task T when in situation C" is considered an r-norm iff the following conditions are satisfied (see [6] for a detailed discussion):

- *promulgation* condition: N has been issued by an authority;
- *accessibility* condition: the agents are aware that N is in force;
- *pervasiveness* condition: many members of G perform T in C;

- *motivational* condition: some of the agents that perform T do that because they believe that they ought to perform T in C;
- *sanction* condition: there are sanctions applied when N is violated.

In the case of an s-norm, the following conditions should be satisfied:

- *acceptance* condition: there is a mutual belief in G to the effect that the members of G ought to perform T in situation C;
- *pervasiveness* condition: many members of G perform T in C;
- *motivational* condition: some of the agents that perform T do that because they believe that they ought to perform T in C and that is what is expected by other members of G;
- *recognized sanction* condition: there are social sanctions applied when N is violated.

There are two main cases where s-norms and r-norms coexist: parallel norms (norms with the same content) and conflicting norms (norms with conflicting content). Tuomela considers that in both cases r-norms override s-norms but which one or ones of these kinds of social norms wins empirically is a factual issue not to be decided a priori.

Tuomela shows further that s-norms characterize the high-trust societies whereas r-norms are norms for low-trust, or business-like societies.

Since Tuomela's theory of social norms stands for human societies we will try to adapt it to be applied to artificial societies of agents. Therefore we propose in this article to use two different but coexisting settings that correspond to the use of r-norms and s-norms.

The first setting is related to the use of r-norms. We will reconsider the definition of an r-norm, that we will call simply a *rule* in the rest of the article. A rule R of obligation is described by using the following notation:

$$rule(C, T, S_+, S_-)$$

which says that in the context described by C, T ought to be executed. If T is the case the agent is rewarded with S_+ otherwise it gets sanctioned with S_-.

In addition to the adoption of such a notation for rules, the setting we propose should satisfy the other conditions given in the definition of an r-norm. The architecture we describe in the following section contains as main ingredients:

1. authorities responsible to create independent sound sets of norms (promulgation condition) and to inform the autonomous agents about them (accessibility condition);
2. ordinary autonomous agents that receive the norms and that are observed and controlled if they are norm compliant;
3. monitoring or control structures that evaluate the behavior of the agents and sanction or reward them according to the normative content (sanction condition).

The pervasiveness condition in the definition of an r-norm accounts for the supposed fact that people in human societies tend to obey the norms. In the setting we propose, the pervasiveness condition is relaxed and is sometimes obtained by applying the sanctions. But it is not guaranteed because of the hypothesis we made to respect the autonomy of the agents. The motivational condition is also very strong, because it considers that i) the agents have cognitive abilities and that ii) they adopt the normative behavior rationally. The hypothesis we adopt on the agents we use is hence that they are autonomous decision-makers able to decide by themselves what to do next, given their internal state, the normative information and the current state of their environment.

The second setting is about s-norms. In a similar way, we propose to re-adapt the definition of an s-norm that we will simply call *convention*. The notation we use for the conventions of obligation is as follows:

$$convention(C, T)$$

This notation says that in the context where C is true an agent ought to do the task T.

As in the case of rules, the setting we propose should allow a community of agents to create and manipulate conventions. The conditions that define an s-norm are therefore partially preserved. For instance, the acceptance condition is obtained by introducing a protocol that allows some agents to exchange information about the current mutual convention. Concerning the recognized sanction condition, since this setting coexists with the setting for rules, we will use the same monitoring structures to help an agent observe the behavior of the other agents. However, the decision on how to sanction or reward the others is made only by the concerned agent, and can not be known in advance. For the pervasiveness and motivational conditions, we make the same hypothesis that we made for rules.

1.2   Reputation as Sanction or Reward

One of the differences existing between rules and conventions consists in the application of sanctions. As shown above, two explicit sanctions are defined in the specification of a rule: a positive sanction applied when an agent respects the deontic constraint and a negative sanction applied in the contrary case. In most of normative systems, these sanctions are material, for instance a fee. In our case, we do not use material sanctions because it implies that there is a way to enforce an agent to pay a fee or at least a physical means of pressure on the agent. This assumption is contradictory with the property of autonomy claimed for agents and it is even more the case for decentralised systems because agents may be deployed on different platforms.

We propose to describe sanctions as a positive or negative influence on the reputation of an agent. Agent reputation is a concept that has been studied in several works [7,2,3,8,4] with different approaches but also with different semantics attached to reputation. The word "reputation" does not have exactly the same meaning depending on the considered approach. Some authors consider that an agent has only one reputation maintained globally by the system [9], whereas others think that two agents can have a different opinion about the reputation of an agent [2,8,4]. Moreover, some works consider that reputation should be relative to a given context [7], to the sources used to build it [10], to the nature of its target [10], to the estimated facet of the agent [2,11], ... A unified view of all these aspects has recently been proposed in a functional ontology of reputation [12]. However, we consider reputation more generally in this paper. Since our contribution is not on the reputation model but on the integration of the concepts of reputation and of norms in a peer-to-peer environment, we only represent reputation by a simple plain value. We will consider using more precise concepts of reputation in future works. The only property that is important here is that two agents can maintain different reputation values for a same target as there is no global view or control of the system.

Thus, reputations are values maintained by other agents and are external to the sanctionned agent. The violation of a rule will cause a decrease of the agent's reputation whereas positive sanction may cause its increase. Sanctions in term of reputation are still an incentive to respect the rules for the agents because one of the consequences of a low reputation for an agent could be the refuse of certain other agents to interact with it (social exclusion). Such sanctions can be viewed as social constraints on the agents.

We consider that the sanction for a rule is defined in terms of reputation and we formalize it as follows:

$$sanction(Applier, Sanctioned, Weight)$$

where *Applier* is the agent applying the sanction, *Sanctioned* is the agent sanctioned and *Weight* represents generally the value of the sanction. We use the last parameter to affect the reputation of an agent according to a mechanism which is explained in latter sections.

In the case of conventions, the sanction is not represented explicitly because it can not be known a priori. It depends on the agent in cause and it is the expression of an approval or disapproval of the actual behavior. It is up to an agent to sanction or not other agents that violate or respect its own conventions. These sanctions may also impact reputation values but these values should be maintained locally by the owner of the convention. In this case the scope of the sanctions does not cover the whole society but only the relation between one agent and another agent or group of agents.

2   An Overlay System to Sanction the Violation of Rules

Since agents are autonomous, we can not assume that they will respect the rules of their system. There must be a way to observe their behavior, their compliance to the rules and to sanction the violations. If such a mechanism exists and is efficient, rational agents are more motivated to respect the rules in order to avoid being sanctionned. This is achieved by a social control of the system if it is the society of agents that supervises and sanctions its members. Then, there is a need for a control system that can be integrated to an existing multi-agent system. This integration can only be effective if the control system takes into account the

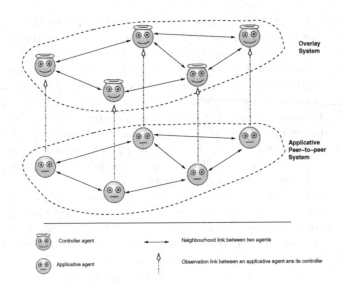

Fig. 1. Overview of the overlay system

specific features of a multi-agent system, in particular the decentralised nature of the system and the autonomy of the agents.

In this section, we propose and describe such a control system for a P2P system of *application agents* in order to control the respect of the rules governing the system. To comply to the features quoted above, the control system is also a multi-agent system where each *controller agent* is associated to an application peer of the controlled P2P system (see Figure 1). The control system is an overlay system in which each controller agent has a partial view of the interactions inside the P2P system. Based on observations on the application agents, a controler agent detects rule violations and cooperates with other controller agents in order to sanction the violators in the P2P system. This solution keeps the decentralised nature of the whole system and is not intrusive for the peers. By "non-intrusive", we mean that there is no constraint on the agent's internal implementation. The observation of the agent's communication is not an intrusion since communications are sent and transit through an interaction medium and we assume that this medium can be observed. This assumption remains realistic because one of the property of communications is that they are public as claimed in [13].

Reputation is used as a mean to sanction the application agents. Thus the reputation of an application agent that violated a rule will decrease for each other controller agent that has observed and detected the violation. Then, the controller agent can share its reputation models with other controller agents or even with its application agent to which it is connected. The reputation of the application agents is hence locally propagated and application agents that do not respect the rules can get bad reputations and be excluded by other application agents from future interactions. We consider that the overlay system performs a social control over the application P2P system and that it aims at excluding the application agents that violate the rules.

2.1 Application Agents

The tasks performed by application agents are completely dependent of the kind of P2P system considered. For instance, in the case of P2P networks used for file sharing, application agents possess some files to share and are able to formulate queries for given files or answer to or propagate the queries from other agents. The behavior of application agents is application-dependent and, since they are autonomous, we do not make any assumption on it. However, inside the system, an application agent may behave or not as it is expected by other application agents.

The goal of the overlay system is to control that application agents respect the rules of the system. The rules only focus on the communicative behavior of application agents. Application agents should be considered as black boxes and there is no way to observe their internal functioning to check if they comply to the rules. The only thing we can control are the external actions of an application agent, which correspond to the interactions with other agents. We therefore make the assumptions that (i) interactions between application agents can be observed by some controller agents; (ii) there exists some rules, formalised as described in section 1, that application agents must respect; (iii) these rules are available for both application and controller agents.

The neighborhood of an application agent is composed of other application agents. We do not study the reason why some application agents are neighbors or not (it also depends on the application) and we note $Neighbors(App_i)$ the set of neighbors of the application agent App_i.

2.2 Controller Agents

The overlay system is composed of controller agents. A controller agent has the capacity to observe the interactions of an application agent, that is the messages sent and received by this agent. It also knows the rules that must be respected by application agents and can detect violations by comparing its observations to the rules. At last, a controller agent has the capacity to sanction an application agent, and to do so, it may have to collaborate with other controller agents. We should also note that we assumed that the controller agents are deployed by a trusted third party and that they are trustworthy.

Each application agent is associated to a unique controller agent in the overlay system described here. This association preserves the autonomy of the application agent and is not very constraining for the P2P system. For example, we can imagine in a P2P file sharing system that controller agents are hosted by internet providers and that they can observe the messages exchanged. From the point of view of an application agent, the existence of a controller is a real advantage since it provides the information about the reputation of the other application agents in its neighborhood. Then the application agent can use this information to choose to cooperate with application agents with good reputation.

The system we propose is caracterized by the fact that for an application agent App_i the neighbors of the associated controller $Cont_i$ is the set of controllers associated to the neighbors of agent App_i:

$$App_j \in Neighbors(App_i) \equiv Cont_j \in Neighbors(Cont_i)$$

The reputation model used by a controller agent considers the reputation value for each application agent in the neighborhood of its application agent. We note Rep_i^j the reputation of an agent $App_j \in Neighbors(App_i)$ computed by the controller $Cont_i$.

2.3   Interaction Between Agents

between application agents. An application agent interacts with its neighbors (other application agents). The nature and the content of these interactions depends on the application and we do not make any assumption over them. However, application agents should respect the rules of the system if they do not want to be sanctionned.

between application and controller agents. An application agent interacts with its own controller agent and can not interact with other controller agents. Such interactions are used by an application agent to get some information related to norms or reputation. Application agents may ask two types of information to their controller agent: (i) the rules that they must respect in their interaction with other application agents; (ii) the reputation value of one or several of its neighbors. These interactions are only possible and not required. Application agents are autonomous and we can not assume that they will interact in a given way with the controller. This possibility of interaction enables an application agent that could reason on norms and reputation to get the information necessary for its reasoning. However, it is also possible to consider different application agents that do not interact with their controller. In this case, if the respect of norms is not hardcoded in their implementation, they are likely to be sanctionned. A controller agent does not need to interact with its application agent but it is able to oversee its interactions and check for violations.

between controller agents. A controller agent interacts with other controller agents to inform them when its application agent violated a rule or behaved well. For instance, when a controller agent detects that its application agent has violated a rule, it sends a message to its neighbors that are concerned by the violation in order to ask them to sanction its application agent using the negative sanction field of the rule. At the opposite, it can also ask its neighbors to apply the positive sanction if the application agent has respected the rule.

3   Experimental Results

The normative system presented here has been implemented and tested on a scenario of a P2P file sharing network.

3.1   The Scenario of P2P File Sharing

We consider a P2P system where each application agent possesses some files to share with other agents and needs to download some files that may be contained by other peers. For simplicity, we used a gnutella-like [14] protocol. According to this protocol, an agent that requests a file formulates a query with the file name and sends this query to each of its neighbors. Each neighbor looks if it owns a file that matches the query. If it does, it responds positively to the agent requester. If not, it does not respond. Then, each neighbor propagates further the query to its own neighbors.

To avoid flooding the network, the queries are enriched with two fields. First, the queries have an unique ID so that an agent does not have to handle twice the same query. The second field is called TTL (*Time To Live*). The TTL corresponds to the depth of propagation of the query in the network. For example a query with a TTL of 3 will be propagated to the neighbors of the neighbors of the neighbors of the requester but not further. When an agent receives a query, it decreases its TTL and it propagates it to its neighbors only if the value of the TTL is at least 1.

3.2   Rules of the Scenario

The correct functionning of a P2P file sharing system requires that the agents propagate the queries of other agents. This is a cooperative behavior, but selfish agents may not behave like this because it would cost them some ressources (CPU time) consumed for the benefit of others. We propose to define the following rule as an incentive to behave cooperatively:

$$rule(asked(Id, TTL, App_b, App_s, App_r, file) \land TTL > 1 \land trusted(App_s),$$
$$asked\_neighbors(Id, TTL - 1, App_r),$$
$$sanction(Cont_r, App_r, HigherRep(Cont_s, S_+)),$$
$$sanction(Cont_r, App_r, LowerRep(Cont_s, S_-)))$$

This rule is an obligation in the context $asked(Id, TTL, App_b, App_s, App_r, file)$ representing that a query about the file $file$ initiated by the agent App_b with the id Id has been received by the agent App_r from the agent App_s with a TTL greater than 1. This context also requires that the sender of the query App_s is trustworthy. This condition is necessary to avoid that an agent that do not want to interact with untrusted neighbors is sanctionned by its controller. The trusted or untrusted nature of a neighbor can be deduced by the controller according to its reputation about App_s, and it may be communicated to App_r if it requests it.

In this context, a task must be achieved to obtain $asked\_neighbors(Id, TTL-1, App_r, file)$ that means that the query Id should be propagated to the neighbours of App_r with a TTL decreased by 1. If this obligation is respected the positive sanction indicates that the controller $Cont_r$ will ask to the controller $Cont_s$ to increase the reputation of App_r by a value S_+. Otherwise the negative sanction $sanction(Cont_r, App_r, LowerRep(Cont_s, S_-))$ is applied. This negative sanction indicates that the controller $Cont_r$ will sanction its application agent App_r by asking to the controller $Cont_r$ to lower the reputation of App_r by a value S_-.

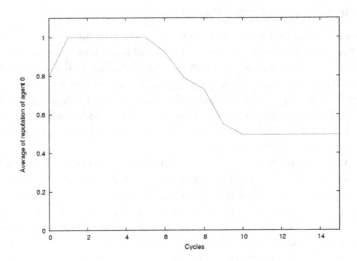

Fig. 2. Average of the reputation of an agent (violations occur at step 5)

3.3   Experiments

Some experiments have been done to observe how the reputation of an agent evolves if it does not respect the rules. We used PeerSim simulator [15] to simulate the P2P protocols, Java to implement the agents and Prolog with JPL [16] to code and interpret the rules.

The tests have been done on a set of 50 agents. Each agent owns from 5 to 10 files taken from a global set of 100 different files. The agents are connected in a network such that each agent has a minimum of 2 and a maximum of 5 neighbors. The simulation lasts 15 cycles. At each cycle an agent formulates from 3 to 5 queries for a file (randomly chosen) and sends on query to its neighbors with a TTL of 2. All queries are propagated according to the gnutella protocol and the agents that own a file matching a received query, answer positively to the requester.

The controller of an agent computes the reputation of the neighbors of its agent by using values in the domain [0:1] with an initial value of 0.8. The positive and negative sanctions associated to the rule are $S_+ = 0.01$ and $S_- = -0.02$. Initially, all the agents behave well and respect the rule. After 5 cycles, one agent (the agent 0 in the figures) changes its behavior: it will not respect systematically the rule and in 50% of the cases, it does not propagate the queries from its neighbors. This violation of the rule is detected by its controller which applies the negative sanction. The impact of the sanction is shown in figure 2 representing the average value of the reputation value of agent 0 kept by the controllers of its neighbors.

The reputation value of an agent is used by an application agent to remove that agent from its neighborhood, for instance, when it has a low reputation. Removal of a neighbor means that queries from it will no longer be considered (neither answered, nor propagated) and that queries from other agents will not be sent further to the neighbor with a bad reputation. This is equivalent to an irrevocable social exclusion, since the removed neighbor will not have the possibility to get positive sanctions and then to recover an acceptable reputation. If we wanted to keep the possibility to "forgive" to an agent, we may have kept the possibility for it to get positive sanctions.

The exclusion of agent 0 can be seen on figures 3 and 4. Figure 3 represents the number of queries sent by agent 0 that are propagated by the rest of the network. We can see that this number decreases when other agents begin to remove agent 0 from their neighborhood (around cycle 9) and that no more queries from it are considered at cycle 12. Figure 4 shows the percentage of files received by agent 0 at each cycle. Since its queries are no more considered, this percentage begins to decrease at cycle 9 and reaches 0 at cycle 11.

The reputation threshold, below which an agent removes a neighbor from its neighborhood, has been set to 0.5 for the simulations. This explains the fact that the reputation value of agent 0 does not continue to decrease in figure 2 after its exclusion, since the agents stop interacting with it and therefore agent 0 can not violate the rule anymore.

4   Convention Dynamics

The control system presented in the section 2 can be used to enforce the respect of the rules of the system. If an agent does not respect these rules, its reputation become lower and lower and other agents will stop cooperating with it. In section 1, we mentioned the distinction we make between two kinds of norms: rules and conventions. The main difference is that a rule is shared by the whole system and its violation should be explicitly sanctionned whereas conventions rather refer to an usage local to a group of agents. Conventions describe the behavior approved and expected by the group. In case of violation of the convention, the sanction is not explicit.

In the example of file sharing P2P networks, described in section 3, a convention can establish, for instance, the initial value of the TTL of a query. The higher is the TTL, the better are the chances to get the required file. But higher values of TTL also means that there will be more communications needed to propagate the query and that the network will be more loaded and that it will be slowed. We can continue to imagine that some agents request rare files difficult to obtain and therefore require a high TTL value, while agents that send many queries for commonly shared files would prefer a low TTL value.

Therefore, we can have many cases showing different conventions needed only by some agents that could regroup in small communities according to their preferences. Our proposal is therefore to use conventions to reorganize the neighborhood links between agents in order to group agents sharing the same conventions. We propose to use the overlay system presented in section 2 to deal with conventions as it follows:

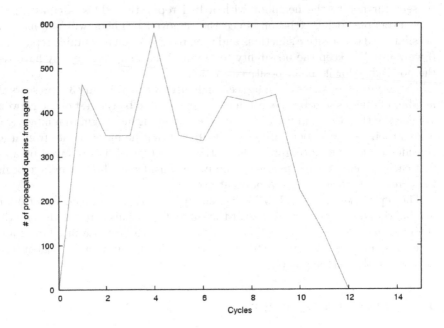

Fig. 3. Number of propagated queries from the agent violator

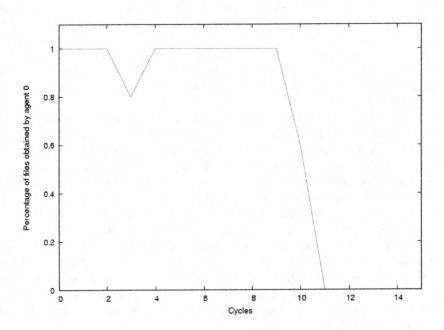

Fig. 4. Percentage of files got by the agent violator

- an application agent App_i sends its own set of conventions $Conventions(App_i)$ to its controller agent $Cont_i$.
- the controller $Cont_i$ informs its neighbors (belonging to the set $Neighbors$ $(Cont_i)$) that its application agent has the set of conventions $Conventions$ (App_i).
- each controller $Cont_j \in Neighbors(Cont_i)$ keeps this information available for its application agent App_j.

The controller $Cont_i$ now observes the behavior of other agents to check if they violate or not a convention of App_i. If a violation occurs, $Cont_i$ does not apply any sanction but inform App_i of this violation. The sanction to apply is up to App_i. We suggest that it also maintains a reputation model about its neighbors. This reputation is attached to conventions and should not replace the reputation based on the respect of rules. Then, two reputation values co-exist for each neighbor of App_i. A violation of a convention may result in a decrease of the corresponding reputation value.

The interpretation by App_i of its reputation model attached to conventions is free, but here again we suggest that it uses it to modify its neighborhood. For instance, App_i could remove agents with a low reputation value for conventions, from its neighborhood and then look for other agents to replace them in its neighborhood. The method used to find new neighbors depends on the kind of P2P network considered and is anyway out of the scope of this paper. The modification of the agents' neighborhood brings a reorganisation of the P2P system and communities of agents sharing similar conventions should be constituted. This reorganisation can also be dynamical because an agent can change its conventions and then progressivly change its neighborhood.

This is ongoing work and an implementation of such a control system that includes conventions is in progress.

5   Conclusion

The work described in this article follows the guideliness proposed by Castelfranchi in [1] who claims that social order in distributed decentralised systems is to be obtained by using social norms and social control. Concerning the use of norms, the adaptation of the concepts of social norms proposed by Tuomela (for human societies) to multi-agent systems seems to satisfy the need of both types of control, centralised and decentralised. We introduced the concept of rules to describe the global norms that constrain globally all the agents of a system, and conventions to describe the rules that could be created and applied locally to a group of agents by mutual acceptance.

We think that this is the main difference between our proposal and related approaches. For instance in [17] the authors propose a formalization of the rules of an ad hoc network which is seen as an instance of a norm-governed system. They also discuss the possibility of a sanction as excluding an agent from the network (i.e. the sanctioned agent loses its roles and therefore its permissions, obligations, etc.). This is in a way similar to what we call "social exclusion". In addition we assure a decentralized control by letting the application agents to decide on-line on the social exclusion of the others (social control).

The notion of controller is also present in works stemming from various domains of research, under names such as wrappers, sentinels [18], controllers [19], governors [20], etc. In general, the controller functions like a filter. It is a sort of interface between the agents and the resources of a system. In our work the notion of controller is used mainly to keep the information about the past behavior of some agents. This information is actually encapsulated in what we call reputation.

Concerning the manifestation of social control, we showed how to obtain it in a P2P network of application agents. Each application agent decides autonomously with whom to cooperate based on the reputation values of other agents. The reputation value depends on the respect or not of the rules and conventions that are currently in force. It is the role of the overlay system to monitor the behaviours and inform the application agents about the reputation of the others. The control of the agents is completely non-intrusive and decentralised.

The experiments showed interesting results, notably the fact that agents with good reputations are rapidly identified and are at the center of communities of agents with similar behaviour. In future works we would like to study the dynamics of open systems when agents come and go and when the content of the norm changes dynamically.

References

1. Castelfranchi, C.: Formalising the informal? dynamic social order, bottom-up social control, and spontaneous normative relations. Journal of Applied Logic 1, 47–92 (2003)
2. Sabater, J., Sierra, C.: REGRET: reputation in gregarious societies. In: Müller, J.P, Andre, E., Sen, S., Frasson, C. (eds.) Proceedings of the Fifth International Conference on Autonomous Agents, Montreal, Canada, pp. 194–195. ACM Press, New York (2001)
3. Conte, R., Paolucci, M.: Reputation in Artificial Societies. Social Beliefs for Social Order, vol. 6. Springer, Heidelberg (2002)
4. Muller, G., Vercouter, L.: Decentralized monitoring of agent communication with a reputation model. In: Falcone, R., Barber, S., Sabater-Mir, J., Singh, M.P. (eds.) Trusting Agents for Trusting Electronic Societies. LNCS (LNAI), vol. 3577, pp. 144–161. Springer, Heidelberg (2005)
5. Jones, A.J.I., Sergot, M.: On the characterisation of law and computer systems: The normative systems perspective. In: Meyer, J.J.C., Wieringa, R.J. (eds.) Deontic Logic in Computer Science: Normative System Specification, John Wiley & Sons, Chichester (1993)
6. Tuomela, R.: The Importance of Us: A Philosophical Study of Basic Social Norms. Stanford University Press (1995)
7. Castelfranchi, C., Falcone, R.: Principles of trust in mas: cognitive anatomy, social importance and quantification. In: ICMAS'98, Paris, pp. 72–79 (1998)
8. Abdulrahman, A.: A framework for decentralized trust reasoning. PhD thesis, University of London (2004)

9. Zacharia, G., Moukas, A., Maes, P.: Collaborative reputation mechanisms in electronic marketplaces. In: HICSS '99: Proceedings of the Thirty-second Annual Hawaii International Conference on System Sciences, Washington, DC, USA, vol. 8, p. 8026. IEEE Computer Society Press, Los Alamitos (1999)

10. McKnight, D., Chervany, N.: Trust and distrust definitions: One bite at a time. In: Falcone, R., Singh, M., Tan, Y.-H. (eds.) Trust in Cyber-societies. LNCS (LNAI), vol. 2246, pp. 27–54. Springer, Heidelberg (2001)

11. Wang, Y., Vassileva, J.: Bayesian network-based trust model in peer-to-peer networks. In: Proceedings of the Workshop on Deception, Fraud and Trust in Agent Societies, pp. 57–68 (2003)

12. Casare, S., Sichman, J.: Using a functional ontology of reputation to interoperate different agent reputation models. Journal of the Brazilian Computer Society 11(2), 79–94 (2005)

13. Singh, M.P.: Agent communication languages: Rethinking the principles. In: Huget, M.-P. (ed.) Communication in Multiagent Systems. LNCS (LNAI), vol. 2650, pp. 37–50. Springer, Heidelberg (2003)

14. Gnutella: Gnutella 0.48 specifications (2000),
http://rfc-gnutella.sourceforge.net/developer/stable/

15. PeerSim: A peer-to-peer simulator (2005),
http://peersim.sourceforge.net/

16. JPL: A java interface to prolog (2003),
http://www.swi-prolog.org/packages/jpl/java_api/

17. Artikis, A., Kamara, L., Pitt, J., Sergot, M.: A protocol for resource sharing in norm-governed ad hoc networks. In: Leite, J.A., Omicini, A., Torroni, P., Yolum, P. (eds.) DALT 2004. LNCS (LNAI), vol. 3476, pp. 221–238. Springer, Heidelberg (2005)

18. Klein, M., Rodriguez-Aguilar, J., Dellarocas, C.: Using domain-independent exception handling services to enable robust open multi-agent systems: the case of agent death. Journal of Autonomous Agents and Multi-Agent Systems 7(1-2), 179–189 (2003)

19. Minsky, N., Ungureanu, V.: Law-governed interaction: a coordination and control mechanism for heterogeneous distributed systems. ACM Transactions on Software Engineering and Methodology (TOSEM) 9(3), 273–305 (2000)

20. Aldewereld, H., García-Camino, A., Noriega, P., Rodríguez-Aguilar, J.A., Sierra, C., Dignum, F.: Operationalisation of norms for electronic institutions. LNCS, vol. 4386, pp. 156–169. Springer, Heidelberg (2007)

Part V
AUTONOMY, COORDINATION AND SOCIAL ORDER

What Is Commitment? Physical, Organizational, and Social (Revised)

Carl Hewitt

MIT EECS (emeritus)
carlhewitt@alum.mit.edu

Abstract. This paper uses Participatory Semantics to explicate commitment. Information expresses the fact that a system is in a certain configuration that is correlated to the configuration of another system. Any physical system may contain information about another physical system.

For the purposes of this paper, physical commitment is defined to be information pledgedabout physical systems (situated at a particular place and time). This use of the term physical commitment is currently nonstandard.

Note that commitment is defined for whole physical system; not just a participant or process.

Organizational and social commitments can be analyzed in terms of physical commitments. For example systems that behave as scientific communities can have commitments for monotonicity, concurrency, commutativity, pluralism, skepticism, and provenance.

Speech Act Theory has attempted to formalize the semantics of some kinds of expressions for commitments. Participatory Semantics for commitment can overcome some of the lack of expressiveness and generality in Speech Act Theory.

1 Introduction

This paper uses Participatory Semantics [15] as formalism within which to explicate commitment. Participatory Semantics makes use of participations that are 4 dimensional regions of space-time. Participations include both happenings (regions in which things happen, e.g., purchasing, communicating, etc) and participants (regions for things that participate, e.g., people, XML expressions, etc). Participatory Semantics derives from concepts in physics (e.g. quantum, relativistic).

2 Information

Information expresses the fact that a system is in a certain configuration that is correlated to the configuration of another system. Any physical system may contain information about another physical system.

P. Noriega et al. (Eds.): COIN 2006 Workshops, LNAI 4386, pp. 293–307, 2007.

2.1   Information Is Necessarily Incomplete

Although Einstein was one of the first to formulate the necessary incompleteness of quantum physics, he never fully accepted it. Chris Fuchs [9] summed up the reality of the necessary incompleteness of information in quantum physics as follows:

> "Incompleteness, it seems, is here to stay: The theory prescribes that no matter how much we know about a quantum system—even when we have maximal information about it—there will always be a statistical residue. There will always be questions that we can ask of a system for which we cannot predict the outcomes. In quantum theory, maximal information is simply not complete information Caves and Fuchs [5]. But neither can it be completed"

The kind of information about the physical world that is available to us according to [9] is "the potential consequences of our experimental interventions into nature" which is the subject matter of quantum physics.

2.2   Information Is Relational

According to Relational Quantum Physics [18], the way distinct physical systems affect each other when they interact (and not of the way physical systems "are") exhausts all that can be said about the physical world. The physical world is thus seen as a net of interacting components, where there is no meaning to the state of an isolated system. A physical system (or, more precisely, its contingent state) is reduced to the net of relations it entertains with the surrounding systems, and the physical structure of the world is identified as this net of relationships. In other words, "Quantum physics is the theoretical formalization of the experimental discovery that the descriptions that different observers give of the same events are not universal".

The concept that quantum mechanics forces us to give up the concept of a description of a system independent from the observer providing such a description; that is the concept of the absolute state of a system. I.e., there is no observer independent data at all. According to Zurek [25], "Properties of quantum systems have no absolute meaning. Rather they must be always characterized with respect to other physical systems".

Does this mean that there is no relation whatsoever between views of different observers? Certainly not. According to Rovelli [23] "It is possible to compare different views, but the process of comparison is always a physical interaction (and all physical interactions are quantum mechanical in nature)."

3   Actors and Events

Actors are the universal primitives of concurrent digital computation. In response to a message that it receives, an Actor can make local decisions, create more Actors, send more messages, and designate how to respond to the next message received. A Serializer is an Actor that is continually open to the arrival of messages. Messages sent to a Serializer always arrive although delivery can take an unbounded amount of time. (The Actor model can be augmented with metrics.)

Unbounded nondeterminism is the property that the amount of delay in servicing a request can become unbounded as a result of arbitration of contention for shared resources *while still guaranteeing that the request will eventually be serviced.*

Arguments for unbounded nondeterminism include the following:

- There is no bound that can be placed on how long it takes a computational circuit called an Arbiter to settle.
  - Arbiters are used in computers to deal with the circumstance that computer clocks operate asynchronously with input from outside, "e.g..", keyboard input, disk access, network input, "etc."
  - So it could take an unbounded time for a message sent to a computer to be received and in the meantime the computer could traverse an unbounded number of states.
- Electronic mail enables unbounded nondetermism since mail can be stored on servers indefinitely before being delivered.
- Communication links to servers on the Internet can be out of service indefinitely.

This section focuses on just those events that are the arrival of a message sent to an Actor.

3.1 Activation Ordering

The activation ordering $(- \approx \rightarrow)$ is a fundamental transitive ordering that models one event activating another (there must be energy flow from an event to an event which it activates).

3.2 Arrival Orderings

The *arrival ordering* of an Actor $x (-x \rightarrow)$ models the (total) ordering of events in which a message arrives at x. Arrival ordering is determined by arbitration in processing messages (often making use of arbiters).

Hewitt [11], and Hewitt and Agha [1], and other published work argued that mathematical models of concurrency did not determine particular concurrent computations as follows: The Actor model makes use of arbitration for determining which message is next in the arrival ordering of an Actor that is sent multiple messages concurrently. For example *Arbiters* can be used in the implementation of the arrival ordering of an Actor which is subject to physical indeterminacy in the arrival order.

In concrete terms for Actor systems, typically we cannot observe the details by which the arrival order of messages for an Actor is determined. Attempting to do so affects the results and can even push the indeterminacy elsewhere. Instead of observing the internals of arbitration processes of Actor computations, we await outcomes. Physical indeterminacy in arbiters produces indeterminacy in Actors. The reason that we await outcomes is that we have no alternative because of indeterminacy.

According to Fuchs[9], quantum physics is a theory whose terms refer predominately to our interface with the world. It is a theory not about observables, not about *beables*, but about *'dingables'* . *We tap a bell with our gentle touch and listen for its beautiful ring.*

The semantics of indeterminacy raises important issues for autonomy and interdependence in information systems. In particular it is important to distinguish between *indeterminacy* in which factors outside the control of an information system are making decisions and *choice* in which the information system has some control.

It is not sufficient to say that indeterminacy in Actor systems is due to unknown/unmodeled properties of the network infrastructure. The whole point of the appeal to indeterminacy is that aspects of Actor systems can be *unknowable*.

3.3   Combined Ordering

The combined ordering (denoted by $\rightarrow$) is defined to be the transitive closure of the activation ordering and the arrival orderings of all Actors. The combined ordering is obviously transitive by definition.

For all events e_1, e_2 if $e_1 \rightarrow e_2$, then the time of e_1 precedes the time of e_2 in the frame of reference of every relativistic observer.

Law of Strict Causality for the Combined Ordering: For no event e does e $\rightarrow$ e.

3.4   Discreteness

Discreteness captures an important intuition about computation: it rules out counter-intuitive computations in which an infinite number of computational events occur between two events *(à la Zeno)*.

The property of Finite Chains Between Events in the Combined Ordering is closely related to the following property:

Discreteness of combined ordering: For all events e_1 and e_2, the set $\{e|e_1 \rightarrow e \rightarrow e_2\}$ is finite.

Theorem 1 (Clinger [6]). *Discreteness of the combined ordering is equivalent to the property of Finite Chains Between Events in the Combined Ordering (without using the axiom of choice.)*

We know from physics that infinite energy cannot be expended along a finite trajectory. Therefore, since the Actor model is based on physics, the Discreteness of the Combined Ordering was taken as an axiom of the Actor model[1].

---

[1] Discreteness of each of the Arrival Orderings and discreteness of the Activation Ordering together do not imply Discreteness of Combined Ordering *even if there is no change in behavior* (see appendix).

The above described Actor event structures can be used as the basis to construct a denotational model of Actor systems as described in the next section.

4   Denotational Semantics

The task of *denotational* semantics is to construct denotations for concurrent systems that are all the possible behaviors that can be exhibited by the system.

We can use Actor event *diagrams* to help construct denotations where an Actor event diagram is just an initial history of the evolution of a concurrent system making use of the combined ordering.

4.1   Domain of Timed Actor Computations

Related to the work of Clinger[6], we will construct an ω-complete computational domain for Actor computations[2]. In the domain constructed here, for each event in an Actor computation, there is a delivery time which represents the time at which the message is delivered such that each delivery time satisfies the following conditions:

1. The delivery time is a positive rational number that is not the same as the delivery time of any other message.
2. The delivery time is more than a fixed δ greater than the time of its activating event. It will later turn out that the value δ of doesn't matter. In fact the value of δ can even be allowed to decrease linearly with time to accommodate Moore's Law.

The Actor event timed diagrams form a partially ordered set $<$ TimedDiagrams, $\leq>$. The diagrams are partial computation histories representing *"snapshots"* (relative to some frame of reference) of a computation on its way to being completed. For d1, d2 $\in$ TimedDiagrams, d1 $\leq$ d2 means d1 is a stage the computation could go through on its way to d2.

The completed elements of TimedDiagrams represent computations that have terminated and nonterminating computations that have become infinite. The completed elements may be characterized abstractly as the maximal elements of TimedDiagrams. Concretely, the completed elements are those having no pending events.

Theorem 2. TimedDiagrams *is an ω-complete domain of Actor computations i.e.,*

---

[2] ω-complete means that limits exist. The work here stands in contrast to [6] which constructed an ω-complete power domain from an underlying incomplete diagrammatic domain, which did not include time. The advantage of the domain TimedDiagrams constructed here is that it is physically motivated and the resulting computations have the desired property of ω-completeness (therefore unbounded nondeterminism) which provides guarantee of service.

1. If $D \subseteq$ TimedDiagrams is directed[3] , the least upper bound $\sqcup D$ exists; furthermore $\sqcup D$ obeys all the Actor laws.
2. The finite elements of TimedDiagrams are countable where an element x $\in$ TimedDiagrams is finite (isolated) if and only if $D \subseteq$ TimedDiagrams is directed and $x \leq \sqcup D$, there exists $d \in D$ with $x \leq d$. In other words, x is finite if one must go through x in order to get up to or above x via the limit process.
3. Every element of TimedDiagrams is the least upper bound of a countable in creasing sequence of finite elements.

4.2 Power Domains

Definition 1. *The domain* $<$ Power[TimedDiagrams], $\subseteq>$ *(after Clinger [1981] with the crucial difference that in this work the domain TimedDiagrams is ω-complete) is the set of possible initial histories M of a computation such that*

1. M *is downward-closed, i.e.,*
   if $d \subseteq M$, *then* $\forall d \in$ TimedDiagrams, $d \leq d \Rightarrow d \in M$
2. M *is closed under least upper bounds of directed sets, i.e. if* $D \subseteq M$ *is directed, then* $\sqcup D \in M$

Note: Although Power[TimedDiagrams] is ordered by $\subseteq$, limits are not given by U. *I.e.*, $\forall i$, $M_i \subseteq M_{i+1} \Rightarrow U_{i\in\omega}M_i \subseteq \sqcup_{i\in\omega}M_i$

$E.g.$, If $\forall i$, $d_i \in$ TimedDiagrams and $d_i \leq d_{i+1}$ and $M_i = \{d_k | k \leq i\}$ then

$$\sqcup_{i\in\omega}M_i = U_{i\in\omega}M_i\{\sqcup_{i\in\omega}d_i\}$$

Theorem 3. Power[TimedDiagrams] *is an ω-complete domain.*

4.3 Denotations

An Actor computation can progress in many ways.

Let d be a diagram with next scheduled event e and $X \equiv \{e|e- \approx\rightarrow_{1-\text{message}} e\}$, Flow(d) is defined to be the set of all diagrams with d and extensions of d by X such that

1. the arrival all of the events of X has been scheduled where
2. the events of X are scheduled in all possible orderings among the scheduled future events of d
3. subject to the constraint that each event in X is scheduled at least δ after e and every event in X is scheduled at least once in every δ interval after that. (Please recall that δ is the minimum amount of time to deliver a message.) Flow(d) $\equiv$ d if d is complete.

---

[3] A subset A of a partially ordered set $< P, \leq>$ is called a *directed* subset if and only if A is not the empty set and if $a, b \in A$, there exists a $c \in A$ with $a \leq c$ and $b \leq c$ (*directedness*).

Let S be an Actor system, Progressions is a mapping
Power[TimedDiagrams] → Power[TimedDiagrams]
$\text{Progressions}(M) \equiv U_{d \in M} \text{Flow}(d)$

Theorem 4. Progressions *is* ω*-continuous.*

I.e., if $\forall i M_i \subseteq M_{i+1}$ then,

$$\text{Progressions}(\sqcup_{i \in \omega} M_i) = \sqcup_{i \in \omega} \text{Progressions}(M_i)$$

Furthermore the least fixed point of Progressions is

$$\sqcup_{i \in \omega} \text{Progression}_S^i(\perp S)$$

where $\perp S$ is the initial configuration of S.

The denotation Denotes of an Actor system S is the set of all computations of S. Define the *time abstraction* of a diagram to be the diagram with the time annotations removed.

Theorem 5 (Representation Theorem). *The denotation* Denotes *of an Actor system S is the timeabstraction of*

$$\sqcup_{i \in \omega} \text{Progression}_S^i(\perp S)$$

Using the domain TimedDiagrams, which is ω-complete, is important because it provides for the direct expression of the above representation theorem for the denotations of Actor systems by directly constructing a minimal fixed point. In future work it will be shown how the representation theorem can be used as the basis for model checking to verify properties of Actor systems. The previous sections on the Actor model provide a basis for grounding concurrent computation in space-time. This grounding provides part of the foundation for the next sections on commitment.

5   Commitment

Various notions of commitment have been proposed around the notion of *information pledged*.

5.1   What Is Physical Commitment?

For the purposes of this paper, a *physical commitment* PC is defined to be a *pledge* that certain *information* I holds for a *physical system* PS for a *space-time region* R. Note that physical commitment is defined for *whole physical systems*; not just a participant or process. Participants and/or processes might be entangled!

Let K be the expressed knowledge of physical commitment for how a large number of people interact with their information systems. The experience (e.g.

Microsoft, the US government, IBM, etc.) with respect to large software systems (where K consists of tens of millions of lines of documentation, code, and use cases) is that K is inconsistent. Such inconsistencies are addressed in Direct Logic [13], [12], [14].

The use of physical commitment here differs from the previous work of Bratman, Cohen, Durfee, Georgeff, Grosz, Huber, Hunsberger, Jennings, Kraus, Levesque, Nunes, Pollack etc. in that it is not founded on the notion of psychological beliefs, desires, intentions, and goals.

5.2   Physical Commitment and Contracts

A contract C is a *signed* (XML) expression for a *physical commitment* PC that pledges the signers S show certain parties P_s behave. In the course of time the parties P_s can fall into and out of compliance with the contract C.

Since C is a finite and of limited expressiveness there is a great deal of behavior by P_s that is left unspecified or ambiguous by C. Given these limitations, it might be that C is clarified, amended, or even completely revised in the course of time.

Furthermore various participants might actually see things differently as to whether the parties P_s are complying with C. For example violations might not be detected for some time or might not ever be detected. Participants who detect violations may or may not be members of P_s.

Also C might contain escape clauses such that the commitment might become trivialized. For example C might contain a time limit such that it is no longer in force after a certain time.

Sometimes some of the parties P_s do not fulfill C or desire to deviate from C. In some cases violations are innocent, unintentional, or cannot reasonably be avoided. In other cases some members of P_s may deliberately violate C perhaps even concealing what they are doing.

5.3   Organizational Commitments

Organizational commitments are physical commitments that are undertaken by organizations.

Organizational commitments can be represented in contracts by having an organization sign a contract as opposed to an individual. For example, it is common for organizations to sign executable code for computers which commits that the organization is the originator of the code.

Often an organization will not entrust its entire authority to just one signature. So a system of delegation is established in which another signature might be granted a limited amount of organizational authority. This can be accomplished by a contract signed by a higher authority delegating certain specified abilities to another signature. In many cases, this delegation can be revoked at a later time.

5.4   Social Commitments

Social commitments involving permissions and obligations have been the subject of previous research by [3], [4], [22], [8], [16], [19] and [20], etc.

[8] proposed that a social commitment can be characterized by the following attributes:

- *debtor*: owes the content to the *creditor*
- *creditor*: is owed the content by the *debtor*
- *content*: a temporal proposition that at every time instant has a truth value that can be one of the following: *undefined, true, or false.*
- *state*: which is obtained by the actions makeCommitment, setCancel, set-Pending and must be one of the following: *unset, pending, cancelled, fulfilled, or violated.*

Similarly in [24], a social commitment has attributes of *debtor, creditor, condition* the debtor is to bring about, and *organizational context.* A social commitment as characterized in the above work can be considered a special case of physical commitment (as defined in this paper) between information with the required attributes and the physical system of the *debtor* and *creditor* during the time periods in question.

5.5   Inconsistent Social Commitments

Social commitments are analyzed in terms of permissions, obligations, prohibitions, dispensations, and delegations in [17] where meta-policies are used to attempt to remove some inconsistencies. As an example, they describe the recent issue with the passage of the Medicare prescription drug bill in the United States:

$$USGovStaff(p) \Rightarrow obligated(p, answerCongressionalQuery(p))$$

$$USGovStaff(Foster)$$

$$boss(p1, p2) \land order(p1, p2, s) \Rightarrow obligated(p, s)$$

$$boss(Scully, Foster)$$

$$order(Scully, Foster, \neg answerCongressionalQuery(Foster))$$

The above example has Foster faced with inconsistent social commitments when he received a query from the congressional Democrats on the estimated cost of the Medicare prescription drug bill since

$$obligated(Foster, answerCongressionalQuery(Foster))$$

has an inconsistent obligation with

$$obligated(Foster, \neg answerCongressionalQuery(Foster))$$

5.6   Psychological Commitment

Psychological commitment has been studied in Artificial Intelligence by Bratman, Cohen, Georgeff, Grosz, Harman, Huber, Hunsberger, Jennings, Kraus, Levesque, Nunes, Pollack, Sidner, Singh,etc.

Psychological commitmentis subject to certain pitfalls including the following:

- *omniscience of deductive consequence*: Typically psychological commitment has been based on psychological beliefs. However, an Agent cannot be expected to be psychologically committed to all the deductive consequences of their beliefs because of combinatorial intractability.
- *mentalism*: Psychological commitment has been widely criticized as being based on mentalism which makes it subject to great uncertainty because the current state of development in Artificial Intelligence. Such mentalism was the subject of great controversy in the 1991 AAAI Fall Symposium on Knowledge and Action at Social and Organizational Levels.

The notion of physical commitment as defined in this paper is not making the kind of psychological assumptions that are involved in psychologically based accounts of commitment [22], etc.

5.7   Electronic Institutions

[10] presented an analysis in terms of a normative framework of obligations, permissions, prohibitions, violations, and sanctions, which can be formalized in terms of physical commitment.

For example consider the commitment to be a *Fishmarket* in which buyers submit bids to an auctioneer in a Dutch auction to purchase round lots of fish. A proper *Fishmarket* provides that

- its participants have particular obligations, permissions, and prohibitions
- that certain violations may occur
- if violations occur, what sanctions are imposed

It is possible to implement an actual *Fishmarket* in the form of an electronic institution (e.g. as described in [21]) in which information technology plays an important role in the operations of obligations, permission, prohibitions, and sanctions. Once this has been done (e.g. in Blanes) we can look at the physical commitment that the fish market in Blanes operates as a proper *Fishmarket* at some particular time (e.g. 12 December 1997). In this regard, it would be possible to have every participant take part in a full audit on 13 December 1997 of what happened the previous day and then sign a contract that to the best of their knowledge all of the *Fishmarket* obligations, permissions, prohibitions, and violations had been obeyed on the previous day. However, although they are evidence, just by themselves, these contracts may not definitely settle the question as to whether a proper *Fishmarket* operated in Blanes on 12 December 1997. E.g., error or fraud (large or small) may still be a possibility. (See [2] for a flexible extension of electronic institutions to allow for a flexible enforcement of norms and manners.)

6 Speech Act Semantics

Speech Act Theory has been developed by philosophers and linguists to account for the use of language beyond simply stating propositions as in mathematical logic. Speech Act Theory encompasses *perlocutionary* and *illocutionary seman-tics.*

6.1 Limitations of Perlocutionary Semantics

The perlocutionary semantics of a speech act the effect, intended or not, achieved in an addressee by a speakers utterance, e.g., persuading, convincing, scaring, insultng, getting the addressee to desire something, etc.. However, perlocutionary semantics is limited in scope to mental state of the addressee. In terms of physics, the addressee is a dingable! In fact the speaker and addressee may be entangled and even privately interacting unbeknownst to an observer.

6.2 Limitations of Illocutionary Semantics

The illocutionary semantics of a speech act is the basic purpose of a speaker in making an utterance, *e.g.*, *Assertive, Commissive, Declarative, or Expressive* as follows:

- *Assertive*: The speaker expresses that the state of affairs described by the propositional content of the utterance is actual.
- *Commissive*: The speaker expresses that they are committed to bring about the state of affairs described in the propositional content of the utterance.
- *Declarative*: The speaker expresses that they are bringing into existence the state of affairs described in the propositional content of the utterance.
- Directive: The speaker expresses that they are attempting to get someone to bring about the state of affairs described by the propositional content of the utterance.
- Expressive: The speaker expresses that they are communicating an attitude or emotion about the state of affairs described in the propositional content of the utterance.

Illocutionary semanticsis limited in scope to the psychological state of a speaker. However, it is unclear how to determine psychological state! Also com-mitments dont fall neatly into the pigeonholes specified by speech act theorists. Furthermore the speaker and addressee may be entangled.

6.3 Web Services

FIPA attempted to promote Agent Communication Languages based on Speech Act Theory. This pioneering effort ran into many difficulties including the prob-lem of trying to pigeonhole communications into the FIPA prescribed illocution-ary performative communicative acts whose semantics are expressed terms of psychological beliefs [7].

Subsequently attention has turned to Web Service standardization. However the current Web Services standards lack formal semantics.

7   Prospects and Future Work

On the 40th anniversary of the publication of Moore's Law, hardware development is furthering both local and nonlocal massive concurrency. Local concurrency is being enabled by new hardware for 64-bit many-core microprocessors, multi-chip modules, and high performance interconnect. Nonlocal concurrency is being enabled by new hardware for wired and wireless broadband packet switched communications. Both local and nonlocal storage capacities are growing exponentially. All of the above developments favor the Actor model.

The development of large software systems and the extreme dependence of our society on these systems have introduced new phenomena. These systems have pervasive inconsistencies among their documentation, implementations, and use cases. There is no prospect for eliminating these inconsistencies. Furthermore, there is no evident way to divide up the information into consistent microtheories. Organizations such as Microsoft, the US government, and IBM have tens of thousands of employees pouring over hundreds of millions of lines of documentation, code, and use cases attempting to cope. Also it would be fair to say that our society is becoming increasingly "committe" to these large software systems. Implications of this circumstance are on the agenda for future research.

Prospects for Agents are difficult to estimate. Currently Web Services do not assign any large role to Agents. On the other hand the semantics of commitment whose development is furthered in this paper are crucial to the future development of Web Services. So one issue before us is what science, technology and terminology will Web Services use for these concepts going forward. For our future Agent systems research, we will need to take the following measures:

– Make extensive use of monotonicity, commutativity, pluralism, skepticism, and provenance.
– Use (binary) XML to express commitments organizing them in viewpoints (theories, contexts) making use of inheritance and translation.
– Further develop semantics and pragmatics for processing expressions for commitments.
– Develop formal semantics for Web Services.
– Study how human individuals, organizations, and communities process expressions for commitments using psychology, sociology, and philosophy of science.
– Prepare for the semantic consequences of massive concurrency both local (many-cores) and nonlocal (Web Services).

Acknowledgments. Mike Huhns, Hidey Nakashima, and Munindar Singh provided comments on the abstract of this paper. Sol Feferman, Mike Genesereth, David Israel, Ben Kuipers, Pat Langley, Vladimir Lifschitz, John McCarthy, Fanya Montalvo, Ray Perrault, Mark Stickel, Richard Waldinger, and others provided valuable feedback at seminars at Stanford, SRI, and UT Austin in which I presented earlier versions of the material in this paper. The AAAI Spring Symposium'06, AAMAS'06, KR'06, and COIN@AMAS'06 reviewers made valuable comments. Substantial comments and suggestions for improvement were contributed by Lalana Kagal, Hidey Nakashima, Pablo Noriega, Munindar Singh, and Richard Waldinger. Unfortunately because of illness, I was unable to attend AAMAS'06. Carles Sierra kindly volunteered to deliver my talk in Hakadote. Sindhu Joseph generously converted this paper from MS Word to LATEX for these proceedings.

References

1. Agha, G.: Actors: A Model of Concurrent Computation in Distributed Systems. PhD thesis, MIT (1986)
2. Aldewereld, H., García-Camino, A., Noriega, P., Rodríguez-Aguilar, J.A., Sierra, C., Dignum, F.: Operationalisation of Norms for Electronic Institutions. In: Noriega, P., Vázquez-Salceda, J., Boella, G., Boissier, O., Dignum, V., Fornara, N., Matson, E. (eds.) COIN 2006. LNCS(LNAI), vol. 4386, pp. 163–176. Springer, Heidelberg (2007)
3. Bergeron, M., Chaib-draa, B.: Acl: Specification, design and analysis all based on commitments. In: Proceedings of the Workshop on Agent Communication (AAMAS 2005) (2005)
4. Castelfranchi, C.: Practical "permission": Dependence, power, and social commitment. In: 2nd Workshop on Practical Reasoning and Rationality, Manchester (April 1997)
5. Caves, C.M., Fuchs, C.A.: Quantum information: How much information in a state vector. In: The Dilemma Of Einstein, Podolsky and Rosen - 60 Years Later, vol. 12, pp. 226 – 257. Annals of the Israel Physical Society (1996)
6. Clinger, W.: Foundations of Actor Semantics. PhD thesis, MIT Mathematics (1981)
7. FIPA. Communicative act library specification (2000),
   http://www.fipa.org/specs/fipa00037/
8. Fornara, N., Vigan, F., Colombetti, M.: Agent communication and institutional reality. In: Workshop on Agent Communication. AAMAS (2004)
9. Fuchs, C.A.: Quantum Mechanics as Quantum Information (and only a little more). In: Quantum Theory: Reconstruction of Foundations. Växjö University Press (2002)
10. Garcia-Camino, A., Noriega, P., Rodriguez-Aguilar, J.A.: Implementing norms in electronic institutions. In: AAMAS (2005)
11. Hewitt, C.: The challenge of open systems. BYTE Magazine (April 1985)
12. Hewitt, C.: Inconsistency is the norm. Submitted for publication (October 2006)
13. Hewitt, C.: The repeated demise of logic programming and why it will be reincarnated. In: Papers from the, Spring Symposium, Menlo Park, California, March 2006. American Association for Artificial Intelligence (2006)
14. Hewitt, C.: Will logicists accept that 'inconsistency is the norm' and 'logic programming is not universal'? Submitted for publication (October 2006)
15. Hewitt, C., Manning, C.: Synthetic infrastructures for multi-agency systems. In: ICMAS '96, Kyoto, Japan (1996)
16. Jennings, N.R.: Commitments and conventions: The foundation of coordination in multi-agent systems. The Knowledge Engineering Review 8(3), 223–250 (1993)
17. Kagal, L., Finin, T.: Modeling conversation policies using permissions and obligations. Journal of Autonomous Agents and Multi-Agent Systems (December 2006)

18. Laudisa, F., Rovelli, C.: Relational quantum mechanics. The Stanford Encyclopedia of Philosophy(Fall 2005 Edition) (2005)
19. Louis, V., Martine, T.: An operational model for the fipa-acl semantics. In: Workshop on Agent Communication. AAMAS (2005)
20. Mallya, A., Singh, M.: A semantic approach for designing commitment protocols. In: Workshop on Agent Communication. AAMAS (2004)
21. Noriega, P.: Agent Mediated Auctions: The Fishmarket Metaphor. PhD thesis, IIIA-CSIC (1997)
22. Brahim Chaib-draa Roberto, A., Pasquier, P.: Conversational semantics with social commitments. In: JAAMAS (January 2005)
23. Rovelli, C.: Relational quantum mechanics. International Journal of Theoretical Physics 35, 1637–1678 (1996)
24. Singh, M., Huhns, M.: Service-Oriented Computing: Semantics, Processes, Agents. John Wiley & Sons, Chichester (2005)
25. Zurek, W.: Physics review letters. Journal of the american physical society D26, 1862 (1982)

Appendix: Discreteness of Each of the Arrival Orderings and Discreteness of the Activation Ordering Together Do Not Imply Discreteness of Combined Ordering Even if There Is No Change in Behavior

Clinger in [6] surprisingly proved that the Law of Finite Chains Between Events in the Combined Or-dering is independent of the discreteness of the arrival or-derings and arrival ordering. The following result generalizes the result of Clinger because it shows that change in behavior is not required for the result to hold.

Theorem 6. *The Discreteness of the Combined Ordering is not implied by the individual discreteness of the Activation ordering and the Arrival orderings **even** if there is no change in behavior.*

It is sufficient to show that there is an Actor computation that satisfies the previously stated laws but violates the Law of Finite Chains Between Events in the Combined Ordering. Such a computation can be generated by $Initial.Start\lceil\rceil$ where [4]

```
Initial ≡
    receiver
Start⌈⌉ →
    let initialGreeter = Greeter.Create⌈⌉
        then send InitialAgain⌈initialGreeter⌉
Again⌈oldGreeter⌉ →
    let nextGreeter = Greeter.Create⌈⌉
```

---

[4] The program uses messages expressed in XML using the notation $< name >_{tag} \lceil < element >_1 \cdots < element >_n \rceil$ for" $< $ " $< name >_{tag}$ " $> $ " $< element >_1 \cdots < element >_n$ " $< $ "$/< name >_{tag}$" $> $" For example, PersonName⌈First⌈"Kurt"⌉Last⌈"Godel"⌉⌉⌉ prints as follows: <PersonName><First>Kurt</First><Last>Godel</Last></PersonName>

> *then* {*send* InitialAgain⌈nextGreeter⌉
> *also send* nextGreeter SayHelloTo⌈oldGreeter⌉}

The above program which defines the Actor Initial makes use of the following program for Greeter:

> Greeter ≡ *receiver* Request⌈Create⌈ ⌉customer⌉ →
>   *send* customerReturned⌈ *serializer* SayHelloBehavior()⌉
>
>   SayHelloBehavior() ≡
>   *behavior*
>   SayHelloTo⌈oldGreeter⌉ → { *send* oldGreeterHello⌈ ⌉
>   *also* SayHelloBehavior()}
>   Hello⌈ ⌉ → SayHelloBehavior()

Consider a computation which begins when an actor *Initial* is sent a Start⌈⌉ message causing it to take the following actions:

Send Initial the message Again⌈$Greeter_1$⌉. Thereafter the behavior of Initial is as follows:

> On receipt of an Again⌈$Greeter_n$⌉ (which we will call the event $Again_n$) create a new actor $Greeter_{n+1}$ which is sent the message SayHelloTo⌈$Greeter_n$⌉ and send *Initial* the message Again⌈$Greeter_{n+1}$⌉

Obviously the computation of *Initial* sending itself Again messages never terminates. The behavior of each Actor $Greeter_n$ is as follows:

- When it receives a message SayHelloTo⌈$Greeter_{n-1}$⌉ (which we will call the event $SayHelloTo_n$), it sends a Hello⌈ ⌉ message to $Greeter_{n-1}$
- When it receives a Hello⌈ ⌉ message (which we will call the event $Hello_n$), it does nothing.

Now it is possible that $Hello_n$ → $Greeter_n$ → $SayHelloTo_n$ every time and therefore $\forall n Hello_n$ → $SayHelloTo_n$.
   Also $Again_n - \approx \to Again_{n+1}$ every time and therefore $\forall n Again_n \to Again_{n+1}$.

All of the Laws for the Activation Ordering and Arrival Orderings Individually Are Satisfied.

However, there are an infinite number of events in the combined ordering between $Again_1$ and $SayHelloTo_1$ as follows:

$$Again_1 \to \cdots \to Again_n \to \cdots \infty \cdots \to Hello_n$$
$$\to SayHelloTo_n \to \cdots \to Hello_1 \to SayHelloTo_1$$

Modelling and Monitoring Social Expectations in Multi-agent Systems

Stephen Cranefield

Department of Information Science, University of Otago
PO Box 56, Dunedin, New Zealand
`scranefield@infoscience.otago.ac.nz`

Abstract. This paper reports on issues confronted and solutions developed while implementing the author's previously proposed hyMITL$^{\pm}$ logic for expressing social expectations as conditional rules. A high level overview of hyMITL$^{\pm}$ is presented, along with a discussion of new features and implementation issues. In particular, the importance of using human-oriented descriptions of time points is argued, along with the need to explicitly take time zones into consideration when defining rules, and a syntax for date/time expressions based on ISO standard 8601 is proposed. A new, more detailed, model for tracking the state of social expectations is also presented, based on the utility of enabling clients of a monitoring service to be notified of multiple instances of the violation or fulfilment of an expectation.

1 Introduction

A significant amount of research in the field of multi-agent systems is currently focused on the theory, design and implementation of *electronic institutions* [1]. This work adapts the mechanisms that keep human society orderly to provide a framework for building open systems of self-interested software agents that are subject to explicitly defined rules of behaviour. Some key requirements in this area are languages for expressing the norms or expectations that apply to agents' interactions and actions, techniques for detecting violations of these rules of society, and mechanisms to prevent or discourage such violations. This paper focuses on the first two requirements, and in particular discusses issues and solutions arising from one previously proposed approach.

The hyMITL$^{\pm}$ logic [2] is a form of temporal logic that allows social expectations to be expressed as rules that are conditional on observations of the past and present, with consequences that impose constraints on future states of the world. The logic and its restricted rule syntax were designed to be amenable to run-time compliance monitoring. This is achieved using an algorithm that keeps a history of observed facts and events, determines when rules are triggered, and applies the technique of *formula progression* [3] to incrementally evaluate and simplify the resulting instantiated consequences (the current expectations) as new states and their associated facts are appended incrementally to the history. When a progressed formula reduces to *true* or *false* this means that a

P. Noriega et al. (Eds.): COIN 2006 Workshops, LNAI 4386, pp. 308–321, 2007.

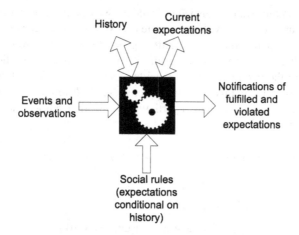

Fig. 1. Overview of the compliance-monitoring process

social expectation has been fulfilled or violated (respectively), and a notification is sent to the clients of the compliance monitor[1]. Figure 1 gives an overview of this process.

The structure of this paper is as follows. A brief overview of hyMITL$^\pm$ is given in Section 2, and some implementation choices in maintaining world states for atomic formula evaluation are discussed in Section 3. Section 4 discusses the concept of social expectations as applied to hyMITL$^\pm$ and other approaches to modelling electronic institutions. Section 5 advocates the use of a human-oriented time scale in social expectation modelling languages, presents a date/time expression language for hyMITL$^\pm$ based on ISO standard 8601, and demonstrates the need for explicit time zone information in date/time expressions involving relative times. The lifecycle of social expectations is discussed in Section 6 and a distinction between local and global compliance is proposed. Some observations are then made in Section 7 on the trade-off between the expressiveness of a social expectation modelling language and the types of decision procedure it admits, before a discussion of some related work is presented in Section 8.

2 Overview of hyMITL$^\pm$

hyMITL$^\pm$ is a temporal logic that includes unary temporal operators (including standard abbreviations) meaning *in the next/previous state* (X^+/X^-), *eventually in the future/past* (F^+/F^-), and *always in the future/past* (G^+/G^-), as well as binary *until* operators for the future and past directions (U^+/U^-) and a *for all possible future sequences of states* operator (A). The F, G and U operators are qualified by temporal intervals to constrain the states that must be considered when evaluating the argument (or the second argument in the case of U^+/U^-). The default interval (if one is omitted)

---

[1] To provide useful information to clients, it is necessary to associate each current expectation with the initial rule instantiation that produced it and the state in which it was fired. This is straightforward, but has not yet been implemented.

is $(-\infty, +\infty)$. An interval may also appear on its own as a formula to express the constraint that the current state is within that time period. There is a "current time" binding operator ($\downarrow$) that is qualified by a time unit (e.g. week) and a time zone, and binds the following variable to a term that names the current time in the specified time zone, rounded down to the beginning of the specified unit of time. The following is an example rule expressed using this language, where p, c, *publication*, *price* and t are terms denoting a service provider, a client, a particular publication, a price and a specific date and time, respectively:

$$\mathbf{AG}^+ \mathrm{done}(c, \mathrm{buy\_sub}(publication, p, price)) \wedge [t, t + \textsf{P1W} \,|\, \textsf{z}) \;\rightarrow$$

$$\downarrow_\textsf{z}^\textsf{week} \mathrm{w}.\mathbf{G}^+_{[\mathrm{w}+ \textsf{P1W} \,|\, \textsf{Z}, \; \mathrm{w}+ \textsf{P53W} \,|\, \textsf{Z})}$$

$$\downarrow_\textsf{z}^\textsf{week} \mathrm{cw}. \downarrow_\textsf{z}^\textsf{now} \mathrm{n}. (\neg \mathbf{X}^-[\mathrm{cw}, \mathrm{n}] \;\rightarrow$$

$$\exists \mathrm{d}\,(\mathrm{date\_time\_to\_date}(\mathrm{cw}, \mathrm{d}) \wedge$$

$$\mathbf{F}^+_{[\mathrm{n}, \; \mathrm{cw}+ \textsf{P1W} \,|\, \textsf{Z})} \mathrm{done}(p, \mathrm{send}(c, publication, \mathrm{d}))))$$

This rule states that if client c has bought a subscription to *publication* from provider p for *price* and this happens within a week of time t (the price is only valid for a week), then at all times within the interval beginning a week after the start of the week that the payment is made (w) and ending immediately before 53 weeks after w, if the current state is the first within a given week (encoded as the constraint that the previous state wasn't between the start of the week and now, inclusive), then between now and the end of the week the provider will send the current edition of the publication. In other words, once the payment is made, the publication will be sent every week for 52 weeks.

This example includes some additions and specialisations to the syntax compared to the previous description of hyMITL$^\pm$ [2]. In particular, relative times (e.g. P1W) are expressed in a notation based on ISO standard 8601, and time zone annotations (the Zs) are added. These are motivated and discussed in Section 5.

Rules such as this are used by matching the left hand side against a history recording the current and previous states in terms of the events that were observed and the facts that were known to hold in those states[2]. The matching operation results in an instantiation of the right hand side. For example, the rule above will match a state in which the specified *buy_sub* operation has been performed if the date/time associated with that state is less than a week after, or is at, the time t. The resulting instantiated right hand side then represents a social expectation that an expectation monitoring tool can monitor over time. First the new expectation is partially evaluated—in the example this will result in the outer $\downarrow$ operator and its variable being removed and the variable w being instantiated to a term denoting the date/time at which the current week began in the timezone Z. Each time a (relevant) event in the world is observed, a new state is created, atomic formulae describing the observed event and the known facts that hold in that state are asserted into the history, and all expectations being monitored are "progressed" to the new state and partially evaluated, which generally will result in them

---

[2] The rules may contain past modalities and even future modalities (if nested within past ones), but they should be designed so that the left hand sides can be evaluated using a finite history.

being simplified. If an expectation becomes *true* or *false* on progression, it can be determined that the expectation was fulfilled or violated (respectively). The progression algorithm is not presented formally in this paper, but a high level description is given in Section 6.

3   Representing Events and Facts

The semantics of hyMITL$^{\pm}$ rely on the standard notion of satisfaction of an atomic formula in a first order model representing a state of the world. When integrating a compliance monitor with an agent platform or institutional middleware, propositions representing observed events and known facts must be asserted into the history of present and past states. While the representation of facts can be based on the ontologies used in the multi-agent system, some convention needs to be adopted for stating that events have just occurred—the example above uses a *done* predicate. A domain model is needed to declare (amongst other things) the event types that are considered relevant to the system and the properties of predicates, e.g. in the example the predicate *date_time_to_date* is used to represent a function that truncates a date/time expression to leave just the date, and this can be implemented as a built-in or user-supplied state-independent predicate. The compliance monitor may also need a way of calculating which facts persist from one state to the next, given the events that have just occurred. A mechanism for fact persistence may not be needed if there is middleware that provides an interface for accessing the public institutional state (as in AMELI [4]). However, for more loosely coupled systems the monitor may need to infer the facts that hold in each state based on the facts that held in the previous state and the actions that have occurred. This is precisely the problem that AI planning has addressed with the development of action description formalisms such as STRIPS rules [5] and the situation and event calculi [6,7]. The domain model could include action descriptions in some existing action description language (such as the event calculus approach of Farrell et al. [8]). Alternatively the hyMITL$^{\pm}$ rule language itself can be used to express this information. Such rules describe the 'physics' or causality of the domain, and their conclusions need to be interpreted not as expectations, but as facts to be asserted into the current state's fact base.

4   Social Expectations

Unlike other languages for defining social rules in electronic institutions, hyMITL$^{\pm}$ does not include concepts from deontic logic such as obligation, permission and prohibition, nor does it include any formalised notion of commitments between agents. Including these concepts in a logic allow the fulfilment and violation of norms by agents to be explicitly stated and reasoned about within the language (rather than at the meta-level), as well as allowing the directed social relationships underlying these concepts to be explicitly represented.

While there would be some benefit in adding these features to hyMITL$^{\pm}$, there is also utility in allowing the expression of rules that are not explicitly defined in terms of deontic concepts. The social expectations that an agent has may come from a number of sources. While an electronic insitution will have published rules with official force—in which case terms such as obligation, permission and prohibition seem appropriate, an agent may usefully maintain its own set of rules expressing social regularities that it has learned, even though these might not have any official status in the institution. Also, rules could be used to express the effects of actions, as discussed above.

In this paper we use the term "social expectations" to encompass any constraints on the present and future that result from rules intended to express social regularities, whether normative or not. We believe that the issues we discuss are relevant to all approaches to modelling and monitoring social expectations.

5   A Human-Oriented Time Scale

One of the motivations for the development of MAS technology is to allow humans to decrease their workload or increase their efficiency by delegating work to trusted autonomous software agents (subject to appropriate constraints and policies). Therefore, while some multi-agent systems (e.g. those controlling nuclear reactors or chemical processes) may only need to consider time as a metric quantity measured in (e.g.) milliseconds, many applications of multi-agent systems will require agents to work within human society, and in particular to understand dates and times expressed using human calendar systems. For example, agents may need to understand deadlines expressed in terms of units such as days, weeks and months.

The theory and practicalities of using a human time scale have been addressed to various degrees in the MAS literature. Mallya et al. [9] present example commitments between agents that include relative time expressions such as $t + 7\,days$, but no syntax and semantics for a date/time language are presented. Verdicchio and Colombetti [10] present a detailed account of the syntax and semantics of date/time expressions and date arithmetic within an agent content language. The normative specification language of Vázquez-Salceda et al. [11] allows the use of absolute and relative deadlines represented in terms of dates and standard time units, but no formal details are presented. Farrell et al. [8] discuss ecXML: a version of the event calculus using an XML syntax, which (based on the examples presented) uses human-oriented date and time units, but this is not explicitly discussed. In our initial presentation of the hyMITL$^\pm$ language [2], we showed how a date/time language in the style of Verdicchio and Colombetti can be integrated into a temporal logic in which time intervals and a date/time binding operator are first class elements of the language, rather than being axiomatically defined.

In contrast, other research has treated times as (essentially) real numbers. The IS-LANDER e-institution editor [12] and the associated AMELI [4] middleware for governing agents in an institution allow timeouts to be specified in protocol-based norms, and the implementation [13] uses the Java system time in milliseconds for its timestamps. SOCS-SI [14] and the formalism of García-Camino et al. [15] use explicit time variables, arithmetic time expressions, and time inequality constraints, but only numeric time stamps are considered.

In this section we discuss the use of a human-oriented date/time scale in our implementation of the hyHITL$^\pm$ logic, in particular, the date/time language used and the qualification of time expressions by time zones.

5.1   A Date/Time Language Based on ISO Standard 8601

ISO standard 8601 [16] defines standard textual representation formats for dates and times. The defined formats are used (generally in a restricted form, and possibly with some changes) by various Internet and Web standards, such as RFC 3339 [17] for date/time timestamps on the Internet and the XML Schema definition of date and time datatypes [18]. In the implementation of hyMITL$^{\pm}$ we use the formats from ISO 8601 for expressing points in time in terms of date/time units, and for expressing durations in time as *periods*. We also allow new date/time points to be calculated by adding or subtracting relative times to date/time points.

Date/time strings. Instances in time are represented using the following syntax:

$$YYYY\text{-}MM\text{-}DD\mathtt{T}hh\text{:}mm\text{:}ss.fffz$$

where *YYYY* is the four-digit number of the year (we assume only AD dates are of interest), and *MM*, *DD*, *hh*, *mm*, *ss* are two-digit representations of the month[3], day, hour (using a 24 hour clock), minute and second, respectively. *fff* represents up to three optional digits for fractions of a second—the preceding decimal point is omitted if there is no fractional part. The T separates the date and time components. *z* represents a time zone in terms of an offset to Universal Coordinated Time (UTC). It can be either the character 'Z' (representing the "zero meridian", i.e. an offset of 0), or a '+' or '−' followed by an hour and minute offset in the form *hh*:*mm*.

We assume the Gregorian calendar is used and that the usual constraints on the number of days in each month for a given year are respected.

We do not currently support various abbreviations and variations to this notation allowed by the ISO standard (such as omitting the field separators) or the use of week-of-year or day-of-year expressions.

Period strings. An offset in time can be expressed using one of the "period" notations in the standard representing "a duration not associated with any start or end". The notation is:

$$P\,years\mathtt{Y}\,months\mathtt{M}\,weeks\mathtt{W}\,days\mathtt{DT}\,hours\mathtt{H}\,minutes\mathtt{M}\,seconds\mathtt{S}$$

where lower case text stands for the desired number of each unit, and the capital letters are unit indicators[4]. Fields and their following unit indicators can be omitted, but the 'T' separator must be present if there are any time fields. The seconds field can include a decimal point. The leading 'P' indicates that this is a 'period', and this can be followed by an optional '+' or '−'.

Date/time arithmetic. We allow expressions denoting the addition or subtraction of periods to date/time points. This is useful when defining date/time points as offsets to date/time variables. The addition of periods to date/time points is complicated as it involves knowledge of the calendar, and it is necessary to have well understood conventions for handling issues such as the variable number of days in a month when adding

---

[3] Unlike the Java Date class, months are numbered from 1.

[4] This format is a slight generalisation of the ISO one as it allows months and weeks to appear together.

months to a date and the occurrence of leap years when adding years. Although the ISO standard is not freely available, an algorithm for adding durations to date/time points appears in an appendix of the XML Schema datatypes definition [18]. Our implementation relies on the Joda Time Java library [19] to perform this computation.

A further complication is that the addition of periods to date/time points can only be defined relative to a particular time zone. This issue is discussed in the following section.

5.2   The Need for Time Zones

A period defined in terms of units such as months, weeks and days does not define a fixed length of time. In particular, the addition of months involves an addition to the month component of a date followed by a "rounding down" of the resulting day to an allowed value. This means that the time zone in which the computation is performed can be significant. Consider the following examples, where the subscript to the '+' indicates the timezone used for the addition:

$$2006\text{-}02\text{-}28T23\text{:}00\text{:}00Z +_Z \text{P1M} = 2006\text{-}03\text{-}28T23\text{:}00\text{:}00Z$$

$$2006\text{-}02\text{-}28T23\text{:}00\text{:}00Z +_{+01\text{:}00} \text{P1M} = 2006\text{-}04\text{-}01T00\text{:}00\text{:}00+01\text{:}00$$

This shows that, given the starting date of 11pm, 28 February 2006 (UTC), the addition of a month can result in a difference of three days depending on whether the calculation is performed with respect to UTC or UTC+01:00. To align with people's experience of time, changes to and from summer time must also be reflected in date/time arithmetic.

In the above example, the time zone was provided as a separate annotation to the addition. As an alternative, the timezone associated with the date/time argument could be used ("Z" in both cases above). However, hyMITL$^{\pm}$ can include interval expressions with variables that become instantiated at an outer level of the formula. To ensure that the time zone in which an addition or subtraction is to be performed is explicit in the formula, we use the syntax $date\_time + period \mid time\_zone$ as an abbreviation for a ternary addition operator taking an explicit time zone argument. Without this, in the following formula the time zone for the calculation would not be known until the variable cd (current day) becomes bound:

paid(cust426, order77867) $\rightarrow$
   $\downarrow_Z^{\text{day}} cd. \, F_{[cd+\text{P1D} \mid Z, \, cd+\text{P2D} \mid Z]}^{+}$received_goods(cust426, order77867)

This formula states that once a particular customer has paid for a particular order, delivery will be made at some time during the next day. Note that the time binding operator $\downarrow$ must also be qualified by a time zone as well as a time unit.

In practice, for some applications it may be possible to omit time zone annotations and simply use an agent's current time zone. However, in other cases where agents are distributed across different time zones it will be crucial to ensure this information is explicitly provided for expressions involving temporal arithmetic. It follows that adapting systems based on real number time points to use a human-oriented time scale is not just a simple matter of changing the data type used to represent time points and plugging in a different time arithmetic module—the syntax of the temporal language used may need to be changed in a more fundamental way.

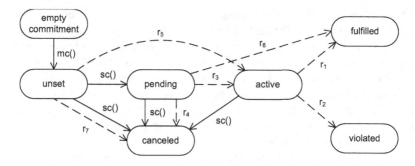

Fig. 2. Fornara and Colombetti's commitment lifecycle [20]

6   The Lifecycle of a Social Expectation

A system that monitors future-oriented social expectations, whether these are obligations, commitments or learned patterns of behaviour, must have some underlying model of the lifecycle of an expectation. For example, various formalisms and practical tools based on commitments have been proposed with differing accounts of the dynamics of a commitment. Figure 2 shows the commitment lifecycle proposed by Fornara and Colombetti [20]. This diagram defines a state space for conditional commitments and the possible transitions between those states, with solid arrows indicating operations (mc for make commitment and sc for set commitment) that occur as a result of agent communication, and dashed arrows indicating state changes that occur as a result of a change in truth value of the commitment's precondition or content propositions. Further constraints on the legal transitions are defined by rules (r_1 to r_7, not shown here) and some "basic authorizations" that restrict the performance of each sc transition to be performed by either the debtor or the creditor of the commitment. The unset state allows an agent to create a commitment for which another agent is the debtor. This can then be set to the pending state by the debtor (if the commitment is accepted), or set to the canceled state (if not accepted).

The *commitment machine* formalism of Yolum and Singh [21] can be viewed as defining a similar state machine, with some additional operations possible on commitments: the release of the commitment by its creditor, the assignment of an alternative agent as the creditor (performed by the original creditor) and the delegation of a commitment by its debtor to an alternative debtor. Because a commitment machine is used to specify protocols in which all commitments are fulfilled, the violation of commitments is not modelled in this formalism. In contrast to the approach of Fornara and Colombetti, a commitment machine does not explicitly represent commitments as propositions with a temporal component—instead, the semantics of commitment assertions directly constrain the possible future paths that conform to a commitment in terms of the satisfaction of the commitment content in some future state. This is in contrast to the earlier work of Venkatraman and Singh [22] which used the same lifecycle but with particular patterns of CTL formulae as the content of commitments.

In general, a tool to monitor social state will need to track two types of transition in the state of a social expectation: those triggered by interactions between agents (the solid lines in the figure) and those triggered by changes in truth value of the logical content of the expectation (the dashed lines). The ability to monitor the former relies on an ability to overhear communication between agents [23] or the use of group multi-casting [24] or a group message redistribution agent [25] when sending messages with important social consequences. Detecting transitions triggered by changes in truth value requires determining whether particular propositions hold or actions have occurred in each state. Vásquez-Salceda et al. [11] have proposed practical implementation techniques for managing this process, and suggested the inclusion of specific detection mechanisms within norm descriptions.

Currently, hyMITL$^{\pm}$ does not include any notion of commitments or obligations, and thus a compliance monitor for hyMITL$^{\pm}$ rules is not concerned with monitoring changes of social state. Its focus is on the right hand side of the state diagram in Figure 2. The content of a social expectation having a temporal aspect can have three possible values when an attempt is made to evaluate it. Its value may be unknown (corresponding to the active state in the figure), *true* (the fulfilled state) or *false* (the violated state). As time passes, the compliance monitor's trace of observations and events is extended and expectations with an unknown value may remain in that state or their content may be reduced to a value of *true* or *false*. The hyMITL$^{\pm}$ compliance algorithm presented previously follows this approach using an iterative process of partial evaluation and formula progression [2]. Once a formula has been reduced to *true* or *false*, a fulfilment or violation is reported and the (now trivial) formula is removed from the set of current expectations.

While this may seem an obvious outcome of applying three-valued logic to the evaluation of expectations with a temporal nature, our experience in implementing hyMITL$^{\pm}$ has demonstrated to us that monitoring the transitions between the three states active, fulfilled and violated is not sufficient for compliance monitoring. This is based on the need to allow a wider range of notifications from the compliance monitor to an agent using its services. For example, consider an expectation that an agent will perform a particular operation every day for a year. A client of a compliance monitor tracking this expectation may wish to be notified after every day that the required operation is not performed, not just the first time (which is when the expectation becomes logically false). Any resulting sanctions may depend on the number of repeated violations. The client may also wish to be notified every time the expected action *is* performed, rather than being notified at the end of the year that the expectation as a whole was fulfilled. These examples suggest that a compliance monitor needs distinct notions of *global* versus *local* compliance, and that its clients may wish to control the notifications they receive in a flexible by specifying *notification policies*. These policies would allow clients to specify, for particular patterns of formulae, their interest or disinterest in single or repeated violations or fulfilments of social expectations that match the patterns.

Figure 3 shows a UML 2.0 state machine giving a more detailed account of the possible states of an expectation's content formula, designed to allow more flexible notification to clients of a compliance monitor. The Active state is decomposed into two orthogonal sets of substates: those indicating the global state, i.e. whether the expectation is logically false, true or unresolved (e.g. if its value depends on the evaluation of future modalities), and those indicating its local state—whether it is true or false when evaluated at the current point in time, ignoring any past violations and requirements

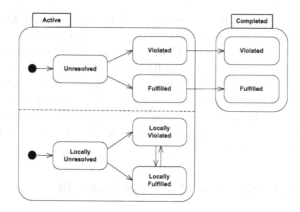

Fig. 3. A more detailed state space for social expectations

on the future. The Completed state represents an expectation that no longer has any relevance, e.g. one that was bounded by a particular time interval that has now passed.

Of course it is still necessary to precisely define the notion of local compliance, and one possible definition follows from the technique of formula progression used in the hyMITL$^\pm$ monitoring algorithm. Paraphrasing Kerjean et al. [26]:

> *The idea behind formula progression is to decompose a linear temporal logic formula into a requirement about the present, which can be checked straight away, and a requirement about the (as yet unavailable) next state.*

As hyMITL$^\pm$ includes temporal modalities that refer to the past, the compliance monitor keeps a history of past states, and for our purposes Kerjean et al.'s "requirement about the present" becomes a requirement about the present and past. This component can then be evaluated to determine the local compliance of the formula.

The computation is, in fact, a little more complex than the above description suggests. Unlike planning, for which the technique of formula progression was developed, our compliance monitor cannot generate a new state whenever it is ready to progress a formula. It must wait until a new observation is made, which generates a new state. However, it is desirable to deliver any fulfilment or violation notifications about the previous state in a timely fashion. Therefore, we split the progression algorithm into two steps. The first step is a partial evaluation step that recursively evaluates the formula, resolving to *true* or *false* any subformulae that have no future modalities and applying the progression rules to those that do, with any resulting "requirements about the next state" wrapped by the X^+ operator. It also performs Boolean simplifications. The second step is applied when a new event is observed and the next state is generated. This basically involves removing the outermost X^+ operators. Given a formula p, the result of the first step, $peval(p)$ determines the local compliance status of the social expectation that this formula is the current value of: if it is *false* the expectation has been locally violated; otherwise (if it is *true* or involves X^+ formulae) the expectation has been locally fulfilled. If the expectation is globally unresolved, then a *peval* result of *true* causes the expectation to become globally fulfilled, and a value of *false* causes it to become globally violated.

A social expectation that has just become globally violated or fulfilled would normally be removed at the next progression step as the current value (*true* or *false*) would have no future-oriented component. However, further local fulfilments or violations can be checked for by progressing the future-oriented part of *peval*(p) before any Boolean simplification is applied. For example, if *peval*(p) evaluates to *true* $\land$ X^+p, or to *false* $\lor$ X^+p, then X^+p could be progressed to the next state, giving p. However, further research is needed to find a general formulation of this idea and a suitably expressive way for clients to specify their desired policies on when this technique should be applied and to what patterns of formula.

7 Expressive Power Versus Inference Capability

hyMITL$^\pm$ was designed to allow the expression of social rules with complex temporal properties (relative to other approaches), while still being amenable to run-time compliance monitoring. However, the compliance monitoring process is concerned solely with the application of rules and the satisfaction and violation of their consequences, given the history so far. It cannot detect violations of liveness properties, and it does not detect inconsistencies between rules or expectations that are inconsistent, until they have resolved to *true* or *false*. For example, the algorithm will progress both F_I^+p and $G_I^+\neg p$, where I is a future interval, until I is reached and one of these formulae is found to be violated. Other approaches to run-time monitoring of expectations have similar limitations [8].

As well as run-time monitoring, there are other decision procedures that may be useful for social expectation modelling languages, e.g.:

- Is a set of rules, or a set of current expectations, consistent?
- Given two sets of rules, which one has the most utility for me?
- What set of rules would ensure that my current goals in society are met?

While there may not be feasible approaches to answering these questions for an expressive language like hyMITL$^\pm$, it would be possible to define templates of social contracts that have known properties, with particular parameters that can be varied. Analysis and negotiation could then take place in terms of the parameter space, just as in human society a negotiation over a house purchase usually focuses on the price and occupancy date rather than the fine print of what is often a standard contract.

8 Related Work

The hyMITL$^\pm$ logic combines aspects of CTL$^\pm$ [27], Metric Interval Temporal Logic (MITL) [28] and hybrid logic [29]. A discussion of these and a comparison of the hyMITL$^\pm$ approach with some previous research on modelling and run-time monitoring of social norms have been presented previously [2]. This section discusses some additional related work that was not addressed by the previous paper or in the preceding sections of this paper.

The rules we use for describing social expectation have the form '*past-and-present-occurrences* $\rightarrow$ *future-constraints*', where the expression *future-constraints* is a linear temporal logic formula. This is similar to the rules used to create programs in the METATEM programming language [30]. The execution cycle for checking the compliance of a sequence of observations with hyMITL$^\pm$ rules is essentially the same as the METATEM interpreter loop. The main difference is that METATEM applies rules to generate a sequence of new states to append to the history—a process that involves choosing between different ways to make *until* formulae true, and which may therefore require backtracking to explore all choices. In contrast, each iteration of the hyMITL$^\pm$ compliance checker is triggered by the arrival of a time-stamped observation, which creates a new state and causes the progression of existing expectations and the application of any rules with antecedents that match the newly extended history. Therefore this is a passive monitoring process. However, agents also need a mechanism to help them decide when they should proactively initiate actions when required by social expectations, and an adaptation of the METATEM approach may be useful for this (although backtracking would not be an option for a run-time process). Also, the techniques used in METATEM for compressing the history representation could be applied to a hyMITL$^\pm$ compliance checker.

Stratulat et al. [31] have developed an approach for using first order logic to describe normative agent systems, which includes the ability to state that predicates hold within intervals of (real-valued) time. Norms are conditional obligations, permissions and prohibitions of an agent with respect to an action type during an interval, and these are modelled as fluent properties that hold over particular intervals of time. A notion of violation is defined, and a Prolog implementation of the approach allows violations to be detected when given the norms and facts asserting the occurrence of events. This model was also used to provide a technique based on temporal constraint satisfaction for an agent to schedule its activities so as to incur the least cost from norm violation. As discussed above, such a scheduler would be a useful addition to a hyMITL$^\pm$ compliance checker, but hyMITL$^\pm$ is probably too expressive for a constraint satisfaction approach to be viable.

9   Conclusion

This paper has discussed a number of issues related to the modelling and run-time monitoring of social expectations that have arisen from implementing a monitoring tool for the hyMITL$^\pm$ logic. Further details on this formalism and its implementation have been presented, and in particular a date/time language based on ISO standard 8601 was described, and the use of explicit reference to time zones in such a language was advocated. The lifecycle of social expectations was analysed and a proposal was made for a more detailed account of violation and fulfilment, in order to support a wider range of notifications to clients of a compliance monitor.

Acknowledgements

Thanks to Carles Sierra, Marco Colombetti and Ulises Cortés and their colleagues at IIIA-CSIC, the University of Lugano and Universitat Politècnica de Catalunya (respectively) for their hospitality and thought-provoking discussions during the author's visits in 2005.

References

1. Cortés, U.: Electronic institutions and agents. AgentLink News 15, 14–15 (2004)
2. Cranefield, S.: A rule language for modelling and monitoring social expectations in multi-agent systems. In: Boissier, O., Padget, J., Dignum, V., Lindemann, G., Matson, E., Ossowski, S., Sichman, J.S., Vázquez-Salceda, J. (eds.) Coordination, Organizations, Institutions, and Norms in Multi-Agent Systems. LNCS (LNAI), vol. 3913, pp. 246–258. Springer, Heidelberg (2006)
3. Bacchus, F., Kabanza, F.: Using temporal logics to express search control knowledge for planning. Artificial Intelligence 116, 123–191 (2000)
4. Esteva, M., Rosell, B., Rodríguez-Aguilar, J.A., Arcos, J.L.: AMELI: An agent-based middleware for electronic institutions. In: Proceedings of the 3rd International Joint Conference on Autonomous Agents and Multiagent Systems, vol. 1, pp. 236–243. ACM Press, New York (2004)
5. Fikes, R., Nilsson, N.: STRIPS: a new approach to the application of theorem proving to problem solving. Artificial Intelligence 2, 189–208 (1971)
6. McCarthy, J., Hayes, P.: Some philosophical problems from the standpoint of artificial intelligence. In: Meltzer, B., Michie, D. (eds.) Machine Intelligence, vol. 4, pp. 463–502. Edinburgh University Press (1969)
7. Miller, R., Shanahan, M.: The event-calculus in classical logic - alternative axiomatizations. Electronic Transactions on Artificial Intelligence 3, 77–105 (1999)
8. Farrell, A.D.H., Sergot, M.J., Sallé, M., Bartolini, C.: Using the event calculus for tracking the normative state of contracts. International Journal of Cooperative Information Systems 14, 99–129 (2005)
9. Mallya, A.U., Yolum, P., Singh, M.P.: Resolving commitments among autonomous agents. In: Dignum, F.P.M. (ed.) ACL 2003. LNCS (LNAI), vol. 2922, pp. 166–182. Springer, Heidelberg (2004)
10. Verdicchio, M., Colombetti, M.: Dealing with time in content language expressions. In: van Eijk, R.M., Huget, M.-P., Dignum, F.P.M. (eds.) AC 2004. LNCS (LNAI), vol. 3396, pp. 91–105. Springer, Heidelberg (2005)
11. Vázquez-Salceda, J., Aldewereld, H., Dignum, F.: Implementing norms in multiagent systems. In: Lindemann, G., Denzinger, J., Timm, I.J., Unland, R. (eds.) MATES 2004. LNCS (LNAI), vol. 3187, pp. 313–327. Springer, Heidelberg (2004)
12. Esteva, M., de la Cruz, D., Sierra, C.: ISLANDER: an electronic institutions editor. In: Proceedings of the First International Joint Conference on Autonomous Agents and Multiagent Systems, pp. 1045–1052. ACM Press (2002)
13. IIIA-CSIC: Electronic Institutions Development Environment Web site. Accessed 2006-02-01, http://e-institutions.iiia.csic.es/software.html
14. Alberti, M., Chesani, F., Gavanelli, M., Lamma, E., Mello, P., Torroni, P.: Compliance verification of agent interaction: a logic-based software tool. In: Trappl, R., (ed.) Cybernetics and Systems, vol. II. Austrian Society for Cybernetics Studies, pp. 570–575 (2004)
15. García-Camino, A., Rodríguez-Aguilar, J.A., Sierra, C., Vasconcelos, W.: A distributed architecture for norm-aware agent societies. In: Baldoni, M., Endriss, U., Omicini, A., Torroni, P. (eds.) DALT 2005. LNCS (LNAI), vol. 3904, pp. 89–105. Springer, Heidelberg (2006)
16. Wikipedia: ISO 8601. Accessed 2006-02-01, http://en.wikipedia.org/wiki/ISO_8601
17. Klyne, G., Newman, C.: Date and time on the internet: Timestamps. Request for Comments 3339. The Internet Society (2002)
18. W3C: XML schema part 2: Datatypes 2nd edn. (2004), http://www.w3.org/TR/2004/REC-xmlschema-2-20041028/

19. Joda.org: Joda Time - Java date and time API, Accessed 2006-02-01,
    http://joda-time.sourceforge.net/
20. Fornara, N., Colombetti, M.: A commitment-based approach to agent communication. Applied Artificial Intelligence 18, 853–866 (2004)
21. Yolum, P., Singh, M.P.: Commitment machines. In: Meyer, J.-J.C., Tambe, M. (eds.) ATAL 2001. LNCS (LNAI), vol. 2333, pp. 235–247. Springer, Heidelberg (2002)
22. Venkatraman, M., Singh, M.P.: Verifying compliance with commitment protocols: Enabling open web-based multiagent systems. Autonomous Agents and Multi-Agent Systems 2, 217–236 (1999)
23. Kaminka, G., Pynadath, D., Tambe, M.: Monitoring teams by overhearing: A multi-agent plan-recognition approach. Journal of Artificial Intelligence Research 17, 83–135 (2002)
24. Cranefield, S.: Reliable group communication and institutional action in a multi-agent trading scenario. In: Dignum, F., van Eijk, R.M., Flores, R. (eds.) AC 2005. LNCS (LNAI), vol. 3859, Springer, Heidelberg (2007)
25. Heard, J., Kremer, R.C.: Practical issues in detecting broken social commitments. In: Dignum, F., van Eijk, R.M., Flores, R. (eds.) AC 2005. LNCS (LNAI), vol. 3859, Springer, Heidelberg (2007)
26. Kerjean, S., Kabanza, F., St-Denis, R., Thiébaux, S.: Analyzing LTL model checking techniques for plan synthesis and controller synthesis (work in progress). Electronic Notes in Theoretical Computer Science 149, 91–104 (2006)
27. Verdicchio, M., Colombetti, M.: A logical model of social commitment for agent communication. In: Proceedings of the 2nd International Joint Conference on Autonomous Agents and Multiagent Systems (AAMAS 2003), pp. 528–535. ACM Press, New York (2003)
28. Alur, R., Feder, T., Henzinger, T.A.: The benefits of relaxing punctuality. Journal of the ACM 43, 116–146 (1996)
29. Blackburn, P., de Rijke, M., Venema, Y.: Modal Logic, pp. 436–447. Cambridge University Press, Cambridge (2001)
30. Fisher, M., Owens, R.: From the past to the future: Executing temporal logic programs. In: Voronkov, A. (ed.) LPAR 1992. LNCS, vol. 624, pp. 369–380. Springer, Heidelberg (1992)
31. Stratulat, T., Clerin-Debart, F., Enjalbert, P.: Temporal reasoning: an application to normative systems. In: Proceedings of the 8th International Symposium on Temporal Representation and Reasoning (TIME 2001), pp. 41–47. IEEE Computer Society Press, Los Alamitos (2001)

Influence-Based Autonomy Levels in Agent Decision-Making

Bob van der Vecht[1,2], André P. Meyer[1], Martijn Neef[1], Frank Dignum[2],
and John-Jules Ch. Meyer[2]

[1] TNO Defence, Security and Safety, The Hague
{bob.vandervecht, andre.meyer, martijn.neef}@tno.nl
[2] Department of Information and Computing Sciences, Universiteit Utrecht, Utrecht
dignum,jj@cs.uu.nl

Abstract. Autonomy is a crucial and powerful feature of agents and it is the subject of much research in the agent field. Controlling the autonomy of agents is a way to coordinate the behavior of groups of agents. Our approach is to look at it as a design problem for agents. We analyze the autonomy of an agent as a gradual property that is related to the degree of intervention of other agents in the decision process. We define different levels of autonomy in terms of inter-agent influences and we present a BDI-based deliberation process in which different levels of autonomy can be implemented.

1 Introduction

This research is motivated by a perspective on automation of distributed systems. As systems are becoming more capable of performing complex tasks, a number of new applications can be thought of where different actors collaborate to reach joint goals. Collaboration can be achieved in several ways and coordination of action always plays an important role. In *mixed-initiative systems* several types of collaboration occur in a dynamic manner. Mixed-initiative means that the initiative for actions of the system comes from multiple actors.

If we look at the engineering of mixed-initiative systems, an agent-based approach seems logical and appropriate. Concepts that are used in the agent community like *situatedness* and *proactiveness* [1] are recurring themes when dealing with the design of such systems. We believe that the concept of *autonomy* of the actors plays a crucial role as well. Actors in mixed-initiative systems need to perform tasks on multiple levels of autonomy during the collaboration.

Mixed-initiative systems can consist of human and artificial actors. Human beings can collaborate with agents, or several types of agents with each other. In this paper we will analyze some engineering issues of agents for mixed-initiative systems and more specifically the concept of autonomy in agents. We propose a decision model that includes different levels of autonomy. We deal with the problem of autonomy in agent design by introducing inter-agent influence types in the reasoning process. In Sect. 2.1 and 2.2, we describe the function of autonomy in mixed-initiative system, and define the concept of autonomy itself.

P. Noriega et al. (Eds.): COIN 2006 Workshops, LNAI 4386, pp. 322–337, 2007.

Section 2.3 addresses related work on agent autonomy. In Sect. 3 we present a deliberation loop for autonomy-aware BDI agents. We show how different levels of autonomy can be defined and how they relate to the agent decision model. Section 4 explains our practical approach and illustrates it with an experiment. We give some conclusions in Sect. 5.

2   Autonomy

The first part of this section describes the function of autonomy of actors in mixed-initiative systems in a general way. In the second part, we focus on autonomy in artificial agents, and we present the definition of autonomy as used in this research.

2.1   Mixed-Initiative Systems

A property of mixed-initiative systems is that the system makes use of different types of collaboration among the actors. We have tried to identify some system requirements of mixed-initiative systems and we try to meet these requirements using an agent-based approach. Figure 1 shows some of the concepts that actors in mixed-initiative systems should be aware of in order to handle different coordination types dynamically. In this paper we focus on the issue of autonomy, although neither autonomy, nor any of the other requirements can be studied in isolation. The various concepts interact and influence each other and add to the complexity of this research topic.

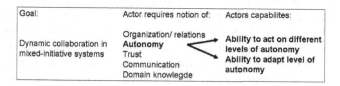

Fig. 1. Important issues concerning dynamic collaboration in mixed-initiative systems

The concept of autonomy is related to the ability of taking initiative. In human cooperation, people readily change their level of dependence with respect to others. This can be regarded as adaptation of their autonomy level. This ability is also essential for agents in mixed-initiative systems, and is currently still lacking. In this paper we will introduce a solution for implementing different levels of autonomy in agents.

2.2   Agent Autonomy

The term autonomy is used in many definitions of agents and is regarded as one of the key features of an agent [1]. Being autonomous means that the agent has control over both its internal state and its behavior. By assuming that agents are autonomous entities, we expect to know something about the way they are internally constructed.

However, the fact that an agent is autonomous does not imply that it has to make all its decisions by itself. In the context of this paper, we look at autonomy as a relational property. We consider the levels of agent autonomy with respect to a certain goal and with respect to other agents. Therefore the degree of autonomy can be defined as the degree of intervention by other agents on the decision making process of how to reach that goal. Barber defines autonomy in a similar manner [2]: *An agent's degree of autonomy, with respect to some goal that it actively uses its capabilities to pursue, is the degree to which the decision-making process, used to determine how that goal should be pursued, is free from intervention by any other agent.*

We have adopted Barber's definition of autonomy for the purpose of this research. It states that an agent can have complete internal autonomy, but deliberately restrict or limit its autonomy in the decision-making process when it is pursuing a certain goal. This means that it allows influences of other agents in its decision-making. In the reasoning process of an agent, the level of autonomy is relevant at every point where the agent actually makes a choice. We consider only agents that are more or less deliberate, since they are aware of their choices. We will present examples of different levels of autonomy in the decision-making process and describe how autonomy can be included in the decision model of agents.

It is widely recognized that the ability of an agent to make decisions autonomously is a strong feature [3]. In some settings it is inevitable to allow autonomous decisions, for example if communication with others fails, or if there is no time to negotiate actions. On the other hand, some tasks require coordination, and then it is necessary to be able to predict an agent's actions, in order to avoid mistakes or conflicts. By limiting its autonomy the agent becomes (partly) dependent of others. At the same time the agent uses capabilities of others. The level of autonomy of agents in the decision-making process with respect to a certain goal is important for cooperation in groups of agents. Controlling and adjusting the agent autonomy can be used in coordination principles.

One perspective on autonomy is that it is an internal feature of an agent, such that it controls its own internal state and its behavior. Another perspective is to look at autonomy as a relational property and consider an agent's autonomy with respect to a certain goal and with respect to other agents. Then autonomy becomes a gradual property of the decision-making process of the agent. We would like to argue here that a truly internally autonomous agent should be able to reason about its level of autonomy in the decision-making process and should be able to adjust its autonomy with respect to a certain goal and to other agents. In the following sections, we first evaluate the use of agent autonomy in other research, and then propose our reasoning model.

2.3   Related Work on Agent Autonomy

Although agent autonomy has been subject to a lot of research, there is no agreement on one definition. Reason for this could be that autonomy is often seen as a property of agents, but it is possible to look at it from different perspectives. Carabelea et al. [4] have given an overview of those perspectives and have tried to classify them. They call the property of an agent being autonomous *self-autonomy*. They distinguish three main types of autonomy in the relation between an agent and its surrounding: *user-autonomy*, *social-autonomy* and *norm-autonomy*. Our approach of agent autonomy is from a relational perspective, and fits in their definition of *social-autonomy*.

Controlling the autonomy of an agent is a way to coordinate the behavior of groups of agents. This coordination can be achieved by explicitly implementing the relations between agents inside their behaviors, e.g. by predefined protocols. We want to argue that this undermines the *self-autonomy* of an agent; the agent does not control its internal state anymore. Agent organizations are an approach to improve coordination without touching the *self-autonomy* as feature of agents. Several researchers propose ways for defining organizational relations, for example by using norms. The Opera model proposes an expressive way for defining organizations in terms of an organizational model, a social model and an interaction model [5]. It uses norms in the description of roles and interaction schemes to define obligations and permissions of an agent. In its approach it explicitly distinguishes between the organizational model and the agents who will act in it. Another example is Moise+, which provides an organizational middle ware for agents, which checks whether actions of agents are allowed or not according to the governing organizational rules [6]. Both approaches separate the organizational model from the agent model. This choice is very legitimate for their goal of developing organizational models. We believe that we can make the concept of agent organizations more powerful by designing agents that can handle different levels of autonomy in the decision-making process. The freedom an agent should get in its decision making can be described in organizational rules and norms.

Sichman [7] has introduced dependence networks to express dependencies between agents in multi-agent systems. Using those dependencies he distinguishes two notions of agent autonomy with respect to a certain goal; relative to actions and relative to resources. Knowledge about the dependencies can be used in plan selection and coalition formation. The dependence theory focuses on dependencies of goal achievement and action execution. In our work we look at interactions and influences between agents as well, but our focus is on goal selection and decision making.

Work on *adjustable autonomy* of agents is done by Scerri [8] and Barber [9]. Their work is motivated by issues on development of human-agent collaborative systems. Scerri's work includes an implementation of a classification task, where humans and agents work together in a dynamic manner. The agent reasons about when the human or when the agent should perform the task. This is a kind of reasoning about autonomy by using *transfer-of-control* strategies. However, the strategies that Scerri uses, are specifically developed for this classification domain. The system shows mixed-initiative behavior, but only in this domain. The general concept of autonomy is not included in the reasoning process of the agents. In the approach of Barber [9] different levels of autonomy are related to styles of decision making. The focus of their work is on decision strategies for organizations and on the interaction that comes from the choices of autonomy levels. Their aim is to make the agents select the best organizational structure autonomously as a group. Our view on autonomy comes close to theirs, but, in contrast, we use the notion of autonomy for the design of a decision model for single agents and allow them to reason about it individually.

3   Decision Making on Different Levels of Autonomy

In this section we will introduce the concept of autonomy in the reasoning model of an agent. First we will briefly explain the deliberation process of the agent. Then we analyze how we can distinguish different levels of autonomy in the decision-making process and we will integrate autonomy in the agent deliberation.

3.1   Agent Deliberation: Introducing the OODA-Loop

In the agent deliberation process we distinguish four sub-processes: 1. do observations and receive messages, 2. process the observations and messages, and determine their semantics 3. decide on the next action and 4. perform the selected action. These processes can be recognized in the four phases of agent deliberation: Observe, Orient, Decide and Act (OODA). We borrowed these terms from the OODA-loop as it is used in decision-making processes in the military command and control domain [10]. In its generalized form, the OODA-loop can be seen as a cycle for all sorts of decision-making processes. It is comparable to Perceive-Reason-Act cycles that are used in the agent reasoning domain. The reasoning phase has been split into two phases, one for information processing and the other for deciding on actions.

The four phases in the OODA-loop can be implemented in a sequential or in a parallel way (cf. Fig. 2). When parallel they can be seen as separate processes sharing resources, but each with its own frequency.

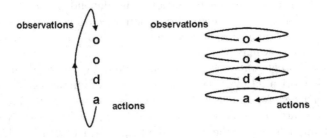

Fig. 2. Sequential and parallel OODA-processes

The Orient phase prepares a world model for the agent to reason with. It transfers raw observation data to data structures that are used in the Decide phase. The designer has some freedom in defining how much information processing takes place in the Orient phase. For example, if certain higher-level information processing is seen as an optional action, the choice for higher-level information processing should deliberately be made in the Decide phase. In the Decide phase, the agent reasons about the actions to take.

We believe that reasoning mechanisms using cognitive notions like beliefs, desires and intentions (BDI) are a good approach for agent reasoning. Several BDI reasoning models have been proposed. For example, 3APL [11], [12], provides the designer with a formalized programming language which is designed for BDI-agent programming. In order to reach its goals, the agent reasons about its beliefs and plans. We use 3APL reasoning in the Decide phase of our deliberation model.

Since we use a BDI-reasoning model in the Decide phase, we will translate both the observations and the content of the messages to beliefs and goals in the Orient phase. These are the data with which the agent can reason properly. Summarizing the four OODA-phases as we use them:

- **Observe.** In the Observe phase, the agent observes the environment with its sensors and receives incoming messages. Observations and messages contain the *presented world state*, i.e. the world as presented by the sensors. There is no connection yet with the agent's beliefs.

- **Orient.** In the Orient phase, the observations and messages are processed. The beliefs of the agent are updated with those observations and messages. Result of the orient phase is an *interpreted world state*; the world as the agent interprets it. The belief base may include knowledge that the agent derived and that is not observable by the sensors. In the Orient phase, the Decide phase will be prepared; the interpreted world state is the world state with which the agent will continue its reasoning. All concepts that are necessary for the BDI-reasoning process need to be defined. Figure 3(a) shows that the belief base and the goal base of the agent are updated.

- **Decide.** The Decide phase is the actual reasoning phase as proposed by 3APL and other BDI programming-languages. The agent reasons with its beliefs and goals and decides upon the next action. Figure 3(b) shows the constructs that are used; Beliefs, Goals, Basic Actions and Practical Reasoning Rules [12].

- **Act.** In this phase the action that has been selected will be executed. Actions can be internal actions of the agent (i.e. the capabilities in the 3APL program) or external actions that take place in the environment.

We use the OODA loop to illustrate how different kinds of influences take part in the agent deliberation. In our definition, the agent's level of autonomy is related to the degree of influence of other agents in the reasoning process of the agent. In the next section we will define different levels of autonomy by relating inter-agent influences to the different phases of the reasoning process.

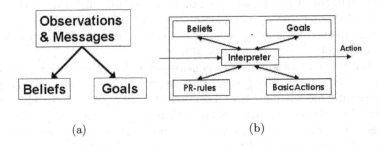

Fig. 3. Two phases of the OODA-loop: (a) the Orient phase, and (b) the Decide phase

3.2   Inter-agent Influences

There are three types of influence between agents to be distinguished, [3], [9]: influence by environmental modification, influence by belief alteration and influence on goal/task determination.

All three types of influence can come together and all types of influence can change the decision on the actions selected. We will explain the types of influence and show how they can be integrated in the decision-making process of an agent. The OODA-cycle as we previously introduced is used to demonstrate this.

Influence by Environmental Modification. Influence by environmental modification is achieved by modifying the agents' environment. It influences the agent via its observations. This type of influence affects the Observe phase of the agent deliberation. What is done with those observations and how they are processed is up to the agent itself.

Influence by Belief Alteration. Influence on beliefs between agents occurs when one agents informs another by sending a message. Belief influence implies that the agent receives a message and processes the information, i.e. integrates the content with its beliefs. The contents of a message can contain knowledge about the environment or an opinion of the best action to take. Belief influence is based on communication, and therefore it implies that the agents have a shared ontology about the concepts they communicate about. Belief influence reaches upto and including the Orient phase of the OODA-loop. The decision on actions is completely up to the agent itself.

Influence on Goal/Task Determination. Influence on goal/task determination occurs when an agent determines the tasks or goals for another agent. The selection process of goals and tasks takes place in the Decide phase of the OODA-cycle and therefore this type of influence reaches to this phase. If agent A has influence on the goal/task determination of agent B it implies that agent B considers suggestions for next actions proposed by agent A, or even stronger, agent B just follows commands of agent A without any doubt. In order to receive a command from another agent or to get someone's opinion about the best next action, agents need to communicate about *goals* and *plans* and need to be able to send *commands* and *opinions* to each other. Therefore a certain level of belief influence between the agents is required.

Barber [2] has identified a spectrum of decision-making styles on goals and tasks as shown in Fig. 4. The spectrum ranges from completely autonomous to completely command driven. In between there are several types of joint decision making, with *true consensus* as the ultimate form of cooperation.

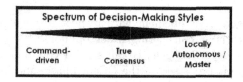

Fig. 4. Spectrum of Decision Making Styles by Barber,[2]

With completely autonomous decision making, there is no influence on goal/task determination. The agent will determine its goals and its actions all by itself, no possible solutions coming from other agents will be considered in the decision-making process. In a fully command-driven decision-making style, there is a full influence on goal/task determination. The agent is dependent on the commands of its partner in the hierarchical relation. With joint decision making styles different types of influences of other agents are possible, for example, an agent can collect opinions of other agents and use them for its decision making.

3.3 Influence-Based Levels of Autonomy

Table 1 summarizes how the influences are linked to the phases in the OODA cycle. We can implement the OODA cycle in such a way that only the required types of influences from other agents take effect.

We will relate inter-agent influences to levels of autonomous decision making. We can design reasoning profiles for agents in an agent organization in terms of the influence types. Some basic examples of those profiles:

- *Solipsistic*: An agent with a solipsistic personality does not care about other agents. Messages from others are ignored. Also the goal/task determination is free from influences. The agent creates and selects its own goals and plans. Influence via environmental modification is still possible. By manipulating an agent's environment, it is possible to influence the agent's behavior. In a solipsistic agent the direct influence of other agents affects the Observe phase of the reasoning process.
- *Trusting* or *naive*: A trusting or naive agent will process messages from others and belief the content. It is under belief influence of others. The decision of which action to perform next is made by the agent itself. The influence of other agents reaches to the Orient phase of the reasoning process.

Table 1. The inter-agent influences in the deliberation process

Type of influence	OODA-phase	Corresp. function
Environmental Modification	Observe	observe()
Belief Influence	Observe	receive_messages()
	Orient	process_messages()
Goal- Task determination	Observe	receive_messages()
	Orient	process_message()
	Decide	commit to commands

- *Obedient*: If Agent A is obedient with respect to agent B, it will do what agent B says without considering other opinions. Its tasks and goals are determined by agent B. Agent B can send a command message to agent A. This message is processed in the Orient phase, and in the Decide phase agent A commits to the command. In the Orient phase, there is influence on beliefs of agent A: it now believes it received a command from agent B. And in the Decide phase there is influence on goal/task determination. This can be done via pre-defined plans in the deliberation cycle of agent A, that demand that if there is an Obedience relation with agent B and a command from agent B then the agent has to commit to the command. In hierarchical decision-making the direct influence of other agents reaches to the Decide phase.

These are a few examples that use extreme forms of some inter-agent influences. Of course more complex profiles are possible as well. All the reasoning profiles can be implemented using our model of influenced-based autonomy levels. In some sense the profiles provide a basic interaction protocol embedded internally in the agent's deliberation process.

3.4   Towards Adjustable Autonomy

Mixed-initiative systems have the property of using different types of collaboration among the actors. The ability of switching dynamically between those types of collaboration is still lacking in agents. We have introduced levels of autonomy in agent reasoning and a next step would be to make the agent reason about its autonomy and allow it to adjust its autonomy level. An agent can not fully control its own level of autonomy. An agent's autonomy is *bilateral adjustable* [3], which means that the level of autonomy can be adjusted by the agent itself as well as by other agents. For example, an agent asking for help instructions chooses to consider options generated by others and therefore it becomes dependent of other agents and lowers its degree of autonomy while pursuing its goal. In a hierarchical relation the master can tell the assistant to solve a problem on its own. Then the assistant becomes autonomous in solving the problem.

We want to look at agents reasoning about their own autonomy. Question is where in the agent-reasoning model the decision about the desired autonomy level should be made. Dastani et al. [13] have analyzed autonomy in the deliberation of BDI agents. Several choices on the deliberation level of an agent influence the agent's autonomy in its decision for new goals and tasks. They propose a meta-language for agent deliberation, which allows the construction of different deliberation cycles. Switching between autonomy levels then could be done in the deliberation cycle itself.

In order to make agents adjust their own autonomy, we need to find rules for switching between autonomy levels. In the next section we will describe experiments that show us some properties of agents collaborating at certain autonomy levels. On basis of the performances in different situations we want to find rules about which autonomy level would be desired in which situation.

4 Experiment

In this section we introduce an experiment for illustrating the concept of autonomy levels in agent decision-making. We have defined an agent organization, in which the agents can operate on different levels of autonomy. We want to observe properties of the organization in the different compositions and compare the performances.

4.1 Organizational Description

The general setting is a fire brigade organization. There is a world with fires, firefighters and a coordinator. The aim of the organization is to extinguish the fires as fast as possible. In the agent organization two roles have to be fulfilled: Coordinator and Firefighter.

- *Coordinator*: Plan which fire is to be extinguished by which fireman, and send commands to the firefighters.
- *firefighter*: Move around randomly to look for a fire, select a fire and extinguish the selected fire.

The agents playing the roles have been implemented following the decision model described above. The phases of the OODA-loop have been implemented sequentially and the 3APL-reasoning mechanism is used in the Decide phase. Goals, beliefs, plans, and basic actions have been made explicit.

In our simulation, firefighters are situated in an environment, where fires can pop up. A firefighter can move to the fire and extinguish it. Fires are growing gradually in time, except for when they are being extinguished, then the fire size decreases and they will disappear. The firefighters have a limited view. The coordinator agent has a global view, it can see all fires. The only action the coordinator can take is sending commands to the firefighters, telling them which fire they should extinguish. The coordinator has one handicap, which is that he can send only one message per time interval.

We have equipped the firefighters with three different profiles: *solipsistic, trusting* and *obedient*. All required influence types are represented in a single OODA-loop. We can create a profile by activating or de-activating the functions corresponding to the influence types as shown in Table 1. As variable we consider only influence on beliefs and on goal/task determination. In all profiles influence via environmental modification is possible, so the observe()-function is always active.

- *Solipsistic*: Solipsistic firefighters observe the fires and select the fire they want to extinguish all by themselves. Influence by environmental modification is possible, for example when a firefighter observes that a fire is getting smaller, because another firefighter is extinguishing it. The agents do not process any message from each other or from the coordinator agent.
- *Trusting*: Trusting firefighters are communicating with the other agents. If they see a fire while they are busy extinguishing another fire, they send a message to the other agents to inform them that there is a fire that needs to be extinguished. The receiving agent processes the message. The information of the particular fire is added to its beliefs. There is still influence by environmental modification by other agents extinguishing fires. There is belief influence by sending messages to each other informing them about fires. The receive_message()-function is active, as well as the process_message()-function.
- *Obedient*: Obedient firefighters are commanded by another agent, who tells them which fire they have to extinguish. They do not take initiative by themselves. There is still influence by environmental modification by other agents extinguishing fires. There is belief-influence by the other agent commands and possibly informing about unknown fires. Therefore both functions receive_message() and the process_message()-function are both active. There is influence on goal/task determination by following the 3APL plans constructed for the obedient relation. A 3APL rule that makes a firefighter agent to follow a command to extinguish a certain fire, could be:

```
<- (obedient(Boss) AND
    command(Boss, fightFire, FireX))
 | fightFire(FireX)
```

It can be read such that the agent no matter what goal it has, if it has an obedient relation with *Boss* and has received a command from *Boss* to extinguish *FireX*, it will adopt the plan *fightFire(FireX)*. *Boss* and *FireX* are variables. The command *fightFire* is written as a constant. This assures that the agent only adopts commands that it knows.

In our experiment we used an organization consisting of two firefighters and one coordinator. We have varied the organizational composition by varying the reasoning profiles of the firefighters with respect to the other agents. We have created three different organizations, as shown in Table 2. In the *solipsistic* organization the firefighter agents ignore all other agents, their profile with respect all other agents is *solipsistic*. In the *trusting* organization the firefighters trust each other, but ignore the coordinator agent. In the *obedient* organization the firefighters are obedient to the coordinator and ignore each other. Note that the difference between the organizations has been created purely by constructing

Table 2. Reasoning profiles of firefighters in their relation with the other agents. Three different organizations.

Organizational characteristic	Profile firefighter regarding firefighters	Profile firefighter regarding coordinator
Solipsistic	Solipsistic	Solipsistic
Trusting	Trusting	Solipsistic
Obedient	Solipsistic	Obedient

different levels of autonomy for a firefighter agent with respect to other agents in the organization.

Furthermore we used environments with different characteristics. The firefighters started in a world containing five fires. In on situation the fires were spread randomly over the field. In the second situation the five fires were clustered in a group. The performance of the organizations was evaluated by measuring the time it took to extinguish all the fires.

4.2   Results and Discussion

What we wanted to show is that the organizations perform differently in environments with other characteristics. We have run several simulations of the different implementations of the firefighter organization. In our results we show the results of 100 runs in six situations (three organizations in two environments). Figures 5(b) and 5(a) show the average extinguish times and the corresponding standard deviation.

Comparing the results of the clustered and random environments, we see the biggest difference in performance for the *trusting* firefighters. They perform worse in the situation of randomly spread fires. This can be explained by the fact that they will only view the fires one by one. They are not able to take advantage of their communication, since tn their behavior it was specified that they would inform each other in the situation when they saw more then one fire. They have to search for each fire individually, which explains the growing standard deviation. As a result they perform comparable with the *solipsistic* firefighters.

If we consider the only clustered environment, the results in Fig. 5(b) show a difference in performance of all three organizations. The *obedient* firefighters perform best. They get orders from the coordinator agent, which has a global view, so all fires are known from the start and the coordinator just sends the firefighters to the right places. In the *solipsistic* and *trusting* organizations the firefighters do not process messages from the coordinator agent. They have only a local view, so they first need to look for the fires. When one firefighter has found a fire, he will see the other fires as well in the clustered situation. The *trusting* firefighters exploit this knowledge by telling each other about the fires, so the second firefighter immediately joins to help. *Solipsistic* firefighters do not have this ability of information sharing. As an illustrative example we show the results of a typical run in the clustered situation in Fig. 6. On the x-axis the

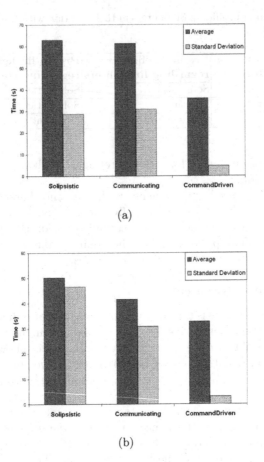

(a)

(b)

Fig. 5. Extinguish times over 100 runs; average and standard deviation. a) Random fire distribution and b) Clustered fire distribution.

time is given and on the y-axis the total fire size in the environment for all three organizational types. It is visible that once the *trusting* firefighters have found the first fire, the fire size decreases faster than for the others. In the *obedient* organization the fire size decreases most constantly.

In the above presented simulations, the *obedient* organization outperformed the other two on average. The organization uses the global view of the coordinator agent. The firefighters follow the orders of the coordinator and it does not really matter how the fires are distributed. However, this type of organization has limitations as well. The organization works by a centralized approach and is very sensitive to the performance of the coordinator agent. The restriction on the number of messages that the coordinator agent can send, is not a big issue in the small organization we use here, but it will be in larger organizations. Another problem is that the observations of the coordinator agent play a very important

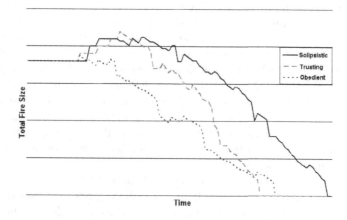

Fig. 6. Total fire size over time, fires are clustered

role, since he determines which fire is to be extinguished by which firefighter. Failure of the observations of the coordinator has big consequences. We have run the same test with randomly distributed fires and the *obedient* organization, but with the restriction that the coordinator could only see two third of the field. The average extinguish times of successful run were comparable of the results in Fig. 5(a), but of the 100 runs the organization failed in 87 cases, because the coordinator missed at least one of the fires. This test shows the necessity of at least some autonomy of the actors in a distributed system.

All results of our experiment are explained by analyzing the information flow in the agent organization. We want to point out that the goal of this experiment was mainly a proof of concept. We have defined different organizations by making the agents reason on different levels of autonomy with respect to the other agents. In our experiment the organization was still static. By defining the autonomy levels internally in the agents in one reasoning model we also create possibilities for switching between autonomy levels at runtime, and therewith allow dynamic organizations. We feel that we need some more experiments to define rules for the agents for switching between autonomy levels.

5 Conclusion and Future Work

This research is motivated by the belief that mixed-initiative and adjustable autonomy are important aspects of future distributed systems and require specific attention. Autonomy of actors is one of the key features when we talk about *mixed-initiative*. The actors should be able to handle several levels of autonomy with respect to a certain goal and with respect to others. We believe that an agent-based approach is a promising way for developing such systems. We have analyzed the concept of autonomy in the decision-making process of agents. Our aim here is to add the notion of autonomy to the reasoning model of an agent.

The level of autonomy is related to the degree of intervention of other agents in the decision making process. We have proposed four phases in the agent deliberation: *Observe, Orient, Decide* and *Act* and we have described three types of influence between agents: environmental influence, influence on beliefs and influence on goal or task determination. We have linked the different influence types to the first three phases of the agent deliberation. Autonomy levels have been defined in terms of inter-agent influences and we have shown how they can be implemented in the agent's reasoning. In our experiment using a fire-brigade organization, we have created three reasoning profiles for the agents based on the autonomy levels. The three organizational types have performed differently in environments with other characteristics.

As future work, we want to formalize the concepts we used in our reasoning model. We want to construct a mechanism to allow agents to reason about their autonomy. By extending our experiments we want to find rules for the agent to decide on switching between autonomy levels. Furthermore, we are interested in including human interaction in our simulation environment in order to conduct experiments concerning adjustable autonomy in the human-agent interaction domain.

Acknowledgement. The research reported here is part of the Interactive Collaborative Information Systems (ICIS) project, supported by the Dutch Ministry of Economic Affairs, grant nr: BSIK03024.

References

1. Jennings, N.R.: On agent-based software engineering. Artif. Intell. 117(2), 277–296 (2000)
2. Barber, K.S., Martin, C.E.: Agent autonomy: Specification, measurement, and dynamic adjustment. In: Autonomy Control Software Workshop, Autonomous Agents 99, pp. 8–15 (1999)
3. Falcone, R., Castelfranchi, C.: The human in the loop of a delegated agent: the theory of adjustable social autonomy. IEEE Transactions on Systems, Man, and Cybernetics, Part A 31(5), 406–418 (2001)
4. Carabelea, C., Boissier, O., Florea, A.: Autonomy in multi-agent systems: A classification attempt. In: Agents and Computational Autonomy, pp. 103–113 (2003)
5. Dignum, V.: A Model for Organizational Interaction: based on Agents,founded in Logic. Utrecht University, PhD Thesis (2004)
6. Hübner, J.F., Sichman, J.S., Boissier, O.: A model for the structural, functional, and deontic specification of organizations in multiagent systems. In: Bittencourt, G., Ramalho, G.L. (eds.) SBIA 2002. LNCS (LNAI), vol. 2507, pp. 118–128. Springer, Heidelberg (2002)
7. Sichman, J.S., Conte, R., Castelfranchi, C., Demazeau, Y.: A social reasoning mechanism based on dependence networks. In: ECAI, pp. 188–192 (1994)
8. Scerri, P., Sycara, K., Tambe, M.: Adjustable autonomy in the context of coordination. In: AIAA 3rd.
9. Barber, K.S., Han, D.C., Liu, T.-H.: Strategy selection-based meta-level reasoning for multi-agent problem-solving. In: Ciancarini, P., Wooldridge, M.J. (eds.) AOSE 2000. LNCS, vol. 1957, pp. 269–283. Springer, Heidelberg (2001)

10. Boyd, J.: A discourse on winning and losing. Maxwell Air Force Base, AL: Air University Library Document No. M-U 43947 (unpublished collection of briefing slides and essays) (1987)
11. Hindriks, K.V., de Boer, F.S., van der Hoek, W., Meyer, J.J.C.: Agent programming in 3apl. Autonomous Agents and Multi-Agent Systems 2(4), 357–401 (1999)
12. Dastani, M., van Riemsdijk, B., Dignum, F., Meyer, J.J.C.: A programming language for cognitive agents goal directed 3apl. In: Dastani, M., Dix, J., El Fallah-Seghrouchni, A. (eds.) PROMAS 2003. LNCS (LNAI), vol. 3067, pp. 111–130. Springer, Heidelberg (2004)
13. Dastani, M., Dignum, F., Meyer, J.-J.C.: Autonomy and agent deliberation. In: Agents and Computational Autonomy, pp. 114–127 (2003)

Centralized Regulation of Social Exchanges Between Personality-Based Agents

Graçaliz Pereira Dimuro, Antônio Carlos da Rocha Costa,
Luciano Vargas Gonçalves, and Alexandre Hübner

Escola de Informática, PPGINF, Universidade Católica de Pelotas
96010-000 Pelotas, Brazil
{liz,rocha,llvarga,hubner}@ucpel.tche.br

Abstract. This paper presents a centralized mechanism for solving the coordination problem of personality-based multiagent systems from the point of view of social exchanges. The agents may have different personality traits, which induce different attitudes towards both the regulation mechanism and the possible profits of social exchanges. A notion of exchange stability can be defined, and the connections between agents' personalities and deviations of social exchanges from the stability point can be established. The model supports a decision procedure based on Qualitative Interval Markov Decision Processes, that can solve the problem of keeping the stability of social exchanges, in spite of the different personality traits of the agents. The paper deals only with transparent agents (agents that allow the external access to their balances of exchange values), but we hint on the case of non-transparent agents. The model is analyzed theoretically and contextualized simulations are presented.

1 Introduction

Social control is a powerful notion for explaining the self-regulation of a society, and the various possibilities for its implementation have been considered, both in natural and artificial societies [1,2]. As mentioned in [3], social control, or coordination mechanisms, vary according to the structure of the society: hierarchy, market or network-oriented societies tend to coordinate activities through, respectively, authority supervision, price mechanism or collaboration mechanisms. Our work aims at the simulation of network-oriented societies with collaboration based social control. However, up to now, we are dealing with a hierarchical model, and the system of exchange values that constitutes the basis of the social control model that we adopted seems to be a price mechanism, although one based on qualitative values, as we show presently.

The centralized social control mechanism that we introduced in [4], concerning small social groups, is based on the Piaget's theory of *exchange values* [5], where a variety of social norms (moral, juridical, even economic rules) are rooted in the qualitative economy of exchange values that emerges when individuals evaluate their interactions. That control mechanism is performed by a *social equilibrium supervisor* that, at each time, decides on which actions it should recommend

P. Noriega et al. (Eds.): COIN 2006 Workshops, LNAI 4386, pp. 338–355, 2007.

agents to perform in order to lead the system towards the equilibrium, regarding the balance of the exchange values involved in their exchanges.

The qualitative exchange values are represented using techniques of Interval Mathematics [6]. The *equilibrium point* of the exchanges between a pair of agents is defined as a pair of intervals, each enclosing the value zero, meaning that benefits and losses in exchanges, for each agent, compensate one another. Then, the equilibrium supervisor builds on *Qualitative Interval Markov Decision Processes* (QI-MDP), where states are represented by intervals, actions are interval operations [6], and equality of intervals is interpreted as a loose equivalence relation (two intervals are equivalent if their midpoints are "approximately" equal).

In general, however, since the agents may have different objectives, it may happen that the exchange balance of a given agent, regarding its exchanges with another agent, becomes stable (after a certain period of time) around a value different from zero. That is, in general, agents stabilize their exchanges in non-equilibrated ways, thus keeping the society disequilibrated, as a whole. Given two agents, the *pair of exchange values* in which they stabilize their respective exchange balances is called the *stability point* of the exchanges between them. Such stability point may vary with time.

In this paper, trying to advance the development of a future model of *decentralized* social control, we extend the centralized control architecture presented in [7], in order to consider a society with *personality-based* agents. We propose a social control mechanism coordinated by a *stability supervisor*, whose duty is: (i) to determine, at each time, the target stability point for each pair of agents in the system (which is not necessarily around the value zero); (ii) to decide which actions should be recommended for each pair of agents in order to lead them towards that stability point; (iii) to maintain them stable around that point, until (for some reason) another stability point for some pair of agents is required.

As explained in [8], a realistic account of agent interactions has to consider that agents may have different *interaction personalities*, in order to allow for the agents to participate in different ways in social interactions, depending not only on the way tasks were delegated to them, but also on the way the agents assess their own contributions and the contributions of the other agents to the interaction. So, in this paper, we allow for the agents to have different personality traits, which induce different attitudes towards the social control mechanism (blind obedience, eventual obedience etc.) and the possible profits of social exchanges (egoism, altruism etc.). As a consequence, the agents may or may not follow the recommendations given by the stability supervisor, thus creating a probabilistic social environment, from the point of view of the social control.

Also, we allow the agents to control the supervisor access to their internal states, behaving either as *transparent agents* (agents that allow full external access to their internal states) or as *non-transparent agents* (agents that restrict such external access). In the paper, however, we focus on the supervisor dealing only with transparent agents. Then, it has full knowledge of the agents' personality traits and has access to all current balances of exchange values, and so it is able to choose, at each step, the adequate recommendation for each agent.

We note, however, that the motivation for establishing a social control mechanism (for instance, social stability, social equilibrium or disequilibrium etc.), is usually not inscribed in the details of the social control mechanism itself. That motivation usually lies in the agents themselves or in the application context of the system. Thus, the social control mechanisms that we are developing are neutral with respect to those motivations, serving any of those purposes.

Section 2 shows our modeling of social exchanges. The regulation mechanism of exchanges is introduced in Sect. 3. Section 4 presents the QI-MDP model for the regulation of exchanges between transparent personality-based agents, and the stability analysis. Section 5 shows a sample simulation. Related work is discussed in Sect. 6. Section 7 is the Conclusion and discussion of further work.

2   The Modelling of Social Exchanges

According to Piaget's approach [5], the evaluation of an exchange by an agent is done on the basis of a *scale* of *exchange values* (that are of a qualitative, subjective nature, like those everyone uses to judge the daily exchanges he has: *good, bad, better than* etc.). In general, those values cannot be faithfully represented quantitatively, due to the lack of neat objective conditions for their measurement. Then, following the approach introduced in [4,9], techniques from Interval Mathematics [6] are used to represent any exchange value[1] as a real interval $X = [x_1, x_2] = \{x \in \mathbb{R} \mid x_1 \leq x \leq x_2\}$, with $-L \leq x_1 \leq x \leq x_2 \leq L$, x_1, x_2, for a bound $L \in \mathbb{R}$, $L > 0$. The set of such intervals is denoted by $\mathbb{IR}_L$.

Analogously to [4,7], consider a reference value h (an anchor for the stability point) such that $-L < h < L$, and a tolerance $\epsilon \in \mathbb{R}_+$. We build an *h-centered scale of exchange values* as an algebraic structure $\langle \mathbb{IR}_L, +, \mathbf{X}_h, ' \rangle$, where: (i) the *L-bounded interval addition* operation $+$ is well defined; (ii) $\mathbf{X}_h = \{X \in \mathbb{IR}_L \mid mid(X) \in [h-\epsilon, h+\epsilon]\}$ is the set of *h-reference intervals*, where $mid(X) = \frac{x_1+x_2}{2}$ is the mid point of X; (iii) an *h-compensation interval* of an interval $X \in \mathbb{IR}_L$ is any interval $X' \in \mathbb{IR}_L$ such that $X + X'$ is an h-reference interval; (iv) the least compensation interval of X is given by $[-mid(X) + h - \epsilon, -mid(X) + h + \epsilon]$.

A *social exchange* between two agents, α and β, involves two types of stages. In stages of type $I_{\alpha\beta}$, α realizes an action on behalf of (a "service" for) β. The *exchange values* involved in this stage are the following: $r_{I_{\alpha\beta}}$, which is the value of the *investment* done by α for the realization of a service for β (this value is always *negative*); $s_{I_{\beta\alpha}}$, which is the value of β's *satisfaction* due to the receiving of the service done by α; $t_{I_{\beta\alpha}}$ is the value of β's *debt*, the debt it acquired to α for its satisfaction with the service done by α; and $v_{I_{\alpha\beta}}$, which is the value of the *credit* that α acquires from β for having realized the service for β. In stages of type $II_{\alpha\beta}$, α asks the payment for the service previously done for β, and the values related with this exchange have similar meaning.

The values $r_{I_{\alpha\beta}}$, $s_{I_{\beta\alpha}}$, $r_{II_{\beta\alpha}}$ and $s_{II_{\alpha\beta}}$ are called *material values* (investments and satisfactions), generated by the evaluation of *immediate exchanges*; the

---

[1] Our choice makes the representation operational and the decision process computationally viable, without being unfaithful to Piaget's approach [4].

values $t_{I_{\beta\alpha}}$, $v_{I_{\alpha\beta}}$, $t_{II_{\beta\alpha}}$ and $v_{II_{\alpha\beta}}$ are the *virtual values* (credits and debts), concerning *deferred exchanges*, which are expected to happen in the future [4,5].

The exchange values are undefined if either no service is done in a stage I, or no credit is charged in a stage II. Also, it is not possible for α to realize a service for β and, at the same, to charge him a credit. A *configuration* of ex-values is specified by one of the tuples of well defined values: $(r_{I_{\alpha\beta}}, s_{I_{\beta\alpha}}, t_{I_{\beta\alpha}}, v_{I_{\alpha\beta}})$, $(r_{I_{\beta\alpha}}, s_{I_{\alpha\beta}}, t_{I_{\alpha\beta}}, v_{I_{\beta\alpha}})$, $(v_{II_{\alpha\beta}}, t_{II_{\beta\alpha}}, r_{II_{\beta\alpha}}, s_{II_{\alpha\beta}})$, $(v_{II_{\beta\alpha}}, t_{II_{\alpha\beta}}, r_{II_{\alpha\beta}}, s_{II_{\beta\alpha}})$.

A *social exchange process* is composed by a sequence of stages of type $I_{\alpha\beta}$ and/or $II_{\alpha\beta}$ in a set of discrete instants of time. The *material results*, according to the points of view of α and β, are given by the sum of the well defined material values involved in the process, and are denoted, respectively, by $\mathbf{m}_{\alpha\beta}$ and $\mathbf{m}_{\beta\alpha}$. The *virtual results* $\mathbf{v}_{\alpha\beta}$ and $\mathbf{v}_{\beta\alpha}$ are defined analogously.

A *stability point* is a pair of balances of exchanges that is desired that a pair of agents should maintain for a certain period of time, established according to conditions and constraints imposed by the system's external and internal environments (see Sect. 3). A social exchange process is said to be in *material stability* if in all its duration it holds that the pair of material results $(\mathbf{m}_{\alpha\beta}, \mathbf{m}_{\beta\alpha})$ encloses a given stability point $(\omega_{\alpha\beta}, \omega_{\beta\alpha}) \in \mathbb{R} \times \mathbb{R}$. It is said in *material equilibrium*[2] if both $\mathbf{m}_{\alpha\beta}$ and $\mathbf{m}_{\beta\alpha}$ enclose the zero.

Let $H = \{-L, -L + \frac{L}{n}, -L + 2\frac{L}{n}, \ldots, L - 2\frac{L}{n}, L - \frac{L}{n}, L\}$ be the set of possible reference values induced on $\mathbb{IR}_L$ by a given $n \in \mathbb{N}_+^*$, and $\kappa_n = \frac{L}{n}$ be the *accuracy* of the stability supervisor. Given a target stability point $(\omega_{\alpha\beta}, \omega_{\beta\alpha}) \in \mathbb{R} \times \mathbb{R}$ for the exchange process between the pair of agents α and β, occurring during a certain period of time, a pair of reference values $(h_{\alpha\beta}, h_{\beta\alpha}) \in H \times H$ is chosen such that $\omega_{\alpha\beta} \in [h_{\alpha\beta} - \epsilon, h_{\alpha\beta} + \epsilon]$ and $\omega_{\beta\alpha} \in [h_{\beta\alpha} - \epsilon, h_{\beta\alpha} + \epsilon]$, for a tolerance $0 < \epsilon < \frac{L}{n}$ and machine numbers $h_{\alpha\beta} \pm \epsilon$, $h_{\beta\alpha} \pm \epsilon$. The stability supervisor builds two scales of exchange values, one that is $h_{\alpha\beta}$-centered (for the agent α) and other that is $h_{\beta\alpha}$-centered (for the agent β). The index $\alpha\beta$ ($\beta\alpha$) of a reference value $h_{\alpha\beta}$ ($h_{\beta\alpha}$) will be omitted when it is not relevant in the context.

3 The Social Exchange Regulation Mechanism

Figure 1 shows the architecture of our social exchange regulation mechanism, which extends the one proposed in [7] with (i) a module for the evaluation of stability points and (ii) a learning module based on Hidden Markov Models (HMM) [10]. The *stability supervisor*, at each time, uses an *Evaluation Module* to analyze the conditions and constraints imposed by the system's external and internal environments (not shown in the figure), determining the target equilibrium point. To regulate *transparent* agents, the supervisor uses two *Balance Modules*, $\Sigma_{material}$ and $\Sigma_{virtual}$, to calculate their material and virtual results of the performed exchanges. To regulate *non-transparent* agents, the supervisor uses a *HMM Module* to observe their behavior in exchanges and then

---

[2] Notice that Piaget's notion of equilibrium has no game-theoretic meaning, since it involves no notion of game strategy, and concerns just an algebraic sum.

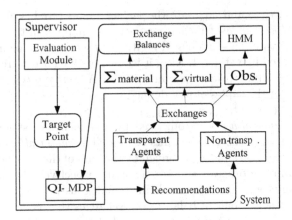

Fig. 1. The social exchange regulation mechanism

recognize and maintain an adequate model of the personality traits of such agents, generating *plausible balances* of their material exchange values.

Taking both the directly observed and the indirectly calculated material results, together with the currently target stability point, the supervisor uses the module that implements a personality-based QI–MDP to decide on recommendations of exchanges for the two agents[3], in order to keep the material results of exchanges stable. It also takes into account the virtual results of exchanges for deciding which type of exchange stage it should suggest. This paper is concerned only with the QI–MDP module. The HMM Module was studied in [13].

4 Personality-Based QI-MDPs

4.1 The States

Consider an h-centered scale of exchange values built as explained in Sect.2. Let $\hat{E}_h = \{E_h^{-n-\frac{sn}{L}}, \ldots, E_h^{-1}, E_h^{0}, E_h^{1}, \ldots, E_h^{n-\frac{sn}{L}}\}$ be the set of $2n+1$ equivalence classes of intervals, where, for each value $i = -n - \frac{sn}{L}, \ldots, n - \frac{sn}{L}$:

$$
E_h^i = \begin{cases}
\{X \mid h + i\frac{L}{n} \le mid(X) < h + (i+1)\frac{L}{n}\} & \text{if } -n - \frac{hn}{L} \le i < -1 \\
\{X \mid h - \frac{L}{n} \le mid(X) < h - \epsilon\} & \text{if } i = -1 \\
\{X \mid h - \epsilon \le mid(X) \le h + \epsilon\} & \text{if } i = 0 \\
\{X \mid h + \epsilon < mid(X) \le h + \frac{L}{n}\} & \text{if } i = 1 \\
\{X \mid h + (i-1)\frac{L}{n} < mid(X) \le h + i\frac{L}{n}\} & \text{if } 1 < i \le n - \frac{hn}{L}.
\end{cases}
$$

---

[3] We consider systems composed by two agents for simplicity. The results are readily extended for more than two agents using the matrix-like notation introduced in [4], where we assumed that the exchanges performed by any two agents are totally independent and cause no interference in any other exchanges. Thus, subQI–MDPs for any two agents can be solved individually and an optimal global supervisor recommendation realized by concurrent execution of the optimal local recommendations; solution time is determined by the size of the subQI–MDPs [11,12].

The classes $E_h^i \in \hat{E}_h$ are the supervisor representations of classes of material results that are either intervals around the reference value h ($i = 0$), or down scale intervals ($i < 0$), called unfavorable results, or up scale intervals ($i > 0$), called favorable results. Whenever it is understood from the context, we shall denote by E^- (or E^+) any class $E_h^{i<0}$ (or $E_h^{i>0}$). The range of the midpoints of the intervals that belong to a class E_h is called the *representative* of the class E_h. In the following, we identify a class E_h with its representative.

The *states* of a QI–MDP model are pairs $(E_{h_{\alpha\beta}}, E_{h_{\beta\alpha}})$ of equivalence classes representing the material results of the social exchange process between the agents α and β, from the point of view of α and β, respectively, considering their respective $h_{\alpha\beta}$-centered and $h_{\beta\alpha}$-centered scales of exchange values. The set of states is denoted by $\mathbf{E}_{h_{\alpha\beta}, h_{\beta\alpha}}$. $(E_{h_{\alpha\beta}}^0, E_{h_{\beta\alpha}}^0)$ is the *terminal* state, representing that the system is stable around the reference point $(h_{\alpha\beta}, h_{\beta\alpha})$ that encloses the stability point $(\omega_{\alpha\beta}, \omega_{\beta\alpha})$. In the following, for simplicity, a class $E_{h_{\alpha\beta}}$ is denoted by $E_{\alpha\beta}$, whenever $h_{\alpha\beta}$ is clear from the context.

4.2 The Actions

An *action* is a pair of intervals $(A_{\alpha\beta}^i, A_{\beta\alpha}^j)$ that induces a state transition of the form $(E_{\alpha\beta}^i, E_{\beta\alpha}^j) \overset{(A_{\alpha\beta}^i, A_{\beta\alpha}^j)}{\longmapsto} (E_{\alpha\beta}^{i'}, E_{\beta\alpha}^{j'})$, such that $mid(E_{\alpha\beta}^i + A_{\alpha\beta}^i) \in E_{\alpha\beta}^{i'}$ and $mid(E_{\beta\alpha}^j + A_{\beta\alpha}^j) \in E_{\beta\alpha}^{j'}$. An *interval* $A_{\alpha\beta}^i$ (analogously for an interval $A_{\beta\alpha}^j$) is of one of the following types: (i) a *compensation interval* $C_{\alpha\beta}^i$ of a class representative $E_{\alpha\beta}^i$; (ii) a *go-forward-k-step interval* F_k^i, such that $mid(E_{\alpha\beta}^i + F_k^i) \in E_{\alpha\beta}^{(i+k)\neq 0}$, $i \neq L$; (iii) a *go-backward-k-step interval* B_{-k}^i, such that $mid(E_{\alpha\beta}^i + B_{-k}^i) \in E_{\alpha\beta}^{(i-k)\neq 0}$, $i \neq -L$. The sets of compensation, go-forward and go-backward intervals are denoted by $\mathcal{C}$ (Table 1), $\mathcal{F}$ and $\mathcal{B}$, respectively.

For example, considering a class E_h^i, with $1 < i \leq n - \frac{hn}{L}$, a *go-forward-k-step interval*, with $k \leq n - \frac{hn}{L} - i$, is given by $F_k^i = [k\frac{L}{n} - \epsilon, k\frac{L}{n} + \epsilon]$. And, for a class E_h^i where $-n - \frac{hn}{L} \leq i < -1$, a *go-backward-k-step interval*, with $k \leq n + \frac{hn}{L} + i$, is given by $B_{-k}^i = [-k\frac{L}{n} - \epsilon, -k\frac{L}{n} + \epsilon]$.

Given a target stability point $(\omega_{\alpha\beta}, \omega_{\beta\alpha}) \in \mathbb{R} \times \mathbb{R}$ (which specifies the pair of reference values $(h_{\alpha\beta}, h_{\beta\alpha}) \in H \times H$), the stability supervisor has to find, for each state $(E_{h_{\alpha\beta}}, E_{h_{\beta\alpha}})$ representing the current material results, the action that may achieve the terminal state $(E_{h_{\alpha\beta}}^0, E_{h_{\beta\alpha}}^0)$ (representing that the system is stable

Table 1. Specification of compensation intervals

State	Compensation Interval $C_h^i \in \mathcal{C}$
$E_h^{i, -n \leq i < -1}$	$[-(\frac{2i+1}{2}\frac{L}{n}) - \epsilon, -(\frac{2i+1}{2}\frac{L}{n}) + \epsilon]$
E_h^{-1}	$[\frac{1}{2}(\frac{L}{n} + \epsilon) - \epsilon, \frac{1}{2}(\frac{L}{n} + \epsilon) + \epsilon]$
E_h^0	$[0, 0]$
E_h^1	$[-\frac{1}{2}(\frac{L}{n} + \epsilon) - \epsilon, -\frac{1}{2}(\frac{L}{n} + \epsilon) + \epsilon]$
$E_h^{i, 1 < i \leq n}$	$[\frac{(1-2i)}{2}\frac{L}{n} - \epsilon, \frac{(1-2i)}{2}\frac{L}{n} + \epsilon]$

around $(h_{\alpha\beta}, h_{\beta\alpha}))$ or, at least, another state from where the terminal state can be achieved, with the least number of steps.[4] Such action generates an *optimal exchange recommendation*, consisting of a partially defined exchange stage that the agents are suggested to perform (see Sect. 4.4). This partial definition shall be completed by the analysis of the virtual results, which allows the specification of which particular types of exchange stages (I or II) should be considered.

4.3   Exchanges Between Personality-Based Agents

We define different levels of obedience to the supervisor that the agents may present: *blind obedience* (the agent always follows the recommendations); *eventual obedience* (the agent may not follow the recommendations, according to a certain probability); and *full disregard of recommendations* (the agent always decides on its own, disregarding what was recommended).

The agents may have different personality traits that give rise to different state-transition functions, which specify, for each obedience level, and given the current state and recommendation, a probability distribution $\Pi(\mathbf{E}_{h_{\alpha\beta}, h_{\beta\alpha}})$ over the set of states $\mathbf{E}_{h_{\alpha\beta}, h_{\beta\alpha}}$ that the interacting agents will try to achieve next. In the following, we illustrate some of those personality traits:

Egoism: the agent is mostly seeking his own benefit, with a high probability to accept exchanges that represent transitions to favorable results;

Strong Egoism: the agent has a very low probability to accept exchanges that represent reduction of its material results even if the agent is maintained in favorable results;

Altruism: the agent is mostly seeking the benefit of the other, with a high probability to accept exchanges that represent transitions toward states where the other agent has favorable results;

Strong Altruism: the agent has a very low probability to accept exchanges that represent reduction of the other agent's material results even if the latter is maintained in favorable results;

Fanaticism: the agent has a very high probability to accept exchanges that lead it to its reference value, avoiding other kinds of transitions;

Tolerance: the agent has a high probability to accept exchanges that lead it to its reference value if his material results are far from that state, but it accepts other kinds of transitions;

Prudence: the agent has a high probability to avoid exchanges when the values involved are higher than a specified limit.

Let $E_h = \{E^-, E^0, E^+\}$ be a simplification of the set $\hat{E}_h$ of the classes of material results, where E^+ and E^- denote the subsets of classes of unfavorable and favorable results, respectively, related to the reference value h. Table 2 presents a pattern of the probability distribution $\Pi(E_h)$, considering individual agent

---

[4] The choice of actions is constrained by the rules of the social exchanges. Since some transitions are *forbidden* (e.g., both agents increasing results simultaneously), the supervisor has to find alternative paths to lead the agents to the stability point.

Table 2. A pattern of probability distribution $\Pi(E_h)$ for agent transitions

$\Pi(E_h)$	Egoist agents			Altruist agents		
	E^0	E^+	E^-	E^0	E^+	E^-
E^0	low	very-high	very-low	low	very-low	very-high
E^+	low	very-high	very-low	low	very-low	very-high
E^-	low	very-high	very-low	low	very-low	very-high

$\Pi(E_h)$	Fanatic agents			Tolerant agents		
	E^0	E^+	E^-	E^0	E^+	E^-
E^0	very-high	very-low	very-low	high	low	low
E^+	very-high	very-low	very-low	high	low	low
E^-	very-high	very-low	very-low	high	low	low

Table 3. A pattern of distribution $\Pi(T)$ for the set T of transitions $E_h^i \mapsto E_h^j$

$\Pi(T)$	$E_h^i < E_h^j$	$E_h^i = E_h^j$	$E_h^i > E_h^j$
Strong Egoism	very-high	low	very-low
Strong Altruism	very-low	low	very-high

transitions, characterizing egoist/altruist and fanatic/tolerant agents. Observe that, for an egoist agent, transitions ending in favorable results (E^+) occurs with very high probability, whereas, for an altruist agent, the most probable transitions are those ending in unfavorable results (E^-). For a fanatic agent, the least probable transitions are those not ending in the terminal state E^0 (around the stability point). In contrast, a tolerant agent accepts transitions to states other than E^0, although with a low probability.

Table 3 shows a pattern for the probability distribution $\Pi(T)$ for the set T of individual agent transitions $E_h^i \mapsto E_h^j$, for strong egoism/altruism. Observe that strong egoist agents presents a very high probability to increase their material results in any exchange, whereas strong altruist agents behave in a completely opposite way.

Table 4 shows parts of sample state-transition functions **F** for systems composed by (a) two tolerant agents and (b) two egoist agents that always disregard the supervisor's recommendations. The mark **X** indicates that the transition is forbidden according to the adopted social rules (both agents increasing results simultaneously). In (b), the highest probabilities appear in the transitions ending in the state (E^+, E^+), representing increasing results for both agents, or in the states $(-, E^+)$ or $(E^+, -)$ when the transitions to the state (E^+, E^+) are not allowed. The probability of 100% in the last line of (b) indicates that the agents refuse to exchange (which would lead both to unfavorable results), remaining in the same state (E^-, E^-). This shows that this system presents an absorbent state, (E^-, E^-), meaning that the system is not able to leave that state if it reaches it, and so it may never achieve the desired target stability point. In

Table 4. Parts of state-transition functions **F** for pairs of agents that always disregard recommendations

(a) (tolerant, tolerant) agents

F (%)	(E^0, E^0)	(E^0, E^+)	(E^0, E^-)	(E^+, E^0)	(E^+, E^+)	(E^+, E^-)	(E^-, E^0)	(E^-, E^+)	(E^-, E^-)
(E^0, E^0)	63.90	X	13.70	X	X	2.90	13.70	2.90	2.90
(E^+, E^-)	49.20	10.50	10.50	10.50	2.20	2.20	10.50	2.20	2.20
(E^-, E^-)	X	X	37.85	X	X	8.10	37.85	8.10	8.10

(b) (egoist, egoist) agents

F (%)	(E^0, E^0)	(E^0, E^+)	(E^0, E^-)	(E^+, E^0)	(E^+, E^+)	(E^+, E^-)	(E^-, E^0)	(E^-, E^+)	(E^-, E^-)
(E^0, E^-)	X	X	0.00	X	X	0.00	15.00	85.00	0.00
(E^+, E^+)	2.20	12.00	0.70	12.00	64.10	4.00	0.70	4.00	0.30
(E^+, E^-)	2.20	12.80	0.00	12.00	68.00	0.00	0.70	4.30	0.00
(E^-, E^-)	X	X	0.00	X	X	0.00	0.00	0.00	100.00

Table 5. Parts of state-transition functions **F** for pair of agents with 50% of obedience

(a) (tolerant, tolerant) agents

F (%)	(E^0, E^0)	(E^0, E^+)	(E^0, E^-)	(E^+, E^0)	(E^+, E^+)	(E^+, E^-)	(E^-, E^0)	(E^-, E^+)	(E^-, E^-)
(E^0, E^0)	81.95	X	6.85	X	X	1.45	6.85	1.45	1.45
(E^+, E^-)	74.6	5.25	5.25	5.25	1.10	1.10	5.25	1.10	1.10
(E^-, E^-)	X	X	18.92	X	X	29.05	18.92	29.05	4.06

(b) (egoist, egoist) agents

F (%)	(E^0, E^0)	(E^0, E^+)	(E^0, E^-)	(E^+, E^0)	(E^+, E^+)	(E^+, E^-)	(E^-, E^0)	(E^-, E^+)	(E^-, E^-)
(E^0, E^-)	X	X	0.0%	X	X	25.00	7.50	67.50	0.00
(E^+, E^+)	51.10	6.00	0.35	6.00	32.05	2.00	0.35	2.00	0.15
(E^+, E^-)	51.10	6.40	0.00	6.00	34.00	0.00	0.35	2.15	0.00
(E^-, E^-)	X	X	0.00	X	X	25.00	0.00	25.00	50.00

(a), one observes the more uniform behavior of tolerant agents, even though the transitions to the states (E^0, E^0), $(E^0, -)$ and $(-, E^0)$ being the most probable.

We remark that even if the agents present a certain level of obedience, there may be a great deal of uncertainty about the effects of the supervisor's recommendations. Considering an obedience level of 50%, the state-transition functions shown in Table 4 become the respective ones shown in Table 5, showing an increase in the probability of the transitions ending in (E^0, E^0) and also the absence of an absorbent state.

For example, for two agents α and β and classes of material results given by $(E^i_{h_{\alpha\beta}}, E^j_{h_{\beta\alpha}}) \equiv ([h_{\alpha\beta} + i\frac{L}{n}, h_{\alpha\beta} + (i+1)\frac{L}{n}], [h_{\beta\alpha} + (j-1)\frac{L}{n}, h_{\beta\alpha} + j\frac{L}{n}])$, with $-n - \frac{nh_{\alpha\beta}}{L} \leq i < -1$ and $1 < j \leq n - \frac{nh_{\beta\alpha}}{L}$, a *compensation–compensation* action $(C^i_{h_{\beta\alpha}}, C^j_{h_{\beta\alpha}}) \equiv ([-\frac{2i+1}{2}\frac{L}{n} - \epsilon, -\frac{2i+1}{2}\frac{L}{n} + \epsilon], [\frac{(1-2j)}{2}\frac{L}{n} - \epsilon, \frac{(1-2j)}{2}\frac{L}{n} + \epsilon])$, should be chosen by the stability supervisor; then, if the agents are obedient, and under certain conditions (see Sect. 4.5), the resulting state transition would be one of the following, with $-n - \frac{nh_{\alpha\beta}}{L} \leq i < -1$ and $1 < j \leq n - \frac{nh_{\beta\alpha}}{L}$:
$(E^i_{h_{\alpha\beta}}, E^j_{h_{\beta\alpha}}) \mapsto (E^0_{h_{\alpha\beta}}, E^0_{h_{\beta\alpha}})$ or $(E^{-1}_{h_{\alpha\beta}}, E^0_{h_{\beta\alpha}})$ or $(E^0_{h_{\alpha\beta}}, E^1_{h_{\beta\alpha}})$ or $(E^{-1}_{h_{\alpha\beta}}, E^1_{h_{\beta\alpha}})$, in increasing order of probability. If one of the agents is not obedient, then there is a probability that none of the above transitions occurs.

4.4   Optimal Value Recommendations

A reward function $\mathbf{R} : (\mathbf{E} \times \mathbf{A}) \rightarrow \mathbb{R}$ must conform to the idea of supporting a recommendation function that is able to direct pairs of agents into the stability point, according to the model of social exchanges (see, e.g, [7]). One sample reward function is partially sketched in Table 6, illustrating some requirements that should be satisfied by such functions. For instance, if the current state is of the type (E^-, E^+), then the reward function must state that the best action to be chosen is a *compensation-compensation* action (C, C), which may result in a state transition $(E^-, E^+) \mapsto (E^0, E^0)$. On the other hand, if the current state is of type (E^-, E^-), then it must prevent the choice of a *compensation-compensation* action (C, C) that would generate a recommendation of exchange of *satisfaction-satisfaction* type, which is forbidden in the model, because it considers impossible to get a satisfaction from no service.

Table 6. Partial schema of the reward function R

R	(C, C)	(B_{-1}, F_{+1})	(F_{+1}, B_{-1})	(B_{-3}, C)
(E^-, E^+)	30	-5	3	20
(E^+, E^+)	30	0	0	20
(E^-, E^-)	-30	30	30	26

The *optimal recommendation* associated to an optimal policy π^* is an operator ρ_{π^*} that gives, for each state $(E^i_{\alpha\beta}, E^j_{\beta\alpha})$ and optimal action $\pi^*(E^i_{\alpha\beta}, E^j_{\beta\alpha}) = (A^i_{\alpha\beta}, A^j_{\beta\alpha})$, partial definitions of recommended exchange stages, consisted by either $(r_{\alpha\beta}, A^i_{\alpha\beta})$ and $(s_{\beta\alpha}, A^j_{\beta\alpha})$, or $(s_{\alpha\beta}, A^i_{\alpha\beta})$ and $(r_{\beta\alpha}, A^j_{\beta\alpha})$, where $(r_{\lambda\delta}, W)$ means the realization, by the agent λ, of a service with investment value W, and $(s_{\delta\lambda}, W')$ means δ's satisfaction with value W', for receiving the service. The optimal recommendation ρ_{π^*} is partially sketched in Table 7.

Finally, the stability supervisor has to decide which types of exchange stages (I or II) should be recommended. This is done by the analysis of the virtual results. For example, if $\mathbf{v}_{\alpha\beta} > 0$ ($\mathbf{v}_{\beta\alpha} > 0$), then α (β) is able to charge β (α) the credit for services previously done. In this case, an exchange stage T^1 (T^2) of type II$_{\alpha\beta}$ (II$_{\beta\alpha}$) should be recommended. However, if $\mathbf{v}_{\alpha\beta} \leq 0$ ($\mathbf{v}_{\beta\alpha} \leq 0$), then the agent α (β) does not have any credit to charge α (β). Therefore, the service done by the agent β (α) must be spontaneous. In this case, an exchange stage T^3 (T^4) of type I$_{\beta\alpha}$ (I$_{\alpha\beta}$) should then be recommended. Some stage recommendations and their combined effects with the optimal value recommendations are sketched in the simplified state transition diagram shown in Fig. 2, where the dot lines represent alternative paths that were not considered as optimal recommendations since they may seem unfair according to social rules.

4.5   Formal Definition and Analysis of the Stabilization Process

Definition 1. *A Qualitative Interval Markov Decision Process (QI–MDP), for keeping the social exchanges in a multiagent system stable around a reference value h, is a tuple* $\langle \mathbf{E}_{h_{\alpha\beta}, h_{\beta\alpha}}, \mathbf{A}, \mathbf{F}, \mathbf{R} \rangle^{L,n}_\epsilon$, *where:*

Table 7. Partial schema of the optimal value recommendation ρ_{π^*}

State	Optimal policy	Recommendation	Label
$(E^i, E^j)^{1<j\leq n}_{-n\leq i<-1}$	(C^i, C^j)	$((r_{\beta\alpha}, C^j), (s_{\alpha\beta}, C^i))$	R_1
$(E^i, E^j)_{1<i,j\leq n}$	(C^i, C^j)	$((r_{\alpha\beta}, C^i), (s_{\beta\alpha}, C^j))$	R_2
		or $((r_{\beta\alpha}, C^j), (s_{\alpha\beta}, C^i))$	R_3
$(E^0, E^j)_{1<j\leq n}$	$([0,0], C^j)$	$((r_{\beta\alpha}, C^j), (s_{\alpha\beta}, [0,0]))$	R_4
$(E^0, E^i)_{-n\leq i<-1}$	$(B^0_{-1}, F^i_{+(-i+1)})$	$((r_{\alpha\beta}, B^0_{-1}), (s_{\beta\alpha}, F^i_{+(-i+1)}))$	R_5
$(E^{-1}, E^j)_{1<j\leq n}$	$(F^{-1}_{+1} \vee C^{-1}, C^j)$	$((r_{\beta\alpha}, C^j), (s_{\alpha\beta}, F^{-1}_{+1} \text{ or } C^{-1}))$	R_6
$(E^1, E^i)_{-n\leq i<-1}$	$(B^1_{-1} \vee C^1, C^i)$	$((r_{\alpha\beta}, B^1_{-1} \vee C^1), (s_{\beta\alpha}, C^i))$	R_7
(E^{-1}, E^1)	$(F^{-1}_{+1} \vee C^{-1}, B^1_{-1} \vee C^1)$	$((r_{\beta\alpha}, B^1_{-1} \vee C^1), (s_{\alpha\beta}, F^{-1}_{+1} \vee C^{-1}))$	R_8
(E^1, E^{-1})	$(B^1_{-1} \vee C^1, F^{-1}_{+1} \vee C^{-1})$	$((r_{\alpha\beta}, B^1_{-1} \vee C^1), (s_{\beta\alpha}, F^{-1}_{+1} \vee C^{-1}))$	R_9
$(E^i, E^1)_{-n\leq i<-1}$	$(C^i, B^1_{-1} \vee C^1)$	$((r_{\beta\alpha}, B^1_{-1} \vee C^1), (s_{\alpha\beta}, C^i))$	R_{10}
(E^{-1}, E^0)	$(F^{-1}_{+1} \vee C^{-1}, B^0_{-1})$	$((r_{\beta\alpha}, B^0_{-1}), (s_{\alpha\beta}, F^{-1}_{+1} \vee C^{-1}))$	R_{11}
(E^0, E^{-1})	$(B^0_{-1}, F^{-1}_{+1} \vee C^{-1})$	$((r_{\alpha\beta}, B^0_{-1}), (s_{\beta\alpha}, F^{-1}_{+1} \vee C^{-1}))$	R_{12}
	$(F^i_{+(-i+1)}, B^j_{-1})$	$((r_{\beta\alpha}, B^j_{-1}), (s_{\alpha\beta}, F^i_{+(-i+1)}))$	R_{13}
$(E^i, E^j)_{-n\leq i,j<-1}$	or $(B^j_{-1}, F^i_{+(-i+1)})$	or $((r_{\alpha\beta}, B^j_{-1}), (s_{\beta\alpha}, F^i_{+(-i+1)}))$	R_{14}

- *The set of states of the model is* $\mathbf{E}_{h_{\alpha\beta}, h_{\beta\alpha}} = \{(E^i_{\alpha\beta}, E^j_{\beta\alpha}) \mid E^i_{\alpha\beta} \in \hat{E}_{h_{\alpha\beta}}, E^j_{\beta\alpha} \in \hat{E}_{h_{\beta\alpha}}\}$ *of pairs of classes of material results as specified in Sect. 4.1.*
- *The set of the actions of the model is the set* $\mathbf{A} = \{(A^i_{\alpha\beta}, A^j_{\beta\alpha}) \mid A^i_{\alpha\beta}, A^j_{\beta\alpha} \in \mathcal{C} \cup \mathcal{F} \cup \mathcal{B}\}$ *of pairs of compensation, go-forward and go-backward intervals.*
- $\mathbf{F} : \mathbf{E}_{h_{\alpha\beta}, h_{\beta\alpha}} \times \mathbf{A} \to \Pi(\mathbf{E}_{h_{\alpha\beta}, h_{\beta\alpha}})$ *is the personality-based state-transition function, that gives for each state and each action, a probability distribution over the set of states* $\mathbf{E}_{h_{\alpha\beta}, h_{\beta\alpha}}$.
- $\mathbf{R} : \mathbf{E}_{h_{\alpha\beta}, h_{\beta\alpha}} \times \mathbf{A} \to \mathbb{R}$ *is the reward function, giving the expected reward gained by choosing an action* $(A^i_{\alpha\beta}, A^j_{\beta\alpha})$ *when the current state is* $(E^i_{\alpha\beta}, E^j_{\beta\alpha})$.

The analysis of the stabilization process is concerned with the number of steps that are necessary to achieve the target stability point. Since the decision process is non-trivial (due to: (i) the qualitative nature of exchange values, (ii) the restrictions imposed by the definition of exchange, that always requires a service be done in any stage, and mainly (iii) the stochastic nature of the agents' behaviors), an analytical study was only possible for agents with blind obedience (after a certain number of free exchanges). Then, the supervisor accuracy $\kappa_n = \frac{L}{n}$ can be adjusted to have the system stable in *at most four steps*, as we show here.[5] Let $\mathbf{m}^\tau_{\alpha\beta}$ and $\mathbf{m}^\tau_{\beta\alpha}$ be the material results of an exchange process performed by the agents α and β, at step τ, and $h_{\alpha\beta}$ and $h_{\beta\alpha}$ be the reference values that approximate a target stability point. For a tolerance ϵ, it holds that:

Proposition 1. *If* $\mathbf{m}^0_{\alpha\beta} \in E^{-1}_{h_{\alpha\beta}}$ *and* $\mathbf{m}^0_{\beta\alpha} \in E^1_{h_{\beta\alpha}}$, *then the target stability point is achieved in one step if and only if* $1 < \frac{\kappa_n}{\epsilon} \leq 3$.

Proof. ($\Rightarrow$) Since $h_{\beta\alpha} + \epsilon < mid(\mathbf{m}^0_{\beta\alpha}) \leq h_{\beta\alpha} + \frac{L}{n}$ and the optimal recommendation (Table 7, R8) gives the action $C^1_{h_{\beta\alpha}} = [-\frac{1}{2}(\frac{L}{n} + \epsilon), -\frac{1}{2}(\frac{L}{n} + \epsilon)]$ (Table 1), it

---

[5] For other levels of obedience, the analysis is based on simulations, as shown in Sect. 5.

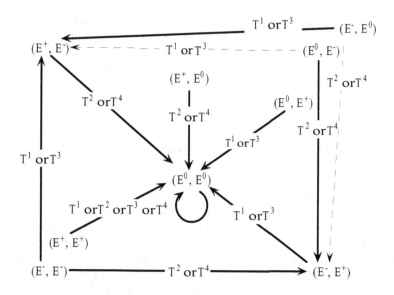

Fig. 2. Effects of stage and optimal value recommendations

follows that: $h_{\beta\alpha} + \epsilon - \frac{1}{2}(\frac{L}{n} + \epsilon) < mid(\mathbf{m}^0_{\beta\alpha}) - \frac{1}{2}(\frac{L}{n} + \epsilon) \leq h_{\beta\alpha} + \frac{L}{n} - \frac{1}{2}(\frac{L}{n} + \epsilon) \Rightarrow$ $h_{\beta\alpha} + \frac{1}{2}(-q\epsilon + \epsilon) < mid(\mathbf{m}^1_{\beta\alpha}) \leq h_{\beta\alpha} + \frac{1}{2}(q\epsilon - \epsilon)$, where $\frac{L}{n} = q\epsilon, q > 1$. If the system achieves the stability point in the step 1, then $h_{\beta\alpha} + \frac{1}{2}(q\epsilon - \epsilon) \leq h_{\beta\alpha} + \epsilon$, $1 < q \leq 3$, and thus, $1 < \frac{\kappa_n}{\epsilon} \leq 3$, since $\kappa_n = \frac{L}{n}$.

Proposition 2. *(i) If $\mathbf{m}^0_{\alpha\beta} \in E^i_{h_{\alpha\beta}}$, $1 < i \leq n$, then it is possible to get $\mathbf{m}^\tau_{\alpha\beta} \in E^0_{h_{\alpha\beta}}$ in at most $\tau = 2$ steps if and only if $1 < \frac{\kappa_n}{\epsilon} \leq 3$; (ii) If $\mathbf{m}^0_{\beta\alpha} \in E^i_{h_{\beta\alpha}}$, $-n \leq i < -1$, then it is possible to get $\mathbf{m}^\tau_{\beta\alpha} \in E^0_{h_{\beta\alpha}}$ in at most $\tau = 2$ steps if and only if $1 < \frac{\kappa_n}{\epsilon} \leq 3$; (iii) If $\mathbf{m}^0_{\alpha\beta} \in E^i_{h_{\alpha\beta}}$, with $1 < i \leq n$ and $h_{\alpha\beta} + \frac{2i+1}{2}\frac{L}{n} - \epsilon \leq mid(\mathbf{m}^0_{\alpha\beta}) \leq h_{\alpha\beta} + \frac{2i+1}{2}\frac{L}{n} + \epsilon$, then $\mathbf{m}^1_{\alpha\beta} \in E^0_{h_{\alpha\beta}}$.*

Proof. (i)($\Rightarrow$) Since $h_{\alpha\beta} + (i-1)\frac{L}{n} \leq mid(\mathbf{m}^0_{\alpha\beta}) < h_{\alpha\beta} + i\frac{L}{n}$ and the optimal recommendation (Table 7, $R2/R3$) is the action $C^i = [\frac{(1-2i)}{2}\frac{L}{n}, \frac{(1-2i)}{2}\frac{L}{n}]$ (Table 1), it follows that: $h_{\alpha\beta} + (i-1)\frac{L}{n} + \frac{(1-2i)}{2}\frac{L}{n} < mid(\mathbf{m}^0_{\beta\alpha}) + \frac{(1-2i)}{2}\frac{L}{n} \leq h_{\alpha\beta} + i\frac{L}{n} + \frac{(1-2i)}{2}\frac{L}{n} \Rightarrow h_{\alpha\beta} - \frac{1}{2}\frac{L}{n} < mid(\mathbf{m}^1_{\beta\alpha}) \leq h_{\alpha\beta} + \frac{1}{2}\frac{L}{n}$, and thus $\mathbf{m}^1_{\beta\alpha} \in E^1_\alpha$. From Prop. 1, with one more step we can get the result.

It follows that an individual transition from E^i ($1 < i \leq n$ or $-n \leq i < -1$), to the stability point can be done in at most two steps ($E^i \mapsto E^1(\text{ or } E^{-1}) \mapsto E^0$). However, combined transitions departing from a state (E^i, E^j) or (E^j, E^i), with $1 < i \leq n$ and $-n \leq j < -1$, may result in a state different from (E^1, E^{-1}), (E^{-1}, E^1) or (E^0, E^0). The worst case is when the system is in the state (E^i, E^j), with $-n \leq i, j < -1$, since two simultaneous positive compensation actions are not allowed. In this case, which occurs very often in exchanges between altruist agents, the optimal recommendation (Table 7) leads the agents to the stability point in at most four steps, by one of the transitions: (i) $(E^i, E^j)_{-n \leq i,j < -1} \overset{R13}{\mapsto} (E^1, E^j)_{-n \leq j < -1} \overset{R7}{\mapsto} (E^0, E^{-1}) \overset{R12}{\mapsto} (E^{-1}, E^1) \overset{R8}{\mapsto} (E^0, E^0)$ or (ii) $(E^i, E^j)_{-n \leq i,j < -1} \overset{R14}{\mapsto} (E^j, E^1)_{-n \leq j < -1} \overset{R10}{\mapsto} (E^{-1}, E^0) \overset{R11}{\mapsto} (E^1, E^{-1}) \overset{R9}{\mapsto} (E^0, E^0)$.

5   A Sample Simulation

We show a simulation of part of the scenario analyzed in [14], extending the application to consider personality-based agents. The situation is a political one, with politicians and voters interacting for the purpose of electing politicians to governmental positions. Politicians are expected to fulfill the promises they have made to voters before the election, by making decisions that favor the voter's interests. After reaching governmental positions, politicians may or may not fulfill their promises. In the positive case, they are entitled to charge the voters for their re-election in the next polling. On the other hand, voters are expected to choose politicians that best represent their interests, and give them votes. After the election, they are entitled to charge the politicians for coherent behavior with the promises they made. Frustration of any of those expectations entitles the frustrated agent to refrain from behaving in a positive way toward the others.

An equilibrated political society is one where both voters and politicians do not accumulate neither benefits nor losses, which is an idealization that may never occur in practice. On the other hand, a stable political society is one where both voters and politicians behave as respectively expected by the others during a considered period, or the regulation of the behaviors of politicians and voters is such that significant deviations from the expected behaviors of any of them get each of the agents to be either enforced to backtrack from the deviated behavior or allowed to look for other partners with different interests. In our simulations, such regulation actions are not allowed, so that agents are doomed to misfortune if the stability supervisor fails in being effective.

Exchange values can easily be associated with each action, of voting and governmental decision. Voters and politicians can thus successively build a balance of such values, as elections are successively performed. Considering this as an open society, at each election new voters and new politicians may appear in the process, behaving as non-transparent agents for the supervisor.

In a realistic simulation, both politicians and voters would have their own decision procedures about the actions they have to take at each election. Such procedures can be seen as stability supervisors that were internalized at each agent, and that restrict themselves to give recommendations specifically for the agent where each one is internalized. Having been internalized, the supervisors can easily be seen to operate under the condition of partial observation, since the internalization makes it not possible for the agents to fully grasp the exchange values accumulated by the others. We are leaving for future work the problem of tackling such situations, also because it could involve the analysis of interactions between groups of agents, where the results of the exchanges between a pair of agents may influence the exchanges performed by the others.

Here, the stability supervisor is a centralized agent that makes recommendations for a pair of transparent agents: a politician and an elector. The simulations were developed in the Python programming language, generating (i) tables with the configurations of exchange values and material results at each time $t \in T = 0, \ldots, 1000$, and (ii) graphics showing the trajectory of the mid points of the material results of the exchanges. The material and virtual values that the electors and politicians could use at each exchange were set to vary in $-100 \ldots + 100$. The target stability point was set at $\omega = 1000$ for both agents, meaning that both agents get positive material results from the interactions. A tolerance of $\epsilon = 25$ was adopted for the definition of the reference value.

At each election and successive governmental period, the elector β assigns a value $r_{\beta\alpha}$ to its vote for the politician α and concludes a value $v_{\beta\alpha}$ for his credit over his election. Correspondingly, the politician α assigns a value $r_{\alpha\beta}$ to the decisions he makes while in the government, after the election, and a credit $v_{\alpha\beta}$ for the benefits he thinks are received by the elector β due to those decisions. Satisfaction and debit values $(s_{\alpha\beta}, s_{\beta\alpha}, t_{\alpha\beta}, t_{\beta\alpha})$ are correspondingly assigned.

First, we considered successions of elections where the elector and the politician *always disregard the supervisor's recommendations*. In those simulations (Fig. 3(a), exchange values bound to $[-3000, 2400]$), the exchanges were totally guided by the agents' personality traits, characterized by the *egoism* of the politician and the *altruism* of the elector. The politician profited from the interaction much more than the elector, which kept the latter in unfavorable results (related to the stability point), resulting that the system was unable to be stabilized.

In successive experiments, we increased the level of obedience to the recommendations, generating the following simulations: (1) obedience during 2% of the elections (Fig.3(b), with exchange values bound to $[-850, 1800]$ and range of exchange values equals to 2650); (2) obedience during 25% of the elections (Fig. 3(c), exchange values bound to $[500, 1500]$, maximal deviation of 500 around the stability point); (3) obedience in 100% of the elections (Fig. 3(d), exchange values bound to $[900, 1100]$, maximal deviation of 100 around the stability point).

Figure 3(b) shows a succession of elections, with a level of obedience to the recommendations of 2%. Observe that just such level of obedience was enough to make the politician and the elector alternated their kinds of behaviors, thus avoiding that one of them profited from the interaction at the expense of the other. The system was able to pass through the stability point in various opportunities (e.g., at $t = 180$ and $t = 365$), but was unstable almost all of the time. Figure 3(c-d) shows the effects of the increasing level of obedience. The range of deviations of the results from the stability point was progressively reduced as the politician and the elector progressively adhered to the recommendations.

The simulations that we produced seem to agree with the theoretical predictions derived from the model (in Sect. 4.5). Thus, considering agents with *blind obedience* (Fig. 3(d)), the deviation around the stability point stayed stable between -100 and 100, the maximum variation allowed at each interaction.

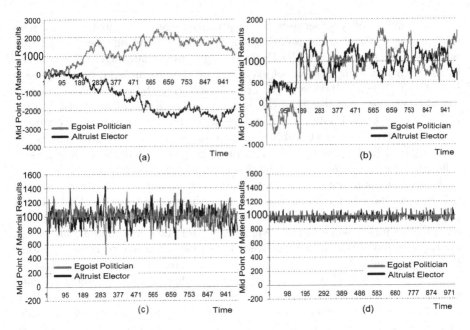

Fig. 3. (a) Agents always disregarding recommendations; agent obedience in (b) 2% of the elections, (c) 25% of the elections and (d) 100% of the elections (blind obedience)

6   Related Work

Values have been extensively used in the MAS area, through value-based and market-oriented decision, and value-based social theory (see, e.g., [15,16,17]), as well social norms (e.g., in [18,19]), the latter considering that knowledge sharing between agents is supported by social contracts and rules.

However, the approach based on social exchange values, which gives rise to a qualitative analysis of the interactions based on the individual evaluations of the exchanges, appeared only in 2003 [20], its formulation becoming stable only after [4]. Since them, the merits in using Piaget's notion of exchange values to the analysis of social organization, and applications to problems like that of partners selection, formation of coalitions and collaborative interactions have been discussed [14,21,22]. In particular, the application of this approach applied to the analysis of successful/uncessful cooperative interactions in the bioinformatics domain was presented in [22].

On the other hand, the study of personality-based agents can be traced back to at least [23], while its study in the context of multiagent systems goes back to [8,24], where advantages and possible applications of the approach were extensively discussed. In both works, personality traits were mapped into goals and practical reasoning rules (internal point of view). Modeling personality traits from an external (the supervisor's) point of view, through state transition matrices as we do here, seems to be new.

7 Conclusion

The paper leads toward the idea of modeling agents' personality traits in social exchange regulation mechanisms in open societies, also extending the previously proposed concept of equilibrium supervisors to consider the stability of social exchanges in points that may be different from the equilibrium and may vary in time. Then, the notion of equilibrium is a particular case of stability [4].

We studied two sample sets of personality traits: (i) blind, eventual obedience, and full disregard of recommendations (related to the levels of adherence to the regulation mechanism), and (ii) fanaticism, tolerance, egoism, altruism and prudence (in connection to preferences about balances of material results).

The regulation mechanism implements a Qualitative Interval Markov Decision Processes for the coordination of the exchanges between transparent agents (agents that allow full external access to their internal states). A theoretical analysis of the Qualitative Interval Markov Decision Process was realized, and simulations of performances of a stability supervisor were presented, considering different levels of obedience, which conformed to the theoretical analysis.

We point out that the regulation of the interactions between non-transparent agents (agents that restrict such external access) was done in [13], with the help of personality-based Hidden Markov Models, so that the supervisor is able to recognize and maintain an adequate model of the personality traits of such agents, based on observations of their behaviors. In that work, the set of personality traits was enlarged with the agents' tendencies in the evaluation of their virtual results, which is then observed by the supervisor.

In our future work, we expect to advance the internalization of the stability supervisor into the agents themselves, going toward the idea of self-regulation of exchange processes, not only distributing the decision process (like, e.g., in Multiagent MDP [11,25]), but also considering incomplete information about the balances of material results of the exchanges between non-transparent agents, in the form of a *personality-based qualitative interval* Partially Observable MDP (POMDP) [26,27], a kind of decentralized or distributed POMDP [28,29,30].

Acknowledgements. This work has been partially supported by FAPERGS and CNPq. We would like to thank the referees and the participants of the COIN@ECAI 2006 workshop for their valuable comments.

References

1. Castelfranchi, C.: Engineering social order. In: Omicini, A., Tolksdorf, R., Zambonelli, F. (eds.) Engineer. Societ. in Agents World, pp. 1–18. Springer, Berlin (2000)
2. Homans, G.C.: The Human Group. Harcourt, Brace & World, New York (1950)
3. Dignum, V., Dignum, F.: Coordinating tasks in agent organizations or: Can we ask you to read this paper? LNCS, vol. 4386, pp. 30–45. Springer, Heidelberg (2007)

4. Pereira Dimuro, G., da Rocha Costa, A.C., Palazzo, L.A.M.: Systems of exchange values as tools for multi-agent organizations (Special Issue on Agents' Organizations). Journal of the Brazilian Computer Society 11(1), 31–50 (2005)
5. Piaget, J.: Sociological Studies. Routlege, London (1995)
6. Moore, R.E.: Methods and Applic. of Interval Analysis. SIAM, Philadelphia (1979)
7. Pereira Dimuro, G., da Rocha Costa, A.C.: Exchange values and self-regulation of exchanges in multi-agent systems: the provisory, centralized model. In: Brueckner, S.A., Serugendo, G.D.M., Hales, D., Zambonelli, F. (eds.) ESOA 2005. LNCS (LNAI), vol. 3910, pp. 75–89. Springer, Heidelberg (2006)
8. Castelfranchi, C., Rosis, F., Falcone, R., Pizzutilo, S.: Personality traits and social attitudes in multiagent cooperation. Applied Artif. Intelligence 12, 649–675 (1998)
9. Pereira Dimuro, G., da Rocha Costa, A.C.: Interval-based Markov Decision Processes for regulating interactions between two agents in multiagent systems. In: Dongarra, J.J., Madsen, K., Waśniewski, J. (eds.) PARA 2004. LNCS, vol. 3732, pp. 102–111. Springer, Heidelberg (2006)
10. Rabiner, L.R.: A tutorial on Hidden Markov Models and selected applications in speech recognition. Proc. of the IEEE 77(2), 257–286 (1989)
11. Boutilier, C.: Sequential optimality and coordination in multiagent systems. In: Proc. XVI Intl. Joint Conf. Artificial Intellig. IJCAI'99, Stockholm, pp. 478–485 (1999)
12. Puterman, M.L.: Markov Decision Processes. Wiley, Chichester, UK (1994)
13. Pereira Dimuro, G., da Rocha Costa, A.C., Vargas Gonçalves, L., Hübner, A.: Regulating social exchanges between personality-based non-transparent agents. In: Gelbukh, A., Reyes-Garcia, C.A. (eds.) MICAI 2006. LNCS (LNAI), vol. 4293, Springer, Heidelberg (2006)
14. Rodrigues, M.R., da Rocha Costa, A.C.: Using qualitative exchange values to improve the modelling of social interactions. In: Multi-Agent-Based Simulation III. LNCS, vol. 2927, pp. 57–72. Springer, Heidelberg (2003)
15. Antunes, L., Coelho, H.: Decisions based upon multiple values: the BVG agent architecture. In: Barahona, P., Alferes, J.J. (eds.) EPIA 1999. LNCS (LNAI), vol. 1695, pp. 297–311. Springer, Heidelberg (1999)
16. Miceli, M., Castelfranchi, C.: The role of evaluation in cognition and social interaction. In: Dautenhahn, K. (ed.) Human cognition and agent technology, pp. 225–262. John Benjamins, Amsterdam (2000)
17. Walsh, W.E., Wellman, M.P.: A market protocol for distributed task allocation. In: Proc. III Intl. Conf. on Multiagent Systems, Paris pp. 325–332 (1998)
18. Castelfranchi, C., Dignum, F., Jonker, C., Treur, J.: Deliberate normative agents: Principles and architecture. In: Jennings, N.R. (ed.) ATAL 1999. LNCS, vol. 1757, pp. 364–378. Springer, Heidelberg (2000)
19. López y López, F., Luck, M., d'Inverno, M.: Constraining autonomy through norms. In: Alonso, E., Kudenko, D., Kazakov, D. (eds.) Adaptive Agents and Multi-Agent Systems. LNCS (LNAI), vol. 2636, pp. 674–681. Springer, Heidelberg (2003)
20. Rodrigues, M.R., da Rocha Costa, A.C., Bordini, R.: A system of exchange values to support social interactions in artificial societes. In: Proc. II Intl Conf. on Autonomous Agents and Multiag. Systems, AAMAS'03, Melbourne, pp. 81–88. ACM Press, New York (2003)
21. Rodrigues, M.R., Luck, M.: Analysing partner selection through exchange values. In: Sichman, J.S., Antunes, L. (eds.) MABS 2005. LNCS (LNAI), vol. 3891, pp. 24–40. Springer, Heidelberg (2006)
22. Rodrigues, M.R., Luck, M.: Cooperative interactions: an exchange values model. LNCS, vol. 4386, pp. 344–360. Springer, Heidelberg (2007)

23. Carbonell, J.G.: Towards a process model of human personality traits. Artificial Intelligence 15(1-2), 49–74 (1980)
24. Castelfranchi, C., Rosis, F., Falcone, R., Pizzutilo, S.: A testbed for investigating personality-based multiagent cooperation. In: Proc. of the Symp. on Logical Approaches to Agent Modeling and Design, Aix-en-Provence (1997)
25. Boutilier, C.: Multiagent systems: challenges and oportunities for decision theoretic planning. Artificial Intelligence Magazine 20(4), 35–43 (1999)
26. Kaelbling, L.P., Littman, M.L., Cassandra, A.R.: Planning and acting in partially observable stochastic domains. Artificial Intelligence 101(1), 99–134 (1998)
27. Lovejoy, W.S.: A survey of algorithmic methods for Partially Observable Markov Decision Processes. Annals of Operations Research 28(1), 47–65 (1991)
28. Bernstein, D., Zilberstein, S., Immerman, N.: The complexity of decentralized control of Markov Decision Processes. In: Proc. of the 16th Conference on Uncertainty in Artificial Intelligence, Stanford, pp. 32–37 (2000)
29. Nair, R., Tambe, M., Yokoo, M., Pynadath, D., Marsella, S.: Taming decentralized POMDPs: Towards efficient policy computation for multiagent settings. In: Proc. 18th Intl. Joint Conf. on Artificial Intelligence, IJCAI'03, Acapulco, pp. 705–711 (2003)
30. Scerri, P., Pynadath, D., Tambe, M.: Towards adjustable autonomy for the real-world. Journal on Artificial Intelligence Research 17, 171–228 (2002)

Cooperative Interactions: An Exchange Values Model

Maíra R. Rodrigues* and Michael Luck

School of Electronics and Computer Science, University of Southampton, Southampton, UK
{mrm03r,mml}@ecs.soton.ac.uk

Abstract. In non-economic cooperative applications with resource constraints, explicitly motivating cooperation is important so that autonomous service providers have incentives to cooperate. When participants of such applications have different skills and expectations over services, it may be that an agent receives less than expected from a cooperation. A decision-making strategy over interactions in this context must consider not only the motivation to cooperate, but also which interactions to perform to cope with resource limitations. In this paper, we present a computational approach for modelling non-economic cooperative interactions based on the theory of *exchange values*. Here, exchange values are used to motivate cooperative interactions, and to allow agents to identify successful and unsuccessful cooperations with others, in order to limit service provision and to improve the number of successful interactions. We also present a scenario in which agents participate in a cooperative application in the bioinformatics domain, and show how agents can improve their interactions using the proposed approach.

1 Introduction

According to [1], it can be useful in certain contexts to view a society as a market, in which individuals exchange goods, services and ideas to achieve their goals. While markets typically involve monetary exchanges, many do not necessarily involve economic capital. For example, in computer-supported scientific communities like bioinformatics, different types of information and tools can be exchanged in a cooperative way in order to improve individual or global results [2].

Although examples of systems that support cooperative bioinformatics applications already exist [3,4,5], there are still issues to be addressed to allow effective cooperation between participants [6]. In particular, resources need to be managed sensibly because they are provided free of charge. This is because services in bioinformatics generally require the processing of large amounts of data, so that responding to a request involves significant computational resources. In addition, the kind of automated experiments that arise in this domain tend to generate more service requests than if they were performed manually. Thus, both the increasing number of requests that automated experiments can generate, and the large amount of computation resources that these requests need, place a heavy overload on service providers, which can limit the number of requests that can

---

* The first author is supported by Coordenação de Aperfeiçoamento de Pessoal de Nível Superior (CAPES) of the Brazilian Ministry of Education.

P. Noriega et al. (Eds.): COIN 2006 Workshops, LNAI 4386, pp. 356–371, 2007.

be processed. These issues provide the context in which we consider non-economic cooperative interactions.

Explicitly motivating cooperation is also important for non-economic exchanges. Considering a system with self-interested entities, a service provider has an incentive to cooperate if it receives a service in return from the requester, either immediately or in the near future. Cooperation with immediate reciprocation is easier to model and to check whether the cooperative interaction is genuine (mutual), since it involves concrete actions that can be clearly observed by both entities. However, immediate reciprocation is not always possible since the provider may not need any service by the time the interaction takes place, or the requester may only be available to provide a service in return in the near future.

Cooperative situations in which reciprocation is not immediate raise interesting issues for modeling cooperative agents. First, there is no guarantee that the requester agent will reciprocate in the future. Second, the provider must receive some *value* in return from the requester, so the provider is motivated to cooperate even in the lack of a concrete, immediate return. Third, if we consider that in a multi-agent system agents might have different perspectives of the same service due, for example, to individual preferences and the relevance of each service to goals, a provider can evaluate a service it gets in return in the future as being of less quality than the service it provided in the past; that is, it may be that an agent receives less than expected from a cooperation.

In this context, the focus of this paper is on cooperative applications in which interactions are based on *deferred reciprocity*, and deal with the issues of modeling cooperative agents that act in such applications. We propose a model based on *exchange values* [7] to motivate such cooperative interactions, and to allow agents to identify successful and unsuccessful cooperations with others, in order to limit service provision. We also analyse the different reasons why interactions succeed as a result of personal influences, such as personal goals and preferences, on the evaluation of services, and how agents can react to improve the quality of their cooperative interactions.

Here, exchange values represent the agents' individual evaluation of provided and received services, and are associated with their interactions, indicating the effort, cost, or satisfaction to each agent. We believe that this approach is suitable for addressing the issue of motivating interactions in cooperative, non-economic applications, especially in cases of deferred reciprocation, in the sense that exchange values provide a system of credits and debts that motivates interactions by giving expectations of future gains (for example, a credit that is gained by performing a service can be charged in the future). Moreover, exchange values allow agents to analyse the outcome of interactions in terms of whether services they receive compensate for services they provide, and use this information to decide about future interactions, which is important when there are different types of services available and there is a need to limit service provision.

The key contribution of this paper is a computational approach for motivating and modelling non-economic cooperative interactions, based on the theory of exchange values.

The paper begins with an introduction to the theory of exchange values, including its advantages for modelling cooperative autonomous agents, followed by an analysis of the different cooperative interactions that can occur between autonomous agents in a non-economic cooperative scenario. We end by presenting an experimental simulation of this scenario and discussing obtained results.

2   Exchange Values

The application of exchange values for modelling interactions between agents was first proposed in [8], in which the mechanism for reasoning over interactions is based on Piaget's theory [7].

In previous work [9], exchange values have been used for addressing the problem of partner selection in dynamic and resource-constrained environments. Here, agents reduce their effort in finding available interaction partners by identifying those that are more likely to accept requests. However, the analysis of interactions in terms of whether the services that agents receive give some compensation for those that they provide, which is relevant to the kind of applications we focus on this paper, is not addressed.

In response, this paper proposes the use of exchange values in agent interactions not only to motivate service provision, but also to allow agents to analyse the outcome of their interactions in terms of gains and losses. We argue that this approach has the following advantages for cooperative and non-economic applications:

– autonomous agents can reason about continuing or stopping cooperative relations, instead of assuming indefinite cooperation, which is only possible with benevolent agents; and
– agents are motivated to provide good quality services to ensure that they are valorised by requesters.

Piaget's theory of exchange values, and the dynamics of exchange values — the way they vary according to gains and losses of values during interactions — are introduced in the next sections.

2.1   Piaget's Theory of Exchange Values

Social exchange is the particular interaction in which an individual performs an action on behalf of another and vice-versa. The *theory of exchange values* was proposed by Piaget [7] as an analysis of human social exchanges and the reasons for their persistence or discontinuity. More specifically, Piaget argues that in all social interactions in which one individual acts on behalf of another there is an *exchange of values* between them. These values result from each individual's evaluation of the provided or received action over a common scale of values.

According to Piaget, every action and reaction of two interacting individuals towards each other has an influence on their values: if the action is useful and beneficial it increases their values; if the action is harmful and disadvantageous it decreases their values; and if the action is neutral their values remain the same. Thus, when two individuals interact and one provides a service that is valuable to the other, three situations can happen as described below.

1. The individual that received the service can *pay back* the provider by giving an object or providing another service in return (*immediate exchange*). This is the

case, for example, if a researcher who is submitting a paper to a conference receives comments on his paper from a colleague, and returns comments on his colleague's paper which is being submitted to the same conference.

2. The receiver just *valorises* the provider by expressing gratitude or approval, instead of giving something immediately in return (*deferred exchange*). Using the same example as above, the researcher who receives the comments on his paper expresses gratitude and *valorises* his colleague's action.

3. The receiver neither returns a service to nor valorises the provider (*no exchange*).

All reactions of the receiver have also an effect on the provider's values. In the immediate exchange, the receiver returns a material action to the provider (comments on a paper), which constitutes an *actual*, concrete value for the latter (the comments are valuable to improve the quality of the paper). In the deferred exchange, the receiver returns an abstract action to the provider (a word or a gesture of approval, gratitude, etc), which constitutes a *virtual* value for the latter, in the sense that his valorisation gives him reputation, respect and authority, which are values he can use to get some benefit in future interactions (next time he is writing a paper, he can then ask the receiver for comments). The third reaction, however, was disadvantageous for the provider since the receiver did not reciprocate the action in any way, and the latter is ultimately devalorised by the provider as ungrateful or unjust.

The values that are exchanged between individuals are clear when concrete objects are involved in the exchange, like the immediate exchange described above. However, when the exchange involves virtual values, like in the *deferred exchange*, a more detailed analysis is needed. When two individuals α (the provider) and β (the receiver) interact, the performed action is for α an *actual renouncement*, since it requires the expenditure of time and effort, while for β it is an *actual satisfaction* or gain. Now, if β immediately performs an action in return to α, β has an actual renouncement and α has an actual satisfaction. At the end of this interaction, both individuals had an actual satisfaction (they received a concrete action). If there is a valorisation of α by β instead, as a reaction for the received action, this valorisation is for α a reward, a *virtual credit* that it can draw upon in the future, and for the receiver the valorisation constitutes a promise, a *virtual debt*, in the sense that the receiver feels obliged to return the favour to the provider in the future. At the end of this interaction, both individuals acquire virtual values, instead of only actual values as in the immediate cooperation. When the exchange is not immediate, the exchange values in an interaction between two individuals α and β are, therefore, the following as shown in Figure 1:

- the *renouncement* of the provider α on performing a service to β (r_α),
- the *satisfaction* β with the received service (s_β),
- the acknowledged *debt* of β as a consequence of his satisfaction (t_β), and
- the *valorisation* of α by β (v_α).

In the future, α can make use of this credit v_α and ask β to perform a service on its behalf; that is, α can realise its virtual values in actual values, as illustrated in Figure 2. Nothing forces β to accept the request, but it returns the favour to α not only because it feels gratitude and recognises its debt t_β, but also because it is a way to persevere with interactions with α when these are successful (otherwise, α will devalorise β as

Fig. 1. Exchange of values between interacting individuals α and β: acquisition of virtual values

Fig. 2. Exchange of values between interacting individuals α and β: realisation of virtual values

ungrateful and will not interact with it again). On the other hand, if β's expectations were not fulfilled by α, β may not reciprocate the action since it is not interested in continuing the relationship with α.

If β agrees to perform an action for α in return, this action is an actual renouncement for β (r_β) since it requires investment of time and effort, and a satisfaction for α (s_α). After the realisation of virtual values, the exchange is *complete*: α provided a service to β and, later, β provided a service to α.

2.2 Dynamics of Exchange Values

The dynamics of exchange values, or the way they are accumulated and spent by individuals, is based on the premise that in every interaction in which an action is provided or received, something is lost and something is gained: the provider α *renounces* its time and resources for providing an action (r_α) but gains a credit as a result of his *valorisation* (v_α), and the receiver β gains *satisfaction* with the benefits of the received action (s_β) but loses in acquiring a *debt* with the provider in return (t_β). What follows is that, if the gains and losses of participants according to their individual evaluations are equivalent (if $r_\alpha = s_\beta$, $s_\beta = t_\beta$, $t_\beta = v_\alpha$ and, consequently, $v_\alpha = r_\alpha$), the interaction between them is said to be in *equilibrium* regarding the acquisition of virtual values (provided that the participants' evaluations are estimated over the same scale of values). We represent the equilibrium situation for interactions in which virtual values are acquired in the form of the equation below:

$$(r_\alpha = s_\beta) \wedge (s_\beta = t_\beta) \wedge (t_\beta = v_\alpha) \Rightarrow (v_\alpha = r_\alpha) \tag{1}$$

After the values of credit and debt are acquired and α requests an action from β in return, the exchange values change as follows: α loses its credit (v_α) but gains satisfaction with the received action (s_α), while β gains by paying its debt (t_β) but loses effort for performing the action (r_β). Again, if losses and gains are equivalent, the interaction between α and β is said to be in equilibrium regarding the realisation of values. The equilibrium situation for interactions in which virtual values are realised is represented in the form of the equation below:

$$(v_\alpha = t_\beta) \wedge (t_\beta = r_\beta) \wedge (r_\beta = s_\alpha) \Rightarrow (s_\alpha = v_\alpha) \tag{2}$$

In summary, the dynamics of exchange values is based on what is gain and what is lost in every interaction. However, since individual evaluations are subjective and individual interests can influence the valorisation of actions, other situations are possible in addition to the *general equilibrium* of exchange values. These situations are described in the next section.

3   Analysing Cooperative Interactions

3.1   Scenario

In the bioinformatics domain, different types of information are available, such as genome sequences and annotations, protein sequences, structure and interaction maps, as well as metabolic pathways and phylogenetic trees [10]. Each of these information sources can be associated with a particular organism, tissue, cell, disease, etc, resulting in a large variety of information that can be exchanged in a cooperative manner. Thus, since all types of information in bioinformatics is related in some way, the cooperation between users to exchange this information may facilitate some of the tasks they perform, such as validation of new discoveries against existing data, or even help them to gain insights on what path to follow towards a new discovery.

Bioinformatics data and services vary in terms of quality or performance, for example, genome annotations made by one group can be more accurate and described in more detail, while annotations from another group can be poor in detail and ambiguous. The same can happen for services: some may have a better response time and more precise algorithms, while others may take longer to perform or give poor quality results.

Despite sharing similar services or information, users can have very different goals and preferences towards service quality. Developing an automated cooperative system with all this variety is a challenge, mainly because it has consequences for the way in which agents evaluate the services and information they receive from others, and the way providers evaluate the service they provide.

3.2   Cooperative Situations

In our approach, exchange values represent the gains and losses of agents in each interaction. Thus, we define the success of an interaction in terms of the *balance* of the agent's values: a *successful interaction* for a generic agent is when its losses and gains are equivalent, or when its gain is greater than its loss, and an *unsuccessful interaction* is when the agent's gain is less than its loss.

It is important to note that, based on the outcome of interactions, an agent can decide whether it should continue with the cooperation (in cases of successful interactions), drop the cooperation, or review the quality of its services to adjust its evaluation to that of the partner in an attempt to improve its valorisation (in cases of unsuccessful interactions).

When two agents α and β interact, and α provides a service to β, their individual evaluations of the service involved can coincide (as in Equations 1 and 2) or can be different, since individual evaluations are subjective and individual interests such as goals and preferences can influence the evaluation of services. In the following we analyse how different individual perspectives over service evaluations can lead to successful or unsuccessful interactions, and discuss possible causes of each situation and how they affect the cooperation between agents.

Successful Interactions. A successful interaction is the one in which the balance of the exchange values of an agent is in equilibrium (its gains and losses coincide) or is positive (its gains are greater than losses). Examples of successful interactions are presented below.

1. *The provider's effort and the receiver's satisfaction coincide.* This is represented by the relation $r_\alpha = s_\beta \Rightarrow r_\alpha = v_\alpha$, which means their values are in equilibrium and the provider is valorised by the receiver in correspondence to its effort. Possible causes for the equilibrium of exchange values are that:

   (a) the service result was as expected for both provider α and requester β; or
   (b) α's and β's expectations are at the same level.

2. *The provider's effort is less than the receiver's satisfaction.* This is represented by the relation $r_\alpha < s_\beta \Rightarrow r_\alpha < v_\alpha$, which indicates that the receiver valorises the provider more than the latter valorises its efforts. This means that the interaction was successful for the provider, since it did not have to make much effort to satisfy the other agent. Possible causes for the high-valorisation of α's service are that:

   (a) α is over-skilled and can perform the service with a small effort;
   (b) β has a low expectation for the service result and thus over-values even a fairly poor service; or
   (c) even though the service is trivial, it helped β to achieve an important goal and thus had a higher value for the latter.

3. *The receiver valorises the provider more than its real satisfaction.* This is represented by the relation $s_\beta < t_\beta \Rightarrow r_\alpha < v_\alpha$, which means the interaction is successful and the provider is valorised more than it valorises its efforts. The cause for the high-valorisation of the provider can be the following:

   (a) the requester β wants to persuade provider α to continue the cooperation by valorising the service higher than its real satisfaction either because β is in a lower social position than α, α is the only provider for the service that β needs, or α is a busy provider and may have to limit its provision in the future.

4. *The debt is recognised by β and paid by spending similar effort.* This is represented by the relation $t_\beta = r_\beta \Rightarrow v_\alpha = s_\beta$, which means α's satisfaction with the service provided by β was equivalent to the credit it charged. This interaction is in equilibrium regarding the values gained and lost and the cooperation between α and β is therefore successful (since there was reciprocal cooperation).

   The causes for the equilibrium can be that β is compelled to return the favour to α not only because it recognises its debt t_β, but also because reciprocating is a way to persevere with cooperation with α when this cooperation is successful.

Otherwise, α will devalorise β as a bad cooperative partner and will not interact with it again.

In all situations described above — when there is either high-evaluation of β by α, equilibrium of α and β's evaluations, or reciprocation by spending similar effort — agents are successful in their interaction and, as a consequence, the cooperation between them tends to continue.

Unsuccessful Interactions. An unsuccessful interaction is the one in which the balance of the exchange values of an agent is negative (its losses are greater than gains). Examples of unsuccessful interactions are described as follows.

1. *The provider's effort is greater than the receiver's satisfaction.* This is represented by the relation $r_\alpha > s_\beta \Rightarrow r_\alpha > v_\alpha$, which indicates that if the satisfaction of β is less than the effort of α, the valorisation of α is less than its effort. This means that the interaction was not beneficial for α, since its *valorisation* did not compensate for its efforts. The disequilibrium of evaluations happened because β was not satisfied with the service it received, for which possible causes are:

   (a) that α's service had poor quality and did not meet β's expectations; or
   (b) that β had very high expectations and thus under-valued even a good service.

   In the bioinformatics example, this situation can occur when β requests from α the annotation data related to a specific tissue, but the data is only partially annotated and with poor descriptions. In this case, β's evaluation of the received service is less than expected. The consequence of this situation can be that:

   - α can either continue cooperating with β and improve the quality of its service to get a better evaluation;
   - α can cease its cooperation with β if the latter is not being fair in its valorisation;
   - β can continue cooperating with α and lower its expectations on service evaluation; or
   - β can cease the cooperation with α if the latter is providing a poor service and search for another partner to cooperate with.

2. *The receiver valorises the provider less than its real satisfaction.* This is represented by the relation $s_\beta > t_\beta \Rightarrow r_\alpha > v_\alpha$, which means that even though β was satisfied with the received service, its does not valorise α accordingly and, as a consequence, the latter's efforts are greater than its valorisation (this interaction is unsuccessful for α). The possible causes for the under-valuation of the provider in this case are that:

   (a) β has authority over α and thus does not feel obliged to reciprocate the service;
   (b) β wants to exploit α and to have as few debts as possible; or
   (c) β is busy and does not want to compromise its future time with α.

   In the bioinformatics scenario, this situation can arise, for example, when a new agent provides a service to an existing agent in the collaborative community, and even if the new agent provides a good service, the existing agent valorises it less. The effects of the under-valuation in α and β's cooperative relation is that:

- α stops the cooperation with β if it thinks the interaction is not beneficial for it;
- α maintains the cooperation despite the under-valorisation if it needs β's service for achieving a goal in the future (either because there is no other agent to provide the service, or because β provides the service with best quality);
- β tends to keep the cooperation since it is beneficial for it (the debt it acquires as a result of α's valorisation is less than its gain from the received service).

When agent α is successful in its action, and achieves $v_\alpha = r_\alpha$ or even $v_\alpha > r_\alpha$, α's valorisation constitutes a credit for it. In the future, α can make use of this credit v_α and ask β to perform a service on its behalf. Nothing forces β to reciprocate and accept the request, since there is no formal or legal commitment between them, and thus the following situations are possible.

3 *The debt is recognised by β but paid by spending less effort than the worth of the credit.* This is represented by the relation $t_\beta > r_\beta \Rightarrow v_\alpha > s_\alpha$, which means that α's satisfaction with the service provided by β was less than the credit it charged (the service α provided to β in the past was highly valued than the service it received from β in return). Thus, the interaction was not beneficial for α since it lost more than it gained. A possible cause for the disequilibrium is that β wants to exploit α by asking more than it is willing to return, or because β does not have enough skills to perform a good service. As a consequence, α tends to stop the cooperation with β if it has other possible partners to cooperate with.

4 *The debt is not recognised by β.* In this case, the interaction does not take place. Possible causes are that β just wants to take advantage of interactions and does not share or provide services to others, or that β's expectations were not fulfilled by α in the previous interactions, and thus β may not reciprocate the action since it is not interested in continuing interacting with α. It is clear in this case that there is no more cooperation between both agents.

In summary, when agents have different perspectives over service evaluations (such as different levels of expectation towards service results), or are influenced by personal interests (like providing a service with less effort in return for another received previously to reduce losses), interactions may not always be successful in terms of gains and losses of exchange values. Therefore, in a resource constrained environment in which agents take autonomous decisions about interactions, it is important that they avoid repeating unsuccessful interactions and try to maintain successful ones instead. To show this approach to decision-making over interactions, we set an experimental testbed with a similar scenario, which is described in the next sections.

4 Experiment

4.1 Scenario

Cooperative applications in bioinformatics are characterised by different types of available services, which can vary in terms of performance and quality (since providers have different skills to perform services). Because service providers are resource-bounded, they must limit the number of services they provide. In addition, service users have different perspectives over service quality.

In this context, agents cooperate by providing services to and requesting services from each other. Since services are free, providers receive from requesters a *valorisation*, based on the requesters evaluation of the received service, as an incentive for cooperation that the former uses as credit for asking something in return in the future. However, since agents have different perspectives of the same service — providers have different skills and users have different preferences — it may be that an agent receives less than expected from a cooperation (so that its interactions are unsuccessful, as described in Section 3.2).

We want to determine whether the analysis of cooperative situations can reduce the number of unsuccessful interactions, but without decreasing the number of interactions between participants, which would be expected if agents increase the restrictions on desirable interactions.

In seeking to determine that, we observe the *difference between the number of unsuccessful and successful interactions* for agents using two different decision-making strategies: *simple reciprocation*, and *analysis of cooperative situations*. Our hypothesis is that by analysing cooperative situations the agents can improve the number of successful interactions in the society, without significatively reducing the *number of achieved interactions*.

4.2   Strategies

Both strategies for selecting among alternative interaction partners are based on the analysis of exchange values. The difference is that, in the simple reciprocation, agents take into account only the credits and debts they have with other agents, as described in previous work [9], while in the analysis of cooperative situations, agents also take into account the balance of each interaction in which they participate to decide whether to cooperate and to which partner to send a request.

Consider the set of possible providers as $P = \{p_1, .., p_n\}$ for a service sr_i, and the set of received requests as $Q = \{q_1, .., q_m\}$. For *simple reciprocation*, the decision-making strategy is as follows.

1. For an agent α requesting a service:

   (a) remove from P agents that did not pay their debts in the past;
   (b) let P_o be an ordered sequence of the elements in P according to the credits α has with each agent in P, with higher credits first (since providers with debt are more likely to cooperate);
   (c) send a request to the first agent in P_o;
   (d) while the request is refused, send the request to the next agent in P_o.

2. For an agent β providing a service:

   (a) remove from Q requests from agents that did not pay their debts previously, since they are likely not to reciprocate in the future;

(b) let Q_o be an ordered sequence of the elements in Q according to the debts β has with each agent in Q, with higher debts first (so that β can reciprocate for services received previously);

(c) accept requests in order, until reaching maximum capacity, and refuse the remaining requests.

In the *analysis of cooperative situations* strategy, decision-making complements items 1(b) and 2(b) by avoiding repetition of unsuccessful interactions, as described in Section 3.2. This strategy is presented below:

1. For agent α:
   (b) reorder sequence P_o by moving the candidate providers with which α had unsuccessful interactions previously to the end of the sequence, such as cases in which α's satisfaction is smaller than its debt, $s_\alpha < t_\alpha$ (indicating that α received a service under its expectations).

2. For agent β:
   (b) deny requests from agents from which β received an unfair evaluation in previous interactions causing its renouncement to be greater than its credit, $r_\beta > v_\beta$; and reorder the requesters in Q_o with equivalent debt with those with which β had higher satisfaction from previously received services first.

Thus, by analysing the balance of their exchange values in previous interactions, requesters try to avoid sending requests to agents that provided a poor service in the past (resulting in $s_\alpha < t_\alpha$), and providers try to avoid continue cooperating with agents that did not reciprocate in the past and also those that are under-evaluating the service they are providing (resulting in $r_\beta > v_\beta$).

4.3 Simulation Configuration

To simulate cooperative interactions between agents with different perspectives over service evaluations, we require: first, that agents have different skills to provide services, and second, that agents have different expectations towards received services. Thus, every provider has an associated skill from the set $k = \{0.5, 1, 2\}$, where 0.5 means the provider has *low* skills; 1, *medium* skills; and 2, *high* skills. Also, every service an agent needs is associated with an expected quality of result $exp = \{0.5, 1, 2\}$, where 0.5 means the requester has *low* expectations; 1, *medium* expectations; and 2, *high* expectations.

Each service sr_i is associated with an execution effort eff_{sr_i} (for the purpose of comparison, we assume that all agents invest the same effort to perform the same service), and the relation between the effort to perform the service and the skill of the provider determines the service result, represented by res_{sr_i}. The service result is informed to the requester after execution and calculated as follows:

$$res_{sr_i} = eff_{sr_i} \times k_{sr_i}$$

A simulation in our experiment consists of a number of iterations. In each iteration, all agents perform an action: they can request a service or provide a service. They use their decision-making strategy to decide whether to provide a service and to whom to send a request. An *interaction* occurs when the request is accepted and a service is received. After every interaction, the agents determine their individual evaluation of the service. The requester (α) evaluates service sr_i as follows:

$$Eval_\alpha(sr_i) = \frac{res_{sr_i}}{exp_{sr_i}}$$

The provider (β) evaluates the performed service sr_i as follows:

$$Eval_\beta(sr_i) = \frac{eff_{sr_i}}{k_{sr_i}}$$

Based on these evaluations, α and β determine their exchange values, as described in the next section.

In real applications, evaluations might be determined in a straightforward way through an objective evaluation process. More specifically, the provider's evaluation ($Eval_\beta$) could be based on a *cost* function (which would include an effort measure related, for example, to processing time or memory usage), and the receiver's evaluation ($Eval_\alpha$) based on a *utility* function (which would consider the actual service result and an expected result).

In every simulation run, we fix the number of total requests the agents can send, and record the *total number of interactions* that occurred, and the *number of unsuccessful interactions*.

4.4   Determining Exchange Values

After agent α receives a service sr_i from another agent β, α determines its satisfaction (s) and debt (t) values. The satisfaction is determined by α based on its evaluation of the received service. We assume that the debt acknowledged by α is always 1 to represent the situations in which the result of the service provided by β achieved α's expectations ($\frac{res_{sr_i}}{exp_{sr_i}} = 1$). Therefore, α's satisfaction and debt values are:

- $V_{\alpha,\beta}(s) = Eval_\alpha(sr_i)$
- $V_{\alpha,\beta}(t) = 1$

Regarding the balance of α's exchange values, if α's evaluation of the service is less than expected, $V_{\alpha,\beta}(s) < V_{\alpha,\beta}(t)$, the interaction is considered unsuccessful for α. After determining its exchange values, α communicates its satisfaction to β to represent its valorisation of the latter.

After agent β provides a service to α, it determines its renouncement (r) and credit (v) values. The renouncement of β to perform sr_i is determined according to its evaluation of the service, and the valorisation of β by α is stored by β as a credit. Thus, β's renouncement and credit values are:

- $V_{\beta,\alpha}(r) = Eval_\beta(sr_i)$
- $V_{\beta,\alpha}(v) = V_{\alpha,\beta}(s)$

If β's renouncement is greater than the credit it gained, $V_{\beta,\alpha}(r) > V_{\beta,\alpha}(v)$, the interaction is considered unsuccessful for β.

Table 1. Population variation for Experiment 1

characteristic	percent in population
providers skills	low(20%), medium(60%), high(20%)
requester expectations	low(25%), medium(60%), high(15%)

Table 2. Results

Strategy	(U) Interactions (%)	Total interactions
SR	26.4	769
ACS	6.9	756

4.5   Results

All simulations used a society with 30 agents, which provide and request services from a set of 4 available services. We fixed the provider capacity at a maximum of 2 simultaneous services, and the total number of sent requests at 800. Services that are needed and provided are distributed equality over the agent population, so that no provider is busier than any other. The variation of the population of agents in terms of skills and expectations follows the proportions in Table 1.

We performed two different experiments: in the first one, we vary the agents' characteristics (skills and expectations) but keep the proportions in Table 1; and in the second one, we keep the proportions for requester expectations and vary the proportion of low-skilled providers.

In the first experiment, we performed 50 simulations for both decision-making strategies, varying the agents' characteristics but keeping the proportions in Table 1, to provide variation to the agent population from one simulation to another, guaranteeing that both decision-making strategies were simulated over the same agent population sample. In each simulation, we recorded the *total number of interactions* that occurred between agents, and the *number of unsuccessful interactions* (U) for each strategy. The average results for the 50 simulations are shown in Table 2.

According to the results, when using the simple reciprocation strategy (SR), of the 800 sent requests, an average of 769 actually resulted in an interaction and, from this total, 26% of the interactions were unsuccessful. However, when using the analysis of cooperative situations strategy (ACS), an average of 756 requests actually resulted in an interaction and, of this total, *only* 6.9% of the interactions were unsuccessful.

We observe that by analysing the balance of the exchange values when deciding over cooperative interactions, agents can significantly reduce the number of unsuccessful interactions. The decrease in the number of total interactions is justified by the increase in the number of constraints that agents make on desirable interactions, when they analyse the balance of exchange values. However, interactions were reduced by only 1.6% in contrast with the significant reduction in the number of unsuccessful interactions.

In the second experiment, we test the behaviour of both strategies when we increase the proportion of low-skilled providers in the agent population. To that end, we keep the proportions for requester expectations in Table 1, fix the proportion of high-skilled providers at 10%, and vary the proportion of low-skilled providers from 5% to 40%

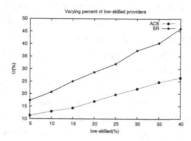

Fig. 3. Percentage of unsuccessful interactions for different proportions of low-skilled providers in the population

(the proportion of medium-skilled providers decreases proportionately with the increase of low-skilled providers). The results are shown in Figure 3.

According to the results, when there are more providers performing poor quality services (40%), the number of unsuccessful interactions can reach a critical amount (almost 50%) if agents rely on simple reciprocation. However, by analysing cooperative situations agents can reduce this amount to less than 30%.

We can see from the results that, when there is a significant number of poor quality services, it becomes more critical to identify unsuccessful interactions, so that successful ones can be maintained instead.

5   Related Work

Related work on exchange values [11] has proposed a centralised approach to coordinate the balance of interactions in terms of exchange values, in which a social equilibrium supervisor uses exchange values and social rules to coordinate exchanges between agents. An extension of this approach to address coordination of social exchanges in spite of different personality traits of agents is presented in [12].

The valorisation of agents that act cooperatively to motivate cooperation in a multi-agent system is used in [13] in the form of *brownie points*. Agents that perform tasks for the group gain brownie points and agents that defect from group tasks lose brownie points. Although it is applied to cooperative group work and our model focuses on one-to-one cooperations, the brownie point approach is similar to the valorisation through exchange values proposed in this paper in the sense that the credits earned by agents are a motivation for providing services with no monetary return, which is the case of the cooperative applications we focus on this paper. However, brownie points represent an agent's self-valorisation (the agent rewards itself for cooperating in a team) and not the valorisation an agent receives from others in retribution for the provided service.

The analysis of reciprocal interactions as a criterion for deciding whether to cooperate with other agents is proposed by [14,15] in the form of an expected utility-based decision-making. According to this approach, agents agree to cooperate if the cost of helping the requester agent is smaller than the expected benefit of receiving help from the requester and other agents in the future. By considering expected future help in the providers's utility function, agents are motivated to cooperate with each other since the probability of receiving resources increases with the number of times they helped others. Similar to this approach, the decision-making based on exchange values also provides a motivation for agents to cooperate with others and to maintain reciprocal relations as a guarantee for future benefits. However, the utility based decision-making does not consider the success of the cooperative relations in terms of the balance between the effort spent by the provider and the satisfaction of the receiver, which is important to consider if the environment has agents with different preferences and perspectives, or even agents that reciprocate but by providing low quality services.

Alternatively, cooperation and reciprocity supported by norms and organisations is proposed by [16], in which knowledge sharing between agents is supported by social contracts and rules inside a virtual organisation framework. Agents that request information from a provider have to offer a service in return that is of interest of the provider by means of a formal contract, which is monitored by an organisation-related agent that checks whether the agreement is followed. Although this approach uses reciprocity to motivate cooperation, it differs from our approach in the way reciprocity is achieved. Instead of using formal social contracts to enforce reciprocal relations, the exchange values approach relies on the informal commitments represented by virtual credits and debts which influence the chance of future interactions. Also, their approach does not consider the evaluation of services neither the influence of the outcome of interactions for the maintenance of cooperative relations.

6   Conclusion and Future Work

We have presented a computational approach for modelling non-economic, autonomous cooperative interactions based on the theory of *exchange values*. Here, exchange values *motivate* agent interactions and their maintenance through a system of credits and debts. Moreover, the credits and debts acquired by agents during interactions are based on their individual evaluation of the service being performed or received, and the balance of these evaluations indicates whether an interaction was successful for each agent involved. We argue that, by analysing the *balance* of exchange values in past interactions, autonomous agents can identify situations in which the cooperation with other agents is unsuccessful and decide whether to maintain this cooperation.

We presented a scenario in which agents participate in a cooperative application in the bioinformatics domain by requesting and providing services to each other with bounded resources, and with different perspectives over service evaluation. Agents have two different cooperative strategies, one based on simple reciprocation of credits and debts, and another based on the analysis of cooperative situations. We use an experimental testbed to compare the number of unsuccessful interactions that occur when agents use both approaches, and show that agents can *reduce the number of unsuccessful interactions* by analysing cooperative situations and still keep a high number of achieved interactions.

Future work aims to combine the analysis of exchange values and their balance with the analysis of service dependencies between agents to improve the decision-making strategy, as proposed in [8]. We also aim at developing a qualitative representation for exchange values to which quantitative evaluations are mapped, to facilitate their application to different scenarios (with different evaluation scales).

References

1. Burt, R.: The network structure of social capital. In: Research in Organizational Behavior, vol. 22, JAI press, Greenwich, CT (2000)
2. Stein, L.: Creating a bioinformatics nation. Nature 417, 119–120 (2002)
3. Gao, H.T., Hayes, J.H., Cai, H.: Integrating biological research through web services. IEEE Computer 38, 26–31 (2005)
4. Goble, C., Wroe, C., Stevens, R.: the myGrid consortium: The mygrid project: services architecture and demonstrator. In: UK e-Science All Hands Meeting 2003, pp. 595–603 (2003)
5. Overbeek, R., Disz, T., Stevens, R.: The SEED: A peer-to-peer environment for genome annotation. Communications of the ACM 47(11), 47–50 (2004)
6. Foster, I.: Service-oriented science. Science 308(5723), 814–817 (2005)
7. Piaget, J.: Sociological Studies. Routlege, London (1973)
8. Rodrigues, M.R., da Rocha Costa, A.C., Bordini, R.H.: A system of exchange values to support social interactions in artificial societies. In: Second International Joint Conference on Autonomous Agents and Multiagent Systems, Melbourne, pp. 81–88 (2003)
9. Rodrigues, M.R., Luck, M.: Analysing partner selection through exchange values. In: Sichman, J.S., Antunes, L. (eds.) MABS 2005. LNCS (LNAI), vol. 3891, pp. 24–40. Springer, Heidelberg (2006)
10. Campbell, A.M., Heyer, L.J.: Discovering Genomics Proteomics and Bioinformatics. Benjamin Cummings, San Francisco, CA (2002)
11. Dimuro, G.P., Costa, A.C.R.: Qualitative Markov decision processes and the coordination of social exchanges in multi-agent systems. In: Gmytrasiewicz, P., Parsons, S. (eds.) Workshop on Game Theoretic and Decision Theoretic Agents at IJCAI Conference, Edinburgh (2005)
12. Dimuro, G.P., Costa, A.C.R., Gonçlves, L.V., Hübner, A.: Centralized Regulation of Social Exchanges between Personality-based Agents. In: Boissier, O., Padget, J., Dignum, V., Lindemann, G., Matson, E., Ossowski, S., Sichman, J.S., Vázquez-Salceda, J. (eds.) Coordination, Organizations, Institutions, and Norms in Multi-Agent Systems, Springer-Verlag, Berlin (2006)
13. Glass, A., Grosz, B.: Socially conscious decision-making. In: Proceedings of the fourth international conference on Autonomous agents, pp. 217–224. ACM Press, New York (2000)
14. Sen, S., Dutta, P.S., Saha, S.: Emergence and stability of collaborations among rational agents. In: Klusch, M., Omicini, A., Ossowski, S., Laamanen, H. (eds.) CIA 2003. LNCS (LNAI), vol. 2782, pp. 192–205. Springer, Heidelberg (2003)
15. Banerjee, D., Saha, S., Dasgupta, P., Sen, S.: Reciprocal resource sharing in p2p environments. In: Fourth International Joint Conference on Autonomous Agents and Multiagent Systems, Utrecht, Netherlands (2005)
16. Dignum, V., Dignum, F.: Knowledge market: Agent-mediated knowledge sharing. In: Third International/Central and Eastern European Conference on Multi-Agent Systems, Prague (2003)

Author Index

Lecture Notes in Artificial Intelligence (LNAI)